1809: Thunder on the Danube

1809

Thunder on the Danube: Napoleon's Defeat of the Habsburgs

VOLUME II: ASPERN

JOHN H. GILL

FRONTLINE BOOKS, LONDON

This volume is dedicated to

Gunther E. Rothenberg (1923–2004)

For Guidance and Light

1809 Thunder on the Danube: Napoleon's Defeat of the Habsburgs, Vol II
First published in 2009
and reissued in this format in 2014 by
Frontline Books
an imprint of
Pen and Sword Books Ltd
Yorkshire - Philadelphia

ISBN: 978-1-84832-758-0

CIP data records for this title are available from the British Library and the
Library of Congress

Typeset by JCS Publishing Services Ltd, www.jcs-publishing.co.uk
Printed and bound in the UK by CPI Group (UK) Ltd, Croydon, CR0 4YY.

The Publisher's authorised representative in the EU for product safety is
Authorised Rep Compliance Ltd., Ground Floor, 71 Lower Baggot Street, Dublin
D02 P593, Ireland. | www.arccompliance.com

For a complete list of Pen & Sword titles please contact

PEN & SWORD BOOKS LIMITED
47 Church Street, Barnsley, South Yorkshire, S70 2AS, England
E-mail: enquiries@pen-and-sword.co.uk
Website: www.pen-and-sword.co.uk

or
PEN AND SWORD BOOKS
1950 Lawrence Road, Havertown, PA 19083, USA
E-mail: uspen-and-sword@casematepublishers.com
Website: www.penandswordbooks.com

Contents

Key to Map Symbols

John H. Gill © 2013, all rights reserved

Stars indicate fortresses, forts, and blockhouses: ★

Units types are indicated by the following symbols. As in the text, units known by their proprietors' or commanders' names are printed in italics.

Sample cavalry unit: Austrian *Liechtenstein* Hussars No. 7 = *Liechtenstein*

Sample infantry unit: Austrian *Hiller* Infantry No. 2 = *Hiller*

Sample artillery (all sides): ▮▮

Nationality is shown by colour: white for Austrians, black for French, and grey for Napoleon's German allies.

Bavarian 3rd Division = 3 Div   **French 1st Cavalry Division =** 1

Austrian movements (advance and retreat) are shown with dashed lines, while those of the French and allied German troops are solid.

Austrian movement = ‑‑‑‑‑‑▶   **Allied movement =** ——▶

Where helpful for clarity, the following units size symbols have been used.

      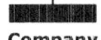

Regiment   **Battalion**   **Company**
               or Squadron

Maps, Charts, and Tables

MAPS

CHARTS

TABLES

Illustrations

Except where noted, all illustrations are from the author's collection. ASKB is the Anne S. K. Browne Collection.

Sources and Conventions

First, complete source citations are included in the endnotes, but for reasons of space a full bibliography is planned for the concluding volume of this series. Second, to deliver a clear and accurate account while retaining something of the flavour of the age, I have adopted the following conventions:

+ French, German, and Austrian rank titles are preserved insofar as this is feasible and convenient, a table after this section relates these to current U.S. and British ranks and lists abbreviations;
+ 'Ligne' and 'Léger' refer respectively to French line and light infantry;
+ I have followed contemporary practice in designating Austrian regiments, using the titles derived from their *Inhaber* ('patrons' or 'proprietors') rather than their numbers (*Kaiser* Cuirassiers No. 1, not the 1st Cuirassier Regiment), although numbers are included where appropriate for clarity ('EH' abbreviates 'Erzherzog' as in Infantry Regiment *EH Ludwig* No. 8);
+ To minimise confusion between individuals and units, units known by the names of their *Inhaber* or their commanders are presented in italics (Württemberg Oberst Karl von Neuffer commanded Jäger-Bataillon *von Neuffer*);
+ I have used Arabic numerals for the French corps d'armée (Davout's 3rd Corps) and Roman numerals for the Austrians (Bellegarde's I Corps);
+ Battalions or squadrons of a regiment are designated by Roman numerals (II/*Jordis* indicates the 2nd Battalion of *Jordis* Infantry Regiment No. 59);
+ The term 'Rheinbund' refers to the Confederation of the Rhine;
+ The terms 'Allied' and 'Allies', when capitalised, refer to the French and their German confederates, while 'German' refers to the host of small states between the Rhine and the Prussian border;

+ In most cases, modern German/Austrian, Italian, and Polish spellings have been used for geographical names so the reader can locate these on a present-day map or road sign (e.g., Eggmühl instead of Eckmühl), however, conventional Austrian names have been retained for terrain features and towns in the Czech Republic, Slovakia, and Hungary to minimise confusion; geographic names are included in the index for ease of locating places on the various maps;

+ All dates are given according to the Gregorian calendar rather than the Julian calendar then in use in Russia.

This work has been a long labour, and progress has only been possible with the generous assistance of many others as noted in the opening of Volume I. I would be remiss, however, not to cite the particular assistance of my father, Herbert J. Gill, for reading the draft and offering emendatory suggestions, and of my family (Anne Rieman, Grant Gill, and Hunter Gill) for reading segments (repeatedly), discussing 1809 (interminably), and indulging me in my pursuit of this war's campaigns. I hope that they, and the several audiences for whom this series is intended, will enjoy reading it as much as I enjoyed writing it.

Table of Comparative Military Ranks and German Noble Titles

Austrian and German Ranks (Abbreviation)	French Ranks (Abbreviation)	Modern British or U.S. Equivalents
Feldmarschall (FM)	(no equivalent rank)	Field Marshal or General
Feldzeugmeister (FZM) or General der Kavallerie (GdK)	(no equivalent rank)	Lieutenant General
Feldmarschall-Leutnant (FML) or General-Leutnant (GL)	Général de Division (GD)	Major General
General-Major (GM)	Général de Brigade (GB)	Brigadier General
[staff] Oberst	Adjutant-Commandant	[staff] Colonel
Oberst	Colonel	Colonel
Oberst-Leutnant (OTL)	Major	Lieutenant Colonel
Major (MAJ)	Chef de Bataillon or Chef d'Escadron	Major
Stabs-Hauptmann	Adjoint	[staff] Captain
Hauptmann, Rittmeister (cavalry), or Kapitän	Capitaine	Captain
Oberleutnant (OLT) or Premierleutnant (PLT)	Lieutenant	Lieutenant, First Lieutenant
Leutnant	Sous-Lieutenant	Subaltern, Second Lieutenant

Notes:
a. All comparisons are approximate, protocol and functions could vary widely.
b. The rank of Feldmarschall-Leutnant was unique to the Austrian military (the Germans used General-Leutnant), but Feldzeugmeister, General der Kavallerie (or Infanterie), and Feldmarschall were occasionally used by Napoleon's German allies.
c. In the French Army, the title 'Major Général' indicated a function rather than a rank and was unique to Berthier. Similarly, the title 'Generalissimo' was unique to Archduke Charles. Technically, the French title of 'Marshal' was also an appointment rather than a rank.

GERMAN NOBLE TITLES

German (Abbreviation)	English
Erzherzog (EH)	archduke
Freiherr	baron
Fürst	prince
Graf	count
Grossherzog	grand duke
Herzog	duke
Kaiser	emperor
Kaiserin	empress
Kronprinz	crown prince

Note: the prefix 'Erb-' was sometimes used to indicate an hereditary title (Erbgrossherzog).

Prologue

I will take my satisfaction in Vienna, I know the road.

Emperor Napoleon to the Bavarian ambassador, 23 March 1809[1]

After a lengthy gestation, the Franco-Austrian War of 1809 erupted on 10 April with the Austrian invasion of Bavaria under the Archduke Charles. A mere two weeks, however, sufficed for Napoleon and his urgently assembled Army of Germany to batter the Habsburg Hauptarmee in a series of bruising defeats. The battles of Abensberg, Landshut, Eggmühl, and Regensburg left the Austrian army demoralised and broken into two pieces: Charles retreating north towards the safety of the Bohemian mountains, and FML Hiller attempting to restore order among the formations of the army's left wing along the Inn River. The initiative lay with Napoleon. The first campaign, as related in the first volume of this history, was over, the second about to begin.

This volume opens with Napoleon astride the Danube at Regensburg. He faces a critical strategic choice: whether to pursue the injured Austrian Main Army north into Bohemia, or to march directly for Vienna south of the Danube in an attempt to force Charles into a battle in defence of the Habsburg capital. Napoleon decides on the latter option, incurring thereby the opprobrium of many subsequent commentators for seeming to direct his operations towards a geographic objective rather than against the enemy's forces. Moreover, to the Emperor's annoyance, Charles, weary and wary, refuses to come south of the Danube. Denied the decisive battle he desires and expects, Napoleon pushes for Vienna. Along the way, his men best Hiller in a number of small engagements and Marshal Massena throws the Austrians across the Traun in the bitter, brutal Battle of Ebelsberg. Still seeking a fight with the Hauptarmee, the Emperor enters Vienna on 13 May—one month to the day after he had departed Paris. If Charles and his army remain at large, the conquest of the Austrian capital represents a significant accomplishment that will do much to deflate the aspirations of excited German patriots and eager Prussian activists who are pressing their king to intervene on Austria's side.

Where the first two chapters of this volume cover the drive for Vienna, the third recounts the Battle of Aspern–Essling, one of the greatest battles in an age of great battles. This two-day affray of high casualties and desperate heroics ends with a repulse for Napoleon, but one that the Austrians are unable to exploit. The French are defeated but not demoralized and the check only strengthens Napoleon's determination to attempt a second crossing of the Danube as soon as his army has recuperated. While he rests, refits, and reinforces the Army of Germany, a month-long operational pause settles over the central theatre of the war, the two principal armies cautiously but quietly observing one another across the rolling expanses of the great river.

Meanwhile, Napoleon is clearing his strategic flanks, so the pause in the centre allows us to catch up on the secondary theatres. These are many and varied. Of foremost importance is the Austrian invasion of Italy in April and the French counter-offensive that carries Viceroy Eugene's Army of Italy into Habsburg territory. Foreshadowing the next volume, this will lead to French penetration of Hungary and Eugene's victory at Raab on 14 June, a triumph that eliminates the threat to Napoleon's right flank and allows Eugene to join his step-father outside Vienna. The French also reverse a limited Austrian incursion into the Balkans, so that General Marmont can bring his small Army of Dalmatia to Vienna as well. Along the Vistula, Napoleon's Polish allies fight a remarkable war of manoeuvre against Archduke Ferdinand, while Russian forces, putatively allied with the French, equivocate and delay, struggling mightily to avoid involvement in any actual action. Most of these operations, along with minor rebellions in Germany and a robust insurrection in the Tyrol, are to be covered in the next volume, but it is important to keep the entire spectrum of combat in mind as we focus on each specific facet of the war in sequence.

This, then, is the story of the second phase of the war: a rapid thrust for Vienna punctuated by vicious fighting and culminating in a grand battle of uncommon ferocity on the banks of the Danube. Impelled by the need to end the war quickly, Napoleon lunges forward, hounding his men down the Danube valley and pressing across the river on rickety bridges only to be halted in the wash of blood at Aspern. In the six weeks that follow, while the Austrians vacillate, he applies his enormous energy to gathering every available man, horse, and gun around Vienna, setting the stage for the gigantic spectacle and cyclopean fury of the Battle of Wagram.

PART I

From Victory to Repulse

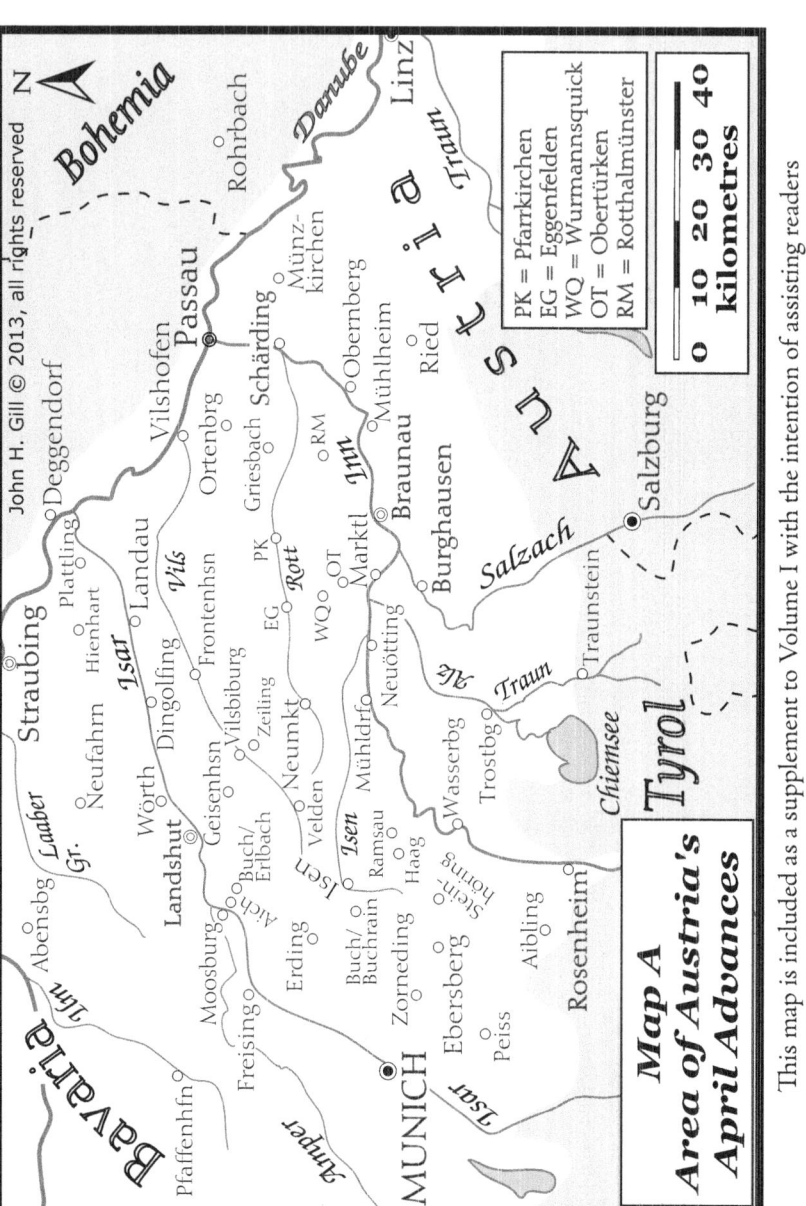

Map A
Area of Austria's
April Advances

This map is included as a supplement to Volume I with the intention of assisting readers in following the complex Austrian movements during the April campaign in Bavaria.

PK = Pfarrkirchen
EG = Eggenfelden
WQ = Wurmannsquick
OT = Obertürken
RM = Rotthalmünster

0 10 20 30 40
kilometres

CHAPTER I

On to Vienna!

'In one month we will be in Vienna!' proclaimed Napoleon in a 24 April order praising the army's performance in the Regensburg campaign.[1] This clarion call repeated the electrifying words of his 17 April proclamation, but this time the inspirational phrase also reflected the emperor's strategic thinking.

With the fall of Regensburg and the apparent, if not yet confirmed, withdrawal of Charles and the Hauptarmee into Bohemia, Napoleon had to decide on the future thrust of his operations. He was inclined[2] to march straight up the Danube valley for Vienna rather than undertake a direct pursuit of Charles, but the larger strategic situation would play a key role in determining his next moves. As he surveyed the political-military horizon from his headquarters in the Carthusian convent in Prüll, his concerns included the possibility of Prussian collaboration with Austria, popular discontent in some parts of Germany, and the potential for an English descent along the Channel or North Sea coast. The Tyrol was already in open rebellion, severing his direct communications with Viceroy Eugene in Italy. He could guess that Austrian troops had probably entered the Kingdom of Italy, but only learned on 25 April that Eugene had suffered a defeat at Sacile on the 16th. He did not yet have any news from Poland, but he knew that substantial Habsburg forces had been committed to that front as well. All of these considerations militated for bold new advances that would capitalise on the string of recent victories to keep the initiative firmly in his hands, transmit that initiative to the other theatres of war, and produce a psychological impact favourable to his interests on the international stage. He decided to march on Vienna.

At Eggmühl on 22 April, just before the French attacks went in, Napoleon described his vision of the coming battle and told Massena, 'One of two things will happen: either the archduke will fight a second battle before that place [Regensburg] and the war will end beneath its walls, or he will cross over the Danube and we will drive straight for Vienna.'[3] Charles having retreated towards Bohemia, the emperor now turned his attention to the Habsburg capital. At first glance, this decision to march on Vienna rather than launching a direct pursuit of the shaken Hauptarmee seems inconsistent with one of the distinctive features of Napoleonic strategy: that the predominant goal of operations should be the elimination of the opponent's armed forces, after which the enemy would be incapable of resisting the victor's political demands. Many commentators, benefiting from hindsight, have therefore regarded the focus on Vienna as a major strategic error and a violation of Napoleon's own principles of war. General Henry Bonnal and Commandant Edmond Buat, two of the most articulate critics, argue that Napoleon, blinded by his pride, chose 'an essentially geographic objective' when he should have pursued the bleeding Hauptarmee to destruction.[4] In common with many other observers, they contend that the Austrian Main Army and its commander, damaged and partly demoralised, would have collapsed if pushed vigorously and in sufficient force.[5] With the principal prop of the Habsburg state thus removed, Napoleon would have been able to dictate terms to Kaiser Franz.[6]

Napoleon, however, was thinking more broadly in April 1809. Viewed through the lens of subsequent events—the costly repulse at Aspern–Essling and the sanguinary but incomplete victory at Wagram—the emperor's decisions can certainly seem questionable if not outright mistaken. He himself reportedly later mused that objections could be raised to his actions as a *commander*, but that he 'contemplated the situation in Europe and the impression it would make if I would enter Vienna rapidly'.[7] An analysis based on the larger political-military situation and on what Napoleon knew at the time, therefore, leads to a conclusion different to that espoused by Bonnal and Buat.

In selecting Vienna as his immediate goal, Napoleon was not reverting to the norms of eighteenth-century warfare; that is, the Habsburg capital was not an end in itself. Rather the emperor founded his decision on an array of persuasive considerations completely congruent with his own military philosophy. In the first place, his objective remained the destruction of the Austrian army, but it was by no means clear that this could be achieved by pursuing Charles north of the Danube. The Austrians already had a lead of one day, perhaps two, ahead of the Allies and the pursuit would be slowed by the exhaustion of both troops and commanders (including Napoleon himself). Getting the Army of Germany over the Danube would impose additional delays, especially considering that the stone bridge at Regensburg constituted the only extant crossing point between Neustadt and Passau.[8] By the time that sufficient French forces were across the river and concentrated for a decisive battle, Charles could either ensconce himself in a good defensive position in the rugged terrain on the Austro-Bavarian frontier or escape over the Bohemian mountains. If the Austrians succeeded in eluding battle, they would draw the Allies over poor mountain roads deeper into Bohemia and a potentially protracted pursuit. Napoleon might even find himself facing the embarrassing prospect of Charles re-crossing the Danube and establishing himself on the *south* bank in a dangerous reversal of the strategic situation. Rather than adopt this potentially risky course of action, Napoleon aimed for the capital, a target he believed the archduke would have to defend. The Austrian army would then be crushed in a grand battle somewhere between Passau and Vienna on the south bank of the river.[9] If Charles left the way to Vienna open, the emperor might be able to repeat the manoeuvre of 1805: seizing the city, passing over the Danube, and finding his decisive engagement on the north bank in a 'vast operation *sur les derrières*' with the river covering his flank against Austrian incursions.[10] In either case, Vienna was 'only a point on his trajectory towards the archduke's army'.[11]

Furthermore, a direct advance on Vienna would place a French wedge between the Hauptarmee and Archduke Johann's army in Italy, giving Napoleon a central position from which he could deal with either Austrian force as circumstances permitted. Indeed, in his analysis, General Hubert Camon terms this a '*double manoeuvre sur les derrières*' as it would, in effect, place the Army of Germany in the rear of both key Austrian armies.[12] In the process, the emperor's thrust down the Danube valley would force Johann to abandon his gains in Italy. If he were not ordered to withdraw to shield Vienna, he would certainly have to pull back for fear of being outflanked.[13] Meanwhile, the presence of the principal Allied army south of the Danube would protect Bavaria and might serve to induce caution if not submission in the rebellious Tyrol.

Napoleon was also considering the larger political-strategic impact of his actions when he decided to strike for Vienna. Although rapid capture of Vienna was unlikely to decide the war, it would reinforce Prussian fears of French power, dampen potential unrest in Germany, and undermine any doubts among the Rheinbund states. This was, above all, a war that Napoleon wanted to finish quickly. Pursuit of Charles under the existing conditions, however, could easily result in extended operations in Bohemia—a campaign that could drag on for weeks, prolonging the conflict and creating opportunities for the Prussian court or disgruntled Germans (or both) to intervene.[14] As we will see, the desire to forestall outside actors by bringing the war to a rapid conclusion will also be significant in the emperor's calculations when the Austrians offer a ceasefire after Wagram.

Similarly, logistical and administrative considerations were major factors in Napoleon's April decision, as they would be in July. In contrast to the rich Danube valley, Bohemia was poor in resources, and as a line of communications, the Danube was far superior to the second-class roads that wound through the snow and pine forests of Bohemia. Napoleon had focused his attention on Passau for just this reason in the weeks prior to the war and he continued to stress the importance of the river as an invaluable supply route.[15] Occupation of the Danube valley and Vienna, however, would also disrupt the administrative apparatus, logistical connections, and communications of the Austrian Empire, hampering its ability to raise new troops, shift forces, and conduct operations. Moreover, Vienna was 'the most important point, the key to the monarchy', in Archduke Johann's words. In particular, it was a vast Habsburg arsenal, so its seizure would at once deprive Austrian forces of significant resources while adding its stores of clothing, shoes, food, wine, ammunition, artillery, and other supplies to Napoleon's side of the ledger.[16]

There is nothing to indicate that Napoleon thought Austria would sue for peace upon the fall of Vienna. He doubtless considered this as a possible outcome and would have welcomed such a swift end to the war, but he did not expect to achieve his war aims merely by taking the Austrian capital. Rather, everything leads to the conclusion that he expected and hoped for triumph in a major battle that would settle the issue and allow him set the terms of peace. If he was realistic in his appreciation of likely Habsburg political reactions, however, he underestimated Austria's military resilience. He did not recognise the improvements in the Austrian army since 1805. He denigrated its performance during the Regensburg campaign, and overstated its losses in men, material, and morale during the first two weeks of the war.[17] This deprecation of Austrian military prowess, especially their lack of energy and agility, contributed to Napoleon's willingness to take risks but did not blind him to possible threats. As we shall see, he kept a close watch on the Hauptarmee even while pushing for the Inn after the fall of Regensburg, and he left major forces along the Danube inside Bavaria until he was confident that Charles had truly withdrawn into Bohemia.

HILLER AND BESSIÈRES: BETWEEN ISAR AND INN

While Napoleon and the bulk of the Army of Germany were bringing the first phase of the war to a close beneath the walls of Regensburg, Marshal Bessières was pursuing the defeated Austrian left wing towards the Inn. Bessières, the son of a well-to-do surgeon, had risen to prominence through his friendship with Murat, his battlefield bravery, and his loyalty to Napoleon. Despite his participation in the wars of Revolutionary France, he maintained an *ancien regime* demeanour, powdering his hair, harbouring a definite sense of his social superiority, and retaining a deep individual piety. 'Tall and straight, impeccably uniformed, rigorous in discipline, cold and dry in speech,'[18] he was known for cool courage, honesty, persistent elegance, and administrative ability, but he was not above the petty intrigues that splotched the marshalate. One of these left a bitter enmity with Lannes that would hobble co-operation between the two men during the ongoing campaign.[19] Moreover, his military record was mixed. He had won a notable victory with a small force of conscripts over a numerically superior Spanish army at Medina del Rio Seco in 1808 and had done well enough when under the emperor's eye, but he was cautious to a fault: 'personally brave, but hardly capable of leading an army corps.'[20] As will be seen here in southern Bavaria and in the pursuit into Austria, he was not the ideal man to command an independent force or an aggressive advance guard.

The marshal's small command consisted of Wrede's 2nd Bavarian Division and Marulaz's division of four chasseur regiments (minus the 14th Chasseurs and the Baden Light Dragoons), to which Napoleon soon added Molitor's division (just north of Landshut).[21] Of these, only Marulaz and two squadrons of the Bavarian 3rd Chevaulegers were actually on Hiller's trail on the evening of 21 April. Assembled around Geisenhausen, this light cavalry was pushing patrols south to Vilsbiburg while Wrede gathered his infantry and artillery at Landshut. GM von Preysing, Wrede's cavalry commander, and the other six chevaulegers squadrons of the division, however, were in Moosburg, having been sent to reconnoitre towards Munich.

The Allied pursuit continued on the 22nd as Hiller fell back to the safety of the Inn's south bank. Around 10 a.m., the Hessian Leib Chevaulegers, supported by 3rd and 19th Chasseurs, fought a brief skirmish at Egglkofen

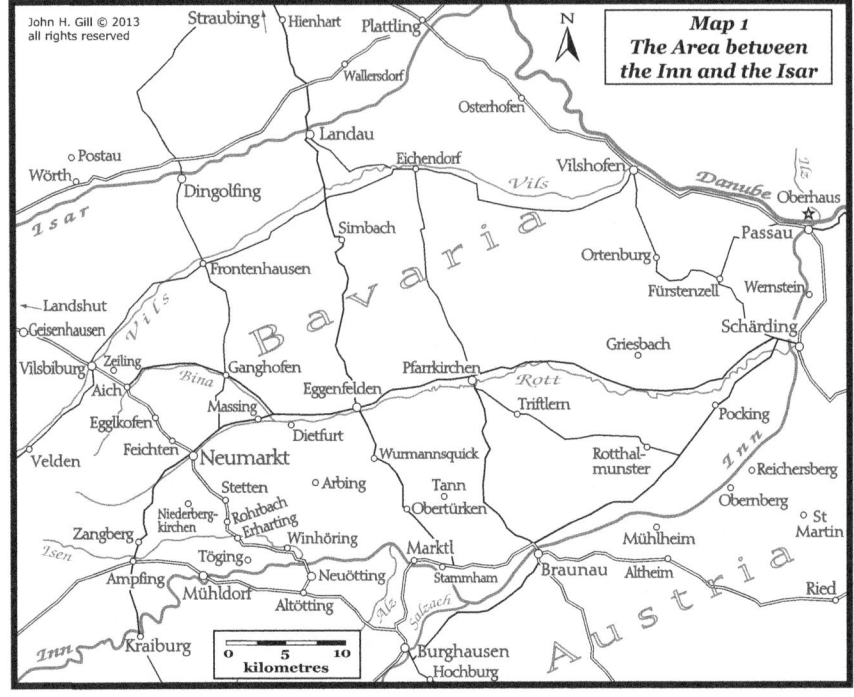

Map 1
The Area between
the Inn and the Isar

with Radetzky's *EH Karl* Uhlans and some stragglers. Otherwise there was little combat and Bessières concluded the day by occupying Neumarkt with Wrede's division, Jacquinot's light cavalry brigade, and part of 8th Hussars.[22] The two Bavarian squadrons watched the left flank at Eggenfelden. Marulaz was north of Erharting with 3rd and 19th Chasseurs. At the marshal's direction, he had sent the Hessian light horse to scout the crossings at Kraiburg and Mühldorf, but the anxiously alert *Kienmayer* Hussars, charged with protecting the bridges, set both afire after exchanging a few shots with the Hessians. Marulaz's other regiment, 23rd Chasseurs, had discovered Oberstleutnant Steigentesch and his three wandering battalions of Vienna Volunteers north of Vilsbiburg. The chasseurs called for infantry assistance and GM von Beckers with the Bavarian 7th Infantry was dispatched to help, but Steigentesch, as we have seen, eluded his pursuers.[23] As a result of this excursion, evening found 23rd Chasseurs at Simbach and the Bavarian regiment at Frontenhausen.

Bessières had not infused his command's actions with much energy during 22 April and the pursuit slackened palpably on the 23rd. Convinced that the

Austrians would evacuate the area north of Inn in any event, the marshal was complacent. The numerous prisoners and other signs of disorder, combined with the ease with which his command had mastered Neumarkt, left him with the impression of an utterly defeated and demoralised foe. He therefore contented himself with sending the Bavarian 6th Light and the French 2nd Chasseurs to Rohrbach and Stetten respectively in support of Marulaz.[24] That general, accompanied by the marshal, probed carefully towards the river, skirmishing with *Kienmayer* Hussars and *Brod* Grenzer under GM Mesko between Erharting and Winhöring, but halting for the day on reaching a position where he and Bessières could see a large body of infantry on the far bank. Bessières recognised that the Austrian force was beyond the capacity of his available troops, but concluded that 'everything indicated the enemy was moving to retire.'[25]

The day was equally uneventful for the rest of Bessières's command. At Mühldorf, the Hessians seized the town and captured ninety prisoners in a bold charge, but could not locate any means to cross the river. Wrede and Jacquinot stopped at Neumarkt, where they were joined by Preysing, Beckers, and 23rd Chasseurs during the course of the afternoon and evening. The two squadrons of the Bavarian 3rd Chevaulegers remained at Eggenfelden. Molitor reached Vilsbiburg at 9 a.m., but Bessières, overly sanguine and fearing some confusion in orders, told the general to halt, as his exhausted division would only be called upon 'in a case where this is necessary.'[26]

Hiller, on the other hand, had decided to act. The feeble Allied pursuit had allowed him to grant his men the 23rd as a rest day behind the shelter of the Inn. At the same time, he kept substantial rear guard forces on the north bank and took steps to protect all of the potential crossing sites with his own troops or Landwehr from Oberst MacDermott's brigade.[27] Confusion and disorder bedevilled Austrian efforts to organise a comprehensive defence of the river and to determine a new course of action. Baggage trains, stragglers, marauders, and lost units criss-crossed the countryside, sowing rumour and panic, ills to which the raw Landwehr and brand-new recruits were especially vulnerable. Moreover, after the shocking reverses of the previous several days, Hiller and his commanders were nervous. His rear guard generals had little real sense of the enemy, sent exaggerated reports, and expressed anxiety about being surrounded or outflanked at every turn. Completely ignorant of the larger strategic situation, Hiller hesitated to recall Jellacic from his now dangerously isolated post at Munich. He informed his subordinate of the disaster at Landshut, but his note only urged increased vigilance without specifying that Jellacic should abandon the Bavarian capital.[28]

To his credit, however, Hiller was already considering a return across the Inn when he and Archduke Ludwig received a message from Kaiser Franz on the night of 22 April or early on the 23rd. This communication, sent from the imperial court at Schärding, related the latest information from Charles: that the Hauptarmee was preparing to launch an offensive against Davout on 22 April. Hiller, of course, did not know that this 'offensive' had never really begun and that the Hauptarmee was now in disorganised retreat to Bohemia. Instead, the Kaiser's letter and the perceived weakness of the pursuing force reinforced his inclination 'to be across the Isar again by the 25th and to take my advance towards the Hauptarmee through Dingolfing'.[29] In addition to his sense of duty, it is very likely that Hiller was also motivated by a desire to burnish his reputation in the eyes of his monarch, particularly if he could impugn Charles in the process. Circumstances had placed him in a position to report directly to the Kaiser and he was not about to forsake the opportunity.[30]

Hiller made thorough, indeed elaborate, preparations for his advance, indulging in the Austrian proclivity for issuing lengthy 'general dispositions' with minute details for every subordinate.[31] As a prelude, he organised three 'advance guards' north of the Inn and set them in motion on the afternoon of the 23rd. Each composed of a Grenz regiment, a light cavalry regiment, and half of a cavalry battery, these forces were to cover the army's deployment, protect its flanks, and gather intelligence. On the right, Radetzky pushed forward to Wurmannsquick, followed by GM Reinwald, whose brigade would occupy Wurmannsquick on the 24th while Radetzky advanced to Eggenfelden. Nordmann led a similar force to Töging on the left; he was to reach Zangberg the following day and establish contact with Jellacic. Additionally, Vincent and the *Rosenberg* Chevaulegers, one of Hiller's meandering commands, rode into Arbing (south-west of Wurmannsquick) at around 11 p.m. that night.[32]

Mesko commanded the advance guard in the centre: *Brod* Grenzer (1,300) and *Kienmayer* Hussars (900). Collecting outlying detachments and arranging his advance took longer than anticipated, but when his hussars advanced around 7 p.m., they struck with fury and success. Falling on the 3rd Chasseurs, whose security seems to have been remarkably lax, the hussars inflicted considerable casualties and threw the French horsemen back to Erharting, where the 19th Chasseurs intervened to blunt the Austrian advance. As Marulaz hastened to withdraw his two chasseur regiments, Mesko's troops encountered the Bavarian 6th Light in their position above the Isen. In a brief but earnest engagement, the 6th Light lost forty casualties but halted the Austrians and earned Marulaz's praise: 'The retreat was supported by a Bavarian battalion that comported itself with extreme valour.'[33] Covered by the Bavarians, Marulaz withdrew through Neumarkt to Feichten, where he was joined by the Hessian Chevaulegers.[34] The 6th Light retired to the hills south of Neumarkt, extending an outpost line formed by the 13th Infantry, while the French 2nd Chasseurs established a screen of pickets between Stetten and the Isen.[35]

As Hiller was advancing, Jellacic was retiring. His distant patrols had skirmished with the enemy at Unterbruck on the 21st, and more small encounters occurred in that village and at Freising on the 22nd after he sent GM von Provenchères to Erding with a battalion and two squadrons to guard his flank and unsettle the French.[36] These scattered brushes with the Allies left him feeling most uncomfortable, and Hiller's message reporting the retreat from Landshut only heightened his anxiety. Leaving their watch fires burning, his men slipped away towards Wasserburg on the night of 23 April.[37]

24 April: The Battle of Neumarkt[38]

The Inn valley is broad and flat, but the land rises sharply north of the Isen, and the region between that river and the Rott is a confusion of low but steep hills, many covered with forest. The battlefield was speckled with tiny hamlets and farmsteads, but the only substantial manmade features in 1809 were Neumarkt, the cloister of St Veit just on the south-eastern edge of town, and the main road from the Inn to Landshut, carried over the Rott on the town's lone bridge. The Rott was not a major obstacle, but it precluded the passage of formed units and would prove a serious embarrassment at the tactical level.

Consistent with Austrian practice, Hiller's plan for his 24 April advance called for the formation of three 'columns', each with its own advance guard above and beyond the three advance guards already across the Inn.[39] The first column, composed of V Corps troops under FML Reuss-Plauen, would march on the right (east of the Landshut highway), while the second, VI Corps units commanded by FML Kottulinsky, pushed directly up the highway on Neumarkt in the centre.[40] The third column, VI Corps troops under GM von Hoffmeister, was assigned a secondary road on the left. Kienmayer's II Reserve Corps, reduced to five grenadier battalions, four dragoon squadrons, and twenty guns, would follow as general reserve.[41] The three columns were to begin moving at 2 a.m. to establish a position stretching from the St Veit cloister to Niederbergkirchen. Hiller expected little interference from the Allies. Should Bessières offer significant resistance on the Rott, the three Austrian columns would advance with their left wing refused (that is, held back) while Radetzky and Nordmann outflanked the enemy position. Once the French were out of the way, Mesko would push north to the Bina and the entire force would prepare for an advance to Dingolfing on the 25th. As for Jellacic, Hiller sent him contradictory orders requiring him to somehow slide closer to Hiller's force while simultaneously protecting the Munich–Rosenheim road and sending Provenchères from Erding towards Freising and Moosburg.

Hiller's offensive started an hour later than planned and almost immediately encountered further delay when the main body came upon Mesko's advance guard. Mesko had misunderstood the disposition and his troops were not yet prepared to march. To accelerate the advance, therefore, Hiller instructed Reuss to keep his column on the main road with Kottulinsky following behind. In this configuration, Mesko pushed back Jacquinot's vedettes and collided with outposts of the Bavarian 13th Line just north of Stetten between 7 and 8 a.m.

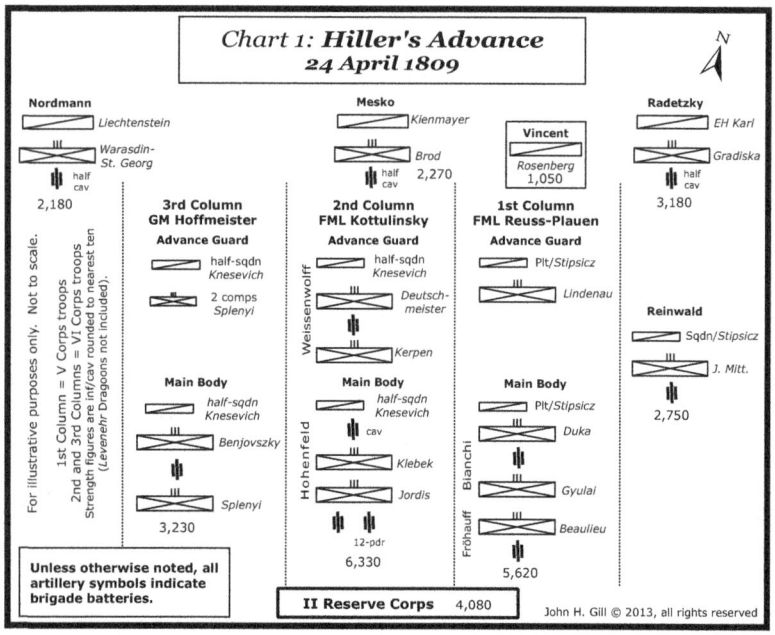

Chart 1: **Hiller's Advance** 24 April 1809

The French cavalry had advised Bessières of Hiller's unexpected advance at about 4 a.m. and the French marshal, hoping to defeat the overbold Austrians, ordered Wrede to form his division on the hills south of Neumarkt. When Jacquinot's staff officers reported his concern about the size of the Austrian force, Bessières replied: 'The more there are, the more we will take,' and, slipping into local patois, exclaimed, 'We will mash them up like rocamadour cheese!'[42] Wrede was far less sanguine. In his eyes, the situation was dangerous: the Rott was only spanned by the highway bridge and a narrow footbridge, and these could only be approached through the town's twisting and narrow alleys. If withdrawal became necessary, Wrede feared congestion, confusion, and heavy losses. Bessières nonetheless ordered the Bavarians south of the stream and sent couriers hastening to Molitor at Vilsbiburg. Wrede thus brought the 3rd, 6th, and 7th Infantry Regiments across the Rott at around 7 a.m., leaving his cavalry and 12-pounder battery north of the stream with Marulaz. By 9 a.m., the Bavarian division was deployed with 13th Infantry and two batteries perched on the narrow ridgeline astride the main road between Strass and Oberscherm; one company of 3rd Infantry in the woods on their left; 6th Light and a battery in the woods north-west of Reit; the rest of 3rd Infantry on the left flank. Jacquinot's two chasseur regiments covered the approaches west of the 13th Infantry. GM von Beckers deployed his brigade across the main road in reserve with two companies of 7th Infantry detached to hold St Veit. These deployments took some time, however, and Beckers's men were still moving up when the battle began in earnest.

Off on the Austrian right, Vincent and the *Rosenberg* Chevaulegers had arrived near Reit at about 8 a.m. Vincent had small detachments execute some minor attacks and manoeuvres, but their influence was insignificant. Along the main road, the *Kienmayer* Hussars were bolder, but their attempts to brush past the 13th Infantry were quickly driven off by the accurate fire of the Bavarian artillery. Their infantry supports (*Brod* Grenzer and eight companies of *Lindenau*) could do no better. Help was soon at hand, however, as GM von Bianchi advanced up the constricted valley toward Oberscherm. The *Duka* Infantry suffered badly under heavy fire and stalled, but Bianchi got some of his guns up and sent two battalions of *Gyulai* into the wood that formed the seam between the 13th and 6th Light. Despite a determined defence, the Hungarians of *Gyulai* advanced quickly, outflanking Oberscherm as the reinvigorated men of *Duka* stormed it from the front. By 10 a.m. the tiny village was in Bianchi's hands and the 13th Infantry's left was unhinged. To make matters worse, Hohenfeld's brigade was deploying west of the main road near Strass.

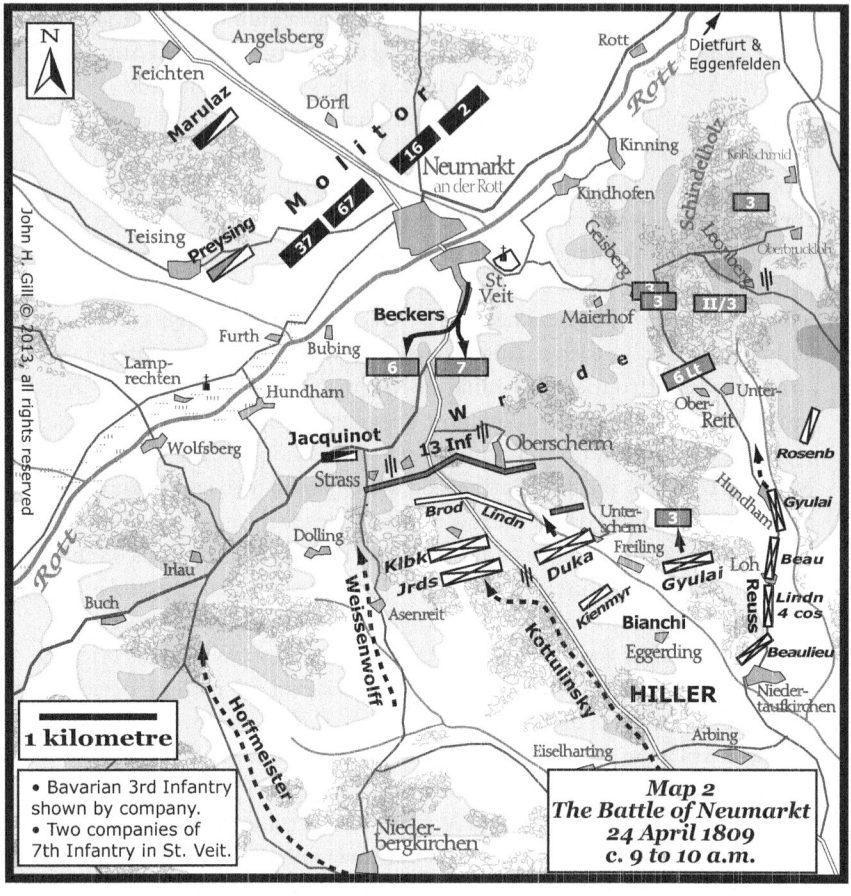

• Bavarian 3rd Infantry shown by company.
• Two companies of 7th Infantry in St. Veit.

Map 2
The Battle of Neumarkt
24 April 1809
c. 9 to 10 a.m.

Wrede was equal to the crisis, committing three companies of 6th Infantry to hold Hohenfeld in check, while his guns battered *Duka's* left with a storm of shot and canister. Shaken by this gunnery and disordered by their advance through the village and broken terrain, the Hungarians were unable to resist a sudden counter-attack by four other companies of 6th Infantry. Bianchi's men were soon stumbling to the rear in disorder and, by about 10.30 a.m., the Bavarians once more controlled Oberscherm.

Almost immediately, a new danger arose. While Bianchi was moving on Oberscherm, Reuss was leading the rest of his column—a battalion each of *Gyulai* and *Beaulieu*, as well as the four remaining companies of *Lindenau*—

off to the right to outflank Wrede (the other battalion of *Beaulieu* remained near Loh in reserve). Reuss's force came under heavy artillery fire but pressed ahead despite the crashing shot, the *Gyulai* battalion peeling off left towards Geisberg, the men of *Beaulieu* toward Leonberg on the right. The 6th Light and the combined Schützen of the 3rd Infantry halted *Gyulai's* attack, but the *Beaulieu* battalion forced 3rd Infantry to pull back. Nevertheless, Reuss's troops, disordered by the fighting and difficult ground, made slow progress and the Bavarian left re-established itself near St Veit.

At the monastery, the Bavarians received welcome reinforcement from Molitor. The French general had arrived north of the Rott around 9 a.m. and deployed his division in line along the heights. At Wrede's request, he had immediately detached four companies of 2nd Ligne to Dietfurt to back up the two Bavarian squadrons near Eggenfelden and now, perceiving the threat to Wrede's line of retreat, he sent the rest of 2nd Ligne across the stream to support the Bavarian left.

The hour was now approaching noon and the situation on Wrede's right was deteriorating rapidly. The *Beaulieu* battalion that Reuss had deposited at Loh had managed to stabilise the Austrian centre after Bianchi's retreat, and Weissenwolff was advancing on Hohenfeld's left, south of Strass. Weissenwolff, ideally placed to outflank the entire Bavarian line, diverted his lead battalion (*Deutschmeister*) and his brigade battery to attack Strass. Johann Schnierer of *Deutschmeister* wrote:

> The regiment now began to deploy by battalions, then by companies we had to pass through the woods in front of us; here in thickets we heard and saw the branches fall from the trees as they were struck; there was someone already carrying wounded back; one had his foot smashed, another his arm. Now musket balls whistled past our tense ears. And after we put the woods behind us, there stood the enemy deployed as skirmishers.[43]

Fortunately for the Bavarians, Weissenwolff adhered strictly to Hiller's disposition and pressed on for Furth with his remaining infantry. The Austrian penchant for focusing on terrain objectives and blindly following instructions thus once again assisted their enemies. Nonetheless, Schnierer and his comrades added to the growing pressure on the Bavarians. With his left and centre in serious trouble, it was high time for Wrede to withdraw and, at about noon, he gave the signal to retire over the Rott.

The Bavarian withdrawal coincided with a renewed Austrian attack as Kottulinsky finally decided to commit his men to the struggle. Wrede was again fortunate in that the Austrian general only risked one battalion (I/*Klebek*), but it pushed into Strass after skirmishing with the Bavarian rear guard. The loss of Strass, however, made the position at Oberscherm untenable and the remaining elements of the 6th and 13th Regiments had to retreat. Oberscherm and its dominant ridge again fell into Austrian hands. Wrede had to call on all of his coolness and tactical skill to extricate his division from this new crisis. With support from 2nd Ligne and three 16th Ligne voltigeur companies, however, 7th Infantry held the enemy at bay. Wrede was everywhere, giving orders, directing movements, inspiring his men by his presence and competence. He repeatedly led the men of the 7th Infantry forward to gain time for the rest of his division to escape. In one of these counter-attacks, Oberst Friedrich Graf von Thurn und Taxis, who had only commanded the regiment for five days, was mortally wounded and captured. Thirteen other officers also fell wounded. Although his hat was pierced by a musket ball so that 'the feathers flew about like snow flakes', Wrede left the battle unscathed.[44] Kottulinsky, throwing *Jordis* into the fight on the right of *Klebek*, pushed the remaining Bavarians back into the town, but this obstinate resistance allowed most of the Allies to escape.

By now the scene in Neumarkt was chaotic. The tight confines were crammed with men, horses, guns, and wagons—all under the fire of Austrian artillery and skirmishers. Jacquinot's cavalrymen, jammed amongst the buildings, were thus unable to defend themselves when Austrian infantry broke into the streets. 'Near the outer houses of the little town of Neumarkt', wrote Oberst Emmerich von Bakonyi of *Duka* Infantry, 'I noticed that the enemy cavalry, hindered by the retreating infantry, had shoved itself all together in the narrow alley before the bridge and in the city gate; united with 200 to 300 men of *Klebek* Infantry, I attacked this cavalry.'[45] Shot, bayoneted, or dragged from their horses into captivity, the 2nd Chasseurs took especially heavy losses and fugitives fleeing this disaster greatly increased the disorder at the bridge. Wrede, however, gradually gathered his troops north of the Rott and, at about 3 p.m., the Bavarians fell back on Aich under the protection of Molitor's regiments.

Hiller did not pursue. Weissenwolff, still following the original disposition, put his brigade across the Rott at Furth but halted there, deterred by a lone battalion of 37th Ligne. The third Austrian column arrived long after the battle had ended, to cross the river above Furth and bivouac south-west of Teising. Reuss posted some vedettes across the river and Mesko, after much stalling and complaining, set out to follow Bessières at about 6 p.m. By then it was too late to inflict any further injury on the Allies. Mesko's patrols went as far as Egglkofen, but found it occupied and so they retired to Feichten for the night.

East and west of the main engagement, the Austrian flanking movements had proceeded more or less as planned. Radetzky had marched for Neumarkt from Eggenfelden along the south bank of the Rott as ordered, but the two Bavarian squadrons, soon joined by the four companies of 2nd Ligne, conducted an exemplary delaying action throughout the day. The Allies even managed to capture about 150 of their attackers before breaking off the engagement. Radetzky halted north of Massing, his evening patrols to Ganghofen unsettling the by-now-bewildered Bessières.[46] Behind Radetzky, Reinwald moved to Wurmannsquick and placed the four companies of III/*Mittrowsky* in Eggenfelden. On the Austrian left, Nordmann had had almost no contact. With patrols out towards Velden, his command spent the night at Zangberg.

The battle at Neumarkt was a startling setback for Bessières and a costly one for the Bavarian 2nd Division. The marshal's insistence on fighting south of the Rott with a difficult defile choking its retreat route placed the Bavarians in a dangerous position, and it was only thanks to Wrede's abilities and the steadfastness of the Bavarian and French soldiers that the defeat was not a disaster. The Bavarians had performed coolly in a trying situation, showing great tenacity in defence and demonstrating admirable tactical flexibility. Hiller acknowledged that 'the Bavarian troops under Wrede had fought with extraordinary bravery', and concluded that 'there was no hope of their joining with us.'[47]

The Austrian soldiers had also done well, attacking 'with rare impetuosity', in Wrede's words, and frequently advancing in skirmish order over the choppy, wooded terrain. Habsburg leadership, on the other hand, had contributed little to the success. Although Hiller can be credited with considerable determination in organising his demoralised wing and attacking his pursuers, there is no evidence that he made any effort to control the battle once it began. His subordinate commanders were equally unimaginative and there appears to have been almost no co-ordination among the various attacking columns. It was a battle won by superior numbers and soldier-level courage.[48]

Both sides had paid heavily for their valour. The Bavarians lost between 1,000 and 1,200 men (including some 880 prisoners), and Molitor's casualties totalled approximately 200. Jacquinot's exact losses are not known; we have only Bessières's report that some 200 were *hors de combat* after the battle. Combining these figures gives a total of 1,400–1,600 casualties for the

Allied command as opposed to Austrian losses of approximately 1,400.[49] 'Our regiment's loss of prisoners, missing, and dead was considerable,' wrote Leutnant Franz Joseph Hausmann of the 7th Infantry in his march journal, 'According to the admission of our enemy prisoners, their loss was also very great, as could not be otherwise in a scene of murder where neither side wanted to give in.'[50]

Hiller was unable to exploit his success. During the night he received word of Charles's retreat into Bohemia and, early the next morning, his columns headed back towards the Inn. Bessières, chastened by the events of the 24th and confused by contradictory reports thereafter, kept his force in the vicinity of Vilsbiburg until the fiery Lannes got the pursuit moving again at midday on the 26th. The Battle of Neumarkt, otherwise of little significance in the larger course of the campaign, thus allowed Hiller to retire behind the protection of the Inn and Salzach rivers unmolested.[51]

24–30 APRIL: FROM REGENSBURG TO BURGHAUSEN

Hiller established his headquarters in the St Veit monastery late on the afternoon of 24 April, pleased with the results of the battle and planning to continue his advance the following morning. Around midnight, however, a messenger from the imperial court arrived to report the Hauptarmee's defeat and retreat. This note placed Hiller in command of all forces along the Inn–Salzach line and directed him 'to manoeuvre so that you are not hindered in the defence of the Inn and can secure the right flank of the victorious army in Italy.'[52] Hiller hastened to comply. For the next two days, therefore, he pulled his command south back the way it had just come. 'With what saddened expressions did we observe one another the following day as the march began again,' observed Schnierer, 'but this time with our faces turned inwards towards Austria rather than outwards!'[53] While the bulk of V and VI Corps passed through Neuötting to Burghausen, Radetzky and Kienmayer crossed at Braunau; Nordmann, fearful of being cut off, headed south-west towards Wasserburg.

On arriving in Wasserburg, Nordmann was alarmed to learn that Jellacic was still far to the west. The latter, as we have seen, had left Munich on the night of the 23rd and had marched as far as Steinhöring when Hiller's messenger reached him around midday on 24 April with the order to cover the Rosenheim post road. Jellacic had dutifully turned about and retraced his steps towards Munich, arriving in Zorneding by the evening of the 25th.

His patrols once again probed into Munich's suburbs. Urgent messages from Nordmann finally reached Jellacic at midnight on 25/26 April. He reacted at once, turning his tired troops around and crossing the Inn at Wasserburg on the afternoon of the 26th with his regulars, while directing his Landwehr to retire beyond the Salzach.[54] By the evening of 26 April, therefore, Hiller's entire wing was safely behind the two rivers. The French had done nothing to disturb its movement.

Hiller's two principal corps received substantial reinforcements during this withdrawal as missing third battalions (that is, those not present with their regiments earlier), Landwehr, volunteer battalions, and new drafts of replacements arrived (see Appendix 2).[55] Although their numbers were welcome, the quality of most of these troops was low. The third battalions and replacement detachments were full of raw recruits, many of whom had never fired their muskets, while the Landwehr was ill-trained and only minimally equipped. The volunteer battalions had similar problems; in one case, Hiller sent a newly arrived half-battalion of the 1st *Karl* Legion back across the Danube rather than encumber his army with more untrained and unequipped men to feed.[56]

As his men marched, Hiller occupied himself with the development of a grand scheme for the defence of the Inn. He intended to assemble his principal force east of Braunau on 28 April with Jellacic watching the Salzach south of Burghausen on the left and Dedovich guarding the lower Inn on the right. He apparently thought that he would have considerable time to prepare as he even requested a large body of Insurrection cavalry to make up for his lack of mounted troops! By the time his men were bedding down for the night, however, Massena's advance down the Danube had entirely unhinged Hiller's careful plans.

Oberhaus Interlude

FML Josef von Dedovich comes into the picture at this point because Austria lifted the blockade of the little fortress of Oberhaus on the night of 25/26 April. Sitting on a bluff on the north bank of the Danube, Oberhaus overlooks the confluence of that great river with the Inn coming from the south and the Ilz flowing down from the north. It was and is a dramatic view. Though itself commanded by heights on the eastern side of the Ilz, it dominated Passau and was in a position to interdict any traffic on the Danube. Napoleon intended to make the entire area a grand fortified bridgehead that would afford passage across either the Inn or the Danube while serving as a central logistics depot. He had therefore dispatched a senior engineer, GB Dominique André Chambarlhiac, with seven other engineer officers and a detachment of fifty sappers in late February to oversee construction work.[57] GL Friedrich Freiherr von Montigny commanded the fortress and its garrison: a provisional infantry battalion of 750 men and 100 artillerymen with forty-four guns, howitzers, and mortars.[58]

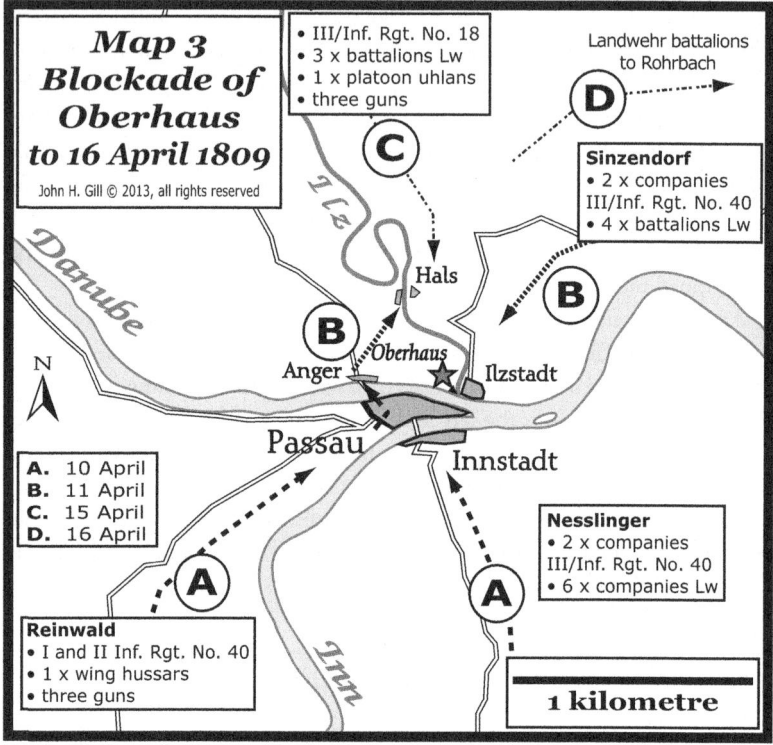

Map 3
Blockade of
Oberhaus
to 16 April 1809

John H. Gill © 2013, all rights reserved

- III/Inf. Rgt. No. 18
- 3 x battalions Lw
- 1 x platoon uhlans
- three guns

Landwehr battalions
to Rohrbach

D

C

Sinzendorf
- 2 x companies III/Inf. Rgt. No. 40
- 4 x battalions Lw

Ilz

Hals

B

B

Anger   *Oberhaus*   Ilzstadt

N

Danube

Passau   Innstadt

A. 10 April
B. 11 April
C. 15 April
D. 16 April

A

A

Nesslinger
- 2 x companies III/Inf. Rgt. No. 40
- 6 x companies Lw

Reinwald
- I and II Inf. Rgt. No. 40
- 1 x wing hussars
- three guns

Inn

1 kilometre

Charles initially envisaged a simple blockade of Oberhaus, a task that could be left to the Landwehr. Several detachments of regulars from II and IV Corps, however, were detailed to conduct the opening phases of this mission along with more than fourteen Landwehr battalions, all under Dedovich's command.[59] Approaching Passau from both sides of the Inn, the Austrians easily secured the city on 10 April and, by the following day, they had thrown a ring around the fortress on both banks of the Ilz as well. The French and Bavarians, taken by surprise, succeeded in escaping into the fortress with little loss, though Chambarlhiac was nearly captured in the process.

The Bavarians rejected the requisite call to surrender, and the blockade proceeded from day to day with little incident beyond a few skirmishes and occasional artillery fire of a more or less perfunctory nature. Bavarian attempts to destroy the Danube bridge by bombardment proved abortive, but a howitzer shell that exploded amid Sinzendorf's Mühlviertel Landwehr east of the Ilz killed one man, wounded four others, and caused the entire brigade to disintegrate. Three hundred men vanished in the confusion and the brigade was only reassembled with difficulty. Indeed, the Landwehr played at best a small role in the blockade and most were soon recalled. Dedovich only asked for three of Richter's ten battalions, and Richter himself never appeared because he was diverted to quell a mutiny in the 1st Prachin Battalion.[60] Three battalions duly arrived north of the fortress on 15 April (2nd, 3rd, and 4th Prachin), but displayed such reluctance to serve outside Austria that Dedovich immediately sent them back to Rohrbach inside Habsburg territory. More useful was the small detachment of regular troops (III/*Stuart* and a platoon of *Merveldt*) who also marched in from the north on 15 April. On 16 April, Oberst Franz von Gratze arrived with *Wallach-Illyria* Grenz Regiment No. 13 to relieve GM von Reinwald's brigade. Reinwald and his regulars left to join IV Corps the following day.[61] By 17 April, therefore, Dedovich was reduced to some 3,400 infantry in three regular battalions (all north of the Danube) and Nesslinger's two Landwehr battalions (occupying Passau and Innstadt), plus thirty-one uhlans, and five field guns. Survey and construction of a series of siege batteries began, and after a week's work and the arrival of siege guns, Dedovich announced that he could probably begin the bombardment on the night of 24/25 April.[62] It was not to be. The dire news from Regensburg made the entire blockade untenable and all now bent their attention to escaping the advancing French. Sending the unused heavy guns back into Austria, Dedovich hastily brought his entire command across the Danube and the Inn to array them in defensive positions opposite Passau under Oberst Gratze. Dedovich himself rode off to set up a new headquarters in Schärding. By 26 April, the only elements of the original blockade force still north of the Danube were Richter's three Prachin Landwehr battalions at Rohrbach. This brigade, and all of the troops between Passau and Braunau, now came under Dedovich's orders as part of Hiller's wing of the army.[63]

The French Advance

Elements of the Allied army had been in motion towards the Inn since 23 April, but the urgency and pace increased as they neared the river. Napoleon in Regensburg did not omit from his calculations the possibility that Charles would return to the offensive, but he assumed the Austrians north and south of the Danube were in full retreat. He therefore oriented the bulk of the Army of Germany to the Habsburg capital, while Davout followed the Hauptarmee towards Bohemia. The emperor arranged the army in three general groups for this drive to the Inn: on the left, Massena was already moving on Passau along the south bank of the Danube, while Lefebvre (1st and 3rd Bavarian Divisions) was in the process of swinging to the right through Freising and Munich. Lannes and Bessières, focusing on Braunau and Burghausen, constituted the centre. Napoleon was now able to place Lannes at the head of 2nd Corps as he had intended since March, and the marshal, with St Hilaire, Tharreau, and Colbert, immediately marched south, accompanied by Piré's light cavalry brigade.[64] Lannes also picked up Demont's small division. Demont had moved to Landshut with Lefebvre, but had been left behind as a support to Bessières when the Bavarians shifted up the Isar towards Munich. The Württembergers (minus detachments)[65] with the 1st and 2nd Heavy Cavalry Divisions served as a general reserve. Reports from Davout showed that Bellegarde no longer posed a threat to the western reaches of the Danube, so the forces there were free for other employment. Boudet, who had occupied Regensburg on the 24th, thus moved to Straubing, and Rouyer's Germans began shifting east to replace him. Bernadotte, approaching from Dresden with the Saxon 9th Corps, received instructions to enter Bohemia. Dupas's small division, GB Pierre Joseph Bruyère's light cavalry brigade, and the Guard were all hastening to join the army and would reach the immediate theatre of operations within a week.

News arriving in his headquarters on the 25th, however, caused Napoleon to re-evaluate the situation and consider the possibility that the Austrians might assume an unexpectedly aggressive posture. Not only did the emperor learn of Hiller's surprising turn-about at Neumarkt, he also received an assessment from Davout stating that Charles could be considering a move to Passau to unite with Hiller. A skirmish at Nittenau, Jellacic's march back towards Munich, and troubling (but erroneous) intelligence from Boudet in Straubing contributed to this impression.[66] Rather than lapse into caution, however, Napoleon responded by accelerating the offensive in the Danube valley. Reading the Austrian situation more accurately than Davout, he reasoned that a rapid invasion of Habsburg territory would upset any plans harboured by Charles and would force the Austrian Main Army into precipitous retreat to the east. On the other hand, thrusting Bernadotte into Bohemia now appeared too risky, so the marshal was directed to march for Regensburg and cover that city against any Austrian threat from the north.[67] Davout was to join the army south of the Danube as soon as Bernadotte arrived 'because it is important that you be present for the battle that will take place between Passau and Vienna.'[68] Similarly, Boudet would remain in Straubing until the situation clarified; Württemberg GM Christian von Stettner was sent to Straubing with the Leib Chevaulegers Regiment to provide Boudet with a mounted reconnaissance capability. Napoleon, however, rode to Landshut, taking himself—as usual—to the area where he expected the decisive action to occur.

Along with their emperor, almost 130,000 Allied soldiers were thus on the road to the Austrian frontier. Whether through chilling downpours or choking dust, their march left its mark both on the countryside and on those who traversed it. One of these was Henri Beyle, better known by his pen name Stendahl, a commissary official who 'studied the curious disorder that war leaves behind it':

The most striking thing was the large quantity of excellent straw, quite fresh and still quite crisp, that was scattered over the fields. Every half hour we came upon a bivouac; but, even apart from these straw huts, the fields were covered with it. There were caps, shoes, a lot of jackets of cheap cloth, wheels, shafts of hand-carts, and many little squares of paper that had been wrapped around packets of cartridges.

From time to time we came to the top of a hill from which we could survey two or three miles of road. We could descry, in a stifling cloud of dust, two files of cuirassiers slipping through the convoys, sometimes at a walk but more often at a trot, and deviating as often as they could onto the fields on either side. In the middle of the road there was an artillery convoy, and at the sides there were hundreds of vehicles carrying regimental baggage, together with officers' carriages . . . As you can suppose, the bacchanalia was still more hellish in a little town of two thousand souls which at present harbours a population of forty thousand men who have not dined and don't give a damn for anything in the world.[69]

Despite its numbers and the seeming 'bacchanalia' of its march, the army moved rapidly. Lannes's men, for example, covered seventy to eighty kilometres in two days to reach Vilsbiburg and Geisenhausen by the evening of 25 April. Lannes himself arrived in Vilsbiburg in the early hours of 26 April. Here he found that Bessières, trammelled by caution after the rebuff at Neumarkt, had lost touch with the enemy. Lannes injected new vitality into his fellow marshal and his ad hoc command moved out during the afternoon. Probing gingerly south, however, Molitor and two of the light cavalry regiments only reached Erharting and Rohrbach, north of the Isen, by evening. The other two cavalry regiments rode towards Ampfing, followed by Wrede's division.[70] The energetic Wrede, on the other hand, pushed ahead to Mühldorf and had restored the bridge by early morning of the 27th. Lannes, recognising that his troops were exhausted and that it was too late to catch the Austrians north of the Inn, granted his corps a much-needed rest day and used the opportunity to recall Jacquinot's troopers from their scattered outposts. Behind Lannes, Vandamme[71] and the two heavy cavalry divisions had reached the area around Landshut along with GD Frédéric Henri Walther and initial elements of the Imperial Guard (970 cavalry, 1,800 infantry, one battery).[72]

On the far right flank, Jellacic's surprising return towards Munich occasioned momentary alarms and excursions.[73] These included an unpleasant experience for King Max Joseph, who was in the process of re-occupying his capital when news of Austrian patrols on the outskirts of the city forced him and his tiny escort to decamp in great haste. On the morning of 26 April, however, Crown Prince Ludwig led his division into Munich, where his men had the pleasure of receiving food, drink, cheers, and the full attention of a grateful citizenry. 'But we were not allowed to halt,' wrote a disappointed artilleryman, 'rather on and on it went, so that we soon came into enemy territory.'[74] Deroy moved his main body to Erding and Lefebvre endeavoured vainly to bring Wrede back into the fold of 7th Corps. The latter, however, existed in a command limbo for the next several days, remaining in contact with Bessières, sending reports to Lefebvre and army headquarters, but taking his instructions from Berthier in most cases.

Massena's corps made the most important move on the 26th.[75] Pushing down the Danube valley from Vilshofen via Fürstenzell, the 4th Corps advance guard (4th Cuirassiers and 14th Chasseurs) arrived in Passau at 8 a.m., followed at midday by Carra Saint-Cyr, Claparède, and 6th Cuirassiers.[76] They were greeted by Montigny and Chambarlhiac, who had hurried to re-occupy the city as soon as they had learned of the Austrian withdrawal.

Massena wasted no time in seizing the vital bridge. Though the Austrians had removed the flooring on evacuating the city, the pilings and many of the beams were still intact. It was defended by two companies of I/*Wallach-Illyria* (perhaps 350 men), who had fortified themselves within the small, wall-enclosed suburb of Innstadt. The Grenzer were well posted, but there were few nearby supports to assist them against the sort of assault Massena was about to mount.[77] The marshal sent several hundred of Claparède's men down the Danube on boats with the task of landing east of Innstadt and attacking the suburb from the rear. Simultaneously, three companies of the Bavarian garrison began crossing the Inn on boats above and below the town to assault the north and south gates.[78] As these flanking columns distracted the defenders, Claparède was to launch other troops directly across the partly-demolished bridge. He selected the Tirailleurs du Po for this key mission, but this veteran battalion did not wait for the other elements to get into position.[79] The flanking units were still clambering out of their boats when the tirailleurs attacked. Dashing across the remaining beams of the bridge 'like the furies and passing one by one under a most terrible fusillade', the tirailleurs stormed into Innstadt as citizens opened the town's gates for the other attackers.[80] The Grenzer surrendered after a brief struggle. Massena, observing the assault from a nearby building, was so impressed with the performance of the Tirailleurs du Po that he asked Napoleon to transfer the battalion and its sister unit, the Tirailleurs Corses, to Boudet's weak division.[81] Having captured 227 officers and men in the town, GB Coëhorn launched an immediate pursuit and took another 150 prisoners from the Grenzer and III/*Stuart* as the surprised Austrians scrambled east towards Münzkirchen. Total Austrian casualties were 400 to 450; French and Bavarian losses were negligible.[82] By nightfall, Claparède's division and 14th Chasseurs were on the far bank and, thanks to Massena's unrelenting determination, the bridge was passable for artillery and other wheeled vehicles by 2 a.m. on the 27th.[83] 'All has gone well,' wrote Coëhorn to his wife, 'and we are now in the land of our enemies.'[84]

Upstream at Schärding another little river-crossing drama was in progress. Dedovich, having been awake all night with the evacuation of Passau, was refreshing himself from his exertions when an excited Landwehr officer burst into his room near midday to announce the approach of a large enemy force. This was the Baden Light Dragoons and a French cuirassier regiment, the vanguard of Legrand's division. The division, accompanied by the Baden light horse and the 2nd Brigade of Espagne's division, had swung away from 4th Corps at Fürstenzell to march directly on Schärding. Fear and confusion immediately broke out among the raw troops of the town's temporary garrison, and the mood edged towards hysteria when Legrand arrived with his main body at around 2 p.m. French and Baden horse artillery trotted forwards to open fire while the Baden Jäger Battalion and French voltigeurs skirmished with Austrians in the houses along the river. Dedovich only had three guns and his 6,500 infantry were almost all Landwehr and untrained recruits.[85] Their anxiety exploded into panic and pandemonium as the shells began to fall. Colonel François René Pouget of the 26th Léger noted that 'the enemy displayed some artillery and sent us some shells and balls that did us no harm', and the Baden battery commander reported that Allied artillery fire silenced the handful of Austrian guns within ten minutes.[86] Legrand demanded Schärding be evacuated or it would face bombardment, but the harassed Dedovich refused, despite the unpromising circumstances. Legrand therefore unlimbered two of his division's foot batteries and opened fire as threatened. 'Before long, thick clouds of smoke rose up out of the roofs and wrapped the town in a dreadful darkness; suddenly flames leaped up brightly from many places at once and spread in all directions.'[87]

Although he was personally anxious and his shaky command hardly seemed capable of resisting a serious attack, Dedovich hung on until a courier brought a message from Gratze announcing that the French were across the Inn. Around the same time, he received word from Nesslinger in Wernstein that his Landwehr had largely fled. With his flank in danger, the town afire, and his force about to disintegrate, Dedovich put Schärding's remaining grain stores to the torch and withdrew towards Eferding in disorder. Legrand immediately sent the 26th Léger across the Inn in boats to chase off the nervous Austrian rear guard and protect the crossing site while he set to work repairing the bridge. Losses among the regular troops were small: other than a wounded Baden gunner, the Allies reported none, and the Austrian total among the line recruits and a tiny detachment of Grenzer came to no more than fifty. Landwehr losses were another matter. There is no record of exact casualties at Schärding, but desertion reduced these battalions to shadows during the next several days. Three of Sinzendorf's battalions lost 25 per cent of their men between 26 and 29 April, while the fourth (2nd Mühlviertel) seems to have dissolved entirely. Nesslinger's two battalions, numbering some 1,600 men in March, had hardly seen any combat, yet counted barely 550 by the end of April. The morale of the remainder could hardly have been exemplary. The formerly charming town, turned to ashes, paid dearly for being the site of this brief engagement.[88]

The day thus came to a close with the Inn barrier breached before it had even been established. Munich had been restored to its monarch, Bessières had closed on the Inn opposite Neuötting, and Wrede was across the river at Mühldorf. The French situation, however, contained its own vulnerabilities. Napoleon had directed Massena 'to take in the flank the corps that debouched from Braunau' (Hiller) if at all possible. The marshal, having unhinged Hiller's intended defensive line, was therefore planning to march for Schärding on the 27th along the east bank of the river 'to join with General Legrand and seek out the enemy'.[89] His 4th Corps, however, was nearly isolated, straddling a major river and far from any hope of timely support. Napoleon recognised the danger and urged Lannes 'to pass the Inn and the Salzach promptly to make a diversion for the Duke of Rivoli', but for several days Massena would be on his own.[90]

Hiller from 27 to 30 April: Vacillations in the Rain

Though he knew little of the enemy, during the 27th Hiller likewise concluded that the French across the Inn might be vulnerable. Massena indeed shifted south to Schärding, but as far as the Austrian commander could tell, the Allies were otherwise quiescent. Fortunately for the French, Hiller had his own problems: his troops were tired, the quality of the Landwehr and recruits left much to be desired, logistics were unsatisfactory, and the weather had again turned cold and rainy. On the other hand, Hiller feared (quite correctly as it turned out) that he would be censured if he abandoned the line of the Inn too readily. After a period of vexed vacillation, therefore, he decided to attack on the morning of 28 April. His discomfort with his situation led him, however, to adopt a half-measure. Rather than launch an all-out attack or pull his entire force back towards the Traun, he placed FML Schustekh in charge of Mesko, Radetzky, Hohenfeld, and Reinwald (approximately 10,000 men), with orders to move against the French at Schärding, while he marched the bulk of his army east towards Ried. But the attack never occurred. Hiller's time line was unrealistic and it proved impossible to assemble the attack force on the 28th. Schustekh was thus forced to postpone his advance until the following day. By then, the situation had changed and the Habsburg generals, fearing they could be taken in the rear, called off the move entirely. Any opportunity to injure Massena's corps or throw it back across the Inn was thereby lost.

Similarly, Massena cancelled the attack he had planned for 28 April. After concentrating his available troops on both banks of the Inn around Schärding on the 27th, he learned that Lannes and Bessières were still north of the river. With the rest of the army so far away and floating chunks of

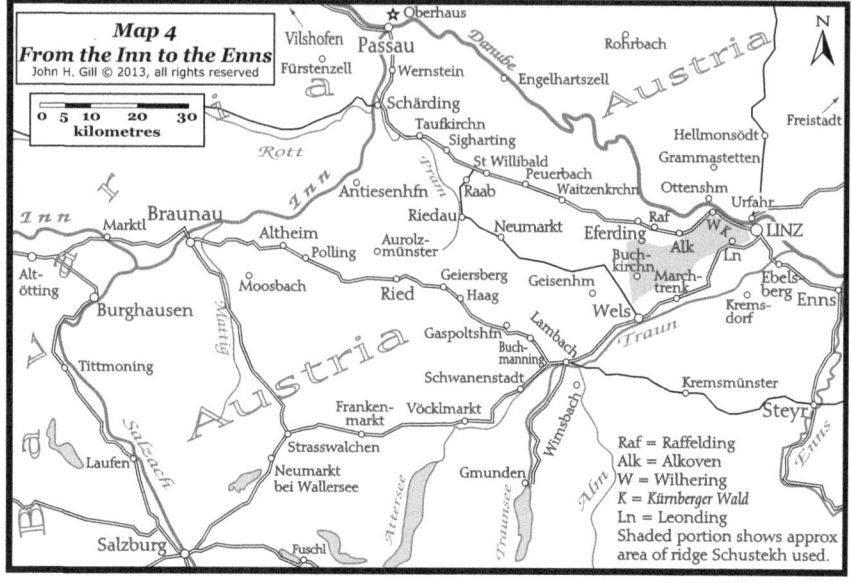

charred wood on the river indicating that the bridges upstream had been burned, Massena rescinded his attack order and situated his corps to await developments.[91]

In the meantime, Napoleon had reached the Inn with the main body of the army. By nightfall on 27 April, Lannes had halted north of Mühldorf with the first echelon of the Guard, the heavy cavalry, and Vandamme crowding the road all the way back to Neumarkt. Other elements of the Guard were approaching Landshut. Bessières, serving more or less as advance guard for Lannes, had crossed the Inn at Mühldorf; he now had Molitor around Altötting and his cavalry (Marulaz, Jacquinot, and Piré) between that town and Burghausen. Wrede, no longer under Bessières but not truly commanded by Lefebvre either, conducted a personal reconnaissance with Napoleon and received direct orders to push south for Laufen on the Salzach in an effort to intercept the retreating Jellacic. Lefebvre, urged by the emperor to send 'strong parties to Kufstein so that the siege might be lifted', detached II/4 Infantry, a squadron of the 1st Dragoons, and one gun under Chef d'Escadron Montélégier to accomplish this mission.[92] The rest of the 1st and 3rd Bavarian Divisions had closed on the Inn at Wasserburg. The 7th Corps, however, was much diminished by stragglers left behind during the gruelling marches of the previous several days (averaging thirty-four kilometres per day since 23 April). As an artilleryman remembered: 'Half rain, half snow fell from the heavens under storming winds, icy cold . . . I mixed in with the infantry and marched on, stomping the mud into the consistency of thin dough . . . My shoes were softened rags, my gaiter straps hung in ruins, the gaiters themselves were soggy with mud.'[93]

The bulk of Hiller's command was around Moosbach on the night of 27/28 April, but Kienmayer's small corps was already at Ried, and Dedovich was about two kilometres south-east of St Martin.[94] Hiller also established a screen of light troops towards the Inn, but one that changed in composition and mission on a daily basis. In a bewildering series of marches and counter-marches, the brigades of Radetzky, Reinwald, Hohenfeld, Mesko, Nordmann, and Bianchi all played a part in this covering force between 26 April and 2 May, as did Oberst Gratze's *Wallach-Illyria* Grenzer and Oberstleutnant Steigentesch with his weary two companies of the 2nd Vienna Volunteer Battalion at Engelhartszell.[95] Some of the newly arrived battalions were assigned to these brigades, and 'orphan' units that belonged to other corps (such as III/*Czartoryski*) were also involved, making the order of battle a complete mare's nest. Hiller compounded the potential for misunderstanding by repeatedly changing the various chains of command and by continually shifting subordinate units about. Most of Schustekh's troops were quickly stripped away, for instance, so that his command soon dwindled to Hohenfeld's brigade and part of the *Kienmayer* Hussars. Besides representing an inefficient use of resources, these shifting arrangements meant that potentially dangerous gaps appeared in the army's command procedures: units were forgotten, reporting was disordered, and Hiller often had little idea of the true composition of his screening force.[96]

Of the more distant flanking forces, Jellacic's division on the far left was behind the Alz between Altenmarkt and the Chiemsee. At Hiller's direction, he had also placed a detachment of four *O'Reilly* Chevaulegers squadrons at Laufen under Oberstleutnant Simon von Sardagna.[97] Richter's three Prachin Landwehr battalions were still north of the Danube on the extreme right.

Having decided not to attack on the 28th, Hiller moved the Austrian main body to Ried under rain that fell 'in rivers, all day without pause.'[98] Oppressed by such conditions, Hiller's men spent the next several days pulling back towards Linz via Haag, Lambach, and Wels. Charles had issued orders to this effect on the 24th, directing Hiller to cross the Danube at Linz to rendezvous with the Hauptarmee; he was also to ensure that a proper bridgehead was constructed so that the army would have easy access to the south bank of the river. Hiller was sceptical. He seems to have believed that the French were already headed for his destination and personally doubted that he would be able to reach Linz ahead of the enemy. He knew that the 'bridgehead' existed only on paper and that its garrison consisted of a Landwehr battalion and two infantry regimental depots. He was thus inclined to seek safety behind the waters of the Enns or in the mountains to the south—in other words, away from the Hauptarmee. A meeting with Archduke Maximilian on the 29th changed his mind. The archduke, sent from the Hauptarmee to help organise the defences around Linz, knew the importance that Charles attached to uniting with Hiller as quickly as possible. He also carried a letter from Franz expressing great imperial displeasure that the Schärding–Linz road had been left completely unprotected. The Kaiser's note, augmented by Maximilian's verbal arguments, persuaded Hiller to march for Linz in accordance with Charles's instructions and the Kaiser's intentions.[99]

Hiller moved the bulk of his army to Lambach on the 29th under the soaking cold rain, while his screening forces sparred with Allied advance troops. A small skirmish flared near Riedau, where exploring Baden Dragoons overthrew a platoon of *Stipsicz* Hussars before being chased off by two squadrons of *Kienmayer*. More serious was a probe Massena launched through Antiesenhofen towards Altheim. One French column, led by Coëhorn, pushed almost as far as St Martin, forcing the Austrian screening troops (Radetzky and Reinwald) to withdraw to Aurolzmünster and Ried for fear of being trapped too close to the Inn. The other French force, the 14th Chasseurs, the voltigeurs of Legrand's division, and a regiment of cuirassiers reached the outskirts of Altheim, scattering two companies of the 5th *EH Karl* Legion that were trying to withdraw from their outposts along the river. The rest of the Legion battalion and III/*Czartoryski* barely escaped a similar fate, apparently owing to inadequate zeal on the part of the chasseurs.[100] The French were unable to exploit their momentary advantage, however, and most of the Austrian soldiers reassembled during the night. Losses in killed, wounded, and missing during the day were relatively minor—approximately 118 Austrians and a few dozen French.[101] Massena, having learned that 'the enemy is retiring on Linz, Wels, and Lambach', withdrew his troops and awaited 'with impatience the order to advance'.[102] Boudet and the Württemberg Leib Chevaulegers reached Schärding that evening, and the marshal pulled the rest of 4th Corps back towards the Inn and remained in place on 30 April. When the Austrians sent patrols towards Altheim on the morning of 1 May, therefore, they were surprised to find the area free of French forces.[103]

Little of note occurred on 30 April as the weary Habsburg soldiers trudged through the drenching rain. Austrian reconnaissance was lame and the reports reaching Hiller in Lambach that evening and on into 1 May led him to a completely mistaken view of the situation. The lack of activity by the French and some bad intelligence suggested that 'the enemy will not undertake anything serious against us any time soon.'[104] A report forwarded by Nordmann was especially misleading as it stated that the Salzach was fordable above Burghausen.[105] Nothing could have been further from the truth, but Hiller accepted it and thus concluded that the French must be very weak indeed if they chose not to cross such a 'minor' obstacle. Moreover, Hiller was keenly aware of the Kaiser's desire to see the Inn defended and was acutely anxious about being blamed for leaving the river too soon.[106] An angry message he received from Franz on the morning of 1 May doubtless sharpened the edge of his fears. Pointedly rebuking Hiller for not attacking, the Kaiser sternly instructed him 'to ensure the safety of Linz, then exert every effort to gather reliable information about the enemy, attack him, if a favourable opportunity should still arise, and maintain yourself at Linz for as long as possible'. Arriving at the same time that morning was a letter from Charles that also stressed the importance of closing on the Danube.[107] In response to these instructions, Hiller marched the main body of his force to Wels on 1 May, while his rather hotchpotch collection of light troops screened the army's flank towards the west.

As they sought their sodden bivouacs north-west of Wels on the road to Eferding that evening, Hiller's three corps were tired, wet, and gloomy. Poor logistical support compounded the miseries inflicted by the weather. Much of the army's train had been lost at Landshut or had already been sent east to safety, and acquisition of provisions in the narrow confines of the bivouacs proved difficult. Privations were especially severe among the Landwehr, and several officers complained that their men had:

> no greatcoats, no trousers, nothing that could protect them from the cold and wet; in addition, the troops have already gone without a warm meal for four days because they lack kettles, lack canteens, lack the minimum they would need to bivouac; and now that such wretched weather has begun they no longer have a single stitch of dry clothing.[108]

The numerous untrained and partially equipped recruits also caused consternation, being unruly and difficult to control.[109] Hiller thus intended to give his army an extended rest at Wels before marching it to Eferding and committing it to combat against the supposedly weak Allied force around Schärding.[110] He anticipated no French action in the near term. Here, again, we encounter a senior Austrian general who expected the French to grant him several days' respite to rest, feed, re-equip, and reorganise his forces before renewing the campaign. As with Charles at Regensburg or Hiller himself after Neumarkt, the Habsburg commander south of the Danube was about to be rudely disabused of this illusion.

Operational Pause at Burghausen

Hiller had been fortunate that difficulties in repairing the bridge at Burghausen imposed a frustrating operational pause on Napoleon and thereby restrained Massena as well. The French had occupied Burghausen on 28 April. The three Landwehr companies guarding on the eastern bank 'threw away their muskets and abandoned their post,'[111] but Nordmann had been most thorough in his destruction of the bridge: 'of all that wooden bridge, we could only perceive the upper portions of some of the charred pilings.'[112] Moreover, the Salzach here was more than 100 metres broad and its waters very swift in the wake of the spring rains. Bertrand and his engineers,'harassed by the marshal and all of the troop commanders', worked ceaselessly to restore the span but made slow progress. Lannes was especially agitated. He 'stormed around the workers with a truly southern impatience', remarked one of Bertrand's staff officers.[113] Napoleon's discontent may well be imagined.

In addition to impatience, the army suffered from lack of victuals. Lannes, Bessières, and parts of the Guard were packed together between Burghausen and Mühldorf in a region already exhausted by Hiller's extended stay. 'We are dying of hunger', Berthier wrote to Daru on 30 April.[114] The weather, of course, was no more clement to the French than to their Austrian adversaries, and the men grumbled under the 'horrible deluges' and 'violent, glacial winds' as they waited to renew their advance.[115]

Impatience, discomforts, shortages, and tactical demands notwithstanding, Napoleon also gave his attention to strategic considerations. From Eugene in Italy, the emperor had learned that his Army of Italy had suffered a serious reverse and had withdrawn behind the Piave. In stinging letters, he admonished the viceroy in the sternest terms, condemning the lack of detailed reporting from Italy and Eugene's exaggerated anxieties of being outflanked through the Tyrol: 'The more I reflect, the more I am persuaded that my affairs in Italy are ruined and that you do not dare to tell me.' In the absence of more precise information, he could at best proffer general operational guidance and, in a tone of resignation, suggest that Eugene consider relinquishing command of the army to Murat. For his part, the emperor sent orders to Lefebvre to press strong detachments deep into the Tyrol, Styria, and Carinthia as soon as possible to quell the rebellion and to force an Austrian evacuation of the region.[116]

The rebellion in the Tyrol also drew Napoleon's eye as a potential threat to the army's lines of communication and to the stability of his German allies. Worries expressed by his ambassador in Berlin and news of a brief uprising in Westphalia (Dörnberg's revolt, 22–4 April) led him to accelerate measures to protect his strategic rear. Marshal François Kellermann was thus placed in command of a new formation entitled 'the Observation Corps of the Elbe'. With his headquarters at Hanau and 12,000 to 13,000 troops (three of the reserve demi-brigades from eastern France and Beaumont's dragoons from Strasbourg), Kellermann was told to 'take yourself wherever may be necessary to give succour to the King of Westphalia and to re-establish tranquillity'.[117] He would thus augment King Jerome's 10th Corps and be available to react to any English threats to the coast as well as disturbances within Germany. To guard the southern border of the Rheinbund, Napoleon wrote to Friedrich of Württemberg, requesting deployment of a force of 2,000 men on the Vorarlberg frontier to 'prevent the insurrection in the Tyrol from spreading'.[118] Bavaria was already in the process of forming six reserve battalions for internal defence and would soon resort to other emergency measures to counter the dangers from the Tyrolian rebels.[119] Napoleon had no illusions about the quality of these raw forces, but, as with Jerome's 10th Corps, he counted on deception to bolster their physical presence and to deter unrest. Kellermann, for example, was told 'to spread the rumour that you are going to Hanau with an observation corps of 50,000 men'.[120] Furthermore, he was confident that 'the news of our victories will calm heads a bit' and that the impending capture of Salzburg and his arrival 'under the walls of Vienna' in a few days would suffice to deflate insurrectionary tendencies in Germany.[121]

Defending the Danubian Monarchy

Austria's leaders also reviewed their strategic situation as Napoleon fumed on the banks of the Salzach. They wavered between shock at the defeats in Bavaria and hopeful illusion about the condition of the Allied army. Their actions, therefore, were a combination of prudent defensive measures and wishful thinking on the operational front.

The illusions among the Habsburg hierarchy stemmed from residual pre-war assumptions, reluctance to acknowledge a policy gone badly wrong, and a less pessimistic appraisal of the state of the Hauptarmee. The courier who arrived in Schärding on the morning of 24 April bearing Charles's grim description of the defeat at Regensburg, was said to have cried 'All is lost!'[122] Five days later, the initial dismay had faded. The Hauptarmee 'has not suffered as much as was at first believed'[123] and the French appeared to be doing nothing: Charles had been permitted to escape and there was little to report from the Inn. Charles, Hiller, and the imperial court all drew the same false conclusion: Napoleon's army, weary and reduced by the recent fighting, required a rest to restore itself. Moreover, many senior Habsburg officers and officials assumed that the French emperor would have to wait for more reinforcements to arrive from Spain, particularly the Imperial Guard.[124] They took for granted that these reinforcements would come in the form of complete divisions and corps. None of this speaks very well for Austrian strategic intelligence, but the central error was the assumption that the enemy would behave as they wished and would therefore vouchsafe the Danube monarchy the time it needed to recover from Regensburg.

Prudence, however, was not forgotten in Franz's court. The defeats in Bavaria had undermined public morale, the army needed to reconstitute itself, and the war had now come to the monarchy's borders, so a number of defensive steps, some quite desperate and urgent, were taken in the final days of April. One of the top priorities was to fortify Linz and allot a garrison. As there were no trained regulars available and only one Landwehr battalion around the city, Austrian officers resorted to the expedient of using the depot 'divisions' (two companies each) of *Klebek* and *Jordis* to provide some security for Linz and its immediate vicinity; by the end of the month, they would be joined by the 9th Jägers depot company, two late-arriving companies of *Lindenau*, a replacement detachment, and the remaining two serviceable squadrons of the *Levenehr* Dragoons. All of these odd bits and pieces were to be lashed together under the command of Oberst Anton Graf Hardegg.[125] Five more Landwehr battalions were to march to Linz to assist with construction work and a pontoon bridge was to be established to augment the existing span. Hiller sent FML Kottulinsky to lend urgency to preparations in the city and, as we have seen, Archduke Maximilian arrived from the Main Army with a similar charter. Behind the archduke came Stutterheim with the *Vincent* Chevaulegers, the *Ferdinand* Hussars, and a cavalry battery, sent by Charles to secure or destroy the bridges at Linz and Mauthausen. Stutterheim was to come under Hiller's orders on his arrival, giving Hiller a much-needed supplement to his cavalry.[126] Hiller did not get any replacement for his lost bridging assets. A new bridging train was indeed established with remarkable speed but, after considerable rolling back and forth in different directions, it was sent trundling off to Charles in Bohemia.

Among other problems, Austria south of the Danube was awash with stragglers, marauders, and deserters. One officer estimated that 10,000 such men had crossed the Traun heading east by the end of April. They 'roam about, commit excesses, and disturb the entire region', he complained. Collection points commanded by senior officers were thus established in Enns, Steyr, and several other cities, but these marauders continued to pose a serious threat to internal order and welfare.[127]

As Austria looked to its defences, the Landwehr received a great deal of attention. The Habsburg authorities placed considerable faith in a large 'corps' of Landwehr to be collected behind the Traisen at St Pölten under FML Andreas Graf O'Reilly. This would comprise thirteen Upper Austrian, nineteen Lower Austrian, and twelve Moravian Landwehr battalions (presumably some 36,000 men) and, it was hoped, would be supplemented by the six Vienna Volunteer battalions and by two regiments of Insurrection cavalry. These would constitute the core of a force entrusted to Archduke Maximilian, who was now charged with overseeing defensive preparations both in Lower Austria and in Vienna. Receiving his new orders on 30 April, Maximilian found there was much to do. He was told, however, that the threat he would have to face was likely no more than cavalry raids or light detachments with no artillery; he thus addressed his daunting tasks with considerable confidence.[128]

Confidence was not the predominant sentiment in the Habsburg capital in late April. News of victory—spread by an official bulletin after Charles's over-hasty note to Franz before the disaster on the 22nd—prompted exuberant demonstrations in the streets: 'All Vienna was in a frenzy of joy.'[129] Rumours spread that Napoleon himself had been beaten. 'I hope he will lose his head entirely', wrote the 17-year-old Archduchess Maria Louise to her father on 25 April.[130] Correspondingly, 'the disappointment was dreadful!' when subsequent couriers brought more accurate accounts.[131] 'It is impossible to depict', wrote one diarist, 'how this dismayed everyone, how it crushed every hope.'[132] A proclamation released by Archduke Rainer to soothe public anxiety had the opposite effect.[133] Discussion of defensive preparations and the departure of the imperial family, though kept as quiet as possible, only intensified popular fears. Before departing Vienna on 8 April, Franz had instructed his family to be ready to move to Ofen in Hungary 'at a moment's notice.'[134] That moment had now come and Kaiserin Maria Ludovica, accompanied by the youthful Maria Louise, headed south on 4 May. Those with money and means soon followed.[135]

THE FALL OF SALZBURG

On 29 April, as the Habsburg imperial family was rolling out of Vienna and Napoleon was reassuring Jerome about the salutary impact of the Army of Germany's imminent advances, Allied forces were approaching Salzburg. Although temporarily stymied by the need to repair the Burghausen bridge, some elements of the army remained active. Bessières, for instance, sent some of his light cavalry probing south along the Salzach on the morning of the 28th. Two squadrons, one each from the 1st and 2nd Chasseurs, came upon the 1st Hausruck Landwehr as it was trying to cross the river at Tittmoning. Chasing the hapless militiamen into a wood, the French surrounded them and persuaded their commander to surrender by telling him that a powerful column of infantry was approaching. Some 500 Austrians thus went into captivity as the French troopers returned to Burghausen.[136]

The direct threat to Salzburg, however, came from further to the army's right, where Wrede, pushing his division hard, drove down the west bank of the Alz to Trostberg in a night march on the 27th and forced a crossing of the river at 6 a.m. on the morning of 28 April. After a brief rest, he continued east to reach Tittmoning at 2 p.m. The French chasseurs and their captives had already departed, but, probing south from Tittmoning, a squadron of the Bavarian 3rd Chevaulegers overthrew a half-squadron of O'Reilly Chevaulegers at Fridolfing and collected the intelligence Wrede needed to continue his advance.[137] Granted permission from Napoleon 'to act as you judge appropriate to do as much damage as possible to the enemy', Wrede immediately sent Preysing off into the darkness towards Laufen with six squadrons.[138] They appeared outside the town at 9 p.m. to find the bridge in flames, but the citizens opened the gates for their countrymen, and the troopers, chasing off a few Austrians, were able to save many of the local salt boats from destruction. The Bavarians immediately set to work repairing the bridge. Meanwhile, at Tittmoning, GM von Beckers with 6th Light and 6th Infantry paddled across the Salzach in boats during the night. Before dawn

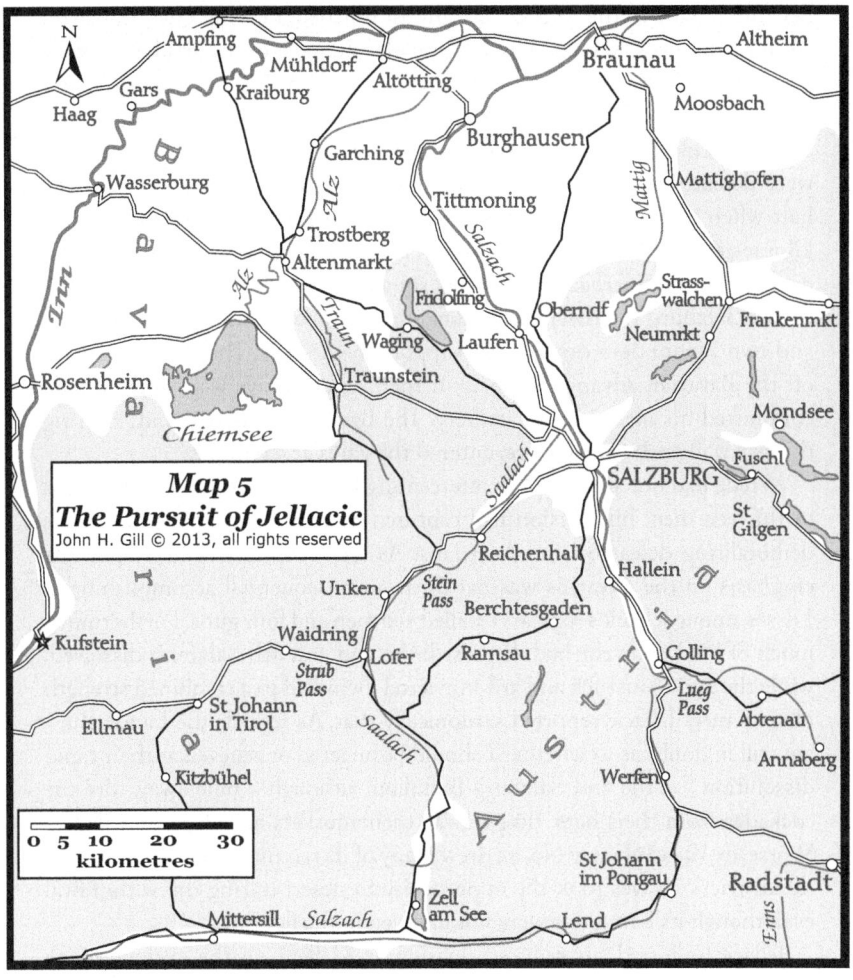

Map 5
The Pursuit of Jellacic

on the 29th, he was headed for Laufen along the eastern bank while the rest of the division marched on the western side.

The Austrians that Preysing's men had struck at Fridolfing were from Oberstleutnant Sardagna's four squadrons at Laufen. Sardagna had been reinforced by two companies of II/*Esterhazy* and a replacement detachment of the same regiment, but he withdrew to Salzburg in the night.[139] When Wrede's troops reached Laufen along both banks of the Salzach on the morning of 29 April, therefore, the enemy had long since fled and repairs to the bridge were almost finished. Leaving GM Franz von Minucci on the west bank with his brigade and most of the artillery, Wrede pressed on for Salzburg along the east bank with Beckers, Preysing, and his light battery. Sardagna, reinforced to six squadrons, attempted to halt the advancing Bavarians at Acharting around 1 p.m., but his chevaulegers were defeated and Preysing's men surged ahead. They were brought to a halt when they reached the main Austrian position near Bergheim, four kilometres north-west of Salzburg. Here Sardagna had deployed his detachment of *Esterhazy* and his six squadrons of chevaulegers, as well as the 1st Salzburg Landwehr; the remaining four companies of II/*Esterhazy* and two 3-pounders came up in support to the rear. The Austrians held off the Bavarian advance troops, but their defence gave way when Wrede committed his infantry and artillery. The Bavarians pursued and, clearing the city wall with canister fire, entered the gates at 5 p.m.

Wrede had not succeeded in intercepting Jellacic's retreat, but for the loss of thirteen men, his division had captured Salzburg and inflicted a sharp, demoralising defeat on the Austrians. As we have seen from Napoleon's emphasis on the city, this was hardly an inconsequential accomplishment. Losses among Jellacic's regulars totalled 350 men and four guns. Furthermore, much of his Landwehr had dispersed: the 2nd and 4th Salzburg dissolved, while the 2nd Hausruck and 3rd Innviertel dwindled to a combined strength of sixty men. Jellacic reported sardonically that, 'As regards the Landwehr, I am still in doubt as to whether I should be angered or relieved at their rapid dissolution . . . the 2nd Salzburg Battalion, although a mile away, tore the cockades from their hats, threw away their muskets and flags, and fled.'[140] Worse, *de Vaux* Infantry No. 45 drew many of its recruits from Salzburg, and the district's natives took the opportunity to desert during the withdrawal even though its battalions were not involved in the fighting.[141]

Jellacic collected his reduced division at Hallein on the evening of 29 April and withdrew through Lueg Pass the following day to cover the key avenues into Styria.[142] The 1st of May found him with his headquarters in Radstadt and detachments scattered across the mountains from St Gilgen through Lueg Pass to Lend in the Salzach valley. Cavalry and heavy guns being of limited utility and difficult to support in the mountains, Jellacic sent seven of the chevaulegers squadrons, his 6-pounder position battery, and the remnants of the two Austrian Landwehr battalions—some 700 men in all—east to the Enns valley under Provenchères. This detachment reached Liezen on 4 May and, after many wanderings, some of these men would participate in the coming Battle of Aspern.[143]

As for Lefebvre, coming from Wasserburg (1st Division) and Traunstein (3rd Division), his advance guard had exchanged a few shots with Landwehr west of Salzburg during 29 April before Wrede's men made their appearance, but the 1st and 3rd Divisions did not actually enter the city until the following day.[144] Lefebvre immediately sent GM Karl von Stengel's brigade (three battalions, one squadron, and two guns) to Hallein to follow Jellacic, but granted most of his weary men a well-deserved rest.[145] All three Bavarian divisions were now concentrated together for the first time since Abensberg. The reunion was brief. That same day, Wrede moved out to Neumarkt am Wallersee to protect the main army's right flank. Other than Wrede's actions on the periphery of the main army during the first week of May, however, the scene now shifts back to the decisive venue and the movements of the principal forces.

Davout and Charles between Regensburg and Bohemia
(see Map 14)

The last two days of April saw Davout's lead elements south of the Danube as the 3rd Corps began its march to rejoin the army. From the 24th to the 28th, the marshal had cautiously followed—his movements could hardly be termed a 'pursuit'—the retreating Hauptarmee. Several factors inhibited him. First, the available force was inadequate to the task of imposing a punishing pursuit on a shaken, but still viable enemy through difficult terrain. With only three infantry divisions and three light cavalry regiments (5th and 7th Hussars, 11th Chasseurs), Davout ran the risk of being overwhelmed if he was caught dispersed on the march. Second, delays in passing through Regensburg on the 24th meant that the French lost contact with the enemy, and Montbrun, leading the advance with Pajol's light cavalry, did not know at first which directions to explore.[146] Third, the lack of information about the Austrians was especially acute in regards to Bellegarde's I Corps. For the initial days of the 'pursuit', therefore, Davout harboured worries that the missing and untouched Austrian corps would fall on his left flank if he extended himself too far towards the Bohemian border. Prudence remained the order of the day and Davout kept the bulk of 3rd Corps infantry within one day's march of Regensburg.[147]

As a result of these considerations, the burden of the chase fell predominantly on Montbrun. That general, uncomfortable in the undulating, wooded landscape without infantry, had requested the services of the 7th

Léger that had worked so effectively with his command south of the Danube. He received instead two battalions of the 13th Léger from Morand's division, but this was sufficient for him to undertake more active advances. His intelligence gathering again proved superb and his reports remain exemplary in their thoroughness, detail, and frequency.[148] Of combat, however, there was little. Montbrun encountered Kolowrat's II Corps emplaced on the hills north of the Regen at Nittenau on the 25th and proceeded to occupy the town once Gudin arrived in support, but the 'engagement' was in reality hardly more than a cannonade.

The same transpired on the 26th when the French ran into Fresnel and a body of I Corps light troops at Bruck in der Oberpfalz a few kilometres north of Nittenau. This time, Gudin was not on hand and Montbrun had no guns, so the fight consisted only of skirmishing. A number of other brushes between outlying detachments and patrols flared during this period, but the French 'pursuit' failed to inflict any serious harm on the Hauptarmee and did not even compel Charles to haste in his movements or decisions. The French did sweep up a large number of stragglers and deserters, but it was clear from the encounters at Nittenau and Bruck that the Austrians were 'fully rallied'.[149] The 12th Chasseurs, for so long the sole opponent to Bellegarde's corps, rode into Burgenlengfeld on the 26th, but were hardly sufficient to change the imbalance in forces between the putative pursuer and pursued.[150] The true benefit of Davout's movements lay in the intelligence Montbrun, Pajol, and others gathered and in the collateral caution they induced in Austrian thinking.

Napoleon had allowed Davout considerable latitude to decide when to join the main army, but he had also repeatedly stressed the importance he attached to 3rd Corps' participation in the major battle expected between Passau and Vienna.[151] Intelligence from Montbrun finally convinced the reluctant marshal to shift south of the Danube on 28 April. Even with his decision made, Davout remained cautious. Two battalions of 48th Ligne marched that night from the Trinity Hill above Stadtamhof for Straubing, and Morand decamped early on the morning of the 29th, taking the road through Regensburg to reach Pfatter that evening. Friant and Gudin only followed on the 30th. By 1 May, 3rd Corps was strung out in stages along the post road from Vilshofen to Straubing, headed for Passau and Austria. Behind it, Rouyer had assembled most of his division in Regensburg on 28 April and Dupas arrived in the ruined city from Ingolstadt on 1 May; both would depart almost immediately for Straubing. Montbrun's light horse and his two attached infantry battalions were left on the Bohemian frontier to watch for any change in Austrian activity.

To supplement Montbrun's efforts, Napoleon sent a 54-year-old cavalry major named Auguste J. J. G. Ameil. Ameil, 'a good soldier but a difficult character', had been in prison in Paris for rather overheated 'discussions' with his colonel when Napoleon ordered him to Montbrun's division. 'This major will distinguish himself and overcome his mistakes.'[152] Marbot held Ameil's talents in high regard, calling him 'with all his faults . . . undoubtedly the best light cavalry officer in any European army.'[153] Like so many officers, Ameil had reached the army only a few days earlier.[154] Napoleon now sent him to Montbrun to take command of a detachment of 150 troopers from the 12th Chasseurs. With these men, Ameil was 'to cause great anxiety to the enemy on the frontiers of Bohemia between Furth and Passau, and to procure news of the enemy's movements for us'. Collecting his detachment from Montbrun, Ameil headed off towards Zwiesel on Montbrun's right to 'spread different rumours . . . and, in fine, to employ all the ruses of the partisan.'[155] The major and his men would continue to monitor the Bohemian border as the rest of the army began to slip east into Austria.

Charles was certainly not planning any shifts in his operations as May began. Focused on reuniting with Hiller, the archduke was hoping to reach Linz no later than the 10th, and trusted he would find there a solid bridgehead and the other third of his army. The Austrian commanders could be pleased that the French pursuit had been so hesitant and the few encounters so insignificant. With the exception of I Corps, all of the troops remaining with the Hauptarmee were able to close into a strong defensive position along the Regen south of Cham by the morning of 26 April. Bellegarde, on the other hand, withdrew through Schwarzenfeld and then turned east to camp around Schönthal. Charles rested and reorganised his army in this position during the next two days: Rottermund's dragoon brigade returned to I Reserve Corps and Vécsey's brigade went back to II Corps. Simultaneously Lindenau's division of V Corps was broken up, with two regiments (*EH Karl* and *Stain*) going to III Corps to replace Thierry and two (*Hiller* and *Sztaray*) assigned to IV Corps in lieu of Reinwald's missing brigade.

Such organisational alterations were the easy measures. Much more difficult was the restoration of manpower, morale, and discipline. The army's strength reports gave a sad picture, with III and IV Corps listing only 6,800 and 10,000 effectives respectively. In contrast, Kolowrat's II Corps, hardly engaged in the Regensburg campaign, still had 23,110 fit for combat. Counting these three and I Reserve Corps, Charles reported to Franz that he had only slightly more than 50,000 effectives at hand during the first day or two at Cham. First Corps, essentially untouched by the war thus far, added another

28,000 or so to the total for the army as a whole (a point Charles did *not* highlight in the letter to his imperial brother) and was the only corps that had not been involved in the demoralising events south of Regensburg.[156] Fortunately for the Habsburg leaders, reinforcements were already en route in the form of third battalions and replacement detachments. Additionally, large numbers of stragglers and lost souls returned to the ranks as the army retired into Bohemia.

The army's poor discipline was perhaps more troubling than its physical weaknesses. Thousands of straggler soldiers roamed over Bavaria: 'Countless marauders of all regiments and corps, with—or largely without—muskets, coursed on and beside the roads, plundering, abusing the inhabitants, and paying no attention to the voices of their officers . . . they spread fear and terror everywhere.'[157] Many officers faulted the more humane regulations Charles had introduced as part of his reforms. The archduke found it necessary to issue a stern order of the day and many of his subordinates returned to older, more familiar methods during the retreat: 'Those found off the road will be punished with 100 blows as an example,' read a IV Corps order of the day.[158] Given these conditions, it is hardly surprising that Charles found his personal demoralisation compounded by the worrisome state of the army as it struggled north from Regensburg.

With these impressions of his retreating troops and the disastrous battles south of the Regensburg fresh in his mind, Charles examined his options. The war had now assumed an entirely different character. As he had predicted before hostilities commenced, what had begun as an offensive to restore and secure Austria's place among Europe's great powers had turned into a desperate defence: 'A decisive victory will lead him [Napoleon] into the heart of Austria, will destroy public support and the inner defensive resources of his enemy—in a word, it could result in the dissolution of the Austrian state.'[159] For Charles, the army—battered though it might be—was now the only pillar of the state, the only shield for the House of Habsburg. To preserve those institutions, above all else, the army must remain intact and capable of offering resistance to Napoleon. This fundamental conviction led him to two key strategic conclusions. First, in the military-operational realm, he would not undertake a new offensive against Napoleon's rear as some of his advisers advocated. The Hauptarmee was not only temporarily crippled and lacking a bridging train; it had proven itself clumsy in offensive operations. Accepting a defensive battle in the advantageous position at Cham would exploit the army's strengths and might give Austria a limited victory, even if this consisted of nothing more than successfully repulsing a French attack. Retreat, if this were necessary, would be difficult with the Bohemian mountains at his back, but at least Charles could be assured of withdrawal into friendly territory. Defeat in a renewed offensive against Napoleon, on the other hand, would probably mean retreat away from Austrian lands and the likely destruction of the army. The immediate need was recovery and this could only be accomplished by a defensive posture.

His second strategic conclusion concerned the political-military arena. With the army injured but still intact, Charles was convinced that Austria should enter into immediate negotiations with Napoleon 'before the enemy crosses our borders and Russia declares against us.'[160] The Kaiser and his confidants did not agree. In a response to Charles's dejected missive of 23 April, Franz wrote, 'you may take upon yourself to attempt a negotiation that takes advantage of the successes my brother Johann has gained in Italy and of the movements of the powers who had decided to tie themselves to those successes.'[161] As courier, however, the court selected Friedrich Lothar Stadion, the foreign minister's elder brother and a committed adherent of the war party. This by itself was an unmistakable signal to Charles. The elder Stadion arrived in Cham on 28 April and informed Charles that Franz and the imperial court were by no means persuaded of the need for an appeal to Napoleon. Franz had only acceded to the archduke's request to avoid the appearance of rejecting a chance at peace. In the opinion of the court and the Kaiser, Stadion emphasised, the monarchy still had large numbers of regular troops available and would hasten the formation of the Landwehr and Hungarian Insurrection. Stadion's instruction placed special importance on what were seen as dramatic victories in Italy: 'Through Italy we can align ourselves with the policies of the English, Sicilian, and Sardinian courts as well as with the success of the Spanish. Italy is Napoleon's most vulnerable point and already offers us a bargaining chip vis-à-vis the French emperor.'[162] Such reasoning was virtually delusional, but the war party, inspired by these hopes, believed that entry into negotiations at this point would represent a dangerous admission of weakness.

As Charles doubtless foresaw, his desire for an approach to Napoleon also opened the door for new accusations of cowardice and incompetence against him. His standing with his brother, already shaky, suffered increased erosion.[163] The archduke, however, was resolved to try. The result was an abject letter to Napoleon drafted by Grünne and transmitted to the outposts of the 5th French Hussars on 29 April by Rittmeister Josef Victoris of the *Klenau* Chevaulegers. Commanding the French troops in the area was Capitaine Adjutant-Major d'Espinchal. He initially suspected an Austrian ruse designed to discover the strength and seriousness of the French pursuit. On learning that Victoris bore a letter to the emperor, however, he had the messenger blindfolded and sent him to the rear with a small escort 'as I was not with the vanguard to talk but to act'.[164] The letter proposed an exchange of prisoners as a pretext for much broader negotiations.

> Your Majesty has announced to me His arrival with cannon shots without leaving me time to offer my compliments. I had hardly been informed of Your presence when I could guess it by the losses that You inflicted on me. You have taken many of my men, Sire, and my troops have likewise made many prisoners in the areas where You were not in command. I propose to Your Majesty to exchange them man for man and grade for grade and, if this proposition is agreeable to you, let me know Your intentions and the place where this exchange may occur.
>
> I am flattered, Sire, to have crossed swords with the greatest captain of the century. I would be happy if Destiny has chosen me to assure my country the benefits of an unalterable peace. Whatever the hazards of war or the reconciliations of peace, I beg Your Majesty to believe that my ambition always leads me towards You and that I will always believe myself equally honoured to treat with Your Majesty with either the sword or the olive branch in my hand.[165]

As this odd note was making its way to Napoleon, the lead elements of the Hauptarmee were already on the road east. Recognising from the quality of the French pursuit and other intelligence that Napoleon had taken himself and the major part of the Allied army towards the Inn, Charles had decided 'to march to Budweis, to reach the Danube in forced marches, unite myself with V and VI Corps, and begin a new offensive against Napoleon'. Dismissing possible operations towards Regensburg or Swabia(!) as unrealistic, he saw the Danube option as 'the most secure' and the one 'that could be most effective in the rescue of the state'. But he did not relent in pressing for talks and took the opportunity to undermine those who flaunted Johann's successes as reasons for optimism:

> I can only leave to Your Highness' judgment whether Your Majesty can take some comfort concerning the future fate of the monarchy from these measures, and whether it will be possible under these conditions to negotiate with the conqueror once he has established himself in the heart of the monarchy and thereby paralysed and reversed the advances of the Italian army.[166]

Union with Hiller and a secure bridgehead from which he could threaten Napoleon's march on Vienna were his operational priorities, but his outlook was hardly hopeful: 'The outcome of a battle is so uncertain that I wish the pen would begin to do its part.'[167]

The halt at Cham, however, made a difference for the better as far as the army was concerned: 'The two days of repose that we have taken here have restored some order,' noted Charles.[168] The Hauptarmee still had far to go to recover its former self-confidence and combat capability, but it had benefited from its brief respite and could hope to collect new equipment and additional manpower as it made its way back into the monarchy. Undisturbed by the French, Charles and his army marched away from Cham on the morning of 28 April, heading for Budweis and Linz. Echoing Schnierer's words after Neumarkt, Corporal F. A. Brandner of *EH Johann* recorded: 'Herewith closed the eighteen-day campaign in Bavaria that had begun with such great hopes and ended with the bleakest prospects.'[169]

Montbrun's patrols thus found Cham empty of enemy on the 29th. The French light cavalry continued to press into the mountains, one detachment advancing through Waldmünchen, the other via Furth, but these could do no more than collect information and periodically harass the enemy. Both detachments skirmished with Austrian rear guards on 30 April and both pushed boldly into Bohemia: beyond Klentsch in the west and as far as Neumark in the east. On 2 May, however, Montbrun finally received orders to rejoin the army. Leaving Colonel Mathieu Désirat with his 11th Chasseurs and a battalion of the 13th Léger at Cham and Ameil further east, Montbrun assembled the rest of his small command and marched for Passau.[170]

As for Charles's letter, the French emperor received it on 1 May in Burghausen. His reaction was less than favourable:

The Emperor to the Duke of Auerstädt, Burghausen, 1 May 1809
My Cousin, I have received your letter and the one you forwarded from Prince Charles. I will respond to the latter when I have the time. In the meantime, retain the envoy. In the next eight days, we will give a response. These people are as vile in adversity as they are arrogant and haughty at the least glimmer of prosperity. We have succeeded in repairing the bridges on the Salzach. We march on Lambach and Linz.[171]

Napoleon never did find time to reply.

1–3 MAY: INTO AUSTRIA

Bertrand and his harried work crews finally restored the bridge at Burghausen late on the afternoon of 30 April. The bridge exhibited 'a frightful oscillation up and down' as artillery rolled over it, but it sufficed to carry the army across the Salzach.[172] Indeed, using captured Austrian pontoons and some scrounged local craft, Bertrand's men managed to construct a pontoon bridge as well. With Marulaz in the lead, Bessières's light cavalry clopped carefully over onto Austrian soil at around 4 p.m. Six hours later, the entire force, some 50,000 to 60,000 men, was on the eastern bank; by nightfall, they were crowded around Braunau. The Württemberg Light Brigade and the two Jäger regiments were across the river from Braunau, while the remainder of the contingent halted at Marktl.[173] The Guard and Imperial headquarters remained on the Bavarian side of the Salzach at Burghausen. The men were in good spirits despite the dismal weather. Chef de Bataillon Bial awoke under a light blanket of snow, but, 'I shook off the snow and, after restoring myself with some excellent bouillon brought to me by my servant, I departed refreshed and content "to seek peace in Vienna", as our soldiers said.'[174]

Scouts from Marulaz's division pushed into Altheim, skirmishing with Austrian outposts as Marulaz set up his headquarters in the town. The French horsemen could see campfires burning to the east, but in the darkness they could not make out any details of numbers or types of troops. Patrols towards Schärding and up the Mattig valley also ran into enemy vedettes and duly reported their findings, but could make no further progress in the night. Down to the south, Wrede reported his presence in Strasswalchen that evening, announced the capture of some sixty disheartened troopers of the O'Reilly Chevaulegers, and related the 'inconceivable consternation' that the local population had observed among the Austrian troops.[175]

During the day, Napoleon learned that Davout was en route from Regensburg and that Bernadotte was at Rudolstadt. Bernadotte's letter included a detailed summary of the Austrian invasion of Poland on 15 April, the Battle of Raszyn on the 19th, and the surrender of Warsaw.[176] From a strategic perspective, the situation in Poland added to Napoleon's concerns, but he remained confident that success on the principal front would repair these in short order.

His men reflected this confidence, as in this letter written by Colonel Bernard Pierre Castex, commanding 20th Chasseurs under Colbert:

Burghausen, 30 April 1809

Three battles, three combats and as many victories and I am doing well. Bavaria is entirely evacuated and we are marching on Vienna where we will without a doubt arrive in less than a month. The newspapers will give you the other details, until then I am mounting up to be the advance guard of the army.[177]

1 May: Encounters at Polling, Riedau, and Waizenkirchen

As we have seen, Hiller was also confident. Indeed, by 30 April, the lack of French activity to his front had led his sense of self-assurance to assume dangerous proportions. On the morning of 1 May, utterly unaware that Napoleon was on, let alone across, the Salzach with more than 50,000 men, and believing that the French force at Schärding numbered only some 10,000 (Massena's strength was well over 30,000), the Austrian commander decided that the enemy must be withdrawing behind the river barrier. Accordingly, he ordered his covering troops to advance, imagining that his main body would rest for a day or two and then position itself on the highway running from Schärding to Linz. In the meantime, his flank screen could discover where the enemy had gone.

Early that morning they found out. A force consisting of the lone remaining battalion of *Brod* Grenzer (half of the regiment had been destroyed on 20 April), an attached replacement detachment from 6th Jägers, and a half-squadron of *Kienmayer* Hussars advanced towards Altheim to gauge the strength of the French force that had unexpectedly appeared the previous evening. Halting just east of Polling, the Austrians were suddenly engulfed by the 7th and 20th Chasseurs of Colbert's *Brigade Infernale* and forced to surrender. The hussars managed to escape this minor fiasco, but nearly 1,200 Grenzer and Jägers went into captivity. While the French chasseurs were encircling the hapless Croatians and inexperienced Jägers, the 9th Hussars were surging towards Ried. Tharreau's infantry was close behind. The energetic Oudinot was commanding the French advance guard and, when outposts of Radetzky's *Gradiska* Grenzer delayed his light cavalry at Ried, he used his foot soldiers to outflank the defenders to the south while the horsemen pushed them from the front. The Grenzer and uhlans, repeatedly turned, fell back in haste. When they stopped just west of Geiersberg that evening, the weary French light cavalry had covered some fifty kilometres and, combined with Tharreau's infantry, had inflicted a small but startling defeat on the Austrian covering troops.[178]

This scene practically repeated itself slightly to the north in a sharp action at Riedau. Massena, like Lannes and Oudinot, was on the move early in the day. While his main body marched up the highway towards Waizenkirchen, the marshal sent a strong force to shield his right flank. He placed one of his staff officers, Adjutant-Commandant Anne Alexis Jean Trenqualye, in command of a detachment composed of 4th Ligne, the Baden Light Dragoons, and the Württemberg Leib Chevaulegers for this mission. Riding from Sigharting through Raab to Riedau, Trenqualye crossed the little Pram stream and chased off pickets of *Kienmayer* Hussars just east of the town, but soon encountered infantry skirmishers. The Austrian foot soldiers were two companies of III/*Jordis*. That battalion, together with two squadrons of *Kienmayer* Hussars, were the rear guard of one of Schustekh's covering detachments. Schustekh had not yet received the order to advance, so the main body of his group (Hohenfeld's brigade) was in Neumarkt preparing to retire to the east. The hussars and III/*Jordis* had positioned themselves to protect this withdrawal when Trenqualye hit them. The French commander ordered two squadrons of Württemberg chevaulegers ahead to clear the way, supported by the three voltigeur companies of the 4th Ligne. Holding the other two Württemberg squadrons in reserve, he skilfully sent the Baden Light Dragoons to outflank the Austrians, directing half of the regiment north of the road and the other half south. As these flanking squadrons were making their way forward, the French infantry swept the Austrians out of a small wood, allowing Rittmeister Friedrich von Bismark to advance with his squadron of Leib Chevaulegers into the open terrain on the road to Neumarkt. Bismark's troopers immediately came under effective fire from the Austrian infantry. With no orders to advance and unwilling to retreat, Bismark soon lost his patience and led an impetuous charge against the skirmishers to his front.[179] Fortunately for the bold Bismark, Oberstleutnant Friedrich von Heimrodt appeared near Erlach behind the Austrians at this point with the southern two Baden squadrons. Heimrodt swiftly swung his troopers to their left and charged. The doomed skirmishers and their immediate supports, attacked from front and rear in open terrain, were soon dead, captured, or scattered to the four winds.

The rest of the Austrian rear guard endeavoured to assist the skirmishers. Oberstleutnant August Edler von Becke advanced with the remaining four companies of III/*Jordis* and the two squadrons of hussars leaped to the attack. Bismark's men bravely stood the Austrian charge but would have been overwhelmed had not Stettner led two other Württemberg squadrons against the Austrian right in a timely manner. Held in front and taken in the

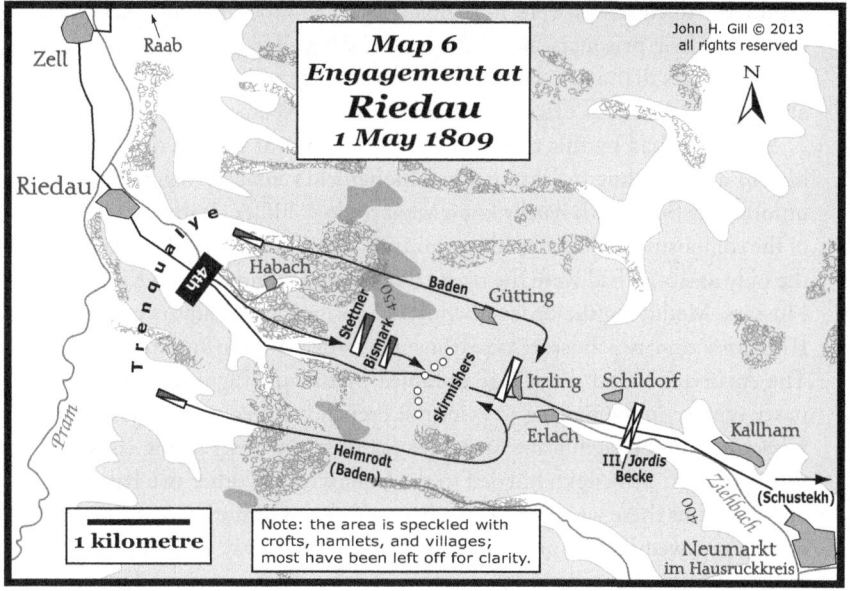

Map 6
Engagement at
Riedau
1 May 1809

Note: the area is speckled with crofts, hamlets, and villages; most have been left off for clarity.

1 kilometre

flank, the hussars fled when the remaining two Baden squadrons appeared from the north. While this cavalry fight was in progress, Heimrodt noticed Becke's four companies, previously hidden by an undulation of the terrain. The Austrian commander, seeing the negative turn of affairs, had formed his men in square and was attempting to withdraw behind some hedges and other obstacles. Heimrodt instantly decided to attack and, calling on the closest thirty or forty dragoons, charged at Becke's square. The remaining men of his two squadrons hurried to join him. Although outnumbered (500 infantry to at most 160 light dragoons), the Badeners fell on the Austrians in a fury. Becke's men got off an ineffective volley, but the square contracted under the ferocious attack and the inexperienced infantrymen, jammed together and disordered, could no longer fire. Heimrodt's horse and several others were pierced by bayonets as the dragoons pressed in, but several Badeners were able to create a gap in the square by grabbing Austrian muskets and shoving them aside. With a hole made, the defence collapsed, the badly wounded Becke falling to the ground and asking to be killed to expunge his disgrace.[180] In all, the Baden dragoons took 706 prisoners. The Württembergers claimed another ninety-seven from III/*Jordis*. Adding in some forty or fifty hussar casualties gives a total of more than 800 Austrians dead, wounded, or captured. Allied losses were negligible.[181] As Heimrodt and his men were collecting their prisoners and the battalion's flag, Trenqualye pursued the fleeing hussars to the east, but called off his advance and retired to Riedau on observing Hohenfeld's brigade assembled around Neumarkt.

Schustekh had by this time been handed a copy of Hiller's order telling him to advance, but to leave behind Hohenfeld's infantry regiments. The unfortunate Schustekh hardly knew what to do.[182] Hiller clearly had no idea of the composition of Schustekh's command: other than Hohenfeld's brigade, the only assets he had were the tired troopers and mounts of the *Kienmayer* Hussars. Modifying the orders, Schustekh formed a new advance guard of III/*Klebek* and two hussar squadrons and ordered them towards Riedau. The Austrians found the village occupied by the 4th Ligne and suffered a nasty repulse in attempting to evict the French between 3 and 5 p.m., III/*Klebek* sustaining significant casualties (at least 165 men) in the course of this fighting.[183] Schustekh hurried to the front with the other two battalions of *Klebek*, but these were barely able to retain their position east of the town against renewed French pressure.[184] The firing faded away as darkness came on and Trenqualye, called back to 4th Corps later that evening, abandoned the village and marched for Raab.

The Austrians experienced another surprise slightly further north, along Massena's principal line of march. Hiller had few forces here, on the high road from Schärding to Linz, just Major Scheibler with his two squadrons of *Rosenberg* Chevaulegers and Gratze's *Wallach-Illyria* Grenzer. Steigentesch was still at Eferding with his two companies of 2nd Vienna Volunteers. Scheibler's troopers had scuffled with French outposts during the afternoon, but the major and his fellow Habsburg commanders were astonished when a considerable commotion arose late that night. Carra Saint-Cyr's men were the source of the nocturnal din. The French division had already marched between fifteen and twenty kilometres during the day to occupy Raab, when, late in the afternoon, Saint-Cyr received orders to press ahead to Waizenkirchen. By the time the division was assembled, therefore, night was falling. What followed was a remarkable advance into the darkness. Saint-Cyr seems to have believed that speed, surprise, and audacity offered the best chances of success and, later reinforced by 14th Chasseurs, he led his division east through the dank gloom at a breakneck pace with none of the normal reconnaissance or march security.[185]

Scheibler reported that 'They seemed to be drunk, singing, shouting, shooting into the air in all directions, and bringing along their regimental bands.'[186] To the major's disgust, the Grenzer showed no interest in defending the bridge at Waizenkirchen, even though from the attacker's viewpoint this was a location where 'the enemy could have repelled our nocturnal advance with great advantage.'[187] Gratze and his men withdrew in fine order despite the sudden appearance of the Allies, but Scheibler could not forgive their lack of firmness.[188] Saint-Cyr's reckless audacity had paid off. At almost no cost in casualties, his division had gained the heights on the Austrian side of Waizenkirchen and had thrown outposts five kilometres further east. Around 1 a.m., the French finally settled down in hopes of snatching some rest in the few remaining hours of darkness. Trenqualye's Baden and Württemberg regiments did not even have this minimum luxury. On reaching Raab from their tidy victory at Riedau, the German horsemen had been assigned to the advance guard and rode all night to arrive opposite Waizenkirchen at 4 a.m. on 2 May.

Behind these tactical successes, of course, the bulk of the Allied army had also advanced. Massena's corps extended from Waizenkirchen back to Taufkirchen. Marulaz, reassigned to 4th Corps, left Altheim and rode into Riedau late that night just in time to preclude the Austrians from re-occupying the village. On the other flank, Wrede remained in Strasswalchen. In the main column, poor regulation of the march somewhat diminished Oudinot's success with the advance guard. Although Jacquinot and Piré were in Ried, the lead infantry division, Molitor's, had started relatively late and halted just west of the town. The trail units, the two heavy cavalry divisions, had proceeded no further than Altheim. In between were St Hilaire and Demont.

Many Allied troops were also approaching from the rear. The Guard was now across the river at Braunau, as was Bruyère's light cavalry brigade, finally arrived from north Germany. Vandamme was also in Braunau where yet another regiment (*Camrer*) was detached as garrison. He had already painstakingly shipped much of his infantry and artillery across the river, but would not finish the laborious crossing until early on 2 May. En route from Munich were the Hessian Leib Regiment, the 3rd Baden Infantry, and a large French march brigade (5,000) under GB Charles Marion. Dupas arrived in Regensburg, 4th Rheinbund was marching to Straubing, and Davout's lead division would reach Passau on the 2nd along with the Württemberg *Phull* Infantry.

On the Austrian side, Nordmann had pulled most of his brigade back across the Traun east of Lambach, leaving only three hussar squadrons on the western bank. Here he received the unwelcome news that he was to place his four strongest squadrons at Hiller's disposition and yet, with this reduced command (two Grenz battalions, four hussar squadrons, and the remaining two companies of *Brod* Grenzer), he was to extend his outpost line south along the river as far as the Traunsee. Radetzky had his outposts just east of Gaspoltshofen with Schustekh on his distant right at Neumarkt. Between Schustekh and the Danube, Gratze and Scheibler had fallen back towards Eferding. A glance at the map will illustrate Schustekh's predicament. He did not yet realise it, but French advances during the day, especially Carra Saint-Cyr's adventurous night thrust to Waizenkirchen, placed him in danger of being cut off.

The danger to Schustekh and the rest of the Hiller's force was particularly acute because Hiller's command style during the preceding several days had revealed a number of potentially catastrophic weaknesses. Not all of this was exactly 'his fault'. External pressures from the Kaiser and the generalissimus certainly taxed him as he tried to reconcile their orders with his own preconceptions and preferences. Moreover, his troops and subordinate commanders, even the normally reliable Radetzky and the energetic Scheibler, were not providing the accurate intelligence he needed (in part, no doubt, owing to exhaustion). The lack of timely and reliable information is especially surprising given that the Austrians were now fighting on their home soil and should have enjoyed the advantages of popular sympathy and the loyalty of the state's administrative apparatus. It is nothing short of astonishing, for example, that Hiller was still unaware of Napoleon's presence across the Salzach. Many of Hiller's problems, however, were of his own making. The daily changes of plans, the constantly shifting order of battle, the increasingly confused command arrangements, the illusion that the foe would grant him a respite to rest his command: all of these stemmed from Hiller's conceptions of the operational situation and his own efforts at higher-level leadership. As a result, co-ordination was often missing, commanders did not know to whom they should report, and units were forgotten.[189] Stress, exhaustion, and heavy responsibility only exacerbated the challenges. Similar weaknesses also appeared in Napoleon's army, but the competence and experience of generals and troops alike allowed the Allies room to compensate. In the Austrian structure, there was a much narrower margin for error.

2 May: Engagements at Wels, Eferding, and Neumarkt

In Wels that night, Hiller completely misread the French dispositions and true strength, but slowly came to recognise that he was outnumbered and thus at last gave up the notion of pushing the French back across the Inn.[190]

He knew that there was not even a bridgehead, let alone a 'position' at Linz, but saw no alternative to directing his three corps towards Leonding in compliance with the repeated orders from Franz and Charles. The light troops, on the other hand, he instructed to occupy the outer rim of the intended 'position', essentially an imaginary defensive line running from the Danube at Wilhering to the Traun south of Ebelsberg. The Austrian penchant for detachments was allowed full expression in Hiller's dispositions for 2 May, leaving his two line corps with few combat troops. With the *Kienmayer* Hussars detached to Schustekh, Bianchi on the right flank and Radetzky on the left, the 'main body' of V Corps thus consisted of a single infantry regiment (*Beaulieu*) and the corps' reserve artillery. Similarly, 'VI Corps' translated into the brigades of Weissenwolff and Hoffmeister, effectively an infantry division plus artillery.

As Hiller was issuing his orders to his covering force commanders, the French were already on the move. The weather had finally changed for the better, with sunshine replacing the oppressive cold rain of the previous week. Bessières, however, seems to have laboured under a cloud of reprimand, having been upbraided by Napoleon for his sluggishness the preceding day. The marshal now led the advance on Lambach with Jacquinot and Piré, supported by some of Oudinot's infantry. Radetzky, gaining time through a ruse, withdrew hastily behind Lambach.[191] Oudinot quickly occupied the town, while the French light horse, pressing ahead with great élan at 3 p.m., overthrew Radetzky's rear guard. Radetzky employed his Grenzer and uhlans with great finesse, however, delaying this French onslaught as he fell back on Wels. Jacquinot attacked again at dusk, but Radetzky administered a severe repulse, driving the French back into the darkness and taking sixty or seventy prisoners. Jacquinot retired in confusion and action along the Traun came to an end. Though his counter-stroke had been successful, Radetzky could see he was heavily outnumbered and withdrew north into the night. No one on the Austrian side thought about the Wels bridge until the last minute and the hasty departure did not allow for a thorough job of destruction. As a result, this important span had suffered only superficial damage when Lannes, Bessières, and Oudinot rode into town at approximately 8 p.m.[192]

The fighting on Massena's line of advance was more intense and more costly for the Austrians. Carra Saint-Cyr's division again led the 4th Corps march with Trenqualye commanding an advance guard composed of 24th Léger and 14th Chasseurs. Stettner and the two German cavalry regiments accompanied Saint-Cyr. Having arrived at 4 a.m. after an all-night march in the drizzle, they only had time to feed their mounts before climbing back into their saddles. The morning, however, brought a welcome change in the weather: 'around and before us a laughing spring', wrote surgeon Meier.[193] Trotting forwards into this beautiful dawn, the French encountered Gratze and Steigentesch west of Eferding. With the addition of three voltigeur companies from the division, Trenqualye attacked and cleared the road by 9 a.m., the 24th Léger capturing a sizeable number of Grenzer with an energetic pursuit.

The Grenzer, retreating in some disorder, found succour at Raffelding, where Bianchi had arrived at 8 a.m. with instructions to cover Gratze's withdrawal. Bianchi posted II/*Gyulai* behind a small stream west of Raffelding and placed I/*Gyulai* in the town itself; the 3rd Battalion was in a support position to the east and *Duka* further to the rear. Scheibler's two squadrons were also on the scene east of town. The skittish Grenzer, continuing their retreat, left anxiety in their wake as they passed through Bianchi's lines, and the arrival of more French infantry and artillery made Bianchi nervous as well. His men repelled a hasty charge by two Baden squadrons and a platoon of 14th Chasseurs, but extended resistance was not part of his mission and he decided to pull back in the face of the growing French strength.[194] This proved difficult. When Trenqualye observed the Austrians withdrawing, he ordered all of his available cavalry to attack. Overthrowing a platoon of *Rosenberg* Chevaulegers, the German and French horsemen dashed through the village and caught I/*Gyulai* before it could form square, with the result that the third Austrian battalion in two days fell to bold Allied light cavalry. In this case, at least, many of the men apparently escaped and rejoined their battalion that night. But, for a few moments, the situation was dicey in the extreme for the Austrians. Bianchi himself only evaded capture because Scheibler led a timely counter-attack that gave the general time to recover and allowed his brigade to retire in good order to Wilhering without further incident. Saint-Cyr followed, but called off his pursuit east of Alkoven with Trenqualye's light horse forward and the combined Hessian Schützen occupying a dominant hill south of the highway (the Annaberg). As with the engagements on 1 May, these running battles along the highway from Waizenkirchen to Alkoven cost the Austrians far more than the Allies: at least 600 Habsburg troops were killed, wounded, captured, or missing at the end of the day.[195] The Allies lost less than fifty.[196]

Schustekh, too, came under French pressure during the day. Marulaz, who had reached Riedau late on the night of 1/2 May en route to link up with Massena, 'wanted to use his movement to reconnoitre along the right flank of the 4th Corps'.[197] With 3rd Chasseurs in the lead, he advanced towards

Neumarkt on the morning of the 2nd. Schustekh's command was already retiring to the east, so Marulaz's men only encountered rear guards as they covered the ground where Trenqualye's detachment had conducted itself so effectively the previous day. By means of platoon-size attacks, 3rd Chasseurs steadily pushed the Austrians back towards Neumarkt. The division's attempt to pass beyond Neumarkt, however, was poorly orchestrated and the Hessian Chevaulegers were sent reeling by a blast of musketry from *Klebek* Infantry posted east of the village.[198] Marulaz, his command in confusion, contented himself with the numerous prisoners he had swept up during the day and decided that 'it was not appropriate to continue the pursuit any further'.[199] Turning north, his division rode to Eferding to rejoin 4th Corps during the night.

Having rebuffed Marulaz, Schustekh marched his men back to Geisenheim undistressed by the enemy, and betook himself to a nearby chateau feeling quite secure. As night fell, however, the *Kienmayer* Hussars reported chasing off French cavalry patrols on the Wels–Eferding road *behind* Schustekh's position. Around the same time, some of his hussars brought in a captive Baden lieutenant who had been carrying dispatches from Massena to Napoleon. His peril suddenly revealed, Schustekh hurried to move his command out of danger. He gave orders to pull back to Buchkirchen in the hope of using the rugged ridge that divides the Danube and the Traun as an avenue to reach Linz. With only rough secondary roads available, his weary little command set out into the darkness sometime after 10 p.m.[200]

Night of 2/3 May: Positions and Intentions

On the evening of 2 May, Napoleon's forces were arrayed in two long, narrow columns. One was along and approaching the west bank of the Traun. Here, Piré and Colbert were north-east of Wels with Tharreau just behind them. Jacquinot's brigade seems to have been out of action, recovering from the repulse it had suffered at Radetzky's hands, but Molitor was north of Lambach, the two cuirassier divisions on the western approaches to that town, St Hilaire near Buchmaning, and Demont at Gaspoltshofen. Bruyère's light cavalry brigade had reached Haag. On the other axis, Massena's 4th Corps had its lead elements on the eastern side of Alkoven and its trail division (Boudet) near Eferding. Vandamme, with his light troops at Riedau and his line infantry and foot artillery at Aurolzmünster, was to close the gap between these two columns. The Guard, foot and horse, was at Ried and Wrede's division was covering the far-right flank with his headquarters at Strasswalchen and detachments as far as Vöcklamarkt. On the Inn, the Hessian Leib Regiment and the Baden 3rd Infantry had finally reached Braunau, where the Württemberg *Camrer* Infantry had remained as garrison. Downstream, Davout was in Passau with Morand's division and the *Phull* Infantry; the rest of 3rd Corps was not far behind. Montbrun, as we have seen, had departed Cham with most of his division, leaving Désirat and Ameil to watch the borders of Bohemia.

Napoleon did not know whether Hiller would choose to defend Linz south of the Danube, retreat north across the great river to join Charles, or withdraw to the east over the Traun to the Enns. In any of these cases, Massena's mission was clear:

> you will take yourself to Linz with all diligence; seize a bridge over the Traun and, if it is possible, a bridge over the Danube ... If the enemy wants to defend the Traun, he will certainly occupy the position at Ebelsberg which is to his advantage; but he will be chased out because the Emperor will pass that river at Lambach.[201]

Bessières would support Massena by advancing towards Linz with his small force (Piré's light brigade and Jacquinot's recuperating troopers) on the west bank of the Traun on the morning of 3 May, while Lannes collected his corps at Wels. The latter was only to send his infantry north to assist Bessières 'if you hear cannon.'[202] As a consequence of these 'supple' dispositions, Napoleon was prepared for any likely eventuality: 'they prejudged nothing, but responded to everything.'[203] If Hiller made a stand south of the Danube, he would be subjected to a powerful attack by Massena with assistance from some light cavalry coming up the Traun, followed, albeit in the mid-afternoon at best, by some infantry (Tharreau's division). If Hiller retreated north of the Danube or east towards Enns, Massena could proceed along the south bank of the Danube while Lannes, crossing at Lambach or at Wels (where Lannes had repaired the bridge by 7 a.m. on 3 May), would press for Steyr, outflanking possible Austrian positions on the Traun or Enns rivers.[204]

On the Austrian side, Hiller had decided to retreat over the Traun. This decision contravened, at least in part, the guidance he had received from both the Kaiser and the generalissimus, but it was entirely in accord with his assessment of the immediate situation and his own personal predilection.[205] From his perspective, Massena's strong column already presented a direct threat to the crossing at Linz, construction of defences had hardly begun, the Hauptarmee would not reach Linz for another week, and Hiller's own troops were both weary and ill supplied. Even the sturdy Radetzky had reported that 'the fatigue of the horses is such that they lay down in their ranks under their riders.'[206] The chances of a successful stand south of the Danube in these conditions were small and he was likely to lose his rear guard at the minimum during the inevitable withdrawal to the northern shore. He was already leaning towards a retreat to Ebelsberg in the late afternoon, therefore, when Radetzky's report on the day's fighting reached him. With enemy forces now pressing both of his flanks, Hiller was convinced that he had no choice but to 'select the lesser of two evils' and 'take my position tomorrow at Ebelsberg behind the Traun.'[207]

Most of Hiller's force was arrayed in an arc south of Linz on the night of 2/3 May, V Corps on the right facing west, VI Corps on the left oriented to the south, Dedovich in the centre, and Kienmayer in reserve. Three of the Austrian rear guards, however, were still far forward of the Linz 'position': Bianchi was posted at Wilhering on the far right holding the narrow defile between the ruggedly hilly Kürnberger Wald and the Danube; Radetzky was at Marchtrenk; and Schustekh was making his way towards Leonding along

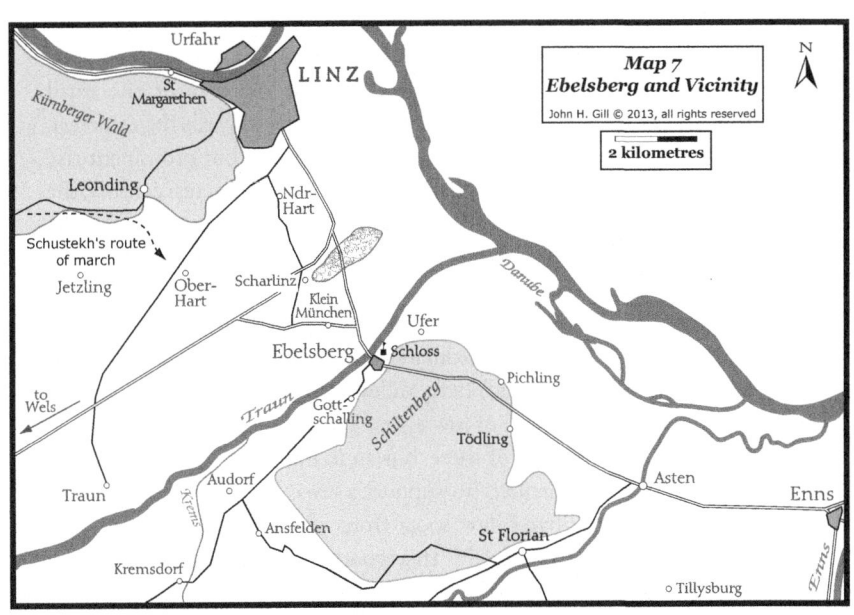

Map 7
Ebelsberg and Vicinity

2 kilometres

the difficult ridge southwest of Linz. On the far side of the Traun, three of the Vienna Volunteer battalions (4th, 5th, and 6th) were just east of Ebelsberg, the four *Liechtenstein* Hussar squadrons sent by Nordmann were riding through Kremsdorf to the north, and the rest of Nordmann's tiny command was stretched in outposts from Wels to the south following the Traun to Wimsbach and then along the Alm. Further to the rear, GM Emanuel von Ulbrecht commanded three Landwehr battalions near Enns. North of the Danube, Oberst Hardegg had two companies and two squadrons opposite Bianchi at Ottensheim and detachments at Gramastetten and Hellmonsödt. Off to Hardegg's right were Richter's three Prachin Landwehr battalions, and Stutterheim's cavalry brigade had reached Freistadt (see Map 4).

3 MAY: THE BATTLE OF EBELSBERG

One of the most vicious battles of this war and one of the most grisly scenes of the entire Napoleonic epoch occurred on 3 May at Ebelsberg, a small town on the eastern bank of the Traun. Coming from Linz, the post road to Vienna crossed the Traun on a long wooden bridge, passed through an open gate tower, and traversed Ebelsberg's broad market square, to enter a second gate (Enns Gate) that gave onto the Vormarkt, or eastern portion of town. As it exited the town, the highway bent sharply north and ran through a deep defile. The Austrian troops that would soon encamp on the Schiltenberg, east of town, would not be able to see either the highway or the small secondary road that led from Ebelsberg up to the slope towards the cemetery. A Schloss (in this case a walled chateau) topped a small but prominent rise immediately adjacent to the town. Dating from the late sixteenth century, the Schloss with its sturdy granite walls was a veritable redoubt, protected on its northern and eastern sides by a ditch and only approachable from Ebelsberg via a confined path some four metres wide, leading to a barred door in the side of the structure.[208] To the east, the landscape rose at a fairly gentle slope to define the Schiltenberg (approximately 320 metres high). To the west, the Traun ran through a broad, deep valley, up to 1,500 metres in width, cut up by millstreams, and full of low eyots. The recent rains had raised the river's level and covered some of these, but an island near the western shore did afford a position for artillery to support a crossing. The terrain left the defenders, on the other hand, few spots from which they could cover the bridge with effective artillery fire.[209] This wooden trestle bridge, 550 metres long, would become the object of the day's fight.[210]

Opening Actions West of the Traun

Hiller began his retreat during the pre-dawn hours of 3 May. Dedovich's mixed division of recruits and Landwehr filed off towards Ebelsberg first, followed by V Corps, II Reserve Corps, and VI Corps. The Landwehr battalions and depot divisions (*Klebek* and *Jordis*) that had been in Linz and north of the Danube also joined the long, tangled line of troops and vehicles making its way east. Behind the marching columns, the Danube bridge was burning. Confusion and friction soon arose, largely because Hiller had neglected to move the trains and other rear area assets across the river the previous evening. These elements, belatedly shaken into action, quickly snarled themselves into a jumble at the entrance to the bridge. The poor march discipline of the Landwehr created additional delays and irritation. These problems prolonged the army's transfer to the eastern bank and introduced unnecessary confusion into an already difficult movement.

Massena's men were marching by 5 a.m. With Marulaz in the lead (minus 3rd Chasseurs, detached to scout to the south-east), 4th Corps pressed towards Linz along the river road. Hardegg attempted to retard Massena's advance by having his two *Lindenau* companies fire at the French columns from the northern bank of the Danube, but this long-distance musketry proved only a minor nuisance. Claparède's troops, following the light cavalry, simply filed off to the flank, fired a volley or two and swiftly moved on. Bianchi, who had begun moving well before dawn, did succeed in delaying the Allied light cavalry for a short time at St Margarethen, but the Austrians withdrew as soon as Coëhorn's foot soldiers appeared. Moving quickly themselves, Bianchi's troops escaped and the French entered Linz without resistance, Massena accepting the salute of the municipal guard as he rode in and began issuing new orders.

It was now between 9 and 10 a.m. and the sun shone in a clear sky on what was already becoming a warm spring day. Probing forward along the Ebelsberg road under this welcome sunshine, chasseurs from Marulaz's advance guard came under fire from Austrian skirmishers posted in the woods north-east of Scharlinz. These were men of the *Benjovszky* and *Splenyi* Infantry Regiments from Hoffmeister's brigade. The bulk of the brigade (five battalions) was deployed across the highway in a line with its skirmishers forward and III/*Splenyi* ensconced in the scattered homes that constituted Klein München. The *Rosenberg* Chevaulegers were behind the infantry with a platoon on the right between the woods and the Danube and a half-squadron on the left just beyond Scharlinz. This half-squadron was to maintain contact with the left wing of the rear guard: Radetzky's ubiquitous brigade of uhlans and Grenzer. Radetzky had withdrawn from Marchtrenk untroubled by the French and now placed his uhlan regiment astride the road and his Grenzer in the wooded water meadows between Klein München and the Traun. He had a squadron and two companies forward at the fork where the Wels road splits to go towards Linz or Ebelsberg. Commanded by Vincent, this Austrian rear guard thus comprised eight battalions and sixteen squadrons supported by one full battery and one half-battery. Marulaz, faced with infantry and woods, probed the Austrian flanks unsuccessfully, but could really do little; he deployed his division to await the arrival of Claparède.

At this point, approximately 10 a.m., several things happened at once. Claparède's infantry began to arrive behind Marulaz, Piré's light cavalry brigade appeared on the road from Wels, and Schustekh came into view near Oberhart with his exhausted column. Piré's troopers made two abortive attempts to intercept Schustekh's march, but both were parried by Habsburg hussars and uhlans. With no numerical advantage and no support at hand, Bessières was unable to halt Schustekh's hurrying detachment, and most of the Austrians made it to the relative safety of Klein München.[211] Schustekh's rear guard, however, II/*Klebek* under Major Jamez, had fallen far behind during the long night march. Surrounded by French cavalry in the open ground near Oberhart, Jamez and his weak battalion suffered heavily and surrendered.[212]

Meanwhile, without waiting for Jamez, Vincent had ordered a withdrawal, and Claparède, perhaps encouraged by the beginnings of the Austrian retreat, ordered his leading brigade (Coëhorn) to attack. Driving the Austrian skirmishers before them, the French infantry pushed through the woods to find that most of Hoffmeister's men had decamped, leaving only the two battalions of *Splenyi* to cover their retreat. Marulaz, swinging to the left at the head of 19th Chasseurs, cut off the Austrian chevaulegers near the Danube and forced *Splenyi* to form masses. The unfortunate whitecoats took heavy casualties when three of Claparède's guns, coming through the thin wood, played upon their packed ranks with shot and shell. Pressed by Coëhorn, the two battalions held together back to Klein München, but Marulaz sounded the charge and led the 19th into the village, so that the Austrian infantry, 'scattering into the gardens, threw away their arms and dispersed by platoons.'[213] The chaos in Klein München was compounded because Radetzky, whom Vincent had neglected to notify of the retreat, was also hastening to get his brigade across the Traun: 'I was entangled in a disadvantageous engagement at Ebelsberg and fell into a bloody pell-mell with Massena's troops at the bridge.'[214] Vincent's men, trying to retire over the bridge, had founded it jammed with vehicles, in part because the market square in Ebelsberg was so full of stalled wagons, soldiers seeking food, and farriers shoeing horses that the crowd on the span could not exit. By the time traffic was able to move again, a disordered knot of soldiers and equipment of every description blocked the entrance on the western shore. Now, pressed by the determined French, this wild mass of men, horses, and guns surged towards the bridge in a swirl of hand-to-hand combat, confusion, and panicked flight. The deep boom of artillery added its sombre tone to this maelstrom scene as Austrian guns on the far bank opened up and Massena unlimbered eighteen of his pieces on the western shore downstream from the village.

It was now approximately 11.30 a.m. Although both sides had had approximately equal numbers at hand, the Austrian rear guard had collapsed with terrifying rapidity.[215] Casualties among Hiller's troops west of the Traun already amounted to more than 3,200.[216] Astonishingly, the Austrians succeeded in getting all of their guns and all but one of their standards to safety. Additionally, although many drowned in the attempt, some individuals managed to save themselves and their horses by swimming the river. Many hundreds of others, however, wounded included, fell from the narrow span or found themselves mercilessly shoved off by the press of compatriots whose only concern was getting to the far side. The frenzied crowd also stymied Hiller's belated efforts to destroy the bridge. Though fifty men of the 5th and 6th Pioneer Divisions were lost (most of them pushed into the river) during the confusion as they prepared the bridge for destruction or endeavoured to set it afire, it was still very much intact when the furious French attack reached its western end.[217]

Vigorous and Murderous: The Storming of Ebelsberg

Hiller, not really expecting a fight, arrayed his forces for the defence of Ebelsberg with V Corps on his right (north) and VI Corps in the centre and left directly behind the town. Oberst Gratze, given the task of holding the town with his Grenzer, placed his 1st Battalion in the buildings overlooking the bridge and the 2nd in the upper portion of Ebelsberg (the Vormarkt).[218] The defence of the Schloss fell to three companies of III/*Lindenau*. Although the position was extraordinarily strong by nature, Hiller did not anticipate

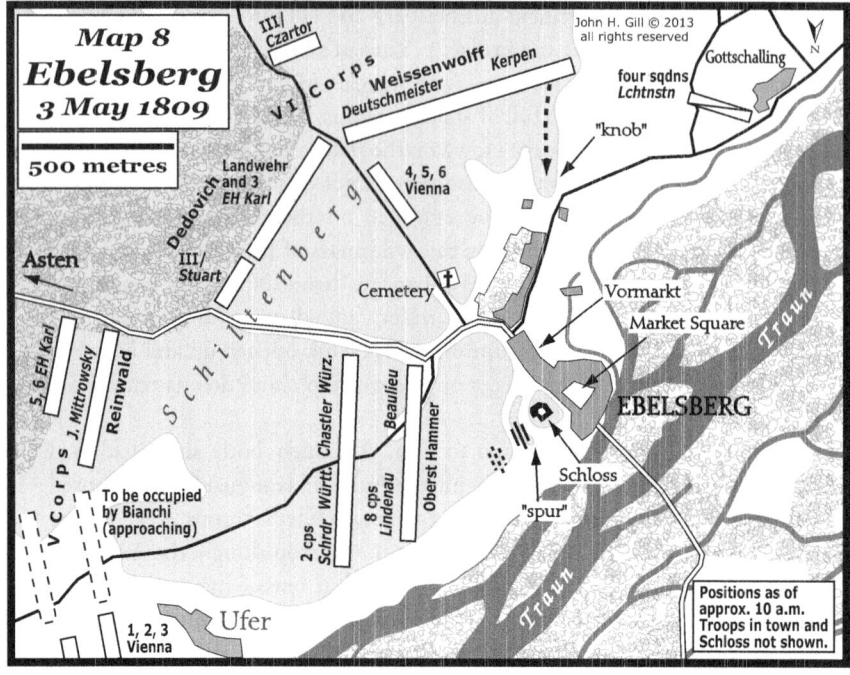

a serious action, so little was done to prepare the town or the Schloss for defence.[219]

Outside the town and Schloss, Oberst Hammer's men and three of the recruit-filled third battalions were wedged between the highway and the Traun with the more experienced regulars (*Beaulieu* and *Lindenau*) in the first line and the recruit units in the second; two companies of *Beaulieu* under Leutnant Pirquet were posted ahead of this line to protect three howitzers on a small spur north of the Schloss. Some 700 metres to the rear of these troops, Bianchi's brigade straddled a small road with the first three Vienna Volunteer battalions on the right behind Ufer and Reinwald's five battalions on the heights to the left up to the post road. In long white- and grey-coated lines, VI Corps stretched across the gentle open slope of the Schiltenberg. Dedovich's right flank rested on the highway, on his left was Weissenwolff's brigade and III/*Czartoryski*.[220] In front of these VI Corps troops were the 4th, 5th, and 6th Vienna Volunteers under the command of the senior battalion commander, Oberstleutnant Johann Küffel von Küffelstein. Having been consistently forgotten in army orders, they had marched across the

Traun on 2 May and encamped east of town on their own volition. No one saw a need to shift them. The four squadrons of *Liechtenstein* Hussars that Hiller had requisitioned from Nordmann covered the low ground on the extreme left from the edge of the Schiltenberg to the river. For artillery, the defenders initially had only the three howitzers on the spur near the Schloss and a battery of 6-pounders near the waterline just downstream from the bridge. It is hard to envisage a more perfect situation for a defender, given the tactics and technologies of the Napoleonic era. 'Our position was superb,' remembered Leutnant Pirquet.[221]

As for the remainder of his command, Hiller sent II Reserve Corps east to Asten in case the French crossed the Traun south of Ebelsberg and sought to cut his retreat route.[222] The trains and heavy artillery were on the road to Enns along with the three Landwehr battalions of the Linz garrison. The rest of the artillery parked temporarily along the main road just east of the Schiltenberg under the protection of III/*Stain*.[223] Finally, one of the *Jordis* depot companies was sent to guard the bridge at Kremsdorf, where it was later joined by two companies of the regiment's 2nd Battalion.[224]

Most of these troops were resting, cooking, eating, caring for their horses, or otherwise engaged in routine bivouac chores, their muskets stacked in pyramids as their comrades struggled to hold the rampaging French on the far bank. They expected to see the bridge burst into flames at any moment.[225] 'In the Schloss, the table was prepared for the headquarters and the high-ranking gentlemen were about to set to their meal when the French stormed the bridge,' recounted the local curate. 'The care-taker thus lost all of the tableware and silver that he had brought out of hiding to serve the senior guests.'[226]

On the far side of the bridge, Coëhorn, 'an officer of singular intrepidity', seized his opportunity.[227] Immediately at hand were his two superb light infantry battalions, the Tirailleurs du Po, who had scrambled over the bridge pilings at Passau, and the Tirailleurs Corses from Napoleon's native island. Coëhorn, without waiting for orders, rode to these two veteran units, placed himself at their head and ordered them forward at double time. Pushing the panic-stricken Austrians before them, his troops lunged forward with great élan, jogging over the crowded bridge through musketry and canister fire. The French were literally on the heels of the whitecoats, some grasping Austrian backpacks and leather gear in their rush. Dozens of men—dead, wounded, and unhurt, friend and foe alike—toppled into the roaring Traun as the brigade rammed its way towards the eastern shore. The Tirailleurs Corses, who made up the head of the column, hurled themselves into the town where the melee became general,' remembered Chef de Bataillon Jean Castillon of IV/76th Ligne.[228] It was a chaotic scene of struggling, shoving, shouting men under fire, but Coëhorn kept his horse and his brigade kept its order. An Austrian howitzer unlimbered beneath the Ebelsberg gate tower and opened fire straight down the bridge, but neither this gun, nor the supporting pieces near the castle, nor the Grenzer firing from the buildings near the gate could delay the determined assault. 'The attack was vigorous and murderous,' remembered Castillon.[229] Coëhorn and his men were soon masters of the lone howitzer and the structures near the riverside. It was about noon and a brief pause ensued as the brigade collected itself, and its commander decided what to do next. He did not delay long, but launched most of his men across the empty market square to secure the town while two smaller columns turned left and right to protect his flanks and to silence the annoying guns near the Schloss.

The Grenzer of II/Wallach-Illyria were shocked. Resting in the Vormarkt on the eastern side of Ebelsberg, the Croatians, like the Habsburg troops in the Schiltenberg, had paid no heed to the snapping musketry and rolling artillery fire beyond the river. Caught unawares as Coëhorn's impetuous attack burst through the Enns Gate between the square and the Vormarkt, some fought back bravely along with scattered remnants of Hoffmeister's brigade, but many fled and many others quickly gave up and found themselves being led away into captivity or worse. Coëhorn, his horse now shot out from under him, instantly saw that possession of the square and of the Vormarkt did not equate to possession of the town. He would have to control the rim of high ground to the east. Despite heavy fire from disparate groups of Austrians nestled in the surrounding buildings, he forged ahead. As his men trotted out of the deep defiles formed by the roads east of town, however, they suddenly saw Hiller's entire army camped on the slopes above them.

Meanwhile, action was developing to Coëhorn's flanks and rear. The column he had sent to his right was chasing the fleeing Grenzer, and beginning to deploy on the southern edges of town. His left-hand column had immediate success in forcing the Austrian battery at the riverside into hasty flight and even managed to seize one of the guns. Leutnant Pirquet, however, boldly leading his two companies in a sudden counter-attack, threw back the French, and captured several of the structures near the water. Despite this little victory, his efforts to reach the bridge failed. With his men 'all jumbled up', all the officers down, and facing French reinforcements, the two companies broke and fled as Pirquet took a grave wound in the neck and stumbled to the rear, dazed and incapable of speech.[230]

The new French troops were from Ficatier's brigade. While Coëhorn was driving through Ebelsberg's marketplace, Claparède was rushing reinforcements across the Traun as fast as traffic on the bridge would permit. Austrian artillery rained on the running battalions because Hauptmann Simbschen, Radetzky's subordinate, had moved three guns into position atop the small plateau north-east of the Schloss on his own initiative; three more soon unlimbered in the same spot. Shot and canister thus knocked dozens of men out of the ranks, but the French did not slow. A pair of guns came first, followed by Lesuire and Ficatier. Claparède placed the two guns in the main square and sent Lesuire directly into town to bolster Coëhorn and to cope with the scattered but determined Austrians still in the buildings around the plaza.[231] The 8th Line Demi-Brigade also moved into the town, but Claparède dispatched the 7th (only some 800 to 900 men in two thin battalions) to the left of the bridge to deal with Pirquet. The Elite Company of the 19th Chasseurs, hurled across by Marulaz, somehow managed to negotiate the bridge and maintained itself in Ebelsberg for a short time before finding its presence both unhelpful and costly.

The arrival of these French reinforcements was most timely. The speed and audacity of Coëhorn's charge had caught the Austrians on the Schiltenberg completely off guard, but the nearest units, Küffel's Vienna Volunteers, reacted with desperate haste. Küffel got his men in line and ordered an advance with admirable promptitude: 4th Battalion on the right (north), 5th on the left and 6th in the middle, directly towards the cemetery. French fire quickly brought this initial assault to a halt and shattered a fumbling effort by III/*Würzburg* and III/*Beaulieu* to advance in concert with the volunteers. These latter two battalions, utterly astonished to see Coëhorn's men appear like magic in the sunken portion of the highway, broke and fled to the rear. Coëhorn's right column on the southern side of Ebelsberg, however, was in trouble. Oberst August Freiherr Vécsey's *Kienmayer* Hussars and parts of Radetzky's uhlans (about two squadrons) were trotting over to reassemble in front of the *Liechtenstein* Hussars when French skirmishers unexpectedly appeared from town. Vécsey, 'inspired by a truly heroic spirit' according to Radetzky's report, lost no time in launching this group of horsemen against the enemy 'at full gallop in dispersed order'.[232] The 5th Vienna, slipping to its left, joined in the battle here and I/*Kerpen*, deploying with a battery on a knob on the edge of the Schiltenberg, sent three companies to assist. The French skirmishers gave way and the Austrians made painful but steady headway in bitter close-quarters fighting. Simultaneously, Küffel renewed the attack with the 4th and 6th Battalions. This time, he was supported by the eight companies of *Lindenau* and I/*Joseph Mittrowsky*; III/*Stuart* and III/*Joseph Mittrowsky* were also moving up. The key advance was that of I/*Joseph Mittrowsky* as it cut behind the French defenders in the Vormarkt and forced many tirailleurs to surrender.[233] The French, however, held on to every house, fence, and garden with grim tenacity and the Austrian push only ground forward slowly. Some of the most obstinate resistance came from the many men who had dispersed into homes and shops in search of loot.

On the northern edge of town, the Austrians were fortunate that another junior officer selected exactly the right moment to demonstrate personal initiative. The 7th Line Demi-Brigade, having crushed Pirquet's little command, had tried and failed to storm the Schloss from the south and west. Elements of the 7th, however, swung through the ditches north of the castle and threatened (albeit by accident) to strike the Austrians that were in the Vormarkt from behind. Instead, the French found themselves trapped when Hauptmann Heinrich von Siegler brought his two companies of *Schröder* against their flank and rear while part of I/*J. Mittrowsky* held them in the front. The French attack collapsed in a confused struggle of musket butts and bayonets. Subsequent attempts to revive their assault proved fruitless.

It was now 2 p.m. and Claparède was facing disaster. On his right, the 5th Vienna and the three I/*Kerpen* companies had reached the Traun and were pressing for the bridge. The Austrians had thrown back his centre, retaken the Vormarkt, and were threatening to penetrate into the main marketplace. On his left, the French attack had stalled and his young troops were nervously looking towards the bridge as they learned about the Austrian push into town. Losses in killed and wounded were heavy, at least 700 men had been captured, and many of his troops were fleeing in disorder towards the bridge. Moreover, the men were exhausted. They had been up and moving well before dawn, had marched thirty kilometres, had fought in the action west of the Traun in the late morning, and had endured a brutal, often hand-to-hand, battle for nearly three hours since crossing the dreadful bridge.

Claparède and Coëhorn, however, were not the sort of men to give in easily. On the French right, a coherent line was established to hold the 5th Vienna in check, while Coëhorn stationed himself at the gate tower near the bridge to turn back fugitives. For his part, Claparède placed the two guns to cover the Enns Gate and arranged his infantry in the square and the surrounding houses. The first Austrians who attempted to pass through the Enns Gate were thus greeted with a blast of canister, and French cannon shot quickly dismounted the first gun the Austrians brought up. Halted but sensing opportunity, the Austrian commanders in and around the town called urgently for reinforcements to finish off the French. Hiller would not send any. He once again found himself in a most uncomfortable situation. He had hoped to rest his command east of the Traun for at least one day before retiring to the position behind the Enns. Now Austrian stumbling and Coëhorn's impetuosity had breached his newest defensive line before it was even established. As the Austrian official history points out, he must have felt an overwhelming weight of responsibility crash onto his shoulders: not only had he disappointed the Kaiser by abandoning the line of the Inn prematurely, not only had he skirted Charles's desire that he cross the Danube at Linz, but now his independent decision to retreat behind the Traun was devolving into a new calamity. Worse, he finally learned that he was facing Napoleon himself and an Allied army of at least 60,000 men.[234] Hiller thus saw no option but retreat at the earliest possible moment. Mindful of the catastrophe at Landshut and the chaotic scene that very morning as the cumbersome trains attempted to cross the river, he wanted to hold on long enough to get his baggage and artillery safely over the Enns. He did not yet know that French troops had passed over the Traun at Wels,[235] but he was probably chary of throwing any more men into the brutal struggle in the confined space in and around the town. Although he had at least twenty battalions at his disposal on the Schiltenberg to augment the thirteen already embrangled in Ebelsberg, he was too cautious and too worried about his coming retreat to risk wrecking his army by committing any of them to the savage fight.[236] Instead, he ordered Kienmayer to post his corps in a covering position at Asten, pushed his trains and some of the less combat-worthy troops over the Enns, and ordered engineers to begin improving the roads as far east as Melk.[237] The requests for reinforcements in Ebelsberg would go unanswered.

Cruel Fire: The Destruction of Ebelsberg

Hiller's decision meant that the grit and determination of the French soldiers and the superb leadership of their officers were not in vain. Pressure on Claparède and his men did not ease perceptibly, but neither did it increase. Massena had just enough time to throw another division into the vortex of combat in the little town.

Although there was plenty of Allied cavalry on the west bank, the horsemen were worse than useless in street fighting, and the next available infantry was delayed in arriving. These men, Legrand's 1st Division, had been held up by confusion in the long march column—especially the careless and disruptive movements of the cuirassier regiments. Yet more problematic were the liquid attractions of the cloister at Wilhering. While officers took their breakfast in the refectory, many French soldiers availed themselves of the rich store of wine. When tapping seemed too tedious, men used bayonets, musket butts, and musket balls to speed delivery of the local vintages. Such activity introduced delay, disorder, and tipsy straggling into the advance, but the Badeners following behind, though annoyed to find most of the wine gone by the time their battalions reached the cloister, could not help but marvel at the 'unique rhythm' of the French under such circumstances.[238] In fits and starts, the division's march proceeded, halting just short of Linz to order the ranks so that the city could be traversed in a disciplined manner.

Just beyond the city, however, 'we heard near Ebelsberg on the Traun a lively cannonade and musketry; many wounded already began to pass us.'[239] By now several of Massena's adjutants had ridden up to hasten Legrand's approach, but Colonel Pouget, whose 26th Léger was leading the divisional column, was not about to be recklessly rushed. 'You can see', he told an agitated staff officer, 'that we cannot go any faster, I will not force this march whatever your orders.'[240] Pouget's care and circumspection, however, masked the speed at which Legrand's men were driving for Ebelsberg. 'We followed in all haste,' wrote Chef de Bataillon Pierre Pelleport of the 18th Ligne.[241] For the Badeners, 'muskets were loaded while running and the rapid movement alternated from time to time with a more normal pace as it was necessary to let the troops catch their breath.'[242] Adjutants carried equally urgent orders to the other divisions, while Massena and Legrand pulled all available guns out of the line of march and arrayed them on the islands and banks along the western edge of the river to add their deeper thunder to the wild cacophony of the battle.

The crash and chaos of combat so absorbed the French that they did not notice an Austrian artilleryman as he stole towards the buildings on the western edge of town. Corporal Johann Gabella of Radetzky's battery managed to start a fire by tossing a bundle of incendiary material into one of the structures near the bridge. He escaped unharmed as the flames started to gnaw at the wooden building and his daring won him the Silver Medal of Bravery, but it would soon turn Ebelsberg into an intolerable inferno.[243]

Legrand led Ledru's brigade across the bridge at approximately 2.30 p.m. Moving at the run, the column forced its way over the span against the oncoming fugitives from Claparède's division. Numerous wounded soldiers were pitilessly pushed aside to fall to their deaths in the river below.[244] Legrand, reaching the far bank, sent Ledru with his lead regiment, Pouget's 26th Léger, to the left to seize the Schloss, while he personally led 18th Ligne directly into the town.[245] The sudden onslaught of the 18th swept the Austrians away from the Enns Gate and carried the regiment into the Vormarkt, but a counter-attack soon threw the Frenchmen back into the market square. At the same time, Pouget's attack on the castle also stalled. With no time for reconnaissance, he found his regiment trapped in the narrow way leading from the town to the castle. 'The dead accumulated in a frightening manner' as his men courageously but futilely attempted to force the barred door.[246] In short order, therefore, Legrand's initial rush was blunted, his momentum lost.

To revive the attack, Legrand formed two flanking columns, sending III/18th Ligne to the right (south), and calling up the Baden Jäger Battalion to swing to the left (north).[247] The Badeners were delayed because the rapidly spreading fire in the town had set the eastern end of the bridge alight and threatened to detonate several munitions wagons that Massena had brought across the river. Hustling the caissons to safety and making temporary repairs to the bridge meant that the Jägers did not cross over until shortly after 3 p.m.

By this time Hiller had had enough. Observing the action from somewhere east of the Enns Gate, he could see that the bridge was intact and out of reach, that more Allied troops were arriving by the minute, and that his own men were running short of ammunition. Contrary to his later account, he did not yet know that Lannes had crossed the Traun at Wels, but as he was unwilling to commit any fresh troops to the hellish struggle, withdrawal was the only remaining option. A new instance of panic among his troops may have lent urgency to his decision. Dedovich, looking for a battalion to replace III/*Stuart* (which was out of ammunition), found the reformed III/*Beaulieu* behind the village and endeavoured to lead it forward. Blasted with a hail of musketry, however, the battalion dissolved and fled to the rear despite the desperate pleas of its officers. Around the same time, Dedovich was thrown out of the saddle when his horse stumbled on a heap of corpses near the Enns Gate. With one foot still in a stirrup, he found himself being dragged along behind his terrified mount. Only the quick thinking and bravery of two soldiers preserved the battered general from imminent capture.

Despite the order to withdraw, the Austrians put up obstinate resistance to Legrand's renewed advance. The fighting was grim, intense, and costly, but by approximately 4 p.m. Ebelsberg was finally in French hands and the first two battalions of 18th Ligne were beginning to push beyond the gardens on the eastern edge of town. 'I have rarely participated in such a hot action,' wrote Pelleport.[248] Resistance in the Schloss also collapsed around this time. Pouget, observing how ineffective his men were at hitting the Austrians firing from the castle's windows, called up a voltigeur lieutenant named Guyot, who was a renowned hunter. With other soldiers loading and handing him muskets, Guyot kept up a sustained, accurate fire against any Habsburg head that appeared. He was soon joined by other skilled marksmen, some firing from behind the piled-up bodies of their comrades. Under cover of these sharpshooters, bold officers led their men into the now-burning Schloss through basement windows while sappers assaulted the stout wooden door blocking the passage. Scattering through the rooms and corridors, the French found the Austrians trying to evacuate the castle. The withdrawal, however, was poorly organised and the 26th captured a large number of whitecoats— as many as 400, according to Legrand's report.[249]

As with Pelleport, Ledru and Pouget did not long delay in pushing the 26th Léger out of the Schloss onto the open ground to the east. Here the regiment found itself threatened by Bianchi's brigade, which was advancing to protect the withdrawal of the Austrian right wing. Simultaneously, *Deutschmeister* and the Austrian cavalry (coming from Hiller's left wing) posed a danger to the regiment's right flank where there was a large gap between 26th Léger and 18th Ligne. Fortunately for Ledru, the Baden Jägers arrived at precisely the right moment to fill the gap and cover the 26th's right. The battalion's voltigeur company, on the other hand, slipped to the left to bolster the French flank along the river. The Austrians did not press their numerical superiority and Ledru, though he estimated the enemy's strength to be nearly 15,000, believed that 'our audacity had demoralised them to the point where their officers could no longer decide to take the offensive.'[250]

As afternoon wore into evening, Hiller's army retreated towards the Enns, 'their retreat soon nothing more than a rout' in Ledru's eyes.[251] Ledru may have exaggerated, but many Austrian units were in poor shape following the brutal struggle. 'There was nothing to do but flee in general dissolution,' wrote a soldier of *Deutschmeister*, 'I leaped down the slope like a qualified voltigeur.'[252] Other elements of *Deutschmeister* offered tough resistance along the edge of the woods atop the Schiltenberg, slowing Legrand's pursuit and losing their colonel in the process. Many of the units that had been embroiled in the heated fighting, however, were hardly combat-worthy: III/*Stuart*, for example, had only fifteen men and a Hauptmann around its colours as it exited the forest. Those who had been spared the battle also suffered.[253]

Fleeing Habsburg cavalry from the left wing crashed into the retreating 2nd and 3rd Battalions of *Kerpen* so that the whole disordered mass staggered back through the woods and only managed to reassemble itself on the far side. Moreover, as at Landshut, Major O'Brien and I/*Kerpen* were once again forgotten in the confusion. The battalion, cut off and harassed by French skirmishers, made its own way back to St Florian.

Followed more than pursued by the exhausted and outnumbered French, Hiller retired to the east as fast as confusion and weariness would permit. Kienmayer covered the withdrawal by posting two of his grenadier battalions, three and one-half squadrons of *Knesevich* Dragoons, and the *Rosenberg* Chevaulegers across the highway at Bruck bei Tödling. At St Florian, a third grenadier battalion and a half-squadron of dragoons received the retreat of I/*Kerpen* and repulsed probes by French and Baden light infantry.[254] As V and VI Corps made their escape over the Enns, Kienmayer pulled back to Asten, where the *Scharlach* and *Scovaud* Grenadiers and the 1st Moravian Volunteers waited in a support position. With no light artillery, few fresh infantry units, and little cavalry, Massena and Legrand were understandably cautious. Napoleon had sent one of his staff generals, GD Antoine Durosnel, north from Wels along the east bank of the Traun with Jacquinot's brigade and 9th Hussars, but this small reinforcement was hardly enough to overcome Kienmayer's rear guard and turn the Habsburg retreat into a rout. Durosnel's force did suffice to overthrow the detachment of *Jordis* at Kremsdorf: of the 600 to 650 men in the two depot and two line companies, some 310 were casualties (mostly missing/captured) after a short fight.[255] Combat between the principal forces, however, was confined to lively skirmishing that petered out around 9 p.m. By 11.30 that night, the Austrians and their discouraged commander were safely across the Enns, watching the bridge at Ennsdorf go up in flames.

Flames also consumed Ebelsberg. What Pelet called 'this cruel fire' spread through the town and the castle, destroying sixty-seven of the eighty houses that made up the market area. Wounded men who had crept into buildings to escape the fighting were burned to death in the most horrible fashion. 'Ebelsberg offered a frightful spectacle; the streets were full of cadavers mostly consumed by fire, and burned wounded who had endeavoured to leave the houses.' Markgraf Wilhelm remembered that the charred corpses in the windows 'seemed to beg for pity from the passers-by'.[256] Dr Meier of the Baden contingent entered the wreck of the town late that afternoon: 'Never did I see, not even in great battles such as Wagram, corpses and wounded lying so thickly next to and atop one another as here.'[257]

The effect on the combatants was profound. Major Charles Faré of IV/69th Ligne described the battle in a letter to his mother as 'one of the most terrible that one could imagine'.[258] 'I was covered with the blood of my brave men who fell near me,' wrote GB Ledru.[259] The hideous aftermath also left an indelible impression on everyone who passed through the town in the following days. The smouldering desolation and the hundreds of charred human bodies trampled by skittish horses and crushed under the wheels of hastening guns and caissons left 'a feeling of intense horror and disgust, of which I have never been able to shake off the memory', recalled Lejeune.[260] Weeks later, Ebelsberg was still nothing but a blackened spot on the landscape, 'a mass of smoking ruins and cadavers'.[261]

Many officers and men, captured by curiosity, visited this morbid site the following day: 'Tears rolled from all eyes and no one dared to proffer a word.' 'I have never seen anything more frightening than those burned cadavers that no longer bore any resemblance to the human,' recalled bandsman Girault of the 93rd Ligne, 'I have walked many fields of battle, but I have never been stricken by such emotion.'[262] Napoleon, visibly disturbed, told his staff as he viewed the carnage on 4 May, 'Every war agitator should see a parallel monstrosity; they should know what their projects cost in evil to humanity.'[263]

The cost to humanity was high indeed. Hiller's casualties totalled some 8,200, or approximately 16 per cent of his combat strength that day, while Massena's corps lost an estimated 3,550 men. On the Austrian side, Infantry Regiment No. 40, the former *Josef Mittrowsky*, took the worst losses, leaving behind 1,046 of its officers and men, or approximately one-third of its effectives. Curiously, Gratze's *Wallach-Illyria* Grenzer suffered only ninety-one casualties, suggesting that their resistance against Claparède's initial onslaught was less than tenacious and that they contributed little to the subsequent combat. The heaviest French losses came from Claparède's division: approximately 850 dead, 1,200 wounded, and 800 prisoners for a total cost of more than one-third of the division's strength. Coëhorn's two tirailleur battalions were especially devastated. Legrand, on the other hand, paid the comparatively low price of 700 casualties.

The most remarkable aspect of the casualty figures, however, is the gross disparity between the antagonists' losses. Where the numbers for dead and wounded on each side were fairly close (2,870 Austrian against 2,750 French), the Austrian total for missing and captured came to some 5,330 as compared to 800 French. Approximately 40 per cent of these fell into Allied hands on the west side of the Traun when disaster struck Vincent's rear guard, but more than 3,000 were taken in Ebelsberg or during the ill-organised retreat to the Enns. Even regiments on the fringes of the fighting had significant numbers of missing and captured.[264] These results are all the more astonishing when one considers that the French were attacking a numerically superior enemy in an extremely strong defensive position. The large percentage of green recruits in the raw third battalions partly explains the tally of missing and prisoners, but it seems clear that the fabric of Hiller's army was wearing very thin. The long retreat from Bavaria, repeated setbacks, wretched weather, poor logistical arrangements, and weak senior leadership sapped Austrian strength. The men fought with dogged ferocity and junior officers displayed bravery, initiative, and skill, but the army frayed rapidly when forced to displace in the face of the aggressive French.

Hiller's pathetic performance compounded the army's problems.[265] Leaving aside the question of his decision to retreat behind the Traun, his arrangements for the withdrawal from Linz were sloppy and he was lackadaisical towards the rear guard, making little effort to co-ordinate its actions with the main body. Vincent made matters worse with his panicky conduct of the rear guard fight. These errors by senior Austrian commanders allowed the French to surprise the main body with their courageous but rash crossing of the river, rapidly gaining a foothold on the far bank and an important psychological edge: 'this audacity stupefied the Austrians,' wrote historian Buat.[266] Once the French were in Ebelsberg, Hiller rejected the opportunity to destroy Claparède's division but otherwise did little to manage the battle. Finally, the retreat was badly handled. Had the burning town not delayed French reinforcements, especially cavalry and artillery, Hiller could have suffered a much more serious defeat.

On the French side, officers and men had done all that was asked of them and more. Co-ordination between Claparède and Legrand seems to have been weak, but otherwise the senior French commanders demonstrated superb leadership.[267] They exploited Austrian vulnerabilities, created opportunities, and rallied their troops in extraordinarily challenging circumstances.[268] Massena praised Legrand for executing his instructions 'with infinite precision' and all of the French commanders were constantly in the heat of the action.[269] As for the men, veteran units such as the two tirailleur battalions and Legrand's regiments exhibited their wonted competence and valour, but even the thrown-together battalions of Claparède's division comported themselves with great courage. Savary called the storming of the bridge and the seizure of Ebelsberg 'a feat of arms that can be regarded as one of the most grand extravagances of courage in military history'.[270]

The military value of this exemplary gallantry and enormous sacrifice has been questioned. Napoleon paid tribute to the men of Massena's corps in general and Coëhorn in particular, but he excoriated the marshal in a note to Lannes on 4 May for having 'the stupidity to attack that renowned position with full force'.[271] With Ebelsberg already turned by the crossing at Wels, the emperor assessed the 4th Corps' struggle as a waste of good men for little gain. Most commentators agree. Buat, for example, argues that Massena should have limited himself to keeping the Austrians engaged west of the Traun to allow the rest of 4th Corps to catch up and to await the development of a flanking manoeuvre from the south.[272] Having hesitated at Landshut on 21 April, however, Massena, Claparède, and Coëhorn may have wanted to redeem themselves, boldly pushing their men and themselves to capitalise on any opportunity. Moreover, once the impetuous Coëhorn had thrown his brigade across the bridge, it is hard to see how Massena could have left him unsupported. Additionally, the rash assault did preserve the bridge for the French where a more restrained approach likely would have granted Hiller time to complete its destruction. Given the severe challenge of traversing the Traun along the post road, the problems Napoleon had already experienced in crossing major rivers, and the lack of a French pontoon train, the ability to employ the Ebelsberg bridge was not a small consideration.

While Hiller's and Massena's men grappled in the hellish alleys of Ebelsberg, Napoleon waited for news. The French emperor had ridden north from Lambach in the morning but, hardly expecting Hiller to retreat over the Traun, he had halted north of Wels to gain more information before making his dispositions for the afternoon. If Hiller made a stand south of the Danube, Napoleon wanted every available bayonet and sabre at Linz. If, on the other hand, the Austrians either retreated over the Danube to join the Main Army or withdrew behind the Traun, the emperor would want to press on for Vienna to outflank the Ebelsberg position and draw Archduke Charles into battle south of the Danube. When cannon fire became audible around 10 a.m. as Claparède's division lanced into Vincent's rear guard, he sent Oudinot north with Tharreau's division in accordance with the plan he had outlined the previous evening. This left only Marshal Lannes and the light cavalry brigades of Colbert and Jacquinot around Wels. St Hilaire, Molitor, Nansouty, St Sulpice, and Demont were all en route to Wels but would not arrive for several hours. Other than the distant rumble of artillery, however, Napoleon had no information upon which to base his decisions and he waited impatiently for word from Massena or Bessières. Initial reports, arriving an hour later, specified that Hiller was retreating behind the Traun, so around midday Napoleon set the available troops in motion towards the Enns. Durosnel with the 9th Hussars and Jacquinot's men would ride up the east bank of the Traun to reconnoitre.[273] Bessières would take Tharreau's division and Piré's brigade to the town of Enns, while Lannes moved on Steyr with Colbert, St Hilaire, Molitor, and Nansouty. Around 4 p.m., therefore, when he finally learned that Massena was embroiled in a battle for the Ebelsberg bridge, Napoleon had no troops at hand. He immediately recalled Molitor and Nansouty, placed himself at their head, and marched north on the east side of the river with all speed. 'We heard the cannon to our left, where one could see a great deal of smoke,' remembered François Joseph Jacquin of the 37th. 'The Emperor, having looked at his map, gave the order to our colonel to direct himself to that point with his regiment; we began a forced march at once; but we arrived too late.'[274] The battle was long over when the column arrived south of Ebelsberg late that night.[275]

The end of 3 May thus saw the French still arrayed in two broad columns south of the Danube. On the right, Lannes had Colbert's two chasseurs regiments between Steyr and Kremsmünster, his headquarters and St Hilaire in the latter town, and Demont at Lambach. Molitor and Nansouty were just one or two kilometres south of Ebelsberg, as was Napoleon's headquarters. On the left, Massena's and Bessières's troops were mixed together on the road generally from Asten to Scharlinz: Durosnel and most of Marulaz's squadrons at Asten with Legrand just behind; Tharreau and Claparède bivouacked on the Schiltenberg east of Ebelsberg; Piré, Espagne, Carra Saint-Cyr, and Boudet just west of the Traun on the road to Linz. St Sulpice, Bruyère, and Vandamme were in and west of Wels, while Davout had his three divisions stretched along the road from St Willibald to Passau. Most of the Guard was in Lambach.[276]

Colbert had aggressively pushed Nordmann's scattered brigade (only some 1,400 men) from the Alm and Traun well beyond Kremsmünster during the day. The French pursuit eventually relaxed and Nordmann's weary force crossed the Enns at Steyr around midnight without further trouble from the enemy.[277] Here he found Oberst MacDermott with his brigade of 3,090 Upper Austrian Landwehr. Although there were no major engagements, the Austrians had suffered considerable loss and Nordmann felt harassed, isolated, and threatened by superior forces. Towards morning, he personally ignited the flammable material on the bridge and hastily headed for Weyer with his weak brigade and MacDermott's Landwehr.[278] He left behind a small, anxious detachment to watch the crossing site.[279]

Map 9
From Linz to Melk
John H. Gill © 2013, all rights reserved

North of the Danube, Hardegg withdrew to Grein. Hiller had hoped to bring Hardegg south of the river, but he learned on reaching Enns that some ships had accidentally crashed into the pontoon bridge at Mauthausen, damaging it severely, and leaving Hiller no choice but to have it dismantled and transferred to Krems.[280]

4–11 MAY: RETREAT AND PURSUIT

Fortunately for Hiller, the thorough destruction of the bridges at Enns and Steyr imposed another operational pause on Napoleon. Despite feverish efforts, the French were unable to construct a bridge at either site for two days. A small Austrian detachment hindered the efforts of the French engineers at Ennsdorf on 4 May, but the principal problems were high water and lack of materials.[281] Hiller used this respite to move his army towards Krems, the next major crossing point on the Danube. He once again entrusted his rear guard to Schustekh with Radetzky's tired brigade, Mesko's men (under Oberst Vécsey in place of the wounded Mesko), and Reinwald. His main body reached the Ybbs around Neumarkt on 5 May, spurred by a sharp remonstrance from the generalissimus. Charles, on learning that Hiller planned to retire behind the Traun, sent an angry reply in which he accused Hiller of disobeying direct orders and thereby thwarting the planned union of their two armies north of Linz. He then proceeded to instruct Hiller to 'cross the Danube at Mauthausen without the least delay, effect your junction with me at once and act as you see fit according to the instructions you have already received from me'. Hiller was also reminded of the order to leave between 8,000 and 10,000 men in the Danube valley 'to place as many obstacles as possible in the enemy's way by removing all bridges'.[282] Stunned by the pointed critique, Hiller responded with prevarication. He implied that enemy action precluded his planned crossing at Linz and exaggerated the damage to the Mauthausen pontoon bridge to excuse his further retreat south of the river. This tendency towards evasiveness would manifest itself again when he came to forming the detachment that was to remain on the right bank of the Danube.

Hiller certainly overstated some of his problems, but others were real enough. Logistical inadequacies were especially severe and these brought with them grievous breaches of discipline. The army was thus caught in a vicious cycle. On the one hand, the failure of the official supply apparatus, compounded by the recent defeats and retreats, left men and horses weak, discouraged, and sometimes desperate, so that many troops turned to marauding. On the other hand, fear of these Austrian marauders as well as the approaching enemy caused most local residents to flee their homes with everything they could carry. This left the army painfully short of food, fodder, and transport, all of which were drawn in part from local resources. The land was empty, the villages abandoned, and many stragglers heedlessly succumbed to base urges of greed and violence. The rear guards endured the worst shortages as they had to traverse areas already devastated by the leading elements of the army. 'The worst barbarians could not behave as cruelly as our infantry stragglers,' lamented Mesko.[283]

Among the stragglers afflicting the countryside were hundreds of Landwehr. Rampant desertion had reduced most Landwehr companies to a mere twenty to forty men, and in some cases all of the enlisted men had simply disappeared. The troops from Upper Austria were especially prone to leave the ranks. As the army had departed their home province on crossing the Enns, many of them no longer felt obligated to serve and took the first opportunity to return to their homes. Even those who remained with the colours caused problems. At the head of the retreating column, they were first in line to draw from the magazines along the way and not infrequently made off with more than their share. The troops coming behind, with only irregular supplies from army sources, often took what they needed or wanted from the local population by force.[284]

The French, of course, passing through the same sad towns and villages, found even less sustenance than their foes. In instructions to Daru written on 4 May, Berthier highlighted the problem, directing the intendant general to bring forward all of the bakers from the rear areas and to hurry the preparation and transport of biscuit as 'The army, having only a single road to carry it to Vienna, is in great need of food as it is experiencing tremendous difficulties sustaining itself.'[285] Nor were the French any more clement to the population. Guardsman Chevalier remarked on the lovely towns, beautiful forests, and industrious inhabitants of the region, but observed that: 'Unfortunately, all of these villages were pillaged and re-pillaged by the bands of marauders that infested our army.'[286] 'Terror preceded us, devastation followed in our wake,' noted pharmacist Charles Louis Cadet de Gassicourt.[287]

Operational Pause on the Enns

Napoleon, chafing at the delay imposed by the burned bridges, found outlets for his enormous energy in arranging matters in the rear areas. Among other things, he conducted numerous reviews, with special focus on the two divisions that had fought at Ebelsberg.[288] These reviews produced some of the enduring memories of the campaign as Napoleon demanded that commanders name the bravest men in their regiments and rewarded these individuals grandly. Dismounting before Pouget's 26th Léger to begin his customary walk through the ranks, for instance, the emperor called for the sapper who had landed the first axe blows on the door of the Schloss and presented Corporal Hattin with the cross of the Legion of Honour. He then demanded that Pouget name the bravest officer in the regiment. Nonplussed, Pouget stumbled.

'Now then, did you hear me?'
'Yes, Sire, but I know many who . . .'
'No phrases, answer!'

Pouget hastily called for Lieutenant Nicolas Guyot, the sharpshooter 'who had shown no fear even though exposed to the greatest peril'. When the embarrassed lieutenant appeared, Napoleon told him: 'You have been designated by your commanders as the bravest officer of the regiment; I name you baron and grant you an endowment of 4,000 livres.' In response to the emperor's request for the regiment's most valiant soldier, the officers nominated a carabinier with the ideal martial name of Bayonette. Napoleon made this common private a chevalier of the Legion of Honour with a hereditary endowment of 1,500 francs. 'It is impossible to describe the effect produced by these last two nominations on those who were the recipients and on the entire regiment,' wrote Pouget.[289] Napoleon almost always included detailed personal inspections of the soldiers in such a grand review and capped the entire affair by putting units through a series of manoeuvres to satisfy himself of the level of training. In one event, therefore, he could distribute rewards to the deserving, display his personal concern for the common soldier, and impose demanding standards of administrative competence and tactical proficiency on individuals and units.[290]

In addition to reviewing his men, Napoleon took steps to guard the army's lines of communication. Of immediate interest was Linz, as he wanted to deprive Charles of the opportunity to strike his rear from that direction. He selected the Württemberg contingent for this mission, and Berthier sent orders to Vandamme to occupy the city, rebuild the bridge, and construct a bridgehead on the north bank. Vandamme received these instructions at Ebelsberg on the afternoon of 4 May. The 8th Corps had already passed through the grisly town when this order arrived, so the men were subjected to an extended experience of 'the most terrifying scene of war's destruction and human misery' as they made their way back through the town.[291] Exhaustion compounded the stark images of horror. The troops had already covered some 125 kilometres during the preceding two and a half days, but Vandamme immediately started them on the road to Linz. 'After a very difficult march during which, among other things, I fell asleep and tumbled in the ditch along the road, we arrived in Linz this morning at two hours after midnight,' wrote one officer. 'We were quartered at once, but could not enjoy our rest for long.'[292]

Despite the exhausting marches, the restive Vandamme lost no time in executing his task. When the Austrian defenders and local officials refused his demand that they evacuate the northern suburb of Urfahr and deliver to him all available shipping, he arrayed his Württembergers along the south bank of the Danube in full view of the Austrians. In an imposing martial display, the troops deployed with rolling drums and blaring trumpets at 4 a.m. on the morning of 5 May. The Austrians on the far bank were ten companies of the 3rd and 4th Prachin Landwehr under GM von Richter. Combined with a mixed bag of stragglers from various regiments and a squadron of *Vincent* Chevaulegers sent by Stutterheim, they made a total of some 1,500 infantry and 100 horsemen. Richter rejected another demand for submission, but had no artillery and could not reply when Vandamme's twenty guns opened up.[293] Fires broke out in Urfahr as two companies of *Neuffer* Jäger made their way across the great river on rafts at approximately 8 a.m. The Landwehr, poorly posted and terrified by the artillery fire, had done nothing to watch the river upstream from Urfahr and were thus completely unprepared when Oberst von Neuffer and his men charged into the town from their flank and rear. The bold Württembergers, at most 250–300 Jägers, captured 180 Austrians in a brief struggle at the cost of a few wounded. Richter and a colonel were among the prisoners. The rest of the Landwehr dissolved and fled. By evening, all four light battalions were across the river along with two squadrons of *König* Jäger-zu-Pferd. These troops fanned out in all directions, occupying Ottensheim and pushing outposts towards Hellmonsödt, Gallneukirchen, and Steyregg.[294]

Meanwhile, the army was assembling between the Traun and the Enns. To do so, most men and horses had to pass through the ruins of Ebelsberg, as pharmacist François Duriau noted in his journal: 'the streets were full of roasted cadavers . . . obliged to wait for two hours in the midst of the most appalling spectacle . . . a day I will never forget.'[295]

This gruesome hindrance notwithstanding, by the evening of 5 May, Bessières, Massena, Oudinot, and the Guard were concentrated west of Enns. Several organisational adjustments were introduced, so that all three heavy cavalry divisions came under Bessières along with Jacquinot, Piré, and Bruyère. Molitor returned to Massena's corps but the marshal retained Claparède, leaving Oudinot only in charge of Tharreau's division. Expecting to cross in force on 6 May, Napoleon ordained that Bessières would lead the advance, supported by Oudinot and detachments of sappers and pontooneers. In an effort to eschew another Ebelsberg, however, the emperor instructed Bessières that 'if it is perceived that the enemy army is still in position, you will limit yourself to reconnoitring and reporting back without going any further.' The 24th Léger was sent across the Enns in boats to secure the far bank and protect the final stages of bridge construction.

At Steyr, Lannes made faster progress. He put five voltigeur companies across the river late on 4 May and, by 11 a.m. the following morning, the bridge was restored. Colbert's two chasseur regiments crossed at once and pushed out to St Peter; lead elements of St Hilaire's division joined the cavalry that evening with the rest of the infantry stretched out to the west along the road. Warned by Napoleon to take no risks until the rest of the army was over the Enns, Lannes replied with his usual cheek: 'Your Majesty may rest easy, I will not engage in anything without being sure that your troops have passed the river at Enns.'[296]

In the army's immediate rear, Davout's lead divisions (Morand and Friant, 15,500 men and thirty guns) joined Vandamme at Linz on the evening of 5 May. Gudin was due the following day and Montbrun's detachment would arrive on the 7th. Dupas held Passau, reinforced by 12th Chasseurs, and Rouyer's troops were distributed from Passau to Regensburg. Bernadotte's Saxons were at Nabburg.

Napoleon also took further steps to protect his strategic rear. Innsbruck had fallen to the Tyrolian insurgents on 13 April in an engagement that included the embarrassing surrender of some 6,000 French and Bavarian troops. The venturesome Tyrolians, with some support from Austrian regulars, then laid siege to Kufstein, occupied Füssen and Immenstadt, and launched a spate of raids into southern Bavaria. They also sent emissaries to ignite the fires of rebellion in the Vorarlberg. These insurgent activities, though not truly co-ordinated with one another, endangered Napoleon's line of communications and undermined the stability of his key German allies. The rebel raids also threatened to supply disaffected factions in Germany with an example of anti-French resistance. Jellacic's division beyond the Lueg Pass represented an additional concern.

None of this was tolerable to the emperor and he designed counter-measures to contain the threat without detracting from his principal strategic and operational focus: the Austrian Main Army. He adopted a two-pronged approach. On the defensive side, he directed GD Beaumont to assemble a reserve division at Augsburg. Beaumont would use five of his six provisional dragoon regiments as the basis for his new command (6th Provisional Dragoons continued to Hanau to join Kellermann). Baden and Berg cavalry, Bavarian and Württemberg infantry, and transiting French march units were to comprise the rest of the division with which Beaumont was to repel Tyrolian raiders, repress any domestic unrest in the southern Rheinbund states, and prevent Austrian intrusions into Bavaria from Bohemia. As usual, Napoleon relied heavily on deception and the aura of power. 'It is necessary that the aspect of your forces in the Vorarlberg maintains the tranquillity of the land,' he told Beaumont. He optimistically estimated that he would soon have as many as 10,000 to 12,000 men in Augsburg upon whom Beaumont could draw to overawe the enemy.[297]

The offensive arm of Napoleon's strategy was 7th Corps. Lefebvre, calling on Wrede if necessary, was directed to teach the insurgents 'a fine lesson': 'The intention of the Emperor is that, on the 8th, you will march yourself with all of your forces to eliminate the rebels, burn the villages in revolt, and execute all of the rebels you capture.'[298] Wrede, enjoying his independence, had been guarding the army's right flank with detachments as far north as Lambach. Now recalled by Lefebvre, he marched south on 8 May, leaving behind, as directed, one cavalry regiment (2nd Chevaulegers under Preysing) to cover the line of the Traun as far as the Traunsee. The disgruntled general arrived in Salzburg on 9 May and the next day saw 7th Corps open what would become its first, but by no means last, offensive into the Tyrol.[299]

6–8 May: Blindenmarkt and Beyond

By 6 May Hiller's confidence had recovered from the severe blow suffered at Ebelsberg. Although he now knew that he faced the dreaded French emperor in person, the lack of enemy activity on the 4th and 5th left him feeling buoyant enough to write 'I believe I can maintain myself in the position near Göttweig against an equal force until the arrival of the main army and can cover the capital city from this flanking position.'[300]

The French had other ideas. Napoleon finally crossed the Enns on the morning of 6 May, pushing east with Bessières in the lead followed by Oudinot, Massena, Nansouty, and St Sulpice. Lannes, who had passed over the river at Steyr on 5 May, was driving north-east from St Peter to join the emperor's column on the post road at Amstetten. Constrained by the terrain, the entire French army would thus find itself using this one road from Amstetten to Vienna between 6 and 10 May. The resultant congestion not only posed challenges in traffic management, but also compounded the army's logistical troubles as it passed over a region already picked clean by the retreating Austrians. Despite these problems, despite bridges burned by Hiller's men, and despite several days of vile weather, the French surged ahead, the emperor eager to bring on the battle he expected west of Vienna.

The morning of 6 May thus found GB Colbert questing north from St Peter along the left bank of the Ybbs. Colbert had his two chasseur

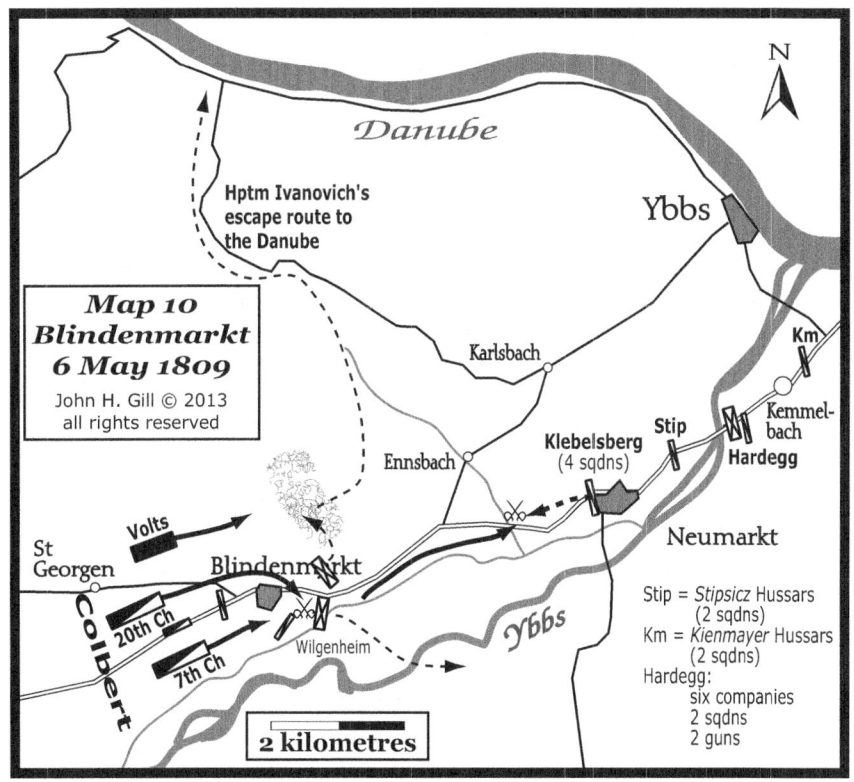

Map 10
Blindenmarkt
6 May 1809

John H. Gill © 2013
all rights reserved

Hptm Ivanovich's escape route to the Danube

Danube

Ybbs

Karlsbach

Km

Kemmel-bach

Stip

Klebelsberg
(4 sqdns)

Hardegg

Ennsbach

Neumarkt

Volts

St Georgen

Blindenmarkt

Colbert

20th Ch

7th Ch

Wilgenheim

Ybbs

Stip = *Stipsicz* Hussars
(2 sqdns)
Km = *Kienmayer* Hussars
(2 sqdns)
Hardegg:
six companies
2 sqdns
2 guns

2 kilometres

regiments and a composite light battalion assembled from the fifteen voltigeur companies of St Hilaire's division, making a combined force of at least 1,100 cavalry and 1,500 infantry.[301] The Austrians did not recognise the strength of the approaching French, and Mesko told the local rear guard commander, Major Wilgenheim of the *Karl* Uhlans, that only some 200 enemy cavalry had shown themselves. Wilgenheim therefore decided to set a trap for the French. He deployed most of his men (approximately 450–500 foot and 150 horse in five companies and two uhlan squadrons) just north of Blindenmarkt, leaving a small detachment on the main road to the south as bait. When the French approached, this detachment would withdraw through the town and lure the enemy into an unpleasant surprise.

It was Wilgenheim, however, who received the nasty surprise, when Colbert's main force began to appear around 10 a.m. that morning.[302] The French voltigeurs swept off to the left and drove the Austrian infantry out of the small wood north of town while the chasseurs, wisely deciding not to follow the bait through the streets of Blindenmarkt, repulsed a desperate charge launched by Wilgenheim's uhlans between the town and the river. Fortunately for Wilgenheim, Hauptmann Basil Ivanovich von Kolinensieg commanding his infantry was a leader of some quality. He formed up the 430 men in the woods and retreated north to the Danube in good order. The remaining infantry escaped by fording the Ybbs. Wilgenheim and his troopers, on the other hand, had no choice but to retreat hastily towards Neumarkt, where his regimental commander, Oberst von Klebelsberg, waited with four more squadrons of uhlans (300 men).[303] Klebelsberg, supported by the available *Stipsicz* Hussars, charged and administered a sharp check on the 20th Chasseurs.[304] The Austrians, however, could not fend off the inevitable. The 7th Chasseurs dashed up in support of their countrymen, and by late afternoon the French were across the Ybbs.[305]

The little engagement at Blindenmarkt punctured Hiller's revived sense of confidence. Casualties had been relatively heavy, especially for a cavalry skirmish, with the much-used *Karl* Uhlans losing a total of 145 men (more than one-quarter of its diminished strength).[306] 'The road', reported St Hilaire, 'was strewn with their lances.'[307] The *Gradiska* Grenzers had gotten away with only eight wounded and missing, but most of the men had fled north to make an adventurous escape by boat across the Danube under the persevering Ivanovich. Nearly half of the regiment was thus out of action for the time being. The French were east of the Ybbs and had again demonstrated their aggressive energy.

Hiller, who had been planning to cross the Danube at Krems on 8 May in accordance with instructions from Charles, now hastened his departure to avoid another clash with the relentless enemy. The weary whitecoats thus broke camp at 3 a.m. on the morning of the 7th for another exhausting slog: V Corps marching on the secondary road along the river, while VI Corps, II Reserve Corps, and all of the artillery took the highway to St Pölten before turning north to Krems. The march was made more miserable by the return of foul weather. A cold combination of snow and rain notwithstanding, Hiller's command was safely across the great river by the afternoon of 8 May. That evening, to avoid a repeat of Landshut and Ebelsberg, he had the bridge partly dismantled and even pulled his rear guard to the north bank; only a few pickets with boats were left on the southern shore.[308]

Hiller was finally north of the Danube as Charles desired. He was able to reunite with Hardegg's detachment (swollen to 1,534 men from collecting up stragglers) and granted his troops 9 May as a rest day.[309] As the Austrian official history caustically notes, however, his decision to occupy the Ebelsberg position rather than retire over the Danube at Linz as ordered had cost the Austrian army some 12,000 men over five days without contributing anything to delaying the French drive on Vienna. Burned bridges stalled the French advance, not Hiller's relatively large but exhausted force, and the destruction of the bridges could have been accomplished by the division of 8,000 to 10,000 men that Charles had directed Hiller to leave south of the river, in any case.[310] Psychologically, his command had suffered two jolting setbacks and, on a personal level, his evasion and equivocation had widened the already dangerous rift with Charles.

Empty Ostentation: The Fall of Vienna

When Hiller withdrew across the Danube, he left behind a congeries of mismatched units destined to join the Vienna garrison. Archduke Maximilian, responsible for the defence of the capital and Lower Austria, placed a premium on the 'detached corps of 8,000 to 10,000 men' that Charles had ordered Hiller to provide for Vienna's protection. Hiller, on the other hand, decided to preserve his core formations and thus formed this division from Landwehr and from line units that did not belong to his army. These 'regulars' were almost all recruit-filled third battalions with little training, little experience, and little equipment. Furthermore, several were drawn from Austrian Galicia and were thus composed of recalcitrant Poles

N

Emmersdrf

Krems

Mautern
Göttweig

Traismauer

Danube

Stockerau

Knbg
Le

Tulln

Klosterneuburg

Diening

Jd

Ried

St
Pölten

Melk

Kapelln

Sieghartskirchen

Nussdorf

VIENNA

Traisen

Purkersdf
Schönbrunn

Traisen

Lilienfeld

Altenmarkt
an der Triesting

Baden

Triesting

Pottenstein

Türnitz

A u s t r i a

Piesting

Annaberg

St
Aegyd

Mariazell

Schwarza

Wiener
Neustadt

Leitha

Neunkirchen

Seewiesen

Mürzzuschlag

Gloggnitz

Semmering
Pass

S t y r i a

Aspang

Mürz

Bruck
an der Mur

Friedberg

Kbng = Korneuburg
Le = Langenzersdorf
Jd = Jedlersdorf

Graz

Steinamanger

Map 11
From Melk to Vienna
John H. Gill © 2013, all rights reserved

0   5   10   20   30
kilometres

L o w e r

whose enthusiasm for the Habsburg cause was decidedly unsatisfactory. Placed under Dedovich, this division left the army at St Pölten and arrived in Vienna on 9 May. The state of these troops, however, did little to inspire Maximilian's confidence: some lacked shoes and other important gear, while many of the Poles had replaced their flints with bits of horn so that their muskets would not fire. The condition of Dedovich's Landwehr was equally discouraging. Although they had not been involved in any combat, desertion and attrition had reduced the six and one-half battalions from more than 3,000 (3 May) to barely 1,000 effectives in the ranks (8 May). They were consolidated into a single battalion.

If Hiller was unhappy about detaching Dedovich's men, the loss of the six Vienna Volunteer battalions was almost painful. Kaiser Franz had specifically designated these to defend the imperial capital, but Hiller had come to value them, especially after their gallant performance at Ebelsberg. Pointed promptings from Maximilian finally led Hiller to send them off as he crossed the Danube. The 4th, 5th, and 6th split off at St Pölten and arrived in Vienna on 8 May; the other three, marching with V Corps, crossed at Krems and moved north of the Danube to reach Vienna on 9 May. Also marching in on that day were the remnants of Nordmann's brigade, reduced to only 500 Grenzer and 200 *Liechtenstein* Hussars along with his half-battery. Nordmann, whom we last saw hastily departing Steyr on 4 May, had reached Weyer on the 5th. From here he sent MacDermott's Landwehr south up the Enns valley and made his own way east via Lilienfeld to Vienna. In addition to Nordmann, Hiller rather parsimoniously proposed that Provenchères detach one squadron of *O'Reilly* Chevaulegers to Maximilian. Provenchères had reached Liezen on 4 May, but events intervened and he ended up at Pressburg instead of Vienna. This did not prevent Hiller from hopefully listing the detachment in a summary he sent to Charles on 8 May as evidence of his putative open-handedness in supporting Maximilian.

In addition to the units extracted more or less willingly from Hiller's army, Maximilian had under his command some depot troops and O'Reilly's twelve Lower Austrian Landwehr battalions. He brought ten of these (some 8,000 effectives) to Vienna on 7 May, but sent the other two south to Mariazell. The commanders of these battalions, Majors Josef Graf Breuner and Albert Graf Clary-Aldringen, had large land holdings around the town and Maximilian hoped that they would enflame the population and thus pose a threat to the French flank. They would thereby give substance to a proclamation he had issued calling out the Landsturm, or local civilian militia, throughout Lower Austria west of Vienna.

Maximilian gathered in two Lower Austrian battalions that had been escorting prisoners and received six Moravian Landwehr battalions under GM Johann Freiherr Wodniansky (approximately 5,500 men) between 8 and 11 May. Six others, however, were diverted, leaving Maximilian in considerable frustration. Equally irritating was his cousin Joseph's refusal to contribute any Insurrection cavalry. Combining the Landwehr contingents with his regulars, depot units, and 2,700 municipal troops, therefore, the archduke had some 34,400 infantry and cavalry by 11 May. Even adding the 1,200 artillerymen in the city, Maximilian believed the number of defenders inadequate to their task, especially as their level of training and organisation left so much to be desired.[311]

The quantity and quality of the available soldiery were not the archduke's only problems. Though equipped with zeal, determination, and the requisite imperial rank, he was young and inexperienced, ill-prepared for the daunting task he faced. The clutch of available generals were 'old and fragile', hardly the sturdy souls needed to inspire soldiers and population to a stout defence.[312] Their dithering, sloth, and incapacity, combined with a dearth of competent staff officers and grossly inexperienced troops, meant that basic military procedures were neglected in a welter of orders, counter-orders, and errors. Moreover, the archduke issued several pompous proclamations and behaved in an overbearing manner that irritated his subordinates. The city's fortifications, in poor repair, could not compensate for the absence of capable forces, and the mood of the citizenry swung from resolution to despair on a daily basis. Archduke Rainer and other leading citizens urged a rapid capitulation to preserve the city should the French appear in force.[313] Franz himself vacillated between a visceral desire to preserve his capital and a realistic assessment that he would likely lose it for the second time in four years. Charles merely hoped that Maximilian could hold on until 18 or 19 May, when the Hauptarmee would be in a position to cross the Danube in the vicinity of the city. This was a pipe dream. Leadership, troops, popular will, and fortifications would all prove inadequate when the French came knocking at Vienna's gates. And they came sooner than Charles and his various relatives thought.

Following the engagement at Blindenmarkt, the two principal French columns (Lannes and Bessières/Massena) had converged west of Melk. Like the Austrians, they were afflicted by the foul weather and the lack of provisions. 'We passed through a devastated land, first by the enemy, then by the army corps that preceded us, so that we found absolutely nothing in the villages we traversed, abandoned as they were by their inhabitants.'[314]

Napoleon drove his straining men with one goal in mind: locating and defeating the Austrian Hauptarmee. Based on Hiller's retreat, Napoleon's fundamental assumption was that the archduke would try to unite with Hiller either north or south of the Danube via the bridge at Krems. Indeed, on 6 and 7 May, he still believed that Charles would endeavour to defend the direct approach to Vienna and that a major battle would therefore occur near St Pölten.[315] He wanted all of his forces available for this decisive struggle, but he could not ignore the possibility that the Austrians might attempt a strike at his line of communications or that Charles might simply march to Vienna. He also gave consideration to crossing north of the Danube himself at Krems to operate on both sides of the river. Hiller's whereabouts would be the critical clue to Austrian intentions and Napoleon's next moves, but the French lost track of their adversary on 6 and 7 May. In part, this gap resulted from the difficulties of collecting intelligence in the desolate landscape. As Colbert complained: 'There are neither people, nor horses, nor letters with the post. All are fled either to Vienna or into the woods.'[316]

Despite these hindrances, Napoleon's light cavalry served him well during these uncertain days and Hiller was soon located. By the night of 7/8 May, for example, Colbert's reconnaissances had expunged all hope of a major battle on the road to Vienna. Skirmishes between his brigade and Dedovich's rear guard (1,000 infantry and 200 cavalry under Mesko) at Sieghartskirchen on 9 May cost the Austrians 205 men and confirmed that there were no significant enemy forces between St Pölten and Vienna.[317] To the south, probes to Traisen and Lilienfeld by Bruyère showed that there was no danger from that quarter; the Landwehr that his advance guard encountered in Lilienfeld 'threw down their muskets and fled into the mountains.'[318] Most important for Napoleon, however, was a message from Savary at Mautern. Sent to the bridge site on the 8th with Piré's cavalry brigade, he reported in the evening that Hiller had definitely retreated north of the river and that the bridge was partially destroyed.[319] The news of Hiller's retreat and the bridge's partial demolition sufficed for Napoleon to decide on his next steps. In a jubilant mood, he wrote to Davout at 6 p.m. on 9 May: 'the enemy has broken the bridge at Krems. Tomorrow at noon I will be before Vienna.'[320] Though he continued to watch the line of the Danube with great care, the emperor's orders for 10 May thus pushed the army towards the Habsburg capital with all speed.

The evening of 9 May found the Allied army stretched along the post road and aimed at Vienna. As advance guard for Lannes and the army, Colbert was north-west of Purkersdorf, closest to the great city. The rest of 2nd Corps was behind the light cavalry from Ried (Tharreau), through Sieghartskirchen (St Hilaire), to Kapelln (Demont); Claparède's division, once more with the corps, was also east of Kapelln. Massena's 4th Corps rested in and around St Pölten (with the exception of Molitor east of Melk), as did Nansouty, St Sulpice, and most of the Guard. Bessières was scattered: Jacquinot at Diendorf intermingled with 2nd Corps and Espagne north of St Pölten. Piré was watching the Danube between Traismauer and Tulln, while Bruyère covered the southern flank at Traisen. Savary was at Mautern with a temporary detachment composed of St Hilaire's combined voltigeur battalion, the Württemberg Leib Chevaulegers, 150 troopers of the *Herzog Heinrich* Chevaulegers (attached to army headquarters since late April), a squadron of 8th Hussars, and Espagne's horse battery. Most of these troops would return to their owning commands on 10 May when Montbrun (just west of Melk) arrived at Mautern to watch the river line. In addition to Montbrun's light cavalry, Davout had a division each at Melk (Gudin),

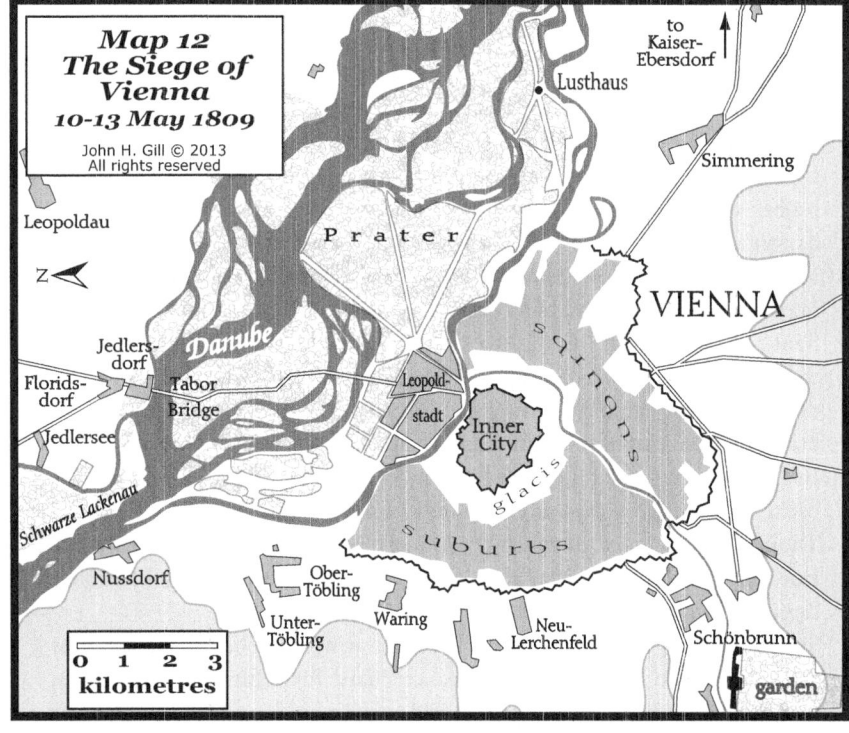

Neumarkt (Friant), and Mauthausen (Morand). Vandamme's Württemberg contingent and the French 17th Ligne remained at Linz.[321] 'All was thus disposed to march on Vienna, to observe the banks of the river and the army's communications.'[322]

The first French troops to arrive in Vienna's suburbs that bright spring morning were Colbert's riders, quickly followed by Tharreau's footsore infantry. Lannes, riding close behind the advance guard, erroneously concluded that the Austrians would not defend the city, and tiny bands of over-curious and over-confident French were soon riding up to the glacis, walls, and gates. Austrian artillery fire and a charge by *Liechtenstein* Hussars chased off the probing French, while pugnacious (and equally curious) Viennese set upon isolated groups of Frenchmen. Several dozen French were captured in these confused melees and GD Tharreau, injured by an angry citizen wielding a wooden plank, had to be rescued from a squad of enraged women.[323]

As embarrassing as this and similar incidents were, they did nothing to slow the French advance. Napoleon occupied Schönbrunn Palace during the morning and by nightfall the hard-marching men of Lannes's and Bessières's commands had surrounded the city. Determined to intimidate but not destroy Vienna, Napoleon instructed Massena to light extra campfires in his bivouacs around Purkersdorf. The scene was memorable: 'The illumination of all the hills, forming a half-circle, provided a lovely view in the deeply black night,' but the seemingly innumerable fires also achieved Napoleon's purpose and the populace rapidly lost much of its ardour.[324] Indiscipline and inebriation characterised Vienna's defenders during the night as many guards deserted their posts and others assiduously fuelled their courage with alcohol. Student volunteers fired their muskets to entertain themselves, wounding several of their countrymen. 'The Landsturm was mostly drunk,' reported O'Reilly as he made the rounds of the walls. 'The students only stopped firing when they were threatened with execution.'[325]

The arrival of Hiller with II Reserve Corps on the morning of 11 May buoyed the city's morale. After resting on the 9th and reuniting with Hardegg's detachment from Linz, he had left Schustekh at Krems with a detachment of nearly 8,000 men, and headed for the capital early on 10 May.[326] Kienmayer's men, covering forty-eight kilometres in twenty-three hours, marched into Vienna the following day to a joyous reception. Unfortunately for Maximilian, Hiller received new orders from Charles that afternoon. Charles specifically forbade the stationing of any troops in Vienna and directed Hiller to focus on guarding the crossing points on the northern shore. Hiller could hardly recall Kienmayer, but he kept the rest of his command on the left bank, posting Vincent near Jedlersee with orders to prepare the great Tabor Bridge for destruction, while directing Kottulinsky and Reuss to Langenzersdorf. Archduke Ludwig placed himself on the sick list and departed the army, so FML Reuss assumed command of V Corps.

While Hiller was marching, Napoleon attempted to force a rapid surrender of 'one of the most beautiful cities of Europe'. On the evening of 10 May, he had Berthier send a letter to Maximilian promising mild treatment if the city capitulated, but threatening 'the ruin of an enormous capital by means of howitzers and bombs' if resistance persisted.[327] Maximilian, partly because Hiller's appearance had bolstered his resolve and partly because he thought the French demand inconsistent with the rules of warfare, dispatched a delegation with his refusal on the morning of 11 May, but returned Napoleon's letter unopened. The French accordingly initiated preparations to take the city by force. All during the day, nervous Austrian gunners and infantrymen fired ineffectually at French activity in the suburbs. Napoleon, on the other hand, assembled twenty of the army's howitzers for the forthcoming bombardment and sent the newly arrived 4th Corps south of the city to seize the Prater island and isolate Vienna from further assistance. By evening, voltigeurs from Boudet's 3rd Léger had chased off a weak detachment of *Wallach-Illyria* Grenzer and established a foothold near the Lusthaus downstream from the city. Massena immediately began working on a bridge. Maximilian, awakening too late to the danger, sent the 2nd and 4th Vienna Volunteers to evict the intruders, but the attack, launched at 9 p.m., failed when the Austrians fired on one another in the darkness. Suffering forty-four casualties, most from friendly fire, the volunteers fled in dire confusion. A second assault came as pre-dawn light was colouring the skies around 3 or 4 a.m. on 12 May. This time the attackers were the *Brzezinski* and *Puteany* Grenadiers led by FML d'Aspre and supported by the two volunteer battalions. The French, however, having reinforced their troops with additional infantry and an artillery battery, halted the grenadiers in their tracks. After a fifteen-minute firefight that cost his force 150 casualties, d'Aspre suddenly broke off the engagement and withdrew towards the city.

D'Aspre's retreat was occasioned by new orders from Maximilian announcing the evacuation of Vienna. The young archduke had ridden to the Leopoldstadt suburb east of the city at 7 p.m. on 11 May before dispatching the Vienna Volunteers to deal with Boudet. Around midnight, he returned to the city. The sounds of fighting near the Lusthaus had diminished, and disturbing reports from within Vienna's walls seemed to call for his personal attention. He was full of enthusiasm and exaggerated expectations, hoping for substantive reinforcement from Hiller, foreseeing success in the Prater counter-attack, and planning in his head a foray outside the city walls to disrupt the French artillery. These fanciful hopes withered as he rode through Vienna's streets. Napoleon had opened the bombardment 'at the stroke of nine', just as Boudet's men were launching their attack on the Lusthaus.[328] Although the French only had twenty field howitzers, the effect was out of all proportion to the number and calibre of their shells. Arcing through the night sky with militant grace, the shells caused a modicum of damage to building and only two dozen or so casualties. They ignited, however, a perfect panic among civilians and militia alike. A predictable swirl of confusion, contradiction, and chaos in the darkness ensued: citizens ran from their homes to check on relatives among the militia, defenders left the walls to see to their families, units were hastily diverted to fire-fighting duties. No one was in charge. Austrian counter-battery fire achieved nothing against the well-positioned French pieces. Fear and uncertainty were palpable and led to a renewed eruption of pointless musketry. Flighty and ill-disciplined, the recruits and militia on the walls fired at shadows and managed to wound seven more of their fellows. On top of these disheartening images, of course, Maximilian knew that Hiller had orders to hold his regular troops on the north bank and that the Main Army could not arrive before 18 May. Furthermore, a council of war convened at 1.30 a.m. on 12 May concluded that Vienna could not be defended and advised him to withdraw all regular troops during the night. Maximilian, doubtless considering his bold proclamations of the preceding week, hesitated. Reports from the Prater indicated that the enemy near the Lusthaus was weak and allowed for the possibility that a swift counter-attack might still retrieve the situation. The result of his deliberations was the order issued at 2 a.m. on 12 May instructing d'Aspre to undertake a strike against the French on the Prater with two of his grenadier battalions and the two Vienna Volunteer battalions.

An hour later all had changed. Somewhere near 3 a.m., a staff officer returned from a mission to Hiller with the discouraging confirmation that Hiller would send no more troops. The bombardment had just come to an end, but the curt reply from Hiller was the last straw for the archduke; he immediately gave the order for all regular troops to evacuate the city. The retreat took place between 3.30 and 6.30 a.m. in a jumble of confusion. D'Aspre, forming the rear guard, retired without opposition because Massena made no effort to interfere with the disordered mass struggling to reach the safety of the far bank. The Austrians thoroughly burned the Tabor Bridge behind them. Owing to the archduke's inexperience and the incapacity of the various staffs in the garrison, however, several units were forgotten in the chaotic early morning hours. O'Reilly, for instance, though he was the commandant of the inner city defences, did not receive the order until 7 a.m.—in other words, after the Tabor Bridge had been set alight.[329] Some 3,000 Austrians, including thirteen generals and the entire 6th Vienna, thus fell into French hands when O'Reilly surrendered the city.[330] Maximilian retired to remote Bukovina in disgrace, haunted by his own boastful verbiage. The patriotic writer Karoline Pichler, whose works had helped stir nationalistic sentiment before the war, lamented: 'Thus were all the efforts, all the lives that had been lost for the idea of the city's defence, so many preparations and decisions, all futile—all was just empty ostentation!'[331]

Manoeuvres, negotiations, and occasional cannon fire occupied the daylight hours of 12 May. Massena, commanding the French troops south of Vienna, had Carra Saint-Cyr, Boudet, and his cavalry near the Lusthaus, but played a cautious hand until all of his divisions were available. Legrand and Molitor did not arrive until almost midday, so Boudet and Marulaz did not advance in force until late morning. Probing north, Marulaz's troopers swept up scattered prisoners but found the Tabor Bridge a smouldering wreck and were greeted with gunfire when they approached the Leopoldstadt suburb. The arrival of these squadrons sealed the fate of the city's much-reduced garrison, however, leaving the unfortunate O'Reilly no choice but capitulation. After consulting his fellow generals and some civilian officials, he sent a deputation to negotiate terms. The citizenry reacted to this alarming news with a mixture of surly resignation, depression, and panic. Some hastened to destroy compromising items such as propaganda about the war in Spain, patriotic sheet music, and anti-French pamphlets, while others, motivated by baser urges, indulged in a spate of looting and thievery. As disorder threatened the city, the Austrian delegates met with Napoleon's representative, the former ambassador GD Andréossy, and, after hours of tedious discussion, the two sides signed an agreement at 2 a.m. on 13 May. Oudinot's men marched through Vienna's gates later that morning, one month to the day after Napoleon's departure from Paris.

CHAPTER 2

Marauders, Militias, and Major Actions

The fall of Vienna did not end the war. Nor had Napoleon ever seriously expected that this would be the case. Intent on coming to grips with the Hauptarmee, he had been thinking of carrying the Army of Germany across the Danube well before the city capitulated; the orders flooding out from army headquarters repeatedly prodded his subordinates to collect boats and other materials along the river for this purpose. From Napoleon's perspective, the probability that he would have to cross the Danube grew after 8 May as the likelihood of an Austrian offensive south of the river faded. He did not ignore the potential threat of an attack between Vienna and Krems, but by 12 May 'everything leads to the conclusion that the enemy is retiring into Moravia.'[1] This brings us to the next stage in the war and the Battle of Aspern–Essling, but first we have to give some attention, as Napoleon and Charles did, to antecedent events in the Danube valley.

THE DANUBE VALLEY AND BOHEMIA, 1–16 MAY: FLANK PRELIMINARIES

The first two weeks of May saw dramatic shifts in the tide of the war as the repercussions of the Austrian defeat in Bavaria were felt in other theatres of operations. Archduke Ferdinand had taken Warsaw and had a detachment pushing towards Thorn, but this seemingly hopeful situation was overshadowed by Johann's decision to begin his long retreat from Italy on 1 May—almost as soon as he learned of the disaster at Regensburg.

Rumours of Russian military movements lurked in the background of the correspondence among senior Austrian leaders, a potential threat from a mistrusted neighbour. In the principal theatre, Napoleon's drive down the Danube valley threatened the northern borders of Styria and the southern frontiers of Bohemia while shattering efforts to organise the Landwehr in the Austrian hereditary provinces. Curiously, Charles's retreat through Bohemia to Vienna mirrored Napoleon's advance on the Habsburg capital. Each side endeavoured to protect an extended flank along the Danube while keeping open the option of crossing the river to seek out the enemy. Neither leader, however, wanted to launch a major operation over the Danube, and each hoped and expected that his opponent would be the one to undertake a cross-river attack with all of its attendant disadvantages. In the meantime, as both lines of march converged on Vienna, each side exerted itself to protect its own communications while threatening those of its adversary.

Davout along the Danube

On 5 May, Napoleon placed Davout in charge of Linz and its environs with a broad charter and extensive powers. The marshal's missions included oversight of local civil administration—with Napoleon especially insistent on the removal of all emblems of the House of Austria—maintenance of order, and expediting logistical support to the army's advance elements. In addition to securing tranquillity in the civilian population, Davout was intent on restoring military discipline in the army's dangerously unruly rear areas. He found the situation appalling. 'There is a mob of soldiers, non-commissioned officers, and even officers in the rear who, on their own authority, have established themselves in refuges and commit much evil,' he exclaimed to Berthier. 'Any tableaux that one could paint for Your Grace concerning the brigandage in this region would not approach the reality.'[2] Others were equally aghast: 'The brigandage of the stragglers is horrible and a quarter of the army is occupied in this infamous business. Many villages are half-deserted and others entirely abandoned, all is broken, burned. It is dangerous to try to oppose their brigandage if one is not superior in numbers.'[3]

This chaotic state of affairs not only eroded military discipline, sapped the army's strength, and turned the population against the French, it also compounded the inherently difficult tasks of foraging and intelligence collection. 'My cavalry is worn out because it has neither forage nor oats, all of the villages are devastated and neither can any means of transport be found to search for subsistence as a result of the frightful disorder committed by the stragglers and marauders,' wrote Montbrun. Davout took immediate steps to curb the criminality and indiscipline: 'Informed that many stragglers existed in the region who perpetrate every sort of disorder, I am forming mobile columns . . . to find and arrest these stragglers and to deliver those who are caught in the act to military commissions as pillagers and assassins.'[4] Napoleon followed with a draconian order of the day issued in 14 May from Vienna: 'Every straggler who, on the pretext of fatigue, detaches himself from his unit to maraud, will be arrested, judged by a military commission, and executed within the hour.'[5] The situation gradually improved, but observers such as Buat regard this as another sign of the marked decline in the quality of the French army by 1809.[6]

As important as discipline, administration, and logistics were, Davout's paramount concern was flank security north along the Danube from Enns to Passau and Regensburg. He was also to observe exits from the foothills of the Alps to the south. For these purposes, Napoleon put the prickly Vandamme under Davout's authority, adjuring the stern marshal to treat Vandamme well and not to quarrel with him.[7] In accordance with their detailed instructions, Davout and Vandamme saw to the completion of a bridge from Linz to Urfahr on 8 May and finished the required bridgehead fortifications on the north bank three days later. During this period, *Neubronn* (9 May) and I/*Camrer* (11 May) had rejoined 8th Corps, and *Phull* arrived on the 12th with its two guns, bringing Vandamme's command to 8,000 infantry and 980 cavalry in thirteen battalions and eight squadrons with twenty-two guns.[8] From 5 to 9 May, Davout could also call on the major combat elements of 3rd Corps as they marched through Linz. Morand's division was the last to depart, heading for Enns on 9 May; at Davout's direction, Morand left 17th Ligne and a battery under GB Lacour behind to support the Württembergers. Vandamme sent Lacour east as well on 10 May, retaining only the 3rd Battalion of the 17th at Linz. Two companies from this battalion departed for Steyr on 10 May with one company from each of the Jäger battalions and 100 cavalry. Commanded by Capitaine Deleau of Vandamme's staff, this detachment sent patrols deep into the mountains as far as Spital, Altenmarkt and Waidhofen 'to find out if there is anything new in this direction.'[9] Finally, Major Ameil's detachment also arrived in Linz on 9 May, having taken an adventurous route from Bavaria by riding through Rohrbach north of the Danube to reach Ottensheim on 8 May.

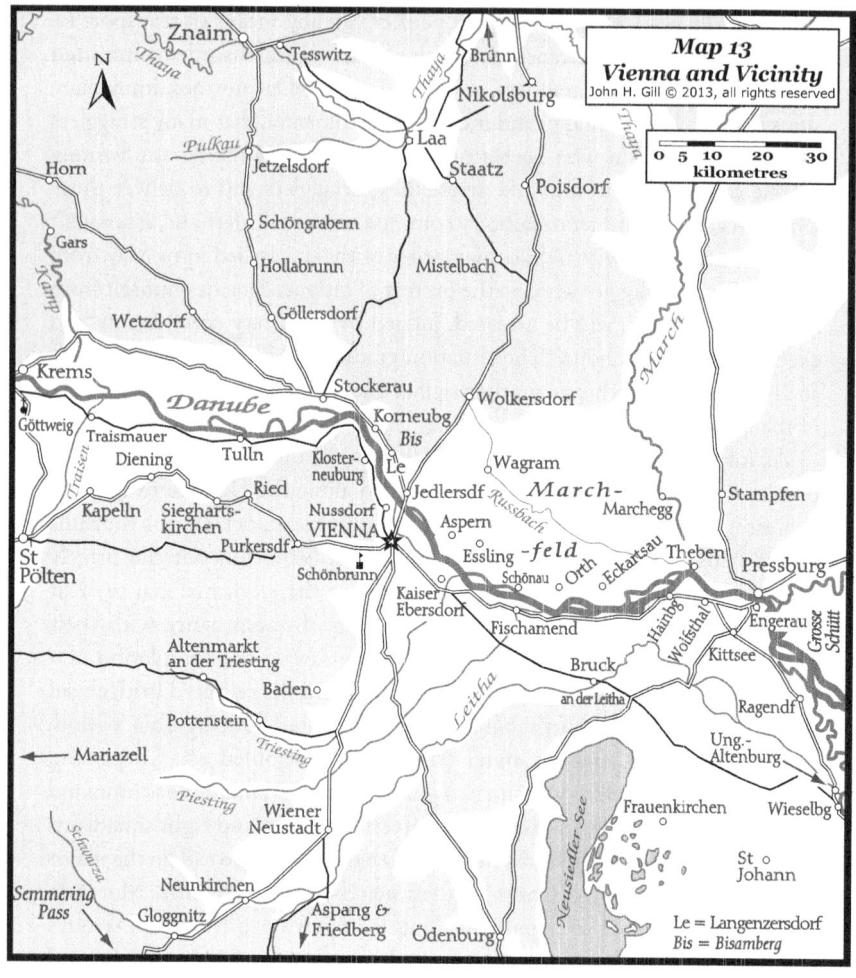

Meanwhile, Davout's 3rd Corps and his responsibilities were shifting to the east. Other commanders had provided flanking detachments along the way as the army marched to Melk, St Pölten, Mautern, and finally Vienna. At Napoleon's direction, Massena thus left small observation detachments in Ybbs and Wallsee (a Hessian fusilier company, fifty German light cavalry, and one gun in each town), Melk was garrisoned by fifty Hessians as well as a French company (first from Demont, later from 4th Corps), and Piré's light brigade remained between Mautern and Tulln after Savary's detachment departed on 10 May.[10] GB Bruyère had his two chasseur regiments in the south around Traisen and Lilienfeld. As the army concentrated at Vienna, however, the entire area from Tulln to Passau/Regensburg came under Davout's purview. He moved his men speedily but with a sure professional hand so as not to exhaust them. Sometimes he resorted to unusual methods, as Lieutenant Espirit de Castellane discovered when he came upon a marching column while carrying despatches back and forth between Davout and imperial headquarters on the night of 8/9 May. 'My night was spent in post carriages shouting for the infantry that covered the roads to open their ranks,' wrote the harried staff officer. 'All of the soldiers had lit tapers or candles in their hands; a most singular illumination.'[11] By 11 May, as far as his own corps was concerned, Davout had his headquarters in Melk, Montbrun at Mautern (still commanding Pajol and two battalions of 13th Léger), Gudin in St Pölten, Friant between Melk and St Pölten, two of Morand's regiments at Ybbs (30th and 61st Ligne), and 17th Ligne split between Enns and Linz. His other varied troops included the Hessian detachments at Ybbs, Wallsee, and Melk, the Württembergers around Linz, and one regiment each of Badeners and Hessians that he had detained at Melk on his own authority.[12] The small Portuguese Legion also came under his orders as it marched through the area. Furthermore, Napoleon used Davout as the superior headquarters for the units that Dupas and Rouyer had posted between Passau and Regensburg. Additionally, he became a principal conduit for orders being passed to Bernadotte. He did not yet know it, but Bruyère would come under his orders (more or less) on 12 May.

Napoleon's careful consideration for security along the river was necessary not only to deter, or at least detect, Charles and the Hauptarmee but also to contain innumerable incursions from the north bank. Davout's area of operations was thus the scene of continuous small-scale actions. Indeed, both sides conducted almost daily raids across the Danube to gather intelligence, to deceive or unsettle the enemy, and, in the case of the French, to forage for food and fodder. Both sides also placed a high priority on river craft, collecting them for their own use as prospective bridging material or destroying them to deny them to the enemy. Most of these actions went unnoticed except by their participants or by the local citizens who suffered the depredations of the intruding armies, but some resulted in minor skirmishes. The French several times employed military displays as a means to provoke Austrian responses and thereby gain intelligence. Savary, for example, had been instructed to force the Austrians to destroy the Mautern–Krems bridge. On the morning of 10 May, he accomplished his mission by marching his force to the riverbank and firing a few artillery rounds over the water. This fire induced panic among the 5th and 6th *Erzherzog Karl* Legion battalions guarding the crossing. The legionnaires dispersed in terror—'like a herd of sheep' said Savary—and an anxious lieutenant at the bridge, thinking that the French were attempting a major attack, set the span afire, destroying it completely.[13] Two days later, the French at Mautern, now Montbrun's so-called 'division', forced Schustekh to deploy by marching out in full view of the Austrians, throwing some round shot over the river, and threatening to bombard Krems to destruction if all of the boats on the north bank were not delivered at once. Montbrun got no boats, but he gained a good appreciation of Schustekh's strength and correctly concluded that there was little to fear from Krems.[14]

Major Ameil, probing east from Linz on the north bank with his small detachment, was equally imaginative, but he paid for his boldness with a potentially disastrous repulse and a serious head wound. Accompanied by a small detachment of 17th Ligne in boats, Ameil spent two days gathering detailed intelligence along the river (telling guileless local villagers that he and his men were a detachment of Hungarian Insurrection troops!) with the intention of using the boats to cross to the south bank on reaching Melk. Unfortunately for Ameil, an Austrian raiding party was also in the area. The Rittmeister commanding the Austrian detachment learned of the French force and ambushed Ameil in a defile near Ebersdorf on the afternoon of 12 May.[15] Ameil was wounded and lost thirty-five of his men, but the steadfast behaviour of his troops allowed him and the rest to escape. Napoleon, in an intolerant mood after the rebuff at Schwarze Lackenau (Chapter 3), excoriated Davout, Vandamme, and Ameil ('This man is a fool') for permitting such a risky patrol, and Berthier sent a gratingly supercilious note reminding Davout that 'War, my dear duke, has its rules.'[16] The emperor, however, soon reconsidered. Within a month he had promoted Ameil to colonel and given him command of a regiment.[17] The Austrian officer, Rittmeister Josef von Menninger, on the other hand, could not capitalise on his success. Although Charles had sent him from the Main Army to disturb the French rear area with cross-river raids, he never found an auspicious opportunity to carry out his task and spent the next ten days complaining about the quality of his troops, while fruitlessly planning and marching about north of the Danube.

The day after Ameil's setback, Davout put a battalion of 15th Léger across the Danube at Emmersdorf. He did not yet know of his subordinate's defeat but was concerned for the safety of the isolated detachment and hoped to effect a diversion in Ameil's favour. Supported by a second battalion on islands in the river, the crossing was a success, but the local Austrian defenders withdrew in haste, setting fire to Emmersdorf to cover their retreat. The only real resistance the French light infantrymen encountered was from the local populace, so they burned the offending village and retired to a defensive position on the north shore. As Ameil was already retreating to Linz, the ashen ruins of the two villages and some twenty captive Austrian soldiers were thus the only results of this well-executed attack. Schustekh reacted on 16 May, but by then the French had withdrawn all but one company from the north side of the river. This company apparently neglected its security: the Austrians surprised and captured more than sixty men while the remnants fled over the Danube in a boat.[18]

In addition to these minor actions by 3rd Corps, Vandamme's Württembergers were energetically vigilant as they protected the bridgehead at Linz–Urfahr. On 7 May, while the bridge was still under construction, a squadron of *König* Jäger and two companies of *Neuffer* Jäger probed north up the Freistadt road and shoved Stutterheim's outpost (a squadron of *Ferdinand* Hussars and 120 men of *Lindenau*) out of its position at Unter-Weitersdorf before returning to Urfahr. Two days later, a stronger detachment pushed as far as Freistadt without encountering resistance and GM von Wöllwarth conducted an extended but uneventful reconnaissance north of the river from 11 to 13 May. The only action of note was a surprise attack by a patrol of *Merveldt* Uhlans on a Württemberg outpost in Freistadt that left ten or so mounted Jägers in Austrian hands.[19]

Other skirmishes were occurring south of the Danube, where Bruyère was engaged with Landwehr, Landsturm, and rag-tag regulars in the rugged Alpine foothills. Bruyère, with his two chasseur regiments but no infantry or artillery, had quickly dispersed some 100 Landwehr when he arrived in Lilienfeld on 8 May. These men belonged to the detachment that Majors Breuner and Clary were leading to Mariazell at Archduke Maximilian's direction in the hopes of raising the countryside and thus threatening the French flank on the approaches to Vienna (Chapter 1). They were part of a chain of small detachments placed on the principal avenues that allowed access over the mountains between the valleys of the Danube and the Mur. This chain of posts not only blocked the entries into Styria, it also served to connect Jellacic at Radstadt with the Habsburg capital. Largely comprised of Landwehr supplemented by a few poorly trained regular recruits and local Landsturm, they more or less took their orders from FML Guido Ferdinand Lippa von Duba und Kosarczow under the overall direction of the Commandant of Inner Austria, FML Wilhelm Freiherr von Kerpen.

From west to east, they were centred on Liezen, Altenmarkt, Mariazell, the Semmering Pass, and Aspang, with a small reserve under Lippa's personal command at Bruck an der Mur (see Appendix 5).[20]

Bruyère was under pressure from Napoleon not only to gather intelligence but also to procure victuals, principally bread, for the army. While explaining to Berthier that there was little or no food to be had, he sent large reconnaissance patrols trotting down the roads leading east and south from Traisen on the morning of 9 May to assess the strength and location of the enemy. Each group consisted of 100 chasseurs led by an imperial staff officer. The patrol to Altenmarkt an der Triesting found no formed Austrian units, but the other detachment ran into Major Clary's men on the road from Türnitz to Annaberg. Clary had some 400 Landwehr and two guns, but a swift French attack scattered his detachment and left the chasseurs in possession of the two cannon. Clary rallied his men later in the day and pressed the French troopers hard in an effort to reclaim his lost guns, but the French retained both their composure and the cannon. Reinforced by 100 chasseurs on foot, they eventually succeeded in repelling Clary's advance. Although Bruyère's men won this little fight handily, rumours that as many as 6,200 Austrians were assembling between Annaberg and Mariazell caused alarms in imperial headquarters. Davout, who had been unaware of Bruyère's position on his southern flank, thus received orders to send some infantry to assist the cavalry. He despatched GB Lacour with two battalions of 13th Léger and two guns for this mission. Lacour's force advanced to Türnitz on 14 May and, thanks to 'incredible efforts on the part of the brave 13th Light Infantry', defeated Breuner's Landwehr the following day near Annaberg after a stiff fight that cost the French at least fifty-five casualties.[21] Despite this tough resistance and 100 reinforcements from Lippa's reserve, Breuner was forced to retreat. Panic broke out during the withdrawal, and within minutes the men vanished into the forests, leaving Breuner almost alone in the middle of the road. He retired as far as Seewiesen and was captured on 16 May, apparently while trying to scout the French positions.

The strength of the French response and Breuner's defeat also deterred another potential militia leader. Rittmeister Anton Freiherr Plächel had organised Landsturm between Purkersdorf and Baden south-east of Vienna. From 9 to 14 May, he caused some commotion by blocking roads, capturing French marauders, threatening to intercept messengers, conducting periodic raids, and occasionally skirmishing with Bruyère's patrols. His activities contributed to the sense that there might be a large agglomeration of Austrian forces between Altenmarkt and Mariazell, but he had little in the way of reliable 'troops', and news of an approaching French column (apparently the reinforcements for Bruyère) forced him to withdraw to the west. On reaching St Aegyd, he learned that Mariazell was occupied by the French and that Breuner was a prisoner. Unable to unite with his comrades as he had hoped, he took his steadily dwindling group south and attached himself to the militia forces at the Semmering Pass on 17 May.[22]

Napoleon, not yet aware of the French successes against Breuner and Plächel, was concerned enough about the possible danger from Styria to order Vandamme to Steyr with 6,000 men 'to disperse those gathering in that direction'.[23] In the meantime, however, Davout had despatched GB Duppelin with 85th Ligne, III/13th Léger, and two guns to reinforce the detachment at Annaberg so as to remove this threat to the army's right. Cavalry being of little use in the mountains, Bruyère left 200 troopers behind and rode for Vienna on Berthier's orders with the bulk of his brigade. Now in charge, Duppelin marched into Mariazell on 17 May and was surprised to come under sudden attack that very afternoon. Lippa seems to have ordered the attack and Clary dutifully obeyed, but the outcome could hardly have been worse for the Austrians: the Landsturm and most of the Landwehr disappeared after a few hours, and Clary beat a hasty retreat towards Bruck. Fugitive Landwehr fled into Styria, robbing, committing crimes, and generally afflicting the population so that senior civilian officials appealed to Archduke Johann for assistance in curbing their excesses.[24] From Duppelin's reports and the statements of deserters and prisoners, therefore, Davout could assure Napoleon that 'Mariazell, St [sic] Gaming, Waidhofen, and vicinity are purged of enemy'.[25] The marshal kept a detachment posted between Lilienfeld and Mariazell for several days, but the threat from the south had evaporated.

The Hauptarmee from 1 to 16 May: Charles in Bohemia

As Napoleon, keeping a wary eye on the Danube, drove towards Vienna, Charles struggled to develop an effective counter-strategy. Considering his situation during the first week of May, he had few good options. His army was sundered in two, the bulk of it was far from the main arena of combat, and it had not yet recovered physically or psychologically from the defeats in Bavaria. In seemingly stark contrast, the news from the subsidiary theatres of war was encouraging: Johann had advanced to the Adige in Italy, Ferdinand had captured Warsaw, the Tyrol had been liberated, and unrest (albeit exaggerated) was bubbling in Germany.[26] Charles and all contemporary observers understood very clearly, however, that the contest between the two main armies, probably in the Danube valley, would determine the outcome of the war. The clarity inherent in the situation invigorated the archduke's enemies at court, as we have seen. It was easy to lay all blame for the Hauptarmee's setbacks at Charles's doorstep, and influential but militarily ignorant persons intrigued for his dismissal, generating enormous pressure on him to do *something* to retrieve the monarchy's fortunes. Charles, of course, saw the army as the last bulwark of the Austrian state and the House of Habsburg. In his eyes, even the safety of Vienna with all of its strategic and psychological importance was not worth endangering the shaken Hauptarmee. Burdened by the weight of his responsibility, he was not about to risk it in some dubious duel with Napoleon and a French/Allied army that had just revalidated its superior qualities. 'In fifteen days everything will be decided—the Austrian monarchy will be saved or lost forever,' he wrote his adoptive uncle on 1 May. 'It is a terrifying idea.'[27]

Once it was clear that Napoleon would shift his focus to the Danube valley rather than pursue the Hauptarmee into Bohemia, Charles's general concept was to retire to Budweis, unite with Hiller, and then seek an opportunity to threaten Napoleon's line of communications on the road to Vienna. At least, this was his stated plan. The junction with Hiller remained his top priority, but by approximately 3 May, he was coming to the conclusion that 'the enemy . . . will probably turn his operations against me.'[28] In other words, he was expecting, and likely hoping for, a defensive battle *north* of the Danube rather than an offensive operation to the south.

Charles arrived in Budweis on 3 May, several days ahead of the army's trail units. Here he was handed Hiller's 2 May evening message announcing his intention to choose 'the lesser of two evils' and retire to the Ebelsberg position rather than cross the Danube at Linz as Charles had ordered. Charles was furious that Hiller had acted 'entirely against my intention and expressed orders', thereby wrecking Charles's plans to combine Hiller's force with the remains of the Main Army. Instead of having the army united near Linz where it could threaten Napoleon's flank and delay a French advance on Vienna, the Austrian forces were still split and a juncture would be 'difficult to achieve before Vienna.'[29] Moreover, Napoleon might now cross at Linz to strike north against the Hauptarmee. This possibility of a French offensive north of the Danube became a central assumption in the archduke's calculations during the coming ten days. It was entirely reasonable, given Napoleon's past practice of ruthlessly pursuing a defeated foe, and was doubly worrisome as Hiller's note did not contain any information about the bridge at Linz. For all Charles knew at that point (3 May), the bridge might still be standing, leaving Napoleon a free passage to the north, and leaving the rump Hauptarmee to face the French alone without Hiller's troops.

At the same time, Charles may have been indulging in some degree of convenient thinking. The archduke viewed a strike south over the Danube as a very risky enterprise because it would require him to force his way across the river and accept a fight with his back to the Danube or to Bavaria with no safe refuge in the event of a repulse.[30] His troops and commanders, moreover, had proven most cumbersome in the offence, and bridging the Danube was no minor proposition. He had, therefore, no desire to hazard his precious army in such an operation unless there seemed no other conceivable option. A French attack across the Danube, on the other hand, would leave Napoleon to undertake the challenge of passing over a major river and entering into battle with attenuated lines of supply and an insecure route of retreat. It would simultaneously exploit the Austrian army's strengths on the defensive. Charles thus had every reason to stay on 'his' bank of the Danube and hope that Napoleon would divert the Army of Germany from its drive on Vienna and come north. This was not only a logical preference for Charles to maintain, it was one that received powerful reinforcement as he interpreted all intelligence through a presumption that the French emperor was actively looking for an opportunity to strike across the great river. The wish, as the Austrian history notes, likely became father to the thought.[31] Though he would consider a move across the river several times during the coming days, this fundamental but false assumption about Napoleon's likely intentions would not vanish from his mind until after the fall of Vienna.

At the tactical level, Charles used the halt in Budweis to address what he perceived as his infantry's fear of French cavalry. Citing the example of Hiller's foot soldiers attacking Jacquinot's helpless troopers in the streets of Neumarkt, the generalissimo issued a lengthy order of the day admonishing everyone from general to private for the poor performance of the infantry when confronted by attacking cavalry. The success of *Klebek* and *Jordis*, he explained, 'shows what determined infantry, aware of its strength, can achieve against cavalry'. He proceeded to specify the tactics to adopt to defeat a mounted enemy:

> The infantry is generally still very clumsy in this. This arises largely from the lack of proper concepts that the generals and staff officers should impress

on the subalterns and these on the non-commissioned officers and soldiers. Infantry that is posted in woods, villages, hedges, gardens, etc. is, in every sense of the word, invincible against cavalry attacks; so is it also in the plains if it retains its prescribed closed order in masses or squares, and no enemy cavalry can withstand its attack.[32]

Had he known of them at the time, the misfortunes of Hiller's foot soldiers on 1 and 2 May would have reinforced Charles in his low assessment of his infantry's capabilities against cavalry. But this was cogent advice for the most senior officers as well. Both Charles and Hiller repeatedly used the superiority of French horse in explicating their setbacks and withdrawals.

In the meantime, the Main Army shifted east at a moderate pace. Poor roads and bad weather delayed the whitecoats as they struggled out of Bavaria through the inhospitable forests and mountains of Bohemia: 'I march through a cold and atrocious countryside on execrable roads, made worse by the downpours of the past two days that have done much damage to our troops and our horses,' wrote the archduke.[33] To the vast irritation and disgust of his critics, Charles then halted in Budweis for three days (3–6 May) to await the arrival of I and IV Corps, whose withdrawals had been particularly arduous.[34]

Kaiser Franz joined Charles in Budweis and differences came to the fore as the two discussed the army's next moves. There is no written record of their deliberations, but Franz wanted to protect Vienna and evidently urged a thrust across the Danube or at least a move closer to the capital to threaten Napoleon's rear. Charles, on the other hand, continued to believe (and hope) that the French emperor would strike north over the river and thus obviate an Austrian crossing to the south. The two men also differed as far as Vienna's fate was concerned. Where Franz was prepared to evacuate the city rather than see it destroyed in a siege, Charles hoped to use it as a secure crossing site (and retreat refuge) if he had to confront Napoleon on the south bank of the Danube. The guidance sent to Maximilian was correspondingly unhelpful and the injunctions for him to hold out until the Hauptarmee arrived on 18 or 19 May were entirely unrealistic. These variant views were not reconciled during the stay in Budweis, but the interim outcome was a decision to march for Krems.[35] On 6 May, II Corps and I Reserve Corps duly departed Budweis, followed by I Corps (from Fraunberg) and IV Corps (from Krumau) on the 7th. Owing to the supposed danger of a French attack—heightened when Ameil's appearance on the Austro-Bavarian border occasioned a rumour that 6,000 French

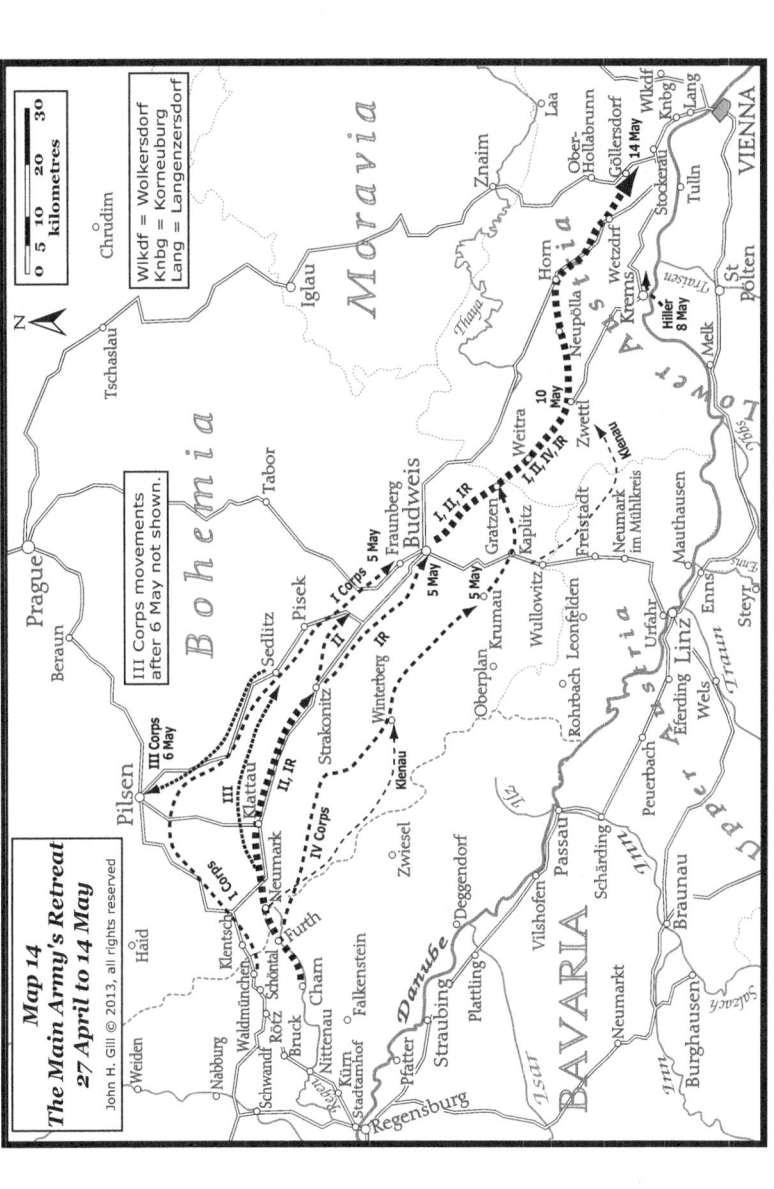

Map 14
The Main Army's Retreat
27 April to 14 May

John H. Gill © 2013, all rights reserved

III Corps movements
after 6 May not shown.

Wlkdf = Wolkersdorf
Knbg = Korneuburg
Lang = Langenzersdorf

0 5 10 20 30
kilometres

were threatening the Linz–Budweis road—a flank guard under Klenau marched along secondary roads south of the main column.[36] At the same time, another Allied threat, Bernadotte's Saxon 9th Corps, had made its presence felt along the western frontier of Bohemia, raising fears of a powerful incursion into the province from another direction. Charles had therefore issued orders on 2 May for III Corps (14,000 infantry and cavalry effectives) to occupy a position near Pilsen from which it could supplement the numerous but unreliable Landwehr and deter or counter any offensive action by Bernadotte.

The army's remaining four corps thereafter marched in deliberate stages from formal 'position' to 'position' through Gratzen and Weitra to Zwettl, arriving in the latter place on 10 May. 'After many sacrifices and strains we reached Upper Austria where the enemy's pursuit was less pressing,' remembered a weary Jäger lieutenant.[37] The anticipated encounter with the enemy slowed the march as the generalissimus wanted to keep his forces close together to oppose Napoleon's presumed attack north of the Danube, but Charles intentionally set a measured tempo because 'the defeated army needed careful handling to recuperate, and time to replace many crucial necessities that had been lost' during the campaign in Bavaria.[38] Some of the campaign's casualties had been filled by the 4,000 recruits waiting in Budweis, but fresh food was in short supply, and inefficient distribution meant that troops often lacked clothing, shoes, and muskets even when these items were available with the army's trains.[39] Marching columns were deranged by disorderly sutlers and vivandières, while the troops displayed an alarming propensity for snatching all available carts and wagons from the local populace.[40] Charles turned to a combination of stern measures and patriotic appeals to restore a degree of order, but part of his plan for recovering the army's discipline and confidence was a return to the comfortable forms and usages of the past. Lengthy 'dispositions' therefore provided the details for each day's march and the troops encamped each evening arrayed in the linear 'order of battle' of a formal 'position' that resembled an arrangement from the Seven Years War rather then the evolving norms of the early nineteenth century. Such measures, of course, while perhaps necessary, also served to stunt any hint of initiative, especially among the senior officers. Reviewing these changes, the official Austrian history of the war remarked: 'While Napoleon south of the Danube demonstrated to perfection the impact of moving an army more rapidly and fluidly according to the new concepts, the pedantic and torpid eighteenth century art of manoeuvre celebrated a resurrection north of the Danube.'[41]

Whatever the benefits or detriments of the return to this old style of command, many critics outside the army were incensed at the seeming lethargy of the march. Some in uniform shared this frustration. Liechtenstein, for one, chafed at the slow pace and volunteered to lead the bulk of the army's cavalry to cross the Danube at Krems with a pair of well-equipped batteries: 'According to circumstances, I would either attempt to strike the enemy's rear, or in co-operation with FML Hiller attempt to prevent the enemy's further advance and thereby preserve the possibility for a crossing by the army.' Charles, impressed by his subordinate's zeal but unswayed by his argument, graciously turned down Liechtenstein's offer.[42]

Freed from immediate pursuit and marching under better weather after Budweis, however, the army began to recover its spirit. As one observer recorded at the camp near Gratzen on 8 May: 'Despite the extremely difficult marches under the worst weather, courage and cheer filled every branch of the army, songs and music echoed through the area, that was illuminated by countless watch fires during the night.'[43]

The troops might be regaining their confidence, but someone had to pay the price for the failure in Bavaria. Charles was inviolate for the moment and he managed to shield his protégé Grünne from the machinations of his enemies. Prochaksa, on the other hand, was vulnerable. He was relieved on 8 May and replaced by the more capable Wimpffen, who was simultaneously promoted to general-major.[44]

It was thus with new leadership and old routines that the Hauptarmee made its way towards the Danube. By the morning of 9 May it was clear that Napoleon was closing on the capital and that a Danube crossing at Krems no longer offered any advantages. The archduke thus decided to make for Vienna, still convinced that the French would assay a crossing at Tulln or Nussdorf. If Napoleon did not attack, Charles hoped that Austrian diversions at Linz and Krems would force the French emperor to make significant detachments 'whereupon I will go against the remainder and, with God's help, drive them from the field'.[45] A council of war held at Zwettl on 10 May with the Kaiser reduced the diversion at Krems from Schustekh's division of 8,000 to Rittmeister Menninger's 220-man detachment, but otherwise left the existing plan in place. Two days later, however, reports from Vienna told a grim tale: the city was encircled, Archduke Maximilian intended to evacuate the garrison on the morning of 12 May, and FML O'Reilly was empowered to negotiate a capitulation. Kaiser Franz refused to believe the report. As long as there was a hope that the inner city was still in Austrian hands, some effort would have to be made to relieve the capital, so

Charles, much against his own will, was forced to initiate serious planning for a Danube crossing.[46] The site selected for the proposed operation was Tulln and the methodical scheme envisaged constructing a bridge during the night of 16/17 May. This concept, of course, was out of date before the ink was dry. At 6 a.m. on 15 May, Charles notified Franz that a spy had just returned with confirmation of the city's surrender. The planned crossing was abandoned without a further thought and the army shifted to a position between Stockerau and Korneuburg.[47] The following day the Hauptarmee and Hiller's command were reunited on the northern edge of the Marchfeld generally between Langenzersdorf and Wolkersdorf. The Kaiser established himself in the latter village for an extended stay.

2–16 May: Kolowrat and Bernadotte, Preludes to Linz

Charles had left behind a strong force of regulars to protect Bohemia while the Hauptarmee marched for the Danube. Most of the troops came from III Corps, but the archduke wanted a more senior commander than Hohenzollern as well as someone who was more knowledgeable about

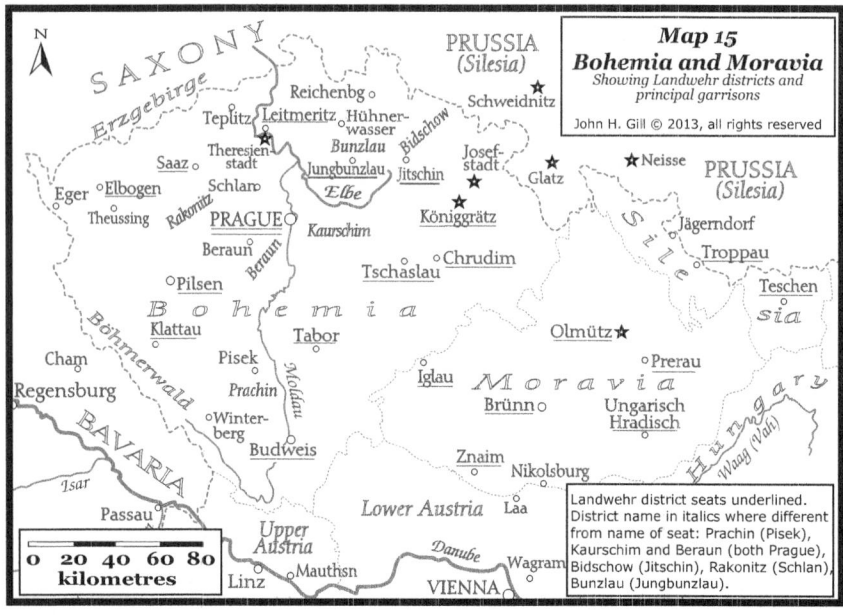

Map 15
Bohemia and Moravia
Showing Landwehr districts and principal garrisons

John H. Gill © 2013, all rights reserved

Landwehr district seats underlined. District name in italics where different from name of seat: Prachin (Pisek), Kaurschim and Beraun (both Prague), Bidschow (Jitschin), Rakonitz (Schlan), Bunzlau (Jungbunzlau).

the region. On 2 May, he therefore assigned FZM Kolowrat, the former commandant general in Bohemia, to take Hohenzollern's place at the head of III Corps and charged him to conduct an aggressive defence of the province. Hohenzollern assumed command of II Corps, whose relatively fresh troops Charles wanted at hand when he next encountered Napoleon. Hohenzollern thus rode off to join the Main Army (bringing along Mayer's brigade as ordered), while Kolowrat moved most of III Corps from Sedlitz (which the corps had reached in its withdrawal) back to Pilsen.

Kolowrat's area of responsibility was extensive and his forces, though largely Landwehr, considerable. The heart of his new command was the restructured III Corps, now consisting of twenty-two regular battalions, sixteen squadrons, and seventeen Landwehr battalions for 21,060 infantry and 1,670 cavalry, supported by fifty to sixty guns. Most of this field force was cantoned at Pilsen, but FML Somariva had a detachment supporting the twenty-four Landwehr battalions and a few regular outfits scattered along the frontier.[48] These troops were to protect more than 500 kilometres of border with Bavaria, Saxony, and smaller German states approximately from the Linz–Budweis road to the junction with the Prussian border near Reichenberg (not counting the border with the Duchy of Warsaw). In addition to these field and frontier forces, Kolowrat was responsible for the fortresses of Prague, Theresienstadt, Josefstadt, and Königgrätz. The garrisons of these places included one regular battalion (the recruits of III/ Josef Colloredo), one dozen Landwehr battalions, twenty-six depot companies, six reserve squadrons, and the newly raised Lobkowitz Jäger Battalion (four companies). In total, his command thus amounted to twenty-five and one-half regular battalions, seventeen and one-half squadrons, and fifty-three Landwehr battalions in addition to depot infantry, reserve squadrons, and the Lobkowitz Jägers.

As to the commander, Kolowrat was certainly very familiar with Bohemia, having been born north of Budweis in 1748 and having served as the province's commandant since 1803. It bears reiterating, however, that he had never led anything as large as a corps in combat, certainly not in the sort of independent operation he was now called upon to undertake.

On 7 May, new orders arrived that would place a premium on his initiative and energy. Charles, fairly confident that Bernadotte's Saxons were headed for the Danube valley, wanted Kolowrat to demonstrate towards Linz to threaten Napoleon's northern flank. A more specific letter reached Kolowrat on 11 May, instructing him to take an active role in staunching the flow of French troops towards Vienna. According to these revised instructions, Kolowrat was directed to seize the bridgehead before it was completed (it was actually finished that very day) and then cross the river via the bridge or on boats 'to make a serious diversion beyond the Danube, which must consist of attacking and dispersing all of the reinforcements and transport following the enemy army . . . and doing the enemy as much damage as possible'. The Allied force on the north bank was assessed as being 'in small numbers and mostly Württembergers or Bavarians'. To magnify the impact of his action, Kolowrat was to give out that he was the avant-garde of the Main Army.[49]

Kolowrat had moved promptly on receiving the 7 May orders, so the new instructions found III Corps' main body in Pisek, marching for Budweis and Linz. With the diminished threat of enemy incursions, Kolowrat withdrew almost all regular units from the frontier, leaving behind GM Paul von Radivojevich with only two battalions of Grenzer, two uhlan squadrons, and two infantry companies to buttress the seven Landwehr battalions covering the long stretch from Oberplan to Eger. Kolowrat complained, however, that the lack of a pontoon train would make his task hard to accomplish, leading the official Austrian historians to comment that 'everything the generalissimus asked of his subordinate had been achieved by General Vandamme, also without a pontoon train, with far weaker forces, and in enemy territory'.[50] Furthermore, although Charles specified 14 May as the date when the diversion operation should begin to have effect, Kolowrat continued south at an ordinary pace: approximately twenty-eight kilometres to Fraunberg (or Frauenberg) on the 12th, but only fifteen on the 13th to camp south of Budweis, and twenty-three on 14 May to Kaplitz with advance troops at Wullowitz on the border between Bohemia and Upper Austria. He then granted his troops a rest day on 15 May to recover from their exertions. Another note from the generalissimus reached III Corps on the night of 14/15 May, re-emphasising the importance of 'setting the diversion on the right bank of the Danube in motion with all zeal and as powerfully as possible' so as 'to defeat the enemy reinforcements that follow the army or, at least, to hold them on the upper Danube'. Despite the urgent tone of the archduke's order, Kolowrat did not change his plans, so it was only on 16 May that III Corps crossed into Upper Austria and moved into positions from which it could attack the Urfahr bridgehead on the following day. By nightfall on 16 May, Kolowrat had his main body at Freistadt with an advance guard under Crenneville at Neumarkt im Mühlkreis. On the left, a flanking column under Saint Julien occupied St Oswald, but a right flank column, Somariva's, was delayed by bad roads and only marched as far as Reichenthal (line infantry) and Schenkenfelden (Grenzer); this limited progress would have serious implications on the following day. Unfortunately for Kolowrat, his extreme right had unexpectedly bumped into a Württemberg outpost near Leonfelden. The Austrian force was not large (5th Jägers, 4th Chrudim Landwehr, and a half-squadron of *Merveldt* Uhlans), but with some 1,300 men it greatly outnumbered the 150 foot and mounted Württemberg Jägers. There was little real fighting and the Württemberg light troops fell back on their supports at Hellmonsödt with the loss of eight men wounded or captured. The regrettable aspect of this little episode from Kolowrat's perspective was that it alerted Vandamme to the approach of the Austrians and allowed him extra hours to prepare for the coming attack.

In addition to warning of the Austrian advance, Vandamme learned on 16 May that significant reinforcements were approaching. We have seen that five infantry battalions had rejoined 8th Corps between 9 and 12 May bringing the number of effectives to approximately 7,700 in Linz and Urfahr, not counting the detachments at Enns and Steyr. Moreover, Vandamme now received news that Marshal Bernadotte was at Eferding (some twenty-five kilometres west of Linz) with the lead elements of the Saxon 9th Corps. Bernadotte and Vandamme were old friends, and Vandamme lost no time in writing to the marshal to apprise him of the impending Austrian attack and request assistance.

The Saxon army of 1809 was an outmoded institution. Though not lacking in courage or good will, the army's organisation, training, education, and outlook made it a relic of the Seven Years War, ill-suited to the rapid, flexible, mobile warfare that Napoleon waged. Tactics were badly obsolete, the troops were not accustomed to extended marches, and the officers were unfamiliar with independent operations as corps and divisions. The Saxon officer corps contained some very fine prospects, but all too often these men, especially at the senior levels, were aged, indolent, and unprofessional, selected for social connections rather than military competence. There were far too many new recruits in all branches and too many new remounts in the traditionally excellent cavalry regiments. The long-neglected artillery was particularly awkward and inexperienced. Above all, standards and expectations were out of tune with the times, the norms of a bygone era when the pace of warfare was slower and more methodical.[51] Even the Saxon uniforms reflected the past. 'These troops . . . with their old-fashioned uniforms, created a general sensation; looking at them, one felt oneself removed to a different century,' commented an officer of the 4th Rheinbund when he saw the Saxons in

Passau.[52] In addition to being stiff and uncomfortable, the Saxon infantry uniforms were white in colour, a fact that would have tragic consequences on the field of Wagram.

For the 1809 war, the Saxon army was organised into a corps of two mixed divisions, each commanded by a general-leutnant and comprising two infantry brigades and a cavalry brigade. The infantry brigades contained five or six battalions, including grenadier battalions composed of elite companies drawn from each infantry regiment on the Austrian style and a composite battalion of Royal Guard grenadiers. The cavalry brigades mixed light and heavy regiments and, owing to the shortage of adequate horseflesh, had several partial regiments and an orphan squadron of *Herzog Albrecht* Chevaulegers. The corps artillery consisted of four four-gun batteries, supposedly 'light' and 'heavy', but this was a distinction without a substantive difference. GL Joachim Friedrich Gotthelf von Zezschwitz served as both the senior Saxon officer and the 1st Division commander.

Consistent with his policy of placing French officers over his allied contingents, Napoleon designated Marshal Jean-Baptiste Bernadotte to command 9th Corps. Bernadotte was an especially complex and controversial character in an era that seemed to abound with such persons. A lawyer's son, he was born in 1763, entered the Royal Army in 1780, and attained the rank of sergeant before the Revolution opened new opportunities. He was soon a général de division, a fervent Republican, and a competitor with General Bonaparte for political power and military reputation. Though hardly brilliant on the battlefield, he had demonstrated considerable military talent, a notable ability to motivate troops, and impressive administrative skills in a career that had run from combat commands in Germany and Italy to service as the governor of the Hanseatic cities from 1807 to 1809. His perplexing behaviour at the double battle of Jena–Auerstädt in 1806, however, cast a dark shadow over his reliability and he made many enemies among the army's senior leaders, including Berthier. He possessed an infamously inflated sense of his own importance, a similar opinion of his own military genius, an often-grating arrogance, and a propensity to let temper overcome prudence in violent verbal outbursts. The man who arrived in Dresden on 22 March to assume command of 9th Corps was thus a competent officer who cared for his troops and received their warm loyalty in return, but also a disputatious, ambitious, and untrustworthy subordinate and comrade, too fond of intrigue and principally concerned with promoting his own interests.[53]

Bernadotte, insulted at being placed in charge of Allied troops and anxious that their deficiencies would reflect poorly on his reputation, immediately asked to be relieved of command. This was the beginning of an extended jeremiad that opened with several requests for reassignment and progressed to incessant complaints about the Saxons and pleading for the attachment of French troops. Despite his misgivings about his command and his injured pride, Bernadotte set about the task of preparing 9th Corps for war with professional thoroughness, eliciting a strong favourable response from his men and the Saxon generals. At one point during the march to the Danube,

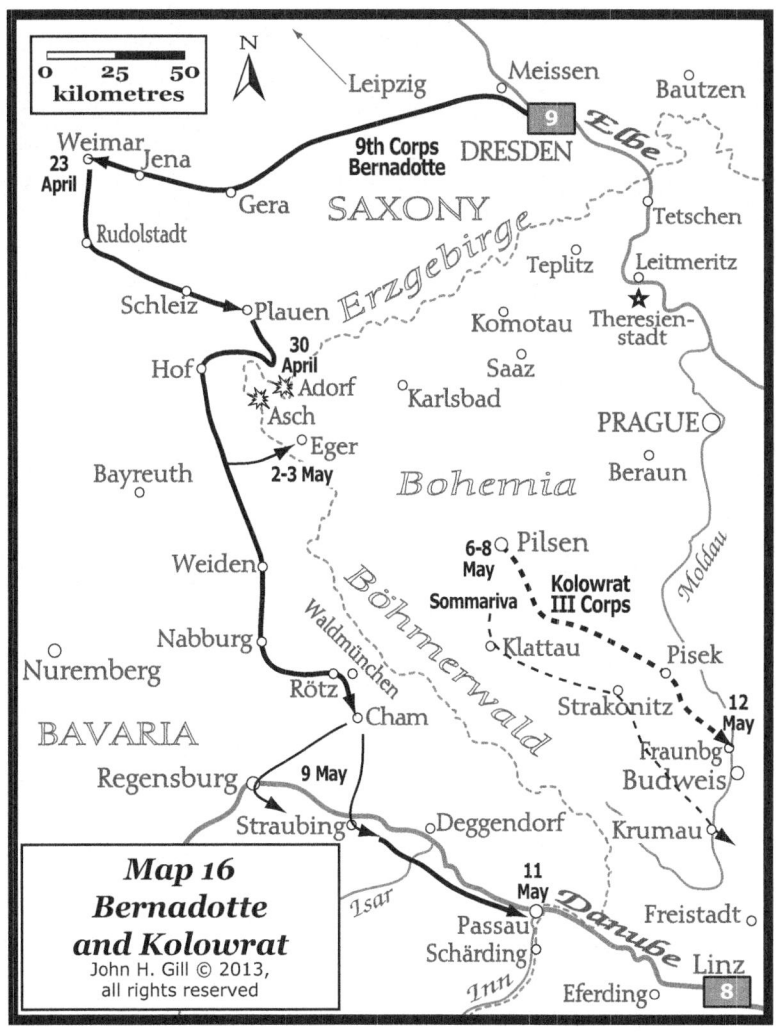

Map 16
Bernadotte and Kolowrat
John H. Gill © 2013,
all rights reserved

he spontaneously stopped to inspect new shoes being issued to the *Prinz Anton* Infantry Regiment and presented a soldier he had questioned with two gold coins, remarking 'that the company should drink his health' with the money. 'Thus did this general seek by every means to earn the goodwill of the Saxons,' noted one beneficiary of this largesse.[54]

The two Saxon divisions departed Dresden for Bavaria on 15 and 16 April, and King Friedrich August, his realm now nearly denuded of troops, removed himself to Leipzig to put some distance between his court and the Austrian border. His uniformed subjects marched via a circuitous route through Thuringia and the Upper Palatinate (Oberpfalz) to reach Weimar on 23 April. Receiving the order to threaten Bohemia, Bernadotte detached a small advance guard towards the border under GM Christoph von Gutschmid, 'the very image of a true hussar; brave to the point of audacity; firmly decisive, circumspect, and sly; in the saddle day and night regardless of weather'.[55] The approach to the frontier led to skirmishes near Adorf and Asch on 30 April between the Gutschmid's troopers and patrols of *Schwarzenberg* Uhlans. Losses were minimal, but these engagements began to alter attitudes among the Saxons, some of whom had been partly sympathetic towards their old Austrian comrades in arms. Having been surprised in one of these encounters, the Saxons now marched with more diligent security and, in several cases, with considerable daring. Gutschmid, for instance, boldly rode into Eger on 2 May with 150 men and spent several hours collecting intelligence and provisions from the undefended town. Another patrol entered Eger on 3 May and probing Saxon cavalry clashed with Austrians on the 5th and 6th as the advance guard screened the march of the main body from Hof (1 May) to Weiden (4 May).[56] Having learned from these actions that the Bohemian border was only lightly guarded, Bernadotte planned an incursion from Waldmünchen for 7 or 8 May to give his men some experience and garner some easy laurels for himself.[57] Before he could launch his raid, however, he received instructions calling him to march to Passau 'as quickly as possible' where he would add Dupas's division to the corps and 'form the left of the army'.[58] Crossing the Danube at Regensburg and Straubing, the Saxons marched into Passau on 11 and 12 May to enjoy a well-deserved rest day. Despite the frailties of the Saxon army and Bernadotte's many idiosyncrasies as a commander, it stands to the credit of both that 9th Corps marched 430 kilometres in twenty-two days (two rest days included) with very few attrition casualties and without losing a single man to desertion.[59] 'Thus does the current style of warfare change our perceptions,' wrote Zezschwitz to King Friedrich August. 'Only a short time ago, one would have considered it impossible to march from Weimar to Passau over a far from direct route without a rest.[60] On 13 May, 9th Corps recuperated in Passau, but the next morning saw the 1st Division on the road into Austria; the 2nd Division followed on 15 May, and Dupas was to march on 16 May. While Kolowrat's III Corps was resting south of Budweis, therefore, Bernadotte and the Saxon 1st Division reached Eferding with the 2nd Division at Waizenkirchen. Here he received orders to halt so as to be available should Lefebvre's Bavarians in the Tyrol require support. By the evening of 16 May, the 1st Saxon Division was some twenty-five kilometres from Linz, with the 2nd Division fourteen kilometres behind and Dupas's French regiments in Passau preparing to march. 'I am ready to move to any point Your Majesty designates,' Bernadotte informed Napoleon.[61] The marshal, having received reports of Austrian patrols near Ottensheim, was already alert to the proximity of Kolowrat's forces and had sent his advance guard to Wilhering with a detachment at Aschach. Vandamme's request for assistance thus found 9th Corps within supporting distance of Linz and its commander aware that action might be imminent.

17 May: The Battle of Linz[62]

The battlefield north of Linz was a narrow strip of lightly rolling farmland no more than 1,000 to 1,500 metres wide, between the Danube and the arc of rugged hills to the north. Brooks flowed across the meadows into the Danube and several small villages were clustered along the highway leading to Gallneukirchen, most notably Katzbach and Dornach. A secondary road ran due north towards Hellmonsödt and another followed the sinuous course of the Danube to Steyregg. A walled church called St Magdalena sat atop a steep hill on the north edge of the field. Above the western edge of the meadows rose the Pöstlingberg, a 539-metre hill that dominated Urfahr and the surrounding lowland, but could only be accessed via unimproved trails. Urfahr itself was largely in ruins, having been badly damaged in the assault on 5 May. The industrious Württembergers, with the help of local workers, had erected a set of fortifications to cover the bridge as directed by Napoleon.[63]

Kolowrat had drafted his plan of attack during the halt on 15 May and had arranged his corps into its three columns on the 16th with this in mind. The central column on the Gallneukirchen road would carry the main weight of the attack, but he hoped that Somariva's force would appear on the

Pöstlingberg above Urfahr between 3 and 4 p.m. to assault the bridgehead directly, cutting off the Allied forces north of the river. Somariva was also to leave a large detachment at Hellmonsödt and send reconnaissance off towards Rohrbach and Ottensheim. Saint Julien's purpose was diversionary: it was hoped that the mere appearance of his column, supplemented by artillery fire and a sham crossing would distract the defenders and cause them to divide their forces. GM von Oberdorf's six Landwehr battalions were to remain in reserve north of Hagenberg. From the start there were several serious problems with this plan. The challenge of co-ordinating multiple independent columns was unavoidable, but Kolowrat diminished his available forces by succumbing to the Austrian proclivity for detachments and reserves. With three battalions at Hellmonsödt and six more near Hagenberg, he placed 4,550 men beyond effective supporting distance of the main force—each group was approximately fifteen kilometres from the anticipated battlefield. Similarly, Saint Julien's mission could have been accomplished with a considerably smaller force; the 2,100 regulars of the *Kaunitz* Infantry might have been especially useful in the advance on the bridgehead. Although he outnumbered the Württemberg contingent by 18,234 to 6,830 in infantry (the Allied total would rise to approximately 13,000 by evening when both Saxon brigades were on hand), Kolowrat thus reduced his numerical advantage by scattering more than 47 per cent of his foot soldiers in secondary tasks and leaving himself only some 9,530 for the primary mission.[64] In fairness to Kolowrat, however, it must be noted that one-third of his infantry force consisted of dubious Landwehr, leaving him only something over 12,000 regular foot soldiers.

On the Allied side, Vandamme took advantage of the warning granted by the skirmish near Leonfelden on 16 May to prepare his corps. He sent an urgent request for assistance to Bernadotte that evening and drew in most of his distant outposts, leaving only a company of *Neuffer* Jägers and a squadron of *König* Jäger zu Pferd several kilometres north along the Hellmonsödt road, where he expected the main Austrian attack. As usual, Hügel's elite light infantry (twelve companies after the detachments to Steyr) had the most important task: covering the approaches to Urfahr. In addition to the company and squadron posted on the Hellmonsödt road, four Jäger companies, a light battery, and both mounted Jäger regiments (seven squadrons) were near Katzbach, both light battalions were at the mouth of the Hellmonsödt valley with a small detachment at St Magdalena, and the remaining company of *Neuffer* Jäger defended a small hill just west of Urfahr. GM Georg von Scharffenstein's brigade (*Phull* and *Neubronn*) occupied

the bridgehead with one light battery and six of the foot guns, while GM
Friedrich von Franquemont's (*Kronprinz* and *Herzog Wilhelm*) remained in
Linz as reserve. The other four guns from the foot battery were positioned
on the south bank. Also on the south bank was I/*Camrer* at Enns.

Bernadotte responded speedily to Vandamme's request for help. Following orders issued on the night of 16 May, the 1st Division's cavalry and the corps headquarters arrived in Linz at approximately 7 a.m. on 17 May. The 1st Brigade followed in the early afternoon and the 2nd reached the city by 6 p.m. The 2nd Division was to follow from Waizenkirchen as quickly as possible. Beyond Vandamme's plea, Bernadotte also had instructions from the emperor to leave Rouyer in Passau and press into Bohemia in support of the upcoming Danube crossing near Vienna, so he directed Dupas towards Linz as well.

As the Württembergers waited and the Saxons marched, Kolowrat's men were approaching the bridgehead. Most had left their cantonments at 2 a.m. as ordered, but Somariva, with the greatest challenges, either started late or encountered severe delays en route.[65] His column did not reach Hellmonsödt until about 11 a.m. Here he left III/*Wenzel Colloredo*, the two Landwehr battalions, and the 3-pounder battery, while sending three *W. Colloredo* companies and almost all of his uhlans towards Rohrbach and Ottensheim.[66] This left him to conduct his main effort with his remaining 3,067 infantry, a platoon of uhlans, and the 6-pounder battery. Turning slightly to the right off the main road, his men, already weary, struggled through a forested and folded landscape on slippery trails made difficult by the preceding day's rain.

Meanwhile, Kolowrat's centre column, led by Crenneville's advance guard, debouched from the hills at about 2 p.m., twelve hours after leaving their encampments. The 6th Jägers at the head of the column ran into Württemberg Jäger zu Fuss and zu Pferd near Katzbach. Here the fight opened in an almost languid fashion during the warm afternoon, the skirmishers of both sides slowly manoeuvring and firing, the Württemberg cavalry waiting dismounted by their steeds. Kolowrat, the success of whose plan hinged on timing, did not want to launch a serious attack until he knew Somariva was in position and was thus hesitant to commit his forces. In this tentative, restrained stage of the combat, the commander of *Herzog Louis*, Major von Waldburg, joked that, having missed breakfast, he would like a sip of wine before the battle. In true light cavalry manner, one of his subordinates, Lieutenant Finckh, rode the 100 or so metres forward to Katzbach in search of an appropriate vintage for his chief. As he took delivery of a flask of Tyrolian wine, he noticed a group of Saxon hussars busily requisitioning quarters and food for the night, completely oblivious to the growing musket fire outside.

In fact, Kolowrat had finally received word that Somariva was en route and a spirited fight quickly developed around Katzbach as the Austrians began to attack in earnest. The Württembergers resisted stoutly, but were soon overpowered and evicted by pressure from Crenneville's advance guard. The eager Saxon quartermasters were mostly bundled up and captured in the ensuing confusion and Lieutenant Finckh barely escaped with his bottle. The Württemberg *König* Jäger managed to regain the village temporarily, but the Austrian 6th Jägers, supported by three companies of II/*Peterwardein*, were soon in control again. The Austrians pressed their advantage. The other three *Peterwardein* companies were moving through Auhof toward St Magdalena, while II/*Schröder* and Crenneville's uhlans deployed beyond Katzbach. With support from skirmishers sent forward from II/*Schröder*, the 6th Jägers and three companies of Grenzer attacked and seized Dornach shortly after 2.30 p.m. Pursuing the retreating Württembergers, some enthusiastic Jägers even pushed into the houses on the eastern periphery of Steeg, threatening the bridgehead entrenchments. Meanwhile, the rest of the vanguard was also advancing. The three Grenzer companies captured St Magdalena from the Württemberg light infantry outpost and II/*Schröder* was gaining ground north of Dornach. So far Crenneville and his advance guard had done well.

Kolowrat judged the time ripe to bring up his main body. Vukassovich had sent I/*Manfredini* far off to the right through the woods to attack St Magdalena (unaware that the Grenzer were about to do so). While this battalion was still poking its way through the wooded hills, the regiment's 2nd Battalion

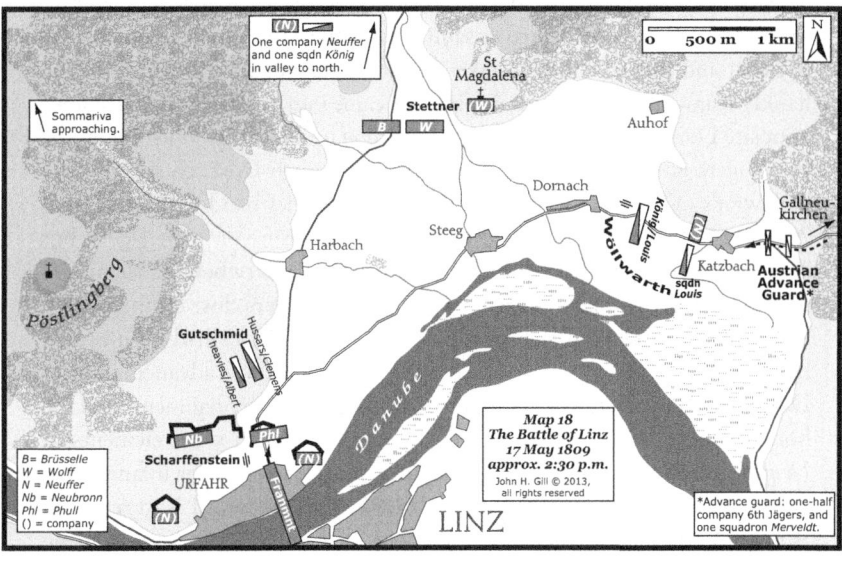

emerged onto the field to occupy Auhof; the 3rd Battalion also came into view, half of it taking up position on a small knoll between Auhof and Katzbach, and the remaining three companies stationing themselves south of Katzbach. Some guns on the heights south-east of Katzbach attempted rather ineffectually to counter the Württemberg pieces south of the Danube, but the rest of Vukassovich's main body (five battalions and four hussar squadrons) waited in battle formation on either side of the Gallneukirchen road east of Katzbach. All was proceeding fairly well from the Austrian perspective, but Kolowrat still had no indication that Somariva was in place and he now observed a great deal of dust and activity around the bridgehead. Correctly concluding that the Saxons had arrived, Kolowrat was unwilling to venture anything in the face of what was clearly a developing counter-attack. He waited.[67]

Vandamme, overcoming his surprise that the Austrians would attack so late in the day, was taking swift counter-measures. The arrival of the first Saxons gave him the freedom to launch a concerted counter-attack and he did not hesitate to do so. The two Württemberg line brigades, supported by the cavalry and the horse artillery, were ordered to attack the Austrian centre while the light battalions were sent against the enemy's right; from the south bank of the Danube, the four guns of the foot battery directed their fire against the Austrian left. These aggressive moves were completely successful. From the valley mouth near the Hellmonsödt road, the light infantrymen of *Wolff* and *Brüsselle* boldly clambered up the steep slope to St Magdalena, followed by the company of *Neuffer* Jäger that had been in the valley. In a well-executed assault, they threw the Grenzer out of the position and turned south to take the Austrians north of Dornach in the flank. Meanwhile, Scharffenstein's brigade came into line across the meadows opposite Dornach, *Phull* on the left, *Neubronn* on the right. With the *König* Fuss-Jägers on their left flank, they stormed through Dornach and pressed Kolowrat's men back towards Katzbach after a brief hand-to-hand fight.[68] Austrian uhlans moved forward to relieve the pressure on their Jägers, but a wild charge by two squadrons of *Herzog Louis* overwhelmed them and sent them flying through Dornach, the Württembergers close on their heels. The time was now approaching 6 p.m. and the Austrians had been beaten back all along the battle line: Scharffenstein's brigade was advancing out of Dornach towards Katzbach, supported by the two cavalry regiments and the horse artillery, while Wolff was moving on Auhof with some elements of *Neuffer*. With great presence of mind, the Württemberg light infantry had detected and halted the advance of I/*Manfredini* and forced it to retire on Auhof. With St Magdalena captured, patrols from *Brüsselle* were scouring the woods north and east of St Magdalena, collecting up Austrian stragglers and posing a potential threat to Kolowrat's line of retreat. In addition, Franquemont's brigade was about to deploy north of Dornach and some of Gutschmid's Saxon cavalry (three hussar squadrons and a half-squadron of *Herzog Albrecht* Chevaulegers) had appeared on the field.

An Austrian battery was situated on the height between Auhof and Katzbach, however, and its fire brought the Württemberg infantry to a halt. Determined to keep the attack rolling, General Wöllwarth sent the *Herzog Louis* troopers forward to deal with these guns, while a squadron of *König* Jäger drove off the protecting infantry of III/*Manfredini* who 'ran into the woods in disorder'.[69] Riding hard, two squadrons of *Louis-Jägers* swung around the hill to the south and charged pell-mell up the steep slope, utterly surprising the Austrian gunners and temporarily silencing the battery. Austrian reserves rushed forward, but the lack of artillery fire had allowed other Württembergers to approach and another squadron of *Herzog Louis* rushed the hill from the north-west while the grenadiers of *Phull* charged the battery frontally. The Saxon hussars and Chevaulegers sent by Bernadotte pounded up to seal the victory. 'Our 3rd Squadron got in amongst some infantry and cut them down,' wrote Rittmeister Karl von Czetteritz und Neuhaus of the Saxon hussars.[70] The Austrians were thrown back to the east and all six guns fell into the hands of the Germans. With the capture of the battery, the fighting in this area slowly came to a close; the Austrians withdrew towards Gallneukirchen, and the Württembergers were too exhausted to send more than harassing patrols in pursuit.

At about this time (approximately 7 p.m.), Somariva put in a belated appearance on the Pöstlingberg after an exhausting march. He had the advantage of surprise—both Vandamme and Bernadotte were completely focused on the fighting by Katzbach—and there were few Allied troops between him and the bridge. Somariva, however, could easily observe the retreat of Kolowrat's column from his vantage point and decided to satisfy his mission and his honour by lobbing a few shells at the bridgehead and retiring. He therefore opened fire from the heights with his 6-pounders, while sending Oberst Ignaz von Leuthner, of the *Peterwardein* Grenzer, towards Harbach with *Würzburg*, his battalion of Grenzer, and fifty Jäger. Leuthner marched through insubstantial resistance from a few surprised Saxons and Württembergers, captured seven of them, and withdrew up the valley to Hellmonsödt in the closing darkness.

Bernadotte, Vandamme, and their staffs, gathered on the eastern slopes below the Pöstlingberg, were shocked by Somariva's unexpected appearance and feared that it betokened the beginning, albeit late, of the main Habsburg attack. 'Fortunately', noted one observer, 'the enemy bestirred himself so little that all available forces could be assembled without disruption.'[71] Bernadotte reacted quickly to reorient the Saxons, who were facing the wrong way to counter Somariva and Leuthner. The two available batteries loosed a few balls at Leuthner, but accomplished nothing with this fire or with the shots they directed towards the Austrian 6-pounders up the slope. As the guns were blasting fruitlessly into the darkness, the marshal turned some of his infantry about and twice personally led I/*Prinz Friedrich August*, I/*Dyherrn*, and a company of II/*Prinz Maximilian* up the rugged slopes in skirmish order with support from the rest of *Prinz Maximilian*. With the best will, however, the Saxons could achieve little in this unfamiliar form of combat.

> The officers of the regiment [*Prinz Friedrich August*] were not a little embarrassed when Marshal Bernadotte rode up during the fight and ordered: 'Forward in skirmish order!' As the trained skirmishers, the Schützen, had been given up to the newly formed Schützen detachments and the other men were not trained in this form of combat, there was nothing to do but give the troops instructions to fan out, remain in their files and press ever forward, 'whereby many a shot was loosed into the blue'.[72]

Vandamme, however, was not about to let the Saxons steal any of the day's glory. Somariva's troops had bivouacked for the night in their strong position and the French general was determined to dislodge them: he ordered GM von Hügel to take the mountain. Although his men were out of ammunition and thoroughly exhausted, the energetic Hügel gathered the *König* Jäger and a company of *Neuffer* and advanced to the attack at about 10 p.m. With fixed bayonets, the weary Jägers struggled up the wooded slopes in utter darkness, the *Brüsselle* Light Battalion following in support. The climb was difficult. 'Finally the column reached a high, open plateau, whose western fringe allowed the outlines of a chapel to be seen jutting up against the firmament in the half-dark of a beautiful summer night.' The Jägers silently overwhelmed the first line of Habsburg pickets with the help of surprise and 'the strength of a bayonet held against the vedette's chest', but their approach was revealed when they came upon the second line and an alert Austrian raised the alarm.[73] Trusting to surprise and audacity, the Württembergers gave a terrifying yell and threw themselves upon the enemy. The shocked Austrians, discovering the danger too late, initially put up a confused and desperate defence, but were soon fleeing through the dark woods in complete panic, chased by the screaming, whooping Jägers. In this bold night action, a few determined companies of Jägers hurled a numerically superior enemy out of an advantageous defensive position and captured close to 400 prisoners. It was a magnificent feat of arms. The threat to Urfahr was eliminated.

It remains to account for Saint Julien's column. This general's forward scouts, about twelve hussars, appeared near Mauthausen early in the morning and were fired upon from the south bank of the Danube by a company of I/*Camrer*. An adventurous *Camrer* lieutenant even took nine men across the river in a small boat to cut off the Austrians, but soon found his own retreat route closed. Although the Württembergers attempted to defend themselves, their cause was hopeless and only two of their number escaped to the south bank. Apparently thinking to fulfil his mission, Saint Julien unlimbered his artillery and opened a bombardment of the *Camrer* company, the only effect of which was to lighten the load of the Austrian ammunition wagons. Saint Julien thus contributed nothing to Kolowrat's plan and returned to Gallneukirchen at dusk, bringing the combat to a close.

The action at Linz/Urfahr on 17 May was a signal victory for Vandamme and the Württembergers. The Saxons, however, had played a critical support role. The mere presence of the 1st Division allowed Vandamme to employ the full force of his command, and the Saxon light horse had fought with dash and skill. King Friedrich's special representative, Oberst von Theobald, was therefore unfair in reporting that 'other than a few Saxon squadrons who did more manoeuvring than acting, no foreign troops were involved.'[74] Nonetheless, the victory belonged to 8th Corps. At a cost of about 320 casualties (the Saxons lost an additional 88), they inflicted 891 on their opponents and took six Austrian guns.[75] The Württembergers had performed splendidly, and their monarch was generous in rewarding his army. Numerous promotions and awards were distributed to all ranks and the *Herzog Louis* Jäger zu Pferd were granted a special Standard of Honour in recognition of their capture of the Austrian battery. Vandamme issued an effusively congratulatory order of the day telling the men that they had 'covered themselves with glory', and Bernadotte said of the Württembergers: 'Their deeds can only be compared with those we are accustomed to achieve with the most experienced French troops.'[76]

In contrast, Kolowrat's performance in this independent role left much to be desired. In the approach to the battle, the questionable rest day on 15 May probably cost him his best opportunity to catch the Württembergers before the Saxons were in a position to provide support. On the day of the engagement, his excessive indulgence in detachments and the allotment of an unnecessarily large force to Saint Julien deprived him of a significant numerical superiority at the decisive point—the open bowl north of Linz. A large portion of his corps was indeed composed of unreliable Landwehr that he was understandably reluctant to commit to serious combat, but placing Oberdorf's reserve fifteen kilometres from the battlefield is still difficult to comprehend. Once the battle was joined, his native caution and the conservative Habsburg military culture prompted a bitter critique by the official Austrian historians:

> Thus at Urfahr as well as elsewhere that spirit predominated which only thinks about blame and never thinks about victory, the spirit that the Generalissimus, despite the most earnest efforts, had not been able to banish in the short time allotted to him. It was opposed to the firm will to victory that was second nature to the contemporary leaders of Napoleon's army.[77]

A bit more nerve on Kolowrat's part might have brought a different outcome. A Württemberg officer, recalling the sudden appearance of Somariva's column and the danger this posed to the bridgehead, came to a similar conclusion in 1809: 'the good thing was that when one was opposing the Austrians, they allowed one time to gather one's wits and recover.'[78]

Kolowrat and Saint Julien both retreated to Gallneukirchen on the night of 17/18 May, and the Habsburg commander decided to unite all of his forces at Freistadt on the 18th. The Austrian main body completed this move at Freistadt with no interference from the Allies. Here GM Schneller joined Kolowrat with III/*Froon*, III/*Josef Colloredo*, two squadrons of *Hessen-Homburg*, a platoon of *Schwarzenberg* Uhlans, and the *Lobkowitz* Jägers. Crenneville remained in Neumarkt with a rear guard.[79] Somariva also headed for Freistadt, leaving a rear guard in Hellmonsödt.

The Allies were too weary to pursue as Kolowrat retreated during the night of 17 May, and the only serious reconnaissance activity on the 18th was an encounter at Hellmonsödt where a small Württemberg detachment under GM von Stettner forced Somariva's rear guard out of its position in a nearly bloodless skirmish.[80] Stettner returned to Urfahr in the evening, leaving an outpost in the town. It was the Austrians' turn to prevail the following morning when Rittmeister von Czetteritz led sixty of his Saxon hussars in a patrol to Unter-Weitersdorf. Vandamme was not satisfied that the hussars had pressed far enough, so he reinforced the rather miffed Czetteritz with twenty-six chevaulegers and twenty-six men of the newly formed *Egidy* Schützen Battalion and instructed the Rittmeister to probe towards Neumarkt. At around 4 p.m., the Saxons pushed back the thin Austrian picket line of Grenzer and *Hessen-Homburg* Hussars near Götschka, but a counter-attack by their supports threw Czetteritz back to Katzbach with a loss of thirty-six prisoners and nine men dead or wounded. GM von Gutschmid was not the sort of commander to accept such a defeat with equanimity. He set off at 6 p.m. with a large detachment consisting of three hussar squadrons, the *Prinz Clemens* Chevaulegers, and the *Egidy* Schützen Battalion. Dropping three chevauleger squadrons and a Schützen company in Gallneukirchen as a reserve, the Saxons pushed north into the darkness and came upon the Habsburg vedettes between midnight and 1 a.m. While the opposing horsemen clashed furiously on the road, Major Christoph von Egidy's Schützen turned the enemy position and forced the Austrians to retire on Neumarkt. Not content, Gutschmid pressed ahead, launched *Egidy's* bold Schützen in an attack against Crenneville just south of Neumarkt at 3 a.m. on 20 May, and again forced the Austrians to retreat. The Saxons occupied the town as dawn was creeping over the hills, and remained there until recalled shortly after dark.[81]

Both sides now prepared for renewed offensive operations and another engagement seemed likely on 22 May. Bernadotte received orders on the 21st to 'enter into Bohemia' and 'manoeuvre either towards Budweis or towards Zwettl depending on circumstances and the movements of the enemy'. 'The principal goal, prince, is always to cover Linz; the second to push the enemy away from the Danube between Krems and Vienna.'[82] The marshal, however, was already raising cautions and objections: the enemy was numerically superior (this was actually accurate), Charles himself might be present, a move into Bohemia would leave Linz vulnerable, and the Saxons suffered from innumerable deficiencies.[83] These pre-emptive hints and anxieties, even if partly true, left the impression in imperial headquarters that Bernadotte was establishing a set of warnings that would excuse any setback and make any success seem all the more noteworthy for having been attained against staggering odds. Recalling Gutschmid from Neumarkt to an advanced post between Katzbach and Gallneukirchen on 20 May, the marshal placed two battalions on the Pöstlingberg, stationed two brigades in the bridgehead, and held Dupas and the rest of the Saxon contingent in and around Linz on the south bank.[84]

The new instructions also called most of 8th Corps south of the Danube. Bernadotte was distressed to lose the energetic Vandamme and his proven Württemberg troops, but Napoleon wanted to assure the security of his southern flank while bringing some of the odd detachments along the Danube back to their owning corps with the Main Army. The emperor, as we have seen, even considered sending Vandamme as far as Mariazell before he learned that GB Duppelin had eliminated this threat.[85] Bernadotte consoled himself by viewing Vandamme's move a temporary measure: 'This expedition seems all the more necessary to me because, being likely to enter into Bohemia soon, we will want, above all, to be certain that there are no more enemy forces behind us on the right bank of the Danube.'[86] By 21 May, Vandamme thus had only three battalions, 200 Jägers, fifty cavalry, and the foot battery in the Urfahr bridgehead, while his headquarters was in Enns and the rest of 8th Corps was distributed between Enns and Ybbs along the Danube and from Kremsmünster to Steyr in the south.[87]

Kolowrat was also planning an advance. Despite the small clashes on the 18th and 19th, most of the Austrians had enjoyed a much-needed rest after the engagement at Linz. GM von Schneller re-occupied Hellmonsödt with a detachment on 20 May and FML Somariva took a newly organised division back to Neumarkt on the 21st. This time, Kolowrat planned to launch his main attack against what he perceived to be the Allies' weakest point, the Pöstlingberg, while Somariva pinned the forces to his front on the Gallneukirchen road. Orders were issued for the main body to march to Leonfelden on 22 May, but mightier events on the Marchfeld brought a change in Kolowrat's plans and the attack never occurred. The Battle of Aspern had intervened.[88]

CHAPTER 3

Aspern

A chronological narrative imposes certain requirements upon the historian to fill in context or discuss subsidiary events, and it is important to have the situation in the Danube valley in mind before turning to the next major event. One must remember, however, that there was, in fact, no pause in operations after the capitulation of Vienna. Certainly there was no pause in Napoleon's thinking. He had Vienna, but 'for the Emperor who wanted, above all, to terminate the war, it meant little to have the city without the bridges.'[1] Charles having been both unwilling and largely unable to come south of the Danube for a decisive engagement, the French emperor immediately began seeking opportunities to carry his army across the river in search of the foe. The first result of this energetic approach was a sharp fight that occurred opposite Nussdorf on the very day Napoleon entered Vienna.

13 May: French Fiasco at the Schwarze Lackenau

'The Emperor's intention, general, is to throw a bridge over the Danube tomorrow or the day after,' wrote Berthier to artillery chief Songis late at night on 11 May as French howitzer shells exploded inside Vienna's walls, 'the pontooneers must be prepared and take all possible measures to have boats, ropes, and anchors.'[2] Personal observation by General Bertrand confirmed that the great Tabor Bridge, the one that Murat and Lannes had captured intact in 1805, had been completely destroyed by the Austrians during their retreat. The French thus redoubled their ongoing reconnaissance efforts and earnest staff officers rode along the riverbanks above and below the capital searching for suitable crossing points. Napoleon had his eye on two:

Fischamend on the road to Hungary and Nussdorf just north of the city. Reports from Songis's diligent officers soon disabused him of his hopes for Fischamend owing to the steep banks and the extraordinary width of the river at that point. Instead, Songis rather unenthusiastically recommended a bridge at Kaiser Ebersdorf if Napoleon intended to establish one downstream between Vienna and Pressburg.[3] Napoleon, who wanted to have two viable crossing sites in hand, accordingly sent orders to Massena to begin work at Ebersdorf at once.[4] Upstream from the city, Songis reported, 'it seems to me that it would be most advantageous to construct one outside of Vienna near Nussdorf.'[5] Napoleon soon learned that Lannes and St Hilaire, entrusted with locating a crossing north of the city, had already explored the Nussdorf site and had sent a reconnaissance detachment across the river in boats.

The French infantrymen who made their way across the Danube on two barges at 10 a.m. found an elongated island separated from the northern (left) bank by an eighty- to one-hundred-metre-wide arm of the Danube known as the Schwarze Lacke (roughly 'the Black Water'). The island, or '*Au*', thus took its name from this branch of the river. It was approximately three kilometres long and ranged from 500 to 1,500 metres in width. The eager French officers had not known that they were landing on an island and were delighted to discover that their proposed crossing site was a natural redoubt. With its size and the protection afforded by the Schwarze Lacke, it

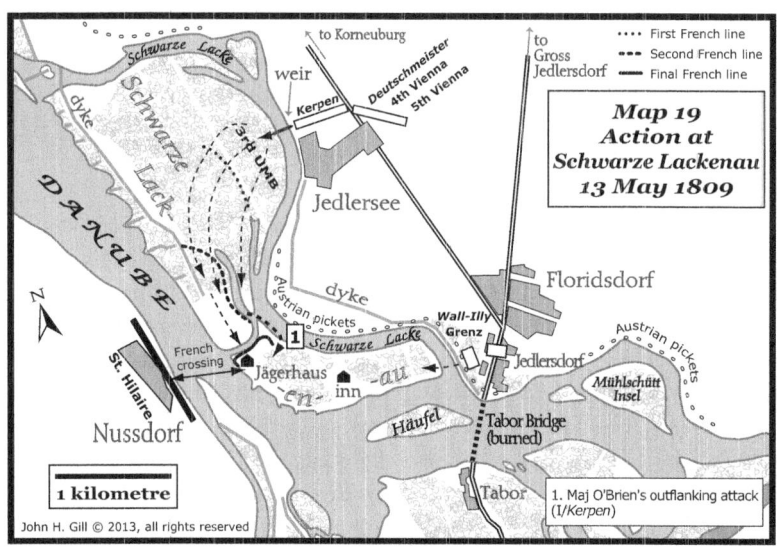

Map 19
Action at
Schwarze Lackenau
13 May 1809

made a perfect staging area for the assault. In addition, the thick woods on the island would conceal their movements from the Austrian pickets on the far bank. Driven off by Austrian artillery fire before they could conduct a thorough examination, however, the French did not notice that a stout weir near Jedlersee connected the island to the Marchfeld.

The French were keen to occupy the island before the Austrians recognised its value, but lack of boats and watermen delayed the crossing. Only at 2 p.m. could St Hilaire begin to send the first troops across the river. For this mission, he selected the three voltigeur companies of 72nd Ligne, but with only three suitable watercraft crewed by French pontooneers the passage was slow and two hours were taken up getting the light infantrymen onto the island. The voltigeurs, numbering perhaps 300 men, landed near a building known as the 'Jägerhaus' and organised themselves before pushing out towards the far side of the island at around 4 p.m. Meanwhile, Lannes hastened to get more troops over the water. The French patrols occasioned some Austrian artillery fire as they emerged from the woods on the northern fringe of the island, but the fire died out almost immediately as the voltigeurs quickly drew back into the trees and vanished. Napoleon, who had now arrived at the crossing site, wanted to send over two guns to support the vulnerable toehold, but only one suitable boat could be found and efforts get this awkward craft to the northern shore proved fruitless. The island, however, was well within artillery range from the south shore and the French unlimbered twenty-six guns, including a pair of 12-pounders, to support the crossing. All the while, French infantry strength on the far bank continued to increase as St Hilaire put more men—now from 105th Ligne—into the three boats to strengthen his tenuous position.

Meanwhile, the Austrians were responding. The brief appearance of 72nd Ligne's voltigeurs led Hiller's chief of staff, Oberst von Csollich, to order a reconnaissance by the nearest available infantry, Major Josef Baron Obergfell's 3rd UMB Landwehr. Crossing over the weir, a group of Landwehr in company strength poked south towards the Jägerhaus and bumped into the growing assemblage of French infantry. The alert voltigeurs drove off Obergfell's men and chased them back towards the dyke near Jedlesee in a rather disorganised pursuit, but the rising sound of firing convinced Csollich that his fear of a serious French crossing was well founded. Using Hiller's authority, he ordered GM von Weissenwolff's brigade to clear the island at once. He also directed Oberst Gratze, whose Grenzer were posted along the riverbank near Floridsdorf, to support the attack by sending a detachment onto the southern end of the Schwarze Lackenau.

Csollich's prompt action set the stage for Habsburg success. At Csollich's direction, Obergfell took most of his battalion across the weir to gain time for the regulars to arrive. This move sufficed, but just barely. By the time Weissenwolff's men reached the scene from Gross-Jedlersdorf, the Landwehr were beginning to disintegrate, many leaving the firing line and throwing themselves into the waters of the Schwarze Lacke in their panic. Substantial help now arrived in the form of the 1,700 men of *Kerpen* Infantry No. 49, while the rest of Weissenwolff's brigade took up covering positions along the northern bank of the Schwarze Lacke.[6] With Csollich at their head, the whitecoats rushed over the dyke in a column only three abreast (the narrow top of the weir would permit no more) and hurled themselves at the French voltigeurs. Major O'Brien's 1st Battalion, joined by the remaining Landwehr, led the attack with the 2nd and 3rd Battalions following in small columns. The voltigeurs of the 72nd put up a stout resistance, but the magnitude of the attack was more than they could withstand and they slowly fell back towards the Jägerhaus. The French commanders on the island threw batches of men from the 105th into the fight as soon as they disembarked, and the light infantrymen, thus reinforced, were able to detain the vigorous Austrian advance for a time along one of the dead-end ditches that broke up the island. Attempts by *Kerpen* officers to outflank the enemy position along the riverside were shot to pieces by the French artillery on the south shore, but the weight of numbers told as the 2nd Battalion and half of the 3rd were injected into the fray. This revitalised assault forced the French back behind another narrow ditch to a relatively strong position just north of their landing spot and the Austrian advance stalled again.

It was now approximately 7.30 p.m. and daylight was fading fast. Major O'Brien recognised that the French would establish an unassailable position if they were allowed to settle in overnight. He was resolved to prevent this and gathered up a band of men for an attack against the French right. While some of his troops occupied the French defenders, O'Brien was able to exploit a lucky circumstance: a fence that skirted the edge of the Schwarze Lacke. Using the fence as cover, the major led approximately fifty men behind the enemy firing line and burst upon the unsuspecting French. This unexpected attack unhinged the stressed French line and the combat dissolved into brief, bitter battles between small bands of Frenchmen and the storming Austrians. Attempts to defend the Jägerhaus quickly collapsed and the French officers, acknowledging the inevitable, surrendered their remaining men to avoid further slaughter. Under fire from the French guns on the south bank, the men of *Kerpen* collected their numerous prisoners, while the two companies of Grenzer who had landed on the southern tip of the island rounded up scattered fugitives.

The first attempt to cross the Danube thus ended in disaster for the French. Although some men, many wounded among them, had been ferried back to the south bank, the three voltigeur companies of 72nd Ligne and six companies from the 105th were eliminated in the evening's struggle for a cost of some 700 men out of the force of approximately 900 to 1,000 that had been put across the river.[7] Austrian casualties in the short battle (three hours) were not insubstantial, some 300 for *Kerpen* and another 50 to 100 for the 3rd UMB Landwehr, but the psychological impact weighed heavily in Austria's favour. Where Napoleon censured St Hilaire ('Everything was very poorly directed'), both O'Brien and Obergfell received promotions in recognition of their roles in this tidy little victory.[8]

The two Austrian majors, as well as Csollich and others, certainly deserved credit for the day's outcome, reacting to the emergency with alacrity and good tactical sense. Their men responded to this leadership with courage and determination. Their French opponents had displayed equal valour but were tactically sloppy. At the company/battalion level, they contributed to their own demise by their over-zealous pursuit of the Landwehr, by failing to organise themselves properly on the island, and by neglecting to establish a reserve near the landing site. Apparently feeding troops into the fight as they arrived on the island, they could not construct a coherent defence. These lapses largely resulted from the haste with which the entire operation was mounted, a sense of urgency that communicated itself down through the ranks from Lannes and St Hilaire. The desire to establish a lodgement on the Schwarze Lackenau before the Austrians could protect it was both understandable and laudable. However, these two senior commanders would have served their emperor better had they taken time to collect more shipping or waited until dark before initiating the crossing. Had they done so, Hiller might have awakened on 14 May to a nasty surprise indeed. Instead, they acted with inordinate haste and suffered a sharp repulse as a consequence. It was the price of impetuosity.

In the broader operational arena, the defeat drew Austrian attention to the Schwarze Lackenau and thus effectively removed it—'the most favourable of all'—from the list of potential French crossing sites near Vienna.[9] With Fischamend unsuitable for technical reasons and the Austrians now alert to the danger at the Schwarze Lackenau, the French turned their focus to the lone remaining possibility in the vicinity of the capital: Kaiser Ebersdorf and the access it afforded to a large island called the Lobau.

14–20 May: Trouble in the Mountains

After the failure at the Schwarze Lackenau, Napoleon had optimistically hoped to see a span at Ebersdorf as early as 17 May.[10] This proved a wildly unrealistic expectation. The daunting technical challenges involved in simultaneously crossing a major river and several of its smaller branches were compounded by a severe lack of the requisite materials. There were shortages of boats, anchors, and cordage. Also in short supply was time. Napoleon was anxious to bring the Austrian army to battle and the war to an end. All of his drive, however, and all of the diligence and ingenuity of the French engineers could not accelerate the bridging project beyond the physical limits of the available material.

As it became apparent that the construction work would absorb more than a day or two, the emperor decided to disperse his cavalry to protect his southern flank and, above all, to ease the logistical problems associated with sustaining thousands of men and horses in Vienna and its suburbs. He thus strung a chain of light horse regiments from Bruck to Neustadt under Montbrun, supported by their heavy brethren closer to the city. Probing as far as Ragendorf and Ungarisch-Altenburg, the French light horsemen were active and aggressive. They caused considerable worry for Hiller and Habsburg authorities in Hungary, who had little means to protect themselves and consequently allowed their imaginations to inflate French strength.

The Austrians felt especially vulnerable in Hungary. There was a political dimension to their worries in that Napoleon had issued a proclamation to the Hungarian people on 15 May, promising independence ('I offer you peace, the integrity of your territory, your liberty, and your constitution') and exciting Habsburg concerns for the loyalty of their Magyar subjects.[11] Military weakness also caused anxiety. Archduke Joseph had his headquarters in Raab, but the Insurrection was far from ready for any serious operations. The cavalry lacked training, harness, uniforms, sabres, pistols, and experienced officers. The infantry was worse, not even capable of outpost duty. There was no artillery until a lone cavalry battery appeared in Raab on 18 May. The Austrians could only hope to mask their weakness while working feverishly to refurbish Raab's defences and constructing an entrenched camp outside the town. The Insurrection troops, however, outnumbered Montbrun. By 20 May, the eve of the Battle of Aspern, 1,400 infantry and 2,500 cavalry were gathered near Raab under FML Janos Freiherr Mecséry, with another 1,100 infantry and 2,100 horsemen stretching south as far as Tuskevar. Against these Montbrun had 2,200 light horse, two guns, and less than 1,000 Hessian infantry (although he could call on more at need).[12] With Montbrun only chartered to screen the upcoming mighty events at Vienna and the Austrians merely hoping to disguise the fragile Insurrection forces, both sides were essentially trying to keep the other at a distance.[13] The result was that a series of tense but ultimately insignificant skirmishes and ambuscades burbled along the Hungarian border until shortly after Aspern. At the same time, fears for Pressburg prompted Habsburg leaders to keep FZM Paul Freiherr Davidovich along the Waag River with most of his troops, while GM Andras Graf Hadik's men remained on Hungary's northern borders following the negative turn of events in Poland.[14]

The enforced pause, however, did allow Napoleon an opportunity to clear out the troublesome pockets to his flank and rear. He issued an edict disbanding the Landwehr and despatched GD Lauriston with the Baden brigade and some of Colbert's troopers to Altenmarkt 'to disperse this gathering of peasants' as a complement to Davout's operations further west.[15] Lauriston arrived in Altenmarkt an der Triesting on the evening of 15 May without encountering any trouble beyond unseasonable heat and the annoyance of removing several undefended abatis along the road. Colbert's men, however, were ambushed by some Landsturm near Pottenstein en route from Neustadt to join Lauriston and returned to their starting point with five troopers wounded. Despite this apparent success, the Landsturm were unreliable, many of them only grudgingly under arms or unwilling to do more than serve brief stints close to their homes. With Altenmarkt clear and Davout prosecuting the expedition to Mariazell, the emperor directed Lauriston to subdue the countryside around the Semmering. Lauriston marched to Neustadt via Pottenstein without incident on the 16th and secured the Semmering on 18 May. In the process, he scattered Plächel's remnants, who had arrived just west of Gloggnitz after a painful march through the mountains that had seen most of his little militia force melt away. Lauriston and the Badeners then overwhelmed the Semmering's defenders with a spirited charge. The Austrian force in the pass consisted of the sad residue of MacDermott's brigade, whom we last saw retreating up the Enns valley from Weyer. After an exhausting and confusing trek through the mountains, MacDermott turned over command of the 'brigade', now reduced to some 500 Landwehr and a few fugitives from regular units, to Oberst Karl Freiherr von Trauttenberg and departed for Vienna. Trauttenberg, however, could do little with this pathetic band. Attacked in the pass by the Baden Jäger and French cavalry, the Landwehr disintegrated and fled, leaving forty-four men in the hands of the pursuing French chasseurs.

Lauriston conducted enough reconnaissance beyond the pass to learn definitively that the only Austrians in Styria were shaky Landwehr, Landsturm, and the scattered shards of broken regular units. With this reassuring news, he returned to Gloggnitz.

There remained one final grouping of militia to suppress. Oberst Leopold Graf Attems, aged 73, was responsible for organising the Landsturm in the vicinity of Aspang, a small town in the valley south of Neunkirchen. The response to his appeals was minimal, but FML Kerpen reinforced him with forty Grenz-Kordon troops and the depots of the 4th and 5th Graz Landwehr Battalions. Attems placed his uncertain little command in Friedberg with posts as far north as Aspang. During the night of 19/20 May, Lauriston sent I/2nd Baden and fifty chasseurs over rough mountain roads to attack Aspang from the west. The column was completely successful in this unusual night move, sweeping up Austrian outposts and clearing a town west of Aspang in a midnight skirmish. Aspang was surrounded and a sleepy Austrian captain captured with his detachment of thirty men. Attems attempted to evict the Badeners on the afternoon of 20 May, but was repulsed with loss, and unrest in the area south-west of Vienna largely came to an end. Isolated groups of Allied soldiers would still be subject to ambush, but from the Semmering to Salzburg there was now no substantial threat to Napoleon's rear from the south. Lauriston, with the Badeners and 20th Chasseurs, established his headquarters in Neustadt and occupied the Semmering Pass, conducting frequent patrols to ensure the region's tranquillity.[16] Colbert and his other two regiments had departed to join the army on Lobau Island and throughout 21 and 22 May, the Badeners could hear 'the powerful, incessant thunder of cannon from the direction of Vienna . . . it was the thunder of the bloody Battle of Aspern.'[17]

Before turning to the roiling conventional struggle on the edges of the Marchfeld, it is useful to highlight several features of the 'unconventional' combat or 'little war' (*Kleinkrieg* or *la petit guerre*) waged on the Styrian frontier by Davout and Lauriston. In the first place, the terrain, as in all military activity, was key. Resistance centred on strategic valleys where forces could gather, move, and sustain themselves, so the French were obliged to control the low-lying areas. At the same time, mastery of the heights was crucial at the tactical level, as demonstrated when the Baden Jägers outflanked and terrified Trauttenberg's men at the Semmering by scaling the mountainsides and attacking from the side. Second, the attitude of the local populace was a determining factor in the fate of military enterprises. The Austrians had only marginal success in recruiting Landsturm from an unorganised, untrained population unaccustomed to notions of a popular militia. The Allies, on the other hand, while certainly unwelcome visitors, seem to have been able to gather intelligence, acquire food, and procure guides with little difficulty. Incidents of active hostility occurred, but co-operation, even if reluctant or under duress, was not uncommon. There was no history of embedded grievance to fuel bitter resistance (as in the Tyrol), and the fall of Vienna and the Hauptarmee's undeniable defeat in Bavaria had a decidedly dampening effect on public spirit. Third, the nature of the combatants put the Habsburg officers at a disadvantage from the beginning. Faced with veteran French and Baden regulars, the hastily enlisted, poorly trained, and minimally equipped Landsturm and Landwehr were prone to flight in battle and evaporated on the march. 'The people called up and placed in the Landsturm along the Austrian border are disheartened and recalcitrant,' reported Oberst von Attems.[18] The various Allied commanders thus accomplished their missions of quelling local unrest on the Austria–Styria border with relative ease. The story would be very different for Lefebvre's Bavarians, who were making their way to Innsbruck with blood and fire even as Davout and Lauriston withdrew most of their men from the valleys south-west of Vienna.

14–19 May: More Bridges, More Delays

In the area around Vienna, the period after the Habsburg success at Schwarze Lackenau passed in relative quiet. The sense of anxiety and tension on the Austrian side of the river, however, was evident in periodic alarms and exaggerated reporting of every Frenchman who showed his uniform on the far bank of the Danube. The city of Pressburg, for example, fell into a panic when a scouting detachment of 3rd Chasseurs appeared in Hainburg and Wolfsthal ten kilometres up the river on 14 May. Work on a strategically important bridgehead on the south bank stopped and the few troops in the city departed with their commandant, GM Andreas Freiherr von Szorenyi. Fortunately for the Austrians, GM Provenchères had arrived from Styria on the 13th with his seven squadrons to provide at least the semblance of a regular troop presence and the French light cavalry, few in number, were only intent on gathering intelligence and forage. Similar jumpiness characterised reporting up and down the river from Pressburg to Langenzersdorf until the union with the Main Army on 16 May. This long stretch of water, previously protected only by Hiller's weakened command, could now be guarded with confidence. The importance of Pressburg for the Hauptarmee's future plans, however, led to the immediate despatch of GM von Hoffmeister with the *Beaulieu* Infantry and his brigade battery to garrison the city; in addition, Provenchères was directed to leave behind two squadrons as he rode off with the rest to join the army on the Marchfeld.[19]

The arrival of Charles and the Hauptarmee meant a reorganisation of the army. While the troops enjoyed the bounty of the local area, the Habsburg commander drafted a new order of battle. Some shifts had already taken place when the army left the modified III Corps behind in Bohemia, but as compared with the army's organisation on 10 April, the biggest changes were the incorporation of the two reserve corps into one large command under Liechtenstein and the transformation of V Corps into a sort of 'holding formation' with only two regular brigades of the standard pattern (Weissenwolff's and Radetzky's). Most of the regular infantry regiments stayed with their original corps, but four former V Corps regiments were distributed to IV and VI Corps, and the assignment of cavalry regiments altered considerably. Reuss was promoted to Feldzeugmeister and retained his post at the head of V Corps (Ludwig never returned to a command position); the other corps commanders remained the same.[20] The volunteer and Landwehr battalions posed a special problem. Proven troops, such as the Vienna Volunteers, stayed with the field army (although the previous brigading was abolished), but many had shown themselves completely unprepared for combat. Four third battalions of regular regiments and nearly 4,000 new recruits destined for regular regiments were also judged unfit for combat. All of these, totalling some 24,100 men in twenty-eight battalions and numerous detachments, were sent into Moravia for further training. Additionally, two third battalions belonging to III Corps (*Würzburg* and *Württemberg*) were sent off to Bohemia. The army (not including V Corps) thus entered the Battle of Aspern with no Landwehr and only nine volunteer battalions. The Hauptarmee received a small reinforcement in cavalry with the arrival of GM Provenchères and his five remaining squadrons of *O'Reilly*. A brigade of two Insurrection hussar regiments, ordered to the Marchfeld 'because the enemy cavalry is greatly superior to ours in number', also joined, riding in from Hungary 1,840 strong.[21] They were considered, however, a liability owing to their state of training and were assigned to the reserve 'because these troops are not practiced in fighting on their own and, although they show much courage, they certainly cannot be left alone.'[22]

The generalissimus now had to decide how he was going to employ his reunited and reorganised army. His enemies at court still called for an early Austrian offensive. They cited the danger to Inner Austria, argued that

Johann would have to abandon the 'gain won' in Italy (he already had), and claimed that Napoleon's resources were ultimately greater than the Habsburg monarchy's. The fall of Vienna, however, had removed the urgency behind demands for an immediate crossing of the Danube, as even Liechtenstein, the most aggressive of the senior commanders, recognised. Charles could thus exploit one of Austria's greatest advantages: time. While Napoleon was 'constantly pressed by time',[23] the Austrians could adopt the delaying strategy of the Roman general Quintus Fabius Maximus ('Cunctator', or 'the delayer') as Wimpffen argued in a lengthy memorandum submitted on 17 May. 'We must imitate this example and conduct the war according to this pattern, that fits our current situation and the condition of our army perfectly,' he wrote.[24] In his view, an extended operational pause would weaken the French, who occupied a hostile and exhausted countryside, while giving the Austrians time to repair the Hauptarmee and organise the Hungarian Insurrection. Additionally, of course, delay meant that Charles did not have to face the difficult decision of how to conduct a risky river crossing in the face of active French opposition.[25]

A waiting game would also allow manifold diversions time to undermine the French position. Charles and most other Habsburg leaders invested a great deal of faith in rebellions and minor military actions that would cause Napoleon to detach major elements of his force around Vienna and thereby make him vulnerable to an Austrian attack. Maximilian had been an early exemplar of this line of reasoning when he called up the Landsturm at the beginning of the month, but Charles, despite his usual aversion to armed citizenry, now began to hope that popular uprisings inside Austria would endanger Napoleon's line of communications and distract his forces. More important than local unrest, the senior Habsburg leadership hoped for great results from military diversions. Kolowrat's expedition to Linz was one branch of this plan. The other manifestation of this thinking was an order prepared by Charles and signed by Franz that called for Archduke Johann to take the bulk of his army 'through Salzburg to the Inn near the Danube or even into Bavaria'. Johann was authorised to involve Chasteler's force in the Tyrol if he wished. It was hoped that these actions, taken in concert, would place the French army in 'the most ruinous situation' and 'punish it for the rashness of advancing into the heart of my states without consideration for its flanks and rear'.[26] Wimpffen hopefully estimated that Johann would arrive on the Inn in ten to fourteen days, that is sometime between 25 and 30 May. At that point, it was assumed, the French would be completely cut off deep inside enemy territory.

Such was the Austrian thinking. Once again, however, it does not take much effort to detect a 'taint of unreality' in these proposals. Orchestrating combined operations by independent forces with the communications available in the early nineteenth century was an enormous challenge, as was demonstrated on a much smaller scale during Kolowrat's attack on Linz. On the other hand, a charitable analysis could assume that these problems were well known and that the Habsburg leaders considered them an acceptable risk, given the monarchy's strategic situation. More interesting is the continued Austrian predilection to believe that Napoleon would remain static and allow his opponents two weeks' repose to implement their plan. They also continued to underestimate the French army that 'has suffered much from forced marches and engagements'.[27] Every pause in Napoleon's operations, such as now occurred as the French gathered materials necessary to cross the Danube, was taken in Habsburg circles as evidence that the enemy was at the end of his tether and vulnerable to a counterstroke.[28]

In the event, these strategic dreams had already been superseded by the practical progress of the war. When Kaiser Franz was signing the order to Johann on 15 May, for instance, the popular resistance founded on the Landsturm that Maximilian had hoped to inspire was already sputtering out in the Styrian mountains. That day also saw the Bavarian 7th Corps enter the town of Schwaz in the Inn valley. After administering a series of sharp defeats on Chasteler and the Tyrolian rebels, Lefebvre and his men were only twenty kilometres from Innsbruck. More important still was Johann's situation. By 15 May, as outlined in the next two chapters, he and his Army of Inner Austria were back on Habsburg soil (near Villach), ejected from Italy and in full retreat. Johann, receiving the 15 May instructions in Klagenfurt on the 18th, was incredulous that he was expected to undertake a major operation 'without prior preparations, without having arranged for logistical support, and with the enemy on all sides'.[29] He wisely continued his retreat. Kolowrat's ineffectual expedition to Linz thus remained the only serious diversionary operation, and it too, as we have seen, was about to conclude in a clear rebuff to Austrian plans.

Napoleon, however, could not ignore the possibility that the Austrians, against their usual practice, would launch an attack against his line of communications. The intelligence he received on the Hauptarmee's movements was frustratingly imprecise and permitted critically variant interpretations. Senior officers captured during the engagement at Linz, for example, told Bernadotte that Charles would retreat towards Brünn unless the attack at Linz was 'a clear success'.[30] This reinforced Napoleon's earlier notion that

Charles was retreating into Moravia, but the prisoners also told Bernadotte that a victory at Linz would have led Charles to cross the Danube. Other news reaching the 9th Corps commander suggested that Kaiser Franz was in Prague preparing a last-ditch defence in Bohemia, while observers along the Danube reported 'the continual arrival of small detachments of infantry and cavalry' as well as 'rumours that the entire Austrian army will assemble in the vicinity of Vienna'.[31] It was difficult to draw a clear picture of enemy movements from these conflicting statements and sightings. By 19 May, however, when he learned of Kolowrat's failed thrust at Linz, Napoleon could conclude that a large portion of the Hauptarmee, perhaps as many as 30,000 men, was still detached in Bohemia even though a major part of the army seemed to be collecting itself on the left bank of the Danube north of Vienna. If these conclusions were correct, the emperor was presented with a problem and an opportunity. The problem was that significant Austrian forces still appeared poised to threaten his rear between Linz and Krems, but the detachment of these formations would mean a reduction in the Hauptarmee's strength and might thus provide an opportunity for the French.[32] Napoleon's planning therefore pressed for an early crossing of the Danube near Vienna, but left adequate forces masterfully echeloned along the river back to Passau to deter any Austrian adventure on the south bank.[33]

Napoleon also addressed the situations in his strategic rear and right flank. With the Bavarians approaching Innsbruck, he hoped that the rebellion in the Tyrol would soon be extinguished, making the troops committed to these operations available for other missions. He therefore directed Lefebvre to 'attack and overthrow everything around Radstadt' (that is, Jellacic) and to be prepared to march on Leoben.[34] General Beaumont in Augsburg with his Reserve Division could turn his attention to ensuring the security of the Palatinate and to preventing raiding parties from passing the Danube between Straubing and Regensburg as long as he was satisfied that the Tyrol was subdued.[35] At the same time, Eugene and the Army of Italy were to pursue Archduke Johann, join the Army of Germany as soon as possible, and prevent Johann from falling on Napoleon's strategic right.[36] The emperor also had good news from the banks of the Vistula where the Poles appeared to be turning the tables on Archduke Ferdinand. In central Germany, he was vastly irritated by what he perceived as a panicked and hasty response to rumours of 13,000 Prussians marching into Westphalia with old General Blücher at their head. Napoleon was confident that Prussia would do nothing and excoriated his minister of war for overreacting to what turned out to be the ride of the renegade Prussian Major Ferdinand von Schill and his band of hussars. Even here, Napoleon believed that the measures he was taking in the formation of Kellermann's Reserve Corps would suffice to maintain calm in the Rheinbund. On the verge of launching his army across the Danube, therefore, the emperor was well prepared for these various operational contingencies. 'The enemy', he wrote to Eugene on 17 May, 'has indeed been defeated on all sides.'[37] His greatest problem was the lack of reliable information on the location of the Hauptarmee and the intentions of its commander. He believed, however, that some portion of the Austrian army 'has assembled on the left bank' between the Danube and Moravia.[38] He was resolved to find it and attack.

Getting the Allied army to the far bank, however, proved a frustratingly tedious and drawn-out process. French cavalry scoured the riverbanks for boats and the innovative engineers resorted to every sort of improvisation to overcome the lack of proper materials. Wooden crates filled with rocks or cannon balls, for example, substituted for true anchors. The technical challenges at the selected crossing site were also daunting. The Danube here was divided into two channels by a wooded isle some 230 metres wide called the Schneidergrund. The first of these gaps (from the right bank to the Schneidergrund) was 460 metres in width. Spanning the second major gap, 230 metres, would connect the Schneidergrund to another irregular island, the Lobgrund, 570 metres wide. Where the former was unoccupied by either side, a company of *Duka* and some Vienna Jägers held the Lobgrund. The Lobgrund was separated from the next major island, Lobau, by a fordable twenty-eight-metre body of water (Lobgrundarm). Finally, the French would have to bridge the 130 metres of the Stadtler Arm of the Danube to reach the Marchfeld. All of these islands were at least partially covered with trees and brush, obscuring the crossing sites from Austrian observers on the Marchfeld.

Austrian forces immediately available to oppose a crossing at Lobau were few. The bulk of the army was back along the hills west and north-west of the Marchfeld, encamped in a great 'L' from Strebersdorf north to Hagenbrunn/Enzersfeld and then east to Pillichsdorf. Though the main body of his corps was ensconced on the southern slopes of the Bisamberg, Hiller was still responsible for the thin line of troops along the Danube. GM Nordmann commanded the units from Langenzersdorf to Aspern: 1st and 2nd Vienna Volunteers, *St Georg/Brod* Grenzer, 4th UMB, and seven squadrons of *Liechtenstein* Hussars. Oberst Bakonyi, whom we last saw leading the attack on the French chasseurs in Neumarkt, had his own *Duka* Infantry, as well as the ubiquitous Major Scheibler with his two squadrons

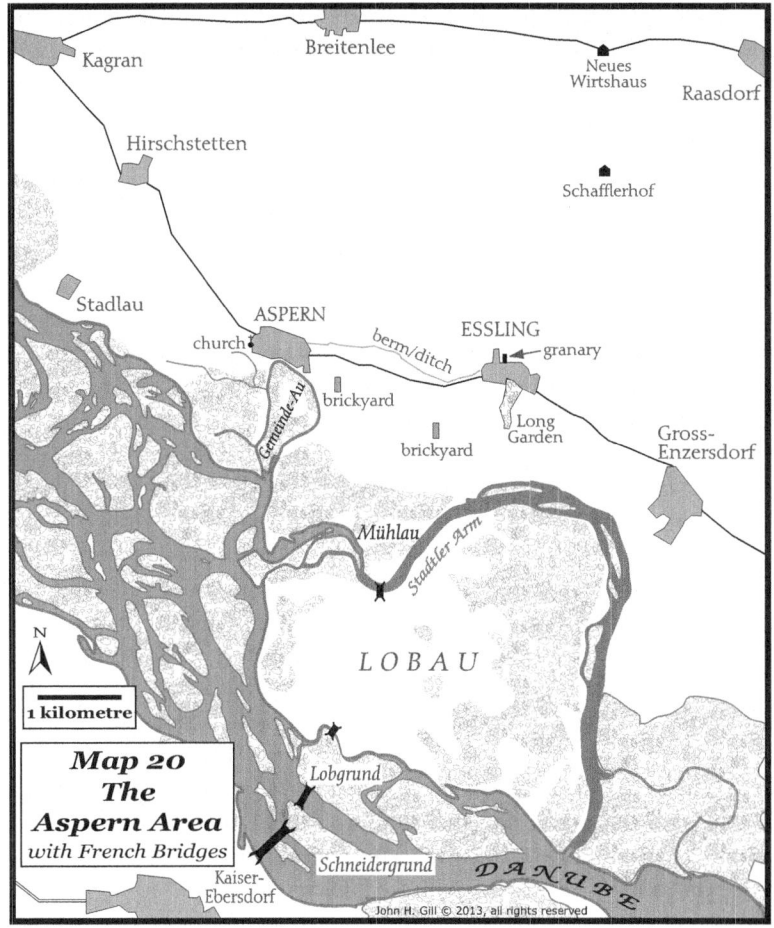

Map 20
The
Aspern Area
with French Bridges

of *Rosenberg* and a cavalry half-battery in the vicinity of Essling and Gross-Enzersdorf. The remaining squadron of *Liechtenstein* Hussars watched the river from the latter place as far as Schönau, opposite Fischamend. Bakonyi's men would therefore be the first ones to greet the French when they arrived on the northern shore.

Notwithstanding the best efforts of the French engineers and their emperor's growing impatience, Oberst Bakonyi and his men would have to wait. Construction of the bridges could not begin until the night of 18/19 May. Molitor, charged with protecting the site, sent several companies across at 5 p.m. that evening to establish a hold on the Lobgrund. 'The Emperor himself oversaw the embarkation of the first battalions that were to take post on the left bank; he himself placed the soldiers in the boats, where he arranged them in such a way as to fit the greatest number possible; he watched the distribution of the cartridges and spoke to almost every soldier.'[39] One may imagine the impression such personal attention left with the men. Mindful of the lessons of Schwarze Lackenau, Napoleon sent two guns with this detachment. Landing at 6 p.m., Molitor's advance force quickly chased off the Austrian company, inflicting sixteen casualties. The French might have taken the entire company, but their mission was simply to secure a landing site for the rest of the division, so they advanced to the Lobgrundarm, built a crossing, and sent patrols into the Lobau. Molitor immediately began shipping over the remainder of his division and the French engineers set to work on the main bridges.

Morning found bridge construction proceeding, albeit slowly, under Napoleon's demanding gaze. 'I went to see the work on the bridge and as I was sitting on a log, I saw the Emperor arrive and he became very angry because the first bridge was not finished,' recalled musician Girault.[40] On the far bank, Molitor was preparing to advance. No one on the Austrian side had thought of attacking the intruders during the morning, even though strong winds temporarily precluded shipping across the river and left Molitor isolated. Despite Molitor's rather vulnerable position, Napoleon ordered him to push forward to the Stadtler Arm. There were only a few *Duka* outposts on Lobau, and these rapidly vanished as the French moved carefully across the island to emerge from the trees along the Stadtler Arm south of Essling at approximately 1 p.m. Skirmishing with the whitecoats of Oberst Bakonyi's *Duka* Infantry, the French infantry and artillery gained the upper hand and drove off the Austrians. By 3 p.m., the firing had faded away, and the rest of the afternoon and evening passed in peace. Hiller, who had ridden to the area on receiving Bakonyi's report of the skirmish, rejected a suggestion from Major Scheibler that the Austrians attack Molitor. Hiller observed that a corps would be required to evict the French, that there was no fixed crossing onto the Lobau, and that the army high command would have to approve any such operation. He returned to his headquarters. On his side of the water, Molitor selected an advantageous crossing site onto the Marchfeld, settled his skirmishers into the woods along the bank to guard it, and put the rest of his troops to work collecting bridging materials, occupying the small islands in the Stadtler Arm, and establishing communications with the Lobgrund.

Molitor's arrival on Lobau Island brought a change of opinion in Austrian headquarters. The generalissimus had been unwilling to view the French activity at Kaiser Ebersdorf as anything other than a demonstration. Although it had been clear that the movements on the far side of the Danube likely presaged a crossing, Charles could not bring himself to believe that Napoleon would use the rather isolated Kaiser Ebersdorf site in preference to Nussdorf with its excellent road network. Molitor's advance, dust clouds thrown up by marching columns south of Vienna, and a spy's report that Napoleon had moved his headquarters to Kaiser Ebersdorf finally convinced the archduke that the attack from the Lobau was real. Even so, as night fell on 19/20 May, he believed the French would simply cross onto the edge of the Marchfeld and then advance north along the Danube to clear the Austrian defences from opposite Nussdorf. He accordingly made his dispositions to stop the French advance along the river with part of his army, while the rest attacked the French flank from the east to drive them into the Danube.

20 May: Onto the Marchfeld

Riding into Aderklaa early on 20 May, Charles was surprised to learn that the French had not crossed onto the Marchfeld from Lobau Island during the night as anticipated. This unexpected development, combined with confirmations of the French concentration at Ebersdorf, led Charles to conclude that Napoleon's main attack would indeed come from Lobau. He correctly guessed that 'the enemy, if he advances into the plains, will probably debouch with a mass of cavalry,' and he decided 'to oppose him likewise with the majority of our cavalry and with superior numbers if possible'.[41] Five mounted regiments and four cavalry batteries from the other four corps were thus sent to join Liechtenstein and the Cavalry Reserve at Aderklaa while the remaining Austrian troops held themselves in readiness further to the rear. An 'advance guard' was formed from this force and placed under Klenau's orders: *Stipsicz* Hussars, *Schwarzenberg* Uhlans, *Erzherzog Karl* Infantry, 1st Jäger Battalion, and a cavalry battery. Scheibler's two squadrons of *Rosenberg* near Essling were also designated to come under Klenau's command.

While Charles was planning and the cavalry were trotting towards Aderklaa, some of the Austrians along the river were also busy. Perhaps most industrious was Oberleutnant Leopold Potier of the General Staff, who was posted on the Bisamberg, 300 metres above the plains to observe French activity. Apparently selected because he owned a powerful telescope, he soon

Table 1: Austrian Cavalry Reserve, 20 May

GdK Liechtenstein

Advance Guard: FML Klenau
Brigade: Oberst Ignaz von Hardegg

Stipsicz Hussars	8 squadrons
Schwarzenberg Uhlans	7 squadrons
EH Karl Infantry	3 battalions
1st Jäger Battalion	1 battalion
one cavalry battery	
Rosenberg Chevaulegers	2 squadrons (Major Scheibler near Essling)

Division: FML Hessen-Homburg
Brigade: GM Kroyher

Liechtenstein Hussars	6 squadrons
Kaiser Cuirassiers	4 squadrons

Brigade: GM Lederer

Hohenzollern Cuirassiers	6 squadrons
Kronprinz Cuirassiers	6 squadrons

Brigade: GM Siegenthal

EH Franz Cuirassiers	6 squadrons
Herzog Albert Cuirassiers	6 squadrons

Division: FML Kienmayer
Brigade: GM Vécsey

Vincent Chevaulegers	8 squadrons
one cavalry battery	
Klenau Chevaulegers	8 squadrons
one cavalry battery	

Brigade: GM Provenchères

Rosenberg Chevaulegers	6 squadrons
O'Reilly Chevaulegers	5 squadrons
one cavalry battery	

Brigade: GM Clary

Knesevich Dragoons	6 squadrons
one cavalry battery	

Brigade: GM Rottermund

Riesch Dragoons	6 squadrons
one cavalry battery	
EH Johann Dragoons	6 squadrons
one cavalry battery	

Brigade: GM Wartensleben

Blankenstein Hussars	8 squadrons
one cavalry battery	

Sources: Krieg, vol. IV, Annex XX.

proved an assiduous reporter, providing a wealth of essential information to the army staff from his perch on the hillside.

Closer to the water, Oberstleutnant Steigentesch on the Schwarze Lackenau had noticed the French troops opposite his positions (Demont's division) marching away to the south and sent a volunteer reconnaissance detachment across the river at 7.30 a.m. With forty-one men from his 2nd Vienna Volunteer Battalion and twenty-two men of *Deutschmeister*, this bold little group landed above Nussdorf and created considerable alarm, capturing twenty-one Frenchmen during their brief excursion. They also made a prisoner of Württemberg GM Reinhard Eduard Ferdinand von Röder, who was returning to Vienna with some ladies after an outing to Klosterneuburg.[42] French troops were soon on the scene and the 33rd Ligne of Friant's division captured twenty of Steigentesch's men before the Austrians could escape. Charles hoped that similar expeditions could be launched elsewhere, but the French were now alert and offered their opponents no further opportunities to probe across the river.[43]

As this miniature fracas north of Nussdorf was ending, the French crossing onto the Lobau was beginning. Napoleon had remained at the crossing site all morning: 'he did not leave until the bridge was completed, and, as several pieces of wood still obstructed the passage and no one was moving fast enough to obey his orders to remove them, he distributed a few strokes of his riding crop and soon all was cleared away.'[44] The bridges were hardly robust and the river water, surging with snowmelt, was rising dangerously, but the spans were finally suitable for passage at midday on 20 May. Napoleon immediately began to feed troops across. Just as Charles was baffled by Molitor's relative lack of activity on the 19th and the morning of the 20th, Napoleon apparently concluded that the absence of a powerful Austrian reaction to Molitor meant that the enemy had no intention of fighting near the river. He may have assessed that the most likely Austrian course of action would be to defend the heights north and west of the Marchfeld, thereby protecting the roads leading to Moravia. In this uncertain situation where the army would face a vast open landscape, he weighted the initial crossings with mounted troops: 'our cavalry will flood the plain.'[45] The light cavalry, soon backed by the heavies, would also serve to mask French movements and could be employed to delay an Austrian withdrawal if the need arose.[46] Lasalle and Marulaz would therefore follow Molitor to place nine light horse regiments on the field. The rest of 4th Corps would then cross, followed by the three heavy cavalry divisions. Marulaz was delayed in recalling all of his outposts and detachments, so Boudet crossed in his stead, followed by

Legrand. Marulaz finally arrived late in the afternoon, but just as his lead regiment, the 3rd Chasseurs, was making its way across the bridges, the first French catastrophe occurred. Perspiring French boatmen had been fending off floating debris all afternoon, but the swelling river released more boats, barges, trees, and other flotsam than these men could handle. At 5 p.m., a large ship crashed into the second bridge between the Schneidergrund and the Lobgrund. Shortly thereafter, the first bridge, the one connecting the south bank with the Schneidergrund, also snapped, stranding Marulaz on the Schneidergrund with one squadron of his 3rd Chasseurs and part of the Baden foot battery that had been at the end of Legrand's column. Ten hours would pass before the bridges were again capable of carrying military traffic.

Napoleon was among the first to cross the bridges shortly after noon. Massena rode with him, as did Bessières and Lannes, even though their respective commands were not scheduled to cross until much later in the

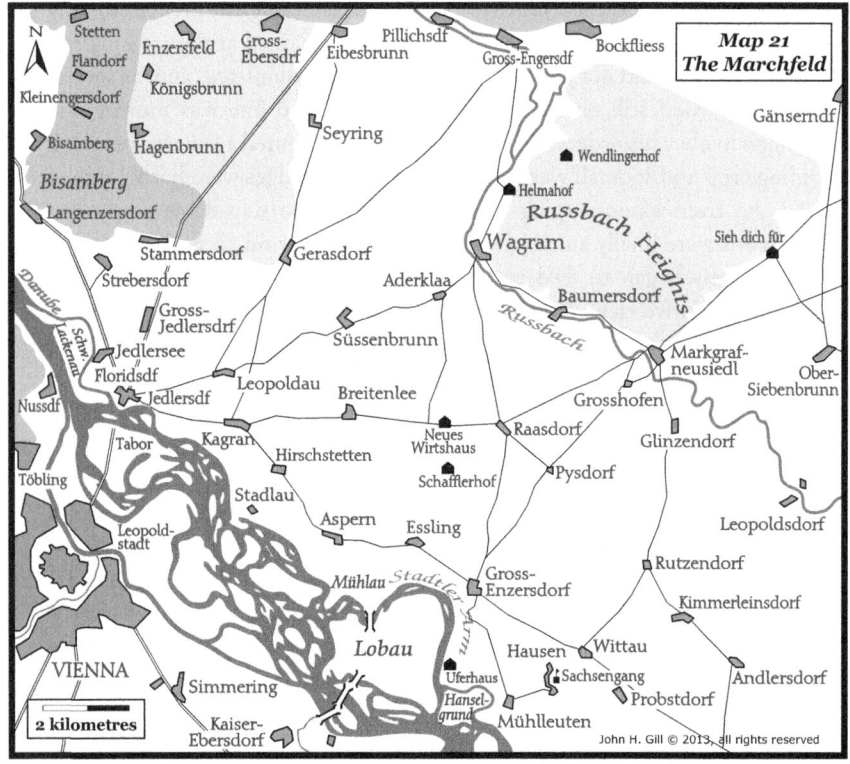

Map 21
The Marchfeld

day. Arriving in the Lobau with his staff and escorting cavalry, the emperor immediately had Molitor begin work on a bridge to the north bank. The rising water impeded construction and the span was still not complete when Oberst Bakonyi advanced against the nascent bridgehead with ten infantry companies around 5 p.m. The Austrian attack was short-lived. French fire was terrible and reinforcements were soon on the scene, scrambling over hastily laid planks to cross the gap in the incomplete bridge. Bakonyi's advance stalled and, when he was badly wounded by a cannon ball grazing his knee, the regiment speedily retreated past Essling. French voltigeurs pressed towards Essling and Aspern as work on the bridge continued. Klenau, sent forward by Liechtenstein with the *Stipsicz* Hussars and *Schwarzenberg* Uhlans (fifteen squadrons) of his 'advance guard', brought the French pursuit to a halt and re-occupied Essling.

It was now 6 p.m. and struggling French engineers, closely monitored by Napoleon, had finished the bridge over the Stadtler Arm onto the Marchfeld. 'Under the eyes of the master, prodigies were accomplished. Everyone worked: officers, generals were in the water almost up to their necks.'[47] Although the challenge was not nearly as daunting as in the principal channel, the rising water and shortage of material made the task difficult and delayed completion beyond expectations. Simultaneously, other troops had erected a small breastwork to cover the crossing site and this sheltered the additional infantry and a few guns that Molitor now sent across to secure the far bank. Lasalle, with Piré's and Bruyère's brigades, was the next to cross. The quintessential hussar, known for baggy red trousers and a cultivated nonchalance, Lasalle was a flamboyant light cavalryman but also a keen-eyed and competent combat leader. He could see Klenau's troopers near Essling, so he edged his command to the left in an effort to get on the enemy flank. This move brought his division near Aspern and he detached GB Piré with 16th Chasseurs to pursue the Austrians retreating in that direction. Piré's chasseurs followed their quarry almost as far as Hirschstetten, skirmishing ineffectually as evening closed in.

With his other three regiments, Lasalle advanced on Klenau's position south of the Schafflerhof.[48] Klenau had seventeen squadrons at hand in his own two regiments and Scheibler's two squadrons of *Rosenberg* Chevaulegers. This made a total of nearly 2,000 troopers, outnumbering Lasalle's 1,600 men. In addition, Klenau's request for support had prompted Liechtenstein to send a lone regiment, the *Hohenzollern* Cuirassiers (600), who took up an advantageous position on his right rear; the *Kronprinz* Cuirassiers (500) were somewhat further back at Neues Wirtshaus. The Austrian commander, however, did not organise his troops to take advantage of their numerical superiority, instead he fussed about arranging them in staggered lines before moving forward. In the end, only four squadrons (two each of hussars and chevaulegers) led the Austrian advance into the growing darkness sometime around 8.30 p.m. Lasalle overwhelmed these with 8th Hussars while 13th Chasseurs charged the uhlans slightly to the rear. Overthrown, the Austrian horsemen tumbled back upon their rearward echelons and carried these away in confusion. Klenau's men rallied behind *Hohenzollern*, but Lasalle now called upon the 24th to charge to the cuirassiers in the flank. Fortunately

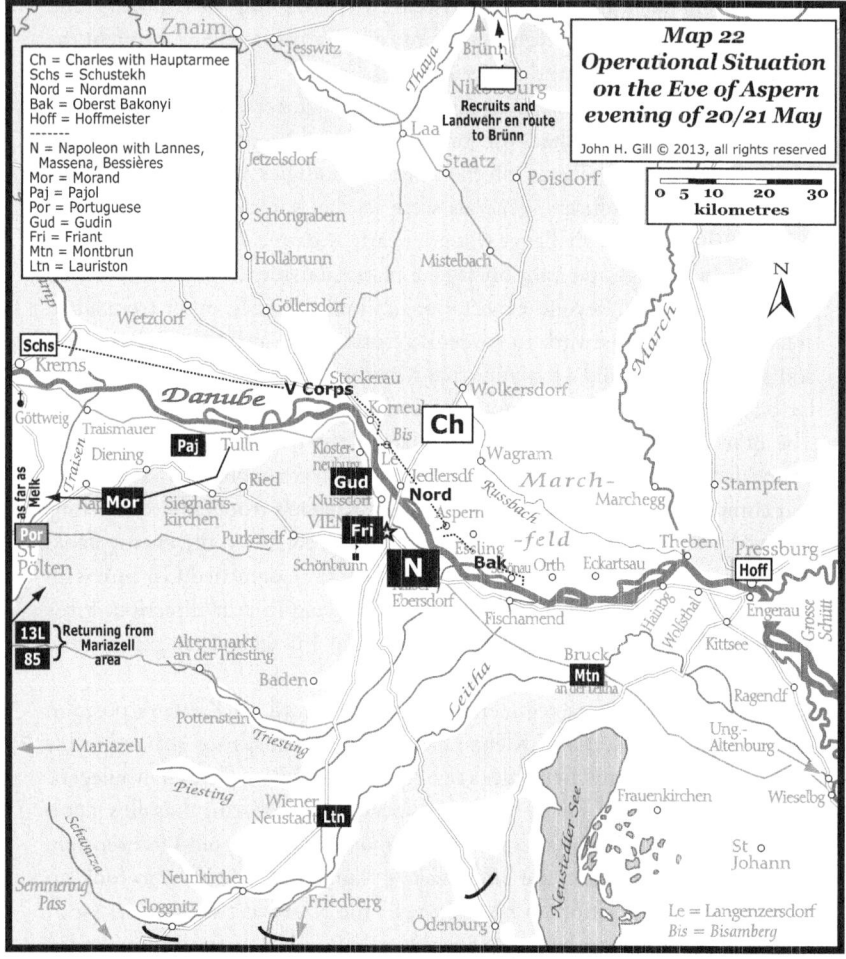

Map 22
Operational Situation on the Eve of Aspern
evening of 20/21 May

John H. Gill © 2013, all rights reserved

Ch = Charles with Hauptarmee
Schs = Schustekh
Nord = Nordmann
Bak = Oberst Bakonyi
Hoff = Hoffmeister

N = Napoleon with Lannes,
  Massena, Bessières
Mor = Morand
Paj = Pajol
Por = Portuguese
Gud = Gudin
Fri = Friant
Mtn = Montbrun
Ltn = Lauriston

Le = Langenzersdorf
Bis = Bisamberg

0 5 10 20 30
kilometres

for Klenau, one whitecoated cuirassier squadron commander demonstrated admirable initiative and spurred his troopers forward to take the 24th in the flank instead. The French attack collapsed and Lasalle, pressed by Klenau's re-formed squadrons, retired behind the protection of the French infantry at Essling.[49] This otherwise minor engagement, that cost each side between 50 and 100 casualties, is significant in two respects. First, it was another example of the Austrian army's tactical weaknesses, especially the want of initiative, the adherence to form over results, and the inability to exploit the potential of its generally fine cavalry. Second, it prevented Lasalle from gathering any useful intelligence that night. While it is doubtful that the French could have learned much in the rapidly falling darkness, their repulse precluded even a limited reconnaissance. Napoleon was thus left with little solid information on his adversary. Indeed, the seemingly limp reaction to Lasalle's limited probe convinced many French leaders that the Austrians to their front were at most a weak covering force. 'The enemy made but a feeble resistance,' Coëhorn wrote his wife. 'In camp everyone asks: where are they?'[50]

The end of 20 May thus came with substantial French forces across the Stadtler Arm (some 19,000 line troops) and the emperor himself lodged on Lobau Island with a large part of the Guard (perhaps 5,500).[51] These forces were, however, isolated until the main bridges could be repaired. The rest of the Allied army waited on the south bank. Crowded around Kaiser Ebersdorf were Carra Saint-Cyr, Marulaz, 2nd Corps, the heavy cavalry, the remainder of the Guard, and Colbert's two regiments. Friant and the Württemberg Leib Chevaulegers were in Vienna and Gudin at Nussdorf. In the army's immediate rear, Morand and Pajol guarded the immense space from Tulln to Melk, while Montbrun and Lauriston watched the frontier towards Hungary and Styria.[52] On the Austrian side, Charles had arrayed the bulk of the Hauptarmee in a long line from Strebersdorf to Seyring: V, VI, II, and IV Corps from right to left. Bellegarde's I Corps was around Hagenbrunn, the grenadiers at Eibesbrunn. The Cavalry Reserve, including Klenau's Advance Guard, stretched itself in long lines across the fields south of Aderklaa. Thus situated, the two armies awaited the dawn.

21 MAY: THE BATTLE OF ASPERN—FIRST DAY[53]

The rising sun shed its light across the broad plain of the Marchfeld on the morning of 21 May. Mists floating up from the Danube and its many ancillary arms obscured the ground during the first hours after dawn, but burned off as the sun climbed into the sky to bring an unseasonably warm day with temperatures exceeding 20 degrees Celsius and pushing up to 30 degrees by afternoon (68 to 86 degrees Fahrenheit). The slowly dissipating fog revealed a battlefield that was bounded on the south by the great river and its sinuous branches. The Mühlau where the French had their bridgehead and the Gemeinde-Au south of Aspern were thick with trees and low vegetation, but the Marchfeld north of the Lobau was a vast expanse of open farmland dotted with villages. Two of these, Aspern and Essling, became the focal points of the coming struggle.

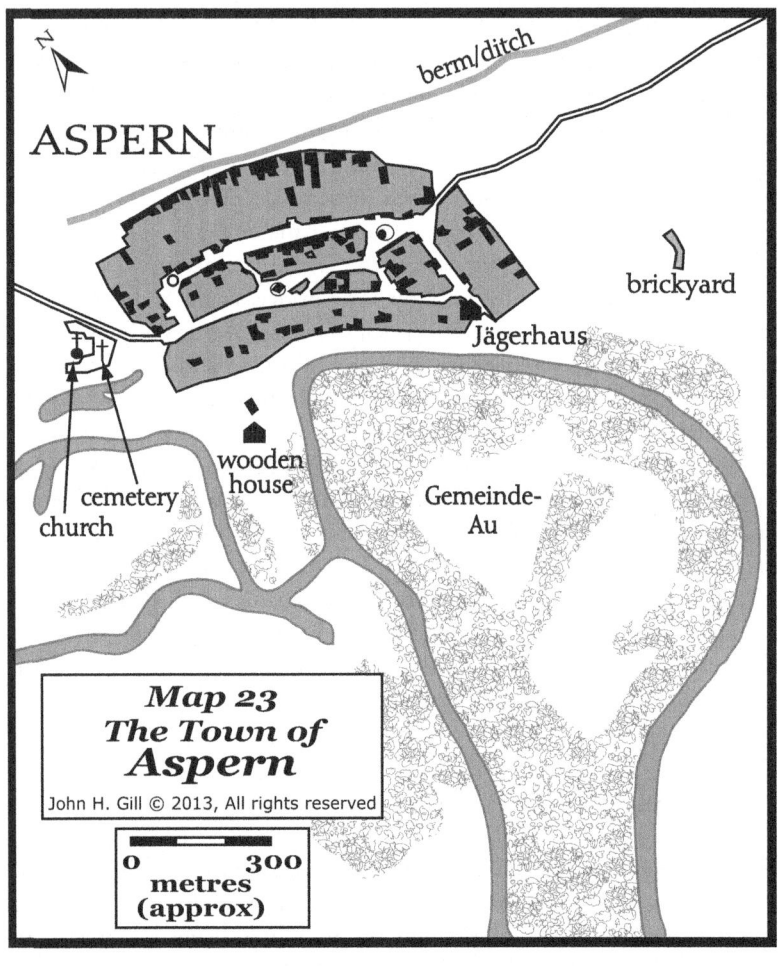

**Map 23
The Town of
Aspern**

John H. Gill © 2013, All rights reserved

0   300
metres
(approx)

On the western side, Aspern consisted of 104 sturdy stone homes. Almost every residence fronted on a fenced garden and was tied to its stalls or barn by a walled farmyard, making each compound a miniature citadel. Most of these homes faced the two principal streets that divided the village lengthwise; they were connected by narrow alleyways, so that a defender could distribute troops with relative facility. Aspern's church complex with churchyard, presbytery, cemetery, and garden dominated the western end of the village. Surrounded by a chest-high wall and sitting atop a four-metre-high knoll, the church with its associated structures formed a virtual redoubt, while the church tower afforded observers a dramatic view far out into the Marchfeld. Separated from the village by a fordable ditch, the Gemeinde-Au to the south appeared to be an impassable tangle, particularly for an army that was highly uncomfortable with irregular tactics, as the Austrian army was. In fact, it was more open than it seemed, but its formidable impression helped to shield Aspern's southern flank from serious assault. The village was thus well suited to defence. As Austrian officers related to a visiting Prussian officer years later: 'We thought we had before us a simple village garrisoned by infantry, but found a fortress that we had to storm without first creating a breach.'[54]

Essling, on the eastern flank of the battlefield, was smaller and rather more open than Aspern. Its fifty-five homes lined a single main street, but the relative openness allowed better control of troops and adherence to more formal combat rules than was possible in tightly packed Aspern. Moreover, its situation afforded better opportunities for all three combat arms to contribute to the defence. The eastern end of Essling was vulnerable, but the western portion represented an excellent defensive position strengthened by the presence of a walled dairy and a walled formal garden on the north side of town, as well as a small tree-lined park (the 'langer Garten' or Long Garden) to the south. Especially noteworthy was the now-famous Essling granary ('Schüttkasten'). The walls of this massive structure were more than a metre thick, its doors were iron, and its windows protected by iron bars. Moreover, the windows were almost two metres from ground level, making it almost impossible for an attacker to see, shoot, or climb inside. Practically impervious to field guns, it also benefited from a tiled roof and would thus be difficult to set afire (unlike the wooden shingles of Ebelsberg or the thatch that covered many buildings in this period). The granary could hold 300 men, 100 of whom could fire from its windows in all directions at any one time. The granary, the walled Master's Garden ('herrschaftlicher Garten') just to its west, and the walled dairy on the opposite side of the narrow street

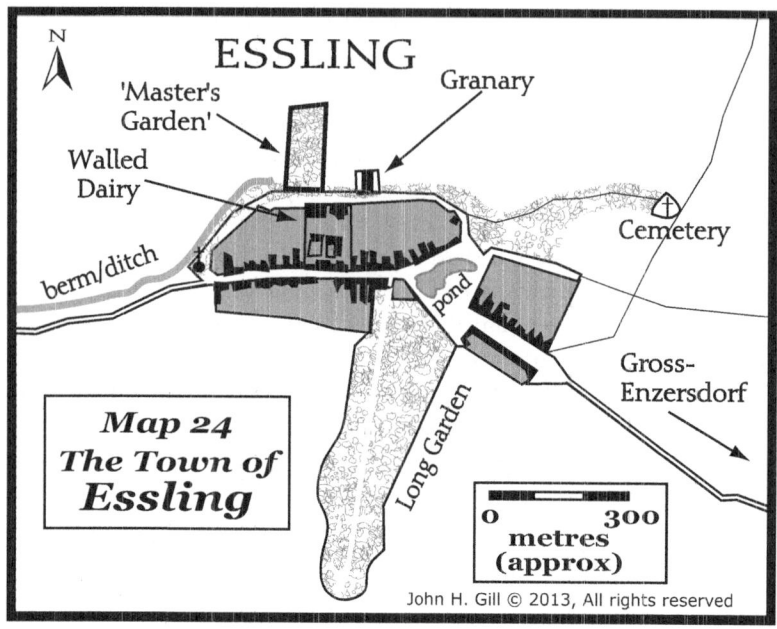

John H. Gill © 2013, All rights reserved

formed a group of three mutually supporting defensive strongpoints on the northern edge of town. Essling, therefore, with these improvised forts and the facility with which all three arms could operate, was arguably a better defensive post than Aspern.[55]

Both Aspern and Essling lay about 2,800 metres beyond Molitor's bridge and both were encompassed by old, worn-down earthen berms that provided some cover for skirmishers and occasionally for an artillery piece or two. The two villages thus resembled the bastions of a fortress, the gap between them protected somewhat by another low dyke or berm and a shallow ditch.[56] The open fields between Aspern and Essling also contained two brickworks: one 800 metres south-west of Essling and one approximately 300 metres south-east of Aspern where Napoleon made his headquarters for much of the battle's second day.

All Quiet in the Morning

The night of 20/21 May brought no clarity to Napoleon's picture of the enemy situation. The available reporting was contradictory and the Emperor was still in a state of great uncertainty, ignorant of whether he had the enemy in front or not.'[57] He ordered Massena to make a visual reconnaissance. Riding into Aspern around midnight in the marshal's company, his staff officers were surprised to find Lasalle 'profoundly asleep'. 'Everyone claimed that there were no enemy for kilometres around.'[58] Massena, left with only one good eye after a shooting accident where he had been wounded by Napoleon, climbed up into the narrow tower with the youthful Markgraf Wilhelm of Baden, and asked Wilhelm to describe the scene. 'As far as the eye could see, the sky was reddened by bivouac fires,' remembered Wilhelm.[59] Interpretations of this imprecise information differed among the marshals and generals around Napoleon. The extent of the fires indicated a large force, but they seemed to be quite distant and the consensus was that they might represent the Austrian army's defensive positions off to the north and north-west. The weak response to Lasalle's foray during the evening reinforced the impression that there were no major Austrian formations in the vicinity of the bridgehead. Some writers have averred that Massena, returning from his visit to the belfry, specifically warned Napoleon that 'the entire Austrian Army was not far away'.[60] This will remain an historical controversy, but whether the anecdote is true or not, the key point was that Napoleon did not have definitive information upon which to base his next moves. He attempted a personal reconnaissance early on the 21st, but alert Austrian cavalry quickly curtailed this imperial patrol and captured an over-confident staff officer. As the morning waxed, therefore, Napoleon's first interest was to penetrate the enemy's cavalry screen and gain detailed intelligence on the whereabouts of the Austrian Main Army. Ordering Massena to occupy Aspern, Essling, and Gross-Enzersdorf, he rode back to the main bridges to hurry their repair and speed the arrival of the heavy cavalry that he needed to pierce the Austrian mask.[61]

Throughout the morning, the French light horse remained quiescent, apparently so as not to draw Austrian attention to the forthcoming advance. The prospect of an imminent offensive move also made defensive preparations seem superfluous and Massena's men did nothing to fortify the villages once they were occupied. Indeed, as 4th Corps moved out of the Mühlau after 8 a.m., the marshal contented himself with posting only small detachments in the villages. Molitor deployed his division along the watercourse south-east of Aspern with a few companies in the village. Legrand did the same, placing his three regiments behind Essling, while Boudet moved on Gross-Enzersdorf. Klenau had withdrawn during the night, but Major Scheibler had remained near Gross-Enzersdorf with his two squadrons and two companies of *Duka*. There was some skirmishing as Boudet evicted these between 9 and 10 a.m., but the firing soon died away and his tirailleurs nestled into the town. Boudet, however, kept the main body of his division in the open ground towards Essling. The light cavalry screened the 4th Corps position with 16th Chasseurs west of Aspern, 8th Hussars north of Essling, and Bruyère's brigade on the right. The Guard Fusiliers and the few available elements of the Guard cavalry covered the bridgehead, while the two Old Guard regiments remained on Lobau.

The Austrians were also moving. Charles needed a victory, at least an *Achtungserfolg*, or symbolic victory, that would shake Napoleon's confidence and, he hoped, open the way to some sort of negotiated peace. He does not seem to have expected or felt the need for a crushing, decisive triumph over the French emperor. A small success, however, would not suffice for his purposes. He had therefore rejected Hiller's proposal for an attack against Molitor on the 20th, and waited to be absolutely certain that the French troops on the Lobau indeed represented Napoleon's main force and that they were in sufficient strength to make a victory of the requisite dimensions. Late on the afternoon of 20 May, the mounting intelligence finally convinced Charles that the time had come. He was not yet sure whether he would attack or defend, he was not even certain that major combat would occur the following day, but he decided to move the Hauptarmee into a position that allowed either defence or offence. According to the 'disposition' issued that evening, the army, marching through the night, was to be arrayed in a defensive stance from Strebersdorf to Wagram by the morning of 21 May: V and VI Corps on the slopes of the Bisamberg as before, but with I Corps behind Gerasdorf, II Corps and the Cavalry Reserve between Gerasdorf and Wagram, IV Corps around Wagram, and the Grenadiers at Seyring. The notion that Napoleon would turn west from the Mühlau and push north along the Danube through Hirschstetten still nagged at the back of Charles's mind, so the new position would also cater for an advance against the French right flank should Napoleon undertake the expected thrust towards Hirschstetten. The disposition reached the corps commanders between 6.30 and 10 p.m., initiating a complex and often-clumsy night movement as the Cavalry Reserve withdrew from Aderklaa while the Grenadiers, along with I, II, and IV Corps, advanced to their designated stations. A picket line stretching from Gross-Enzersdorf through Raasdorf and Süssenbrunn to Leopoldau would keep inquisitive French patrols at a respectful distance.

As it happened, two Austrian actions this night of 20/21 May combined to create an unintentional, but effective deception. First, Klenau's rather timorous response to Lasalle's advance gave the impression that there were no strong Austrian forces in the vicinity. Otherwise, reasoned the French, Lasalle would have had a much tougher fight. Second, with most of the Hauptarmee on the move during the night, the bivouac fires that Massena and Wilhelm espied from the Aspern belfry represented only a fraction of the Habsburg host and did not indicate the advance towards the river. In addition, of course, the delayed completion of the bridge into the Mühlau allowed Lasalle only a few hours for daylight reconnaissance with his small division. It is therefore hardly surprising that the reports reaching imperial headquarters were contradictory and ambiguous. Now, as the sun crept higher in the clear spring sky, Napoleon would not have to exert himself to penetrate the Austrian veil. The Austrians were about to remove it themselves.

21 May: Austrian Advance

With sunrise on 21 May, a Whitsunday, Charles had mounted and ridden out to view his army in its new positions. The troops were formed in battle order and had heard an earnest, if rather vapid, order of the day read out, telling them that 'there can be no choice between eternal shame and undying fame' and that this was a moment 'to conquer or to die'.[62] Morale was good, the army was ready, but as the fog slowly dissolved over the fertile Marchfeld, the enemy had barely moved and the Habsburg commander had not yet chosen his course of action.

Charles did not know that the French bridges had broken. Hidden by night and the morning mist, his observers could see little of what transpired on the river. Moreover, the Hauptmann who replaced Leutnant Potier apparently selected a less auspicious spot from which to make his reports and could not see the bridge at all. From the archduke's perspective, Napoleon's inactivity was inexplicable. Sent to reconnoitre, Wimpffen returned around 9 a.m. and announced that the French were advancing on Hirschstetten as expected! Though conveyed with conviction, this news, of course, was utterly false, apparently the result of wishful thinking by the chief of staff. He seems to have over-interpreted patrolling by Piré's brigade or Molitor's deployment south-east of Aspern in accord with his own desire for an offensive. Whatever the explanation, he persuaded Charles and the archduke decided to advance.[63]

The attack order, read aloud to Bellegarde, Hohenzollern, and Hiller at 10 a.m., envisaged an advance in five 'columns' supported by the Cavalry

Reserve and the Grenadiers. Leaving Reuss to secure the Danube above Jedlersdorf, Hiller would command the 1st Column, advancing directly along the river towards Aspern with the 12,130 men and fifty-two guns of VI Corps. Bellegarde's corps comprised the 2nd Column (23,260 men, sixty-eight guns). He was to march on Kagran and Hirschstetten, while Hohenzollern's 3rd Column advanced on Aspern with the 20,290 and sixty-two artillery pieces of II Corps. As Charles anticipated encountering the French generally along the line Stadlau–Hirschstetten–Breitenlee, the orders for these first three columns were reasonable. Based on the erroneous premise of a French drive on Hirschstetten, however, the attack disposition would lead to an unwieldy agglomeration of troops around Aspern as the battle developed. Liechtenstein and the Cavalry Reserve (6,670 men, eighteen guns) were allotted the space between the 3rd and 4th Columns, where the Austrians assumed 'the main body of the enemy cavalry' would operate. To Liechtenstein's left, the 4th Column would advance against Essling and the 5th Column towards Gross-Enzersdorf, with Klenau's Advance Guard clearing the way for both. These columns numbered 11,320 and 13,150 combatants respectively. Rosenberg was supposed to command the 4th Column, but as the two columns were drawn from his IV Corps, he more or less retained control of both. He rode with the 5th Column, however, and gave it almost all of his attention, leaving the 4th Column to Dedovich's dubious leadership. Held in reserve, the Grenadiers (11,420 men and twenty-four pieces) were assigned a position just north of Gerasdorf. All movement was to begin at noon. The aim of the attack, delineated with some clarity in the disposition, was relatively narrow: 'The principal goal is to throw the enemy over the first arm of the Danube [Stadtler Arm], to destroy his bridges over said arm, and to occupy the banks of the Lobau with a numerous artillery, especially howitzers.'[64] Reflecting the archduke's desire for a symbolic, limited victory, there was no mention of 'destroying' or 'eliminating' the French forces on the left bank.

In addition to the disposition for the formal advance, the generalissimus sought a volunteer to undertake operations against the French bridges. Hauptmann Friedrich Freiherr von Magdeburg of the General Staff immediately stepped forward to claim this mission. Embarking on his task with alacrity and imagination, he rode off for Jedlersdorf and was soon busy preparing boats, floating mills, and other debris to launch down the river against the bridges.

As the attack order made its way down the chain of command, officers formed their units and had the drummers beat 'To Prayers' so that the regimental bands could play a patriotic hymn, 'God Preserve Franz the Kaiser'. Franz himself made an appearance near Süssenbrunn and reviewed the 3rd Column as it marched past cheering lustily. Then, with bands playing and banners unfurled, the 98,000 men of the Hauptarmee started across the rich farmland under the warmth of the midday sun. An observer from the Baden contingent wrote that 'the enemy advanced to battle as if on a grand parade. The men had thrown their greatcoats over their shoulders, their bands played constantly, and we saw the flags with the double eagle waving cheerfully.'[65]

It was not long before this immense movement came to Napoleon's attention. Sometime in the first dawn hours, the bridges over the Danube had been repaired and Marulaz had been able to bring his division across the river, followed by the Württemberg *Herzog Heinrich* Chevaulegers and Espagne's cuirassiers. While the Württembergers trotted off to join the small Guard cavalry detachment in the Mühlau and Espagne rode towards Essling, Marulaz moved his division to cover the army's left flank beyond Aspern. Ordered to relieve Piré's 16th Chasseurs, Marulaz kept his four French regiments in the Mühlau and sent his German brigade west of Aspern. The Badeners and Hessians had just assumed the outposts at around 1 p.m., when they saw Austrian hussars approaching from Stadlau and Hirschstetten. This was the advance guard of Hiller's 1st Column, cautiously making its way along the Danube in the expectation of encountering the supposedly advancing French at any moment. Rheinbund couriers dashed off to report the news to Napoleon, while the Austrians brought up a gun to chase off the German troopers.

Back in the Mühlau, Napoleon apparently received a number of reports almost simultaneously. Not only Marulaz's outposts, but those of 16th Chasseurs observed the approach of significant Austrian forces, as did Pelet and an officer who had clambered up into the Aspern belfry out of simple curiosity. Napoleon's initial reaction was to retreat. A staff officer sent to the Aspern tower by Berthier confirmed the approach of a force he estimated at 80,000. Napoleon, with few troops available and the bridges broken, decided on withdrawal, and issued the initial orders for the army to fall back onto Lobau Island. His marshals and generals, on the other hand, were unwilling to give up so quickly after what had so far been a successful campaign. They argued that Aspern and Essling made excellent defensive posts that the French would only have to hold for a few hours until nightfall. Once relinquished to the Austrians, however, the enemy would fortify them strongly, making a future French breakout from Lobau costly if not impossible. In the short time it took for this discussion to run its course, two things happened: the emperor learned that the bridges were almost repaired, and he heard the sound of cannon fire coming from west of Aspern. These decided the issue. As one of the Württemberg officers in imperial headquarters reported to his sovereign, 'The Emperor could no longer avoid battle as much as he may have wanted to do so.'[66] His course of action selected, Napoleon moved with his accustomed vigour. With only some 22,300 infantry, 7,680 cavalry, and forty guns available on the left bank of the Danube, he had to distribute his men with great care.[67] Aspern seemed the most threatened point and Molitor, who had urged holding onto the Marchfeld position, was assigned to defend it with Legrand to his left rear in reserve. Both of these infantry divisions as well as Marulaz's light cavalry remained under their corps commander, Marshal Massena. Napoleon gave Lannes overall responsibility for the right flank. Lack of troops meant that Gross-Enzersdorf could not be defended, so Boudet left a small detachment in the town and pulled back to ensconce

Table 2: The Battle of Aspern: French Arrivals and Strengths, 21 May

All times approximate. Strength figures are rounded.

Time	French Arrivals	Cavalry	Infantry	Guns
Morning	**Massena, Lasalle, Guard**	2,970	22,300	52
1200	Marulaz	1,980		
	Herzog Heinrich	160		
1300/1400	Espagne	2,570		6
1600	Guiton	1,240		
1700	Lagrange	1,110		6
1800	Carra Saint-Cyr		9,270*	14
1900	Nansouty/3rd Cuirassiers	620		
Total Additional		7,680	9,270	26
Grand Total		10,650	31,570	78
Austrian Hauptarmee (not including V Corps)		14,250	84,010	292

* Figure for Carra Saint-Cyr may be high: some sources give him only 6,000 men (see Appendix 8).

himself in Essling. In addition to Boudet, Lannes's authority included Lasalle and Espagne, both of whom were part of Bessières's Cavalry Reserve. Placing one marshal under another's orders was always a tricky prospect, but the long-standing enmity between Lannes and Bessières made this an especially caustic combination. The Guard Fusilier regiments, the small Guard cavalry detachment, and the four 6-pounders would protect the bridgehead while the Old Guard and the four 12-pounders remained on Lobau Island. As the army had been expecting to advance in search of a retreating or defending foe, neither Aspern nor Essling had been prepared for defence, but the respective commanders set to work to improve their positions as best as they could before the Austrians arrived in force. Worse, there was not enough infantry to hold the vulnerable gap between the two villages in strength; this responsibility would fall to the cavalry until more men could be brought across the fragile bridges.

Aspern: This Horrible Melee

The Austrians were indeed approaching, but the expectation of encountering a powerful French force near Hirschstetten induced extreme caution. Unaware of his advantage, Nordmann, commanding Hiller's advance guard, expended more than an hour driving off the cocky German cavalry vedettes and French infantry outposts west of Aspern. When he finally sent four companies of II/*Gyulai* into the town at 2.45 p.m., it was too late. Molitor, belatedly moving to occupy Aspern with 37th and 67th Ligne, quickly ejected the Hungarians of *Gyulai* and began to advance west beyond the town. Massena, however, immediately recalled the eager general and deployed his division to hold the French left flank: II/67th in Aspern, I/67th and 37th along the watercourse in the Gemeinde-Au, 2nd Ligne east of Aspern along the ditch/berm, and 16th Ligne in reserve. Marulaz deployed his six regiments in an extended line at the north-western corner of the village facing west. The French infantrymen, 'uncommonly clever and skilful in exploiting all local advantages', hastened to make up for lost time in making Aspern defensible.[68] Luckily for Massena, the initial Austrian advances were weak and disjointed. GM Winzingerode, sent by Bellegarde on a wide sweep through Hiller's troops towards the river, managed to lodge himself in a large wooden house on the south-western corner of town at 3.30 p.m., but halted there under a harrowing fire. At approximately the same time, the two battalions of *Anton Mittrowsky* No. 10 advanced from the north-west.

Directing the fight from a stand of old elms near the churchyard, Massena stood 'calmly indifferent to the fall of branches brought down by the showers of grape shot and bullets, keenly alive to all that was going on, his look and voice, stern as the *quos ego* of Virgil's angry Neptune, inspiring all around him with irresistible strength'.[69] He coolly allowed the whitecoats to come within deadly range before blasting them with a whirlwind of musketry and canister. Suffering heavily, the regiment fell back in disorder.

In part these opening attacks were ineffectual because the linear tactics used by the Austrians imposed lengthy delays as they deployed from column of march into battle order. As a consequence, only the advance guards of Hiller's and Bellegarde's columns had come into action thus far. Moreover, Hiller 'did not throw reinforcements into the village, his cautious nature led him to arrange his battalions and squadrons so that they were positioned to cover the retreat of the units in the village if necessary'.[70] By 4 p.m., however, the first three Habsburg columns were deployed and the battle began in earnest. Corporal Brandner was among those approaching the action: 'we soon clearly heard the cannon and musket fire, and from the powder smoke that was visible in great, long, extended masses ahead of us, we could tell that the battle would take place very close to Vienna, as to our right, across the Danube, Austria's capital with the grey tower of St. Stephen's could be seen'.[71] The mistaken assumptions behind the Austrian attack plan meant that these three columns actually got in each other's way, but also resulted in a large number of guns unlimbering north and west of Aspern. The fifty to sixty pieces of these batteries opened a dreadful cannonade. 'We were soon wrapped in thick clouds of black smoke through which the sun, low on the horizon, shone like a blood-red globe of fire, giving a crimson hue to the whole landscape,' recalled Colonel Lejeune. Smiling grimly, the French officers told one another: 'We are going to have hot work.'[72] The Austrian fire forced Marulaz to take his division behind Aspern after leading the Baden dragoons on a futile advance against the guns. Caught in a crossfire, Massena's artillery on the western edge of town had no choice but to withdraw as well. With the French guns out of the way, *Anton Mittrowsky* returned to the attack supported by III/*Klebek* from Hiller's column. At the same time, Nordmann's men pressed the French left back towards the Gemeinde-Au, allowing 2nd Jägers to charge into Aspern from the south. This combined assault gained the churchyard and the western fringe of the town by 4.15 p.m., but was quickly brought to a halt by local French reserves.

While both sides were struggling to assert their control over Aspern, the Austrian cavalry was deploying in two lines out into the broad open area north of Essling. As they came under fire from the French guns lined up along the Aspern–Essling dyke, however, 'everyone got too excited'.[73] Through some misunderstanding and perhaps inadequate training, the entire force lurched forward at the gallop, only to have the second line crash into the first when the first line suddenly halted.[74] The result was a confused tangle of intermixed regiments that momentarily neutralised the Cavalry Reserve as cursing officers endeavoured to sort out the mess. While this was going on, Liechtenstein noticed Dedovich's 4th Column marching up from his left rear and sent GM Karl von Kroyher's brigade of cuirassiers along with his two dragoon regiments off to that flank both to clear some of the snarl and to shield Dedovich's approach.

Bessières, on the French side of the field, apparently noticed the split of Liechtenstein's cavalry or the disorder in the Austrian ranks and ordered Espagne to attack. Four French cuirassier regiments thus trotted forwards at approximately 3.30 p.m. and attacked GM Siegenthal's two regiments just west of the Schafflerhof. A swirling mounted battle was soon in progress and Liechtenstein recalled the four regiments he had sent to his left. These troopers took the French in the flank, but their attack had little effect. GB Albert de Fouler was wounded and captured in the melee, but the four French regiments, now quite outnumbered, held their own against at least six regiments of Austrian heavy cavalry. At about 4 p.m., however, the 4th Column appeared on the scene. Three of its batteries, supported by 1st Jägers and Dedovich's two light regiments, took Espagne's men under fire from the flank and compelled them to retreat. By 4.30 p.m., the French heavies thus were back behind the dyke and the 4th Column could continue its tentative advance on Essling. The material result of this brief but furious engagement was small, but the psychological impact was significant. Where the French prepared for further action, 'the Austrian Reserve Cavalry Corps lost all sense of enterprise and limited itself to defensive movements' for the remainder of the day.[75]

At about this time, the clouds of false assumptions parted for Charles: the enemy was *not* advancing on Hirschstetten and the Austrian army would have to undertake an attack against Napoleon in his defensive position between Aspern and Essling. He hurried to issue new orders calling the Grenadier Corps forward from reserve and shifting Hohenzollern's 3rd Column to the left, both to relieve the pointless congestion north of Aspern and to cover the yawning gap between the two villages. By 5 p.m., these moves were underway in the centre, while on the left Dedovich's guns were setting Essling ablaze and Rosenberg was clearing the small French detachment out of Gross-Enzersdorf. At Aspern, however, the tide had again turned against the whitecoats. Massena was not about to relinquish his hold on Aspern without a fight. Placing himself at the head of 16th Ligne's grenadiers, he led a charge up the flaming streets that cleared the four Austrian battalions from the village. His success was short-lived. Hiller and Bellegarde, evidently each on his own, threw new forces into the struggle. Under a terrific bombardment from the numerous Habsburg artillery, I/*Jordis* and I/*Klebek* of Hiller's column stormed the church, while Bellegarde's *Reuss-Plauen* No. 17 attacked from the north-west. Despite the success of their initial rush, the fighting rapidly devolved into a pitiless grappling among the burning buildings. It was a 'horrible melée', wrote Pelet, 'we disputed in turn the church, the presbytery, every street, every house, every wall.'[76] Astride their mounts, Hiller and Charles watched the apparent success of this renewed assault on Aspern, but Hiller expressed worries about a French effort against the Austrian centre. 'You just hold Aspern for me, my dear Hiller,' Charles told him, 'I will have the reserve brought up at once.'[77]

The Centre: Cuirassiers versus Masses

There was indeed cause for Hiller (and Charles) to be concerned. Napoleon could clearly discern Hohenzollern's column making its way towards the centre of the field and he had no trouble imagining the danger these troops would pose should they attack, as seemed likely, the vulnerable gap between Aspern and Essling. This space, nearly two kilometres wide, was only protected by a screen of skirmishers from 2nd Ligne (from Aspern) and 3rd Léger (from Essling), with most of the cavalry in support. As an initial measure, therefore, Napoleon moved Legrand's two French regiments to a defensive position to the east of Aspern. 'We manoeuvred infantry on the plains to try to make the enemy believe the bridge was not destroyed and to gain time for reinforcements to arrive,' recalled a staff officer.[78] This was clearly inadequate, so the emperor turned to Bessières and his cavalry to delay and disrupt the Austrian deployment.

Bessières called on Marulaz to lead the attack, followed by six regiments of cuirassiers: Espagne's division and Guiton's brigade of St Sulpice's division that had just arrived from the south bank of the Danube. In round numbers, this made perhaps 1,500 light and 3,500 heavy horsemen. Marulaz led his men north in an echeloned formation with 19th Chasseurs leading on the right. Ahead he could see Hohenzollern's gun line wrapped in smoke as it bombarded Aspern and the Aspern–Essling gap. Beyond the cannon, the 3rd Column was marching to the east at right angles to Marulaz's approach. Sounding the charge, the French and German troopers spurred towards the head of the Austrian column. The Austrian artillerymen must have been grossly inattentive because the French caught them completely off guard. Bursting through the smoke like wraiths, the chasseurs scattered the gunners and forced them to abandon as many as fourteen pieces as they fled to the protection of the nearby infantry. Five squadrons of *O'Reilly* that attempted to intervene were handily put to flight by the 19th and 14th Chasseurs, but Marulaz then found himself attacked by the foot soldiers of *Froon*. The French general was almost captured in the ensuing wild struggle and, as his other regiments had made no deeper impression on the Austrian infantry, he retreated back to his starting point.[79]

Napoleon, however, needed to achieve a greater effect and ordered Bessières to renew his attacks and 'charge home'. Arrayed across the trampled young crops in a long line, glistening in the afternoon sunlight, Espagne's and Guiton's cuirassiers rolled towards the battalion masses of the Austrian infantry. With the Austrian guns silenced, an eerie quiet seemed to descend on the field as Habsburg officers rode in front of the bayonet-hedged masses, encouraging their men. To the waiting infantry, time seemed to slow. The cuirassiers halted about 300 metres from the bristling formations and French officers rode forward to demand that the Austrians surrender. The Austrians, of course, rejected these calls and emptied many saddles when the French finally charged. 'With no regard for the monstrous numerical superiority that stood against them,' the horsemen 'fell upon the enemy with rare determination,' wrote an eyewitness.[80] Although the cuirassiers displayed the courage that made them one of the army's elite arms, repeated efforts to break into the Habsburg formations failed in the face of the steadfast Austrian infantry. Frustrated groups of cuirassiers rode among the tight blocks of whitecoats, riderless horses dashed about in confusion, and dismounted French troopers limped back to their own lines to avoid capture, but the Austrians, packed tightly in their masses, held firm. The proximity of other masses inhibited Austrian musketry after the first volley or two, so the casualties among the French heavy regiments were not as severe as depicted in later legendry. Nonetheless, it was clear that the attack had run its course with little impact on the enemy's infantry, and the cuirassiers rode back to their start point, chased by shot from a few hastily re-manned guns. It was now approximately 6 p.m.

In one sense this grand attack had failed. None of the Austrian masses had broken and the whitecoats had learned that they could repel even the dreaded cuirassiers if they remained in coherent, disciplined formations. On the other hand, the charge had accomplished exactly what Napoleon had desired: Hohenzollern's 3rd Column was not only delayed and disrupted, its commander and men were chastened and the corps made no further forward movement until after dark. The weak French centre was thus spared a serious attack by the 20,000 fresh troops. Moreover, this vitally important result was achieved with only 3,500 cuirassiers and perhaps 1,500 light cavalrymen against four to five times their number (a fact often overlooked in the common depictions of this fight as uncounted masses of French horsemen pounding down upon the Austrian foot soldiers).[81] At the same time, one is compelled to ask if Bessières might not have done considerably more damage had he committed the cuirassiers earlier to exploit the initial gains won by Marulaz's troopers. The whitecoats were certainly fortunate that the French did not have enough artillery to dedicate a battery or two of horse guns to support these attacks.

On the Austrian side, the curious absence of the Reserve Cavalry is worth a comment. Liechtenstein had moved his mounted regiments to the rear as Hohenzollern approached, both to make room for the 3rd Column and to support the infantry, at least as Liechtenstein viewed tactical affairs. This position condemned the Habsburg mounted reserve to such 'complete inactivity' that it could not even exploit the disorder and weariness of the French troopers as they retired after the attack.[82]

See-Saw Struggle for Aspern

The vicious battle in Aspern continued to burn as the French cavalry was engaged in its fruitless charges against Hohenzollern's column. Fortunately for Massena, the lead elements of Carra Saint-Cyr's division were beginning to reach the Mühlau when Hiller and Bellegarde renewed their attack at 5.30 p.m. Assured of a reserve, the marshal threw Legrand into the fray. Leading the 26th Léger and joined by parts of Molitor's weary division, Legrand once again retrieved the village for the French, but could not evict the Austrians ensconced in the wooden house. Hiller's chief of staff, the energetic Oberst Csollich, tried to use the structure as a launching pad for a new assault with four companies of I/*Gyulai* brought up from the Gemeinde-Au. Although Csollich distinguished himself by his courage and determination, this thrust, like the earlier one by 2nd Jägers, collapsed in a storm of French musketry. Using the respite gained by Legrand's counter-attack, most of Molitor's exhausted men withdrew out of the village to reorganise and recuperate; some, however, seem to have fought on in Aspern until well after nightfall.

It must have been approximately 6 p.m. when Charles rode over to see Bellegarde, north-west of Aspern. The general seems to have lacked initiative and an adequate 'sense of urgency' in his effort to seize the village. The archduke thus sought to re-energise the assault by telling Bellegarde to take Aspern 'regardless of cost', and sent messengers pounding off across the fields with instructions to Hiller and Hohenzollern to support the coming attack. On Bellegarde's orders, GM Theodor Freiherr Wacquant-Geozelles led his brigade (*Vogelsang* and *Rainer*, 6,500 men) across the corpse-strewn fields to the attack. Riding to the front of I/*Vogelsang* No. 47, Wacquant grabbed the battalion's banner and waved it aloft crying 'Long live Kaiser Franz! Conquer or die!' He then dashed ahead of his men and almost achieved the latter injunction when his horse was shot from under him close to the French positions. He clambered out from under the dead animal, however, lifted the flag and pressed ahead. Charles also appeared at a timely moment to inspire II/*Rainer* when the battalion wavered in the brutal French fire from the cemetery. As the battalion commander was encouraging his men, the archduke rode up and shouted 'Well done, major, lead the battalion to victory!' Assisted by the re-formed *Anton Mittrowsky* from the west and the troops that had taken refuge near the wooden house, Wacquant stormed into Aspern.[83] The tenacious French resisted from every gravestone and wall, but the churchyard and cemetery fell into Austrian hands once again and the whitecoats drove deeper into the village.

Legrand had no intention of giving up so easily. He rallied the 26th and, with support from the 18th Ligne, led a ferocious counter-attack that regained most of the village. 'The noise and confusion were dreadful,' remembered Cadet Höppler of *Vogelsang*, 'the French among us with the bayonet.'[84] Legrand's men, however, could not throw the enemy out of the churchyard, and the Austrians returned to the attack, this time in conjunction with forces from the north. Bellegarde had pushed his remaining infantry along the northern edge of Aspern while Wacquant was attacking. He now turned two battalions to the right and sent them into the blazing wreck of the town. At the same time, Hohenzollern's 7th Jägers advanced from the north-east. Gathering momentum, the Austrian assault seems to have gained complete control of Aspern for a few moments before yet another French counter-attack hurled them back once more. The 46th Ligne from Carra Saint-Cyr's division, arriving just in time from the shaky bridges, led this charge, while 24th Léger deployed to the right of the village (concerned for the safety of the Mühlau bridgehead, Napoleon kept 4th Ligne in the rear; the Hessians were in reserve). The Austrians responded to the 46th's élan with more troops fed in from the fields to the north and revived vigour from the combatants already in the town.[85] Many units were quickly distributed in small packets according to tactical needs. The companies of Brandner's battalion 'were directed to different destinations ... but even the companies had to dissolve themselves into small groups as every house, every tree, every fence was defended by the enemy and had to be won separately; we fought in every house, in every barn; wagons, ploughs, and harrows had to be cleared away to get at the enemy.' 'Every little wall was an obstacle for the attackers and a protection for the defenders,' Brandner recalled, 'and we had hardly seized an alley or a house, when the enemy stormed a different one and forced us to leave what we had taken.'[86] Assault and counter-assault thus swept back and forth over the flaming ruins, but as night fell the combined efforts of the three French regiments sufficed to retain a firm hold on the southern half of Aspern. Fortunately for the French, Hiller was content to annoy the defenders in the Gemeinde-Au with Nordmann's advance guard; he never made a serious or sustained effort to outflank Aspern from this direction.[87]

As the fighting raged in Aspern, Bellegarde's advance along the town's northern fringe allowed him to place two batteries at the north-eastern corner, where they could enfilade the French in the open ground towards Essling and the Mühlau. Napoleon sent three cuirassier regiments to remove this threat: Guiton's brigade and the newly arrived 3rd Cuirassiers. With support from 2nd Ligne and 24th Léger, the French heavies advanced at 7 p.m. They quickly overran the guns and chased off the nearby Austrian light cavalry, but were unable to make any impression on Bellegarde's infantry. Pressed by the returning Habsburg light horse and some heavy cavalry detached from Liechtenstein, the French abandoned the guns they had won and retired to their starting positions.[88]

This brief attack brought no lasting gains, but it silenced the guns temporarily and occupied the Austrian right long enough for Napoleon to send Marulaz on another charge against Liechtenstein's horsemen. The Austrian general had moved his riders from their useless post behind Hohenzollern's column to hold the ground between Hohenzollern and Dedovich. Even though Liechtenstein had detached more then one-third of his squadrons to other parts of the battlefield, the remaining collection of thirty-four squadrons, combined with Hohenzollern's corps, posed a serious threat to Napoleon's thin centre. To pre-empt an attack by this formidable mass, Marulaz formed his light regiments into a deep column with 23rd Chasseurs in the lead and charged the Austrian heavies under the darkening sky. In another hacking wild melee, Marulaz cracked the first line of Austrian cavalry, putting four enemy regiments to flight while some of his rearward squadrons stormed impotently around the stationary infantry masses of Hohenzollern's column. Austrian reserves, however, hit the French in both flanks and forced them to retreat.[89] Marulaz, again in danger of falling into Austrians hands, was rescued by some of his men and hurried to the rear with his division, while heavy fire from French infantry in Essling forced Habsburg pursuers to turn away and seek safety in the distance. Once again, outnumbered French light cavalry led by a determined and energetic general had inflicted a tactical defeat on Austrian heavy horse and succeeded in discouraging any offensive adventurism by the enemy during the closing hours of the day.

Essling Holds

The Austrians also made a number of attempts to seize Essling during the late afternoon and on into the night. Conducted by the 4th and 5th Columns, these attacks were half-hearted and unco-ordinated.

Lannes and Boudet had placed 56th Ligne in Essling with 3rd Léger extending the defensive line along the berm towards Aspern and 93rd Ligne in reserve behind the village along with Piré's light cavalry. They also maintained a detachment of some 100 infantrymen in Gross-Enzersdorf, supported by Bruyère's troopers.[90]

The 4th and 5th Columns did not start their approach marches until around 2 p.m., and the 4th Column was then delayed by the cavalry battle north of Essling, so that it was not until 4 p.m. that Dedovich's 4th Column arrived at the Schafflerhof. Here he waited for Rosenberg to come in line with the 5th Column. Rosenberg, expecting serious resistance at Gross-Enzersdorf, carefully deployed his formation as he approached the town at 4.30 p.m. He did not notice Bruyère's two regiments, however, and these lunged forward to destroy the two companies of inexperienced *Carneville* Jägers before other Austrians could come to their rescue. Having inflicted almost 200 casualties on the unsuspecting Jägers, the French evacuated Gross-Enzersdorf and withdrew to their main defensive position. This miniature disaster appears to have infused even more caution into Rosenberg's outlook.

Observing French cavalry to his front in the open ground between Essling and the Stadtler Arm, the general decided that he could not advance without some heavy regiments in support. While Rosenberg waited for friendly cuirassiers, Dedovich waited for Rosenberg. Edging the 4th Column forward gingerly, Dedovich deployed 1st Jägers as skirmishers towards Essling and had his artillery open fire on the village. Most of the town's wooden structures were soon in flames, but the bombardment had no effect on the granary and the French remained in place. Indeed, from their protected positions, Boudet's men inflicted such heavy losses on 1st Jägers that Dedovich had to reinforce the skirmish line repeatedly with companies from the 2nd Moravian Volunteers.

Other than this exchange of artillery and skirmish fire, the situation on the eastern side of the battlefield remained stagnant until approximately 6.30 p.m. The reinforcements Rosenberg had requested arrived in the form of Lederer's cuirassier brigade, Gross-Enzersdorf was secure, and his deployment was complete.[91] He finally advanced. But, believing himself too weak to launch an attack in earnest, he only moved far enough to unlimber his artillery and take the village under effective fire. Lannes had been reinforced by GB Armand Le Lièvre, Comte de La Grange's cuirassier brigade (1,110) and the *Herzog Heinrich* Chevaulegers (160), but in fact the 13,000 men of Rosenberg's 5th Column and Lederer's 900 cuirassiers alone outnumbered the 8,500 French at the marshal's disposal.[92] Adding 11,000 from the 4th Column, the Austrians had a numerical advantage of approximately three to one over the defenders. The Habsburg commanders proved incapable of exploiting this superiority.

As evening crept over the field and the fighting on his right and centre diminished, Charles could devote some attention to his left wing. 'Now officers of the general staff came to me one after another on the orders of His Imperial Highness Archduke Charles with instructions that I should attack Essling,' recorded Dedovich in his operations journal.[93] The response to these goads, however, lacked all coherence. The *Koburg* Infantry, sent into the northern side of Essling by GM Josef von Grill sometime after 7 p.m., suffered a bloody repulse near the granary. Unaware of Grill's move, Dedovich organised a separate advance by *Reuss-Greitz* No. 55 and III/*Czartoryski* from the north-east, but these also recoiled after a short, bitter struggle. The only success was the capture of the cemetery just beyond the edge of town, which *Reuss-Greitz* successfully defended against French counter-attacks.[94]

The energetic Lannes, noting the Austrian withdrawal and hoping to put an end to threats from the northern flank, sent orders to Bessières to

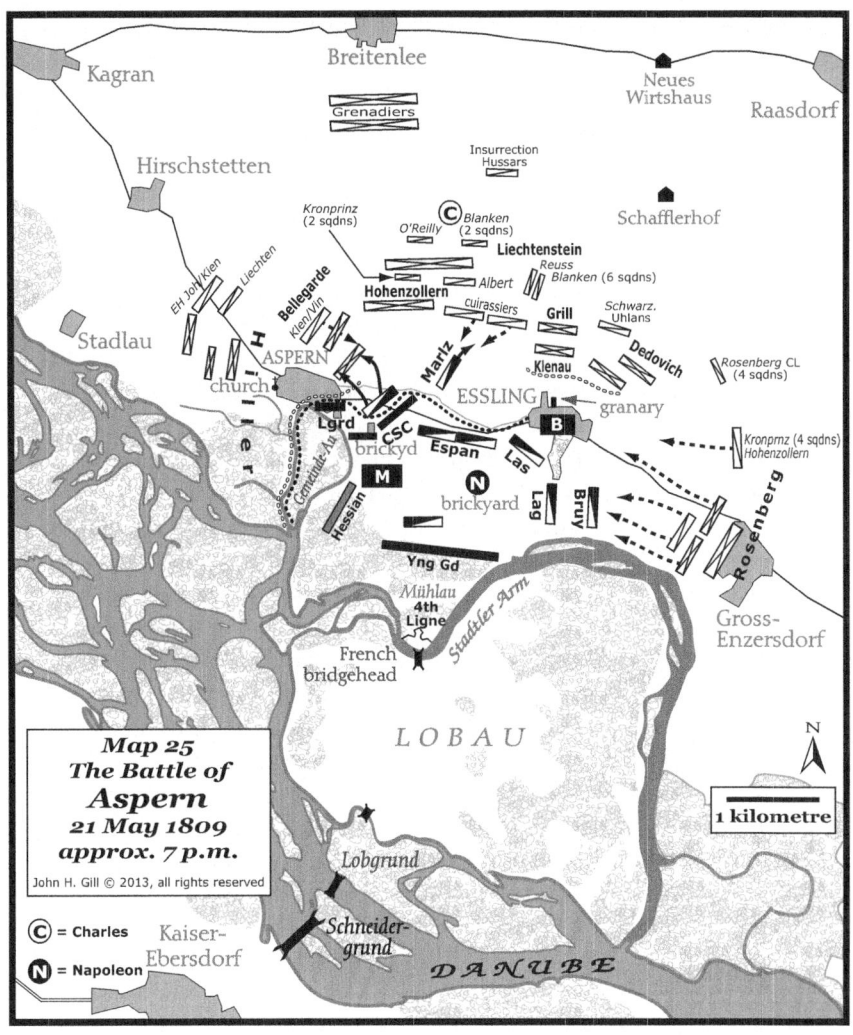

Map 25
The Battle of
Aspern
21 May 1809
approx. 7 p.m.

John H. Gill © 2013, all rights reserved

Ⓒ = Charles
Ⓝ = Napoleon

attack the Austrian forces out on the plains and 'to charge home'. Though dealing with a fellow marshal, Lannes indulged the enmity he bore towards Bessières by using the abrasive words 'orders' and 'charge home'. The first two staff officers to carry these instructions had no desire to communicate in such terms with a marshal of the empire and thus employed circumlocution in delivering their messages. Lannes then called for Capitaine Marbot, directing him to speak the 'order' verbatim and poking Marbot in the ribs for emphasis. Bessières reacted with predictable outrage, but called Espagne's division forward, placed himself at its head, and charged. It was now nearly night and the flames of Essling cast an macabre glow over the twilight landscape as the cuirassiers trotted towards the enemy. Unfortunately for the French, the brief opportunity to catch the Habsburg infantry unawares and in disorder had passed. The formed whitecoats received the cuirassiers with punishing volleys and did not collapse, leaving Espagne's men to ride among the bristling infantry masses in growing frustration and vulnerability. Nearby Austrian cavalry dashed into the fray: *Schwarzenberg* Uhlans from the east, *Blankenstein* Hussars and *Albert* Cuirassiers from the north. The highly regarded Espagne was killed in the swirling melee, and Bessières only evaded capture because Lasalle plunged into the action with Piré's brigade and the Württemberg chevaulegers. Exhausted, bloodied, and grieving at the loss of their commander, the French troopers retired behind Essling. According to Marbot, Lannes was satisfied that his 'stern injunction' had spurred Bessières into action and produced an 'excellent' result.[95] The only real accomplishment, however, was halting and chasing off III/*Rohan*. Hohenzollern, after being directed to support Dedovich's advance, had foolishly despatched this lone battalion to storm Essling with the promise of awarding the commander the cross of the Maria Theresa Order for a successful attack. Isolated on the vast plain and surrounded by French horsemen, the battalion stood firm, but probably owed its survival to the darkness and the distractions that prevented the French cavalry from focusing on its predicament.[96]

The day's concluding actions occurred on Rosenberg's front. That general did not receive Charles's emphatic orders to attack until sometime after 8 p.m., probably as the cavalry battle was ending. It was almost totally dark, but Rosenberg saw no way to refuse his instructions, so the 5th Column lurched forward into the gloom: two battalions of *Bellegarde* along the Stadtler Arm, III/*Bellegarde* towards the Long Garden, and *Chasteler* Infantry towards Essling itself. Stutterheim with the light cavalry and III/*Sztaray* advanced cautiously in the open space south of the garden, but even this intrepid general halted after a curt skirmish with the French outpost line. To Stutterheim's left, the first two battalions of *Bellegarde* drove off some French cavalry but stumbled upon formed French infantry in the gloom, probably fusiliers of the Imperial Guard. The Austrians exchanged a volley with their opponents, but collapsed in panic and fled when hit in the flank by artillery fire from the four 12-pounders of the Guard on Lobau Island. This branch of Rosenberg's advance thus came to a swift conclusion. The battalions aimed at Essling and the garden did little better. Although they succeeded in penetrating the village and garden at about 9 p.m., French reserves threw them out in short order. As Rosenberg's men were retreating into the darkness, Dedovich, prompted by the hopeful generalissimus, attempted another advance on Essling around 9.30 p.m. This thrust also proved abortive, as did a revived effort by Rosenberg's four battalions at 10 p.m. and a final weak advance by III/*Bellegarde* around 11 p.m. The Austrian attacks against the French right flank thus ended in costly failure, a series of unco-ordinated stabs against the skilful, aggressive defence conducted by Lannes and Boudet.

The two armies drew apart as night wrapped itself around the bloody field. 'Along the entire enemy line all of the villages near the Danube were burning brightly and, just as the previous night, everyone bivouacked among the dead and wounded,' wrote Oberleutnant Grueber of the *Albert* Cuirassiers, 'the whimpering and groaning of the latter tore one's heart.'[97] Worried about a French night attack, many Austrian units remained under arms and Liechtenstein's commanders only allowed their men to rest and water their mounts in shifts. Fighting indeed persisted in the twin villages until at least midnight as each side tried to acquire minor local advantages. Conducted in the lurid light of the burning buildings, these small combats did not change the tactical picture except in one small case. At the north-east corner of Aspern, where Bellegarde's two batteries had so discomfited the French, the Austrian gunners had returned to their pieces after the abortive French attack at dusk. Massena called on the 3rd Baden Infantry to remove or reduce this threat sometime around 1 a.m. Creeping forward through the shadows and flickering firelight, the men to the 1st Voltigeur Company surprised and scattered the outposts of Austrian Jägers protecting the two batteries. Nestling themselves into the shallow ditch, the voltigeurs maintained an intolerable fire against the Habsburg artillerymen and repelled several local counter-attacks. Two other Baden companies replaced the voltigeurs when they ran out of ammunition, and the harassed Austrians withdrew their last functioning guns as dawn was brightening the eastern sky.

The Night of 21/22 May

Given the potential catastrophe he had faced all afternoon, Napoleon had every reason to be pleased with the day's outcome. Thanks to extraordinary skill and valour, his army on the north bank had withstood a determined but poorly orchestrated attack by a vastly superior enemy and had preserved the deployment room he needed to launch a major offensive. Here was the opportunity to fight the decisive battle he had sought since Regensburg. As his men desperately searched for food, drink, and a chance to catch some rest in the dreadful night, their emperor therefore turned his attention to organising his army for a grand attack on the morning of the 22nd. Planning back in his tent in the Mühlau while the bridges were functioning, Napoleon envisaged a massive attack against the Austrian centre. He had noted the weakness of the enemy's centre during the day's fighting and knew that Charles would have difficulty reinforcing it from the wings of the extended Austrian deployment. Using Aspern as a pivot, he intended to crack the middle of the enemy line with Lannes's corps and then swing north to push the bulk of the Hauptarmee towards Bohemia. Davout would form the right wing of the army, turning on Essling to protect Lannes's rear and drive the Austrian 4th and 5th Columns south towards Hungary. With any luck, the war could be effectively over by the end of the day. Unfortunately for the emperor, his luck would be in short supply on 22 May.

Napoleon needed to solve three problems to prosecute this contemplated offensive. First, he needed more troops. Second, he needed to replenish the ammunition expended on 21 May and to have an adequate supply for the 22nd.[98] The means to satisfy both of these requirements were at hand on the south bank, but both therefore depended on resolution of the third problem: maintaining the bridges over the Danube. All night long, columns of troops streamed over the shaky spans, ammunition caissons interspersed among the men. All night long, exhausted engineers, pontooneers, and men drafted from infantry regiments strove to preserve the bridges against the rising waters, floating debris, and the strain of supporting thousands of men, horses, guns carriages, and wagons. Riders led their mounts, foot soldiers had to wade over parts of the bridge, and gunners moved their pieces with all possible care. Lanterns and torches cast a wavy illumination over the hectic scene. A ferry service took wounded and others to the Vienna side and small boats were employed to bring additional ammunition to the Lobau. The officers had no need to urge the men to speed and determination: 'We were filled with admiration for the eagerness with which the men pressed on to the assistance of their comrades.'[99]

Interruptions, however, continued. The 12th Cuirassiers had just crossed to complete St Germain's brigade and GB Jean Pierre Doumerc was slowly making his way over the bridges with the 2nd when a large craft crashed through the structure, carrying away a number of startled French troopers and stranding half of the regiment on the south shore. This was apparently the first fruit of Hauptmann Magdeburg's efforts. By the time the bridge was restored several hours later, Napoleon had changed his priorities and ordered infantry, guns, and ammunition to precede the remaining mounted units. The pace of activity was tremendous and the French managed to get at least 32,000 men across the river during the dead hours of the night: the two Young Guard tirailleurs regiments along with the divisions of St Hilaire, Tharreau, and Claparède. Hauptmann Magdeburg intervened again around 3 a.m. This time, the bold Magdeburg and some of his volunteers brought four boats of their dire flotilla to within 1,500 paces of the bridges before releasing them.

The resulting gap was large and the paucity of suitable materials made each succeeding break harder to repair for the weary engineers. Nonetheless, the spans were sufficiently stable for Demont's division and the first two

Table 3: The Battle of Aspern: French Arrivals and Strengths, 22 May

All times approximate. Strength figures are rounded. Casualties from 21 May *not* deducted.

Time	French Arrivals	Cavalry	Infantry	Guns
Morning	**4th Corps, Guard (part)**	10,650	31,570	78
	Cavalry Reserve (part)			
By 0700	Oudinot		21,000*	64
	St. Hilaire		8,900	
	Guard Tirailleurs		2,450	
	12th Cuirassiers	610		12
	part 2nd Cuirassiers	250		
After 0700	Demont		4,800*	
	Colbert/9th Hussars (part)	200		
Total Additional		1,060	37,450	76
Grand Total		11,710	68,720	154
Austrian Hauptarmee (not including V Corps)		14,250	84,010	292

Note: Additional French guns are for all of 2nd Corps (64) and all of Nansouty's division (12). Two 2nd Corps guns were left on the Schneidergrund.
* Oudinot may have had as few as 12,800, and Demont no more than 4,300 (see Appendix 8).

squadrons of Colbert's brigade to cross just before 7 a.m., when yet another break occurred. Thanks to the superhuman efforts of the French engineers, Napoleon thus received a reinforcement of 37,000 infantry, 1,060 cavalry, and seventy-six guns during the night of 21/22 May.[100] Left waiting on the south bank were Gudin's and Friant's divisions of 3rd Corps, the rest of Nansouty's 1st Heavy Cavalry, five squadrons of Colbert's brigade, and the two remaining Guard cavalry regiments. After deducting four battalions left behind as garrisons by Davout, this made a potent additional force of 11,980 veteran infantry, 2,370 heavy cavalry, 1,200 light horsemen, and twenty-six guns.[101] Intended to be the right wing of the French advance, they would remain helpless spectators to the coming combat.

As thousands of French troops surged across the swaying bridges to the north bank, Charles thought Napoleon was moving in the opposite direction. The archduke and his staff, completely misreading the day's action, believed that they had held the field with honour against Napoleon's entire army. They interpreted the cavalry attacks against the Austrian centre as breakthrough attempts and, unaware of the repeated breakages in the bridges, they decided that the French would surely retreat during the night. As indicated in the disposition he issued at 10.30 p.m. from his headquarters in Breitenlee, the only question seemed to be whether the French had left any forces on the north side of the Stadtler Arm.[102] The relative quiet that had settled in around midnight did not last long, however, and the steady snap of musketry along the picket lines was enough to cause him to reconsider his assumptions. He therefore ordered the Grenadiers to move to the weak spot between Hohenzollern and Dedovich. He had not yet decided whether he would assume an offensive or defensive approach to the coming battle when Napoleon removed the decision from Habsburg hands.[103]

22 MAY: THE BATTLE OF ASPERN—SECOND DAY

Napoleon Prepares his Offensive

Neither army had had much sleep during the brief night, clean water was scarce, and the French suffered from a severe shortage of food.[104] 'We had nothing to eat and only water from puddles to drink,' lamented Leutnant Veigl of 8th Jägers.[105] The supply of ammunition was also a concern for the two commanders, especially on the French side when the break in the bridge occurred after Demont's crossing. All of these logistical and human factors would make themselves felt as the battle dragged on into the afternoon, but the day erupted with combat of terrifying ferocity.

The battle opened at Aspern. In rearranging his forces during the night, Charles had withdrawn all of Hiller's men from the village and left its defence in the hands of Bellegarde's troops. His reasoning in this instance is not clear. Given his sensitivity to his river flank, however, it seems likely that he wanted Hiller free to counter any French adventure across the Danube, while his wishful hope that Napoleon would retreat during the night made an attack on Aspern seem improbable.[106] The early hours of 22 May thus found eleven and one-half battalions of I Corps ensconced in Aspern, awaiting the dawn.[107]

They did not have long to wait. Skirmishing was already lively by 3 a.m., and at 4 a.m. Massena launched a sudden, violent assault on Aspern. The town was to play a central role in Napoleon's offensive, and he had ordered the marshal to seize it while the troops of 2nd Corps completed their crossing and arrayed themselves for the thrust against the Austrian centre. Molitor was entrusted with the defence of the Gemeinde-Au, while the rest of 4th Corps undertook to secure Aspern. Legrand on the left with the 18th Ligne and Carra Saint-Cyr on the right with the 4th achieved initial surprise and success, but were thrown back by Wacquant's reserves after an hour's bitter fighting. Massena almost immediately delivered a new blow, hurling 24th Léger and most of the 3rd Baden at the village around 5 a.m. This assault too was at first successful. Eight hundred Habsburg soldiers and six guns were captured in the onslaught, a battalion sent by Bellegarde was swept away in the Austrian retreat, and by 6 a.m. the Allies had driven into the western end of the village. Here Massena's attack came to a halt as GM Bianchi counter-attacked with *Klebek*. The setback for the French was only temporary. Massena's reserves were also at hand and the combined power of Legrand's men and the French regiments of Carra Saint-Cyr's division brought all of Aspern, including the churchyard, into French hands by 7 a.m. Bellegarde and Hiller, distracted by action elsewhere, failed to support Aspern's defenders.

The situation around Essling had also developed to Napoleon's satisfaction. Lannes had surprised Rosenberg by opening a terrific bombardment at 3.30 a.m. Lasalle, deftly exploiting the enemy's shock and the morning mist, charged Stutterheim's cavalry on the Austrian left and sent the Habsburg troopers reeling to the rear. This exposed the left flank of GM Friedrich Freiherr von Riese's brigade. Swinging north to strike the Austrian ranks from the side out of the fog, Lasalle shattered Riese's cohesion and the whitecoats fled east in disorder, to remain out of action for the rest of the morning. Rosenberg counter-attacked at once to restore the situation, sending *EH Karl* No. 3 into Essling supported by I/*Hiller*, and the rest of GM Ferdinand von Reinhard's brigade against the Long Garden and the gap between Essling and the Stadtler Arm around 4 a.m.[108] The men of *Karl* were repulsed but managed to hang onto the very eastern edge of town. To their left, Lasalle held Reinhard's five battalions in check, forcing the Habsburg general to form his infantry into masses. Lagrange's cuirassiers also stormed against Reinhard, but could not break the Habsburg infantry. Taken under fire by French artillery, however, Reinhard's *Hiller* and *Sztaray* regiments suffered heavily in their tightly packed formations; many of the 661 men *Sztaray* lost during the day fell here in the space of two hours. North-east of Essling, the foot soldiers of Dedovich's 4th Column also endured fearful losses in their battalion mass formations. Dedovich, perhaps noticing the movement to his south, also advanced at 4 a.m. As on the first day of battle, his advance was not co-ordinated with Rosenberg's, and he only moved far enough to bring his batteries into action and to put his infantry in range of the French guns. Up to ten men were going down on the impact of a single ball before he redeployed his unfortunate battalions into less vulnerable line formations.

It was now 6 a.m., and Lannes still had not gained enough freedom of action for Napoleon to launch his central offensive. The marshal therefore called on some of his other battalions and the emperor sent the Guard Fusilier and Tirailleur brigades towards the gap south of Essling.[109] Reinhard, his ranks depleted, thought himself incapable of resisting an attack and promptly withdrew to the east with Stutterheim. This displacement left the men of the *Karl* Infantry vulnerable. Attacked by French infantry from the Long Garden, the regiment, its commander wounded, retreated from Essling. When its supporting battalion, I/*Hiller*, unwisely attempted to advance, a well-organised French combined-arms attack forced it to fall back as well. By 7 a.m., therefore, Rosenberg's entire 5th Column had recoiled to the vicinity of Gross-Enzersdorf under pressure from numerically equal, but adroitly handled, French forces.[110] As Dedovich remained inert north and north-east of Essling, the conditions for Napoleon's offensive were fulfilled.

Crisis in the Centre

The confluence of events now seemed to favour Napoleon: his wings were secure at Aspern and Essling, Demont had just crossed to complete 2nd

Corps, and the status of the bridges gave every expectation that Davout and the rest of the cavalry would soon be on hand. Having ridden along the lines early in the morning, he knew the troops were ready: 'every time he appeared he excited a frenzy: all commenced to cry "Vive l'Empereur!"'[111] New but erroneous intelligence indicating that the Austrian centre was composed primarily of Landwehr may have boosted his optimism, but he had taken his decision during the night in any case. Now it was time to execute. 'He told Lannes, who was near him, to commence his movement, indicating with his finger the direction in which he should take 2nd Corps.'[112] Napoleon instinctively chose the most vulnerable point in the Austrian line as the focus of his attack. Lannes was to strike the seam between Hohenzollern's left and the right of Cavalry Reserve. The marshal, placed in command of his own 2nd Corps as well as Bessières's cavalry, rode off to set his men in motion. 'We have a right black cloud ahead of us that I have to penetrate,' he told his chief engineer. 'We will have some work to do.'[113]

Preceded by a long line of guns, 2nd Corps advanced at approximately 7.30 a.m., St Hilaire's veteran regiments on the right with the recruits of Claparède's and Tharreau's divisions echeloned to the left towards Aspern. The heavy cavalry followed behind the right wing, Lasalle stood behind the left.[114] Though his division was not part of Bessières's command, Marulaz was north-east of Aspern and thus effectively behind the left wing of the attacking echelons as well. His charges would apply pressure on Bellegarde north of the village, while Massena and Hiller grappled with one another among the burning houses. Boudet remained responsible for the defence of Essling, but may have moved some infantry north of the village to cover the gap behind Lannes's right until Davout could arrive. The Hessian and Württemberg light horse regiments took Piré's place behind Essling, while the four Guard regiments covered the interval between the Long Garden and the Stadtler Arm. Napoleon made his headquarters in the Essling brickyard.

Looking south from their position in the gentle fields north-east of Essling, Liechtenstein and his officers were surprised when:

the fog that had occurred earlier suddenly vanished; the sun brightly illuminated every feature and one clearly perceived the beginning of the enemy's attack. His entire infantry was deployed in a long, extended line, crowned as usual with an enormous number of cannon and, in the middle of all, his entire cavalry with the armoured men arrayed at the point in thick and deep masses.[115]

Charles was taken aback by the threat to his centre. He had been discouraged to the point of paralysis on learning that he had not contended with the entire French army on 21 May. Moreover, he was, as the Austrian history phrased it, 'under the spell of his great opponent's superhuman influence' and 'thoroughly convinced of the tactical superiority of the enemy army.'[116] He had therefore abandoned all thought of attacking and consigned his hopes to a defensive posture. He did not, though, re-evaluate his assumption that the French would drive up the Danube towards the roads that led to Bohemia, the routes of retreat he was so keen to protect. With Napoleon's plan suddenly revealed in the stark morning light, however, Charles acted quickly to diminish the blow that was about to fall upon his vulnerable centre. He rode at once to Hiller. 'Whatever the cost,' he told the general, 'Aspern must be torn from the enemy's grasp.'[117]

The struggle that now exploded in the centre of the field was intense, confusing, and costly to both sides. Many of the details are obscured by the smoke of battle and conflicting recollections, but the general outlines are clear enough. Lannes drove forward with great élan and consummate skill, St Hilaire's superb veterans leading the way on the right. He steadily pushed Hohenzollern's left back, bending, but not breaking, the Austrian line. Hohenzollern was able to pull wavering battalions out of the firing line and rally disordered troops in the rear, but the relentless pressure forced him to extend his front continually to the left. Casualties were heavy and the Habsburg line thinned dangerously. At the same time, every step that Lannes took to the north brought him deeper into a cul-de-sac of Austrian artillery fire that riddled his ranks with canister and ball. 'Death from all sides!' exclaimed his chief engineer. 'The battalions that one wanted to deploy in this internal angle were cut up and enfiladed; even the most fearless were forced to halt.'[118] Oudinot progressed much more slowly, constrained by the necessity of tying his line to Aspern and the worry that his inexperienced troops, some of whom 'had not the least notion of manoeuvres', would tumble into confusion if ordered to deploy. As with the Austrian masses, the dense columns maintained by most of Oudinot's men resulted in high casualties: 'the enemy artillery ravaged our lines painfully but we gained ground steadily.'[119] Oudinot's strength was dwindling and his advance ground to a halt, leaving St Hilaire somewhat isolated on the right front of the French line. The time was 8 a.m., and Lannes's offensive power was temporarily exhausted. The entire assault settled into a brutal firefight with the French at a disadvantage vis-à-vis the numerous Austrian artillery. Lannes called for reinforcements to continue the attack. Napoleon had none to send. He was not about to commit the Guard and he had just learned that the bridges had suffered another break. Indeed, Napoleon may have ordered Lannes to pause in the hopes that rapid repairs would allow Davout's corps to arrive. 'The pontooneers, their zeal augmented by the army's peril, worked with ardour on the broken bridges,' but their efforts were in vain and Lannes remained agonisingly exposed under a pitiless rain of artillery and musket fire.[120]

Apparently seeking to resolve his dilemma by attacking, Lannes unleashed the massed cavalry at his disposal, sending the heavy regiments to the right against Liechtenstein's horsemen and ordering Lasalle to charge the enemy infantry. The Austrian Reserve Cavalry initially advanced to oppose their foes, but seemed to think better of this and rather ignominiously turned about to seek shelter among and behind the infantry masses. Many individuals even cut away and fled to the rear, causing the Insurrection hussars to rout; these spread terror and disorder among the baggage trains in their turn. The French heavies then directed their attention to the Austrian infantry masses. Some of these, shaken by heavy losses and the flight of their own cavalry, began to show signs of disintegration.

The trial of I/Zach was especially harrowing and led to one of the iconic incidents in the battle. Stoutly confronting the French horsemen, the battalion was shot to pieces when the riders parted to unveil a battery in close support. Canister balls tore into the mass of whitecoats and most fled in terror. Fortunately for the Habsburgs, Charles appeared at precisely the right moment. Riding forward to the 200 or so men huddled around their standard, the archduke grabbed the flag and rallied the men through his personal example. It was only one demonstration of Charles exposing himself to enemy fire during the two days of battle, but his courageous intervention proved a turning point in the French offensive. This irresistible image inspired innumerable artists, including the architect and sculptor who crafted the Charles Monument that still decorates the courtyard of the Hofburg in Vienna.[121]

The French cavalry attacks, of course, continued. As on the previous day, however, the horsemen were not sufficient by themselves to crack Austrian resistance. None of the enemy infantry masses collapsed. A few bands of French broke through to reach Breitenlee or beyond, but these loose groups soon retreated in haste or fell into Austrian captivity. Unable to dislodge the sturdy whitecoats, and counter-attacked repeatedly by Habsburg horse, the French were first contained and then repulsed, the weary troopers eventually turning their lathered mounts about to retire behind their own hard-pressed foot soldiers.

It was 9 a.m. Lannes's assault had stalled, casualties were mounting, ammunition was being consumed at an alarming rate, and the Austrian Grenadier Corps had arrived, closing the gap between Hohenzollern and Dedovich while presenting a new threat to Lannes's open right flank. The marshal sent Chef d'Escadron César de Laville to Napoleon with a report of progress and an urgent request for reinforcements and ammunition. Laville found the emperor near the Essling brickyard, but his arrival coincided with that of another staff officer, this one bearing the grim news that one of the bridges had suffered a new and more extensive break. Demont had finished his passage and Colbert was leading his light cavalry brigade across when a

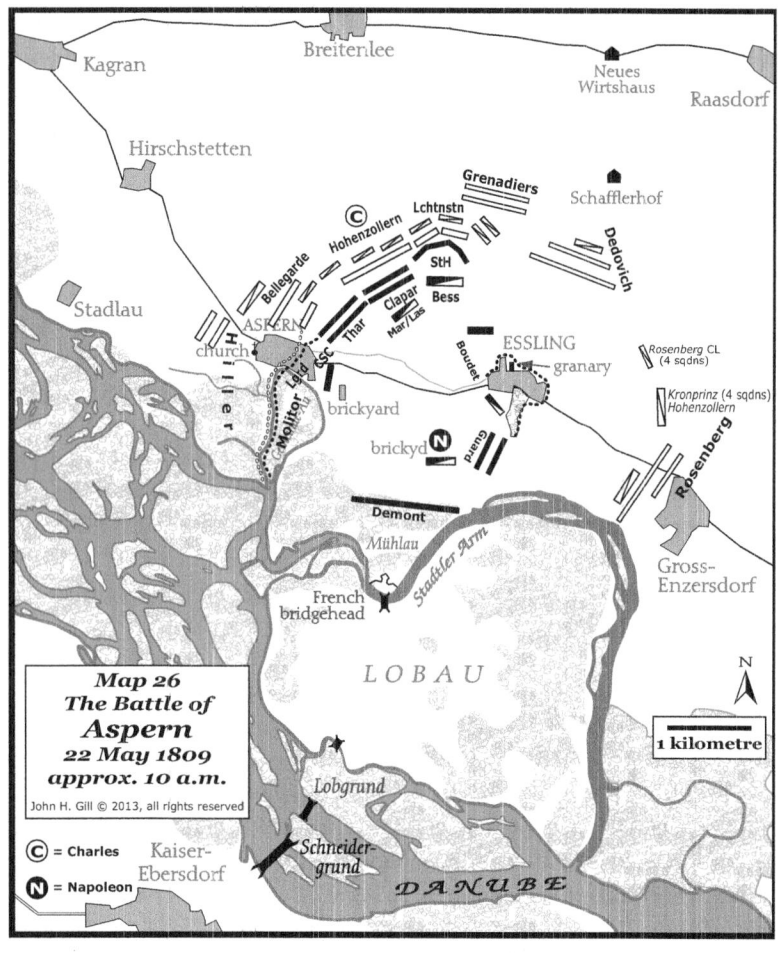

Map 26
The Battle of
Aspern
22 May 1809
approx. 10 a.m.

John H. Gill © 2013, all rights reserved

© = Charles
N = Napoleon

boat carried away a large portion of the span between the Schneidergrund and the Lobgrund. 'I had just passed to the left bank with two squadrons of the 9th Hussars when the bridge was broken,' noted Colbert.[122] He and his two squadrons would be Napoleon's last reinforcements. Faced with this situation, Napoleon ordered Lannes to hold his position, hoping that the bridge might still be repaired.

For the next one to two hours the French 2nd Corps thus stood in a firestorm in the centre of the Austrian line. Charles had succeeded in restoring some order to his battered ranks and began to launch local counterattacks. He sent FML d'Aspre against St Hilaire's right with four grenadier battalions, but St Hilaire, supported by Boudet's 3rd Léger and 93rd Ligne, rebuffed this attempt with heavy loss, and the generalissimus himself had to rally his disordered grenadiers.[123] On the other flank, the 105th Ligne repelled an attack by the *O'Reilly* Chevaulegers into the gap between St Hilaire and Claparède, while Vécsey could not persuade his troopers to charge Tharreau's men near Aspern.[124] Though unsuccessful, these cavalry actions dampened any thought of offensive movement by the French and heralded a possible advance by Bellegarde.

Along with the looming danger to 2nd Corps came a new report from GD Bertrand around 11 a.m. The first bridge, from Kaiser Ebersdorf to the Schneidergrund, had been smashed, carrying Massena's artillery chief, GD Joseph Pernety and a number of sappers a considerable distance downstream before they could rescue themselves on the south bank. Hope vanished and Napoleon issued instructions for Lannes to withdraw to his starting point. But more bad news was in the offing. Marbot, carrying an order to St Hilaire, had just reached the general when a blast of grape-shot hurtled through the air, killing several of the staff, wounding Marbot, and ripping off one of St Hilaire's feet. The chivalrous St Hilaire, 'one of the most distinguished officers of his rank', was carried from the field in great pain and Lannes had to take command of his much-reduced division.[125] Despite heavy losses, the French withdrawal was conducted slowly and in good order. Hohenzollern's troops had raised loud cheers on observing the French retreat and moved cautiously to follow. Assessing II Corps' casualties, confusion, and lack of ammunition, however, Charles decided to replace Hohenzollern with the Grenadier Corps, a process that consumed considerable time. The French thus soon out-distanced the Austrians and, by midday, Lannes and his remaining men were back along the berm between Aspern and Essling from which they had begun their costly advance five hours earlier.[126]

Aspern: Cinders and Cadavers

The dreadful whirlwind of fire in the centre of the battlefield did not reduce the intensity of the struggle for Aspern. Indeed, Hiller, motivated by Charles's urgent order to seize the village at all costs, made every effort to capture and control its smoking ruins. Massena, one of the great generals of the era, was equally determined to retain his grip on Aspern. The result was seven hours of vicious assaults and counter-assaults as waves of shouting, shooting, stabbing combatants washed over the scorched stone and blazing beams that had once been a prosperous town. At times, the inferno was so intense that the best either side could do was to maintain detachments of skirmishers among the flames and smoke in brief shifts. 'We found hideously mutilated French lying about who had crept into the houses and then, as the village had been set alight, burned to death horribly,' observed the appalled Cadet Höppler.[127] Throughout, the numerous Austrian batteries north and west of town kept up a heavy fire, smashing the wrecked homes and blasting back every French attempt to press their attacks beyond the western fringe of buildings. In the end, Aspern was 'nothing but a pile of cinders encumbered with cadavers.'[128]

Hiller began with an assault by eight to ten battalions shortly after 7 a.m., but Massena struck back without delay, throwing some of his last untouched reserves, the Hessians of II/Leib and part of I/Leibgarde, into the village. He had the remnants of Molitor's four regiments strongly posted in the Gemeinde-Au and his other two divisions in the town or in close supporting distance just outside. The combat rocked back and forth, but turned against the whitecoats around mid-morning. A combination of heat and flame, flanking musketry from the Gemeinde-Au, and Bellegarde's withdrawal in front of Oudinot caused Hiller to pull most of his men out of Aspern. At approximately 10 a.m., therefore, a renewed Allied attack drove back the Austrians and once more placed Massena in control of the church and its associated structures. This situation did not last long. With his centre under relentless pressure, Charles sent staff officers galloping to Hiller to order redoubled efforts at Aspern. Hiller responded with vigour. With the support of several other battalions, I/Benjovszky cleared the churchyard and Splenyi charged into the village. At least eleven battalions participated in the assault and, by 11 a.m., Aspern was largely in Austrian hands. To deny the French their bastion in the event of future reverses, Hiller had the church set afire and ordered his pioneers to demolish the enclosing wall. At the same time, his men in the Gemeinde-Au were at last gaining some ground against Molitor's stubborn defence.

Massena, his reserves exhausted, appealed to Napoleon for reinforcements and the emperor turned to his Guard. Led by GD Philibert Jean Baptiste Curial, three battalions of the brand-new Tirailleurs of the Guard, accompanied by the four Guard 6-pounders, crossed the open ground from the French right towards Aspern under punishing artillery fire. Curial displayed a rather haughty demeanour when he reported to Massena, but his young conscripts entered Essling 'in closed columns and in the finest order', flanked by Hessian troops. Driving back the Austrians, the Tirailleurs reached the intersection at the western end of the village and ran into a hail of canister. Stunned, the young Guardsmen immediately turned and retreated in confusion, while their older officers 'wept with rage' at the disgrace of seeing their troops rout.[129] The attack, however, granted Massena and his division commanders an opportunity to revive their veterans and resume their own offensive. Storming forward, the men of 1st and 2nd Divisions once again made themselves masters of the church, while Molitor's regiments threw back the Austrians in the Gemeinde-Au. It was near noon and the French line had more or less stabilised from the Gemeinde-Au through Aspern and along the connecting berm to Essling.

This situation did not endure long and the see-saw struggle resumed. Hiller retook most of Aspern around 1 p.m., only to be hurled back by the Hessians of II/Leibgarde. The Hessians and their French allies, however, could not gain the churchyard, and a new assault by *Duka* put Habsburg troops in control of most of the village as the hour approached 2 p.m. The bitterness and intensity of the fighting left a deep impression on all participants. 'Every time we re-entered, we found new heaps of dead to be climbed,' wrote Pelet. 'The rain of projectiles destroyed the houses above our heads. The fire that devoured the remains could not arrest the fury of the combatants.'[130] Both sides exhausted themselves in brutal, close-range musket duels and desperate hand-to-hand combat. Both of the corps commanders had used up their last fresh reserves. Massena, however, 'seemed to be everywhere. One saw him in the woods, in Aspern, now on foot, now on horseback, sword in his hand, fire in his eyes, conducting the attack and defence.'[131] Through his energy and the dogged determination of his men, he was able to cling to a portion of the town and continually disrupt his adversaries, while Hiller lacked the resources to launch an attack beyond Aspern. The danger to the French left was, for the moment at least, contained.

The Centre: Lannes Holds the Line

Hiller's weakness at this stage deprived Charles of an opportunity. Between 1 and 2 p.m., the archduke had rearranged his forces in the centre so that most of the Grenadier Corps (twelve battalions) was in the first line and Hohenzollern's troops in the rear. On the right, Bellegarde connected the grenadiers to Aspern and Infantry Regiment *Frelich* No. 28 tied the centre to FML d'Aspre with the other four grenadier battalions just north of Essling. Charles knew by this time that the French bridges had suffered serious damage and he decided to attack despite worries among his staff that the enemy would restore the spans and bring reinforcements across the river. At approximately 2 p.m., he ordered the grenadiers forward against the Aspern–Essling berm.

Here again details are sparse, but it is clear that Oberst Josef von Smola opened the action by assembling as many guns as he could locate and directing a devastating barrage at the French centre. At least 100 cannon, and possibly as many as 190, pounded Napoleon's troops in the compact space between Aspern, Essling, and the Mühlau.[132] Men and horses fell on all sides under this harrowing bombardment and the earth was scarred throughout the French position:

> there was not a single point along the battle line or in the terrain to the rear that did not become a target for the artillery crossfire, and I can add that the ground was so furrowed by projectiles that in a number of places the furrows crossed and re-crossed each other in such a way as to form star shapes.[133]

The men of the Old Guard, deployed in line to intimidate the enemy and encourage wavering compatriots, stood as patiently as possible under this galling fire, telling each other grim jokes. 'The balls fell among our ranks, and cut down three men at a time; the shells knocked the bearskin caps twenty feet in the air,' wrote Guardsman Coignet.[134] Napoleon was visibly present. As a Württemberg liaison officer observed, 'Never, not even at the Battle of Eylau, had the Emperor placed himself in such danger.'[135] At one point, the Guard famously declared that they would lay down their muskets if he did not withdraw. Casualties were heavy but the French did not break, and Napoleon replied with his own artillery as far as the dwindling ammunition reserves permitted. In one case, a single shot knocked down twenty-five men in a battalion mass formed by *Frelich* to ward off French cavalry.

Despite the fearful barrage, the Austrian attack faltered shortly after it began. Bellegarde followed Oudinot's retreating divisions, but never truly pressed his opponent. He seems to have been content to manoeuvre while his artillery worked on the French. Lindenau's grenadiers advanced against the French right and almost reached the gun line, but Lannes repulsed them in masterful fashion. Blasting the approaching Austrians with artillery until the last moment, he recalled his gunners and had his infantry loose well-timed volleys at close range. The grenadiers came on a second time only to receive a repeat of this punishing tactic. Lannes followed up by hurling Bessières's weary horsemen at the retreating whitecoats. Although the French cavalry still could not break the solid infantry masses, the casualties inflicted on the grenadiers and the energetic, aggressive nature of Lannes's defence discouraged any further efforts against the French centre for the time being. This was exceedingly fortunate for Napoleon because a new crisis was about to erupt on his right. It was 3 p.m.

Essling: Let Us Charge Them with the Bayonet!

Other than a desultory artillery exchange, most of the morning had passed in relative quiet on the southern edge of the battlefield. Rosenberg, daunted by his experience early in the day, had not stirred from Gross-Enzersdorf. Likewise, Dedovich had done little beyond turn his batteries on St Hilaire during the grand French attack against the Austrian centre.

Charles, astonished and angered that his left wing sat motionless while the rest of the army strained to hold Lannes's offensive, rode to Rosenberg and ordered an immediate attack on Essling. This order sparked a series of four assaults between 11.30 a.m. and 1 p.m., but, as on 21 May, these were unco-ordinated and suffered defeat in detail. Dedovich was first, sweeping into the village with five battalions, only to be ejected after a brief fight.[136] At noon, as he was retreating to the north-east, the *Scharlach* and *Scovaud* Grenadiers charged the granary and the Master's Garden from the north. While riding back towards the centre, Charles had apparently directed FML d'Aspre to support Rosenberg's attack and that general marched four of his battalions towards Essling as the rest of the Grenadier Corps was changing places with Hohenzollern's column. This initial attack achieved nothing and the whitecoats fell back with heavy losses. Shortly thereafter, Rosenberg sent FML Rohan towards Essling with six battalions while FML Hohenlohe protected Rohan's flank with a limited advance south of the Long Garden with five others.[137] Neither of these columns achieved anything. Rohan barely reached the outer fringes of Essling before flooding back in disorder and Hohenlohe, taken under fire by the Guard's 12-pounders on the Lobau, stalled almost as soon as he started. GM Reinhard was wounded in the process. Shortly thereafter, Dedovich's battalions again lurched forward, only to recoil under fire from the granary and walled dairy. Both Dedovich and Grill went down with wounds. This advance was not co-ordinated with Rosenberg's, nor was another futile attack by the two valiant grenadier battalions synchronised with Dedovich's abortive move.

It was now 2 p.m. and Lannes had fallen back to anchor his right flank on Essling. The Guard battalions south of Essling may have helped in the repulse of Rosenberg's most recent attacks, and Marulaz was shifted to the interval between the village and the Stadtler Arm to bolster the defence. Massena had halted Hiller at Aspern and Lannes was fully engaged in fending off the grenadiers in the centre, when d'Aspre moved to assault the north side of Essling yet again. This attack, like its predecessors, was a costly failure. The *Kirchenbetter* and *Georgy* Battalions headed for the Master's Garden, but foolishly halted outside the garden walls to open a fruitless firefight with the well-protected French. Assaulting the granary for the third time, *Scharlach* and *Scovaud* had no more luck than before. All were soon in full retreat. The only result was more dead and wounded Habsburg grenadiers.

Not until 3 p.m. did the Austrian leadership manage to assemble a coherent assault on Essling. Prompted by the energetic Liechtenstein, GM von Riese, the last unwounded general near the north-east corner of the town, organised twelve battalions from Dedovich's former command into attack formation. He placed five battalions of his own brigade and I/*Hiller* to the left of the 4th Column troops, while Liechtenstein directed *Sztaray* and the other two *Hiller* battalions to attack the Long Garden with Stutterheim in support.[138] This powerful advance, with inspiration from Liechtenstein, proved irresistible. The granary remained in French hands and its garrison succeeded in repelling another attack by d'Aspre's four battalions, but the rest of Essling swiftly came under Austrian control.

Napoleon now faced a new crisis, compounded by dire news that the bridge over the Stadtler Arm had been broken as well. Fortunately, his left still held and Lannes had by this time driven off the grenadiers in the centre. The emperor once again turned to his Guard for a solution. Five battalions of Guard Fusiliers and Tirailleurs were at hand near Essling, Napoleon sent three of these towards the village under GD Mouton, the hero of Landshut. Deploying his men in a two-rank line to make their numbers appear greater,

Mouton advanced on a broad front. Remnants of Boudet's regiments joined the attack, but Austrian reserves brought it to a halt. Napoleon called on another trusted staff officer, GD Rapp, gave him command of the last two Guard Fusilier battalions, and told him to disengage Mouton so that the army could attempt an orderly retreat into the Mühlau salient.

Rapp rushed forward with his fusiliers, but thought he perceived an opportunity. The numerous Austrian battalions would probably overwhelm a defensive manoeuvre, but a sudden attack might surprise them and gain the army more time. Catching up with Mouton, he said 'let us charge them with the bayonet and push them back on the advancing columns; if we fail, the responsibility will rest with me.' 'With both of us,' replied Mouton and the sudden French onslaught overthrew the exhausted and disorganised Austrians with surprising rapidity.[139] Both Mouton and the fusilier brigade commander, GB Jean Louis Gros, were wounded, but by 3.30, the Guard battalions and Boudet's weary troops had regained all of Essling, including the cemetery—'heaped with bodies of Hungarians'—on the far north-eastern corner that Dedovich had held since the previous day.[140] 'It seemed that we would be eliminated in an instant, but it turned out otherwise,' Fusilier Faiseau-Sauloy told his family, 'I consider myself very lucky to serve in a corps that brings glory to the French.' 'The enemy seemed astonished by such resistance,' wrote GB François Roguet.[141] It was a stunning success and a grateful Napoleon gave full credit to Rapp and Mouton for the victory they had earned through disobedience.

Thrown out of Essling, d'Aspre's grenadiers soon returned for their fifth and final unsuccessful attack. Rosenberg, however, had had more than enough. Threatened by French cavalry south of the village and a bold charge by the *Herzog Heinrich* Chevaulegers on the eastern side, he withdrew once more to Gross-Enzersdorf.[142] Napoleon had survived another crisis and the fighting on the southern side of the field slowly sputtered into silence after 4 p.m.

22 May: The Most Frightful Day

Napoleon's thoughts now turned to retreat and he rode to conduct a personal reconnaissance of the Lobau with a view to adjudging its suitability. Curiously, retreat was also on Charles's mind. Not only did he forbid a request by the grenadiers to renew their attacks on the granary, he also ordered the entire Austrian centre to retire. He apparently feared a French strike against his left and wanted to withdraw to prevent the middle of his line from being outflanked. The Cavalry Reserve, the grenadiers, Hohenzollern, and Bellegarde had all pulled back as much as 2,000 metres when the archduke changed his mind sometime before 5 p.m. Some of his generals, Liechtenstein most vocally, are said to have importuned him to halt the withdrawal, but the deciding factor was the obvious French retreat.[143] The whitecoats returned to their previous positions north of the berm, but this incident illustrates how the Austrian leadership could be dominated by fears of Napoleon and his army.

Charles was extremely fortunate that Hiller, who had observed to his astonishment that the centre had vanished ('I suddenly found myself all alone'), maintained his position at Aspern.[144] Having received no new instructions, Hiller adhered to his previous orders and thus preserved this critical post for his commander.

Charles may have reversed his decision on the army's withdrawal, but he wanted no more combat. He had achieved the desired symbolic victory and had no interest in risking this success by a hasty evening attack against an enemy that still seemed to be full of fight. Couriers thus dashed off with orders to pursue the enemy with artillery fire but to avoid any action that might lead to serious engagement.

The French troops, hungry, thirsty, and utterly weary, thus had to endure a reinvigorated barrage as the afternoon waned. Along with dozens of other men and numerous horses, this deluge of iron cost the army GB Pierre Charles Pouzet, one of St Hilaire's brigadiers and a close friend of Lannes. Shortly thereafter, probably sometime between 5 and 6 p.m., as he was mourning the death of this old comrade, Lannes himself was struck by a 3-pounder ball that grazed his right thigh and crushed his left knee. His remaining staff officers and some carabiniers of the 10th Léger carried him awkwardly on a litter improvised from muskets and branches to the nearby field hospital where the Guard Surgeon, Dominique Larrey, amputated his left leg. A short time later, the wretched party was attempting to evacuate the semi-conscious marshal to the Lobau when they came upon the emperor at the Stadtler Arm bridge. The ensuing scene of dolour and compassion has many variants, but Napoleon's 'indescribable grief' for his friend's pitiable condition was evident to all who witnessed it.[145] 'None of us could hold back his tears,' recalled one of Napoleon's personal escorts.[146] The two men embraced and exchanged a few words, a tearful Napoleon anxiously trying to hearten the stricken marshal and Lannes telling his leader, 'Sire, you are losing your best friend.' Nine days later, Lannes would be dead. It was a deep personal blow to Napoleon and a 'loss sad and irreplaceable!' for the army.[147]

However painful the loss of Lannes, Larrey had more wounded to treat and Napoleon had to see his army safely across the Stadtler Arm. Thanks to tireless exertions by the dedicated French engineers and a small group of senior staff generals and colonels, the bridge over this branch was repaired after a fashion and the impossible welter of wounded men, wounded horses, skulkers, shirkers, servants, baggage, and other detritus was more or less cleared from the approaches in the Mühlau. 'The young infantrymen took themselves off five or six at a time to carry one wounded fellow,' adding to the disorder.[148] 'We had much difficulty in reducing this chaos into something like order,' wrote Mathieu Dumas, one of the generals assigned to this task.[149] But it was done. Napoleon, returning from reconnaissance of the Lobau and shifting his attention from his dying friend, could begin to plan his withdrawal with confidence.

Combat along the French centre and right settled into a cannonade between 5 and 5.30 p.m. as the sweating Austrian gunners unlimbered their pieces within effective range and opened fire. In Aspern, however, fighting raged anew. About 5 p.m., Hiller pushed four companies of *Duka* and two guns along the northern edge of the town and apparently resumed the struggle in the village as well. This movement unhinged the French defences and Hiller saw an opportunity to gain the berm east of Aspern. Seeking support, Hiller rode to the nearest brigadiers, FML Ludwig Freiherr von Vogelsang and Oberst Josef Weiss von Finkenau, but was angered and dismayed to meet only reluctance and rejection.[150] Spying the generalissimus nearby, Hiller complained vociferously and obtained authority over whatever units he needed to 'ensure the troops advance to the berm'. Supported by at least three battalions of II Corps, Hiller commandeered two of Bellegarde's regiments and led them forward. The exhausted Austrians not only chased off the equally weary French skirmishers to establish themselves along the western end of the berm around 6 p.m., but also exploited their advantage to capture the remaining ruined homes of Aspern from the French and Hessian defenders.[151]

Hiller's conquest may have been facilitated by new orders from Napoleon. Massena, in full battle fury, had been maintaining a defiantly aggressive defence, opposing every Austrian advance with tenacious resistance and local counter-attacks. When Napoleon sent GB Bailly de Monthion to ask if 4th Corps could hang on for four hours till nightfall, the marshal seized Monthion's arm in an iron grip and replied: 'Go and tell the emperor that no power on earth can force me to retreat from here; and that I will stay for four hours! Twenty-four hours! Forever!' Another officer, Chef d'Escadron

Armand Jules de Canouville, arriving a short time later from Napoleon, was treated to a similarly impassioned expression of determination. Eyes flashing, Massena told Canouville: 'Hold? No, no, I am not holding; I am not defending at all; I am attacking! Tell him clearly that I am the one who is attacking and that I will attack till night falls!'[152] Now, however, Napoleon was looking to bring the battle to a close and sent instructions for Massena to retire to the brickyard and maintain his line there until ordered to retreat. Massena, under great pressure, skilfully established this new defensive position, and the Austrians, though masters of Aspern at last, could make no progress beyond its smouldering ruins. With their limited artillery, active skirmishers, and menacing manoeuvres by exhausted cavalry that was no longer capable of charging, therefore, the French held off further Habsburg advances in this sector. 'Simultaneous with this concluding piece of the bloody day's work, night fell and the longest, most frightful day of our lives finally came to an end,' recorded an anonymous Hauptmann of *Zach* Infantry, 'hardly were the pickets posted when everyone ran to the blood-coloured Danube arm to quench their burning thirst.'[153] Between 7 and 9 p.m., the firing on the western flank faded and darkness settled over the field.

At nightfall, the French line ran from the Stadtler Arm to Essling's Long Garden, then from the village west along the berm for a little more than a kilometre before it angled to the south-west towards the Aspern brickyard and the small clump of woods along the Gemeinde-Au. Molitor still held the Au, but Hiller's men had made gains during the afternoon, helping and helped by Austrian progress in Aspern itself. Behind this line, in the open meadows now ploughed by Austrian balls, stood the weary and depleted ranks of the heavy cavalry and the Old Guard. Napoleon held a brief council of war in the lee of his army—more to bolster the spirits of his generals and to persuade them of his decision for a limited withdrawal than to garner their opinions—and issued orders for a retreat under the cover of darkness.[154] 'We must threaten an enemy accustomed to fear us and keep him in front of us,' he told the assembled marshals. 'Before he has made up his mind, before he has begun to act, the bridges will be repaired in a manner to defy all accidents, the corps will be able to unite and fight on either bank.' His subordinates catching his fiery optimism and determination, he turned to Massena. 'You will finish what you have so gloriously commenced,' he said, summoning the memories of their long affiliation. 'No one but you can overawe the archduke to keep him immobile before us.'[155] Massena executed this task with his wonted skill and the army filed over the bridge in orderly silence during the night, while Colbert and his hussars kept the bivouac fires burning. The Austrians, exhausted and uncertain, did nothing to interfere.[156]

Leaving Massena to protect the retreat and police the battlefield, Napoleon departed for the riverbank at approximately 10 p.m. After a stumbling ride through the Lobau's ditches and obstructions in the darkness, he reached the water's edge and learned from his engineers that at least several days would pass before the bridges could be restored. He then boarded a small boat with Berthier and Savary for a rough but uneventful passage to Kaiser Ebersdorf on the south shore. He was exhausted and leaned on Savary as he exited the boat. Before anything else, however, he sent an order to Daru to expedite provisions of every sort to Lobau Island.[157] He went to bed sometime after 1 a.m. on 23 May, but rose early that morning to visit the 3rd Corps troops encamped around Ebersdorf.[158]

At approximately 7 a.m. on the 23rd, as the emperor rode to inspect Davout's men, Massena had the Stadtler Arm bridge dismantled 'and passed the bridge himself last of all'.[159] Two hours later the last French rear guards, voltigeurs of 18th Ligne, paddled across the arm to the temporary safety of Lobau Island. The Battle of Aspern was over.[160]

It took some time before the Austrians realised that combat was not going to resume on 23 May. The stout resistance offered by the French in the late afternoon (especially the sudden reversal of fortune at Essling), the apparent steadiness of the troops deployed in the Mühlau, the looming bearskins of the Guard, and the near-empty Austrian ammunition caissons, all combined to dissuade Charles from pressing his luck. 'The Battle of Aspern was won because we held the field as victors,' noted the archduke's old mentor, FML Lindenau, 'But the French were not scattered, not broken. They stood, as I saw, in lines and masses, their rear resting on the woods.' Moreover, there was no certainty that the French would not launch a new attack in the morning, perhaps directed along the Danube's left bank in accordance with the false expectation the Habsburg staff had harboured for the past several days. With all of these considerations in mind, Charles issued instructions for the army to array itself in battle order and returned to Breitenlee to rest.[161]

Aspern: Casualties and Comments

Contemporaries immediately identified the Battle of Aspern as 'among the most bloody to have been fought from the outbreak of the Revolutionary Wars to the present day'.[162] 'Many hundreds of corpses floated on the Danube and were washed up against the banks,' recalled Corporal Brandner.[163] The carnage was indeed extraordinary. The Austrian list of dead, wounded, missing, and captured topped 22,900, or nearly 24 per cent of the 97,000 effectives on the field during the two days (not considering the Insurrection hussars). One regiment (*Koburg No. 22*) and two of the grenadier battalions (*Puteany* and *Kirchenbetter*) suffered losses amounting to some 50 per cent. The Habsburg casualties included thirteen generals, one of whom, FML Weber, was wounded and captured only to die two days after the battle. Liechtenstein and Hohenzollern sustained slight injuries, but Charles escaped unscathed despite his continual exposure to fire.

French casualties were slightly lower, estimated by the Austrian history as 19,980, or approximately one-quarter of the men who fought on the left bank of the Danube.[164] Where the Austrian tally comes from fairly reliable documentation, the French number is largely estimated using known factors such as the number of officer casualties and likely percentages of wounded to killed as bases for extrapolation. The loss in outstanding senior officers was especially painful for the French and personally tragic for Napoleon. Among the twenty senior officers killed were two superb division commanders, Espagne and St Hilaire, the latter of whom had been promised his marshal's baton. Lannes would prove truly irreplaceable. Intrepid, energetic, insightful, and charismatic despite his moodiness, he was sorely missed by everyone from the lowest private to the emperor himself. Fifteen other generals were wounded, including Legrand, Oudinot, Tharreau, Claparède, Mouton, and Curial. GB Fouler fell wounded into Austrian hands and GD Durosnel was captured uninjured. Like Charles, Napoleon had been under heavy fire much of the battle, but remained untouched as soldiers and staff officers fell around him.

In addition to men, thousands of horses were killed or wounded, but in terms of equipment, the Austrians only lost two cannon, the French three. The artillerymen of the two armies, however, certainly earned their pay on 21 and 22 May. The Habsburg gunners with 292 pieces fired some 53,000 rounds during the battle, while their French and German opponents, whose artillery component grew to 152 by the morning of the second day, loosed at least 24,300.

What had this vast expenditure of blood and iron purchased? The question, in the wake of this ferocious, costly struggle, does not submit to easy answers. On the one hand, Charles had achieved the *Achtungsgserfolg*, the symbolic victory towards which he had been aiming: the French attempt to cross the Danube had been repulsed, leaving the Hauptarmee in possession of the battlefield. Moreover, the success had been gained against an enemy army commanded by Napoleon in person, a major consideration at a point in the emperor's career where he seemed surrounded by an aura of invincibility. This time, unlike Eylau, the setback could not be disguised. Reports of the battle and the French withdrawal, often highly embellished, flashed around Europe, reigniting enthusiasm among Napoleon's enemies outside Austria and reviving exaggerated expectations among members of the Habsburg leadership. 'Mr. Napoleon is in the soup and will find it difficult to get out,' exulted Prussian General Blücher, and Stadion believed that Austria could 'again grasp well-founded hopes' of assistance from 'all of our friends'.[165] 'One regarded all of the favourable prospects that we had entertained before this war began as once again, and more than ever, close to fulfilment,' noted the German patriot Karl August Varnhagen von Ense as he travelled through Silesia to volunteer his services to the House to Habsburg.[166]

On the other hand, the French had fought with their accustomed skill and fury, the French army had not been destroyed, and the troops did not believe themselves defeated. In terms of contemporary metrics for victory, for example, the French had lost only three guns, seven caissons, and one standard despite the challenge of withdrawing a major army over a lone and shaky bridge in the face of a numerically superior enemy. Describing the battle and the destruction of the bridges in a letter to his wife on 23 May, Davout wrote: 'In regard to any other troops, this accident would have had the most serious consequences, but for ours it was only a new occasion to display their valour.'[167] This was perhaps an overly rosy assessment, for several days of anxiety at the army's 'desperate situation' followed the battle, and life for those left on Lobau Island was hungry and grim as the soldiers scrounged for anything vaguely edible—horsemeat stew flavoured with gunpowder and cooked in a cast-off cuirass was one solution.[168] 'The horses had the honour of being our cuisine,' remembered Grenadier Delmarche of the 18th, 'not that we desired it.'[169] Conditions for the pitiable wounded were especially horrifying. 'It is impossible to describe our privations,' wrote one survivor, 'and, in addition, heart-rending shrieks came from near at hand, where Dr. Larrey was making amputations; it was frightful to hear.'[170] Nonetheless, if surprised that the Austrians did not attack, the troops did not despair. A bridge to the south bank was restored during 24 and 25 May, food arrived, the wounded were evacuated, and the French army soon 'regained its old attitude'.[171] 'Days of joy succeeded the days of misery and one heard nothing but happy songs throughout the camp.'[172]

The men on both sides could take justifiable pride in the valour and tenacity they had demonstrated during the two-day battle. For the Austrians this endurance and determination was a sign of the army's resilience, its ability to recover quickly after the stunning blows it had received in Bavaria. If the cavalry had seemed disappointingly hesitant, the infantry and artillery had been stubborn in defence and resolute in the attack. 'I could tell you of acts of bravery that moved me to tears,' wrote Charles to his uncle.[173] Above the level of common soldiers and junior officers, however, the army's persistent and debilitating flaws were also evident. Feeble leadership in the senior echelons remained the most crippling weakness. Although the Habsburg generals displayed individual courage and could inspire their men, they showed little initiative, seldom grasped the larger picture beyond what was directly in front of them, and consistently failed to organise coherent assaults against the often-tenuous French defence. For all of their gallantry, most of their attacks were lone thrusts, unco-ordinated with neighbouring units. The result was the costly but fruitless bravery evident in the repeated attempts to storm the Essling granary. In most cases, Charles had had to intervene personally to ensure co-ordination or to inject energy into the senior generals. His personal example was indeed critical at several crisis points, but among his top subordinates the only one who did not seem to require constant oversight was Hiller. The Austrian army thus remained an inept offensive instrument, cumbersome in movement, difficult to co-ordinate, and inflexible once engaged. Charles, his abilities notwithstanding, could neither alter the army's fundamental character nor overcome by force of leadership its ingrained faults. Indeed, even he seems to have been unable to 'push any attack home'.[174] Despite the personal exertions of its commander and the dogged bravery of its soldiers, therefore, the Hauptarmee proved incapable of crushing its badly outnumbered foe.

On the French side, superior leadership and tactical ability almost brought victory against superior numbers clumsily employed. The first day, from the infantry's defiant resolution and intrepid counter-attacks to the cavalry's self-sacrificing charges, was a superb defensive performance. The second day began with an impressive display of offensive prowess, but the available French forces were insufficient to break the resistance offered by superior numbers of obstinate Austrians.[175] Napoleon needed the men, guns, and ammunition gathered on the south bank of the Danube and there is good reason to conclude that their appearance on the battlefield would have brought a French success. On both days, Napoleon managed the battle in masterful style. He inspired with his personal sangfroid and interjected himself where necessary, but the exemplary quality of the French officers meant that he could entrust Massena, Lannes, and others with crucial missions without constantly looking over their shoulders. The skill and courage of the Army of Germany from the common soldiers to their emperor-commander thus made Aspern–Essling a very close-run affair.[176] The confidence of the French soldiers in their own performance, their recognition of the dire odds against them (especially on the first day), and their awareness of the near-success helps explain why, hungry, tired, and thirsty as they were, they did not see themselves as beaten.[177]

Over the acknowledged talents Napoleon and his men displayed once the battle was joined looms the question of whether the battle should have been fought at all. Many commentators treat this initial attempt to leap the Danube as foolhardy and rash, the result of Napoleon's overweening pride and arrogance.[178] Certainly, the low esteem he harboured for the Austrians in general and his exaggerated estimate of the damage the Hauptarmee had suffered in Bavaria informed his decision to cross the river and bring Charles to battle as quickly as possible once he reached Vienna. However, this was not as unreasonable as often portrayed in hindsight. One need not be an 'apologist' for Napoleon to consider the situation from his viewpoint. In the first place, he knew little of Charles and the Hauptarmee—in enemy territory where he had few if any spies and on the far side of a great river inaccessible to his cavalry. Intelligence, which often appears so pellucid after the fact, is usually much less precise and unmistakable when weighed in the welter of other information leaders have to sift when making crucial decisions. Such was the case here. Napoleon had hints only, nothing definitive. Second, he had the initiative and wanted to exploit it to bring the war to a swift close. As we have seen, he began searching for crossing options as soon as he reached Vienna, and he was doubtless frustrated that a week elapsed between his entry into the city and the completion of the bridge. Endeavouring to capitalise on his army's momentum, he gambled and lost, but it is important not to lose sight of how close he came to success.[179] He returned to Schönbrunn with a revised opinion of Habsburg soldiery and an adamantine determination to prepare the next crossing with infinite care and to execute it with every available musket and sabre.[180]

While Napoleon retired thwarted, the Austrians considered the extent of their victory.[181] This was defensive and tactical rather than decisive, a 'passive success' in the words of the official history.[182] However, even this relatively confined achievement had two important consequences. The first, from a defensive point of view, was what the victory prevented: the possible debasement or dissolution of the Habsburg monarchy. Napoleon had not made up his mind, but he was clearly considering very severe penalties to be imposed on Austria for what he perceived as its recidivist tendency to challenge France repeatedly in spite of solemn treaties and against all logic (as he saw it). Aspern–Essling halted his juggernaut progress and led him to re-evaluate not only his assessment of the Austrian army but also his goals in this unwanted war. The second consequence fell in the offensive sphere: the victory, though limited, opened strategic options for the Habsburg leadership. Politically, Austria might now explore peace from a position of relative strength as Charles hoped. Alternatively, it could inflate the glory of battle and trade on it to garner active allies—both states and insurgents—in further prosecution of the war. In the military arena, the archduke could now transition to the offence if he so desired, conducting his own crossing of the Danube to exploit French material weakness and presumed psychological dislocation in the wake of the battle. Charles had his *Achtungserfolg*. It remained to be seen what he and his Kaiser could do with it.

1   **Archduke Maximilian d'Este** (1782–1863): Disgraced by the rapid fall of Vienna, he withdrew from the army, but the experience of Napoleon's rapid advance down the Danube led him to promote an abortive fortification scheme at Linz during the 1830s.

2   **Heinrich XV Fürst Reuss-Plauen** (1751–1825): Retired to Plauen after the war; returned to serve the Habsburgs in 1813–14.

3   **Maximilian Freiherr von Wimpffen** (1770–1854): Left his post of chief of staff after Znaim; remained in service and returned to active command in 1813–14.

4 **Marshal Jean Baptiste Bernadotte, Prince of Ponte Corvo** (1763–1844): Cashiered from corps command after Wagram, he led French forces opposing the British landings in Holland later in 1809.

Panchery del

5 **Saxon Infantry:** In their stiff white uniforms, the Saxons looked antiquated even to contemporaries (note grenadier at right). (ASKB)

(clockwise from top left)

6   **Austrian Jäger:** These men cut a fine figure in their handsome grey uniforms, but
      with no proper training manual, they were often misused. (ASKB)

7   **Austrian Landwehr and Hungarian Insurrection:** Austrian leaders placed great
      hopes in these second line forces, but were often disappointed (left to right: Vienna
      Volunteer, Lower Austrian and Styrian Landwehr, Hungarian Insurrection).

8   **Imperial Guard Fusiliers:** Two battalions of these veterans (one each of grenadiers
      and chasseurs) helped stem the Austrian tide at Essling on 22 May.

9   **Tirailleurs Corses:** This outstanding light infantry battalion in its distinctive brown
      uniforms played a key role at Passau and Ebelsberg.

10 **Battle of Neumarkt** (24 April): Austrian infantry inflicted heavy losses on French light horse in the close confines of the town. (ASKB)

11 'The last shot': Austrian infantry near Nittenau fends off pursuing French hussars (5th Regiment); naïf image from Brandner's memoirs. (ASKB)

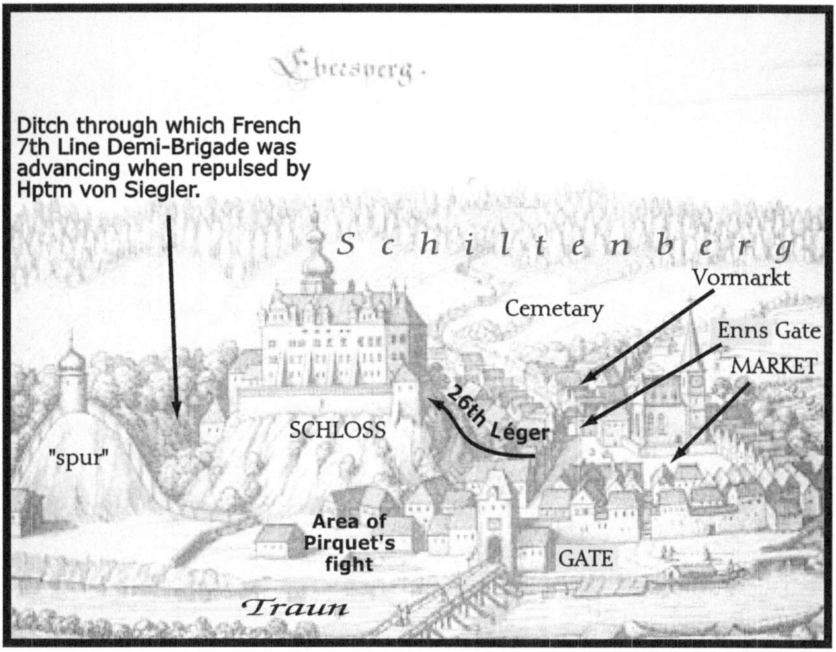

Ebersperg.
Ditch through which French 7th Line Demi-Brigade was advancing when repulsed by Hptm von Siegler.
Schiltenberg
Vormarkt
Cemetary
Enns Gate
MARKET
26th Léger
SCHLOSS
"spur"
Area of Pirquet's fight
GATE
Traun

12 **Ebelsberg schematic:** Shows principal areas of action and the Schloss as it was before the battle.

13 **Battle of Ebelsberg** (3 May): French infantry storm across the wooden trestle bridge. In reality, there was no opposing Austrian column and the bridge side rails had already been removed. (ASKB)

14 Engagement at Blindenmarkt (6 May): Colbert's chasseurs had the better of this running fight with Austrian uhlans.

15 Night Reconnaissance: Austrian infantry prepares for a night patrol across the Danube. Both sides conducted numerous small forays to gather intelligence and provisions. (ASKB)

16 Siege of Vienna (11/12 May): Cleverly concealed French howitzers lob shells into Vienna during the night of 11/12 May.

17 Engagement on Schwarze Lackenau (13 May): Major O'Brien's battalion of *Kerpen* Infantry takes advantage of a fence to outflank French defenders. (ASKB)

18 Aspern Church: Having repeatedly served as a bastion for both sides, the church and its associated buildings were in ruins after the battle.

19 Essling Granary: Boudet's men repulsed numerous assaults from this sturdy fortress.

20 Charles at Aspern: Though doubtless exaggerated in this depiction, Charles's rallying of Zach Infantry help to avert calamity on 22 May. (ASKB)

21 Austrian Artillery at Aspern: Well over 100 guns pummelled the constricted French position on the afternoon of 22 May. (ASKB)

23 French Senior Officer Casualties: (*above*) Two of the French generals mortally wounded on 22 May were Napoleon's friend, Marshal Lannes (seen here in the poignant encounter with the emperor), and (*right*) the promising GD St Hilaire. (ASKB)

(*Opposite*)
22 Fighting at Aspern: Troops from Benjovszky and Klebek Infantry Regiments storm the churchyard on the afternoon of 22 May. Note the Hungarian uniforms (shakos, tight blue trousers) of the former and the 'German' uniforms (helmets, white breeches) of the latter. (ASKB)

84

SAINT-HILAIRE

88

(clockwise from top left)

24 **Archduke Johann** (1782–1859): Though he never held another military command, he led an active life especially promoting commerce, education, and culture in Styria; scandalised the court by marrying a commoner in 1829. (ASKB)

25 **Ignaz Graf Gyulai** (1763–1831): Ban (viceroy) of Croatia, Dalmatia, and Slavonia as well as a general, he commanded several corps in 1813–14 and served as overall commander in Austria during 1815. (ASKB)

26 **Jean Gabriel Marquis de Chasteler-Courcelles** (1763–1835): Belgian by origin, he commanded a division in 1813, but thereafter retired to Venice pained by many wounds suffered in Habsburg service. (ASKB)

27 **Albert Graf Gyulai** (1766–1835): Younger brother to Ignaz and de facto VIII Corps commander, he retired in 1811, but was recalled to command reserve troops in 1813 and 1815. (Austrian National Library)

(clockwise from top left)

28 **Eugene de Beauharnais** (1781–1824): Josephine's son from her first marriage and husband to Bavarian Princess Auguste, he commanded 4th Corps in Russia, a desperate defence in Germany in spring 1813, and the Army of Italy 1813–14; retired to Bavaria with his beloved wife in 1814.

29 **Louis Baraguey d'Hilliers** (1764–1813): Served in Spain 1810–11, then in Russia; arrested for dubious performance, he died in Berlin of fever en route back to Paris for trial. (ASKB)

30 **Etienne Jacques MacDonald** (1765–1840): Appointed marshal on the field at Wagram, served in Spain 1810–11, then commanded several corps from 1812 through 1814; one of those who persuaded Napoleon to abdicate, he presided over dissolution of the army. (ASKB)

31 **Paul Grenier** (1768–1827): Held commands in Germany till wounded in spring 1813, then wing commander in Italy till 1814; younger brother Jean Georges (1771–1832) of 60th Ligne also became a general, leading a brigade at Waterloo. (ASKB)

32 **Italian Royal Guard Infantry:** Grenadiers (dark green coats as shown) and Velites (white coats with dark green lapels) of the Italian Guard performed superbly in difficult fighting on 29 and 30 April. (ASKB)

33 **Italian Mounted Troops:** In the centre are Italy's excellent dragoon regiments (in helmets): Queen's, Napoleon, Guard (from left to right). At left is a mounted gendarme, at right horse artillery of the line (left) and Guard (right). (ASKB)

34 French (*above*) **and Austrian** (*right*) **Dragoons:** Both sides used dragoons as heavy cavalry in Italy, but these regiments also performed a multitude of other tasks. (author/ASKB)

35 GD Emmanuel Grouchy (1766–1847): Commanded cavalry corps from 1812 to 1814, he was made a marshall in 1815 and played a controversial role in the Waterloo campaign.

36 Battle of the Piave (8 May): French infantry storms into the centre of the Austrian line during the afternoon attack on the Piave. (ASKB)

PART II

Clearing the Strategic Flanks

CHAPTER 4

Over the Alps:
Austria's Southern Offensives

With Napoleon stymied in Vienna and the Habsburg leadership weighing its options, it is time to remind ourselves of the other theatres of war. Italy was the second most important arena for Austria. As we have seen, this was not the case in the initial concept developed by Charles and Mayer. They were focused on actions that would be of direct assistance to the Hauptarmee's offensive; consequently, they stressed the Tyrol and Poland. The former because its occupation would threaten French communications from Strasbourg to the Danube valley and would cut the link between Napoleon's armies in Germany and Italy; the latter because they harboured exaggerated hopes that the presence of a Habsburg corps in Poland would force or persuade Prussia to declare against France and then join the Main Army in Germany. For Charles and Mayer, operations on the Italian frontier were thus intended to be limited and primarily defensive. Johann's influence and Stadion's political desire to evict Napoleon's power from the Italian peninsula, however, led to changes shortly before the war: VIII Corps was shifted from the Main Army to the Army of Inner Austria and the youthful Johann was allowed considerable latitude in drafting the plans for his army's operations. Charles, on the other hand, sought to constrain his younger brother's ambitions, using his final instructions to emphasise the need for 'a strong corps' to advance up the Drava River valley (Pustertal) into the Tyrol and suggesting that the Army of Inner Austria need only cover the border with Italy. Johann had other ideas. While detaching a relatively small force of regulars and Landwehr into the Tyrol and allotting a brigade to Dalmatia, he planned a full-fledged invasion of northern Italy.[1]

THE SOUTHERN FRONT: PLANS AND FORCES

Johann's army was inadequate for his ambitions. Once the basic allocation of forces was decided, Johann commanded VIII Corps (27,150), IX Corps (33,280), and a bundle of Landwehr (34,640). The regulars had never operated together in their new division and corps formations, but they were solid units, largely at full strength, well equipped, and generally prepared for combat. The Inner Austrian Landwehr, on the other hand, suffered from the same ills that plagued their brethren elsewhere in the monarchy: inadequate uniforms and equipment, little training, and antique or absent officers. Though some units would prove quite durable, many would also demonstrate the motivational problems that crippled Landwehr in the Danube valley. Nonetheless, most were ready, or nearly so, when the war began. The Adelsberg and Neustadtl battalions, however, owing to the inactivity of the local authorities', were utterly unprepared for war, and Johann, convinced of their 'uselessness', deducted these 6,880 men from his pool of troops available for the opening of hostilities.[2] He was thus left with 88,200 infantry and cavalry (60,430 regulars, 27,770 Landwehr) supported by 148 guns to invade Italy, the Tyrol, Dalmatia, and Istria.[3] Additionally, the small Habsburg fleet under GM Josef Graf l'Espine was to undertake coastal operations against Dalmatia, in co-ordination—hoped Vienna—with elements of the Royal Navy. The Austrians, assuming Russian sympathy and co-operation, had tried in vain to enlist the assistance of a Russian naval squadron in Trieste (a relic of the tsar's Mediterranean imaginings). Lacking orders, however, the commodore, Michael T. Bychenskii, rebuffed the Habsburg entreaties and 'pursued a policy of neutrality'.[4]

The nature of his manifold missions forced Johann to detach important portions of his force from the very beginning. While FML Chasteler advanced into the Tyrol with 13,560 regulars and Landwehr (with another 3,500 Landwehr to follow) on the right, GM von Stoichevich on the left would push into Dalmatia with 8,000 (almost all Grenzer militia); and Major Dominik Freiherr von Cazzan would occupy Istria with a tiny detachment composed largely of Landwehr. Another 17,230 Landwehr would remain in Austrian territory initially. These detachments left the archduke with only 44,720 regulars and 8,170 Landwehr, not quite 53,000 men, to conduct his main effort: the invasion of Italy. Further detachments would become necessary as the Austrians advanced and had to detail units to mask French fortresses in north-east Italy: Palmanova, Osoppo, and possibly Venice. Johann complained bitterly that army high command refused to acknowledge that the French had more than 30,000 men in Italy, and he realised that he would have little, if any, numerical advantage, but he made no attempt to confine his ambitious offensive mission in more manageable bounds or to limit himself to nothing more than to regaining the Tyrol and defending the monarchy's frontiers.[5] His desire for a prominent attacking role in the war thus contributed to the dispersal of Austrian forces and, after some early successes, led to a demoralising, debilitating retreat back into Habsburg lands with the French hard on his heels.

On the other side of the border waited the Franco-Italian Army of Italy and Marmont's Army of Dalmatia, both under the command of Viceroy Eugene. The Army of Italy, totalling 74,922 infantry and cavalry of French and Italian origin, was divided into six French and two Italian infantry divisions, a light cavalry division, two small dragoon divisions, and the Italian Royal Guard. Marmont's Army of Dalmatia was organised in two divisions numbering 11,285 infantry and cavalry, but—imposing title notwithstanding—it was only the size of one of Davout's large divisions. An additional 6,350 infantry (including some unit depots) were committed to the garrisons of Istria, Venice, and Palmanova at the start of hostilities, and four companies of the 92nd Ligne (a further 550 men) would be detached to hold the fortress of Osoppo the day after the war began.

In terms of quality, most of the French and some of the Italian units were composed of seasoned, reliable troops who were confident that 'the *Kaiserliks* would receive another lesson from their masters.'[6] Organisationally, however, there were weaknesses, especially as there was no corps structure at the outset of the war. This was consistent with Eugene's preferences. He respected his generals—who 'do not have the pretensions of the marshals'— and wanted to deal with his subordinates directly rather than cope with the egos of 'marshals and dignitaries.'[7] Napoleon, however, told Eugene that an intermediary command echelon was essential so the viceroy would not have to co-ordinate the plethora of divisions personally.[8] To comply with the emperor's wishes, Eugene was to divide his army into ad hoc 'wings' (rather than the more formal and enduring corps d'armée) to be commanded by GD Louis Baraguey d'Hilliers, GD Paul Grenier, and, at Napoleon's direction, a rehabilitated Republican general named Etienne Jacques MacDonald. This new arrangement, however, would not be implemented until late April. When the war opened, therefore, Eugene was still personally responsible for the direction of eight infantry and three cavalry divisions as well as the myriad other duties attendant upon his simultaneously being an army commander and viceroy of a large kingdom.[9] The profusion of new divisions

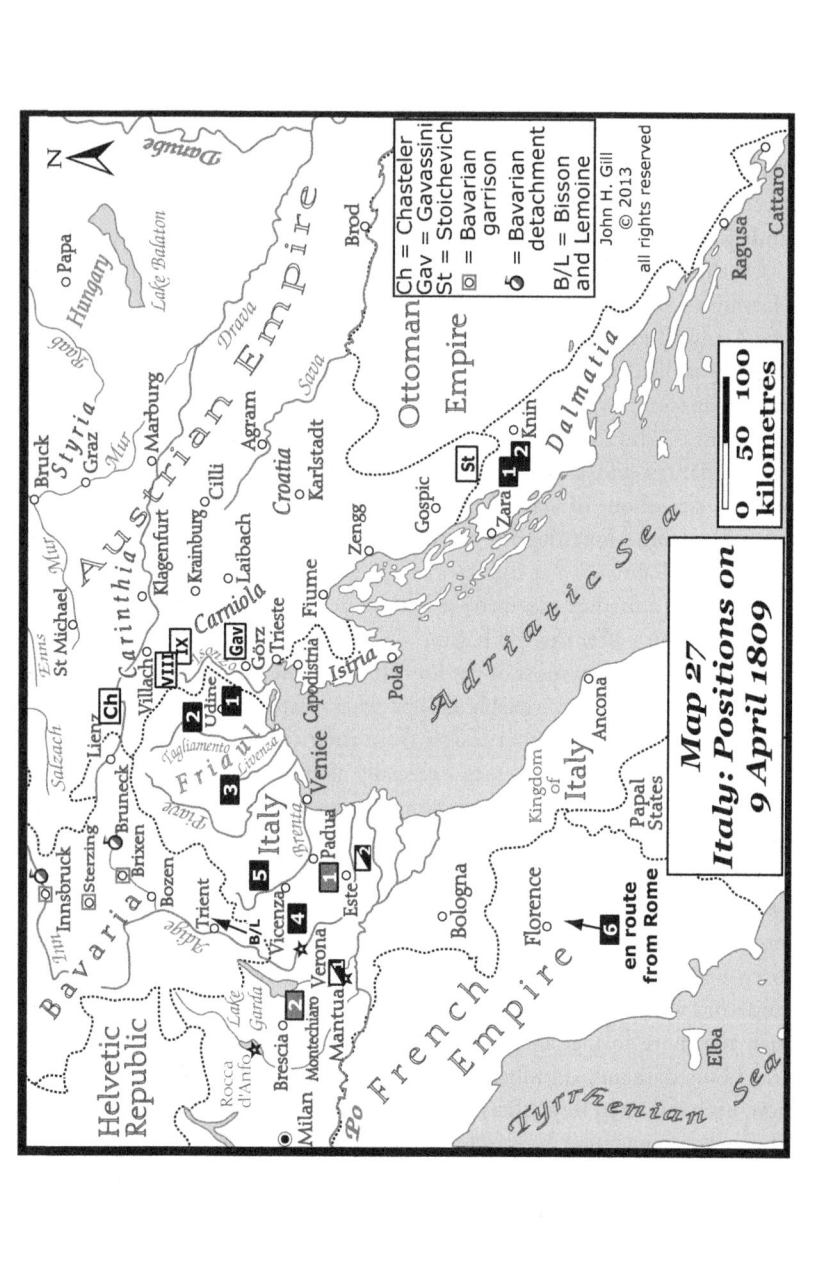

Map 27
Italy: Positions on
9 April 1809

John H. Gill
© 2013
all rights reserved

Ch = Chasteler
Gav = Gavassini
St = Stoichevich
▣ = Bavarian garrison
♦ = Bavarian detachment
B/L = Bisson and Lemoine

and the absence of long-standing corps also meant the French in Italy did not benefit from long pre-war association in higher formations as in the old Grande Armée or the new Army of Germany. At the tactical level, the preponderance of third and fourth battalions in the Italian units reflected the facts that a major Italian contingent was fighting in Spain and that the army was still struggling to complete its transition to the 1808 model infantry organisation. There were not enough officers and NCOs to staff many of these battalions and common soldiers were in short supply, so the average strength of these 'half-regiments' in 2nd Division was just 408 per battalion.[10] The troops, moreover, were largely brand-new recruits.[11] Not sturdy enough to maintain their strength when subject to the erosion of combat and marching, many of these battalion pairs would be amalgamated into single battalions before the war was very old.

Eugene, following Napoleon's careful instructions, had deployed his army defensively 'in a long column from the eastern frontiers of the kingdom to Montechiaro' by early April.[12] The emperor based his orders on the assumption that the Austrians would 'reflect on the abyss that will engulf them' and would thus do nothing before May, if at all.[13] In the meantime, dispersal in the plains reduced the chances of provoking Vienna while easing logistical burdens and sparing the troops the sickness that would ensue if they moved into the mountains under the foul spring weather.[14] Nonetheless, the possibility of an early attack could not be ignored, so the army was arrayed to guard three approaches into rich plains of northern Italy: from the Tyrol in the north, from the area around Tarvis in the north-east, and along the Isonzo in the east. Eugene therefore posted the divisions of GD Achille Fontanelli and GD Jean Maximilien Lamarque west and east of Lake Garda respectively to watch the principal exits from the Tyrol (an area that caused Eugene particular anxiety).[15] GD Filippo Severoli's Italians and the two dragoon divisions, cantoned between Padua and Este, were available for support. East of the Tagliamento, GD Jean Mathieu Seras protected the Isonzo front and the difficult approach from Karfreit (Caporetto), while GD Jean Baptiste Broussier held responsibility for the approach from Pontebba to Osoppo. GD Grenier's division and 6th Chasseurs stood between the Tagliamento and the Piave, close enough to come to the assistance of Broussier and Seras within one day if needed. GD Gabriel Barbou d'Escourières's 5th Division served as a general reserve, capable of moving west, north, or east as the situation demanded. GD Louis Sahuc's four regiments were scattered about, as was the Italian Guard, and GB François Valentin was en route from Rome with the initial components of what would become GD Pierre Durutte's division.

In addition to these deployments for the field forces, Napoleon had ordered the creation of reserve demi-brigades in the French departments of Italy.[16]

Tension was thick and war seemed unavoidable, but the general sense in the French camp reflected Napoleon's belief that the Austrian offensive would not come before the end of April or the beginning of May at the earliest. 'Yesterday evening I saw all my spies and all assert that the Austrians will attack us soon,' wrote Eugene to wife Auguste on 10 April from Udine, 'but nothing is certain and I do not believe it.' 'I have viewed the greater part of the army,' he concluded, 'and you would not believe how splendidly and well everything is placed.'[17] As in Germany, the Allies would be the victims of tactical surprise.

Archduke Johann hoped to compound the surprise by launching his main effort along one of the less likely avenues of approach: the Natsione valley leading from Karfreit to Cividale on the edge of the plains. Furthermore, to mislead the French, the troops on this approach were not to cross the border until the morning of 11 April. The secondary forces would advance first, with Chasteler's 13,500 men marching into the Bavarian Tyrol on the morning of 9 April to make the opening move. Next would come Oberstleutnant Anton von Volkmann pushing through Pontebba along the shorter and less tortuous route to Italy with a small detachment (I/*Johann Jellacic*, I/*Franz Karl*, I/*2nd Banal* Grenz, two squadrons of *Ott* Hussars, and a half-battery) on the morning of 10 April. Johann hoped that Volkmann would distract the French and disguise the fact that the main Austrian force was advancing on Cividale from the north. To buttress the ruse, a General Staff Hauptmann named Eduard von Zuccheri entered into a correspondence with Eugene's chief of staff, GD Henri François Marie Charpentier. Zuccheri, portraying himself as ambitious and disgruntled, passed false information on Austrian dispositions to the French general.[18] Finally, on the Habsburg left, GM Alois Graf Gavassini would lead a division comprised mostly of Landwehr across the Isonzo on the evening of 10 April (the night before the main body moved). With luck, the French would be deceived and the Habsburg forces would be able to complete the difficult march to Cividale before Eugene could gather his dispersed forces and react.

9–15 APRIL: INSURGENT SUCCESS IN THE TYROL

The Army of Inner Austria's operations began with the invasion of the Tyrol by Chasteler's command on 9 April. Napoleon had detached the region from Austria following the victory at Austerlitz in 1805 and had granted it to Bavaria's King Max Josef in recompense for Bavarian support during the war. The Tyrolian population, however, fiercely attached to the House of Habsburg and, imbued with a deep Roman Catholic piety, detested Bavarian rule, especially Munich's interference with cherished local traditions and privileges. Covert contacts with sympathisers in Vienna soon began to grow, many centred around Archduke Johann, who had commanded Austrian forces in the Tyrol during the 1805 war and had rapidly become the most ardent advocate of Tyrolian interests within the ruling family. Youthful and romantically inclined, Johann was drawn to the Tyrol by the region's rugged natural beauty and the simple peasant lives of its hardy inhabitants. His passionate interest was widely reciprocated, many Tyrolians referring to him as 'Prince Hannes' and thinking of him as 'their' Habsburg.[19]

As war approached during the winter of 1808–9, proponents of Tyrolian 'liberty' (i.e. a return to Habsburg sovereignty) sought to exploit the strong pro-Austrian sympathies in the region. At one level, therefore, Chasteler's attack had been well prepared: clandestine meetings and communications between Habsburg officials and Tyrolian representatives had been taking place sporadically since December, including a secret visit to Vienna by a three-man delegation of Tyrolians during January and February 1809. Following a surreptitious audience with Johann and other discussions, the trio returned home to spread the word of an impending uprising against the hated Bavarians and French with the support of the Austrian regular army. With the Spanish example of anti-French resistance clearly in mind, enthusiasts pointed to other factors that favoured a rebellion: especially the difficult mountainous terrain and the ferocious spirit of independence that animated most of the populace. Also working to Austria's advantage was the Tyrol's tradition of self-defence. In many cases, this tradition only manifested itself in groups of poorly armed, poorly disciplined local militia, but the region was also home to many independent, semi-military rifle companies (Schützen-Kompanien), who combined intimate knowledge of the area with expert marksmanship. Although subsequent hagiography has often elevated their fanaticism and talent as riflemen to impossibly legendary levels, the Schützen companies were certainly formidable opponents. Capable of being mobilised at short notice, they not only provided a significant supplement to Habsburg regulars, but also proved sufficiently skilled and motivated to tackle Bavarian and French troops with no support at all from Austrian whitecoats.[20]

In other respects, deficiencies in planning appeared in the first days of the Austrian invasion. In the first place, Habsburg leaders seem to have given little thought to how they would utilise local insurgents. Chasteler, for instance, did not bring stocks of muskets to arm the population and apparently did not consider the problem of co-operation with eager but barely organised locals before he crossed the border. Second, there was no central co-ordination authority or military command structure among the often-fractious Tyrolian leaders, many of whom soon showed themselves to be more opportunistic and personally ambitious than dedicated to the cause of liberation. Although the semi-literate Andreas Hofer, a bearded and colourfully burly innkeeper from St Leonhard in the Passeiertal,[21] would become the icon of the insurgency, he possessed little in the way of 'command authority' in the early days of the insurrection.[22]

Fighting cold temperatures and deep snow, Chasteler's main body reached Lienz on the evening of 9 April, and Sillian on the 10th. Their welcome was ecstatic as Major Franz Karl Veyder von Malberg of Chasteler's staff recorded: 'Triumphal arches were erected in the villages, the streets were strewn with flowers, the sound of crackers and ringing bells echoed from all sides. Doughty Pustertal women armed with halberds joined the ranks of the soldiers to encourage them.'[23] Cheering as these celebrations were, the men were exhausted from slogging through the snow, and Chasteler declared 11 April a rest day. The Tyrolian insurgents, however, had already taken matters into their own hands and the Austrian general soon discovered that events were leaving him behind.

The Bavarian forces in the Tyrol were small and isolated, a total of some 4,450 men and six guns under the aged and indecisive GL Georg von Kinkel. Kinkel had his headquarters in Innsbruck with 11th Infantry, a squadron of 1st Dragoons, and three guns; the 2nd and 4th Light Battalions were divided between Sterzing and Brixen; and 3rd Light was posted in the Inn valley from Hall north to Rattenberg. In addition, Major Maximillian von Aicher held the fortress of Kufstein with a provisional light battalion of 470 depot troops and some ninety-eight artillerymen. Also entering the picture were two columns of French troops marching from their depots in Italy to Massena's 4th Corps in the Danube valley. The first column, commanded by GD Baptiste Bisson, was formed around the third battalions of 2nd Ligne and 3rd Léger with some 350 cavalry, and apparently a pair of guns. GD Louis Lemoine led the second column: the fourth battalions of 67th and 93rd Ligne, a march battalion, 270 cavalry, and three guns. Each column numbered approximately 2,000 men, albeit almost all new conscripts, and

Napoleon thought that they could be 'usefully employed' during their transit of the Tyrol if necessary.[24] At the same time, he worried that they might experience some 'unfortunate adventure' and urged caution in their march.[25] By the time he sent that latter injunction to Berthier, however, it was already too late.

Neither the Bavarians nor the French were surprised by the Tyrolian uprising: the ferment was unmistakable, intelligence on covert contacts with Vienna had been evident for months. As in the main theatres of war, the surprise was in the timing and probably in the strength and swiftness of the insurgent wave that swept over the mountains in the first half of April. A small Bavarian detachment in Bruneck was the first to suffer when rebels captured six men at an isolated outpost in Innichen on 9 April. Sensing his peril, the lieutenant in charge ordered a hasty retreat to Brixen, but lost twelve more of his men during a vain attempt to dismantle the bridge over the Rienz just west of Bruneck before withdrawing.[26] The rest of the detachment escaped to Brixen where Oberstleutnant Dominikus von Wreden of 2nd Light was in command.[27] Recognising the danger, Wreden immediately marched for Innsbruck, attempting to demolish the Eisack bridge near Oberau (the Ladritsch Bridge) en route. Spontaneously assembled peasants had attacked a Bavarian company at the bridge early on 10 April and fighting continued all day, erupting afresh on 11 April as Wreden endeavoured to destroy the span. GB Bisson and his column of conscripts arrived that afternoon, but the French general was not inclined to risk his raw troops in combat so he continued north according to his instructions. Shortly thereafter, the appearance of fifty Austrian Jägers and a few chevaulegers sufficed to revive the Tyrolians' sinking spirits and Wreden, feeling pressured and abandoned, hurried to join Bisson's column.

The Allied commanders thus fled northwards pursued by terrifying numbers of persistent and enthusiastic rebels. As this Franco-Bavarian column was heading up the valley, some 5,000 insurgents, led by Andreas Hofer, were overwhelming the two companies of 4th Light in Sterzing: 40 Bavarians were killed or wounded and 431 taken prisoner. Tyrolians also beset Innsbruck on 11 April, repulsing several bold forays by the Bavarians trapped in the city. Combat around Innsbruck resumed on the morning of 12 April and by 10 a.m. the outnumbered Bavarians had capitulated, so Bisson and Wreden found the city held against them when they arrived the next morning (13 April). Bisson, initially incredulous, surrendered after a conversation with the disconsolate Kinkel convinced him that resistance would be pointless. The two companies of 3rd Light closest to Innsbruck were attacked during the night and also surrendered on the morning of 13 April when they ran out of ammunition. In five days, the Tyrolians, with almost no help from Austrian regulars, had thus driven the Bavarians from their lands and captured two generals, 130 senior officers, 3,860 Bavarians, 2,050 Frenchmen, and seven guns. The only formed Bavarian troops to escape the debacle were the other two companies of 3rd Light, led back to Bavaria by a resolute major.

While the Tyrolians were encompassing the destruction of Kinkel's Bavarians, Chasteler was making his way to the heart of the region. His command having rested in Sillian on 11 April, he sent it on an extraordinary march of some sixty-five kilometres through the snow to reach Mühlbach in the early hours of 13 April, just as Bisson and Wreden were arriving outside Innsbruck. On the way, he dropped off two small detachments at Toblach to guard his left flank and to make contact with Johann's main force to the south: Major Anton de la Notte with a company of 9th Jägers, 200 Landwehr Schützen (2nd Villach), and a few chevaulegers south-east to San Stefano di Cadore, and Major Hieronymus Graf Lodron to Cortina d'Ampezzo with his 2nd Villach and some Landsturm.[28] Chasteler also deposited a battalion of *Lusignan* in Bruneck under Oberstleutnant Dominik von Ertel.

Riding ahead to Brixen as his men were establishing their camps south of Mühlbach on 13 April, Chasteler learned of the insurgent successes on the road to Innsbruck and decided to march north without delay. An advance detachment was thus able to reach Innsbruck on the 14th, and Chasteler made his own triumphant entry the following day. Coincidentally, Oberstleutnant von Taxis of Jellacic's division also arrived in Innsbruck on 15 April, having completed a roundabout march from Salzburg through the Salzach and Ziller valleys with his 800 men.[29] In addition to Taxis, Chasteler now had three infantry battalions, three Jäger companies, one and one-half squadrons, and five guns in and around Innsbruck. He left the bulk of his force in the vicinity of Brixen under GM Ignaz Peter Chevalier Marchal de Berelat and GM Franz von Fenner, with III/*Hohenlohe* posted forward at Klausen under Oberstleutnant Christian Graf Leiningen. Down the Inn valley, an additional force came under Chasteler's orders: Oberstleutnant Reissenfels with his detachment from Jellacic (approximately 650 regulars) had reached Wörgl via the Strub Pass and St Johann in Tirol on the 15th.[30] Chasteler now sent this detachment, reinforced by as many as ten Tyrolian Schützen companies (perhaps 2,000 locals), to lay siege to the little fortress of Kufstein, the last remaining Bavarian outpost in the Tyrol.[31]

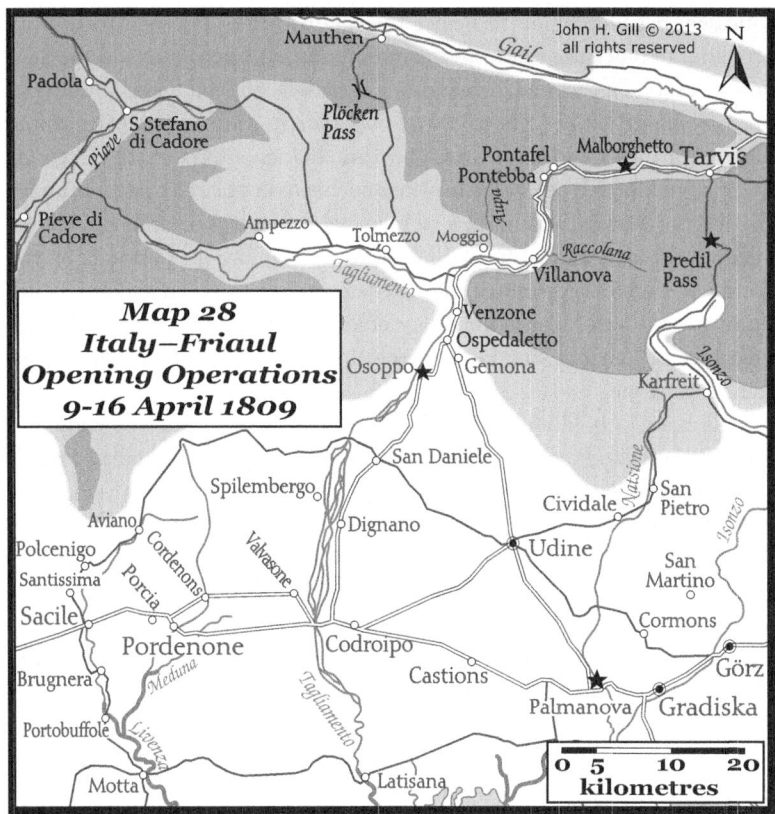

Map 28
Italy–Friaul
Opening Operations
9-16 April 1809

10–14 APRIL: JOHANN INVADES ITALY

While these events were unfolding further north, Johann was launching his invasion of Italy. The weather in the mountains that April was execrable. Heavy snowfalls, cold drenching rain, and bitter winds conspired to impede movements and make the soldiers' lives miserable. 'It has been snowing continually for eight days,' complained Johann.[32] Nonetheless, his offensive began on schedule.

Oberstleutnant Volkmann opened the ball, crossing the border at 6 a.m. on 10 April and capturing ninety French in a skirmish at Villanova at the cost of five Austrian casualties before settling in for the night.[33] The prisoners, infantrymen of 9th Ligne and a few dragoons, were from Broussier's division and that general, informed of the Austrian advance at 2 p.m., sent a messenger galloping off to Prince Eugene in Udine. The viceroy directed Broussier to block the exit from the mountains at Ospedaletto and the division was soon on the road. Leaving two battalions of 92nd Ligne in Osoppo, Broussier marched all night to halt at Ospedaletto early on 11 April, pushing three companies of 9th Ligne, two guns, and his squadron of 24th Dragoons ahead to reinforce I/9th Ligne in Venzone. Broussier placed this force under GB Joseph Dessaix with orders to hold his forward post until the rest of the division could establish itself in the 'very advantageous positions' on the Monte di Comielli just north of Ospedaletto.³⁴ Dessaix left the Grenadier Company of I/9th Ligne in the village of Portis about two and a half kilometres north of Venzone, and kept the remainder of his little command in and behind Venzone.

Volkmann, a bold and energetic officer, had his men moving early and appeared outside Portis at approximately 8 a.m. The outnumbered French grenadiers were overwhelmed after a tough fight, but the Austrians found their pursuit blunted when they came upon Dessaix's men at Venzone. Volkmann sent two companies of *Johann Jellacic* splashing across the Tagliamento and two others into the hills to outflank the French position, but the village was actually captured by the men of *Franz Karl* who charged just as Dessaix was trying to implement an order to withdraw. The Austrian attack bundled the French out of Venzone and introduced an extended combat in the small area of rocky low ground between Venzone and Monte Comielli. The battle rolled back and forth for more than an hour before Dessaix withdrew to the heights, closely followed by his adversaries. Indeed the Austrians, though outnumbered approximately two to one, showed 'extraordinary perseverance' in exerting steady pressure on Broussier's men.³⁵ The combat was hot and the injured included Dessaix, wounded first in the head and then, as he was retiring from the field, struck in the lower jaw by a piece of shrapnel.³⁶ The fighting on the heights did not begin to trail off until 3 p.m., but around that hour the Austrian right, perhaps encouraged by the advance of the two *Jellacic* companies on the far bank of the Tagliamento, surged forward along the main road next to the river.³⁷ Fire from a 12-pounder and howitzer that Broussier had posted near the road soon forced the whitecoats to withdraw, and this proved to be the last serious action of the day. Firing continued until nightfall, when Broussier withdrew to the south in compliance with orders he had received at 2 p.m.

The little engagement at Venzone cost each side approximately 250 to 300 casualties and left both feeling victorious. Volkmann, with only some 3,450 men, could be justly proud of tying down twice his number (Broussier

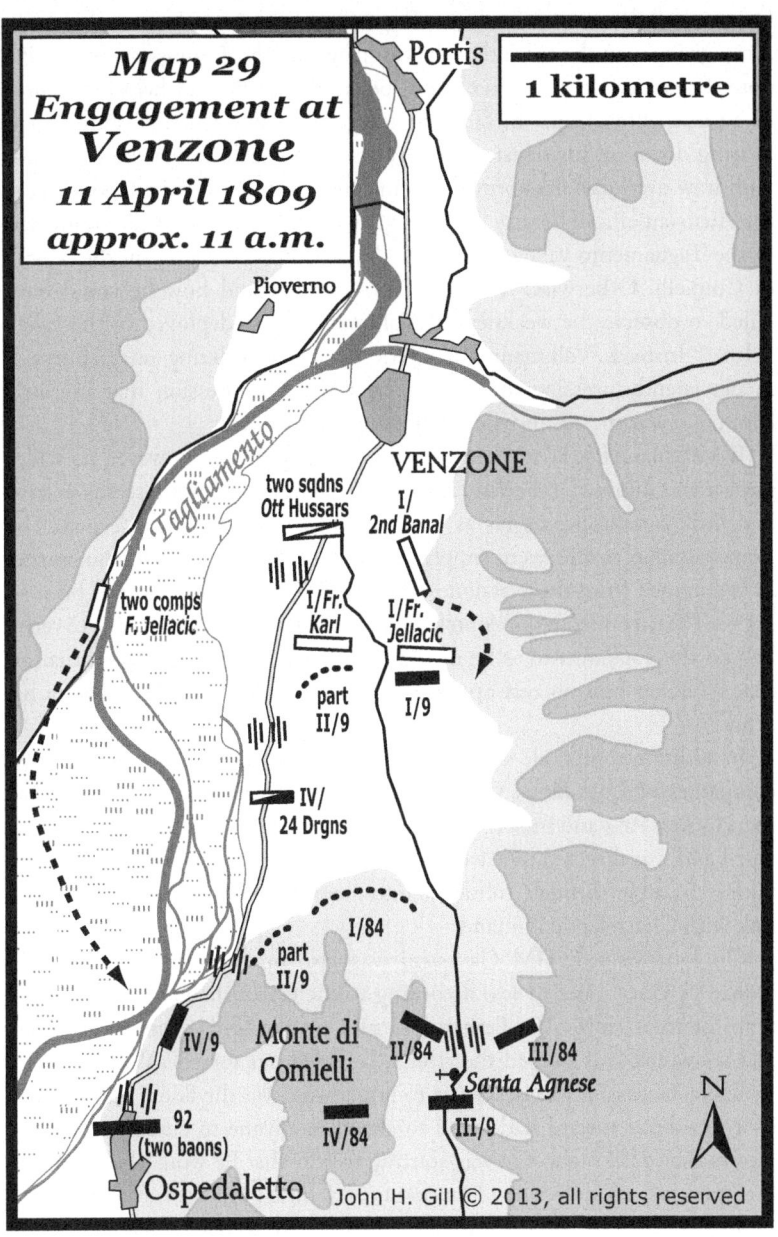

Map 29
Engagement at
Venzone
11 April 1809
approx. 11 a.m.

1 kilometre

Portis

Pioverno

Tagliamento

VENZONE

two sqdns
Ott Hussars

I/
2nd Banal

two comps
F. Jellacic

I/Fr.
Karl

I/Fr.
Jellacic

part
II/9

I/9

IV/
24 Drgns

I/84

part
II/9

IV/9

Monte di
Comielli

II/84

III/84

Santa Agnese

IV/84

III/9

92
(two baons)

Ospedaletto

N

had approximately 7,500 on the field after deducting the battalions at Osoppo) all day for minimal loss. Reports of his success buoyed the entire army, giving men the sense that the campaign was beginning on a promising note. Broussier, on the other hand, believed that he had held off a force of 24,000 elite troops. In fact, the image of a powerful Habsburg corps bearing down on his division led Broussier to conclude that he could not withdraw until darkness provided him some cover. It is entirely possible, as the Austrian official history suggests, that the French commander remained in the Tagliamento valley during the day and never set foot on the Monte di Comielli. Otherwise, it is difficult to understand how he could have failed to observe the weakness of Volkmann's force deployed in the valley below.[38] Instead, Volkmann's energetic daring—bordering on rashness—in persistently pressing the French created the impression that his little command was the advance guard of a much larger host.

If Volkmann's feint succeeded in deceiving Broussier, however, its wider impact was minimal. Likewise, Zuccheri's elaborate deception seems to have had little significance as far as French deployments were concerned. The Franco-Italian troops were simply too scattered to ambush Johann's army as it emerged from the Natsione valley even if Volkmann had not been so active. The threat from the Pontebba valley did not persuade Eugene to retire behind the Tagliamento as he now did, rather it was his strategic situation that truly left him no real option except to withdraw and concentrate his army.

In addition to his role in trying to mislead the French, Zuccheri led two companies of I/*1st Banal* Grenz from Mauthen through thick snow over the Plöcken Pass and into Italy. He reported to Volkmann at Venzone on 11 April and was directed to leave one of his companies with Volkmann while taking the other through Tolmezzo into the upper Piave valley to establish a link with Chasteler's command.

On Johann's left, GM Gavassini was also on the move, crossing the Isonzo at Görz more or less according to the established timetable on the night of 10/11 April. The French had torn up the bridge, and recent rains and snowmelt had swelled the river to a dangerous torrent. With no fords available, Gavassini was desperate to find a way over the flood, but his offer of a 100-ducat reward had failed to convince anyone to enter the swirling waters that dark night. He was starting to fear that he would be unable to maintain his schedule when Hauptmann Heinrich Graf von Faverge of II/*Franz Karl* managed to organise fifty volunteers who made their way across the river through a combination of swimming and wading. Though two men drowned in the crossing, Faverge and his sodden volunteers captured the French pickets on the far bank and held off local counter-attacks long enough for repair work to begin on the bridge. Gavassini was thus able to get his main body across the Isonzo during the morning and began pushing cautiously west. On his left two squadrons of *Frimont* Hussars, supported by two companies of 2nd Triest Landwehr, captured Gradiska, while two companies advanced to San Martino on his right. At the cost of seven dead and wounded, Gavassini had brought his division across the river as planned and collected seventy prisoners in the process.

Johann and the men of the principal Austrian force, cold and wet from the mountain bivouacs they had endured for the preceding several days, made their entry into Italy on the morning of 11 April against very light resistance. Leading troops entered Cividale around midday and by early afternoon VIII Corps was settling itself into quarters in and around the town, while IX Corps found shelter in San Pietro and neighbouring villages. Johann felt that he could ask no more of the wet, weary, and bedraggled men, some of whom had been up and moving since shortly after midnight, and granted them a most welcome respite.[39]

Fortunately for the French, Eugene was in Udine when the war opened, and his adventitious proximity to the border allowed a rapid and co-ordinated response to Johann's advance. He immediately ordered Broussier's and Seras's exposed divisions to withdraw behind the Tagliamento and sent messengers galloping off to the west with orders for the rest of the army. Grenier, Barbou, Severoli, Lamarque, 2nd Dragoon Division (GD Charles Joseph Pully), the light cavalry, and the Italian Guard were to march for the Tagliamento at once, while Baraguey d'Hilliers remained behind to guard the approaches from the Tyrol with the 2nd Italian and 1st Dragoon Divisions.[40]

The rapid implementation of Eugene's withdrawal orders to Broussier and Seras meant that the Austrians found Udine empty when they advanced again on 12 April. The VIII Corps occupied the city, while IX Corps moved to Cividale, Gavassini entered Cormons, and Volkmann moved to Gemona. The 13th brought another day of cautious probing by Johann's command. Ninth Corps and most of Gavassini's regulars (*Reisky* No. 13, II/*Franz Karl*, and six squadrons of *Frimont* Hussars) joined VIII Corps in Udine, but three and one-half Landwehr battalions, four companies of 3rd Garrison Battalion, half of a cavalry battery, and the remaining two squadrons of *Frimont* were left behind to blockade Palmanova under Oberst Franz Freiherr von Tomassich.[41] On the right, Volkmann masked Osoppo with I/*Franz Karl* and some Grenzer, while 1st Görz Landwehr occupied Gradiska on the left and Oberst Andreas von Gyurkovics of *Franz Karl* led a detachment to Castions to shield the army's southern flank.[42] As these moves were taking place in the rear, Volkmann's command, reinforced by two squadrons of *Hohenzollern* Chevaulegers, skirmished with IV/9th Ligne east of the Tagliamento near Dignano.

Further south, FML Johann Freiherr Frimont led a substantial advance guard of five battalions, eight squadrons, and one and one-half batteries towards the river at Codriopo.[43] His men skirmished with French outposts and with a probing force (two battalions, eight squadrons) led by Sahuc, but the French, having ascertained that the Austrians were present in large numbers, withdrew and left Codriopo in Habsburg hands. None of the advance guard scuffles on 13 April had been significant, but the arrival of the Austrians on the Tagliamento in strength determined Eugene's next steps. Though loath to begin the campaign with a retreat, he could not consider tackling Johann until substantially more of his own army was on hand; he sensibly ordered a withdrawal to positions on the Livenza. By the afternoon of 14 April, the French were in place east of the river, some of them having covered thirty kilometres during a difficult night march in driving rain. Johann largely lost touch with the French during the day and only brought his main body as far as Codriopo on the east bank of the Tagliamento. Scouts poked forward across the river, but found little. Gyurkovics reached the river at Latsiana on the Habsburg left and Volkmann's command was across at Spilimbergo on the right. Farther to the right, Hauptmann Zuccheri, now with only one company of *Banal* Grenzer, reached Pieve di Cadore and made contact with the two communications detachments Chasteler had sent south from Toblach (Lodron and la Notte).

15–16 APRIL: TWO AUSTRIAN VICTORIES—
PORDENONE AND SACILE

Viceroy Eugene, considering his situation on 14 April, was actively looking for an opportunity to turn on Johann. His retreat had been undisturbed and Austrian movements seemed extremely torpid, but he expected an attack on 16 April and wanted to anticipate this with an offensive of his own. Two factors influenced his thinking. First, he feared an imperial rebuke for beginning the campaign with a retreat; second, he was very worried about his northern flank, as reporting from the Tyrol indicated that Chasteler had reached Bruneck with 20,000 men. He thus hoped to 'completely defeat' Johann so that he could reinforce Baraguey d' Hilliers to counter the threat from Chasteler. Five of his divisions were now on hand on the Livenza along with Sahuc's light cavalry.[44] The first echelon comprised Broussier on the left at Polcenigo, Grenier (reinforced by IV/11th Ligne) at Sacile in the centre, and Seras on the right at Brugnera with 6th Chasseurs. Barbou (twelve battalions) was four kilometres west of Sacile and Severoli had arrived behind Brugnera to form a second echelon.[45] The two battalions of 79th Ligne and two 3-pounders would guard the extreme left at Santissima, while Severoli sent a company of voltigeurs and twenty-five chasseurs to destroy the bridges at Motta and Portobuffole on the far right. Eugene posted GD Sahuc with an advance guard (6th Hussars, 8th Chasseurs, three battalions of 35th Ligne, four guns) at Pordenone, some twelve kilometres (at least three hours' march) ahead of the main position. As an afterthought, he placed GB Joseph Pagès at Fontanafredda with 1st Ligne and 25th Chasseurs to support Sahuc, but Pagès was neither strong enough nor close enough to offer effective assistance should Sahuc come under heavy pressure on the vast plain where Johann's numerous cavalry would enjoy significant advantages. As for his other forces, Eugene believed, or hoped, that Lamarque and Pully would arrive in time to participate in the coming battle, but he was concerned about the Habsburg superiority in cavalry and had therefore ordered GB François Guérin d'Etoquigny to leave 7th Dragoons with Baraguey d'Hilliers and march with the other two regiments of 2nd Dragoon Division to join the army. 'We expect to see the enemy tomorrow,' wrote trumpeter Jacques Chevillet of the 8th Chasseurs.[46]

15 April: Pordenone

Sahuc was to conduct an active reconnaissance on the morning of 15 April to locate the enemy army, but Johann moved first.[47] The Habsburg commander had learned that the French held a position at Pordenone and he ordered Frimont forward in hopes of inflicting a defeat on what Austrian patrols described as a weak rear guard 'of at most two to three hundred men'.[48] To this end, Frimont organised three columns of attack with his command: two of these would slide to the north to outflank Pordenone and cut off Sahuc's retreat, while the third advanced directly on the town.[49] As Frimont executed this attack, Johann would personally lead the bulk of his cavalry to Roveredo and reconnoitre towards the Livenza. FML Albert Gyulai would bring the rest of VIII Corps along the highway through Cordenons, followed by his brother, Ignaz, with IX Corps. Volkmann was to occupy San Quirino on the right and Gyurkovics would move to Motta.[50] A miserable march through the chill, rain-soaked night brought the lead Austrian elements to Cordenons at 9 a.m. Shaking off the effects of the drenching downpour and near-sleepless night, Johann headed for Roveredo with GM Ignaz Freiherr Splenyi's brigade of hussars (ten squadrons), while GM Ferdinand von Hager moved on San Quirino with his two dragoon regiments and Frimont prepared to attack Pordenone. Frimont hoped that his two flanking columns would be in position before his advance was discovered, but the group pushing directly towards Pordenone from Cordenons (GM Josef von Wetzl with two battalions) encountered a company of 35th Ligne at Torre around 10 a.m. and opened the engagement. Johann, alerted by the musketry, rode towards Torre and saw at once that the French force was much stronger than his lackadaisical scouts had indicated. He immediately sent Oberst Laval Graf Nugent, his chief of staff, to recall Splenyi's hussars and lead them to Talponedo in hopes of cutting off Sahuc's escape.

By this hour, the French were already moving. Sahuc had kept his men on alert all night and a vigilant patrol had reported Volkmann's advance on San Quirino sometime shortly after dawn. The news of an Austrian advance in the north-east forced Eugene to bring his entire command east of the Livenza in order to preserve the offensive he hoped to launch as soon as Lamarque and the dragoons arrived from the rear.[51] He could not afford to have his army straddling the Livenza, so he issued new orders sending Broussier to Vigonovo, Grenier to Fontanafredda, and Seras to Tamai; Barbou was to follow Grenier and Severoli would cross the river behind Seras. This lone report also drew Sahuc's attention to the north when the real danger loomed from the east. French outposts and patrols towards Cordenons apparently neglected their duty for they reported nothing of Frimont's approach. Sahuc was thus taken unawares when Wetzl's men began skirmishing with the company at Torre, but the rest of his command was soon engaged as well.

Sahuc had deployed 35th Ligne with two battalions in front of Pordenone and one to the rear; he had placed 6th Hussars north of the town with 8th Chasseurs on their left towards Rorai Grande.[52] Amazingly, however, he had left the main road uncovered, so Frimont had reached a point due north of Pordenone unnoticed when the firing at Torre became audible. As Frimont advanced, the scope of the enemy manoeuvre became clear to the

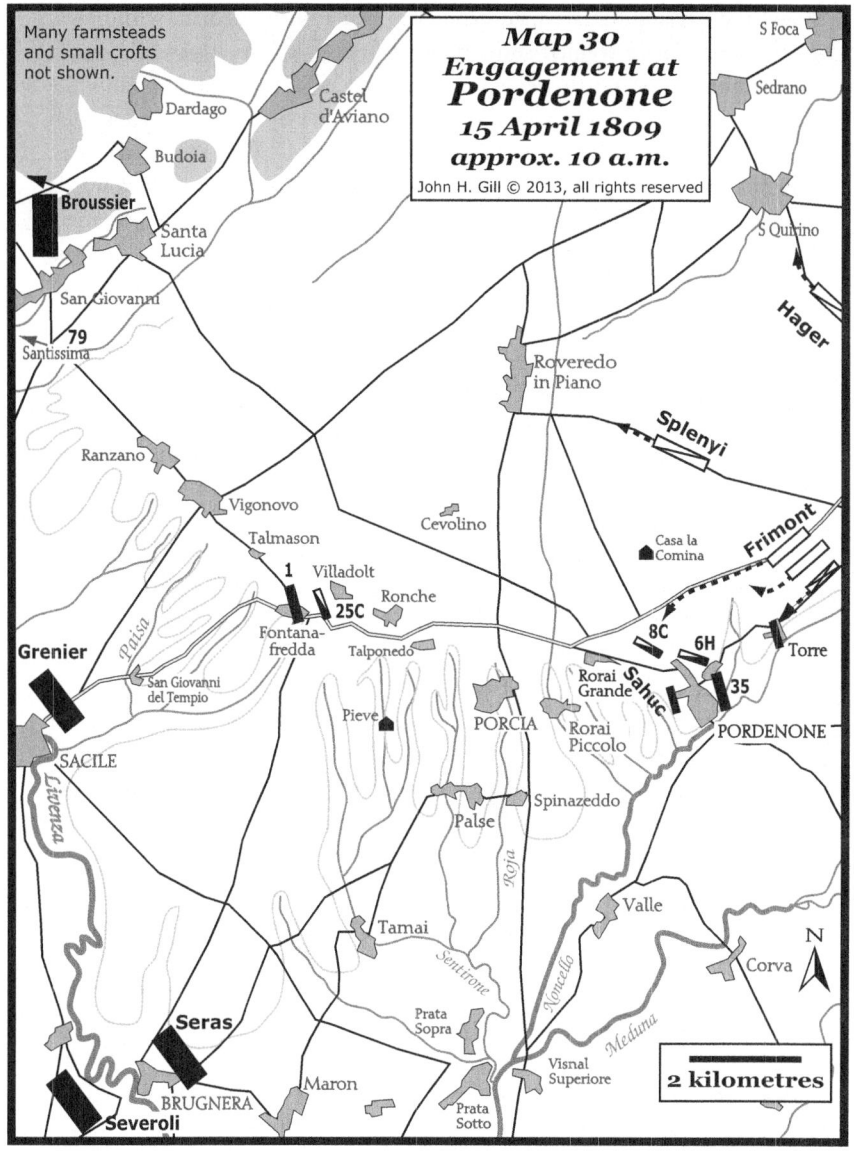

Many farmsteads and small crofts not shown.

**Map 30
Engagement at
Pordenone
15 April 1809
approx. 10 a.m.**

French. Although Frimont had only the slightest numerical advantage in troops at hand (4,610 Austrian to 4,160 French), the Austrian advance along the highway threatened to cut off the French, rendering Sahuc's situation grave and causing the alarmed general to order an immediate withdrawal to the west. There seemed some hope at first. The 35th apparently exited Pordenone to the north-west, attempting to reach the main road, while the French light horsemen easily repelled attacks by two squadrons each of *Ott* Hussars and *Hohenzollern* Chevaulegers. The 8th Chasseurs, however, perhaps misunderstanding the withdrawal order, rode off towards Fontanafredda after their brief success, reducing Sahuc's force by 900 men. Worse, the Austrian cavalry charges had slowed the French, granting time for Splenyi's hussars to join the fight from near Roveredo. The arrival of these ten squadrons, responding to the urgent order from Johann, brought Austrian numbers to 5,800 against 3,190 French. Frimont compounded the enemy's desperation by unlimbering a cavalry battery on the highway north-west of Rorai Grande to pummel the helpless French foot soldiers.

With no hope for succour from their distant countrymen, the situation for Sahuc's troops was hopeless. The harried general sent one battalion with two squadrons of hussars to chase off the whitecoats near Rorai Grande, but Austrian light horse drove the infantry back into the village with a loss of 300 prisoners. The two French squadrons also fared ill. Attacked and sliced up by the *Erzherzog Josef* Hussars, their shattered remnants fled in disorder to the protection of the 8th Chasseurs, 'covered in blood, with sabre cuts on their bodies, their arms, etc'.[53] Two of the French guns were lost around this time, and the defenders of Rorai Grande, encircled by Habsburg foot and horse, succumbed to an overwhelming assault. Sahuc endeavoured to gain space for withdrawal by launching his two remaining squadrons at Frimont's men, but the attack was quickly repulsed and his detachment's fate was sealed. Attempting to gain the temporary safety of Rorai Piccolo, Colonel Joseph Breissand of the 35th found that Grenzer had already reached the hamlet. This was Wetzl's battalion of *1st Banal* that had slipped south of Pordenone to come up behind the French. Other Habsburg troops—I/*Franz Jellacic*, parts of *Franz Karl*, two companies of *2nd Banal*, and the bulk of the cavalry—closed in to complete the circle around the doomed but defiant 35th. Sahuc and his hussars broke through the ring of steel in a desperate charge, but Breissand could not escape. Bleeding from two wounds, he formed his two battalions into a sort of square and held out for a time, but the rain rendered many muskets useless and he soon had no choice but surrender. This proved difficult as enraged Grenzer and hussars fell upon the disarmed French and had to be deterred from further destruction by the threats and blows of their officers. Johann, horrified and ashamed, chastised the army in an order issued later that day: 'As much as I otherwise see the day's action crowned with the happiest success, I cannot repress the observation that it displeases me to note how much some individual persons neglected the humane treatment of prisoners of war.' The archduke chivalrously returned Breissand's sword.[54]

It was now approximately noon; the brief fight had lasted but two hours. While their comrades fell on Breissand's men, two companies of 1st *Banal* had pushed beyond Porcia. These Grenzer, supported by two companies from *Franz Karl*, skirmished with I/1st Ligne that Grenier had advanced along the highway from Fontanafredda. The firing continued through the afternoon and became serious enough that 1st Ligne's Colonel Jean St Martin reinforced his line with his 2nd Battalion around 4 p.m. By the end of the day the regiment had lost more than fifty men.[55] Other than this bloody sparring, however, the muddy battlefield soon fell silent as the weary men of both sides, most of whom had had little food and less sleep the preceding night, sought some rest and refreshment in the rainy afternoon. The short combat cost the French 500 dead and wounded (not including those of 1st Ligne), more than 2,000 prisoners, at least two guns, and one precious eagle.[56] The 35th Ligne was temporarily wrecked and the 6th Hussars badly damaged.[57] Austrian losses amounted to only some 250 (many who had been captured were freed as the battle evolved). Frimont had conducted himself with great skill and Johann had reacted to the unexpected with promptness and aplomb. On the French side, blame for the disaster lay partly with Eugene for posting Sahuc so far from support and partly with Sahuc for neglecting to ensure vigorous patrolling.[58] It was an ominous prologue to the coming battle.

16 April: Sacile, the French Advance (8 to 10 a.m.)

Misperceptions in both camps concerning the rear guard action on the 15th led to a full-scale battle the following day. For his part, Johann assumed the French were retreating and thus ordered a rest day for his weary army. Habsburg headquarters came to this odd conclusion because Volkmann, ordered to advance on Vigonovo, came under fire from Broussier's cannon as he approached the village late on 15 April. Austrian headquarters somehow interpreted these shots as a French withdrawal signal.[59] Eugene, on the other hand, believed that retreat across the Livenza was impossible because Johann was 'commencing to press us closely'.[60] In this he was partly misled by a serendipitous Austrian deception. Volkmann, anxious at being isolated on the Austrian right and badly outnumbered, had his men light a large number of bivouac fires during the night to convince the French that he was stronger than he really was. The trick worked. Eugene concluded that the entire Austrian army was close at hand and that withdrawal over the river would be risky and possibly very costly.[61] Furthermore, Eugene's exaggerated estimate of Chasteler's force in the Tyrol left a gnawing worry in his mind and he may have wanted to inflict a quick defeat on Johann before Chasteler could move down from the north. There were also psychological facets to the viceroy's thinking. He not only disliked 'the idea of abandoning two departments of Your Majesty's kingdom without a fight' and feared Napoleon's censure for retreating too far, but he likely also hoped for a victory to erase the embarrassing stain of Pordenone.[62]

With these considerations in mind, the two leaders arrayed their forces. Johann, expecting a day of recuperation, left Frimont around Porcia with the advance guard and Volkmann west of Roveredo supported by the *Savoy* Dragoons.[63] Eighteen light cavalry squadrons under Oberst Wilhelm von Fulda and GM Splenyi were arrayed between Pordenone and Porcia to back up Frimont.[64] Eighth Corps encamped north-west of Pordenone and IX Corps was stacked up along the main road back towards Cordenons. Eugene had Seras and Severoli at Brugnera and Broussier near Vigonovo with the rest of the army between Fontanafredda and Sacile; concerned for his northern flank, he left the two-battalion detachment at Santissima. The two armies were very similar in total numbers: 40,000 Austrians opposed to 41,900 French and Italians. The Austrians should have enjoyed a considerable advantage in artillery—eighty-three pieces against sixty French—but, for unknown reasons, some twenty of Johann's guns never reached the battlefield. On the other hand, Eugene was painfully cognizant of the Austrian superiority in cavalry, being able to counter Johann's 4,440 horsemen with only 2,800 of his own. Everyone was wet and weary, but the French were famished as well because the army's movements had disrupted food distribution. A hungrily incredulous soldier of the 102nd spoke for many: 'Lack of bread in Italy at the start of a campaign, it was inconceivable!'[65]

Thanks to Volkmann's campfires, Eugene made his dispositions under the false assumption that the bulk of the Austrian force was posted west of Roveredo. He thus planned an attack that would strike the presumed left flank of this position at Porcia, forcing the Austrians away from the post road and leaving Johann little choice but to retire behind the Tagliamento. Seras, commanding Severoli's division and 6th Chasseurs as well as his own division, would launch the main attack on Porcia from the south-west, with Grenier advancing from the west as the battle ripened. All three divisions would then press for Roveredo and Pordenone with Barbou (eight battalions) and Sahuc following in reserve. The French left, comprised of Broussier and 25th Chasseurs, was weak and in the air, but Eugene entertained illusory hopes

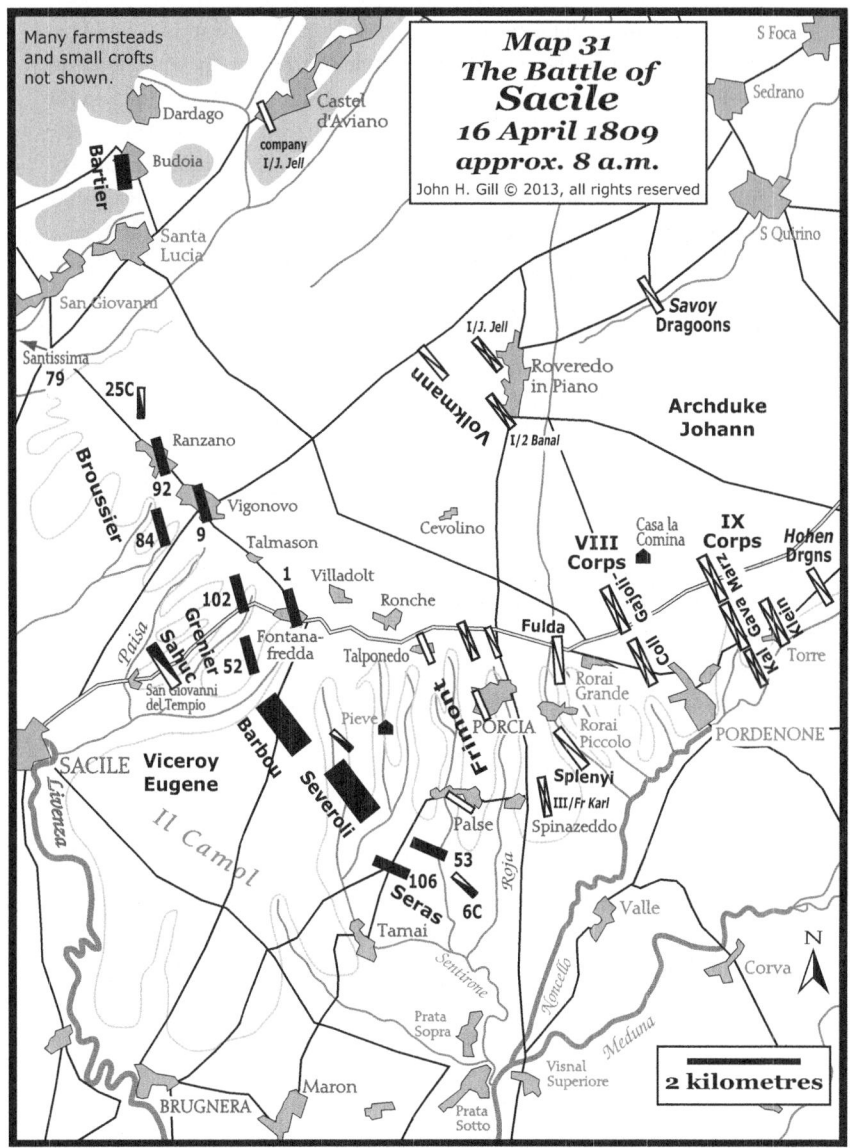

Many farmsteads and small crofts not shown.

Map 31
The Battle of
Sacile
16 April 1809
approx. 8 a.m.

that Lamarque (5,000 infantry, ten guns) and Pully (2,300 dragoons) would arrive in time to reinforce this flank. On the far left, Adjutant-Commandant Jean Etienne Bartier de Saint-Hilaire led a force of four battalions (from Barbou) against Castel d'Aviano.[66] Eugene selected the southern approach for the main attack because the broken terrain on this side of the battlefield—cut up by ravines, irrigation ditches, and marshy lowlands—could be expected to favour the dispersed fighting style of the French, while Johann's superiority in cavalry would give the Austrians a significant advantage in the flat meadowlands north of the highway. However, this difficult ground also impeded French movement and constricted deployment, while the marshy 'Il Camola' south-east of Sacile would preclude mutual support between the right and centre columns until they mounted the plateau and took Porcia.

The sun rose over a bright spring landscape on the morning of 16 April, a welcome change from the preceding days of steady, chilling rain. It was a Sunday, and Johann was dutifully attending the morning service in Pordenone when a courier arrived around 8 a.m. to tell him that Frimont's advance guard was under attack west of Porcia.

The report Johann received and the firing he soon heard were the result of Seras's attack on Palse and Porcia. Seras seems to have moved with considerable formality and deliberation in assembling his two divisions around Tamai. He thus compounded the delays imposed by the irregular terrain and did not begin his advance until 8 a.m., Severoli on the left and the French on the right with 6th Chasseurs protecting the right flank. Contending with the broken ground, the lead regiment, 53rd Ligne, finally charged Palse at 9 a.m. and swiftly evicted the Austrian defenders (two companies). GB Louis Gareau fell, badly wounded in the attack. Seras, however, rather than directing the regiment towards Spinazzedo to outflank Frimont and to make room for Severoli to assault Porcia, turned the 53rd north and left Severoli to shift his young conscripts among the constricting hills and dales. He thereby negated the enormous French advantage in numbers (roughly 12,000 to 4,000) and forced his subordinates to attack on narrow fronts in isolated packets.[67] The battle quickly evolved into two separate fights: first, an extended engagement along the little Roja stream south of Porcia as 53rd Ligne found itself forced to detach strong elements against the Austrians in Spinazzedo and east of the watercourse, and second, the struggle for Porcia itself. While neither side could gain and maintain an advantage along the Roja, the powerful Franco-Italian force quickly mastered Porcia.

Their success was short lived, as Frimont counter-attacked with four companies of Grenzer and sent Fulda's cavalry brigade north-west of the town with a cavalry battery. The Habsburg gunners were soon pouring shot into Severoli's ranks, halting and disordering the inexperienced troops, and a spirited charge by Fulda's troopers sent the Italians flying. Severoli was wounded and his fleeing division carried away the men of the 53rd in front of Porcia as well.[68] Seras brought up 106th Ligne to restore his line and threw his entire command forward as soon as some sort of order had been established. At the same time, Eugene, noticing the confusion on Seras's front, sent one of his senior staff officers, GB Jean Joseph Augustin Sorbier (younger brother of his artillery chief, GD Jean Barthlèmot Sorbier), with three of Barbou's battalions (two of 5th Ligne, one of 23rd) to support the attack on Porcia. This renewed drive gained Eugene Porcia, but Frimont's determined Austrians set themselves in a new defensive position on a low hill just east of the town and stymied French attempts to push further. Efforts by parts of 53rd Ligne to cross the Roja were similarly unsuccessful. It was now between 10 and 11 a.m. Eugene had won Porcia, the key 'tactical point' on the battlefield, but he had invested one-third of his army to take the town, his hold on it was uncertain, Frimont's advance guard was still a viable fighting force, and the bulk of the Austrian army remained uncommitted. That was about to change, as the battle entered a new phase.

Sacile: Battle in the Balance (10 a.m. to 1 p.m.)

Johann's initial reaction to the French offensive was cautious. Unwilling to believe that Eugene would make a major advance over the rough terrain south of the post road, the archduke decided that the assault on Porcia was a demonstration and that the main French attack would come in the open fields to the north. He thus ordered VIII Corps to deploy in front of Pordenone with its two infantry brigades, and posted IX Corps near Casa la Comina to extend his right, but wisely kept the bulk of his army in hand and did not counter-attack. These moves, however, did little to succour the hard-pressed advance guard. Fortunately for Frimont, FML Albert Gyulai responded to an urgent plea by sending GM Hieronymus Graf Colloredo-Mansfeld forward with St Julien Infantry No. 61. The arrival of this regiment not only provided relief to the exhausted Habsburg defenders along the Roja, it also allowed Frimont to retake Porcia, driving out the French with a vigorous thrust.

Eugene's battle plan was now a shambles. The capture of Porcia should have opened the way for an advance on Pordenone, but he found himself forced to commit his centre simply to secure the former town. Grenier therefore received instructions to support the attack on Porcia and pressed forward along the highway, with GB François Teste and three battalions of 1st Ligne in the lead. Halted and disordered by the unyielding Austrian resistance, Teste had to commit two more battalions (I/1st and I/52nd) to revive the attack. Thus reinforced, the 1st Ligne drove some Grenzer out of Talponedo and penetrated into the open area north of Porcia, so stretching Frimont's defences that Seras could seize the town once again. This advance opened a bitter three-hour contest for Porcia, during which the town changed hands repeatedly in intense house-to-house, fence-to-fence fighting. Albert Gyulai threw *Strassaldo* Infantry No. 27 into the fight and Frimont, bolstered by the loan of the *Ottocac* Grenzer from IX Corps, skilfully employed his cavalry and artillery north of Porcia to halt Teste's push.[69] Grenier responded by adding the rest of 52nd Ligne on Teste's left, but his division's advance had stalled completely and the 52nd had to bend its left flank back at a right angle to fend off Frimont's active horsemen. While the struggle for the town raged, cavalrymen from both armies distinguished themselves on the immediate flanks. Splenyi's troopers, deployed behind the firing line, found few opportunities, but Fulda's men aggressively tackled the French, and Grenier's squadron of *Napoleon* Dragoons earned plaudits for its performance, including two charges into Porcia. Austrian gunners also played a key role in blunting the French assault and punishing Grenier's men. Léon Michel Routier of the 102nd watched three entire files obliterated by three consecutive Austrian shots as the enemy's artillery 'ravaged our ranks' with a 'deluge of murderous projectiles.' 'I do not believe I ever found myself in the midst of more lively fire,' he recalled.[70]

In the meantime, more French troops had arrived. Eugene, counting on Lamarque and Pully, ignored the potential danger to his line of retreat to Sacile and ordered Broussier towards Fontanafredda, where he arrived at approximately midday. Almost the entire French army was thus concentrated in the space between Palse and Talmason. Its left flank was in the air, and only Broussier, Barbou (reduced to five battalions), Sahuc, and five of Grenier's battalions remained uncommitted.

Sacile: The Austrian Advance (1 to 5 p.m.)

As the action around Porcia grew in intensity, gradually absorbing most of Eugene's army, Oberstleutnant Volkmann was anxiously observing the

French left flank. Between 10 and 11 a.m., however, he noted that Broussier's division was marching off towards the centre of the battlefield and hastened to report this change to Johann. This news and Grenier's appearance at Porcia convinced Johann and his staff that Eugene's main effort was indeed focused along the post road. The archduke therefore ordered GM Anton von Gajoli's brigade of VIII Corps to join with Volkmann and advance on Vigonovo in order to operate against the French left and rear. Gajoli reached Volkmann around noon and, on learning that the French had departed Vigonovo, decided on his own to threaten the enemy's left by deploying opposite Ronche, Villadolt, and Talmason. With the *Savoy* Dragoons in reserve, he arrayed the rest of his and Volkmann's troops in a long thin line to make an imposing display. Eugene quickly took measures to counter this danger, sending one of Barbou's battalions to Fontanafredda, occupying Ronche and Villadolt with a battalion each of 102nd Ligne from Grenier, and placing Broussier's 84th Ligne north of Talmason with the lone French dragoon squadron.

As reports from Gajoli clarified the situation on the northern flank, Johann saw an opportunity. He rode to IX Corps where he directed FML Ignaz Gyulai to move to Gajoli's right flank and advance through Vigonovo 'to effect an offensive against the enemy's communications, the road to Sacile', while GM Vitalis von Kleinmayrn's brigade remained near Pordenone as army reserve.[71] At the same time, between 1 and 2 p.m., Johann ordered Gajoli to press the French flank while IX Corps marched behind him to assume its position on his right. Gajoli moved slowly—probably wanting to assure himself that IX Corps was close enough to offer support—so his first assault did not occur until 3 p.m. This attack was too weak (one battalion each against Ronche and Villadolt) and the French repelled it easily with well-delivered musketry, Sahuc pursuing the retreating Austrians aggressively until chased off by Habsburg horse.[72] Gajoli's movement, however, sufficed to prevent Broussier from reinforcing Grenier. Ordered to Porcia at 3 p.m., Broussier almost at once found himself forced to swing his two remaining regiments to the left to support the threatened French flank. As he was doing so, Gajoli attacked again, this time with his entire force and this time successfully. After stubborn resistance, brutal close-quarters combat, and a failed counter-attack by IV/11th Ligne, Ronche and Villadolt fell between 4 and 5 p.m. Eugene's situation was now deteriorating rapidly: heavy Austrian columns threatened his left, Grenier's position in the centre was untenable with the loss of Ronche, the Austrians had crossed the Roja and occupied Palse on his right, and the only remaining reserves were Barbou's four battalions. The battle was lost and the viceroy ordered a general withdrawal.

Sacile: French Disaster (5 to 9 p.m.)

The marshy ground forced Eugene to divide his retreating army into two groups: Seras and Severoli were to cross the Livenza at Brugnera, while the remaining troops, protected by Broussier and Sahuc, fell back on Sacile. Heavy Austrian pressure, however, quickly disrupted this plan. Grenier, the most vulnerable, withdrew first. The 1st and 52nd Ligne decamped, 'not without some disorder' according to the division's report, behind the protection of the 102nd and aggressive Franco-Italian cavalry action. GB Louis Abbé and the 102nd, on the other hand, found themselves outflanked on all sides' and had to retire 'with great haste' to Brugnera.[73] Advancing Austrians threatened the French and Italians in front of Porcia as well. Barbou's remaining four battalions suffered heavily in the severe fighting as they intervened to grant the retreating units some breathing room, and Oberst Fulda was killed leading a charge against Barbou's squares. Much of the withdrawal on the right, however, was conducted by echelons in fairly good order. Faced with some intact units and difficult terrain, the exhausted whitecoats of VIII Corps soon abandoned their pursuit, allowing the French right wing to cross the Livenza undisturbed at 8 p.m. Similarly, Bartier's small command retired without incident after having skirmished feebly with the lone company of *Johann Jellacic* in Castel d'Aviano during the day. The story at Sacile was completely different. With great courage and skill, Broussier's infantry and the weary Franco-Italian horsemen made their way slowly back along the post road towards the river, fending off repeated Austrian cavalry charges but suffering heavily from the fire of twenty-two guns that were advancing 'in a veritable artillery attack'.[74] Darkness was closing in as Broussier's squares coolly repulsed a final charge by FML Christian Freiherr Wolfskeel von Reichenberg and the two Habsburg dragoon regiments between Fontanafredda and San Giovanni around 7 p.m. Similarly, Broussier's 92nd Ligne unleashed a terrible volley on Gajoli's lead battalion as the French were crossing the Paisa. The withdrawal then proceeded without interruption.[75]

Unfortunately for Eugene and his army, these abortive charges were not the last Austrian efforts on 16 April. Ninth Corps had reached its assigned position in the fields west of Roveredo around 3 p.m., but did nothing as the battle with Broussier and Grenier reached its climax. Not until 5 p.m. did FML Ignaz Gyulai direct any of his men to advance. Even then, he risked only one of his three brigades, GM Franz von Marziani's, and Johann, who subsequently approved the order, did not deign to increase the force. Marziani was to occupy Vigonovo and 'if possible . . . advance as close as feasible to Sacile and attempt to attack the place', but he moved with ponderous deliberation, halting three times for unknown reasons and depositing half of his command (*Allvintzi* No. 19) in Vigonovo at his corps commander's direction.[76] As they probed gently into the dark, most of Marziani's *Ogulin* Grenzer drifted south towards San Giovanni and ended up skirmishing with 84th Ligne as it retired. Only Oberst Ignaz Freiherr Csivich with four Grenz companies and a battery remained on the road connecting Vigonovo with Sacile. Nonetheless, these sufficed to turn the French withdrawal into a rout.

Confusion reigned in Sacile even before the arrival of the Austrians as horses, wagons, guns, terrified administrative personnel, and crowds of discouraged soldiers attempted to negotiate the narrow streets in the darkness and make their way across the lone bridge. When Oberst Csivich fired a few rounds into the town around 9 p.m. and ordered his four companies to attack, the result was unimaginable chaos. Soldiers who had fought all day with incredible fortitude, now fell prey to wild panic. 'The retreat was a free-for-all' in the words of a cavalry trooper, and infantryman Pierre Robinaux of IV/11th Ligne witnessed the 'great disorder' as discipline dissolved: 'cavalry, artillery, infantry found themselves all pell-mell without ever being able to rally . . . What a painful day!'[77] 'The disorder was total,' wrote Sous-Lieutenant Jean-Claude Barat of the 52nd. 'We followed the flood, receiving the enemy's bullets and balls without replying.'[78] Csivich's bold Grenzer exploited the collapse, pressing all the way to the bridge and taking hundreds of prisoners as the French threw down their weapons and abandoned their vehicles in attempts to escape. When the *Allvintzi* Infantry appeared (having been relieved in Vigonovo by *Reisky*), the regiment was able to capture large groups of French endeavouring to slip away to Brugnera. In addition to a large haul of prisoners and military material, Marziani's men freed numerous Austrians who had been captured earlier in the battle. Perhaps most important, the Austrians seized the stone bridge, effectively precluding a defence of the Livenza and ensuring that the French retreat would continue to at least the Piave. 'Fortunately for us', recalled Sergeant Major Jean-Louis Lacorde of the 84th, 'night had arrived.'[79]

It had been a disastrous day for Eugene and the Army of Italy. French sources give the viceroy's losses in dead and wounded on 16 April as 3,000 with an additional 3,500 captured, so that Eugene's casualties for the two days' fighting approached 10,000—nearly one-quarter of the forces on hand on the Livenza—when those of 15 April are included.[80] Among the wounded were Severoli, Gareau, Teste, and GB Jacques Dutruy; the brave Colonel St Martin of 1st Ligne took three sabre cuts and fell into Austrian hands during the retreat, while GB Pagès was wounded and captured in the chaos of Sacile. In addition, the Austrians took at least fifteen guns and reported retrieving 14,000 muskets from the battlefield. The army, particularly the units that escaped through Sacile, was so disorganised 'that it was not possible to even think of rallying'. Some of the generals were disgusted with their inexperienced commander's performance, while the soldiers were dispirited and humiliated.[81] Eugene courageously reported to his step-father that he had lost the battle and that 'our troops quit the field of battle in the greatest disorder' as he sought to reverse his own discouragement.[82] Johann's casualties were not light: 2,838 killed and wounded (including the talented GM von Wetzl) with another 1,268 captured or missing. Losses were concentrated in the few regiments that fought around Porcia: *Johann Jellacic* (897), *Strassaldo* (829), and *St Julien* (716) alone making up more than half of the total Habsburg casualties. Nonetheless, there was no disguising the magnitude of the French defeat.

Although his decision to fight was understandable given the misconceptions under which he laboured, Eugene erred badly in standing east of the Livenza in 'one of the worst positions in Italy'.[83] Rather than assuring himself of his reinforcements, he had attacked with an unfordable river at his back over a field that divided his army into two mutually unsupportable channels of advance. He demonstrated the bravery and coolness under fire that became a personal trademark, but he allowed Porcia to act as a magnet, drawing almost his entire army into a struggle with a fraction of the Austrian host. He seems to have forgotten Bartier and put his left in great peril by shifting Broussier to the centre. He also failed to build any additional bridges over the swollen Livenza and committed an 'unpardonable fault' by failing to provide any protection whatsoever for the crucial river-crossing sites.[84] A battalion and a pair of guns would probably have held off Csivich's Grenzer to permit a more orderly withdrawal. Overall, sneered one of his detractors, 'it was truly the action of a schoolboy'.[85] At the same time, the viceroy's generals cannot escape reproach. Some of them resented serving under a commander 'whom they regarded as a child' and their performances may have suffered from an excess of personal pique.[86] Seras's attack on Porcia, for instance, was slow and fragmented, Grenier inserted his troops in driblets, and Barbou had to be prevented from burning the bridge at Brugnera while the Italian division was still on the east bank. On the other hand, the result could have been much worse. Once again, the French were the beneficiaries of excessive caution and plodding mental processes on the part of the Habsburg commanders. Had Johann or Ignaz Gyulai committed all or most of IX Corps to a vigorous attack on Sacile instead of sending part of Marziani's brigade forward in a tentative, methodical advance, it is hard to see how Eugene's left and centre could have escaped destruction. Likewise, the Austrian official history chides the archduke for holding back Kleinmayrn's reserve brigade (5,400 men) when a concerted thrust towards Brugnera would almost certainly have caused far more damage to the French right wing. The 'strange passivity' that had the Austrians beginning 16 April as a rest day prevailed in army headquarters for much of the battle.[87] Johann, therefore, had won an important victory, but failed to convert it into something that might have been decisive for the campaign.[88]

STALEMATE ON THE ADIGE

Eugene's battered army stumbled away to the west. 'We marched all through the night,' remembered Sous-Lieutenant Barat, 'encouraging our soldiers to hold on to their weapons, telling them that we were going to unite with two divisions, with our dragoons, with the royal guard.' The weather had again turned foul, the skies opening to drench the weary troops, flood the low-lying fields, and transform every watercourse into a surging torrent, but 'the bad weather and the indolence of the Germans [Austrians] was such that the pursuit was very feeble,' commented Barat. Like the rest of the army, he was bone-weary as well as wet: 'I was exhausted, it had been twelve days since I had taken off my boots.' Burdened by fatigue, hunger, and unceasing rain, Eugene got his army across the Piave on 17 April, gathering up Lamarque and Pully at Conegliano along the way.[89] 'We continued our march in disorder and passed the Piave at noon,' wrote Routier, 'still starving and covered up to our ears with mud.'[90] Eugene had the bridge burned that night and prepared to continue the retreat.

Napoleon was furious when he subsequently learned that the viceroy had abandoned the line of the Piave, but Eugene, concerned about the state of the army and Austrian moves in the Tyrol, saw no realistic option. The army thus resumed its withdrawal on 18 April: Grenier and 8th Chasseurs via Bassano, Sahuc on the road through Castelfranco, and most of the army

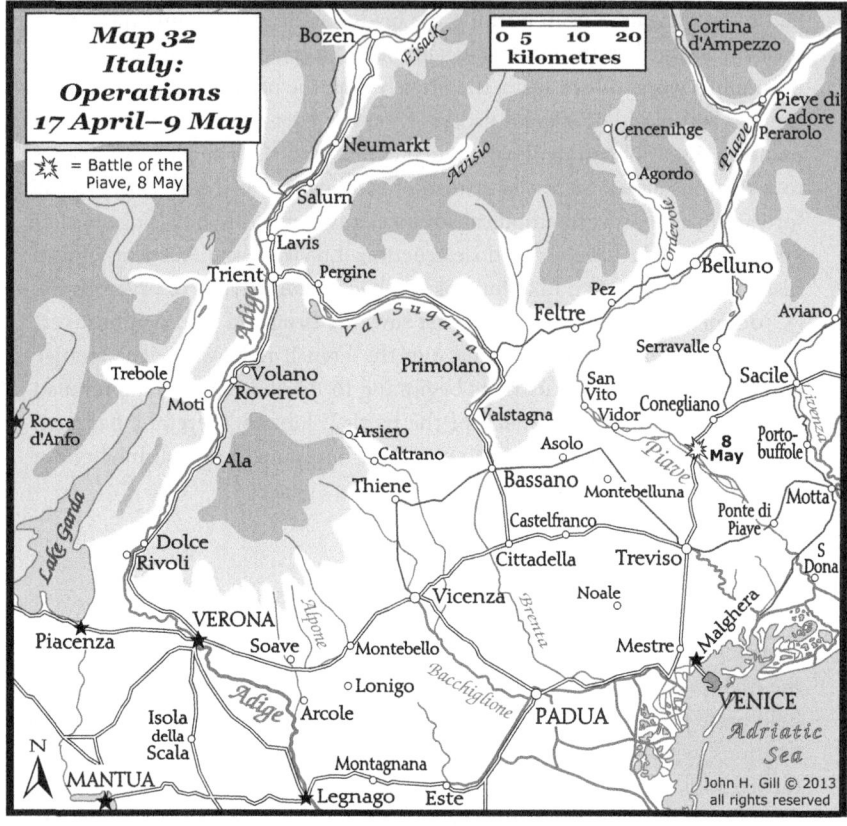

through Treviso and Mestre to Padua. Bartier marched west from Serravalle
with 79th Ligne and apparently went through Belluno where he skirmished
with Zuccheri's ad hoc column.[91] The loss of the Piave line exposed Venice,
rich in strategic, material, and psychological value, to Austrian attack, so
Eugene detailed Barbou to bolster the garrison with thirteen battalions and
the *Royal Italian* Chasseurs (this assignment also removed the apparently
troublesome Barbou from the field army).[92] Barbou's remaining seven
battalions were distributed among the other divisions, while the other Italian
troops, five battalions and half the chevaulegers, were attached to Seras as
a brigade under GB Filippo Bonfanti.[93] The retreat was often difficult, but
proceeded in reasonable stages with little interference from the Austrians,
and the army, reinforced, revictualed, and untroubled by the enemy, soon
began to regain its spirit. Pully, retiring towards Este and Montagnana on

24 April, even sent two squadrons of 28th Dragoons under Chef d'Escadron Aymonin back to Padua to keep an eye on the enemy. These bold dragoons, assisted by some Italian gendarmes, captured Johann's intendant general, Johann Peter Graf von Goës, in a daring pre-dawn raid along with much of the army's administrative staff and a trove of papers full of useful intelligence. The dragoons skirmished with Habsburg hussars east of the city later in the day, but withdrew in the face of overwhelming numbers.[94] Meanwhile, the army was collecting itself around Caldiero east of Verona.[95] It had largely recovered from the calamity at Sacile, and its commander, having regained his own confidence, was preparing to challenge Johann again.

Johann, put off by the inclement weather, the army's losses, and a general sense of exhaustion, did not launch an immediate pursuit after Sacile, even though the crowds of prisoners collected by the morning of 17 April should have given a clear picture of the French army's dissolution. Instead, the archduke contented himself with shifting his main body from Fontanafredda to Sacile (all of six or seven kilometres) and sending Frimont six kilometres beyond the Livenza.[96] Frimont was unable to intercept Bartier (the French moved quickly despite the weather) and did not reach the Piave until 19 April. He fired a few rounds to chase off a small French detachment, but Johann was still in Sacile, so Frimont, unsupported, had to wait for the army to come up. Gyurkovics, who had reached Motta on the Livenza while the battle was raging at Sacile, brought his flanking detachment up to the Piave between Ponte di Piave and S Dona on 19 April. Johann, however, did not stir from Sacile until 20 April, dragging his sodden columns up to the Piave on the 21st and finally crossing the following day. By this time, he had lost all touch with the enemy, so his army made its way slowly and carefully across the skein of rivers that etch the north Italian plains, entering Vicenza on 25 April without encountering any resistance beyond scouts and outposts. In his rear, some Landwehr were becoming available. In addition to those at Palmanova, three Graz battalions were en route to the army under GM Ignaz Freiherr Sebottendorf von der Rose; GM Peter von Lutz took over blockade duties at Osoppo with the two Marburg battalions, relieving I/ *Franz Karl* to join Johann on the Adige.

Johann kept a close eye on developments in the Tyrol and sent Volkmann to Thiene via Bassano on 23 April with a sizeable detachment to protect the army's right flank and make contact with Chasteler and Zuccheri. The latter made a cautious entry into Belluno on 17 April, but had been forced back to Fortogna in a scuffle with a French force and eventually retreated almost to Pieve di Cadore.[97] As the French withdrew, Zuccheri resumed his advance, passing through Feltre on the 22nd and arriving on Volkmann's right (Caltrano) on 25 April. Two weak companies of 2nd Villach and a company of 144 Tyrolians had now joined him, but Zuccheri was not impressed with their utility. The Landwehr only numbered 138 ('the rest have gone home,' remarked Zuccheri) and wanted to flee on hearing that the French were approaching, while the Tyrolians were 'a true burden to me; as, in the first place, they have no powder, and, in the second, they want to eat and drink in each and every place we enter and can never get enough'.[98] Other odd detachments from Chasteler also made their appearance on the main army's flank at this time. Major la Notte with his company of 9th Jägers and several hundred Tyrolian insurgents had followed Zuccheri's route down the Piave valley and reached Arsiero north-west of Volkmann, and Oberstleutnant Ertel had brought his battalion of *Lusignan* to Pergine east of Trient. Behind these miniature commands, Major Lodron's Villach Landwehrmen had made their way to Primolano. Eighth Corps, arriving in Bassano on 24 April, was greeted by ten companies of Tyrolian militia, some 1,600 to 2,000 men with, however, few weapons. Not quite sure what to do with these eager but dubious allies, Johann assigned a pensioned captain to lead them and urged them to move on Trient.[99]

On the Austrian left, Gyurkovics hustled a few French vedettes out of Mestre on 22 April and moved to seal off the Venice garrison. The main army was then at Treviso, and Johann sent III/*Franz Karl*, the *Ottocac* Grenzer, and a position battery to reinforce Gyurkovics for an attempted *coup de main* against the bridgehead at Malghera. The archduke himself rode down to observe the advance against what was adjudged an unready enemy. The French, however, were prepared and the assault turned into a bloody repulse. Chastened, Johann ordered Gyurkovics simply to neutralise the French garrison and returned to his headquarters with nothing to show for the effort except a lengthy casualty list.[100]

Further south and east, an ad hoc Austrian force had overrun Istria and its garrison (II/3rd Italian Light). Departing Triest on the night of 10/11 April, Major Cazzan led his small detachment (less than 1,000 men) to Capodistria and encircled the town from the landside while the Royal Navy blocked the seaward approaches. The town capitulated on 13 April and Cazzan made his way down the coast, subduing minimal resistance in Pirano, Cittanova, and Rovigno before capturing Pola on the 24th. His mission complete, he was called to Italy to bolster the blockade force at Palmanova. In the meantime, the Austrian navy captured three gun-sloops in a successful attack on Grado on 15 April.[101] A Royal Navy squadron of four frigates and a sloop under

Captain Jahleel Brenton was also active in the Adriatic. In addition to showing the flag and harrying Franco-Italian shipping, boats from three of Brenton's ships attacked Pesaro on the Italian coast on 23 April, capturing thirteen merchant vessels and blowing up the fort that guarded the harbour (see Map 44).[102]

As these secondary forces continued their actions and advances on the flanks, Johann was deciding what to do with his main army. Both corps were gathered around Vicenza by the evening of 25 April, but the archduke knew little of the enemy other than the fact that Frimont was reporting—at last, nine days after Sacile—direct contact with what appeared to be the French rear guard in and around Montebello. Johann assumed the French would await him behind the Adige and hoped that Chasteler would push south from Trient to unhinge any defence along the river. But was Eugene's main force due west on the road to Verona, or was it south-west towards Legnago, preparing to strike his flank? For 26 April, Johann reinforced the advance guard and placed Volkmann under Frimont's orders for the difficult task of locating the enemy, but Frimont's overly complex plan to trap the French at Montebello took too long to evolve and Eugene's troops (Sahuc and Seras) safely withdrew during a day of continual minor skirmishes. The following day, Frimont again pushed at Eugene's defences and a fierce fight erupted at San Bonifacio and Villanova where a battalion of 106th Ligne and four guns held the crossings over the Alpone. Oberst Csivich led five companies of his *Ogulin* Grenzer against Villanova, but the Croatians, raked by the 106th's musketry, broke and fled in disorder. Discouraged by this miniature disaster, Frimont called off the offensive, even though eight companies of *Johann Jellacic* had succeeded in capturing much of San Bonifacio on the left. The late hour and renewed rain brought combat to a close without any noticeable success for the Austrians. The two corps, in the meantime, only advanced some ten to twelve kilometres west of Vicenza, Johann anxiously sending GM Splenyi south-west towards Arcole with a detachment to guard the army's left flank and a squadron of *Ott* Hussars to maintain contact with Gyurkovics.[103] Further south, Gyurkovics sent a small detachment under Oberstleutnant Josef Hirsch to probe west through Este to Montagnana.[104]

The 28th passed in relative quiet as the Austrians undertook convoluted manoeuvres to outflank the French rear guard on the Alpone. Most of these only led to confusion and exhaustion in the streaming rain as Seras had withdrawn the 106th to unite with the main army in the strong position at Caldiero. Nonetheless, the day ended with Johann's troops in possession of Soave as well as the crossings over the Alpone and the army dispersed in quarters just east of the river to escape the rain. That afternoon, Johann received the encouraging news that Chasteler had reached Ala on 27 April, placing him on Eugene's left flank only some fifty kilometres up the Adige valley from Verona. With luck, the threat posed by Chasteler and the small communications detachments in the mountains would lever Eugene out of the daunting Caldiero position, sparing the Army of Inner Austria the prospect of a costly assault. When 'dull cannon fire' rolled across the plains from the French position that evening, therefore, many hopefully believed it indicated Chasteler's appearance on the French left. For Johann, however, 'the enemy's composure in his camp and the reduction of the fire clearly showed me that it was a celebratory salute.' It was not long before a French emissary arrived with news that Napoleon had won a great victory in Bavaria. Even accounting for exaggeration in the enemy's report, the recent silence from the Hauptarmee made the archduke uneasy: 'nothing good could be expected.'[105]

16–28 April: Chasteler Moves South

Both Eugene and Johann regarded events in the Tyrol as crucial to their own actions. The viceroy entertained justifiable, if exaggerated, concerns about his northern flank and dispatched GD Baraguey d'Hilliers to Trient with several thousand troops to reinforce Lemoine and block incursions down the Adige. Lemoine's replacement column, as we have seen, consisted of some 2,100 men and, like Bisson's, had been destined for 4th Corps in Germany. Unlike his compatriot, however, Lemoine had turned back when he encountered masses of rebels at Brixen on 12 April and wisely retired to Trient with his crowd of conscripts. Baraguey d'Hilliers arrived in the town on the 17th and grouped his available troops into two divisions: GD Honoré Vial in command of Lemoine's column supplemented by 112th Ligne and a squadron of 7th Dragoons; and Fontanelli's division of nine Italian battalions, two squadrons of 2nd Italian Chasseurs and the remaining three squadrons of 7th Dragoons. The divisions numbered approximately 4,400 and 5,300 men respectively, but most of these were utterly innocent of military experience.[106] Vial, who had fought in the region during the wars of the Revolution, was concerned about the quality of the troops and the region in which they were to fight. 'I know from experience', he wrote Eugene's chief of staff, 'that the Tyrol is a poor place to wage a war.'[107]

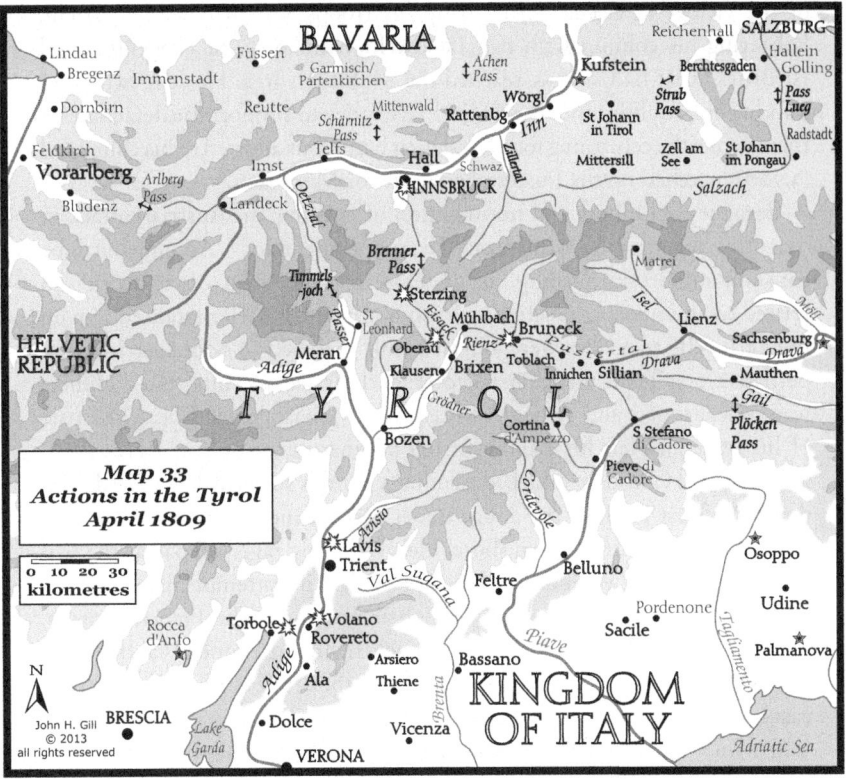

Map 33
Actions in the Tyrol
April 1809

0 10 20 30
kilometres

From his headquarters in Innsbruck, Chasteler considered his options as April passed its midpoint. He held the initiative, but there was little immediate need for his troops in the north: the Tyrolians had freed their land from Bavarian occupation, and the Hauptarmee's offensive, as far as he knew, had not yet matured to a point where his command could make a serious contribution to its success. Indeed, there is nothing to suggest that much co-ordination of any kind occurred between Chasteler and the Hauptarmee. To the south, however, he knew that Johann had invaded Friaul and that the French had occupied Trient. A dash over the Brenner towards Verona could remove this French threat and materially assist the archduke's advance while inspiring additional Tyrolians to take up arms. He therefore ordered his subordinates around Mühlbach to march for Bozen and headed south himself with two battalions, two Jäger companies, a squadron, and a half-battery of cavalry guns. He rode into Bozen on 21 April and, on learning of the victory at Sacile, gathered up his troops and marched for Trient, bolstering his column with two Landwehr battalions (1st Klagenfurt and 1st Bruck) that had already reached the Mühlbach area. He sent two other Landwehr battalions into the upper Piave valley to support the detachments there, while the remaining four Landwehr battalions allotted to his command (3,700) marched up the Pustertal en route for Mühlbach.[108]

Baraguey d'Hilliers had no intention of awaiting an Austrian attack in Trient, a location he considered far too vulnerable.[109] Accompanied by constant minor skirmishing, he therefore left the town on 22 April and retired to an imposing position at Volano, where Chasteler attacked him on the 24th. The two sides were almost evenly matched (8,000 Austrians and perhaps 2,000 Tyrolians against 9,700 French/Italian recruits), but d'Hilliers was concentrated and strongly posted, while Chasteler had detached part of his force and left his Landwehr ten kilometres to the rear in reserve.[110] Nonetheless, Chasteler attacked, sending columns towards Lake Garda and down the west bank of the Adige under GM Fenner while his main force pressed ahead on the eastern shore. Heavy fighting raged all day as the two sides struggled for Volano, but Austrian outflanking attempts failed and the battle ended with the French still in their positions. The French division, under the leadership of the 112th's Colonel Raymond Penne (Vial had been recalled to assume command in Venice), bore the brunt of the fighting on the east bank and the French conscripts and the Istrian Battalion performed fairly well in their first significant action. The 112th Ligne particularly distinguished itself in well-executed counter-attacks and in repeated assaults on Volano: 'It is impossible that the most seasoned soldiers could have displayed greater courage than our soldiers,' wrote a proud sous-lieutenant.[111]

On the other side of the river, Guillaume de Vaudoncourt with an Italian detachment of one and one-half battalions, two squadrons, and two guns held off Tyrolian attempts to seize a bridge in Penne's rear; GB Jean François Julhien was wounded as he came up with a battalion of reinforcements late in the action. The Austrian regulars on this side of the river arrived too late to influence the outcome.[112] Chasteler's aggressiveness cost his command 538 casualties and he was fortunate that d'Hilliers, fighting a defensive battle, did not exploit his numerical advantage when I/112 briefly seized Volano late in the day. The prominent role played by Penne's regiment was evident in the 304 casualties it suffered, and total Franco-Italian losses probably came to between 400 and 500. Minor skirmishing flared on 25 April as Chasteler, undeterred by the abortive efforts the previous day, manoeuvred his command to position it for a complex flanking attack on 26 April. The

Austrian plan came to naught as d'Hilliers, worried by French setbacks in the plains, withdrew to Ala on the 25th and to Dolce just north of the old Rivoli battlefield the next day. A number of small combats ensued as Chasteler followed the retreating French, instructing the communications detachments to support his advance. Major Lodron and his three Landwehr battalions thus joined the main column at Rovereto on 27 April, while Zuccheri and la Notte advanced between Chasteler and Johann.[113] By 28 April, Chasteler seemed well placed to make a direct contribution to the Army of Inner Austria's operations. His impetuous push south, however, had just come to an end.[114]

29 April: Actions on the Alpone—Engagement at Soave

On the edge of the mountains, the two main armies faced one other across the Alpone, each wondering who would move first. Johann, counting on Chasteler, hoped that he could throw the French across the Adige, inflicting one more defeat on his opponent before settling in to a defensive posture. He knew that he was now outnumbered and recognised that he had reached his strategic 'culminating point', the stage in a campaign when the balance of forces begins to tilt in favour of the defender.[115] He also understood that a French victory in Bavaria would render his position in Italy untenable, but he wanted confirmation from Charles before reacting to the French display of jubilation on the evening of the 28th. He therefore declared 29 April a rest day to await either an advance by Chasteler or news from the generalissimus. In his rear, Gyurkovics (joined by Sebottendorf's three Graz Landwehr battalions) maintained the blockade of Malghera, while Lutz watched Osoppo, and FML Anton Freiherr von Zach assumed responsibility for holding the lines around Palmanova against GB Jean Jacques Schilt's active defence.[116]

Eugene, for his part, was waiting for a 'good opportunity' to 'redeem with advantages the defeat at Sacile'.[117] The concentration of the army at Caldiero, the proximity of Baraguey d'Hilliers, and the arrival of reinforcements allowed him to reorganise his forces into wings as Napoleon desired and thereby ameliorate some of the command problems experienced thus far in the campaign. Among the reinforcements was GD MacDonald, an old Republican general being given a second chance after incurring imperial disfavour for associating with Napoleon's political enemies. In his memoirs, MacDonald would later present a canted version of events, taking credit for all of the Army of Italy's successes.[118] His inflated claims

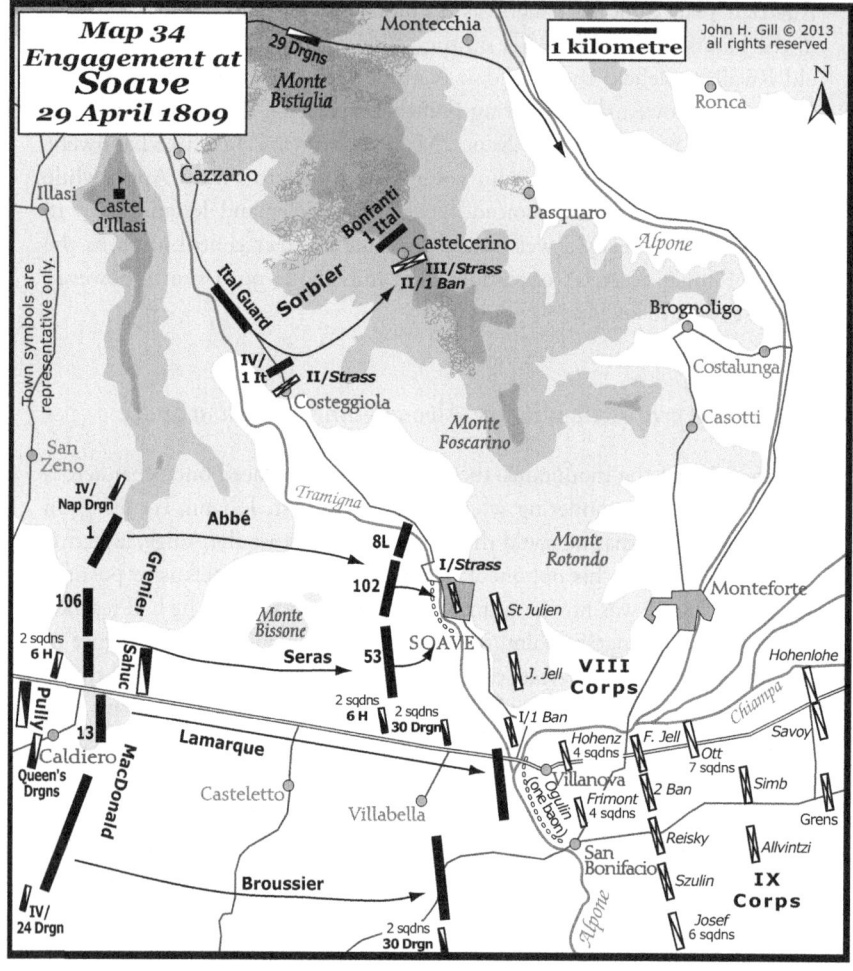

need not detain us here, but in 1809 he was a respected professional soldier whose seniority and familiarity with Italy made him a good choice for a wing commander under the young viceroy. Eugene placed MacDonald in charge of the right wing with Broussier's and Lamarque's infantry divisions, along with Guérin's brigade of dragoons (30th and *Queen's*); while Grenier commanded the centre, consisting of his own division (under GB Abbé), Seras, and 6th Hussars. Baraguey d'Hilliers remained responsible for the left wing, but this would now be composed of a reformed Italian division under Fontanelli and the division in the Tyrol, reorganised and placed under GD Jean Rusca. The 7th Dragoons were also allotted to d'Hilliers. Eugene himself would command the reserve including the Italian Guard, Sahuc's light cavalry, Pully's dragoon division, and various troops approaching from the south who would form a new division slated for GD Durutte. The latter, however, ordered to assemble at Isola della Scala, could not possibly join the army until 2 May. Details would change considerably over the coming two months, but this basic organisational outline remained in place for the rest of the war; there was little evidence of it, however, in the combat that now erupted along the Alpone.[119]

Eugene, eager 'to force the Archduke Johann's retreat and to cut his communications with the Tyrol', decided to seize the heights on Johann's right on 29 April, masking this attack with a reconnaissance in force against the main Austrian position along the Alpone.[120] All was quiet that morning until 11 a.m., when the Austrians, who could clearly see the French army, noted that units were assembling in evident preparation for movement. Before long, three French columns were observed advancing from Caldiero, the troops cheering ardently as they marched.[121] On the right, Broussier moved against San Bonifacio with one brigade and Lamarque against Villanova with 29th Ligne, each supported by two squadrons of 30th Dragoons and all under MacDonald's overall command. Both were directed to capture the bridges in their respective sectors and Lamarque was to occupy Villanova if possible, but Broussier was instructed not to cross the Alpone. In the centre, Grenier would attack Soave with ten battalions, and GB Sorbier was entrusted with the task of capturing Cazzano and Monte Bastiglia on the left with 1st Italian Line under GB Bonfanti and three battalions of Italian Guard. The French right advanced with great élan, but the attack soon stalled as the Austrians had dismantled the bridges and there was no other feasible means to cross the Alpone. As the right wing's move devolved into a standing firefight, the French centre assaulted Soave and gained a foothold on the edge of town but could not dislodge I/*Strassaldo*; the battle here settled into a bloody stalemate of attack and counter-attack.

In the meantime, Sorbier had had unexpected success. Bonfanti's Italians not only evicted five companies of II/*1st Banal* from Cazzano, one battalion took Costeggiola while the other three pursued the retreating Grenzer up the slopes to the east towards Castelcerino. A stiff fight ensued near Castelcerino as the Grenzer found support from III/*Strassaldo*, but the Austrians were driven from this position when Sorbier used a shallow draw to bring the three Guard battalions up behind the enemy. The Austrians retreated to

Costalunga in confusion, perhaps encouraged by the appearance of the 29th Dragoons, who had crossed over the difficult Monte Bastiglia ridge to come down into the Alpone valley threatening the Austrian rear. The French and Italians did not exploit their advantage, indeed Sorbier hardly had enough forces or daylight to do so even if the thought had occurred to him. Instead, he followed the letter of his orders and withdrew his three Guard battalions during the night to secure Monte Bastiglia and the valley near Cazzano. The 29th Dragoons also returned west of the ridge, leaving 1st Line isolated and vulnerable at Castelcerino.

Both commanders played exceedingly cautious hands on 29 April. Eugene did not allot sufficient combat power to his flanking attack to secure permanent gains or to take advantage of opportunities. The rest of his advance was a series of half-measures: rather too powerful for a reconnaissance in force or diversion and yet too weak for a major attack. Johann fed a few additional forces into the combat around Soave, but kept IX Corps out of the action when its intervention at Soave in the late afternoon might have placed the weary French in a dangerous situation. Curiously, neither commander became aware of the 1st Italian Line's presence at Castelcerino until the morning of 30 April.

30 April: Actions on the Alpone—Engagement at Castelcerino

During the fighting on 29 April, Johann, as noted in his campaign journal, finally received a letter from Kaiser Franz concerning the situation in Bavaria: 'Arrival of a courier from the army in Germany with news of its misfortunes!'[122] Although he had not yet made a final decision, his thinking on next steps in the campaign now became a function of Chasteler's actions, and from this point forward, he was increasingly concerned about ensuring a safe retreat for his army.[123] He was therefore doubly shocked on the morning of 30 April, when GM Colloredo in Soave reported the alarming presence of substantial enemy forces on the heights around Castelcerino; that is, in a position to threaten the army's right flank and rear. The archduke, not knowing how strong the enemy was, quickly sent a force of ten battalions straining up the steep slopes to throw the Italians off the ridge 'regardless of cost': *Franz Jellacic, Johann Jellacic,* and *2nd Banal* climbed up to assault Bonfanti's three battalions along the crest, while III/*Strassaldo* and II/*1st Banal,* who had fallen back to Costalunga, swung up the Alpone valley to approach Monte Bastiglia.[124] Additionally, Oberst Ferdinand Fellner led two battalions of *Reisky,* the *Szulin* Grenzer, and a half-squadron of *Josef* Hussars towards Ronca to secure the far right flank, detaching one of his battalions towards Pasquaro as a link to the forces on the ridge. Four other battalions remained in support on the heights above Monteforte.[125] The overwhelming power of this assault took some time to develop and Bonfanti's men held their own until about midday when Sorbier ordered the three battalions of 1st Line to withdraw and advanced with the three Guard battalions to cover the retreat. The guardsmen performed their mission with skill and cool courage: 'these brave battalions made themselves remarkable through the co-ordination of their manoeuvres and the precision of their fire, which they executed as if on the parade field.' They paid heavily for their 'infinitely glorious' day.[126] When finally driven from the ridge late in the afternoon, the three battalions retired in good order but had lost 500 of their 1,800 men. Although the Austrians occupied Cazzano as darkness fell, the re-formed 1st Line blocked any further pursuit and the fighting came to an end.

The engagements at Soave and Castelcerino cost the Austrians 1,822 men in killed, wounded, missing, and captured. Total French and Italian losses are not known but were probably slightly higher given their role as attacker in most cases. The wounded included the highly regarded GB Sorbier: shot in the ankle, he was captured by Feldwebel Silagy of *Johann Jellacic* and died in captivity shortly thereafter.[127]

The two days of combat were disappointing for both sides. Eugene, unaware that his Italian troops had exceeded their orders and made significant gains on 29 April, lost a potentially crucial advantage as there were no supports available to reinforce Sorbier during the tough battle on the 30th. The army, however, had thoroughly proved itself, demonstrating renewed esprit, stamina, and tactical skill. Johann, on the other hand, had become seized with notions of imminent retreat and did nothing to exploit the situation. Another courier with discouraging information had arrived during the day. This time it was a rider from Chasteler who announced that Chasteler had marched for Innsbruck on the night of 29/30 April with the bulk of his force to defend northern Tyrol, leaving behind in the Adige valley only GM Marchal with a squadron and two and one-half battalions. Johann's last hope thus vanished.[128] Furthermore, he learned that most of his Landwehr was being recalled (through a bureaucratic misinterpretation of Franz's intentions) thereby eviscerating Chasteler's command and depriving the main army of the manpower needed to blockade the French fortresses in its rear.[129] Retreat was now the only option and he issued orders for the trains and heavy artillery to begin withdrawing that very night with the rest of the Army of Inner Austria to follow the next day.

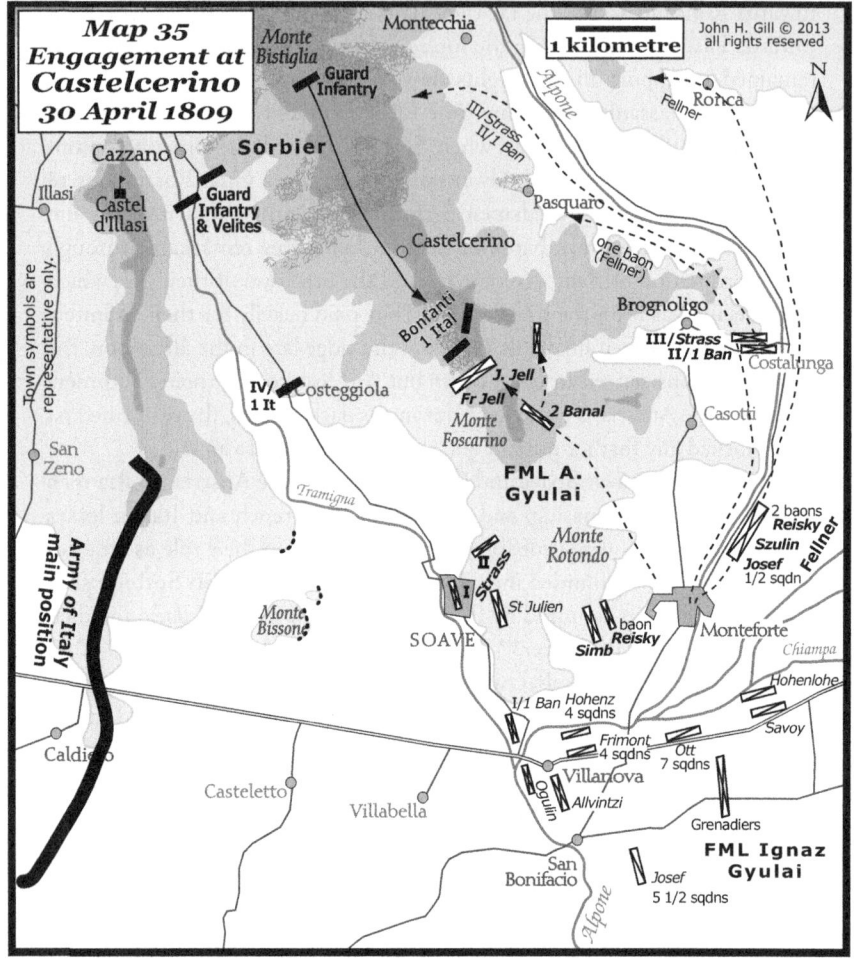

Thus ended an offensive campaign begun with much hope but inadequate forces. Although largely undone by exogenous factors—especially the disaster in Bavaria—torpor, caution, and a certain lack of decision on Johann's part at several key points overshadowed his real accomplishments and precluded the achievement of decisive results. By not exploiting French errors at Sacile and by allowing them to escape after the thrashing they had received in that battle, Johann lost his best chances for a more potent victory. Once he reached the Adige, far from his own bases and facing an enemy whose strength increased by the day, his opportunities narrowed dramatically and only a strong thrust by Chasteler might have remedied his difficult situation. Italy was never going to be the determining theatre in this war, but a crushing victory over Eugene might have slowed Napoleon's progress and would at very least have caused him to respond to a much more dangerous situation on his southern flank. Unfortunately for Austria, Johann now compounded his errors on the offence by envisaging a defensive concept that would scatter his army at the very time when he needed to concentrate. He thereby 'planted the seed of a series of failures' that would cripple the Army of Inner Austria and lead the French into the heart of the Habsburg monarchy.[130]

Eugene, on the other hand, after a stumbling beginning, had recovered impressively. His conduct of the engagements on 29 and 30 April was by no means exemplary, but he had clearly learned from the missteps in the opening days of the campaign and his innate good sense was manifesting itself with increasing frequency to complement his unquestioned courage and sangfroid. Despite his personal inexperience, initially fractious generals, the numerous conscripts in the ranks, and the stain of the early defeats and retreats, he had revived the Army of Italy and was about to win a string of notable successes in a swift offensive campaign that would garner praise even from his demanding step-father.

CHAPTER 5

From the Adige to the Danube: Eugene's Counter-Offensive

Although he had held Eugene's half-hearted thrusts along the Adige on 29 and 30 April, the outnumbered Johann was in no position to resume offensive operations against the viceroy's reinforced army. Moreover, the disaster in Bavaria had drawn away Chasteler's flanking force and made his continued presence in Italy virtually untenable. While these factors militated for retreat, Johann was reluctant to abandon his gains and knew that his brother the Kaiser placed a high value on the seeming advantages achieved thus far in Italy. 'My principal object is not to interrupt Your Grace's successful operations, so long as this is at all possible,' wrote Franz on 24 April. 'The undertaking in Italy, the land where we have established most of our liaisons, where the contact point between Sicily, Sardinia, and England lies, is of the greatest importance to me.' 'We live in a catastrophe where manly vigour leads farther than anxious calculations of mathematical lines,' continued Franz, succumbing to desperation in the immediate aftermath of Regensburg.[1] The imperial court may have clung to these desperate illusions, but Johann's immediate actions were driven by a more pragmatic appreciation of the situation. Leaving Frimont with a rear guard to keep the campfires burning and cover the retreat, the Army of Inner Austria quietly slipped away to the east on the night of 30 April.[2] Thus began seven days of Austrian withdrawal, French pursuit, and running, often surprisingly costly, engagements.

1–7 MAY: RETREAT TO THE PIAVE

The French were utterly surprised and utterly pleased when their morning reconnaissances on 1 May revealed that the Austrians had decamped. Eugene had been planning another advance on his left towards Monte Bastiglia, hoping that capture of this feature, combined with an advance by Rusca through the Val Sugana, would unhinge the Austrian line on the Alpone. Now the viceroy could happily report to Napoleon that 'the Austrians have chosen to beat a retreat' and that he was organising 'a fine advance guard to pursue them'.[3] By the evening of 2 May, the French were on the outskirts of Vicenza. The first day of the month had passed with only minor skirmishing, but 2 May saw a series of small yet bloody actions as Eugene's 'fine advance guard' unceasingly hammered at the whitecoats. The day cost the Austrians at least 200 casualties and probably as many as 500 (perhaps even more as the French swept up many stragglers during their advance). French losses were likely somewhat lower, but the wounded included GB Armand Louis De Broc, commander of the ad hoc vanguard. The following day brought the bulk of Eugene's army to the west bank of the Brenta, with Seras on the left aimed at Bassano. South of the main body, GD Durutte's lead elements reached Padua on 3 May. Reinforced by 23rd Dragoons and three squadrons each of 7th Dragoons and 9th Chasseurs, Durutte had marched from Legnago via Este (2 May), pushing Oberstleutnant Hirsch's little detachment and the lone squadron of *Ott* Hussars steadily east.[4]

The Austrians withdrew generally along three lines. Johann and the majority of the army fell back along the highway through Montebello and Vicenza towards Cittadella, the main body crossing the Brenta on 2 May, followed by Frimont's rear guard on the 3rd. Other than some skirmishing as the French appeared along the river, most of the Habsburg troops were able to rest behind the protection of the Brenta on 4 May. To the south, the outnumbered Hirsch hastened to escape Durutte, pulling back to Noale on the night of 2/3 May and thus uncovering Gyurkovics's blockade force outside Malghera.[5] The latter accordingly retired towards Treviso on 3 May in anticipation of orders. Durutte, who picked up seven battalions of the Venice garrison as he marched east, pressed them hard.[6] Nonetheless, at the cost of 187 casualties, the combined Austrian detachments held off a French attempt to seize Treviso on the 4th, before withdrawing up the highway to the north during the night to join Johann.[7] The Austrian retreat continued on the 5th and several sharp cavalry fights erupted between Montebelluna and Treviso as Eugene's advance guard pressed Frimont; each side suffered between 100 and 200 casualties, but the French were unable to break through and the Austrians retreated safely over the Piave on the 6th, burning the highway bridge behind them.[8]

In the north, Johann had sent GM Josef Freiherr von Schmidt's brigade to Bassano on 3 May with the intention of detaching him to support the weak forces in the southern Tyrol. Vigorous pursuit by Seras and worrisome (though erroneous) rumours from the Tyrol delayed execution of this plan and Johann ordered Schmidt back to the Piave at San Vito. Seras, however, trapped and captured two companies of Grenzer on the west bank of the Brenta at Bassano on 4 May and swept up several hundred additional prisoners as he chased Schmidt east on the 5th. Schmidt left San Vito for Feltre on 6 May to arrive in Belluno the following day. Also on the army's northern flank was Hauptmann Zuccheri with his peripatetic little detachment and a small force of regulars that Schmidt had sent into the Val Sugana on 5 May. Falling back with the army from the Thiene area (30 April) to Primolano (3 May), Zuccheri gathered up Schmidt's detachment and withdrew through Feltre to a position behind the Cordevole covering the approaches to Belluno (7 May).[9]

The first week of May was thus a series of continual retreats and rear guard actions that cost the Austrian army at least 1,000 prisoners as well as several hundred killed and wounded. These withdrawals and casualties notwithstanding, Johann repeatedly concocted schemes to march north into the Tyrol or to counter-attack Eugene. On 4 May, inspired by news of Hiller's victory at Neumarkt and a desire to act offensively, he briefly flirted with unrealistic notions of marching half of his army through the Tyrol to invade Bavaria or threaten Napoleon's southern flank. These fantasies collapsed on the evening of 4 May when he received a gloomy note from Charles, followed by an alarming report from the Adige valley indicating that the small Austrian detachment there would probably have to retreat to Lavis, thereby leaving the Val Sugana open for Rusca to march against Johann's right. These messages seem to have reminded the archduke that he faced a numerically superior enemy to his front and that his left was in danger from Durutte's advance. Nonetheless, he returned to variants of this idea several times before finally deciding to retire behind the Piave on 6 May. Here he planned a lengthy stay, hoping that Schmidt's arrival in the Tyrol would allow GM Marchal to revive the offensive towards Trient with a supporting drive through the Val Sugana.[10]

Johann's interest in marching through the Tyrol had an unexpected benefit for the French. The archduke had informed Chasteler as a matter of course and that general, assuming that troops from the main army would soon arrive, pulled GM Marchal's force from Rovereto all the way back to Brixen. This left only Oberstleutnant von Leiningen with two infantry companies, three Jäger companies, a half-squadron of chevaulegers, and two 3-pounders at Ala opposite French GD Rusca and his 5,300 men at Dolce. Rusca, acting promptly to support Eugene, advanced on 1 May. Using his superior numbers to outflank the enemy, he drove the Austrians back, taking Ala on the 2nd, Rovereto on the 3rd, and breaking in the gates of Trient to seize that town on 4 May. He then turned up the Val Sugana according to his instructions and marched through Primolano to reach the Cordevole on 7 May. Behind him, Marchal re-occupied Trient on the 6th and pushed outposts as far as Rovereto by the close of the next day.[11] This move, however, did little to help Johann in the short term, while Rusca's advance would remain a constant source of worry for the Austrians.

With the Austrians east of the Piave and the highway bridge burned to the waterline, Eugene contented himself with establishing his army along the west bank of the river on 7 May. Both armies now reorganised. On the Austrian side, this was a fairly simple matter of returning the units of Hirsch's and Gyurkovics's detachments to their home regiments and shielding the army's encampments with Frimont's rear guard (five battalions, thirteen squadrons, sixteen guns) towards the river. Detachments, losses, and reorganisations thus far in the war, however, meant that the hussars were scattered between the two corps and that three of the infantry 'brigades' actually contained only one regiment.[12] The viceroy's changes were more extensive. In the first place, he reassembled his dragoon regiments into the original two divisions, with the 1st destined to come under GD Emmanuel Grouchy when he arrived on the morning of 8 May. Second, he returned 6th Hussars to Sahuc and designated Seras as the army reserve, replacing the latter in Grenier's corps with Durutte. Durutte lost his dragoons to Grouchy, while four of his French battalions went to Lamarque and the three Italian battalions from Venice marched into Fontanelli's bivouac. Finally, Eugene created a new advance guard under GB Dessaix (barely recovered from the wound he had received at Venzone) by matching 9th Chasseurs from Durutte with two new combined voltigeur regiments and four guns for a total of at least 4,800 infantry and more than 700 cavalry. With this new structure he planned to force the Piave against what he believed to be the rear guard of an enemy already retreating toward Sacile and Pordenone.[13]

8 MAY: BATTLE OF THE PIAVE[14]

As with Sacile, the Battle of the Piave arose from fundamental misconceptions on both sides. Johann seems to have been complacent, convinced that he would have at least several days to rest his army and perhaps launch a counter-attack if the opportunity arose. His covering troops along the Piave were poorly posted to observe the potential crossing sites and he overestimated both the weariness of the French and the value of the Piave as an obstacle. Eugene, on the other hand, thought he was facing a rear guard of no more than 10,000 men. The viceroy had carefully considered the enemy situation, but all of the intelligence from spies and locals described an Austrian army in retreat, an assessment apparently confirmed by his own observations and by the lack of reaction when 8th Chasseurs made a brief foray across the river on the evening of 7 May. The French troopers had splashed through the ford at San Nichiol, chased off a few Habsburg hussar pickets while probing into the plains, and returned to the south bank without incident as darkness fell. As one French officer observed, 'there was no readiness on the part of the Austrian military authorities, and this was a general fault that has been found with them.'[15] 'A few carbine shots were exchanged without results,' was all trumpeter Chevillet saw fit to note.[16] Additionally, the viceroy felt intense pressure from Napoleon, whose angry letter threatening to replace him with Murat arrived that morning.[17] Eugene's orders for 8 May thus called for a rapid passage of *both* the Piave and the Livenza. Dessaix's advance guard would lead the way, pressing beyond Sacile by evening, with the rest of the army arrayed along the highway from Sacile back to Conegliano where Eugene intended to establish his headquarters. His thinking about the future was evident in his instructions to Rusca: the general was to march from Belluno up the Piave valley and cross the mountains at Mauthen heading for Villach—well inside Austrian territory.[18]

The other key factor shaping the battle was the Piave itself. There were five potential crossing sites in the immediate vicinity of the armies during that time of year; from upstream these were: Nervesa (where the Austrians had dismantled their pontoon bridge), la Priula (site of the wooden trestle bridge that the Austrians had burned), Lovadina (ford), San Nichiol (ford), and Ponte di Piave (where the Austrians had also destroyed the bridge). The nature of the river, however, presented significant challenges to bridging or fording operations at any of these sites. Dangerously mercurial, the Piave could change from fordable to impassable within hours, especially during the spring when melting snow swelled its waters. The Austrians were therefore correct to assume that a major crossing would be difficult, but they were too sanguine in this assumption and neglected routine security. In contrast, the diligent French sounded the river and, sedulously questioning local inhabitants, ascertained that the water level should permit fording near Lovadina and San Nichiol by the morning of 8 May. Although the river was likely to rise as the day wore on, Eugene planned to construct a floating bridge or ferry or both to carry the army and its baggage across by nightfall. Eugene accordingly planned to have Dessaix pass over the river at Lovadina, followed by Broussier and Lamarque, while the cavalry, Abbé, and Durutte crossed at San Nichiol; the remaining troops would follow as the two sites became clear. A feint at Nervesa would divert Austrian attention from the actual crossing points.[19]

The Piave ran in a broad, stony bed among many low islands and sandbars, but beyond its immediate floodplain, the battlefield was broken up by numerous watercourses, retaining walls, vineyards, and villages. These features provided defensive possibilities but also impeded movement and visibility. The terrain, however, was strikingly flat, and from their perch in the tower of the Collalto castle near San Salvatore, Johann's staff officers could observe troop movements in the surrounding area 'as if on a chess board'.[20] A small stream, the Piavesella, generally paralleled the Piave, forming a potential hindrance to the movement of formed bodies of troops as it cut across the fields through Campana and Tezze. Two principal roads ran from south to north towards Conegliano: one crossed the ford near Lovadina; the other led up from the la Priula bridge site.

Perilous Passage: Across the Piave (5 to 9 a.m.)

The Austrian rear guard, under Frimont as usual, was stretched along the river from Vidor to Ponte di Piave, with supports posted slightly back from the river, and a reserve at Barco under GM Splenyi (Table 4). Behind this screen, VIII Corps camped south of Susegana, IX Corps north of Boca di Strada, and Sebottendorf's three Landwehr battalions near Conegliano with the trains. Additionally, two companies of *Szulin* Grenzer were stationed far to the right at Serravalle to maintain contact with Zuccheri and the other alpine detachments. Frimont, who had turned in a sterling performance thus far in the war, now faltered: focused on the potential crossing sites on the Austrian right, he gave little attention to the Lovadina ford and 'utterly neglected' the one at San Nichiol.[21] As a result, when Eugene's 8th Chasseurs conducted their uneventful foray at the latter location late on 7 May, the report took three or four hours to reach Habsburg headquarters and panic ensued when it did because no one knew how strong the French force was or even whether it was still across the river. Furthermore, outposts opposite Nervesa and la Priula reported that the French seemed to be making preparations to throw bridges at these two points. The French chasseurs had long since returned, when urgent orders from Johann shook his army from its rest late on the night of the 7th. The archduke betook himself to Colfosco, which seemed to be the most threatened point, and the Austrians spent the night awake and under arms.[22] As a result, the Habsburg men and horses were weary and their commander in the wrong place when the French splashed across the Piave early on 8 May.

Although awake, the bleary-eyed Austrians were not in position to observe the French crossing in the early hours of 8 May. Thick fog compounded slipshod Austrian surveillance. GB Dessaix was fortunate that the enemy was quiescent, because the passage itself was difficult enough. The first men

Table 4: Austrian Detachments on the Piave, 8 May morning

Location (north to south)	Commander	Units
Vidor	Maj Toperczer	I/*Franz Karl*, wing/*Ott*, 2 x 3-pdrs (division in San Vito)
Serravale	-	2 x companies/*Szulin*
Colfosco	-	baon/*Ogulin*, sqdn/*Josef*, 1/2 cavalry battery
La Priula	Oberstlt Collenbach	III/*Franz Karl*, sqdn/*Josef*, 1/2 cavalry battery
Barco	GM Splenyi	baon/*Ogulin*, 4 1/2 sqdns/*Frimont*, 2 x sqdns/*Josef*, 1/2 cavalry battery
Campana	-	sqdn/*Frimont*, 1/2 cavalry battery
La Grave	-	2 x sqdns/*Josef*
Cimadolmo	-	sqdn/*Frimont*
Ponte di Piave	Maj Ogrissovich	II/*Franz Karl*, wing/*Frimont*, 2 x 3-pdrs (one company in Oderzo)

Note: cavalry 'wing' (*Flügel*) = half-squadron

to enter the water, some voltigeurs from 9th Ligne, were swept away by the current, leading other light infantrymen to exclaim 'Better to die by a bullet storming a village than to go like that!' Volunteers from the 11th, however, made their way across, and Dessaix posted a chain of swimmers just downstream from the crossing site to snare those caught by the frightening torrent.[23] Stripped naked, this string of swimmers and a helpful rope saved many men from drowning, but could not rescue all. Thus Lieutenant Jean Nicolas Auguste Noël, commanding Dessaix's horse battery, lost his 16-year-old trumpeter and a number of others vanished in the rushing flood. Many of the soldiers struggling through the water were also completely nude, carrying their clothes and weapons on their heads, but they quickly dressed and reassembled on the far bank so that Dessaix and his ad hoc vanguard brigade, 'despite the rapidity and depth of the water', were across the river and ready to advance well before 7 a.m.[24]

The Austrians had still seen nothing, and the Habsburg hussars near Campana were shocked when a probing squadron of 9th Chasseurs appeared out of the mist sometime before 7 a.m. The chasseurs were overthrown in a brief clash, but Dessaix pressed up the highway until he encountered artillery fire from the Austrians in the Campana position and had to deploy. The strength of his force told the Austrian commanders that the French were making a serious push, just as the booming cannon fire alerted Eugene that he might be facing more than a simple rear guard. The viceroy hastened to support Dessaix, ordering a battery of 12-pounders to cover each crossing point from the French side of the river and directing Seras to divert Austrian attention by feigning preparations for a crossing at Nervesa.

Johann, at Colfosco, could see nothing in the morning fog, so he covered all contingencies by calling Gajoli forward with *Franz Jellacic* in case the French attempted a crossing at Nervesa, while sending GM Johann Kalnassy von Kalnass to the left towards Cimadolmo and ordering FML Wolfskeel and the dragoon brigade to throw back any enemy forces advancing up the highway in the centre. Wolfskeel, adding his one and one-half batteries to the half-battery at Campana, launched an impetuous cavalry charge at Dessaix, dragoons swinging to strike the French right and three squadrons of hussars seeking the enemy's left. The French, however, quickly and coolly formed two squares with their guns between and 9th Chasseurs to the rear. Delivering deadly volleys with professional precision, Dessaix's men withstood the Austrian charge 'with the greatest intrepidity'.[25] The Habsburg troopers 'fell like flies and retreated in great disorder', in the words of one voltigeur.[26] The 9th Chasseurs, with admirable initiative, attempted to capitalise on the

Austrian confusion with a counter-charge, but were repulsed with loss and retired behind the infantry squares, the voltigeurs firing indiscriminately on friend and foe as the mob of cavalry washed past their ranks. Having donned full dress uniforms for the battle 'to distinguish themselves from the other regiments', the brilliantly plumed and accoutred 9th became the object of scoffing mirth from their fellows as they retreated in a disorganised tumble.[27]

It was now shortly after 8 a.m., and Johann had arrived in the centre from Colfosco, sending orders to bring up reinforcements. The fog had largely dissipated and French officers such as Capitaine Aymar de Gonneville could clearly see the Austrian troops 'opening out upon the plain'.[28] On the archduke's right, GM Splenyi was bringing up the advance guard's reserve (six and one-half squadrons, a Grenz battalion, and a half-battery) immediately along the banks of the river. In the centre, the infantry of IX Corps (eleven battalions) along with three and one-half squadrons of *Ott* Hussars were deploying behind Campana, while one brigade battery joined the twelve cavalry guns already bombarding Dessaix's foot soldiers. Additional danger was approaching as Johann had called up Colloredo to fill the gap between Wolfskeel's cavalry west of Campana and Splenyi's command by the river.

The archduke's intent was to attack Dessaix's left with Wolfskeel and Colloredo as soon as the latter was in position. Luckily for the French, Colloredo marched slowly. In the meantime, the battle settled into a fierce cannonade with the infantry and cavalry on both sides suffering as their respective gunners plied their grim trade. 'The bullets rained and ricocheted on the stony soil,' wrote Lieutenant Noël, and none of the voltigeurs forgot the torment of a harrowing fire to which they could not respond.[29] Dessaix was nearly killed by a cannon ball 'that passed an inch from his shoulder', and Gonneville noted that shot 'literally hailed upon the spot where we were; some could be seen to ricochet, the wind of others could be felt, and there was a continuous hissing that caused very grave reflections.'[30] On the other side of the field, Wolfskeel's hapless dragoons thought themselves the special targets of the French 12-pounders on the far bank.[31]

While these events were unfolding, other French forces were making their way through the roiling Piave. It was a painfully slow process. Broussier, using Dessaix's ford, was collecting part of his division on the left bank, the soldiers wading through water 'up to their shoulders and necks' with 150 swimmers downstream 'to activate the passage and prevent accidents'.[32] The 9th Ligne was already forming square with seventeen guns in the low ground just beyond the ford and three battalions of the 84th were soon to follow. Lamarque, a short distance downstream at a slightly more secure spot, was also preparing to cross. The tension and urgency of the situation notwithstanding, the activity at the fords made a curious scene: 'General MacDonald was in the water on horseback and his sword drawn,' while 'the men of all the regiments, officers and soldiers all entirely naked and crowded together, awaited their turn to cross.'[33] Further downstream, Sahuc and Pully had forged a passage at San Nichiol and headed upstream towards the Lovadina site: 6th Hussars and 23rd Dragoons trotted off to support Broussier, while the other five regiments rode to Dessaix's assistance. Grouchy was also in the process of crossing; his green-clad dragoons would hold the French right, protecting the ford for Grenier's infantry.

On this end of the battlefield, Kalnassy's troops reached their positions at approximately 9 a.m., *Reisky* at Tezze and one battalion of *Simbschen* at Cimadolmo with a squadron of *Frimont*. The other two battalions of *Simbschen* and two squadrons of *Josef* Hussars were to head for San Michele but, passing through le Grave, they were temporarily sucked into the combat in the centre. Their appearance alarmed Eugene as they seemed to threaten Dessaix's right, so he hurled the 23rd Dragoons at the approaching Austrians. The dragoons overthrew the Habsburg hussars, but were repulsed by steady fire from the accompanying infantry. The experience, however, seemed to suffice to quell any aggressive intentions on the part of the Austrians: they marched off for San Michele as ordered, shadowed by the French dragoons.

Defeat of the Habsburg Horse (9 a.m. to noon)

By 9 a.m., Eugene's situation was dangerous in the extreme. The army's dedicated exertions had put some 14,000 men and 30 guns on the far bank of the Piave and another 1,800 were in the process of crossing. Instead of sweeping aside an enemy rear guard, however, he found himself contending with the Army of Inner Austria's main body: at least 20,000 men and 48 guns with an additional 1,300 available.[34] Austrian artillery fire was knocking men out of the ranks with frightful regularity and Dessaix was vulnerable: Splenyi hovered on his left, Colloredo was approaching, and what seemed a threat to his right had just been seen off by the 23rd Dragoons. Moreover, with his back to the increasingly difficult river, a defeat would almost certainly escalate to an irremediable disaster. Some fugitives had already fled back towards the Lovadina crossing point, giving Broussier an additional problem to remedy. 'This is beginning badly, we shall very likely be thrown into the water,' remarked GB Archange Louis Baron Rioult-d'Avenay when he rode

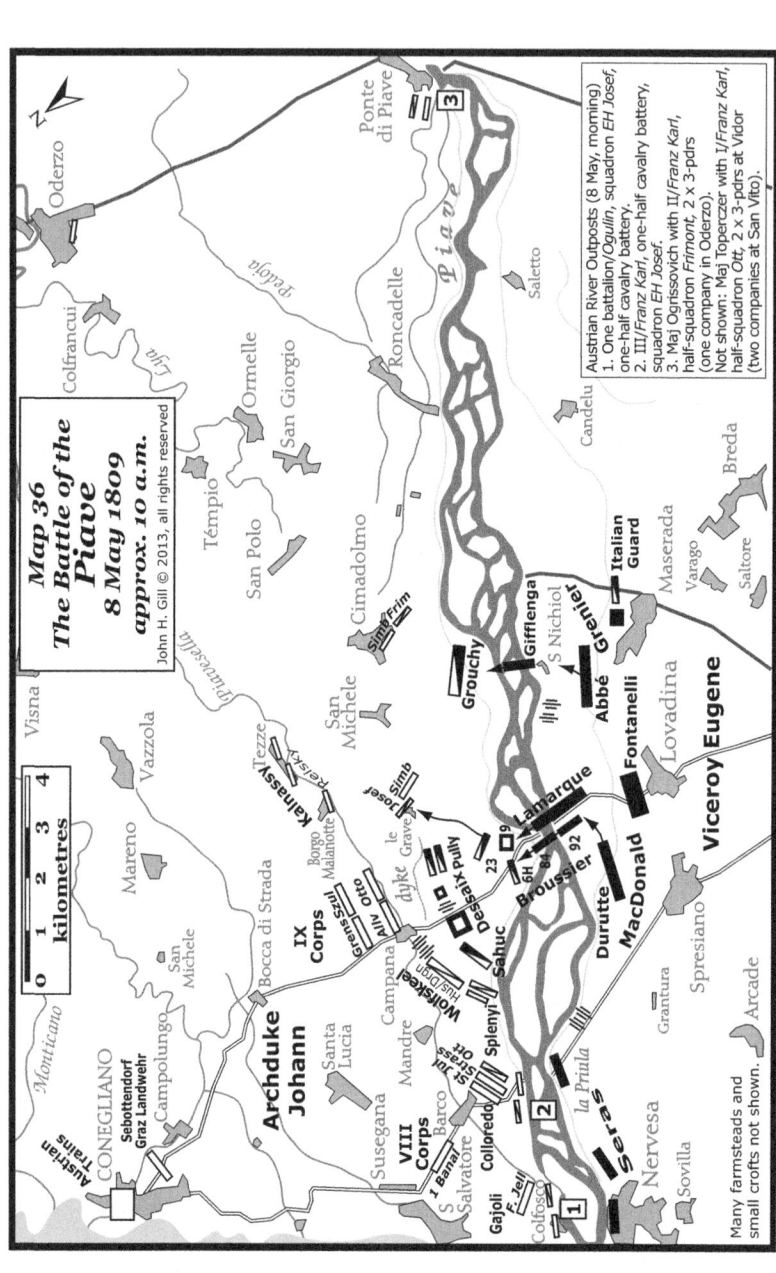

Map 36
The Battle of the Piave
8 May 1809
approx. 10 a.m.

kilometres
0 1 2 3 4

Austrian River Outposts (8 May, morning)
1. One battalion/Ogulin, squadron EH Josef, one-half cavalry battery.
2. III/Franz Karl, one-half cavalry battery, squadron EH Josef.
3. Maj Ogrissovich with II/Franz Karl, half-squadron Frimont, 2 x 3-pdrs (one company in Oderzo).
Not shown: Maj Toperczer with I/Franz Karl, half-squadron Ott, 2 x 3-pdrs at Vidor (two companies at San Vito).

Many farmsteads and small crofts not shown.

Monticano
Visna
Oderzo
Colfrancui
CONEGLIANO
Austrian Trains
Sebottendorf
Graz Landwehr
Piovia
Lia
Campolungo
Santa Lucia
Mareno
Vazzola
San Michele
Susegana
Mandre
Campana
Bocca di Strada
Borgo Malanotte
Tezze
Kalnassy
Peasxy
Ponte di Piave
Roncadelle
Saletto
Candelu
Breda
Saltore
Varago
Maserada
Ormelle
San Giorgio
Témpio
San Polo
Cimadolmo
San Michele
Paruuseele
Sim Frim
Gifflenga
S Nichiol
Grouchy
Abbé Greniér
Italian Guard
Fontanelli
Lovadina
Viceroy Eugene
Spresiano
Arcade
Sovilla
Nervesa
Grantura
la Priula
Seras
MacDonald
Durutte
Broussier
Lamarque
Josef
le Graves
dyke
Desaix Pully
Sahuc
Woristeel
Hus/Dran
Splenyi
Ott
St Tut Stras
1 Banal
F Jell
Colloredo
S Salvatore
Gajoli
Colfosco
VIII Corps
Archduke Johann
Barco
IX Corps
Grens Szul
Allv Otto
9
23
6H
8
92
1
2
3

up near Dessaix's squares at the head of 8th and 25th Chasseurs.[35] Eugene, however, addressed the potential crisis with firm decision and sought to solve his predicament by attacking. Although he was significantly inferior in over-all numbers, half of the French troops on the far bank were cavalry (7,300), more than double the number of horsemen available to Johann (3,000). The viceroy, pressing the passage of his army and taking himself to the far bank, would soon have an opportunity to exploit this advantage.

Around 10 a.m., after nearly two hours of mutual bombardment, the Austrians offered Eugene his opportunity. Both sides were finding the prevailing situation increasingly unbearable, and GB d'Avenay repeatedly pleaded with Sahuc to let him charge the deadly Austrian guns, but it was a Habsburg commander who moved first. Despite the failure of his first attack, Wolfskeel had watched the progress of the battle with mounting impatience. He twice sent officers to Johann requesting permission to charge, only to be told to await the arrival of Colloredo's brigade along the river. A messenger had just delivered a third request and received qualified approval when, to the astonishment of the archduke and his staff, the sound of trumpets in the warm spring air announced a charge and they saw Wolfskeel's squadrons moving forward. To Johann's lasting irritation, someone—apparently FML Ignaz Gyulai, who had no business doing so—gave Wolfskeel the permission he had sought and the Austrian horsemen jogged towards Dessaix. Unfortunately for the Austrians, the attack collapsed almost immediately. It is possible that the troopers, weary from lack of sleep during the night and chastened by their failure in the morning, never charged home in the first place.[36] Whatever the case, Wolfskeel's men recoiled in the face of Dessaix's steady ranks and fell back towards their starting point in confusion.

The stage was now set for a decisive French riposte. Pully and d'Avenay had already reconnoitred the ground they would have to cover and an orderly from Eugene was actually galloping to deliver attack orders when Wolfskeel advanced. Although d'Avenay was carried from the field when an Austrian ball nearly tore his leg off just before Wolfskeel's charge, the veteran French cavalry, 'calm and intrepid', were thus well prepared and eager to 'take their revenge for the Battle of Sacile'.[37] Leading with the 28th, Pully threw his two dragoon regiments at Wolfskeel on the right, while 6th Chasseurs and the 4th Squadron of the 8th attacked Splenyi on the left with the 25th following in support; the 9th Chasseurs advanced in the middle.

Momentarily delayed by a ditch in front of the Austrian guns, 28th Dragoons suffered heavily from a dreadful blast of canister, but the French troopers plunged ahead, capturing fourteen guns, killing, wounding, or dispersing the gunners, and taking prisoner GM Anton Freiherr von Reisner, Johann's artillery chief. Manoeuvring skilfully, the French crushed and scattered the Austrian dragoons and hussars, pursuing the fleeing enemy headlong to within 700 or 800 metres of Conegliano. 'The mob rolled back in the greatest disorder,' recorded the doleful Johann, noting that those who escaped through Mandre 'fled to Conegliano and brought the baggage, the reserve, everything into the greatest disorder so that everyone fled towards Sacile.'[38]

Wolfskeel, refusing to surrender, was killed outside Mandre as he tried in vain to rally his men. Oberst Karl Graf Aichelburg, commander of the *Savoy* Dragoons fell likewise, and GM von Hager was captured. With his men carried away by their enthusiasm, Pully had a difficult time recalling his regiments and a number of French saddles were emptied by Austrian musketry before the weary but elated troopers retired to reorganise. The charge of the light cavalry on the left had been equally successful, the 6th Chasseurs overthrowing first Splenyi's hussars and then smashing Colloredo's four squadrons of *Ott* as the 25th Chasseurs galloped up to join the attack. Trumpeter Chevillet was thrilled by 'the imposing and admirable spectacle' and recounted that 'a species of terror' seemed to seize the enemy hussars.[39] The whitecoated infantry, on the other hand, retained its composure. With the French cavalry swarming on all sides, there was no time to form masses, so Colloredo had the rear ranks turn about and let loose a volley at thirty paces. The infantry's steady demeanour and well-delivered fire sufficed to repel the chasseurs, and the Austrian foot solders were able to reclaim several of the guns lost in the first rush of the French attack.

It was now 11 a.m. The bold French charge had been a resounding success. Unleashed at exactly the right moment by experienced professionals who had studied the terrain in advance, it had shattered the Austrian horse, removing it from the battlefield chessboard as an offensive playing piece for the remainder of the day. Superior numbers had been a key factor in the French victory: although the number of squadrons was equal (twenty-one to a side), the French brought some 3,200 men to the fray as compared to 2,200 or so Austrians.[40] However, courage, skill, and determination were just as important, especially in the case of Pully's dragoons where the French enjoyed little, if any, numerical advantage and the Austrians were supported by a large battery. Pully justifiably remarked that his dragoons were 'the saviours of the army', and a French infantryman proudly stated 'our cavalry executed the most splendid charge.'[41] Johann, on the other hand, could only lament that much of his mounted arm had galloped 'on beyond Conegliano and only a few rallied themselves'.[42]

Both commanders adjusted their forces in the wake of the grand cavalry clash. In addition to Broussier's 9th Ligne, Eugene now had three battalions of 84th Ligne and part of Lamarque's division across the river. He used these to hold his centre while transferring Dessaix to the right to block Colloredo's approach to the fords. The cavalry reordered itself on both flanks of Broussier and Lamarque. Dessaix's shift towards the river, however, allowed FML Ignaz Gyulai to advance. Pivoting on Campana, his line moved up to the sinuous dyke that ran towards the le Grave farmstead; the *Chimani* Grenadiers occupied le Grave to anchor this line on the left.

Action near the San Nichiol ford had been limited thus far. As soon as Grouchy was across, Grenier sent over a pair of ad hoc elite battalions and two guns under Colonel Alexandre de Rége Gifflenga, the two cannon producing 'a marvellous effect by drawing [Austrian] artillery fire that would have ravaged our deep columns terribly'.[43] Supported by two of Grouchy's squadrons, these men pushed back Austrian skirmishers who were trying to edge close to the ford, the dragoons capturing more than 100 prisoners in the process. Shortly before noon, a substantial body of Habsburg hussars apparently sought to drive through to the ford, but the Austrian troopers recoiled in disorder when charged from the front by 7th Dragoons and struck in the flank by 8th Chasseurs. Meanwhile, Grenier was pushing more infantry and artillery behind Grouchy and Gifflenga. The midday sun thus shone on Abbé's division struggling through the water at San Nichiol (two battalions of 1st Ligne and his squadron of *Napoleon* Dragoons joined Gifflenga), while Lamarque's braved the river at Lovadina. Otherwise a lull descended on the battlefield, broken only by smattering of skirmishing and cannon fire as the two armies eyed each other across the fields and vineyards.

Afternoon Attack: Sacile Avenged (noon to night)

The lull in the fighting offered Johann an opportunity for an ordered retreat during the afternoon, but he chose to hold in place. Despite the cavalry debacle, he saw no reason for an immediate withdrawal. The quiescent enemy to his front seemed to pose no imminent threat (he could not see the French troops massing in the low ground along the river), while precipitate withdrawal might endanger the disordered baggage trains, could expose his line of communications to attack from the French at Nervesa, and would

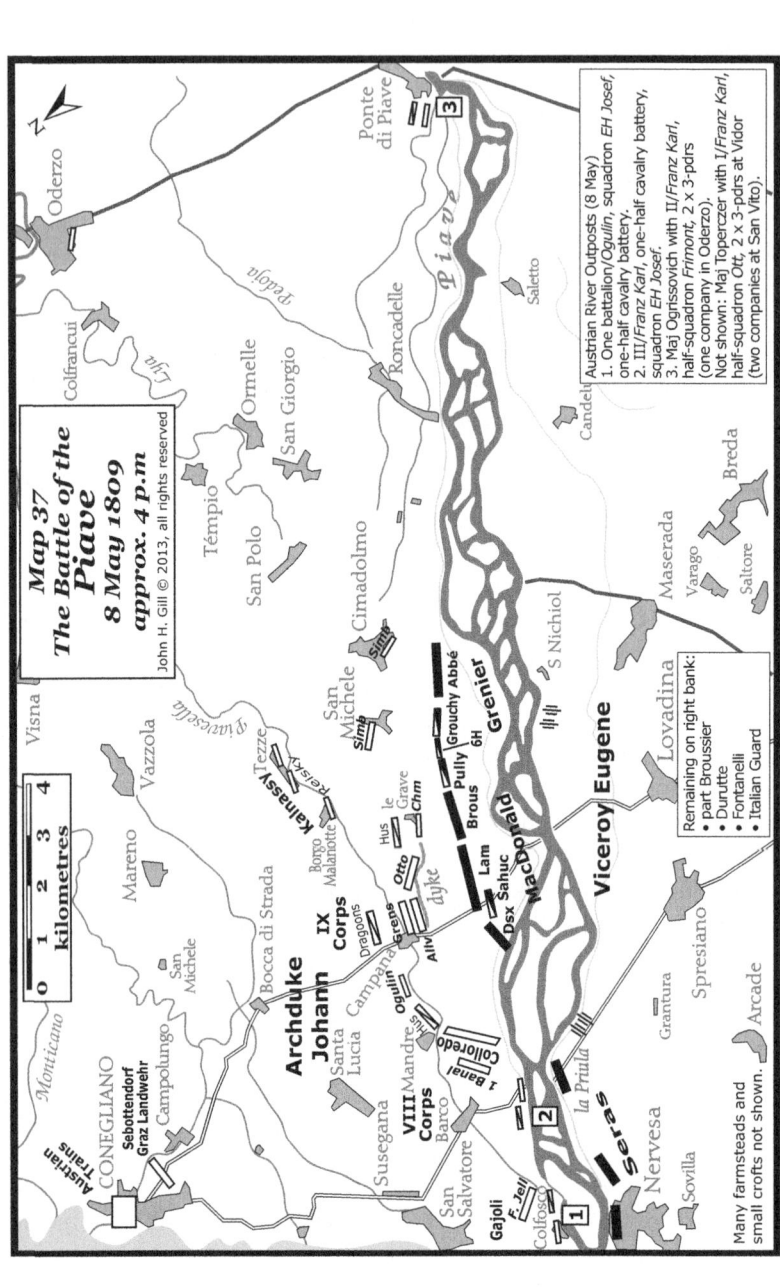

Map 37
The Battle of the Piave
8 May 1809
approx. 4 p.m
John H. Gill © 2013, all rights reserved

kilometres
0 1 2 3 4

Austrian River Outposts (8 May)
1. One battalion/*Ogulin*, squadron *EH Josef*, one-half cavalry battery.
2. III/*Franz Karl*, one-half cavalry battery, squadron *EH Josef*.
3. Maj Ogrissovich with II/*Franz Karl*, half-squadron *Frimont*, 2 x 3-pdrs (one company in Oderzo).
Not shown: Maj Toperczer with 1/*Franz Karl*, half-squadron *Ott*, 2 x 3-pdrs at Vidor (two companies at San Vito).

Remaining on right bank:
• part Broussier
• Durutte
• Fontanelli
• Italian Guard

Many farmsteads and small crofts not shown.

Archduke
Johann

IX
Corps

VIII
Corps

CONEGLIANO

Austrian Trains

Sebottendorf
Graz Landwehr

Viceroy Eugene

MacDonald

Grenier

Seras

Oderzo

Ponte di Piave

Piave

likely create opportunities for the numerous French cavalry to harass his retreating columns.[44] He thus reordered his lines as best he could and waited for darkness, hoping that the presumably exhausted French would permit him an unmolested retreat during the night. The renewal of the battle at 4 p.m. therefore came as a complete surprise to the Austrians, shattering their comfortable assumptions and placing the army in grave danger.

Eugene, with the unbridged and now unfordable river at his back, was in an equally precarious position. Rather than wait for an Austrian counter-stroke, however, he resolutely decided to attack, aiming to break the Austrian left and then drive for the Conegliano road to threaten Johann's principal route of retreat. At the very least, the Austrians would be forced to abandon the line of the Piave and fall back behind the Livenza. Eugene entrusted Grenier and Grouchy with the opening attack, reining in MacDonald to strike the hinge in the Austrian line once Grenier began to bend it back.

Grenier attacked at 4 p.m. Colonel Yves Pastol of the 52nd led his regiment and two battalions of the 1st against the south-western face of Cimadolmo, while Gifflenga advanced on the village from the south with his two elite battalions, the other two battalions of the 1st, and the squadron of *Napoleon* Dragoons. Simultaneously, the 102nd Ligne and 8th Léger assaulted San Michele under Colonel Pierre Espert de Sibra (102nd), as the French dragoons and 6th Hussars pushed into the space west of the village, outflanking it on that side.[45] The lone battalion of *Simbschen* in Cimadolmo and the two in San Michele had no chance of holding long against this sort of pressure. They soon fell back, the two from San Michele withdrawing slowly towards Tezze and holding the French for a time as they withdrew, while the other retired undisturbed to the east. Grenier's advance opened the way for MacDonald. Broussier accordingly wheeled his division to the left to evict the stubborn *Chimani* Grenadiers from le Grave and called on 7th Dragoons to hold a haphazard collection of Austrian hussars in check. As Broussier moved towards the dyke where the determined grenadiers had re-established themselves, Lamarque began wheeling to the left in his turn to advance up the highway with Sahuc on his left flank.

Johann, surprised and alarmed by the unexpected French attack, hastened to react. On his left flank, he ordered Kalnassy to stand firm and sent Major Josef Freiherr Fisson du Montet to Vazzola with his half-baked 4th Inner Austrian Volunteers, the *Szulin* Grenzer, a squadron of *Josef* Hussars, and two guns to serve as a backstop for Kalnassy. On the right, he directed Gajoli to join Colloredo for an attack against Dessaix in the hope of relieving pressure on his endangered left and centre. Two hours elapsed, however,

Table 5: The Battle of the Piave:
French Afternoon Attack, 8 May

Commander (left to right)	Units	Cavalry Squadrons	Infantry Battalions	Guns
Dessaix	Advance Guard	4	6	4
Sahuc	6th, 8th, 25th Chasseurs	12	-	4
Lamarque	18th Léger, 13th, 23rd, 29th	-	12	12
(from Durutte)		-	-	3
Broussier	9th (four), 84th (three)	-	7	12
(from Durutte)	23rd Léger	-	1 1/2	3
Pully	23rd, 28th, 29th Dragoons	11	-	-
Grouchy	7th, 30th, Queen's Dragoons	11	-	4
	6th Hussars	4	-	-
Abbé/Espert	8th Léger, 102nd	-	6	6
Abbé/Pastol	1st (two), 52nd	-	6	4
Gifflenga	1st (two), 2 x elite battalions	-	4	2
	IV/*Napoleon* Dragoons	1	-	-
Total		43	42 1/2	54
Italian Guard artillery (possibly on left bank)				+6

Note: distribution of Abbé's guns is speculative.

before these generals had their brigades (eleven battalions) in position to advance. Following a vicious fight, Grenier threw Kalnassy out of Tezze sometime after 6 p.m., and Johann, who had ridden to VIII Corps to press the counter-attack, dashed to the centre to assess the situation personally. He immediately saw that the battle was irretrievable and issued a new disposition for a retreat behind the Livenza: the VIII Corps attack was recalled, Kalnassy, who had fallen back on du Montet in Vazzola, was to advance again on Tezze, while IX Corps would form a rear guard across the highway to cover the rest of the army in its retreat.

Meanwhile, the battle raged in the centre. Pressure from Broussier and Lamarque forced FML Ignaz Gyulai to pull back behind the Piavesella, but the whitecoats offered stiff resistance and the French advance stalled despite a fierce artillery bombardment and courageous infantry assaults. Colloredo and Gajoli, on the other hand, showered with shot from the French 12-pounders on the far bank, had made almost no progress with their counter-attack when the withdrawal order arrived. Darkness was falling rapidly now and FML Albert Gyulai, breaking off his anaemic advance, was able to lead his corps, the infantry formed in masses, away from the field in good order followed by Dessaix 'at a respectful distance'.[46] In the left-centre, however, a furious struggle ensued as Johann desperately fended off Grenier's thrust towards Conegliano and the highway. Hurled against the French, II/*Ottocac* lost almost all of its officers and many of its men in a brutal half-hour fight.[47] The regiment's 1st Battalion also suffered severely as it marched up, but their efforts, bravely supported by remnants of the dragoon brigade and some *Josef* Hussars, sufficed to block Grenier. This success probably saved the Austrian army, because shortly thereafter the IX Corps rear guard had to yield its position on the Piavesella to the impetuous French infantry and a powerful battery of twenty-four guns Eugene had assembled in the centre.

Shielded by their rear guard, most of Johann's men made good their retreat through Conegliano and across the Livenza towards Sacile. Some troops, however, were not so fortunate. Three companies of *St Julien*, for instance, somehow became lost in the darkness and marched into the French lines, where they promptly surrendered; several of the more distant detachments became separated from the main body of the army. Chief among these was Kalnassy, who received no orders and thus remained east of the Livenza while the rest of the army withdrew. We shall consider the colourful fates of these groups shortly.

Back on the battlefield, 'the enemy retreated so rapidly that he could no longer reply to our fire,' remarked one of Napoleon's personal staff officers.[48] Eugene was content to let them go. Worried about losing control in the darkness and concerned that half of his army was on the far side of the still-unspanned Piave, he called off the weak pursuit around 9 p.m. With Sahuc and Pully screening the area towards Conegliano, the army spent the night stretched from San Salvatore (Dessaix), through Bocca di Strada (Broussier, Lamarque), to Tezze (Grenier, Grouchy). Around 11 p.m., the viceroy retired from the field, taking as his lodgings the Collalto castle just vacated by his opponent.[49] With the benefit of hindsight, the Austrian official history suggests that Eugene's decision to halt for the night was a mistake, that he could have swept up many more stragglers had he loosed his cavalry to press Johann's retreat. Although it is doubtless true that more prisoners would have been seized with a bolder pursuit, Eugene's night was crowded with uncertainties and his prudent orders were entirely consistent with his situation. More telling is the criticism that Grenier should have continued his thrust into the Austrian flank after he had crossed the Piavesella and taken Tezze. A small force would have sufficed to contain Kalnassy and an unrelenting jab towards the highway, in combination with Lamarque and Broussier, might have unhinged Johann's entire line and thrown his army into even greater disarray.[50] These observations notwithstanding, Eugene committed few errors on the banks of the Piave on 8 May and had a handsome victory as his well-deserved reward. Seasoning daring with caution, he made quick, bold decisions and displayed a fine sense of timing to complement his acknowledged personal bravery.[51]

Most of the day's mistakes were made by Austrians. Foremost among the tactical lapses was the neglect of the fords at Lovadina and San Nichiol, but the delays in bringing Colloredo into action, the refusal to use IX Corps' infantry offensively, and the dispersal of Kalnassy's brigade in small, digestible packets from front to rear on the left wing all contributed to the negative outcome for the Habsburg cause. As noted above, the decision to remain in place during the afternoon may also be questioned. The greatest error in judgement, however, was Johann's decision to halt behind the Piave in the first place, when further retreat was all but inevitable given the results on the Danube. As Johann himself later observed, 'the battle could have been avoided.'[52] Instead, he had founded his plans on hopes and illusions, allowed himself to be attacked, and suffered a severe battering. Austrian casualties totalled some 3,900 as compared to something over 2,000 French, losses that Eugene's much larger army could better afford. The Habsburg army that trudged east through the night, the army that would now be called upon to defend the monarchy's borders, was therefore substantially weaker—both psychologically and physically—than it had been when it crossed the Piave two days earlier. In contrast, the French saw 'this brilliant day' as confirmation of their superiority.[53] Already encouraged by the turn of the campaign since their consolidation on the Adige, they now felt vindicated and many echoed Routier's sentiment that 'this brilliant affair' had 'avenged that of Sacile'.[54]

9–17 MAY: TO THE EMPIRE'S BORDERS

Johann spent the next two days getting his army safely behind the Tagliamento. Hesitant French pursuit allowed him to accomplish this task with little interference despite his army's exhaustion and the flooded state of the river. Leaving Frimont at Dignano as rear guard, he collected the bulk of his command around San Daniele, hoping to grant them a morning's rest on 11 May before continuing the retreat back into Habsburg territory.[55]

As mentioned earlier, however, several detachments had lost contact with the army in the confusion following the Battle of the Piave and did not reach the bivouac at San Daniele. Kalnassy's was the most important of these. He had quickly assumed a defensive posture after making a half-hearted advance on Tezze during the evening of 8 May, but his withdrawal orders went awry and he spent the night near Vazzola. Sometime during the night the *Reisky* Infantry and two squadrons of *Josef* Hussars became separated from the brigade and made their way back to the main army, but thanks to lack of enterprise on the part of French reconnaissance, Kalnassy and the remainder (six battalions, one squadron, one battery) were able to reach Udine on 11 May, after blundering about the countryside on both banks of the Livenza for two days. Similarly, Major Michael Ogrissovich's detachment at Ponte di Piave had received no orders whatsoever and spent 8 May utterly unaware that a major battle was blazing only five or six kilometres away. Although a detached company at Oderzo was overwhelmed by Fontanelli's division (112th Ligne) on 9 May, the rest of Ogrissovich's little command escaped through Motta to arrive safely in Latisana on the 11th. The detachment at la Priula was able to retreat with VIII Corps, but the one at Colfosco received its instructions too late and had to turn north into the foothills for two days before rejoining the army at Spilembergo on 10 May. By far the most adventurous was the fate of Major Paul Toperczer's detachment at Vidor. These men marched for Serravale on the 8th, but found themselves trapped between Eugene and Rusca. Sinking their guns and vehicles in a lake, they wandered through the mountains on snow-covered tracks for four days, losing half of their number (including Toperczer) in the process, before reaching Ampezzo on 14 May.[56]

Johann planned to use Kalnassy and Ogrissovich as part of the defensive scheme he issued on 11 May from San Daniele. According to this rather grandiose concept (the official historians called it 'fantastical'), Chasteler would hold the Tyrol, Frimont and Albert Gyulai would defend the border area around Tarvis, and Ignaz Gyulai, the Ban (viceroy) of Croatia, would hold the line of the Isonzo. Jellacic, placed under Johann's command as Hiller withdrew down the Danube, would guard the approaches from Salzburg.[57] Johann himself would command a reserve of fifteen battalions, twelve squadrons and nine Landwehr battalions in a central position near Villach from which he could presumably rush to the assistance of any endangered subordinate.[58] In addition to exaggerating the defensive value of the mountains he was about to enter, the archduke's concept underestimated the damage his own army had suffered and took his energetic enemy for granted: 'the enemy on the Italian front moves more slowly, he will have to divide his forces, that is our good fortune,' he wrote at the time, 'we need some rest, if only that the soldiers may be given shoes, the artillery horses, and that the stragglers may be collected, then I will renew my operations.'[59] Eugene was not about to grant this sort of indulgence.

11 May: Engagement at San Daniele

While Johann was concocting this plan, the French were cautiously following his retreat, gathering up significant numbers of stragglers (more than 700 on 10 May alone) as they moved towards the Tagliamento. Spurred by new orders from Napoleon, Eugene pushed powerful elements across the river on 11 May: Grouchy heading for Udine with most of the cavalry and Dessaix marching north towards San Daniele followed at some distance by Grenier. The cavalry found Udine abandoned and Grouchy located lodgings for his men and Sahuc's on the road to San Daniele, while Pully occupied the city with 7th, 28th, and 29th Dragoons. Despite the tentative nature of their advance, Grouchy's troopers netted between 700 and 1,500 prisoners during the day.

Dessaix, on the other hand, collided with Frimont's outposts south of San Daniele. The highway here passed through a defile and the Austrians were unconcernedly resting and cooking in preparation for an afternoon march to the north. Frimont's patrols had spotted dust columns east of the Tagliamento just after dawn and reported that the French were moving on Udine, so the army ignored the sounds of skirmishing that drifted up from the south around mid-morning. Frimont soon found himself under heavy pressure and sent his ten companies of *Ogulin* Grenzer back to Villanova and his regular battalion (III/*Franz Karl*) to Sacco as his hussars retreated before the impetuous French. Dessaix's 9th Chasseurs, reinforced by 23rd Dragoons and backed by the six voltigeur battalions, however, were more than the Austrian hussars could hold.[60] They fell back in haste, exposing the Grenzer at Villanova. Frimont's reporting must have been sparse, because Johann and his men were astonished when Dessaix suddenly struck the Grenzer, overwhelmed them, and advanced towards the army's bivouacs at around noon. The army's 'idyllic peace' rudely broken, Johann scrambled to react.[61] As the disordered Grenzer fled north, he ordered IX Corps to retreat,

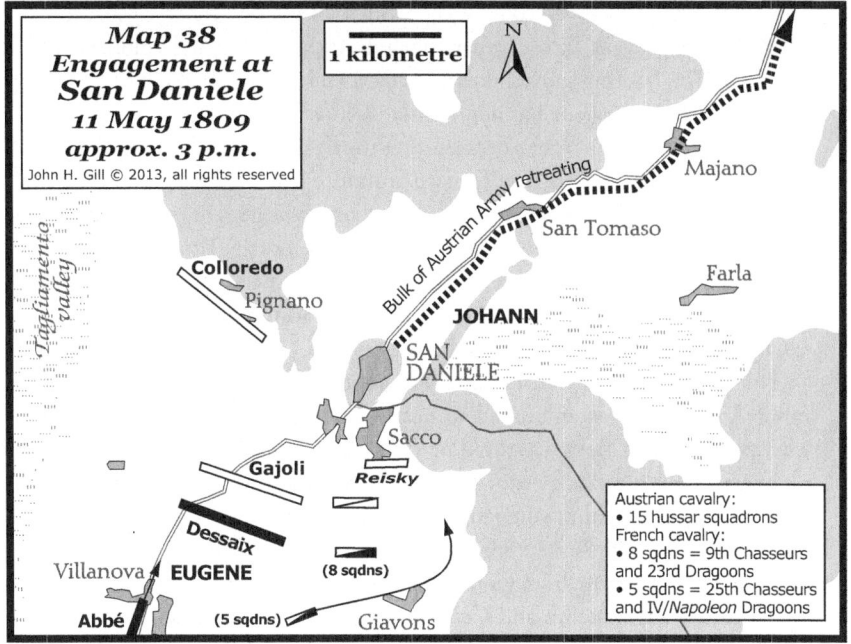

Map 38
Engagement at
San Daniele
11 May 1809
approx. 3 p.m.

1 kilometre

N

Tagliamento valley

Colloredo

Pignano

Bulk of Austrian Army retreating

Majano

San Tomaso

Farla

JOHANN

SAN DANIELE

Sacco

Gajoli

Reisky

Dessaix

Villanova EUGENE

(8 sqdns)

Abbé

(5 sqdns)

Giavons

Austrian cavalry:
• 15 hussar squadrons
French cavalry:
• 8 sqdns = 9th Chasseurs
and 23rd Dragoons
• 5 sqdns = 25th Chasseurs
and IV/*Napoleon* Dragoons

sent Gajoli to counter-attack Dessaix, and directed Colloredo to occupy the heights west of San Daniele. Gajoli's advance stalled almost immediately and the combat settled into a tense, noisy stalemate for several hours.

Eugene reached the battlefield at 2.30 p.m. and decided to 'attack without delay', but had to wait until Abbé's division arrived at approximately 3 p.m. The viceroy then reinforced Dessaix with two battalions each of 1st and 52nd Ligne to attack Gajoli, while the rest of the infantry advanced on the western heights and the cavalry, grown to thirteen squadrons with the appearance of 25th Chasseurs and the squadron of *Napoleon* Dragoons, sought for a weak spot on the Austrian left. The French attack coincided with poorly timed Austrian withdrawals. Colloredo, seeing that IX Corps was almost clear of the defile, ordered his brigade to retire and the Habsburg hussars, fearing encirclement by the encroaching French horse, turned north on their own accord. Gajoli's men were thus left alone to face Dessaix as French troops pushed past both their flanks. They soon broke and fled, streaming to the rear to carry confusion into the congestion of the retreating column. The French, hard on their heels, reached San Daniele before the last IX Corps unit, a battalion of *Reisky*, could escape. Surrounded by French cavalry, the entire battalion went into captivity, including the regimental colonel and standard. The fighting moved north of San Daniele as a charge by Dessaix with the Italian voltigeur battalion broke the last remnant of resistance in the town and Eugene's troops pressed after the fleeing Austrians. The French finally lost momentum at San Tomaso around 5 p.m., when Johann placed the *Sallomon* Grenadiers across the road and ordered the reorganised *Ogulin* Grenzer to hold the flanking high ground to the north. This intervention afforded the army enough breathing space to get away, the long column snaking off to the north to reach Venzone early on the morning of 12 May, exhausted, disordered, and demoralised.

The engagement at San Daniele was another disaster for the Army of Inner Austria. Losses amounted to nearly 2,000 (890 dead and wounded with an additional 1,000 captured or missing), while the French casualties numbered only some 200–250. Almost all of the French losses came from Dessaix's hard-marching voltigeurs; indeed, it seems the Austrian defence collapsed before Abbé's men became seriously engaged. Johann also lost his pontoon train. Fontanelli's division picked up a further sixty prisoners in its march to the Tagliamento and Colonel Gifflenga added to Habsburg woes by a bold stroke during the night. Ordered to inflict further injury on the retreating Austrians, Gifflenga took a squadron each of 6th Hussars and *Queen's* Dragoons to Osoppo late on the evening of 11 May as the Austrians withdrew from their blockade of the little fortress.[62] Here he picked up three companies of 9th Ligne from the garrison and marched on to attack Gemona at 4 a.m. on the morning of the 12th, capturing as many as 700 men and a standard of *Franz Jellacic*.[63]

The rest of the 12th passed with little incident until evening, when Dessaix attacked the Austrian rear guard (Colloredo's brigade) ensconced in Venzone. Conducted with equal ferocity and determination by both sides, this exchange cost the Austrians some 350–400 men (Colloredo was among the wounded) and the French probably a similar number.[64] The whitecoats held off Dessaix's attacks but could not remain in Venzone. As the firing died down sometime between 9 and 10 p.m., they slipped off to the north to join the rest of the rear guard near Moggio, burning bridges as they went. Johann and the army's main body halted at Pontebba. To the east, Kalnassy and his weary men trudged to Karfreit and gratefully accepted a rest day before heading east to Idria and a junction with Ignaz Gyulai as ordered. He left I/*Szulin*, a hussar platoon, and his four guns at Flitsch to secure the upper Isonzo and the approaches to the Predil Pass.

Plans and Illusions

One month and one day after opening his offensive, the archduke was back on home soil facing an almost insoluble strategic problem.[65] Yet he retained a relatively rosy outlook. Despite the severe setbacks of the preceding four days, the acknowledged French advantage in numbers, the clear revival of French morale, and the disturbing evidence of demoralisation among the Habsburg troops, Johann maintained that he would be able to hold the passes from Friaul towards Carinthia with a mere eight line battalions, two Landwehr battalions, and four squadrons under FML Albert Gyulai. The army could thus recuperate, while FML Ignaz Gyulai defended Carniola with a hotchpotch of line troops, unreliable Landwehr, and the as-yet unformed Croatian Insurrection. Even if supported by the archduke himself at Villach with 'the core of my army', it is difficult to see how he could have expected his subordinates to accomplish their missions with exhausted, uncertain troops against a numerically superior foe riding high on a string of recent successes.[66] In part, he seems to have consoled himself with the alluring assumption—so common among Habsburg leaders—that the French would need to rest before undertaking a drive into the mountains.[67]

Johann's thinking was thus wildly optimistic and his underlying assumptions bore little resemblance to reality, but in fairness, it must be stated that he was faced with a nearly insuperable strategic challenge: defending a long border with inadequate numbers of shaken, weary men against an active enemy. Furthermore, the instructions he received from Franz and Charles were often outdated, vague, or hopelessly sanguine. Johann and his army always seem to have been an afterthought in the minds of the Habsburg leadership, and earnest orders were sent directing him to retain as much as possible of his 'advantages' in Italy when the authors of those missives probably knew that what they were asking was utterly unrealistic.[68] The fact that he was in this predicament, however, highlights the bankruptcy of the very notion of adopting an offensive strategy in Italy in the first place and offers yet further evidence that Vienna's choice of war under the conditions prevailing in 1809 was an error of grand-strategic magnitude. Scattering his diminished army and placing his faith in hopeful assumptions, he was simply compounding the empire's problems.

Regardless of his plan's merits, Johann acted quickly to implement it, sending FML Ignaz Gyulai off to Laibach on 12 May with the two dragoon regiments, the *Frimont* Hussars (five squadrons), III/*Franz Karl*, the *Ottocac* Grenzer, and three and one-half batteries. Generals Splenyi and

Gavassini were assigned as Gyulai's subordinates. To speed the march, the infantry were transported in requisitioned wagons, allowing Gyulai's men to reach Laibach on 16 May, a notable achievement.[69] Also headed towards Carniola were FML Zach with the blockade force from Palmanova and GM Kalnassy with his orphaned brigade. Along with Major Ogrissovich's detachment, they were to defend the line of the Isonzo and the fortress of Präwald as part of Ignaz Gyulai's new command. All of these troops were in poor shape: Zach's flighty Landwehr had dwindled to a fraction of its authorised strength, while the regulars were exhausted from long marches and weakened by battle losses (the three *Simbschen* battalions had to be consolidated into two). None of them was in any condition to resist the blows that were about to fall.

For his main force in the tangle of valleys south of Tarvis, Johann sent Frimont to Villach and Arnoldstein with a so-called 'mobile corps' of fifteen infantry battalions, three Graz Landwehr battalions, and twelve hussar squadrons (perhaps 5,000 regulars and 3,000 Landwehr) to serve as a

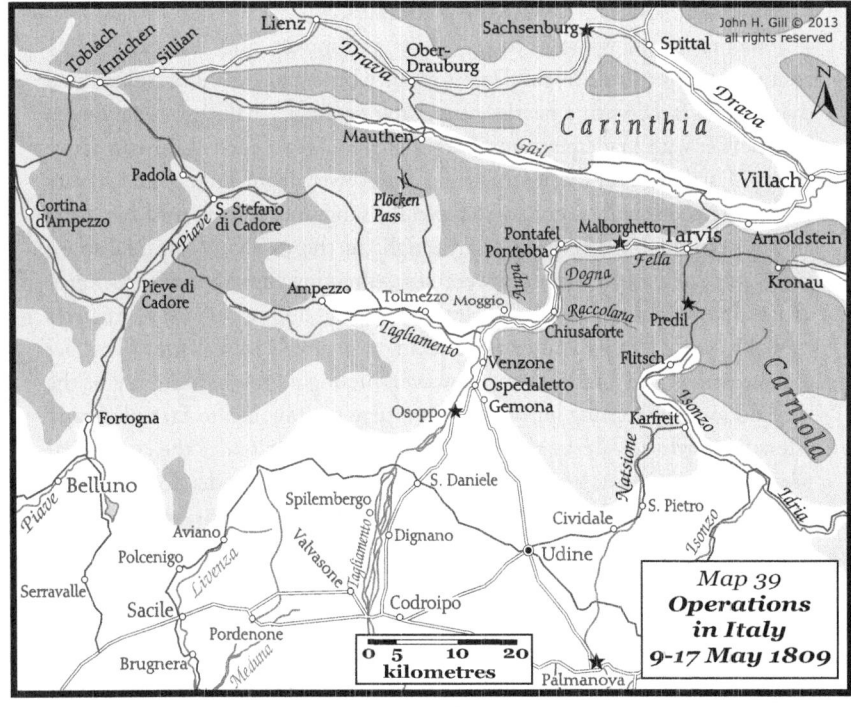

Map 39
Operations in Italy
9-17 May 1809

central reserve. He gave FML Albert Gyulai responsibility for the rear guard: ten battalions, four squadrons, and three batteries (at best 3,000 infantry, 2,000 Landwehr, and 300 cavalry). These would be centred on Tarvis but would rely heavily on the defensive strength of small forts at Malborghetto and the Predil Pass. Eight additional Landwehr battalions and some depot troops were to join Albert Gyulai, but the French did not allow Johann time to complete the reorganisation of the troops at hand, let alone call in reinforcements from Styria.[70] Beyond these assigned troops, Gyulai also had at his disposal the battalion of *Szulin* Grenzer that Kalnassy had left near Flitsch and three companies of *Strassaldo* that had been deposited in the Raccolana valley to cover the rear approach to the Predil Pass.

Eugene, unlike Johann, had a realistic plan and clear guidance from Napoleon. 'I have no doubt that the enemy will be retiring in front of you,' wrote the emperor on 1 May, 'he is to be pursued vigorously with a view to joining me via Carinthia as soon as possible.' 'The junction with my army should take place near Bruck,' he continued. '*It is likely that I will be in Vienna between 10 and 15 May.*'[71] With this guidance in mind and intent on pressing his advantage, Eugene divided his army into three principal elements and pushed his men forward. MacDonald (with Pully's dragoons and 6th Hussars), on the right, would advance on the Isonzo, while Seras made his way up the twisted valleys from Cividale towards Flitsch, and Eugene drove up the Tagliamento and Fella valleys on Tarvis and Villach. The advance began at once.

14–16 May: Engagements around Tarvis—Approach

Dessaix led the way north up the Tagliamento with his slightly modified advance guard (the voltigeur battalions from Seras and from MacDonald's corps returned to their parent formations and were replaced by 8th Léger),[72] followed by Durutte with GB Valentin's brigade (23rd Léger, 62nd Ligne), Fontanelli, GD Michel Pacthod's division (Pacthod had arrived on 12 May to supplant Abbé) and, somewhat farther to the rear, the infantry of the Royal Guard. Owing to the thorough destruction of the bridges and the impossibility of speedy repair, Eugene decided to send Grouchy's dragoons, the Guard cavalry, and most of the artillery after Seras on the road through the Predil Pass. The light horse and a mere six guns remained with the main body. Lieutenant Noël, commanding the battery, gives a sense of the difficulties involved getting the guns across the river:

The bridge at Pietra Tagliata had been rebuilt on the burned piles of the old one. It did not appear strong enough for the weight of the artillery, but time was short. I had the guns dismantled, the limbers and caissons emptied. The guns were securely tied with ropes to beams carried on the shoulders of soldiers positioned on either end. The soldiers also carried the ammunition, the limbers, and the caissons across separately, and the horses were led over one at a time. The whole operation . . . took until nine in the evening . . .[73]

Such challenges notwithstanding, by evening of 14 May, Dessaix had cleverly outflanked the Austrian rear guard (II/*Ogulin*, one hussar squadron) and pushed it back to Malborghetto. Behind him were Durutte at Pontebba, Pacthod further south, and Fontanelli encamped downstream from Chiusaforte, while Seras entered Flitsch on the right flank. In addition, the French had pushed two flanking columns into the mountains to the east of the Fella. The 60th Ligne had moved up the Raccolana valley to cut off the little fortress guarding the Predil Pass in conjunction with Seras's advance,

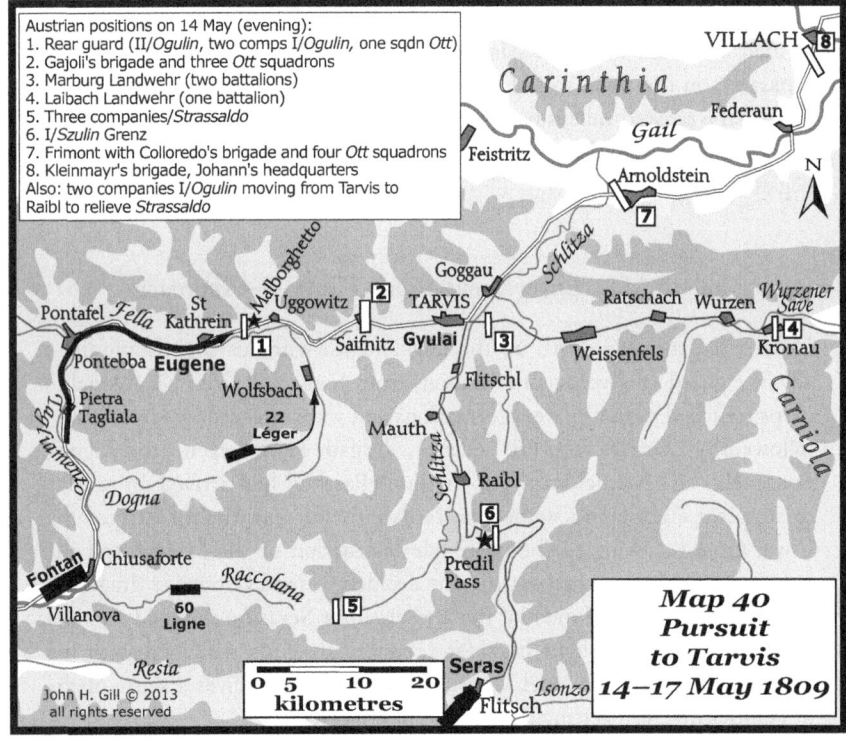

Austrian positions on 14 May (evening):
1. Rear guard (II/*Ogulin*, two comps I/*Ogulin*, one sqdn *Ott*)
2. Gajoli's brigade and three *Ott* squadrons
3. Marburg Landwehr (two battalions)
4. Laibach Landwehr (one battalion)
5. Three companies/*Strassaldo*
6. I/*Szulin* Grenz
7. Frimont with Colloredo's brigade and four *Ott* squadrons
8. Kleinmayr's brigade, Johann's headquarters
Also: two companies I/*Ogulin* moving from Tarvis to Raibl to relieve *Strassaldo*

Map 40
Pursuit to Tarvis
14–17 May 1809

John H. Gill © 2013
all rights reserved

and 22nd Léger had advanced up the Dogna under instructions to keep pace with Dessaix's march. The Dogna valley, however, offered no sustenance and Major Daguzan commanding the 22nd moved his men over a difficult pass to come down in the next valley in the hope of finding food and shelter at Wolfsbach. The two battalions arrived sometime after 10 p.m. but Daguzan neglected basic security, and his command was caught completely unawares by a surprise Austrian attack at 2 a.m. on 15 May. After a silent approach, *Franz Jellacic* charged out of the darkness and scattered the French light infantrymen in every direction, killing some and taking 198 prisoners (including Daguzan) for the loss of one dead and a handful wounded.[74]

During the day, Frimont's new command had withdrawn as directed to Arnoldstein (Colloredo's brigade, Graz Landwehr, *Ott*) and Villach (Gajoli and *Josef* Hussars). The 'rapid and bold' French advance, however, combined with the shaky state of morale in his command, made Albert Gyulai uncomfortable.[75] The unexpected appearance of 22nd Léger on his flank (in terrain the Austrians had deemed impassable) and prisoners' statements that they were the vanguard of a large column only heightened his anxiety. Despite the new command arrangements, therefore, he 'more ordered than asked' Frimont for immediate help and, by the morning of the 15th, the latter's three line regiments were in supporting positions: *Allvintzi* at Saifnitz and Colloredo's other two regiments at Tarvis.[76] To Gyulai's south, I/*Szulin* had fallen back to Predil in front of Seras, and two companies of I/*Ogulin* were en route to relieve the three *Strassaldo* companies blocking 60th Ligne's exit from the Raccolana valley.

As Gyulai's reinforcements were arriving, the French were advancing, Dessaix and Durutte in the forefront along the Fella, while Fontanelli's troops exploited the Dogna and Raccolana valleys. Placed under Bonfanti's command, 60th Ligne drove the three *Strassaldo* companies back to Raibl during the morning and forced the *Szulin* battalion at Predil to evacuate its position to avoid being cut off. Indeed, one company had to turn back to the fort (where a different company had been left as garrison). In the late afternoon, as the rest of Bonfanti's brigade (six battalions) crossed over the pass, the 60th renewed its attacks and pushed the Austrians as far as Mauth despite the intervention of a *Strassaldo* battalion sent by Gyulai. Along the Fella, Dessaix's bold troops, supported by III/8th Léger and three battalions of 23rd Léger, clambered up the trackless crags on both sides of the valley to outflank the Austrian rear guard at Malborghetto.[77] Pressed by the venturesome French, Gyulai left a garrison in the fort and withdrew his entire command to Tarvis as the sun was setting. Dessaix's three voltigeur

Table 6: Advance on Tarvis: French Columns, 15–16 May

Valley (north to south)	Follow-on Units	Follow-on Units	Lead Units
Fella	GD Pacthod (12)	GD Durutte/ GB Valentin	GB Dessaix Voltigeurs (3)
	GD Sahuc	23rd Léger (4)	8th Léger (2)
	Guard Infantry (3)	62nd Ligne (4)	
Dogna		GD Fontanelli	Maj Daguzan
		112th Ligne (3)	22nd Léger (2)
		3rd Italian Line (2)	
Raccolana		GB Bonfanti	Maj Grenier
		1st Italian Line (4)	60th Ligne (2)
		2nd Italian Line (1)	
		Dalmatian Regt (1)	

Note: number of battalions shown in parantheses.

battalions, who had emerged near Uggowitz after their scramble over the mountains, remained where they were while the rest of his command and Valentin's bridge encamped around Malborghetto. Pacthod's men bivouacked just down the valley.

Fortunately for the Habsburg commander, the difficulties of negotiating a crumbling 'goat path' along the heights of the Dogna valley delayed Fontanelli and the other five battalions of his division (7th Italian remained in the Venzone area to prevent incursions from the upper Tagliamento).[78] 'The guides whose services the colonel had acquired conducted the regiment along sheer cliffs surrounded by chasms,' recalled a soldier of the 112th. 'It came to a point where every soldier, his musket slung across his back, had to cling with his hands to complete this arduous ascent, during which two of them found their deaths by falling over a precipice.'[79] Fontanelli halted just west of the pass, but the departure of *Franz Jellacic* from Wolfsbach allowed 22nd Léger to collect its wits around the town during the night and link its outposts with those of Dessaix's voltigeurs.

The situation on the evening of 15 May thus looked grim from the Austrian perspective and pessimism dominated thinking in the archduke's headquarters in Villach. All during the day, he had bombarded the harried FML Albert Gyulai with angry orders directing him to return Colloredo's brigade to Frimont and to detach a company and a squadron to guard the Gail valley against imaginary threats. Out of touch and indignant that his instructions were not being obeyed, Johann warned that Gyulai's insubordination could have the direst consequences for the monarchy. Gyulai dutifully, if regretfully, sent Colloredo's brigade to Villach. During the night of 15/16 May, however, as Gyulai's reports of the day's fighting came in, the mood in Villach sank, exacerbated by news that Chasteler had suffered a severe defeat at Wörgl in the Inn valley on 13 May. Gyulai's description of discouragement and exhaustion among the troops seems to have made a particularly vivid impact on Johann. His report to the Kaiser the following morning thus enumerated the army's many deficiencies, explicated the need to disperse troops along the frontier, and discussed future retreat options. In the meantime, Johann would wait to see 'if perhaps a favourable development along the Danube gives our situation a better outlook'.[80] In contrast to his commander, Albert Gyulai was oddly optimistic, confident that he could hold Tarvis for as long as ten days and hopeful that support from Frimont might permit a fruitful counter-attack.[81] The time for such thinking, however, was long past.

The morning of 16 May found the Austrians in the fortifications east of Tarvis, I/*Szulin* on the left behind a small earthwork (or flèche), *Reisky* in reserve at Klein Kreuth, *Ott* Hussars on the road to Weissenfels, and the remaining infantry spread along the redoubts and earthworks in the centre and right. The position was potentially strong, but the fortifications had been neglected since the advance into Italy and, with only some 3,500 weary and anxious men after Colloredo's departure, Albert Gyulai did not have enough troops to man them properly. Furthermore, his entire force was ensconced south of the Schlitza (Slizza) stream, making any retreat towards Villach and the rest of the army extremely chancy.

The French were on the move early in the Fella valley. Using mountain trails, Dessaix and Valentin led 8th and 23rd Léger past the guns of the Malborghetto fort without loss, followed by Abbé with his brigade (52nd, 102nd). To blockade the fort from the east and to secure the valley against surprise flank attacks, the latter deposited two battalions of 102nd at Uggowitz and stationed himself at Saifnitz with the remainder. Dessaix meanwhile pressed ahead to occupy Tarvis late in the morning, supported by Valentin, who assumed command of the battered 22nd Léger as well as the 23rd. Fontanelli also arrived west of Tarvis from the Dogna valley and Wolfsbach, giving the French sixteen battalions in and around the town. Austrian fire frustrated all efforts to move further, however, and with the Malborghetto fort holding up the French artillery and cavalry, Dessaix did

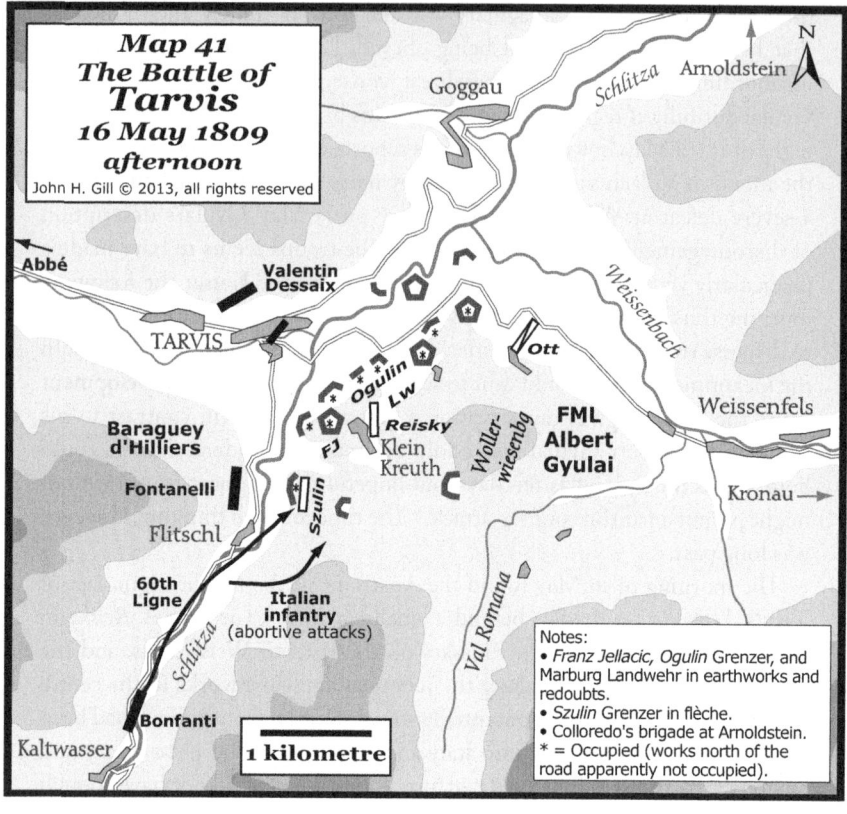

Map 41
The Battle of
Tarvis
16 May 1809
afternoon
John H. Gill © 2013, all rights reserved

Goggau   *Schlitza*   Arnoldstein

N

Abbé

Valentin
Dessaix

Weissenbach

TARVIS

Ott

Weissenfels

**Baraguey
d'Hilliers**

Ogulin

LW

Reisky
Klein
Kreuth

**FML
Albert
Gyulai**

Weissenfels

Fontanelli

FJ

Wollerwiesenbg

Kronau →

Flitschl

Szulin

**60th
Ligne**

**Italian
infantry**
(abortive attacks)

Schlitza

Val Romana

Bonfanti

Kaltwasser

1 kilometre

Notes:
• *Franz Jellacic*, *Ogulin* Grenzer, and
Marburg Landwehr in earthworks and
redoubts.
• *Szulin* Grenzer in flèche.
• Colloredo's brigade at Arnoldstein.
• * = Occupied (works north of the
road apparently not occupied).

not have the resources to press his attack. The afternoon thus passed in desultory skirmishing until around 5 p.m.

At this relatively late hour, Fontanelli, concerned about the safety of Bonfanti's isolated brigade, edged his battalions forward south of Tarvis to the western bank of the Schlitza, almost as far as Flitschl. Bonfanti advanced from Raibl at approximately the same hour and attacked the Austrian right with two battalions (IV/2nd Line, I/Dalmatia). Despite initial progress and the addition of a third battalion (III/1st), Bonfanti apparently engaged his troops sequentially by battalion rather than exploiting his numbers. His attacks stalled. The Austrians were able to hold their own and even regain some lost ground as the fighting swayed back and forth in the woods. These piecemeal tactics seem to have infuriated Major Jean-Georges Grenier (GD Paul Grenier's brother), the commander of the two 60th Ligne battalions, and he appealed to Bonfanti to launch a concerted assault. With supporting fire from Fontanelli across the stream, Grenier led his battalions against the flèche on the left and the Italians renewed their charge on the right. The attack was a complete success, shattering I/*Szulin* and forcing Gyulai to commit his reserves to stave off a complete collapse. Fortunately for the Austrians, darkness prevented the French from exploiting this twilight triumph.

Though Gyulai had preserved his position, there was no disguising that his outnumbered division had suffered another reverse and would be in even greater danger come the morning. The men were exhausted, nervous, and discouraged; food was short and so was ammunition. Even before the evening attack, Gyulai had written Johann 'I will consider myself lucky to hold my position for the rest of the day, but am very worried about my ability to hold against a renewed attack.'[82] Given Johann's peremptory orders of the preceding two days, Gyulai really had little choice, and he disposed his scanty forces to create some offensive possibilities should he receive the reinforcements he had urgently requested. The *Szulin* Grenzer, once rallied, were posted in the woods on the far left to outflank Bonfanti, *Reisky* was in the rear to protect the retreat route, the *Ogulin* Grenzer held the right, and the remaining regulars and Landwehr were stationed around Klein Kreuth in the open ground opposite Bonfanti.

Back in Villach, Johann was watching his plans fall to pieces under relentless French pressure. In some desperation, he wrote to Ignaz Gyulai, directing him to rejoin the main army with his meagre command if at all possible (an order that reveals a complete misreading of the French forces near Tarvis as well as those in the process of invading Carniola), and he warned Jellacic that retreat might be necessary. As for the local scene, however, he did not ride to Tarvis himself and, although he told Frimont to march back with Colloredo's brigade, he kept Kleinmayrn at Villach. Furthermore, Frimont was not to move during the night but to wait for first light. The reinforcements on which Albert Gyulai was relying would not arrive as quickly as he hoped.[83]

On the French side, the soldiers had conducted themselves extraordinarily well in difficult mountain and woods fighting (even if Bonfanti's tactics were poor), and the army was positioned to press its advantages on 17 May. At the operational level, however, Eugene had cause for concern. His men at Tarvis had fought all day without cavalry or artillery because these arms could not safely pass the fort at Malborghetto. With this obstacle in place and Predil blocked by its determined garrison, his forces, strung out in narrow valleys, would be in serious danger if the Austrians slipped a significant detachment over one of the many mountain passes and cut off his lead elements. Bonfanti was especially vulnerable. The viceroy could have halted, consolidating his forces and reducing the troublesome forts, but—as on the Piave—he decided instead to solve this operational problem by attacking.[84]

17 May: Engagements around Tarvis—Decision

The early hours of 17 May passed in inconsequential action around Tarvis. Dessaix's men advanced to the Schlitza to skirmish with the *Ogulin* Grenzer and Baraguey d'Hilliers brought all of Fontanelli's troops to the east side of the stream in support of a half-hearted attempt to gain the Austrian rear via the Weissenbach valley. Gyulai responded by shifting his reserve and Fontanelli called off the flanking manoeuvre before it had truly begun. As Fontanelli's men retired into the woods around 10 a.m., a lull descended on the battlefield. Shortly thereafter, however, to the great alarm and amazement of the Austrians, a large column of French troops, clearly including cavalry, appeared on the road from Malborghetto. This was Abbé coming from Saifnitz, joined by some mounted detachments, but to the Habsburg troops the arrival of so many French, particularly cavalry, seemed inexplicable in view of the strength and dominance of the Malborghetto position. How could they have passed the fort? In addition to the disheartening sight of additional enemy forces, the Habsburg commanders were increasingly anxious about Frimont and their own reinforcements. Frimont had marched for Tarvis with Colloredo's brigade that morning as directed, but halted on the northern side of the mountains some eight kilometres from Gyulai's position, apparently overcome by uncharacteristic timidity. Only at 1 p.m. did he despatch a lone regiment, *Strassaldo*, to Gyulai's assistance. Gyulai would see none of Kleinmayrn's men; Johann had held them in Villach, for the archduke had decided to retreat.[85]

Johann learned that morning that Vienna had fallen and received a bleak assessment of the Hungarian Insurrection's readiness from his brother Joseph. With his rear thus in danger and with Gyulai near collapse at Tarvis, Johann could not remain in Carinthia. He set to work at once drafting new plans, but found that the forces he had so easily scattered could not be reunited with equal facility. Nonetheless, he decided to move the troops under his immediate command to Pettau in the hope of uniting with Ignaz Gyulai and the Croatian Insurrection. Zach, with an unspecified minimal force, was to remain behind to protect the eastern portion of Carniola and somehow maintain control of a seaport to assure a connection with Britain. Jellacic would march to Graz by the quickest possible route, but Chasteler was 'left to his own devices in Tyrol as there is no longer time to pull him out and because it may be suspected that the local population will not let him leave'. He was therefore to 'defend the Tyrol as an independent fortress as long as possible' and, if necessary, 'seek to break out somewhere'.[86] Albert Gyulai was sent an order to retreat down the Sava valley towards Pettau, but the courier did not depart until midday and took his time riding over the mountains via Kronau. As a result, this instruction did not reach Gyulai until after 7 p.m. By then it was far too late.

Increasing numbers of French troops appeared on the road from Malborghetto as the afternoon of 17 May wore on, and anxiety mounted among the Austrians around Tarvis as the enemy movement clearly presaged

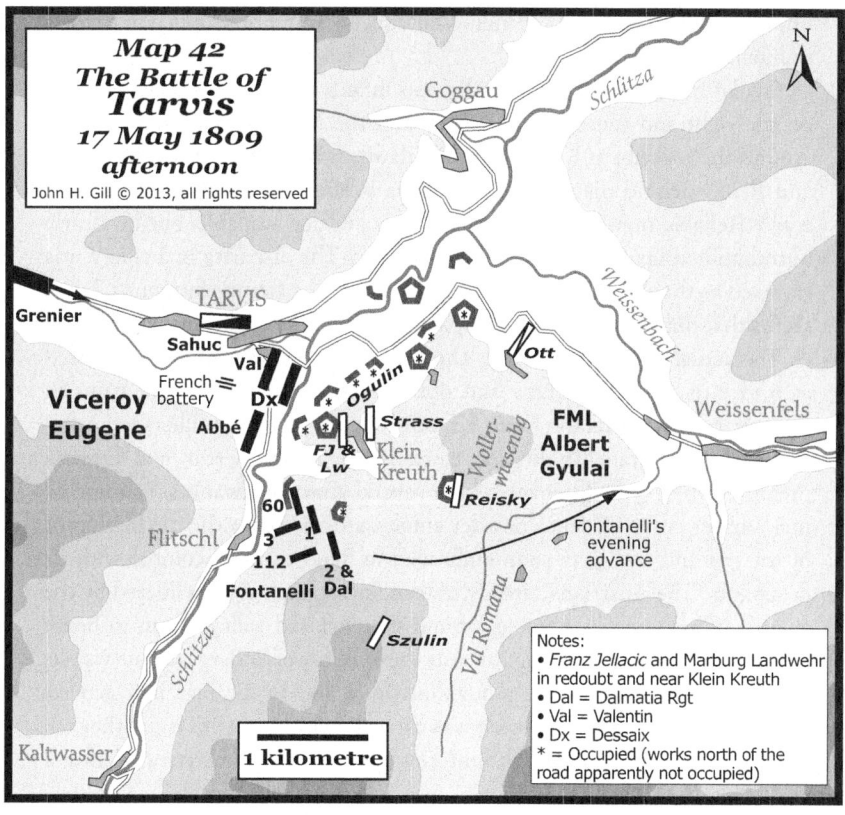

**Map 42
The Battle of
Tarvis
17 May 1809
afternoon**
John H. Gill © 2013, all rights reserved

Notes:
• *Franz Jellacic* and Marburg Landwehr in redoubt and near Klein Kreuth
• Dal = Dalmatia Rgt
• Val = Valentin
• Dx = Dessaix
* = Occupied (works north of the road apparently not occupied)

a new assault. The arrival of the *Strassaldo* Infantry around 5 p.m. brought some relief even though the regiment numbered only 1,200 men, but morale plummeted when Eugene's guns opened fire an hour later. Trusting that the Malborghetto fort would block all vehicular traffic in the Fella valley, the Austrians were shocked that the French had somehow managed to bring guns into action.[87] The Austrians would not learn the details for some weeks, but Malborghetto fort had fallen at 10 a.m. that morning to an overwhelming assault launched with great élan by 62nd Ligne and two battalions of 102nd. The defenders, two companies of *Ogulin* (350 men), earned a place in Austrian military legendary for the great courage they displayed, but their situation was hopeless and the struggle ended after only thirty minutes.[88] Eugene had already had his caissons ready on the road and had pushed his small battery, ammunition wagons, and Sahuc's horsemen forward as soon as the way was clear. Combined with the effects of weariness, hunger, and the obvious numerical superiority of the French, the six pieces that Eugene brought to the field had a psychological impact far out of proportion to their number.

Gyulai had between 4,500 and 5,000 infantry on hand: *Ogulin* Grenzer on the right and centre, *Franz Jellacic* and the Marburg Landwehr in and around the redoubt at Klein Kreuth with *Strassaldo* in reserve behind them, and *Reisky* behind the earthworks on the Wollerweisenberg to protect the rear.[89] Reliable numbers for Eugene's force are not available, but he clearly outnumbered Gyulai by three or four to one. The disparity in artillery was reversed as the Austrians may have had as many as twenty-four guns, but it seems that only a half dozen or so participated in the engagement.[90]

The actual combat was brief. The French and Italian infantry advanced at 6.30 p.m., 1st Italian Line and 60th Ligne making significant gains in the first rush towards the Klein Kreuth redoubt, while d'Hilliers led other elements of Fontanelli's division towards the Austrian rear, and Dessaix pressured the *Ogulin* Grenzer.[91] After several abortive advances, Fontanelli's men, under cover of dense powder smoke, stormed into the ditch in front of the redoubt and were soon embroiled in hand-to-hand combat with its occupants. The Austrians, already shaken and apparently bewildered by the sounds of cannon fire echoing around the enclosed valley, began to break as the Italian infantry driving towards the Wollerweisenberg became visible. Resistance unravelled and the forward units fled to the rear 'in a general panic'.[92] A battalion of *Strassaldo* was carried away by the mob, another fell back in disarray after a failed counter-attack, and the third retreated after a few moments of staunch defence along the brook east of Klein Kreuth. This uncovered the rear of the *Ogulin* Grenzer, and they fell back in haste, adding to the growing confusion and demoralisation.

French cavalry, disregarding the cannon in the redoubts, rode north along the road towards Arnoldstein to prevent any interference by Frimont and doubtless contributed to the sense of Austrian despair. Gyulai was furious, excoriating his men in his report for behaving 'in the most despicable manner' and for 'fleeing in the most disgraceful disorder after only a little shooting and resistance'.[93] He attempted to restore some sort of order at the bridge just west of Weissenfels, but Eugene had sent part of Fontanelli's division in a wide sweep to the right. The appearance of this column, crossing the Weissenbach and emerging from the valley, was enough to end all hope of Habsburg recovery. Gyulai's division collapsed and fled down the valley to Kronau, where their disordered arrival occasioned the disintegration of the Laibach Landwehr battalion stationed there.[94] Throwing down their muskets, the Landwehrmen dispersed in all directions. With the onset of night putting an end to further pursuit, Eugene brought Grenier forward to support Sahuc on the road to Arnoldstein, set Fontanelli to guard the valley towards Weissenfels, and happily composed a report for his step-father: 'a new victory, inflicted on Your Majesty's enemies, has crowned this fine day.'[95]

Once again, the Austrians had been saved by darkness. Not counting the evaporated Laibach Landwehr, Gyulai lost well over 2,000 men and at least eleven guns, perhaps as many as eighteen. His division was temporarily combat ineffective and probably would have suffered more had the Grenzer at Malborghetto not delayed Eugene's cavalry and artillery. This valour notwithstanding, 17 May had been another serious defeat for the Army of Inner Austria. Fortunately for Johann, the little blockhouse at Predil gained him a day's respite by retarding the movement of Eugene's artillery and supply trains, thereby forcing the viceroy to remain encamped around Tarvis on 18 May. Refusing to surrender, the garrison of 242 Grenzer and others was practically annihilated that afternoon in a ferocious assault by Seras's division with support from three battalions that Eugene sent from Tarvis to seal the valley north of the fort.[96] The garrison's desperate heroism, however, could not change the larger picture. Johann, his army demoralised and dispersed, began a long retreat that would not end until he reached Raab on the banks of the Danube and another major contest with Eugene's Army of Italy.

From the Isonzo to Laibach

Events along the Isonzo and in Carniola were also going ill for the Austrians.[97] FML Zach, on learning that Johann was retiring to the north, broke off the blockade of Palmanova during the night of 11/12 May and retired to the Isonzo in accordance with his latest instructions, posting most of his men in Görz, with 2nd Triest and 2nd Adelsberg at Sagrado, and Major Ogrissovich on the far left with 1st Triest. Zach's Landwehr had shown itself unreliable. It panicked when Schilt made a minor sortie from Palmanova on 11 May, and the mere appearance of a French cavalry patrol during the retreat to Görz sufficed to scatter two companies of 2nd Triest. Widespread desertion, already a problem, increased as the units crossed back into Habsburg territory: 2nd Adelsberg, an extreme example, was down to sixty men. It was hardly surprising, therefore, that resistance was light when MacDonald's two divisions arrived on the western bank of the Isonzo on the evening of 14 May. To Ogrissovich's disgust, the Landwehr vanished after firing a few shots and his attempt to intervene with two companies and two guns was repulsed by two of Broussier's grenadier companies. With the river line compromised, Zach and Ogrissovich retreated to Präwald, arriving safe but exhausted on the 16th. Präwald, a complex of small forts guarding the mountain pass through which the main highway to Laibach passed, was occupied by GM Josef von Munkacsy with 2nd Neustadtl Landwehr and 500 untrained recruits slated for the St Julien Infantry.[98] Zach also heard from the wandering GM Kalnassy and directed that general to hold a position at Podkraj (a secondary pass through the mountains) to prevent Präwald from being outflanked. As we have seen, Kalnassy had left a battalion, a hussar platoon, and his four guns in the upper Isonzo valley, so the 'brigade' that arrived in Podkraj on 16 May consisted of only two and two-thirds battalions with three hussar platoons (1,861 infantrymen and 76 troopers).[99]

MacDonald assembled his corps on the eastern bank of the Isonzo on the afternoon of 15 May. He detached Schilt with 79th Ligne, 100 hussars, and two guns to occupy Trieste, a task Schilt accomplished on 18 May without encountering any active opposition. Meanwhile, MacDonald marched via Görz (where he seized eleven abandoned siege guns intended for use against Palmanova) towards Präwald. Dividing his corps on 16 May, he sent Broussier up the main road, while Lamarque marched on the secondary route towards Kalnassy's position at Podkraj, arriving early enough for the 18th Léger to launch several fruitless attacks on Kalnassy. Heavy fighting flared at both locations on 17 May. GB Léonard Huard de St Aubin (18th Léger,

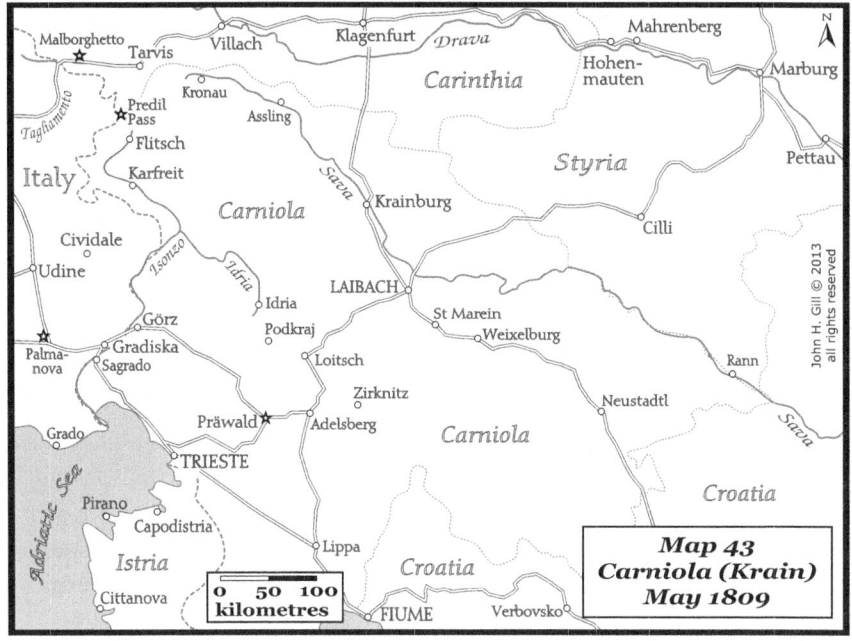

**Map 43
Carniola (Krain)
May 1809**

13th Ligne, one squadron of 23rd Dragoons) broke Kalnassy's defence after a bitter struggle that cost the Austrians at least 400 casualties.[100] Kalnassy retreated towards Loitsch, where further unpleasantness awaited. Gyulai in Laibach had sent III/*Franz Karl* to support Kalnassy, using first boats and then wagons to speed the battalion on its way. Finally on its feet, the battalion collided unexpectedly with II/13th Ligne as the two sides marched on winding roads through the close, wooded terrain. Both sides were equally surprised, but the French recovered quickly to unleash a spontaneous bayonet attack that overthrew the whitecoats completely with hardly a shot fired. The Austrian commander, eleven other officers, and 384 of their men were captured before the remainder were able to escape up the road towards Laibach.[101]

The outcome at Präwald was less embarrassing, but equally unfortunate for the Habsburg cause. Attacked with great vigour and skill by Broussier early on the morning of the 17th, Zach withdrew at 9 a.m. with his hussars and most of the Landwehr, leaving at least 200 prisoners in Broussier's hands and the incomplete little fortress in Major Cazzan's care. Fighting continued for the rest of the day, but the French could not penetrate the fort and Cazzan, with not quite 2,000 men in his garrison, held out until

Table 7: Präwald Garrison, 17–20 May

Commander: Major Cazzan

3rd Garrison Battalion (elements)	430
II/*Franz Karl* (Major Ogrissovich)	865
1st Kordon Company	125
5th Kordon Company	111
2nd Neustadtl Landwehr (Major Albrecht)	286
Pioneers	15
Artillery	63
Stragglers etc. from other units	30
Total	1,925

Source: Sallagar, 'Präwald', ÖMZ, 1908.

20 May when lack of food and water compelled him to capitulate. Combined casualties for Zach and Kalnassy on 17 May totalled at least 1,000, not counting the 2,000 at Präwald whom Gyulai had no hope of rescuing. Moreover, with the Landwehr rapidly dissolving, the loss of what amounted to three precious regular battalions was especially crippling.[102] Leaving a garrison of two and two-thirds battalions in Laibach under FML Johann Ritter von Moitelle, Gyulai retired to St Marein and Weixelburg east of the city. The day had thus been as devastating for Gyulai as it had been for Johann, and neither would be capable of serious offensive operations for some time. Indeed, joined by Zach and Kalnassy's remnants on the 18th, Gyulai left Splenyi with the hussars to watch Laibach and retired to Rann on the Sava, arriving there on 23 May. That day the octogenarian Moitelle (who would be cashiered for his lax defence) surrendered Laibach to MacDonald and the garrison, 1,200 strong, went into captivity.[103] Some of the *Szulin* Grenzer, suitably outraged by the capitulation, managed to march out of the city and join Splenyi. Other than these few Grenzer, the *Ottocac* Regiment, and Kalnassy's shattered troops, Gyulai had almost no trained regular infantry, his cavalry was reduced to squadrons averaging fifty to seventy troopers, and almost none of the Landwehr remained with the colours.[104] His only hope lay with the Croatian Insurrection, a brigade of which was assembling at Verbovsko under GM Ignaz von Kengyel. He thus left Gavassini to manage the command's quotidian affairs and devoted himself to hastening the mobilisation in Croatia. MacDonald, on the other hand, advised that he would 'participate in the operations that will take place on the Danube',

moved part of his command to the Sava north of Laibach in preparation for a rapid march north. By the 27th, lead elements of his wing had united with Grouchy's vanguard at Marburg.[105]

Mountain Marches

We left GD Rusca and Hauptmann Zuccheri facing each other across the cold waters of the Cordevole River on 7 May, with GM Schmidt and his brigade at Belluno under orders to join GM Marchal and threaten Eugene's strategic rear in the Adige valley. Johann, deeply annoyed with Chasteler for taking almost all of his troops north of the Brenner Pass, specifically directed Schmidt not to go north of the Brenner, and the brigade (some of its troops now barefoot) marched off on 8 May through Cortina to reach Toblach on the 10th. He and his troops disappear from our story for the time being and enter into the affairs of the Tyrol. Zuccheri and Rusca, on the other hand, remained in the Piave valley, Zuccheri underestimating Rusca's strength, while the French general entertained an exaggerated notion of Zuccheri's force. Operating under these misunderstandings, the two clashed south of Pieve di Cadore on 10 May when the Austrians (now including the two *Szulin* companies from Serravale) ambushed Rusca's column. Fighting continued into the afternoon, but IV/93rd Ligne conducted a successful charge, Zuccheri fell wounded, and an ensign from the *Szulin* companies was killed. Lacking their leaders, the Grenzer broke and ran, clearing the way for the French. Rusca, however, conscious of his isolation, contented himself with occupying Pieve on 11 May and was doubtless relieved to receive orders recalling him to the main army. He returned down the Piave valley on the 12th, passing through Pordenone (14 May), Udine (18 May), and Tarvis (20 May) to reach Spittal on 23 May. By the 27th, Rusca had pushed his outposts as far as Sachsenburg.

Hauptmann Franz Kuncz of 2nd Banal replaced the incapacitated Zuccheri. Instructed to watch the passes leading north from Piave–Tagliamento valleys, he was therefore the one to welcome the pathetic remains of Major Toperczer's I/Franz Carl when they stumbled into Ampezzo on 14 May (albeit minus the captured major). The battalion, reduced to 400 exhausted men, rested for a day before retiring to Innichen on the 16th. Unbeknownst to them, their meandering movements had created alarming reports that worried Rusca and led Fontanelli to leave 7th Line behind at Venzone as his division marched north to Tarvis.

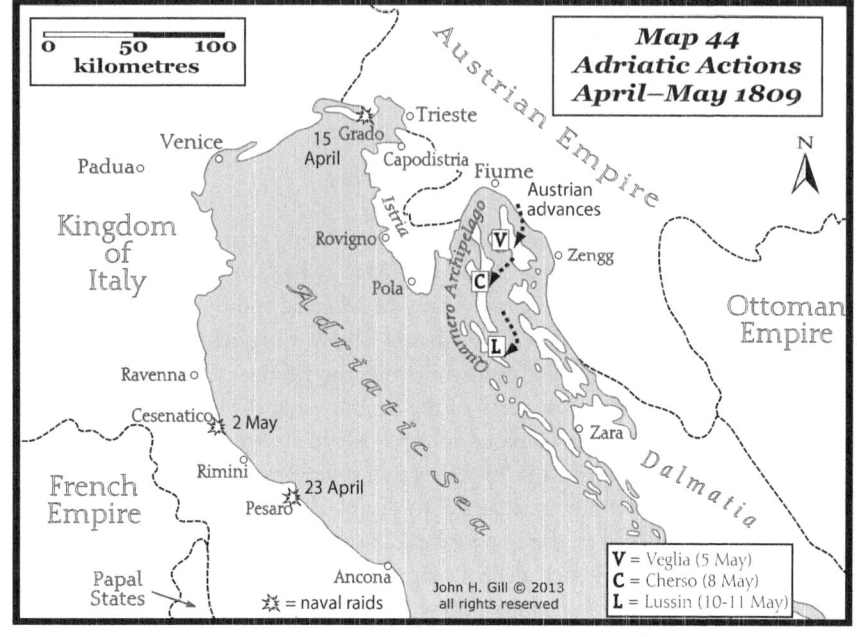

May: Adriatic Actions

While the land campaign advanced, small coastal actions were continuing along the shores of the Adriatic. Captain Brenton, after his success at Pesaro, conducted a similar raid on Cesenatico on 2 May with *Spartan* (38) and *Mercury* (28), seizing twelve vessels and spiking the guns of an enemy battery before sailing off to the other side of the Adriatic. On the Croatian coast, approximately 500 local volunteers under Oberstleutnant Baron Peharnik had occupied Veglia and Cherso in the Quarnero Archipelago between 5 and 8 May. When Brenton arrived on the 9th, he and Peharnik orchestrated the successful capture of Lussin with 170 prisoners (a detachment of IV/Dalmatia carabiniers) and eighteen guns on 10–11 May.[106] These small operations and the Royal Navy's active presence at sea not only presented an annoyance to the French, they secured the line of communications, albeit tenuous, between Vienna and London. They did not, however, 'prevent the army of Dalmatia from passing into Italy by sea' as the British and Austrians had hoped, for the simple reason that Napoleon's intention was for Marmont to join Eugene by land.[107] The French never seriously considered the sea route and Austrian fears of such a movement, as their worries about the Russian squadron in Trieste, proved irrelevant. The British nonetheless established a blockade of Trieste on 24 May (they and the Austrians had evacuated all of their shipping before Schilt's entry on the 18th), an effort they maintained until 5 July.

Kingdom of Italy

Präwald ★

Zirknitz ∘
Adelsberg

N

Grado

∘TRIESTE

Austrian

Pirano ∘
Capodistria

∘ Lippa

Empire

Cittanova ∘

Fiume ∘

Verbovsko ∘

Istria

Archipelago

Adriatic
Sea

∘ Rovigno

Veglia ∘
Veglia

Zengg ∘

Quarnero

Cherso ∘

Pola ∘

Cherso

Arbe

Dalmatia

**Map 45
Istria and the
Quarnero Islands**

Lussin

Lussin-
-piccolo
-grande

Pago

On Habsburg Soil: 20–27 May

As Napoleon and Charles were assessing the results of Aspern, the campaign in Italy came to a close and a new campaign, a French offensive into Styria and Hungary, opened. Johann retired to Graz with his portion of the Army of Inner Austria (8,600 men) on 24 May, while Albert Gyulai (3,000) fell back to Pettau. The archduke, as we have seen, wisely rejected the ill-advised urgings of the Kaiser that he march towards Linz to co-operate with Kolowrat, but French pressure had relaxed since the defeat at Tarvis and he allowed himself to discern some bright points in the near future.[108] He did not yet know that Malborghetto, Predil, Präwald, Trieste, and Laibach had fallen, and he looked forward to union with Jellacic by 27 May to raise his complement of regulars. He also hoped Chasteler would soon escape from the Tyrol to join the main body and, as always, he invested a great deal of faith in the Croatian and Hungarian Insurrections.[109]

Eugene was also looking towards the future with some optimism on 24 May, and with considerably more justification. He had reorganised his army again on 20 May at Villach and during the march to Klagenfurt the following day: the advance guard was dissolved with high praise for its many services, Seras replaced Pacthod in Grenier's corps, the recovered Severoli resumed command of the Italian division, and a number of regiments were moved about (Appendix 15). Eugene also divided the army again, sending Grouchy with Pacthod's division, two chasseur regiments under Sahuc, and Lieutenant Noël's battery on a southerly route to maintain contact with MacDonald; the main body marched north to the Mur valley under his direct command. Grouchy reached Hohenmauthen on the Drava on 23 May and sent reconnaissance patrols in all directions, but found little of the enemy. Leaving Pacthod's infantry in Hohenmauthen, he and his vanguard (light cavalry and two battalions) trotted into Marburg on 26 May, chased off an Austrian rear guard, and began repairing the bridge that the retreating Austrians had demolished.[110] MacDonald's 6th Hussars arrived in Marburg that day, followed by Broussier and Pully (23rd and 28th Dragoons) on the 27th; Lamarque and 29th Dragoons were at Gonobitz.[111]

Likewise, 60th Ligne, sent down the valley through Kronau to Assling on 20 May had nothing to report on its march; its two battalions went to Krainburg the next day before turning north via Klagenfurt to await the army's artillery park at St Veit.[112]

In the Mur valley, Grenier's vanguard chased 1st Judenburg Landwehr out of Judenburg on 23 May, forcing the Landwehr to execute a difficult retreat over the mountains to Köflach during which 655 of its 1,062 men deserted. Grenier's advance troops also encountered Austrians five kilometres west of Judenburg that day. These were 300 or so fugitives from Chasteler's corps that had fled east to Jellacic's division after the defeat at Wörgl (13 May). Rallied under Oberst Joseph Chevalier Ruiz de Rojas of *Lusignan* Infantry, they were attempting to locate Johann's army when they stumbled upon Eugene. The whitecoats repelled the French advance guard, but retired into

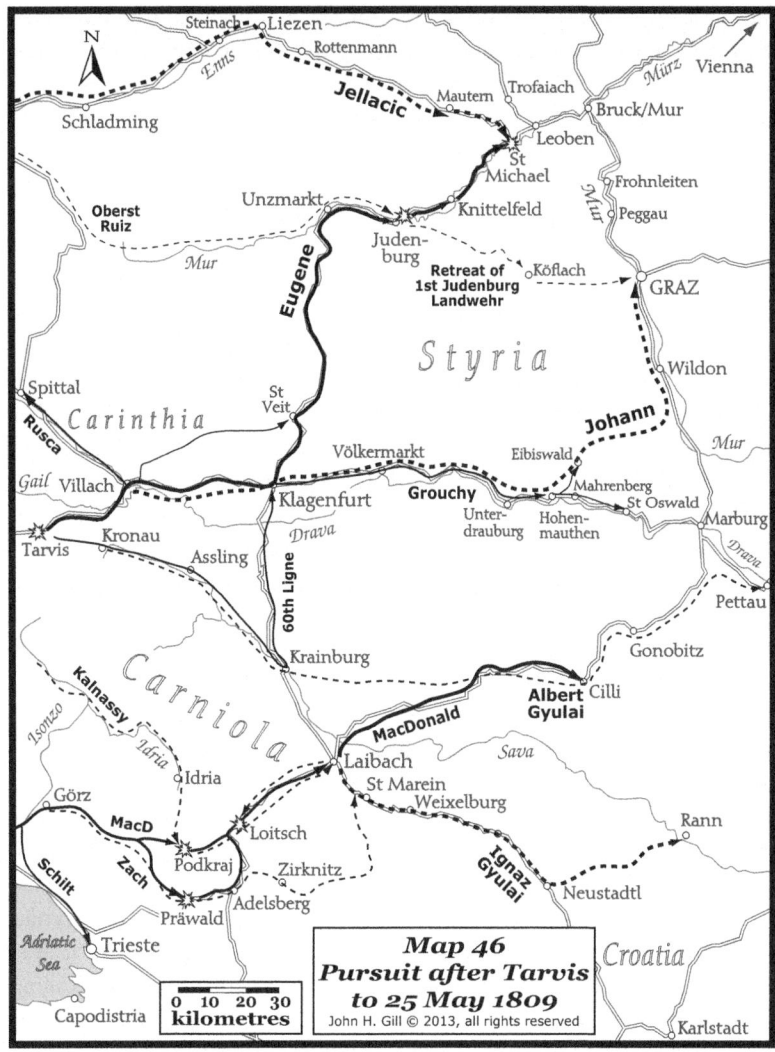

Map 46
**Pursuit after Tarvis
to 25 May 1809**
John H. Gill © 2013, all rights reserved

0 10 20 30
kilometres

the mountains to seek Jellacic as Eugene's main body approached.[113] To the south, Rusca reached Spittal in the Drava valley and pushed his outposts west to observe the fortress at Sachsenburg.

Eugene's lead division (Durutte) marched into Knittelfeld on 24 May, with Seras behind at Judenburg, and the rest of the army stretched out along twenty-five kilometres of twisting road up the Mur. That evening, however,

Eugene learned that Jellacic was approaching from Rottenmann and Mautern with the aim of reaching Leoben. Grasping this golden opportunity to trap the isolated Austrian division, he immediately issued orders for Grenier to intercept the Austrian division on the 25th.

The Anxieties of General Jellacic

The war thus far had gone poorly for FML Johann Jellacic. 'Brave in the face of the enemy, but limited in his abilities', he had been placed in an independent command for which he was not suited. Although his division had successfully entered Munich as ordered during the campaign in Bavaria, he had been badgered by contradictory and imprecise orders from Hiller in the ensuing retreat and found himself unceremoniously evicted from Salzburg as April came to a close. His men repelled Bavarian attempts to force Lueg Pass on 1 May and again on 4 and 5 May, but his division was scattered in dribs and drabs all along the mountainous frontier east of Salzburg trying to cover every access into Styria. This situation became alarmingly worse as Napoleon drove down the Danube valley and opened the province's northern border to possible Allied incursions. Although reinforced by three Landwehr battalions on 12 May (1st Bruck, 1st and 2nd Judenburg, en route back to Styria from Chasteler's command), he did not have enough troops to defend his assigned area, let alone come to Chasteler's assistance when the Bavarians opened their first offensive into the Tyrol on 10 May. His men were thus distant and helpless bystanders as the Bavarians crushed Chasteler at Wörgl on 13 May and could do nothing to preclude Bavarian occupation of Innsbruck on the 19th. With Lefebvre's Bavarians in Innsbruck, Napoleon in Vienna, and French troops probing the Styrian border deep in his rear, Jellacic's situation was now quite grim. He was doubtless relieved therefore on 19 May to receive orders from Johann calling the division to Graz.[114] On the other hand, the archduke's orders placed impossible demands on Jellacic, requiring him somehow to cover the Styrian border while simultaneously keeping his division united on the march to Graz. Jellacic, burdened with logistical headaches ('I have to fight with hunger as much as the enemy') and fearing that his command would dissolve into detachments, tried to comply.[115] Sending 1st Judenburg to Judenburg, 1st Bruck to Bruck an der Mur, and I/*Esterhazy* to Trofaiach to secure his route of march, he departed Radstadt on 20 May and reached the general area of Mautern four days later.[116] In accordance with his instructions, he left behind near Liezen a Landwehr Oberstleutnant named Thomas Graf Plunquet with a mixed bag of some 3,000 Landwehr and other second line troops drawn from the covering detachments at Altenmarkt and Liezen. With blocking forces at Aussee, near Steinach, and towards Radstadt, Plunquet was to fend off Allied incursions into Styria from the north-west.[117]

Jellacic had decided to march to Graz via St Michael, Leoben, and Bruck an der Mur. He expected no interference. Johann's missives contained almost no information about Eugene's forces and Jellacic, despite excellent information from local officials, was supremely confident that he would see no French on the 25th. 'At most, according to his opinion, a skirmish between the advance or rear guards might eventuate,' recorded GM Konstantin von Ettingshausen, one of his brigadiers.[118] Nonetheless, he ordered his vanguard (a battalion of Grenzer) to depart at 3 a.m. to secure the defile at St Michael. Through a concatenation of unwise decisions and unpredictable frictions, however, the battalion was delayed by almost two hours.[119] As a result, the Grenzer and Jellacic's three platoons of chevaulegers reached the little valley east of St Michael at almost the same moment that Seras's lead elements appeared.

The Battle of St Michael

St Michael sits on the north bank of the Mur at a point where the river winds through a narrow defile dominated by steep, forested hills. The pleasant valley of the Mur, approximately one kilometre in width, opens to the west, but the area adjacent to the village presents a starkly delineated plateau called the 'Platte', some fifteen metres higher than the rest of the valley floor. A much narrower valley serves as the channel for the Liesing stream, bending down from the north to join the Mur through St Michael. The Liesing was small, but ran through deeply cut banks and the Austrians considered it unfordable. The little bridge that carried the post road across the Liesing in St Michael was thus Jellacic's only route of escape and consequently assumed critical tactical importance in the coming struggle.

The action opened around 9 a.m. as the two advance guards collided on the Platte. Seras led the French advance that morning, and his men (approximately 7,500) had already mounted this low plateau when Jellacic appeared on the scene with Ettingshausen. The alarmed Austrians were able to hold their own ground, but lacked the strength at first to push Seras off the Platte. Fighting spread up the flanks of the Liesingberg on the Austrian right as Grenzer clashed with French skirmishers in the heavy woods and

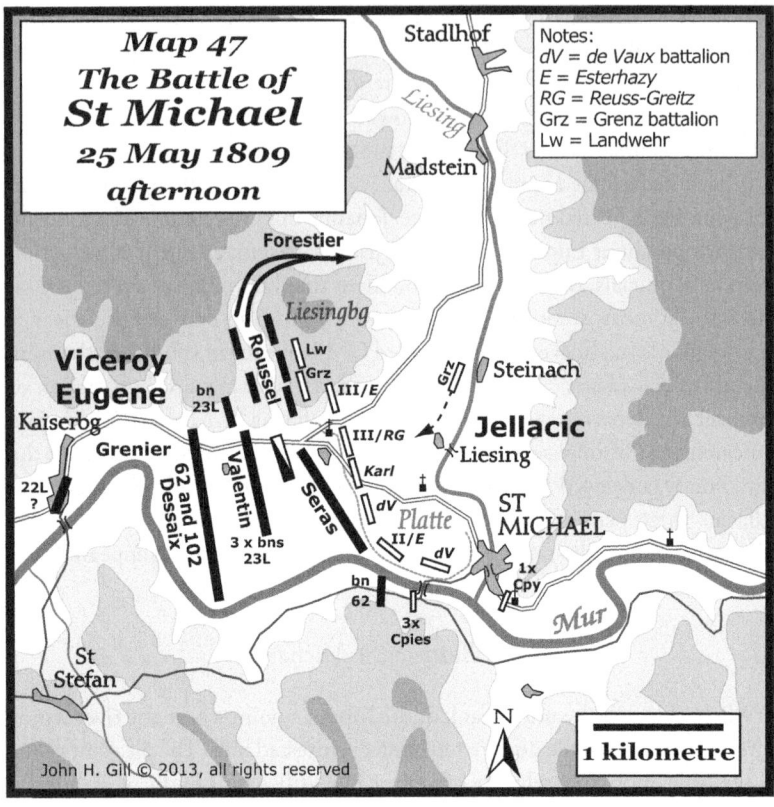

Map 47
The Battle of
St Michael
25 May 1809
afternoon

Notes:
dV = de Vaux battalion
E = Esterhazy
RG = Reuss-Greitz
Grz = Grenz battalion
Lw = Landwehr

Stadlhof

Liesing

Madstein

Forestier

Liesingbg

Viceroy
Eugene

Roussel

Lw
Grz
III/E

Grz
Steinach

III/RG

Jellacic
Liesing

bn
23L

Kaiserbg

Grenier

Valentin

Seras

Karl

ST
MICHAEL

22L
?

62 and 102
Dessaix

3 x bns
23L

dV

Platte
II/E

dV

1x
Cpy

bn
62

3x
Cpies

St
Stefan

Mur

N

1 kilometre

more Austrian troops arrived.[120] Jellacic rushed II/*Esterhazy* to his left to hold the crucial bridge and, by 11 a.m., with most of his division on hand (some 7,000 to 7,500 men), he launched an attack that threw the French back into the valley.[121] Combat in the centre diminished as the French, short of ammunition, sought to conserve their cartridges, but a steady nattering of musketry echoed from the sides of the mountain to the north as Seras's men clung tenaciously to their gains.

Eugene had arrived at about the time that the Austrian attack cleared the Platte, but the enemy's dispositions were clearly visible and he elected to keep the whitecoats engaged while awaiting the arrival of Durutte's division hurrying up from the rear. For his part, Jellacic was content to rearrange his battalions on the Platte and allow his cumbersome train to trundle along the road to St Michael. Though urged to withdraw or at least send troops to secure the dangerous defile in his rear, he did neither, choosing instead to deploy his entire force 'in order to intimidate the enemy until nightfall when he would at once begin the retreat'.[122] He limited himself to placing three companies south of the Mur and, finally, detaching one company to a reserve position near the town.

The long hours of the afternoon thus passed in desultory skirmishing and occasional but ineffectual artillery fire along the edge of the Platte. The steady arrival of French battalions in the valley was clearly visible to the Habsburg troops, however, and Jellacic's officers grew increasingly nervous about their division's fate. Their commander, on the other hand, would not move until he could disengage his right from the Liesingberg and this the dogged French were not about to permit. Indeed, French success on his northern flank forced Jellacic to shift III/*Esterhazy* from his centre to support the fight on the mountainside. This move had dire consequences for the Austrians as Jellacic filled the resulting gap in the centre of his position with the completely green men of III/*Reuss-Greitz* and the *Erzherzog Karl* conscript detachment. His command was now arrayed in a single, brittle line: the combined Salzburg Landwehr battalion, a battalion of Grenzer, and III/*Esterhazy* on his right, the recruits and a battalion of *de Vaux* in the centre, and the other *de Vaux* battalion along with II/*Esterhazy* on the right. The rear guard (the remaining battalion of Grenzer) had also arrived by this time, but its exact location is unclear.[123]

Eugene's intention was to stress his foe's flanks and then launch a powerful attack in the centre. He thus sent a battalion of 62nd Ligne across the Mur to clear annoying Habsburg skirmishers from the south bank and to threaten Jellacic's left, while GB Jean-Claude Roussel with five of Seras's battalions, supported by a battalion of 23rd Léger, pushed against the Austrian right. Two of Roussel's battalions made a wide swing to the French left under Major François Louis Forestier of Grenier's staff, aiming for a saddle on the high ridge of the Liesingberg that would lead down into the Liesing valley behind the Austrian position. Seras's other six battalions were in a line just west of the Platte.[124] Behind him were Eugene's two available cavalry regiments (6th and 9th Chasseurs), GB Valentin with the other three battalions of 23rd Léger, GB Dessaix commanding the remaining three battalions of 62nd Ligne, and finally the three battalions of 102nd Ligne.[125] In total numbers, Grenier's wing counted some 15,000 infantry and cavalry in its ranks as compared to only about 8,000 under Jellacic.

Around 4 p.m., Eugene considered himself ready and launched his attack on the Austrian centre. The fighting did not last long; it was 'all the work of at most ten minutes' in Ettingshausen's recollections.[126] Seras's onslaught broke the untried men of *Reuss-Greitz* and *Karl* in the first rush and the two cavalry regiments dashed forward at once to exploit the panic in the Austrian formations. In moments, Jellacic's entire division was in uncontrollable flight. Roussel drove the Habsburg right wing off the mountainside, while Forestier's two battalions leaped down into the Liesing valley, and Valentin swung his 23rd Léger battalions first onto the Platte and then to their left into the flank of the unfortunate Habsburg troops. Trapped on three sides by these French advances, the Austrian right had no choice but surrender. The rest fled towards St Michael, thousands falling into French captivity as Grenier's cavalry, Dessaix's infantry, and the available troops of Seras's division took up the chase. 'We penetrated into the town at the run,' wrote Dessaix, 'the enemy did not have time to destroy the bridge.'[127] Ettingshausen, swept away in the flood of fugitives, lamented 'it was not possible to correct this disorder as everyone believed the enemy cavalry was at his heels.'[128] Somewhere east of town a platoon of *Frimont* Hussars sent from Bruck managed to induce a temporary halt in the pursuit, in part by blowing up an ammunition caisson. Jellacic's men regained some of their composure, but there could be no thought of stopping and the demoralised mass pressed on for Leoben. As the disordered division passed through this town and headed for Bruck, Jellacic ordered the *Esterhazy* Regiment's 18th Company to hold the bridge over the Mur until the arrival of I/*Esterhazy* from Trofaiach. This battalion reached Leoben around 7 p.m. just as Seras's lead elements were arriving and a bitter fight erupted as two of the battalion's companies sacrificed themselves to shield their comrades' retreat. With a loss of 447 men, the *Esterhazy* men tore up the bridge as best they could and marched hastily off towards Bruck with their two guns. The French soon repaired the span and seized portions of the Austrian baggage train, but the pursuit came to an end as Seras's men, having marched forty-eight kilometres and fought all day, finally collapsed in exhaustion.[129]

The Battle of St Michael was another disaster for Johann and the Habsburg cause. Having suffered 6,573 casualties, Jellacic's division had ceased to exist. Instead of the more than 9,000 relatively fresh troops Johann had expected, only some 2,000 dragged themselves into Graz on the evening of 26 May, hungry, disheartened, and utterly weary. Perhaps another 500 to 1,000 stragglers returned to the colours over the following two or three days. Jellacic was fortunate to have lost only one of his guns. Grenier's casualties, according to French accounts, came to 200 dead, 400 wounded and 70 prisoners, in any case less than 1,000. Compounding this Habsburg calamity, small detachments of Italian troops under bold officers forced the capitulation of Plunquet's Landwehr command on 26 and 27 May. Although some evaded capture and many later escaped to rejoin the army, for the moment an additional 2,350 Austrian troops and two guns had fallen into French hands and several hundred more were scattered about the Styrian countryside, at least temporarily unable to contribute to the war. Total Austrian losses for 25 to 27 May thus came to more than 9,000 men, some two-thirds of whom were regulars: 'this fine corps, on which the archduke had relied...was completely shattered.'[130] Under the physical loss and psychological shock of the defeat, Johann had to abandon any hope of consolidating a new force at Graz and undertaking offensive operations. On the evening of 29 May, he therefore departed Graz and set his shaken command on the road to Hungary.

The reaction on the French side, of course, was rather different. 'More good news, my tender Auguste, but this is truly excellent!' wrote an elated Eugene to his wife on the morning of the 26th in a letter outlining his triumph.[131] The culmination of a difficult campaign, St Michael not only added another handsome victory to the Army of Italy's string of successes, it also opened the road to Vienna. Seras occupied Bruck an der Mur on 26 May and Durutte bivouacked on the road to Graz, while Eugene established his headquarters in Bruck and sent one of his staff officers, the martially named Capitaine Auguste Nicolas Bataille, up the post road towards the Austrian capital. Not knowing what to expect, Bataille was delighted to find GD Lauriston and his Badeners at the Semmering Pass. The general met Eugene in Bruck that very evening and Bataille rode on to report to the emperor at Ebersdorf on the morning of the 27th. Eugene himself arrived in Ebersdorf two days later. The Army of Germany and the Army of Italy were now united and Napoleon could turn his attention to driving the remnants of Johann's army and Joseph's Insurrection troops north of the Danube. As he planned his next moves, however, he did not forget the men who made his strategies possible. 'Soldiers of the Army of Italy, you have gloriously attained the goal I set for you,' he proclaimed, 'I am pleased with you.'[132]

We conclude this chapter with Archduke Johann retreating from another catastrophe, and Viceroy Eugene pleased with a new victory and his step-father's warm congratulations. After an awkward beginning that led to the defeat at Sacile and the long retreat in the rain to the Adige, Eugene had regained his equilibrium and rediscovered his self-confidence. As he told his beloved wife in a affectionate letter written the night of the victory at Tarvis:

> I hope the emperor will be content and I am quite satisfied. I tell you, for yourself alone, that I am all the more content with myself as no one advised attacking, because the enemy had many lines of entrenchments; but I thought the orders given were right, and the results proved that I was absolutely correct: a few more hours and we would have been defeated ourselves. I am doing well; it is true that I have not slept for many nights, but all is going as well as could be.[133]

The Army of Italy had rebounded as well as its commander. Granted a reprieve on the Adige, bolstered by reinforcements and victuals, the men recovered their spirit. 'Hope re-entered our hearts,' as one said.[134] They then sought to erase the stain that the campaign's opening encounters had left on their personal honour and regimental reputations. Thus the sense of 'ferocious joy' experienced by many on the Piave and the repeated references to having achieved a satisfactory 'vengeance' with the battle's outcome.[135] One is left with an impression that the officers and men of the Army of Italy felt that they had restored the proper ascendancy over their Habsburg foes. This attitude gave them a crucial psychological advantage as manifested in the élan, energy, and endurance they displayed consistently during the advance to the Piave and thence to the frontiers of the Austrian Empire. As one soldier described the mood in mid-May: 'Now we had to continue to triumph in response to Napoleon's confidence, as he was advancing on Vienna and counted on us.'[136]

Johann and the Army of Inner Austria, on the other hand, had suffered severely and, in some respects, never recovered fully from the opening campaign. Although the army exhibited the same disabilities as the Hauptarmee—torpor, inflexibility, mediocre leadership, and excessive concern for reserves—it could fight very well indeed, showing all of the steadiness and courage its commanders could desire. After the Piave, however, it began to fray badly. Although Malborghetto and Predil became icons of Habsburg heroism (both, ironically, involving Croatian troops), many units melted away during the weeks of incessant retreats and defeats as the tide turned in favour of the French and Italians. If this was true of proud, old regular regiments, it was painfully evident among the Landwehr. Many of these battalions dissolved without even engaging the enemy and, despite a few bright spots like Präwald, most commanders had few compliments and many complaints to offer about their conduct.

As for Johann, his performance as army commander was neither egregious nor exemplary. He acquitted himself moderately well at the tactical level in most of his engagements, displaying no brilliance but avoiding gross ineptitude. However, of the two largest battles, Sacile could well have been a much greater victory and the Piave need not have been such a debilitating defeat had he acted with greater decision and perhaps shown less concern for maintaining large reserves. On strategic questions, his vision was sometimes clear and pragmatic, such as refusing to take his battered army towards Linz in mid-May. At the same time, he could be 'fantastical' in his conceptions (such as his own plans to head into the Tyrol in early May), and he seemed to ignore the deteriorating condition of his own troops for far too long.[137] His situation in mid-May as he withdrew to Austrian lands was certainly unenviable and possibly irretrievable, but his choices in coping with it were fundamentally flawed. Having scattered his army from Carinthia to Croatia, he found it was impossible to reassemble, and his decision to leave Albert Gyulai at Tarvis without supporting him led directly to that disastrous defeat. He also evinced the same weakness so prevalent among other Habsburg commanders: a tendency to make convenient but unfounded assumptions about the enemy. Though young, he had faced the French before and he had an adequate supply of advisors who knew the Revolutionary and Imperial French armies very well. Yet at several critical points, he assumed—just like Charles, Hiller, and others—that the French would rest, relent, or relax and grant him days or weeks to refurbish his forces. There was already sufficient evidence in the ongoing campaign to demonstrate that such facile assumptions had no basis in reality, but he and several of his subordinates persisted in this sort of analysis. Finally, it is important to remind ourselves that Johann was a key factor behind the adoption of an offensive strategy in Italy. Not content with a defensive role in the coming war, he was instrumental in allotting more forces to the Italian front and in assigning those forces a mission that was beyond their capabilities. The result was the crippling of the Army of Inner Austria and a powerful French invasion into the heart of the Habsburg monarchy that complemented Napoleon's drive down the Danube valley.

Intermezzo

THE SECOND CAMPAIGN

The war now drifts into a period of strategic pause in its principal theatre. In the conflict's first campaign, Napoleon had evicted the invading Austrians from Bavaria; in the second, he took his Army of Germany to Vienna with speed and violence; all this in less than one month, just as he had promised in his opening proclamation to his troops. The second campaign's swift march of triumph, however, ends in slaughter and repulse at Aspern, encouraging not only his immediate Austrian adversaries, but also a spectrum of opponents all across Europe. Though blocked in the first attempt to cross the Danube, the French are neither broken nor bowed, the raging river providing a ready rationale for the absence of success. Nor has Aspern diminished Napoleon's determination to terminate the war with a victory as quickly as possible. Forced to wait, he restores the Army of Germany, gathers reinforcements, and meticulously creates an opportunity to renew his offensive.

On the farther shore, the Austrians ponder their own opportunity. Charles could not save Vienna from occupation, but he had revived the Hauptarmee after the debacle in Bavaria, bringing it to the Marchfeld in time to counter Napoleon's thrust, and leading it successfully through a brutal trial by fire. These were significant achievements and earned him and his soldiers well-deserved accolades. However, there were disturbing signs to be descried by those who looked—as the archduke would—beyond the satisfying glow of accomplishment. The army had displayed great courage and determination in both attack and defence during the battle, but it had also given new proof of its awkwardness in offensive operations even in the open terrain of the Marchfeld when the odds were stacked heavily in its favour. Its actions were marked by poor or nonexistent coordination at the corps and division level, (unless personally animated by Charles), a lack of initiative among subordinate generals, and often painfully slow processes of movement and deployment. Despite the achievement of Aspern, therefore, these worrying signs will colour Charles's thinking as he considers the army's next moves.

Moreover, the Austrian success on the Marchfeld was dimmed by the steep decline in Habsburg fortunes on more distant fields. Johann's defeat of Eugene at Sacile and his muddy march to the Adige had excited enormous enthusiasm among the members of the Kaiser's court, desperate for a victory to balance the Bavarian calamity. The success could not be sustained. In what must have seemed to Franz and his advisers an inexplicably sudden reversal, Eugene had forced the Army of Inner Austria out of Italy in a series of punishing engagements. Back on Austrian soil, his forces scattered and demoralised, Johann has just seen his nascent hopes crushed in the luckless Jellacic's disaster at St Michael. He now stands on the threshold of new decisions, hoping a retreat to Hungary will allow him time to collect reinforcements and regain the initiative, while limiting French occupation of Habsburg lands. Eugene, on the other hand, with clear guidance from Napoleon, has won an impressive series of victories and established a link with his step-father, while his more distant subordinates harry and harass the dispersed Austrians.

As these operations are in progress, the Habsburg court is also learning of other setbacks. In the first place, Chasteler has suffered a crippling defeat in the Tyrol. Though the hardy mountaineers will soon recover to inflict an embarrassing setback on the Bavarian 7th Corps, Chasteler's rout and Johann's retreat have resulted in the loss of Innsbruck and Jellacic's fateful retreat into Styria. Other than the Tyrol, the few sparks of resistance to Napoleon in German-speaking lands have proven ephemeral, quickly quashed by the French and their allies. In the Balkans, General Marmont has pushed Stoichevich's invading detachment out of Dalmatia and is marching north to join Napoleon. Along the banks of the Vistula, initial Austrian success has soured and Polish forces under GD Poniatowski have outflanked Archduke Ferdinand at Warsaw in a brilliant campaign of manoeuvre. They will soon force the archduke, like his cousin in Italy, to abandon his gains and retreat to Habsburg territory. The outcomes of these actions will set the military and political context for the decisions both sides make as the war moves into its concluding stages. Austria's leaders will struggle to craft a coherent strategy to cope with this complex combination of events, while Napoleon, his eye firmly focused on the Hauptarmee, will orchestrate these ancillary actions to support his coming strike across the Danube. As he had told his marshals on the night of the retreat from Aspern–Essling: 'We shall soon be complete masters of our operations.'[1]

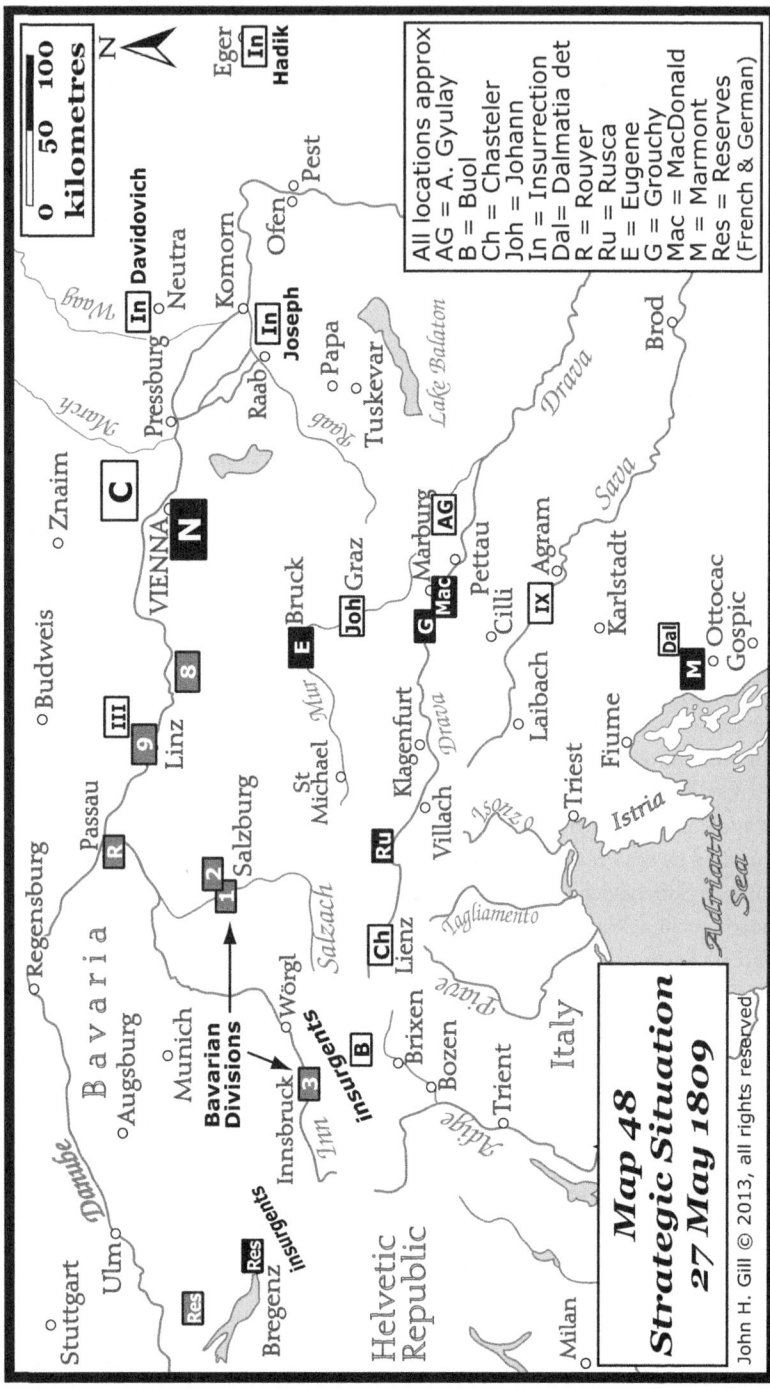

Map 48
Strategic Situation
27 May 1809

All locations approx
AG = A. Gyulay
B = Buol
Ch = Chasteler
Joh = Johann
In = Insurrection
Dal= Dalmatia det
R = Rouyer
Ru = Rusca
E = Eugene
G = Grouchy
Mac = MacDonald
M = Marmont
Res = Reserves
(French & German)

N

0   50   100
kilometres

Eger
In
Hadik

In Davidovich
Neutra

Pest

Ofen

Komorn
In
Joseph

Papa
Tuskevar
Raab
Lake Balaton

Pressburg
Neutra

Znaim

Budweis

C

N
VIENNA

8

III
9
Linz

Brod

Marburg
AG
Joh Graz
G
Mac
Pettau
Cilli
Agram
IX
Karlstadt

Bruck
E

St
Michael

Klagenfurt
Villach
Laibach
Triest
Fiume
Istria

Dal
Ottocac
M
Gospic

Ru

Salzburg
1 2

R
Passau

Regensburg

Augsburg
Munich

Bavaria

Wörgl
3
insurgents
Innsbruck
B
Brixen
Bozen
Trient

Ch
Lienz

Italy

Milan

Stuttgart
Ulm

Res
Bregenz
insurgents

Res

Helvetic
Republic

Bavarian
Divisions

Danube
Inn
Salzach
Mur
Drava
Sava
Drava
Isonzo
Tagliamento
Piave
Adige
Raab
Waag
March

Adriatic
Sea

Appendices

NOTES TO THE READER

1. See Volume I for remarks on the conventions followed in orders of battle.
2. No 'lost battalions'. I have made every effort to avoid the 'lost battalion' phenomenon one often encounters in campaign histories: the unexplained arrival and departure of units in the theatre of operations. Although this is not a compilation of unit histories, it is my hope that careful use of the text, notes, and order of battle appendices will allow the interested readers to track the origin, location, and strength of divisions (at a minimum) during the various phases of the war.
3. As before, a 'c.' (*circa*) indicates the author's estimate.
4. 'Baon' = battalion.
5. '>' indicates an officer who was replaced during the action.

APPENDIX I

Orders of Battle for the Battle of Neumarkt[1]

AUSTRIAN ARMY, MORNING OF 24 APRIL 1809

Wing under the Command of FML von Hiller

Note that this reflects the 'official' order of battle. Hiller arrayed his men in three different 'columns' for the actual engagement.

	baons/ sqdns	present under arms
V Corps: FML Erzherzog Ludwig		
Division: FML Reuss-Plauen		
Brigade: GM von Bianchi		
Duka Infantry Regiment No. 39	3	1,407
Gyulai Infantry Regiment No. 60	3	1,966
Lindenau Infantry Regiment No. 29	2	1,136
Brigade: Oberst Fröhauff		
Beaulieu Infantry Regiment No. 58	2	1,061
Division: FML von Schustekh		
Brigade: GM Mesko de Felsö-Kubinyi		
Brod Grenz Infantry Regiment No. 7	(2)	1,355
Kienmayer Hussars No. 8	6	914
Brigade: GM Radetzky		
Gradiska Grenz Infantry Regiment No. 8	2	2,203
Erzherzog Karl Uhlans No. 3	8	976
III/*Stain*	1	831

Artillery:
1 x 12-pounder position battery
2 x 6-pounder position batteries
1 x 6-pounder brigade battery

1 x 3-pounder brigade battery
2 x cavalry batteries
Infantry: 9,959
Cavalry: 1,890
Guns: 44

Notes:

a. The 3rd Battalion of *Stain* remained with the corps, but was kept out of combat owing to its raw composition.
b. III/*Beaulieu* was still en route to the army; it reached Braunau on approximately 23 April.
c. Three Vienna Volunteer battalions (1st, 2nd, 3rd) retreating separately.
d. The *Brod* Grenz Regiment had lost heavily on 20 April and should be considered either a single, extra-large battalion or two weak battalions.

VI Corps: FML von Hiller
Division: FML von Kottulinsky
Brigade: GM Hohenfeld

Klebek Infantry Regiment No. 14	3	1,676
Jordis Infantry Regiment No. 59	3	1,525
Brigade: GM Weissenwolff		
Deutschmeister Infantry Regiment No. 4	3	1,084
Kerpen Infantry Regiment No. 49	3	1,932

Division: [FML von Vincent] [2]
Brigade: GM Hoffmeister von Hoffeneck

Benjovszky Infantry Regiment No. 31	3	1,534
Splényi Infantry Regiment No. 51	3	1,582
Brigade: GM von Nordmann		
Warasdin-St Georg Grenz Infantry Regiment, No. 6	2	1,372
Rosenberg Chevaulegers No. 6	8	1.049
Liechtenstein Hussars No. 7	8	842

Artillery and Train: — 726
   3 x 12-pounder position batteries
   3 x 6-pounder position batteries
   3 x 6-pounder brigade batteries
   1 x 3-pounder brigade battery
   1 x cavalry battery
Infantry: 10,705
Cavalry: 1,891
Guns: 79

Note: Three Vienna Volunteer battalions (4th, 5th, 6th) en route from Braunau.

II Reserve Corps: FML Kienmayer
Grenadier Brigade: GM d'Aspre

Puteany Grenadier Battalion (14, 45, 59)	1	732
Brzezinski Grenadier Battalion (24, 30, 41)	1	673
Scovaud Grenadier Battalion (4, 49, 63)	1	724
Kirchenbetter Grenadier Battalion (34, 37, 48)	1	769
Scharlach Grenadier Battalion (31, 32, 51)	1	721
Brigade: GM von Clary		
Knesevich Dragoons, No. 3	6	694
Levenehr Dragoons, No. 4	(2)	233
Artillery and Train:	–	348
1 x 6-pounder brigade battery		
1 x cavalry battery		
Infantry: 3,619		
Cavalry: 927		
Guns: 14		

Note: The *Knesevich* Dragoons had been reduced to two squadrons owing to heavy losses. It is unclear whether the dragoons accompanied the corps towards Neumarkt.

From IV Corps
Brigade: GM Reinwald

Infantry Regiment No. 40 (former *Josef Mittrowsky*)	2 2/3	2,659
Stipsicz Hussars No. 10	1+	*c.*150
2 x 6-pounders, 2 x howitzers		

Note: The hussar squadron had been joined by a replacement detachment from the regimental depot. This was formed into two platoons.

FRENCH ARMY, 24 APRIL 1809

Pursuit Force under Marshal Bessières

Note: All strength figures are approximate. A '*c.*' (*circa*) indicates estimated strengths subtracting losses from engagements up to 21 April (inclusive). Other figures have been brought forward from previous orders of battles. Possible losses to non-battle attrition (illness, desertion, march fatigue, etc.) are not included.

	baons/ sqdns	present under arms
2nd Bavarian Division: GL von Wrede		
1st Brigade: GM von Minucci		
3rd Infantry Regiment *Prinz Karl*	2	*c.*1,560
13th Infantry Regiment	2	*c.*1,550
6th Light Infantry Battalion *La Roche*	1	*c.*790
2nd Brigade: GM von Beckers		
6th Infantry Regiment *Herzog Wilhelm*	2	*c.*1,450

7th Infantry Regiment *Löwenstein*	2	1,597
Cavalry Brigade: GM von Preysing		
2nd Chevaulegers *König*	4	*c.*450
3rd Chevaulegers *Leiningen*	4	500
Artillery and Train	–	406
Line (Foot) Batteries: Dorn, Berchem		
Light (Mounted) Battery: Caspers		
Reserve Battery: Dobl		
3rd Division/4th Corps: GD Molitor		
1st Brigade: GB Leguay		
2nd Ligne	2	1,537
16th Ligne	3	2,110
2nd Brigade: GB Viviès		
37th Ligne	3	1,699
67th Ligne	2	1,485
Artillery and Train	–	308
4th Corps Light Cavalry Division: GD Marulaz		
3rd Chasseurs-à-Cheval	2	438
19th Chasseurs-à-Cheval	3	599
23rd Chasseurs-à-Cheval	3	594
Hessian Chevaulegers	3	340
Light Cavalry Brigade: GB Jacquinot		
1st Chasseurs-à-Cheval	3	*c.*470
2nd Chasseurs-à-Cheval	3	749
8th Hussars	2?	*c.*580

Totals

Shows all troops in immediate area, not those actually engaged.

	Austrian	Allies
Infantry	26,942	*c.*13,700
Cavalry	4,858	*c.*4,700
Guns	141	36

Note that the estimated Allied numbers are probably high as they do not include march attrition.[3]

Additional Austrian Forces Under Hiller (not under command of a corps),[4] morning of 26 April 1809

	baons/ sqdns	present under arms
At Rohrbach north of the Danube: (from GM Richter's brigade)		
2nd, 3rd, 4th Prachin Landwehr	3	
Opposite Passau: Oberst Franz von Gratze		
Wallach-Illyria Grenz Regiment No. 13	2	
III/vacant Infantry Regiment No. 18 (formerly *Stuart*)	1	
Stipsicz Hussar Regiment No. 10 (two platoons)		
2 guns		
At Wernstein: Oberst Nesslinger		
1st Innviertel Landwehr	1	
4th Traunviertel Landwehr	1	
At Schärding: FML von Dedovich[5]		
III/*Württemberg* Infantry Regiment No. 38	1	
III/*Chasteler* Infantry Regiment No. 46	1	
III/*Schröder* Infantry Regiment No. 7 (two companies)		
III/vacant (J. *Mittrowsky*) Infantry Regiment No. 40		
(two companies)		700
3rd *Erzherzog Karl* Legion	1	
GM von Sinzendorf		
1st, 3rd, 4th Mühlviertel Landwehr	3	
3rd Hausruck Landwehr	1	

2 x guns, 1 x howitzer
From Radetzky's outpost line along the Inn

Gradiska Grenz Regiment, No. 8	(one platoon)
Merveldt Uhlan Regiment, No. 1	(one platoon)

En route to Altheim:

III/*Würzburg* Infantry Regiment No. 23	1
III/*Reuss-Greitz* Infantry Regiment No. 55	1[6]
1st, 2nd, 3rd Vienna Volunteers	(3)[7]
1st Moravian Volunteers	1

Near Waitzenkirchen:

1st *Erzherzog Karl* Legion (Prag Jägers)	1	800

Note: This was the second tranche of the 1st *Karl* Legion, the initial group participated in the fighting south of Regensburg, suffering heavily in the process. This group arrived in Waitzenkirchen on 24 April along with the 1st Moravian. Hiller ordered the Moravians to join the army at Altheim, but sent the Legion battalion, poorly equipped and utterly untrained, back across the Danube to complete its preparations.

At Obernberg (Oberst von MacDermott):

4th Hausruck Landwehr	1

At Mühlheim (Oberst von MacDermott):

2nd Mühlviertel Landwehr	1

At Braunau (Oberst von MacDermott):

1st, 2nd, 3rd Traunviertel Landwehr	3

At Burghausen (Oberst von MacDermott):

2nd Innviertel Landwehr	1

The following joined the army on 25–26 April:

III/*Czartoryski* Infantry Regiment No. 9	1	
III/*Beaulieu* Infantry Regiment No. 58	1	
5th, 6th *Erzherzog Karl* Legion	2	
4th, 5th, 6th Vienna Volunteers	3	
Replacement detachments for:		
6th Jäger Battalion	–	250
W. Colloredo Infantry No. 56	–	?
Gyulai Infantry No. 60	–	400

Note: a replacement detachment for *EH Ludwig* Infantry No. 8 had also arrived in Braunau by 24 April; its location on the 26th is not clear. Replacement columns for V Corps infantry regiments *Gyulai* (247), *Sztaray* (400), and *Duka* (230) were in Wels along with 800 infantry replacements destined for VI Corps regiments.

En route to Jellacic:
  Replacement detachment for *Esterhazy* Infantry No. 32   –   530

Under FML von Jellacic
In Salzburg: GM von Legisfeld
  1st, 3rd, 4th Salzburg Landwehr   3
Note: Five companies detached escorting prisoners.

Returning from Bavaria (GM von Legisfeld):
  From Wasserburg: 1st Hausruck Landwehr   1
  From Rosenheim:
    2nd Hausruck Landwehr   1
    2nd Salzburg Landwehr   1
    (Only four companies, two detached with Taxis in Tyrol)
  3rd Innviertel Landwehr
    From Reichenhall   (one and a half companies)
    From Traunstein   (one half company)
    From Strasswalchen   (two companies)

Landwehr in 1809

The Landwehr was raised locally and organised regionally. Each battalion was therefore named according to its district (*Kreis* or *Viertel*) and an effort was made to keep battalions grouped by region (Lower Austria, Styria, etc.). This was not always successful, but understanding the regional aspect helps explain the orders of battle. This table shows which districts belonged to which regions and how many battalions each district was *supposed* to form. Note that in some cases (especially Upper and Lower Austria) the battalions never materialised. The abbreviations used in this work for the elaborately titled Lower Austrian battalions are in parentheses.[8]

	baons/ sqdns
Lower Austria (Niederösterreich)	
Viertel unter dem Wiener Wald (UWW)	6
Viertel ober dem Wiener Wald (OWW)	4
Viertel unter dem Manhartsberg (UMB)	4
Viertel ober dem Manhartsberg (OMB)	5
Upper Austria (Oberösterreich)	
Mühlviertel	4
Traunviertel	4
Hausruckviertel	4
Innviertel	3
Salzburg	
Salzburg	4
Styria (Steiermark)	
Graz	5
Judenburg	2
Marburg	2
Bruck	2

Cilli	2
Carinthia (Kärnten)	
Klagenfurt	3
Villach	2
Carniola-Coastal (Krain-Küstenland)	
Laibach	3
Görz	2
Adelsberg	4
Neustadtl	4
Trieste	2
Bohemia (Böhmen)	
Prague (city)	2
Elbogen	3
Pilsen	3
Klattau	3
Tschaslau	3
Tabor	2
Saaz	2
Rakonitz	2
Königgrätz	5
Leitmeritz	5
Kaurschim	2
Beraun	2
Budweis	3
Bunzlau	6
Prachin	4
Chrudim	4
Bidschow	4
Moravia-Silesia (Mähren-Schlesien)	
Brünn	4
Iglau	2
Hradisch	3
Znaim	2
Prerau	3
Olmütz	5
Troppau	3
Teschen	2

Companies per battalion:
Lower and Upper Austria: four companies each, except six companies each for 1st OWW and 1st UMB.

Salzburg: eight companies each for 1st, 3rd, 4th Battalions; six companies for 2nd.
Styria: six companies each, except eight companies for 1st Graz.
Carinthia: four companies each, except five companies each for 2nd Klagenfurt and 2nd Villach, and six companies each for 3rd Klagenfurt and 1st Villach.
Carniola-Coastal: six companies each, except seven companies for 4th Adelsberg. The two Trieste battalions were unique. They were often known together as the 'Trieste Freijägerkorps'. The 1st Battalion was formed from the city militia and included six fusilier and two Jäger companies. The 2nd Battalion (also sometimes called the 'Thurn Jägers') had six fusilier and four Jäger companies.
Bohemia: six companies each.
Moravia-Silesia: six companies each.

APPENDIX 4

Orders of Battle for the Battle of Ebelsberg[9]

AUSTRIAN ARMY, EVENING OF 2 MAY 1809

Wing under the Command of FML von Hiller

	baons/ sqdns	present under arms
Independent Rear Guards (listed north to south)		
Brigade: GM von Bianchi		
Duka Infantry Regiment No. 39	3	1,200
Gyulai Infantry Regiment No. 60	3	1,700
Rosenberg Chevaulegers Regiment No. 6 (Scheibler)	2	170
Stipsicz Hussar Regiment No. 10	1	100
One 6-pounder brigade battery (7 guns)		
FML Schustekh:		
GM von Hohenfeld's brigade:		
Klebek Infantry Regiment No. 14	3	1,460
Jordis Infantry Regiment No. 59	2	1,075
Kienmayer Hussar Regiment No. 8	8	740
One cavalry battery (6 guns)		
Brigade: GM von Radetzky		
Gradiska Grenz Regiment No. 8	2	1,790
EH Karl Uhlan Regiment No. 3	8	850
Merveldt Uhlan Regiment No. 1	(one plt)	30
One-half cavalry battery (3 guns)		
Brigade: GM von Nordmann		
Warasdin-St Georg Grenz Regiment No. 6	2	1,000
Brod Grenz Regiment No. 7	(2 companies)	270

| Liechtenstein Hussar Regiment No. 7 | 8 | 800 |
| One-half cavalry battery (3 guns) | | |

Notes:

a. Four squadrons of *Liechtenstein* were en route to Hiller; joined him on 3 May.

b. Six of Bianchi's guns were sent to VI Corps that night; one was under repair; he was left with one by 3 May.

c. The *Stipsicz* Hussar squadron was comprised of half of the squadron that had been at Oberhaus supplemented by replacements.

V Corps: FML Erzherzog Ludwig

5th Pioneer Division (one and three-quarters companies)		200
Division: FML Reuss-Plauen		
Brigade: Oberst von Hammer		
Beaulieu Infantry Regiment No. 58	3	3,100
Lindenau Infantry Regiment No. 29	2	1,130
III/*Würzburg* Infantry Regiment No. 23	1	1,150
Brigade: GM von Reinwald		
Vacant (former *Josef Mittrowsky*) Infantry Regiment No. 40	3	3,200
5th *EH Karl* Legion	1	1,010
6th *EH Karl* Legion	1	1,100
Not assigned to a brigade:		
1st, 2nd, 3rd Vienna Volunteers	3	1,800
III/*Stain* Infantry Regiment No. 50	1	850

Artillery:
   1 x 12-pounder position battery (6 guns)
   2 x 6-pounder position batteries (12 guns)
   1 x 3-pounder brigade battery (7 guns)
   1/2 x cavalry battery (2 guns)
   1 x 6-pounder brigade battery (5 guns, from IV Corps troops)
Infantry: 13,340
Guns: 32

Notes:

a. The 'two battalions' of *Lindenau* were eleven companies, the remains of the elements that had retreated from Abensberg with V Corps under the regimental commander, Oberst Hammer. The two late-arriving companies of III/*Lindenau* were with Oberst Hardegg north of the Danube.

b. III/*Czartoryski* was assigned to Reinwald's brigade late on 2 May or early on 3 May.

c. III/*Württemberg*, III/*Chasteler*, and the two companies of III/*Schröder* were assigned to Hammer's brigade late on 2 May or early on 3 May.

VI Corps: FML von Hiller

6th Pioneer Division (one and three-quarters companies)		140
Division: FML von Kottulinsky		

Brigade: GM von Weissenwolff

Deutschmeister Infantry Regiment No. 4	3	1,900
Kerpen Infantry Regiment No. 49	3	2,400
III/*Czartoryski* Infantry Regiment No. 9	1	1,000

Division: FML von Vincent
  Brigade: GM Hoffmeister

Benjovszky Infantry Regiment No. 31	3	2,000
Splenyi Infantry Regiment No. 51	3	2,015

  Cavalry:

Rosenberg Chevaulegers Regiment No. 6	6	680
Stipsicz Hussar Regiment No. 10	1/2	50

  Not assigned to a brigade:

4th Vienna Volunteers	1	800
5th Vienna Volunteers	1	900
6th Vienna Volunteers	1	900

Artillery:
  3 x 12-pounder position batteries (18 guns)
  2 x 6-pounder position batteries (12 guns)
  5 x brigade batteries (37 guns)
  1 and 1/2 x cavalry batteries (9 guns)
Infantry: 11,915
Cavalry: 730
Guns: 76

Note: III/*Czartoryski* was assigned to Reinwald's brigade late on 2 May or early on 3 May.

II Reserve Corps: FML von Kienmayer

Grenadier Brigade: GM (FML) d'Aspre

Puteany Grenadier Battalion (14, 45, 59)	1	730
Brzezinski Grenadier Battalion (24, 30, 41)	1	730
Scovaud Grenadier Battalion (4, 49, 63)	1	710
Kirchenbetter Grenadier Battalion (34, 37, 48)	1	720
Scharlach Grenadier Battalion (31, 32, 51)	1	740
1st Moravian Volunteer Battalion	1	1,200

Brigade: GM von Clary

Knesevich Dragoons No. 3	6	620
Levenehr Dragoons No. 4	–	(100)

Artillery:
  1 x 6-pounder brigade battery (8 guns)
  1 x cavalry battery (6 guns)
Infantry: 4,830
Cavalry: 620
Guns: 14

Note: Approximately 100 *Knesevich* dragoons joined the corps on 3 May.

Not assigned to a corps
FML von Dedovich

III/*Stuart* Infantry Regiment No. 18		1	1,000
III/*Württemberg* Infantry Regiment No. 38		1	1,100
III/*Chasteler* Infantry Regiment No. 46		1	800
III/*Schröder* Infantry Regiment No. 7	(2 companies)		450
3rd *EH Karl* Legion		1	800
Brigade: Oberst Nesslinger			
1st Innviertel and 4th Traunviertel Landwehr		2	550
Brigade: GM von Sinzendorf			
1st Mühlviertel Landwehr		1	600
3rd Mühlviertel Landwehr		1	600
4th Mühlviertel Landwehr		1	600
3rd and 4th Hausruck Landwehr		1	700
Cavalry: cuirassier replacement detachments (various regiments)	–		50

Artillery:
1/2 x 6-pounder position battery (3 guns)
Infantry: 7,200
Cavalry: 50
Guns: 3
Note: The *Württemberg* and *Chasteler* battalions and the two companies of *Schröder* were assigned to Hammer's brigade late on 2 May or early on 3 May.

Independent: Oberst Gratze

Wallach-Illyria Grenz Regiment, No. 13		2	1,400
Attached: *Kronprinz Erzherzog Ferdinand* Scharfschützen (1 company)			III

At Steyr: Oberst MacDermott

2nd Mühlviertel Landwehr		1	700
1st Traunviertel Landwehr		1	600
2nd Traunviertel Landwehr		1	650
3rd Traunviertel Landwehr		1	700
2nd Innviertel Landwehr		1	90
4th Hausruck Landwehr	(2 companies)		350

Infantry: 3,090

North of the Danube: Oberst Anton Graf Hardegg

III/*Lindenau* Infantry Regiment No. 29	(2 companies)		710
Depot Company, 9th Jäger Battalion	(1 company)		160
Replacement detachment, *J. Mittrowsky* Infantry Regiment No. 40	–		220
Depot detachment, *Jordis* Infantry Regiment No. 59		–	100
Levenehr Dragoons No. 4		2	210

Infantry: 1,190
Cavalry: 210

Notes:

a. The *Lindenau* companies were those absent from the order of battle at the start of the war.

b. GM Richter's brigade was no longer under Hiller's command (under Klenau as part of Bohemian command).

Linz garrison: GM von Rüffer

Depot division, *Klebek* Infantry Regiment No. 14	(2 companies)	400
Depot division, *Jordis* Infantry Regiment No. 59	(2 companies)	350
1st Ober dem Manhartsberg Landwehr	1	700
5th Ober dem Manhartsberg Landwehr	1	600
3rd Ober dem Wiener Wald Landwehr	1	800
Sapper Company	(1 company)	110
Infantry: 2,850		

Note: The *Klebek* and *Jordis* depot divisions crossed the Danube in time to join their respective regiments on 3 May.

Enns/Mauthausen garrison: GM von Ulbrecht

3rd Ober dem Manhartsberg Landwehr	1	650
1st Ober dem Wiener Wald Landwehr	1	1,200
4th Ober dem Wiener Wald Landwehr	1	900
Infantry: 2,750		

Note: The 1st OWW marched to St Pölten on 3 May to join FML O'Reilly.

FRENCH ARMY PURSUIT FORCES NEAR LINZ, EVENING OF 2 MAY 1809

Note: Only French forces actually engaged at Ebelsberg are shown. All strength figures are approximate, with a 'c.' (*circa*) indicating estimated strengths (subtracting losses from previous engagements). Other figures have been brought forward from previous order of battles and have not been adjusted for possible losses to non-battle attrition.[10]

	baons/ sqdns	present under arms
4th Corps: Marshal Massena		
1st Division: GD Legrand		
1st Brigade: GB Ledru		
26th Léger	3	1,993
18th Ligne	3	2,312
2nd (Baden) Brigade: GB Kister (French) and GM von Harrant (Baden)		
1st Baden Infantry Regiment *Grossherzog*	2	1,696
2nd Baden Infantry Regiment *Erbgrossherzog*	2	1,713

Baden Jäger Battalion *Lingg*	1	572
2nd Division, 2nd Corps: GD Claparède		
1st Brigade: GB Coëhorn		*c.*3,400
2nd Light Demi-Brigade	3	
IV/17th Léger, IV/21st Léger, IV/28th Léger		
4th Light Demi-Brigade	3	
IV/26th Léger, Tirailleurs Corses, Tirailleurs du Po		
2nd Brigade: GB Lesuire		*c.*2,470
5th Line Demi-Brigade	2	
IV/27th Ligne, IV/39th Ligne		
6th Line Demi-Brigade	3	
IV/59th Ligne, IV/69th Ligne, IV/76th Ligne		
3rd Brigade: GB Ficatier		
7th Line Demi-Brigade		
IV/40th Ligne	1	498
IV/88th Ligne	1	498
8th Line Demi-Brigade		
IV/64th Ligne	1	520
IV/100th Ligne	1	383
IV/103rd Ligne	1	395
Light cavalry: GD Marulaz		
3rd Chasseurs-à-Cheval	2	438
14th Chasseurs-à-Cheval	2	*c.*200
19th Chasseurs-à-Cheval	3	599
23rd Chasseurs-à-Cheval	3	594
Hessian Chevaulegers	3	340
Baden Light Dragoons	4	475
Württemberg Leib Chevaulegers	4	565
Reserve Cavalry: Marshal Bessières		
Light Cavalry Brigade: GB Piré		
8th Hussars	3	*c.*800
16th Chasseurs-à-Cheval	3	*c.*600
Arriving in late afternoon under GD Durosnel		
9th Hussars	3	793
Light Cavalry Brigade: GB Jacquinot		
1st Chasseurs-à-Cheval	3	*c.*400
2nd Chasseurs-à-Cheval	3	*c.*700

Austrian Forces in the Danube Valley, 8–9 May 1809[11]

Wing under the Command of FML von Hiller

Note: Strengths as of 9 May (including Schustekh's division as of 10 May).

	baons/ sqdns	present under arms
V Corps		
Advance Guard: GM von Radetzky		
Gradiska Grenz Regiment No. 8	2	1,153
EH Karl Uhlan Regiment No. 3	8	395
Division: FML Reuss-Plauen		
Brigade: Oberst von Mariassy		
Duka Infantry Regiment No. 39	3	1,888
Gyulai Infantry Regiment No. 60	3	2,469
III/*Stain* Infantry Regiment No. 50	1	710
Division: FML Schustekh		
Kienmayer Hussar Regiment No. 8	8	563
Brigade: GM von Reinwald		
Lindenau Infantry Regiment No. 29	2	829
Vacant (former *Josef Mittrowsky*) Infantry Regiment No. 40	3	1,540
5th *EH Karl* Legion	1	880
6th *EH Karl* Legion	1	954

Infantry: 10,423
Cavalry: 958

Note: Bianchi had fallen ill and was replaced temporarily by Mariassy.

VI Corps
Division: FML von Kottulinsky

Brigade: GM von Hohenfeld

Klebek Infantry Regiment No. 14	2	718
Jordis Infantry Regiment No. 59	2	916
3rd *EH Karl* Legion	1	653

Brigade: GM von Weissenwolff

Deutschmeister Infantry Regiment No. 4	3	1,370
Kerpen Infantry Regiment No. 49	3	1,828

Division: FML von Vincent

Brigade: GM Hoffmeister

Benjovszky Infantry Regiment No. 31	3	1,175
Splenyi Infantry Regiment No. 51	3	803
1st Moravian Volunteer Battalion	1	1,004

Cavalry:

Rosenberg Chevaulegers Regiment No. 6	6	851
Liechtenstein Hussar Regiment No. 7	4	439

Infantry: 8,467

Cavalry: 1,290

II Reserve Corps: FML von Kienmayer

Grenadier Brigade: GM (FML) d'Aspre (3,378 for the five grenadier battalions)

Puteany Grenadier Battalion (14, 45, 59)	1
Brzezinski Grenadier Battalion (24, 30, 41)	1
Scovaud Grenadier Battalion (4, 49, 63)	1
Kirchenbetter Grenadier Battalion (34, 37, 48)	1
Scharlach Grenadier Battalion (31, 32, 51)	1

3rd Moravian Volunteer Battalion	1	1,188

Brigade: GM von Clary

Knesevich Dragoons No. 3	6	612

Infantry: 4,566

Cavalry: 612

Under Command of FML Archduke Maximilian

En route to Vienna (north of the Danube):

Vienna Volunteers (arrived 9 May)

1st, 2nd, 3rd Vienna Volunteers	3	2,148

Moravian Landwehr: GM von Wodniansky

1st and 4th Brünn	2(arrived 8 May)
1st and 2nd Znaim	2(arrived 9 May)
3rd Hradisch	1(arrived 10 May)
1st Iglau	1(arrived 11 May)

Total	–	5,500

Note: Six other battalions were diverted to Laa: 3rd Brünn, 1st Hradisch, 2nd Hradisch, 3rd Prerau, 2nd Moravian Volunteers, and 5th Olmütz.

En route to Vienna (south of the Danube):

Vienna Volunteers (arrived 8 May)		
4th, 5th, 6th Vienna Volunteers	3	2,069
FML von Dedovich (arrived 9 May)[12]		
Beaulieu Infantry Regiment No. 58	3	2,800
III/*Czartoryski* Infantry Regiment No. 9	1	1,050
III/*Stuart* Infantry Regiment No. 18	1	802
III/*Würzburg* Infantry Regiment No. 23	1	636
III/*Württemberg* Infantry Regiment No. 38	1	810
III/*Chasteler* Infantry Regiment No. 46	1	486
III/*Schröder* Infantry Regiment No. 7	(2 companies)	230
Landwehr (Upper and Lower Austria)	–	1,477
Brigade: GM von Mesko		
Wallach-Illyria Grenz Regiment, No. 13	2	–
Brod Grenz Regiment No. 7	(1 company)	–
Stipsicz Hussar Regiment No. 10	1 1/2	120
Total infantry (Mesko)	–	*c.*1,000

Infantry: 7,200
Cavalry: 120
Notes:
a. The Landwehr was composed of remnants of 1st Innviertel, 4th Traunviertel, 1st Mühlviertel, 3rd Mühlviertel, 4th Mühlviertel, 3rd Hausruck, and one-half of 4th Hausruck Landwehr.
b. The remnants of the *Brod* Grenzer had been consolidated into a lone company.

Brigade: GM von Nordmann		
Warasdin-St Georg Grenz Regiment No. 6	2	500
Liechtenstein Hussar Regiment No. 7	4	200
One-half cavalry battery (3 guns)		

Vienna garrison:
See 11 May order of battle (Appendix 6)

West and south-west of Vienna:

Vicinity Annaberg/Mariazell: Major Graf Breuner	
1st unter dem Manhartsberg Landwehr (Breuner)	1
2nd ober dem Wiener Wald Landwehr (Clary)	1
Landsturm	
2 guns	

Notes:
a. Other Landsturm groups were gathering north of Vienna (Hauptmann Kohout),

south of Vienna (Rittmeister Plächel), and in the vicinity of the Semmering Pass (Oberst von Attems).
b. Styrian Landsturm and 200 men from FML Lippa's reserve joined later (see below).
c. Two more guns added later in May (after the first two were captured).

At Bruck an der Mur: Oberst MacDermott

2nd Mühlviertel Landwehr	1
1st Traunviertel Landwehr	(2 companies)
2nd Traunviertel Landwehr	1
3rd Traunviertel Landwehr	1
2nd Innviertel Landwehr	1
4th Hausruck Landwehr	(2 companies)
Infantry: 500	

Note: two companies of 1st Traunviertel had been left at Altenmarkt.

Under the Command of FML Kerpen

West and south-west of Vienna:

Vicinity Liezen: Oberstleutnant von Plunquet

III/Reuss-Greitz Infantry Regiment No. 55	1	
Recruit detachment/EH Karl Infantry Regiment No. 3	–	400
4th ober dem Wiener Wald Landwehr	1 (3 companies)	
1st Cilli Landwehr	1	
2nd Cilli Landwehr	1	
depot/1st Judenburg Landwehr	–	c.125
depot/2nd Judenburg Landwehr	–	c.125

Note: the 2nd Company of the 4th OWW was in Vienna.

Vicinity Altenmarkt: Major Fitzgerald

1st Inner Austrian Volunteers (forming)	1	
1st Traunviertel Landwehr	(2 companies)	
two Bruck Landwehr depots	–	c.250
two Graz Landwehr depots	–	c.250

Notes:
a. The two Traunviertel companies soon disintegrated.
b. Oberstleutnant de la Bussière later joined with the 3rd OWW and three companies of the 1st OMB c.13 May.
c. Two guns added later in May.

Vicinity Aspang: Oberst von Attems

Kordon troops	–	41
depot/4th Graz Landwehr	–	c.125
depot/5th Graz Landwehr	–	c.125

Landsturm

Bruck an der Leitha: Reserve under FML Lippa

Depots of *Lusignan* and *Strassaldo* Infantry Regiments	–	500
Depot Division/*de Vaux* Infantry Regiment, Nr. 45	–	?
Reserve Squadron/*Frimont* Hussars Nr. 9	–	31

Note: Two guns added later in May.

SCHUSTEKH'S DIVISION, 10 MAY 1809[13]

	baons/ sqdns	present under arms
Gradiska Grenz Regiment No. 8	1	500
Lindenau Infantry Regiment No. 29	2	1,625
Josef Mittrowsky Infantry Regiment No. 40	3	1,731
5th *EH Karl* Legion	1	880
6th *EH Karl* Legion	1	990
1st Moravian Volunteer Battalion	1	1,113
III/*Stain*Infantry Regiment No. 50	1	710
Levenehr Dragoons No. 4	2	280

One 3-pounder battery (7 guns)
One brigade battery (6 guns)
Brigade commanders: GM von Reinwald, Oberst von Hardegg

Vienna Garrison, 11 May 1809[14]

FML Archduke Maximilian

	baons/ sqdns	present under arms
Division: FML O'Reilly		
Brigade: GM Auer		
Beaulieu Infantry Regiment No. 58	3	*c*.2,800
Brigade: GM Keller		
Kerpen Infantry Regiment No. 49		
(depot division and recruits)	1	
Depot Company/7th Jäger Battalion	(1 company)	
Green Sharpshooters (Grüne Scharfschützen)	–	118
Gray Sharpshooters (Graue Scharfschützen)	–	40
1st Citizens' Regiment (Bürgerregiment)	3	678
2nd Citizens' Regiment (Bürgerregiment)	(elements)	245
Green Grenadiers (Grüne Grenadiere)	(1 company)	62
Universitätskorps	(1 company)	200
Landsturm	1	650
Brigade: Oberst Nesslinger		
Deutschmeister Infantry Regiment No. 4		
(depot division and recruits)	1	
2nd Citizens' Regiment (Bürgerregiment)	2	600
Brigade: GM Egger		
EH Karl Infantry Regiment No. 3		
(depot division and recruits)	1	
Klebek Infantry Regiment No. 14		
(depot division and recruits)	(1 company)	160
Gray Sharpshooters (Graue Scharfschützen)	–	32
Akademiekorps		40
Brigade: Oberst Waldstein		64

Citizens' Cavalry (Bürgerkavallerie)
Mounted Jäger Volunteers (Berittenes Jägerfreikorps)
Division: FML Dedovich
  Brigade: GM Mesko
    Wallach-Illyria Grenz Regiment No. 13   2
    Brod Grenz Regiment No. 7   (1 company)
    III/*Czartoryski* Infantry Regiment No. 9   1
    III/*Stuart* Infantry Regiment No. 18   1
    III/*Württemberg* Infantry Regiment No. 38   1
    Stipsicz Hussar Regiment No. 10   1 1/2   120
  Brigade: GM Nordmann
    St Georg Grenz Regiment No. 6   1
    III/*Würzburg* Infantry Regiment No. 23   1
    III/*Chasteler* Infantry Regiment No. 46   1
    III/*Schröder* Infantry Regiment No. 7   (2 companies)
    Liechtenstein Hussar Regiment No. 7   4   200
    Upper Austrian Landwehr (composite battalion)   1   1,000
  Brigade: GM Paar (Lower Austrian Landwehr)   total   8,000
    1st Ober dem Wiener Wald   1
    1st Unter dem Wiener Wald   1
    2nd Unter dem Wiener Wald (most still escorting prisoners)   1
    3rd, 4th, 5th, 6th Unter dem Wiener Wald   4
    2nd and 4th Ober dem Manhartsberg   2
    2nd, 3rd, and 4th Unter dem Manhartsberg   3
Division: GM Moritz Liechtenstein
  Brigade: Oberstleutnant Steigentesch
    1st through 6th Vienna Volunteers   6   4,217
    Schlegenberg (Wiener) Jäger   (1 company)   150
  Brigade: Oberst Strachwitz—reserve squadrons from the following: 320
    Cuirassier Regiments 3, 4, and 8
    Dragoon Regiments 1, 3, and 4
    Chevaulegers Regiment No. 3   total: 3 1/2 squadrons
Division: GM Wodniansky (Moravian Landwehr)   5,500
    1st and 4th Brünn   2
    1st and 2nd Znaim   2
    3rd Hradisch   1
    1st Iglau   1
Artillery (regular and municipal)   1,200

Gross Totals

	Infantry	Cavalry
Line infantry:	7,500	
Line cavalry:		320
Depot infantry:	5,000	
Depot cavalry:		320

Vienna Volunteers:	4,200	
Schelgenberg Jäger:	150	
Lower Austrian Landwehr:	8,000	
Upper Austrian Landwehr:	1,000	
Moravian Landwehr:	5,500	
Viennese citizen infantry and Landsturm:	2,650	60
Sub-Totals	34,000	700

With artillery: 35,900

Note: It is not clear where the 2nd Company of the 4th OWW was assigned within the garrison

Orders of Battle for the Battle of Linz[15]

AUSTRIAN ARMY, EVENING OF 16 MAY 1809

III Corps under FZM von Kolowrat

	baons/ sqdns	present under arms
Right Column (FML Somariva)		
Merveldt Uhlan Regiment No. 1	2	205
5th Jäger Battalion	1	656
I/*Peterwardein* Grenz Regiment No. 9	1	354
Würzburg Infantry Regiment No. 23	2	795
Wenzel Colloredo Infantry Regiment No. 56	3	2,514
1st and 4th Chrudim Landwehr	2	1,264
One 3-pounder battery (4 guns)		
One 6-pounder battery (4 guns)		
Centre Column (FML Vukassovich)		
Advance guard (GM Crenneville)		
Merveldt Uhlan Regiment No. 1	4	408
6th Jäger Battalion	1	546
II/*Peterwardein* Grenz Regiment No. 9	1	359
II/*Karl Schröder* Infantry Regiment No. 7	1(included below)	
One cavalry battery		
Main Body (FML Vukassovich)		
Hessen-Homburg Hussar Regiment No. 4	4	426

Karl Schröder Infantry Regiment No. 7	2	1,798
Manfredini Infantry Regiment No. 12	3	2,415
Württemberg Infantry Regiment No. 38	2	811
Four batteries (18–24 guns)		

Left Column (FML Saint Julien)

Hessen-Homburg Hussars Regiment No. 4	2	213
Kaunitz Infantry Regiment No. 20	3	2,100
1st, 2nd, and 3rd Pilsen Landwehr	3	1,732
Two batteries (12–16 guns)		

Reserve (GM Oberdorf)

1st and 2nd Prague Landwehr	2	–
1st and 2nd Beraun Landwehr	2	–
1st Kaurschim Landwehr	1	–
4th Königgrätz Landwehr	1	–
Total (Oberdorf)	–	2,890

III Corps Totals
Regular Infantry: 12,348
Landwehr: 5,886
Cavalry: 1,252
Guns: 38–48

Note: The 2nd Königgrätz was found unfit for field duty and sent back to Prague, its place in the reserve taken by the 4th Königgrätz.

En route (did not participate in the battle)

III/*Froon* Infantry Regiment No. 54	1	975
Schwarzenberg Uhlan Regiment No. 2	(platoon)	*c*.25
III/*Josef Colloredo* Infantry Regiment No. 57	1	1,057
GM Schneller		
Hessen-Homburg Hussar Regiment No. 4	2	205
Lobkowitz Jäger	1	430

Frontier Forces
Vicinity of Klattau: GM Radivojevich

Merveldt Uhlan Regiment No. 1	2	*c*.200
Deutsch-Banat Grenz Regiment No. 12	2	799
2nd Klattau Landwehr	1	*c*.800
cavalry half-battery		

On the Bavarian border: Oberst Rosenhayn

II/*Froon* Infantry Regiment No. 54	(2 companies)	307
1st and 2nd Prachin Landwehr	2	1,399

1st Klattau Landwehr	1	*c.*800
3rd Klattau Landwehr	1	746
2nd Budweis Landwehr	1	*c.*550
3rd Budweis Landwehr	1	581
two 3-pounders		

ALLIED ARMY, EVENING OF 16 MAY 1809

Forces near Linz[16]

	baons/ sqdns	present under arms
8th Corps (Württemberg): GD Vandamme		
Infantry Division: GL Neubronn		
Brigade: GM Franquemont		
Kronprinz Infantry Regiment	2	1,333
Herzog Wilhelm Infantry Regiment	2	1,384
Brigade: GM Scharffenstein		
Phull Infantry Regiment	2	1,274
Neubronn Fusilier Regiment	2	1,079
Light Brigade: GM Hügel		
Jäger Battalion *König*	1	*c.*430
Jäger Battalion *Neuffer*	1	*c.*440
1st Light Battalion *Wolff*	1	*c.*440
2nd Light Battalion *Brüsselle*	1	*c.*450
Cavalry Division: GL Wöllwarth		
Brigade: GM Stettner		
König Jäger zu Pferd	4	*c.*430
Herzog Louis Jäger zu Pferd	4	*c.*450
Artillery: 1st and 2nd Horse Batteries, 1st Foot Battery: 22 guns		
8th Corps Totals (approximate)		
Regular Infantry: 6,830		
Cavalry: 880		
Guns: 22		

Notes:
a. One company from each Jäger and light battalion in Steyr.
b. Approximately 300 men from *Neubronn* detached to escort prisoners.
c. I/*Camrer* (*c.*650 men) at Enns.

9th Corps (Saxon): Marshal Bernadotte

1st Division: GL von Zezschwitz		
1st Brigade: GM von Hartitzsch		
combined Leib Grenadier Guard Battalion	1	540
2nd Grenadier Battalion (Major von Bose)	1	509

3rd Grenadier Battalion (Major von Hake)	1	526
König Infantry Regiment	2	876
I/*Dyherrn* Infantry Regiment	1	463
Schützen Detachment	(2 companies)	271
2nd Infantry Brigade: GM von Boxberg		
Prinz Maximilian Infantry Regiment	2	1,064
Prinz Friedrich August Infantry Regiment	2	1,044
Prinz Anton Infantry Regiment	2	1,065
Schützen Detachment	(2 companies)	271
Cavalry Brigade: GM von Gutschmid		
Gardes du Corps Regiment	2	324
Karabiniers Regiment	2	244
Hussar Regiment	3	494
Prinz Clemens Chevaulegers	4	407
Prinz Albert Chevaulegers	1	203
2nd Division: GL von Polenz		
1st Infantry Brigade: GM von Lecoq		
Prinz Clemens Infantry Regiment	2	1,061
von Low Infantry Regiment	2	1,044
von Cerrini Infantry Regiment	2	1,066
Schützen Detachment	(2 companies)	271
2nd Infantry Brigade: GM von Zeschau		
1st Grenadier Battalion (Major von Radeloff)	1	543
4th Grenadier Battalion (Major von Winkelmann)	1	512
von Niesemeuschel Infantry Regiment	2	965
II/*von Oebschelwitz* Infantry Regiment	1	533
Schützen Detachment	(2 companies)	226
Cavalry Brigade: GM von Feilitzsch		
Leib-Garde Cuirassiers	4	593
Prinz Johann Chevaulegers	4	598

Artillery and Train
  1st Heavy Battery (Hoyer): 4 x 8-pounders and 2 x howitzers
  2nd Heavy Battery (Coudray): 4 x 8-pounders and 2 x howitzers
  1st Light Battery (Bonniot): 4 x 8-pounders and 2 x howitzers
  2nd Light Battery (Huthsteiner): 4 x 8-pounders and 2 x howitzers
9th Corps Totals
  Infantry: 12,850
  Cavalry: 2,863
  Guns: 24 (+2 spare)

Note: The individual strength figures for the regiments/battalions are from an appendix in *Krieg*, vol. IV, but seem inconsistent with other Saxon strength returns, in that the authors apparently added the four Schützen Abteilungen (detachments or sections) created on 8 May without subtracting their strength from the contributing units. Discrepancies in cavalry strengths are probably a result of detachments at various stages in the campaign.

Orders of Battle for the Battle of Aspern–Essling

AUSTRIAN HAUPTARMEE,[17] 21–2 MAY 1809

Archduke Charles

	baons/ sqdns	present under arms
First Column (VI Corps), FML Hiller		
Advance Guard: GM Nordmann		
Liechtenstein Hussar Regiment No. 7	7	640
Warasdin-St Georg Grenz Regiment No. 6	1	686
(including remnants of *Brod* Grenz Regiment No. 7	–	–)
(including *Schlegenberg* Jägerfreikorps	–	–)
1st Vienna Volunteers	1	544
2nd Vienna Volunteers	1	610
Gyulai Infantry Regiment No. 60	2*	1,717
Division: FML Kottulinsky		
Erzherzog Johann Dragoon Regiment No. 1	6	700
Brigade: GM Hohenfeld		
Klebek Infantry Regiment No. 14	2*	824
Jordis Infantry Regiment No. 59	2	973
4th Vienna Volunteers	1	269
Division: FML Vincent		
Brigade: GM Mesko		
Kienmayer Hussar Regiment No. 8	7	434
Brigade: Oberst Splenyi		
Splenyi Infantry Regiment No. 51	2*	938

Benjovszky Infantry Regiment No. 31	3	1,130
3rd Moravian Volunteers	1	1,057

Brigade: GM Bianchi

Duka Infantry Regiment No. 39	2*	1,065
3rd Vienna Volunteers	1	547

Infantry: 10,360
Cavalry: 1,774
Guns: 52 (3 1/2 x brigade, 2 x cavalry, 2 x position batteries)

Notes:
a. One *Liechtenstein* squadron on reconnaissance duty towards the March River.
b. One *Kienmayer* squadron detached to V Corps.
c. Asterisk (*) indicates third battalion sent to Moravia for further training.
d. III/*Jordis* destroyed at Riedau.

Second Column (I Corps), GdK Bellegarde

Division: FML Fresnel
Brigade: Vécsey

Vincent Chevauleger Regiment No. 4	8	746
Klenau Chevauleger Regiment No. 5	8	780

Brigade: GM Wintzingerode

2nd Jäger Battalion	1	891
Anton Mittrowsky Infantry Regiment No. 10	2	2,185

Division: FML Vogelsang
Brigade: GM Henneberg

Reuss-Plauen Infantry Regiment No. 17	3	3,313
Kolowrat Infantry Regiment No. 36	3	3,185

Division: FML Ulm
Brigade: GM Wacquant

Erzherzog Rainer Infantry Regiment No. 11	3	3,254
Vogelsang Infantry Regiment No. 47	3	3,202

Division: FML Nostitz
Brigade: Oberst Schaeffer

Argenteau Infantry Regiment No. 35[18]	3	3,397
Erbach Infantry Regiment No. 42	2	2,315

Infantry: 21,742
Cavalry: 1,526
Guns: 68 (4 x brigade, 2 x cavalry, 2 x 6-pdr position, 2 x 12-pdr position batteries)

Note: III/*A. Mittrowsky* and III/*Erbach* in Bohemia.

Third Column (II Corps), FML Hohenzollern

Advance Guard:
Brigade: GM Provenchères

O'Reilly Chevauleger Regiment No. 3	5	665

Brigade: GM Mayer		
7th Jäger Battalion	1	493
8th Jäger Battalion	1	620
2nd *Erzherzog Karl* Legion	1	958
Stain Infantry Regiment No. 50	2	1,062
Division: FML Brady		
Brigade: GM Buresch		
Zach Infantry Regiment No. 15	2	1,548
Josef Colloredo Infantry Regiment No. 57	2	2,164
Brigade: GM Koller		
Infantry Regiment No. 25 (former *Zedtwitz*)	3	2,067
Froon Infantry Regiment No. 54	1 2/3	1,500
Division: FML Weber		
Brigade: GM Wied-Runkel		
Infantry Regiment No. 18 (former *Stuart*)	3	3,037
Rohan Infantry Regiment No. 21	2 2/3	2,874
Frelich Infantry Regiment No. 28	3	3,305
Infantry: 19,628		
Cavalry: 665		
Guns: 62 (4 x brigade, 2 x cavalry, 3 x position batteries)		

Notes:
a. III/*Froon* and III/*J. Colloredo* with III Corps. Two companies of II/*Froon* in Bohemia.
b. Two companies of *Rohan* guarding trains.
c. Two squadrons of *O'Reilly* in Pressburg; one squadron with Jellacic.
d. III/*Stain* with Schustekh.
e. *Zach* formed into two battalions after losses at Regensburg.

Under FML Rosenberg

Fourth Column (part IV Corps), FML Dedovich

Division: FML Klenau		
Brigade: Oberst Ignaz von Hardegg		
Schwarzenberg Uhlan Regiment No. 2	7	917
1st Jäger Battalion	1	770
Division: FML Dedovich		
Brigade: Oberst Gratze		
Wallach-Illyria Grenz Regiment No. 13	1	650
2nd Moravian Volunteers	1	933
Brigade: GM Grill		
Erzherzog Ludwig Infantry Regiment No. 8	3	2,400
Koburg Infantry Regiment No. 22	3	2,368
Brigade: GM Neustädter		
Czartoryski Infantry Regiment No. 9	3	2,140

Reuss-Greitz Infantry Regiment No. 55	2	692
Rosenberg Chevauleger Regiment No. 6	4	450

Infantry: 9,953
Cavalry: 1,367
Guns: 34 (2 x brigade, 1 x cavalry, 2 x position batteries)

Notes:
a. One squadron of *Schwarzenberg* Uhlans in Bohemia.[19]
b. One company of 1st Jägers in Bohemia.
c. III/*Reuss-Greitz* in Styria.

Fifth Column (part IV Corps), FML Hohenlohe
Division: FML Klenau
  Brigade: Oberst Frelich

Stipsicz Hussar Regiment No. 10	8	861
Erzherzog Karl Infantry Regiment No. 3	3	1,330

Division: FML Rohan
  Brigade: GM Carneville

Wallach-Illyria Grenz Regiment No. 13	1	650
Carneville Freikorps (infantry)	(2 companies)	208
Carneville Freikorps (cavalry)	1	115

Division: FML Hohenlohe
  Brigade: GM Riese

Bellegarde Infantry Regiment No. 44	3	1,620
Chasteler Infantry Regiment No. 46	3	1,580

  Brigade: GM Reinhard

Hiller Infantry Regiment No. 2	3	3,050
Sztaray Infantry Regiment No. 33	3	2,470

Division: FML Rohan
  Brigade: GM Stutterheim

Erzherzog Ferdinand Hussar Regiment No. 3	8	821
Rosenberg Chevauleger Regiment No. 6	4	450

Infantry: 10,908
Cavalry: 2,247
Guns: 34 (2 x brigade, 1 x cavalry, 2 x 12-pdr position batteries)

Note: Erzherzog Karl No. 3 was with Cavalry Reserve on 21 May, but returned to Rosenberg during the night.

I Reserve Corps, GdK Liechtenstein
Cavalry Reserve
  Brigade: GM Wartensleben

Blankenstein Hussar Regiment No. 6	8	1,020

Division: FML Hessen-Homburg
  Brigade: GM Siegenthal

Erzherzog Franz Cuirassier Regiment No. 2	6	530
Herzog Albert Cuirassier Regiment No. 3	6	533
Brigade: GM Lederer		
Kronprinz Ferdinand Cuirassier Regiment No. 4	6	518
Hohenzollern Cuirassier Regiment No. 8	6	599
Division: FML Kienmayer		
Brigade: GM Kroyher		
Kaiser Cuirassier Regiment No. 1	4	290
Liechtenstein Cuirassier Regiment No. 6	6	567
Brigade: GM Rottermund		
Riesch Dragoon Regiment No. 6	6	623
Brigade: GM Clary		
Knesevich Dragoon Regiment No. 3	6	644
Insurrection: GM Kerekes		
Primatial Insurrection Hussars	6	767
Neutra Insurrection Hussars	4	582
Cavalry: 6,674		
Guns: 18 (3 x cavalry batteries)		

Notes:
a. Two squadrons of *Kaiser* Cuirassiers guarding trains.
b. Two squadrons of Neutra Insurrection Hussars north of Pressburg.

Grenadier Reserve
Division: FML Lindenau
  Brigade: GM Murray

Leiningen Grenadier Battalion (25, 35, 54)	1	772
Portner [formerly *Hauger*] Grenadier Battalion (40, 44, 46)	1	716
Georgy Grenadier Battalion (17, 36, 42)	1	764
Weiniawsky Grenadier Battalion (10, 11, 47)	1	833
Demontant [formerly *Stark*] Grenadier Battalion (7, 18, 21)	1	764
Legrand [formerly *Peccaduc*] Grenadier Battalion (9, 55, 56)	1	745
Hohenlohe Grenadier Battalion (1, 29, 38)	1	733
Hahn Grenadier Battalion (2, 33, 39)	1	561

Division: FML d'Aspre
  Brigade: Oberstleutnant Scovaud

Brzezinski Grenadier Battalion (24, 30, 41)	1	616
Puteany Grenadier Battalion (14, 45, 59)	1	661
Scovaud Grenadier Battalion (4, 49, 63)	1	694
Scharlach Grenadier Battalion (31, 32, 51)	1	718
Mayblümel Grenadier Battalion (8, 22, 60)	1	701
Bissingen Grenadier Battalion (3, 50, 58)	1	760
Kirchenbetter Grenadier Battalion (34, 37, 48)	1	709
Oklopsia [formerly *Cappy*] Grenadier Battalion (12, 20, 23)	1	676

Infantry: 11,423

Guns: 24 (3 x brigade batteries)

Notes:

a. Scovaud replaced the ill GM Drechsel.

b. The *Nissel* Grenadier Battalion was being re-organised after being destroyed at Eggmühl.

Army Totals
  Infantry: 84,014
  Cavalry: 14,253
  Guns: 292

FRENCH ARMY OF GERMANY,[20] 21–2 MAY 1809

Emperor Napoleon

	baons/ sqdns	present under arms
Imperial Guard[21]		
Division (Young Guard): GD Curial		
Brigade: GB Roguet		
1st Tirailleur-Chasseurs	2	1,334
1st Tirailleur-Grenadiers	2	1,116
Brigade: GB Gros:		
Fusilier-Chasseurs	2	1,272
Fusilier-Grenadiers	2	1,313
Brigade (Old Guard): GB Dorsenne		
Grenadiers	2	1,519
Chasseurs	2	1,324
Cavalry: GD Arrighi		
Chevaulegers	2	414
Chasseurs-à-Cheval	*c.* 1	*c.* 120
Artillery:		160
Attached to Imperial Headquarters		
Württemberg *Herzog Heinrich* Chevaulegers	-	160

Total infantry: 7,878
Total cavalry: 694
Guns: 4 x 6-pounders, 4 x 12-pounders

Note: Approximately *Herzog Heinrich* 160 to 170 troopers participated in the fighting on 21-22 May; 70–80 were apparently performing staff duties in/around Imperial Headquarters, an additional 278 officers and men were on detached service in various locations along the army's line of comunications.[22]

2nd Corps: Marshal Lannes

Under GD Oudinot[23]   21,000

  1st Division: GD Tharreau

    1st Brigade: GB Conroux   6   *c.* 2,500

      1st Light Demi-Brigade (IV/6th Léger, IV/24th Léger, IV/25th Léger)

      3rd Light Demi-Brigade (IV/9th Léger, IV/16th Léger, IV/27th Léger)

    2nd Brigade: GB Albert   6   *c.* 2,600

      1st Line Demi-Brigade (IV/8th Ligne, IV/24th Ligne, IV/45th Ligne)

      2nd Line Demi-Brigade (IV/94th Ligne, IV/95th Ligne, IV/96th Ligne)

    3rd Brigade: GB Jarry   4   *c.* 1,800

      3rd Line Demi-Brigade (IV/54th Ligne, IV/63rd Ligne)

      4th Line Demi-Brigade (IV/4th Ligne, IV/18th Ligne)

  2nd Division: GD Claparède

    1st Brigade: GB Coëhorn   6   *c.* 2,300

      2nd Light Demi-Brigade (IV/17th Léger, IV/21st Léger, IV/28th Léger)

      4th Light Demi-Brigade (IV/26th Léger, Tirailleurs Corses, Tirailleurs du Po)

    2nd Brigade: GB Lesuire   5   *c.* 1,800

      5th Line Demi-Brigade (IV/27th Ligne, IV/39th Ligne)

      6th Line Demi-Brigade (IV/59th Ligne, IV/69th Ligne, IV/76th Ligne)

    3rd Brigade: GB Ficatier   5   *c.* 1,550

      7th Line Demi-Brigade (IV/40th Ligne, IV/88th Ligne)

      8th Line Demi-Brigade (IV/64th Ligne, IV/100th Ligne, IV/103rd Ligne)

  Division: GD St Hilaire

    1st Brigade: GB Lorencez

      10th Léger   3   2,069

      3rd Ligne   3   *c.* 1,970

      57th Ligne   3   *c.* 1,720

    3rd Brigade: GB Destabenrath

      72nd Ligne   3   *c.* 1,750

      105th Ligne   3   *c.* 1,400

      Artillery and Train   -   463

  Division: GD Demont   10   4,800

(Fourth Battalions of 7th Léger, 12th Ligne, 17th Ligne, 21st Ligne, 30th Ligne, 33rd Ligne, 61st Ligne,

65th Ligne, 85th Ligne, 111th Ligne)

Total infantry: 34,700

Guns: 64

Notes:

a. There are no official returns for the 1st and 2nd Divisions for late April or early May, so the figures given here are estimates taken from *Krieg*, vol. IV, Anhang XXIII.

b. St Hilaire's strength figures are from returns dated 1 May and modified as follows. Estimated casualties for Schwarze Lackenau (13 May) have been subtracted from the 72nd and 105th Ligne. Replacements that were to depart Strasbourg on 15 April are assumed to have arrived more-or-less intact for 3rd Ligne (120), 57th Ligne (174), and 72nd Ligne (350) by mid-May (in effect making good the 72nd's losses on 13 May).[24]

4th Corps: Marshal Massena[25]

1st Division: GD Legrand

1st Brigade: GB Ledru

26th Léger	3	1,944
18th Ligne	3	2,161
Baden troops:		
3rd Baden Infantry Regiment *Graf Hochberg*	2	1,445
French Artillery and Train	-	331
Baden Artillery and Train	-	*c.* 250

2nd Division: GD Carra St-Cyr[26]

1st Brigade: GB Cosson

24th Léger	3	2,274

2nd Brigade: GB Dalesme

4th Ligne	3	2,287
46th Ligne	3	2,214

3rd (Hessian) Brigade: GB Schiner (French) and GM von Nagel (Hesse-Darmstadt)

Leib-Garde Regiment	2	*c.* 2,500
Leib Regiment	2	total
French Artillery and Train	-	348
Hessian Artillery and Train	-	*c.* 140

3rd Division: GD Molitor

1st Brigade: GB Leguay

2nd Ligne	2	1,369
16th Ligne	3	1,951

2nd Brigade: GB Viviès

37th Ligne	3	1,535
67th Ligne	2	1,295
Artillery and Train	-	311

4th Division: GD Boudet

1st Brigade: GB Fririon

3rd Léger	2	1,489

2nd Brigade: GB Valory

56th Ligne	3	2,290
93rd Ligne	2	1,401
Artillery and Train	-	354

Light Cavalry Division: GD Marulaz

3rd Chasseurs-à-Cheval	2	321
14th Chasseurs-à-Cheval	3	255
19th Chasseurs-à-Cheval	3	449
23rd Chasseurs-à-Cheval	3	519

Brigade:

Baden Light Dragoons	4	290
Hessian Chevaulegers	3	150
Corps Artillery and park	-	646

Total infantry: 25, 636
Total light cavalry: 1,984
Guns: 56

Notes:

a. The four musketeer companies of II/1st Baden Infantry (some 400 men) were detailed to guard the corps artillery park and baggage; they probably did not cross the Danube.

b. A Hessian detachment was at Bruck an der Leitha with Montbrun; most of the Baden brigade detached to Lauriston. See Appendix 13.

Cavalry Reserve: Marshal Bessières[27]

1st Heavy Cavalry Division: GD Nansouty		
2nd Brigade: GB Doumerc		
2nd Cuirassiers (part)	-	c. 250–300
3rd Brigade: GB St Germain		
3rd Cuirassiers	4	629
12th Cuirassiers	4	615
Artillery and Train	-	300
2nd Heavy Cavalry Division: GD St Sulpice		
1st Brigade: GB Lelièvre de Lagrange		
1st Cuirassiers	4	597
5th Cuirassiers	4	515
2nd Brigade: GB Guiton		
10th Cuirassiers	4	610
11th Cuirassiers	4	637
Artillery and Train	-	173
3rd Heavy Cavalry Division: GD Espagne		
1st Brigade: GB Reynaud		
4th Cuirassiers	4	633
6th Cuirassiers	4	655
2nd Brigade: GB Fouler		
7th Cuirassiers	4	525
8th Cuirassiers	4	766
Artillery and Train	-	267
Light Cavalry Division: GD Lasalle		
Brigade: GB Piré		
8th Hussars	3	679
16th Chasseurs	3	562
Brigade: GB Bruyère		
13th Chasseurs	3	650
24th Chasseurs	2	c. 350
GB Colbert and 9th Hussars (part)	2	c. 200

Total heavy cavalry: c. 6,182
Total light cavalry: c. 2,441
Guns: 24

Notes:

a. Information is from returns dated 15 May except for Bruyère (28 April) and Colbert (early June).

b. From its low officer casualties (five compared to sixteen or more for most regiments) and from the regimental history, it seems that the elements of 2nd Cuirassiers on the north bank engaged in little, if any, combat.

c. Some 180-200 men (one squadron) subtracted from 24th Chasseurs for the detachment at Mariazell.

d. Only two squadrons of 9th Hussars (*c.* 200 with Colbert) actually crossed the river.

Approximate Army Totals: (morning of 21 May)	Approximate Army Totals (morning of 22 May):
Infantry: 22,300	Infantry: 68,720
Cavalry: 2,970	Cavalry: 14,420
Guns: 44	Guns: 154

Units from the above formations that remained on the right (south) bank of the Danube (These are in addition to Davout)

Imperial Guard:
Cavalry: GD Arrighi

Chasseurs-à-Cheval	*c.* 1	*c.* 250
Dragoons	1	254
Grenadiers-à-Cheval	1	219
Elite Gendarmes	-	55

Cavalry Reserve:
1st Heavy Cavalry Division:
  1st Brigade: GB Defrance

1st Carabiniers	4	551
2nd Carabiniers	4	585
2nd Brigade:		
2nd Cuirassiers (part)	-	*c.* 250–300
9th Cuirassiers	4	587

Other:
Light Cavalry Brigade: (GB Colbert)   *c.* 1,200

9th Hussars	2
7th Chasseurs-à-Cheval	3

Forces in the Vicinity of Vienna/Marchfeld During the Battle of Aspern-Essling

AUSTRIAN ARMY,[28] 21–2 MAY 1809

	baons/ sqdns	*present under arms*
V Corps: FML Reuss		
Brigade: GM Weissenwolff (Strebersdorf)		
Kienmayer Hussar Regiment No. 8	1	140
Deutschmeister Infantry Regiment No. 4	3	1,217
Kerpen Infantry Regiment No. 49	3	1,411
3rd Jäger Battalion	1	758
5th Vienna Volunteers	1	407
4th UMB Landwehr	1	605
Brigade: GM Radetzky (Stockerau)		
Erzherzog Karl Uhlan Regiment No. 3	8	486
Gradiska Grenz Regiment No. 8	1	950
4th Jäger Battalion	1	843
Division: FML Schustekh (Krems)		
Levenehr Dragoon Regiment No. 4	3	285
Lindenau Infantry Regiment No. 29	3	2,039
III/*Stain* Infantry Regiment No. 50	1	654
Gradiska Grenz Regiment No. 8	1	652
5th *Erzherzog Karl* Legion	1	832
6th *Erzherzog Karl* Legion	1	913

1st Moravian Volunteers	1	965
Combined Upper Austrian Landwehr	1	1,178
Brigade: GM Hoffmeister (Pressburg)		
O'Reilly Chevauleger Regiment No. 3	2	260
Beaulieu Infantry Regiment No. 58	2*	1,574
Neutra Insurrection Hussars	2	250

Notes:
a. Strength figures from 26 May.
b. The Neutra Hussars detachment was posted at Angern on the March River.
c. III/*Beaulieu* to Moravia for further training (*).

Guarding the Hauptarmee's Baggage Train

Kaiser Cuirassier Regiment No. 1	2	230
Kaiser Infantry Regiment No. 1	1	900
Rohan Infantry Regiment No. 21	(2 companies)	500

In Moravia for further Training

III/*Duka* Infantry Regiment No. 39	1	800
III/*Splenyi* Infantry Regiment No. 51	1	700
III/*Beaulieu* Infantry Regiment No. 58	1	640
III/*Gyulai* Infantry Regiment No. 60	1	900

Training Division

Hiller Infantry Regiment No. 2	(2 companies)	400
Erzherzog Karl Infantry Regiment No. 3	(2 companies)	2,000
Sztaray Infantry Regiment No. 33	(2 companies)	400
Bellegarde Infantry Regiment No. 44	(2 companies)	400

Training Company

EH Ludwig Infantry Regiment No. 8	(1 company)	100
Czartoryski Infantry Regiment No. 9	(1 company)	100
A. Mittrowsky Infantry Regiment No. 10	(1 company)	100
Chasteler Infantry Regiment No. 46	(1 company)	100
Vogelsang Infantry Regiment No. 47	(1 company)	100

3rd *Erzherzog Karl* Legion	1	650
4th *Erzherzog Karl* Legion	1	960
1st through 6th UWW Landwehr	6	2,800
1st OWW Landwehr	1	650
2nd and 4th OMB Landwehr	2	1,230
2nd and 3rd UMB Landwehr	2	1,100
Eleven Moravian Landwehr battalions	11	10,000

Note: All figures rounded.

ALLIED ARMY, 21–22 MAY 1809

	baons/ sqdns	present under arms
3rd Corps: Marshal Davout[29]		
1st Division: GD Morand		
1st Brigade: GB Barbanègre		
13th Léger	3	1,862
2nd Brigade: GB Guiot de Lacour		
17th Ligne	3	2,048
30th Ligne	3	2,173
2nd Brigade: GB L'Huillier		
61st Ligne	3	1,953
Artillery and Train	–	438
2nd Division: GD Friant		8,621
Brigade: GB Gilly		
15th Léger	3	
Brigade: GB Grandeau		
33rd Ligne	3	
48th Ligne	3	
Brigade: GB Gautier		
108th Ligne	3	
111th Ligne	3	
Artillery and Train	–	404
3rd Division: GD Gudin		
1st Brigade: GB Petit		
7th Léger	3	2,442
2nd Brigade: GB Lorencez		
12th Ligne	3	1,862
21st Ligne	3	1,979
3rd Brigade:		
25th Ligne	3	1,410
85th Ligne	3	2,009
Artillery and Train	–	423
Light Cavalry Brigade: GB Pajol		
5th Hussars	3	474
7th Hussars	3	570
11th Chasseurs-à-Cheval	3	589
Attached: Portuguese Legion		
Infantry	3	1,471
Cavalry	1	133

Total infantry: 27,830
Total light cavalry: 1,766
Guns: 45

Note: The 7th Léger was attached to Pajol at Mautern on 20 May.

Covering Detachment: GD Lauriston[30]

20th Chasseurs-à-Cheval (from Colbert's brigade)	3	*c.*500
Baden Brigade: GM Harrant		
1st Baden Infantry Regiment *Grossherzog*	2	975
2nd Baden Infantry Regiment *Erbgrossherzog*	2	1,399
Baden Jäger Battalion *Lingg*	1	463
Baden Artillery and Train	–	103

Total cavalry: *c.*500
Total infantry: 2,837
Guns: 4

Notes:
a. Strength information for cavalry: 1 June; for Baden troops: 13 June.
b. The four musketeer companies of II/1st Baden Infantry were guarding 4th Corps trains near Vienna.

Covering Detachment: GD Montbrun[31]

Light Cavalry Brigade: GB Jacquinot		
1st Chasseurs-à-Cheval	3	444
2nd Chasseurs-à-Cheval	3	444
Hessian detachment: Major Gall		972
Leib-Garde Fusiliers	1	
1st Leib Fusiliers	(2 companies)	
Artillery (French)	–	37

Total cavalry: 888
Total infantry: 972 (Hessian)
Guns: 2

Note: The combined Schützen of the Leib-Garde Musketeer Regiment (approximately eighty men) were attached to Gall's command. The Hessian fusiliers who had been detached in Wallsee, Ybbs, and Melk (two companies and one platoon for some 299 men) had been relieved by Württembergers and were en route to rejoin their fellows.

Vienna Garrison[32]

Württemberg Leib Chevaulegers (city)	4	497

Notes:
a. The Württemberg regiment had been under GM von Röder until his capture on 20 May.
b. Davout was to leave three battalions (Friant) in Vienna and one of the 25th Ligne near Nussdorf.

Orders of Battle for the Opening Campaigns in Italy and Dalmatia

ARMY OF INNER AUSTRIA, 9 APRIL 1809

GdK Archduke Johann[33]

Note: the following reflects actual force allotments, not the 'official' order of battle. Landwehr strengths include small depots left behind inside Austria (c.125 to 250 per battalion).

	baons/ sqdns	present under arms
Right Column: FML Chasteler		
Brigade: GM Marchal		
Hohenlohe-Bartenstein Infantry Regiment No. 26	3	3,314
Lusignan Infantry Regiment No. 16	3	3,265
Hohenzollern Chevaulegers No. 2	3	c.330
Brigade: GM Fenner		
9th Jäger Battalion	1	785
1st Villach Landwehr	1	1,242
2nd Villach Landwehr	1	1,158
1st Klagenfurt Landwehr	1	868
1st Bruck Landwehr	1	1,401
2nd Bruck Landwehr	1	1,173

Artillery:
1 x 6-pounder position battery
1 x 3-pounder brigade battery (minus four guns attached to flanking columns)
1/2 x cavalry battery

Infantry: c.13,230
Cavalry: c.330
Guns: 13

Notes:

a. This was a nominal organisation only. Chasteler continually shifted units among commanders in response to operational requirements.

b. The varying arrival dates of the Landwehr battalions allotted to Chasteler make it difficult to determine his exact strength at any particular point in the early days of the war. Many accounts credit him with only some 10,000 foot soldiers, largely resulting from imprecise accounting regarding the Landwehr. The other two Klagenfurt battalions (2,012) and the two from Judenburg (1,709) arrived in the second half of April to bring his total force to more than 17,000.

Centre Column: Archduke Johann
VIII Corps: FML Albert Gyulai
Division: FML Frimont
  Brigade: GM von Schmidt

1st Banal Grenz Regiment No. 10	2	2,465
2nd Banal Grenz Regiment No. 11 (attached)	2	2,543
I and III/*Erzherzog Franz Karl* Infantry Regiment No. 52 (attached)		
	2	c.1,800
Ott Hussars No. 5	4	c.535

  Brigade: GM von Wetzl

Ott Hussars No. 5	4	c.535
Hohenzollern Chevaulegers No. 2	4	c.440

Division: GM Colloredo
  Brigade: GM Colloredo

Strassaldo Infantry Regiment No. 27	3	3,274
St Julien Infantry Regiment No. 61	3	2,753

  Brigade: GM von Gajoli

Johann Jellacic Infantry Regiment No. 53	3	3,125
Franz Jellacic Infantry Regiment No. 62	3	1,984

Artillery:
  1 x 12-pounder position battery
  1 x 6-pounder position battery
  3 x 3-pounder brigade batteries
  1 and 1/2 x cavalry batteries
Infantry: c.17,900
Cavalry: c.1,510
Guns: 45

IX Corps: FML Ignaz Gyulai
Division: FML Wolfskeel
  Brigade: GM von Marziani

Allvintzi Infantry Regiment No. 19	3	2,710
Ogulin Grenz Regiment No. 3	2	*c.*2,590
Brigade: GM Kalnassy		
Simbschen Infantry Regiment No. 43	3	3,418
Brigade: GM von Splenyi		
Erzherzog Josef Hussars No. 2	8	979
Division: GM Hager		
Brigade: GM Hager		
Hohenlohe Dragoons No. 2	6	714
Savoy Dragoons No. 5	6	766
Brigade: GM von Kleinmayrn		
Szulin Grenz Regiment No. 4	2	*c.*2,760
Sallomon Grenadier Battalion (16, 26, 27)	1	804
Van der Mühlen Grenadier Battalion (53, 62)	1	532
Albeck Grenadier Battalion (13, 43)	1	505
Janusch Grenadier Battalion (19, 52, 61)	1	803

Artillery:
1 x 3-pounder brigade battery
1 x cavalry battery
Infantry: *c.*14,120
Cavalry: 2,459
Guns: 14

Flanking Columns of the Centre
Near Saaga: Major du Montet

Ottocac Grenz Regiment No. 2	1	*c.*1,290
Klagenfurt Landwehr	1	*c.*900
2 x 3-pounders		

Near Karfreit (Caporetto):

Ottocac Grenz Regiment No. 2	1	*c.*1,290
2nd Görz Landwehr	1	782
3rd Laibach Landwehr	1	556
platoon/*Frimont* Hussars No. 9	–	*c.*30
2 x 3-pounders		

Infantry: *c.*4,818
Cavalry: *c.*30
Guns: 4

Left Column: GM Gavassini
Brigade: GM Gavassini

Reisky Infantry Regiment No. 13	3	3,202
3rd Garrison Battalion (four companies)	1	*c.*320
1st Adelsberg Landwehr	1	1,130
1st Triest Landwehr (three companies)		*c.*250
2nd Triest Landwehr	1	1,158

Brigade: Oberst Gyurkovics		
II/*EH Franz Karl* Infantry Regiment No. 52	1	*c*.900
1st Görz Landwehr	1	934
Militär-Grenzkordon	(four companies)	*c*.760
Frimont Hussars No. 9	8	*c*.890
Brigade: GM von Munkacsy		
1st Laibach Landwehr	1	1,171
2nd Laibach Landwehr	1	1,291
Artillery:		
1 x 6-pounder position battery		
2 1/2 x 3-pounder brigade batteries		
1 x cavalry battery		

Infantry: *c*.11,116
Cavalry: *c*.890
Guns: 32

Notes:

a. The four battalions of Neustadtl Landwehr and the other three Adelsberg battalions remained behind at first because they lacked clothing and equipment.

b. A 12-pounder position battery and half of a brigade battery remained in the Präwald fort.

c. FML Knesevich was initially slated to command this column, but was detailed to Agram to organise the Croatian Insurrection instead.

Other Forces under Johann
Istrian Detachment: Major von Cazzan[34]

3rd Garrison Battalion	(two companies)	*c*.160
1st Triest Landwehr	(seven companies)	*c*.570
platoon/*Frimont* Hussars No. 9	–	*c*.30
4 x 3-pounders		

Dalmatian Detachment: GM von Stoichevich[35]

Licca Grenz Regiment No. 1	2	*c*.2,550
Reserve Battalion/*Licca* Grenz Regiment No. 1	1	*c*.1,270
Reserve Battalion/*Ottocac* Grenz Regiment No. 2	1	*c*.1,290
Reserve Battalion/*Ogulin* Grenz Regiment No. 3	1	*c*.1,295
Reserve Battalion/*Szulin* Grenz Regiment No. 4	1	*c*.1,375
Hohenzollern Chevaulegers No. 2	1	*c*.110
Mounted Serezaner	1	*c*.200
Artillery:		
1 x 6-pounder position battery		
1 x 3-pounder brigade battery		

Infantry: *c*.7,690
Cavalry: *c*.310
Guns: 18

Note: The 4th Garrison Battalion (*c*.480) in Fiume also came under Stoichevich.

Austrian Fleet[36]
GM l'Espine
To Dalmatia: Oberstleutnant Maidich

Brig *Dolfino*	1
Schooner *Indagatore*	1
Trabakel *Dromedario*	1
Gun sloops	8
Felucca *Mora*	1

To Venice: Oberstleutnant Flanegan

Corvette *Armonia*	1
Brig *Eolo*	1
Brig *Pilade*	1
Brig *Oreste*	1
Trabakel *Bravo*	1
Trabakel *Camello*	1
Gun sloops	8
Tartanone *Isabella*	1

Distributed among these vessels: two infantry companies = 543 men.

Landwehr in the rear or still organising/equipping

Styria		
Graz	5	5,441
Judenburg	2	1,709
Marburg	2	2,647
Cilli	2	2,270
Carinthia		
Klagenfurt	2	*c*.1,800
Carniola-Coastal		
Adelsberg	3	3,411
Neustadtl	4	3,465

FRENCH ARMY OF ITALY, 9 APRIL 1809

Viceroy Eugene de Beauharnais[37]

Personnel figures for artillery include sappers.

	baons/ sqdns	present under arms
Field Army		
In Friaul		
1st Division: GD Seras (GB Gareau , GB Roussel)		
35th Ligne	3	2,293

53rd Ligne	4	2,912
106th Ligne	4	2,915
		(Total 8,120)
12 guns	–	257
2nd Division: GD Broussier (GB Dessaix, GB Dutruy)		
9th Ligne	4	2,919
84th Ligne	4	2,872
92nd Ligne	4	3,211
		(Total 9,002)
IV/24th Dragoons	1	174
12 guns	–	260
Light Cavalry Division: GD Sahuc (GB Pagès)		
6th Hussars	4	908
6th Chasseurs	4	847
8th Chasseurs	4	964
25th Chasseurs (one company with Marmont)	4	807
		(Total 3,526)
4 guns	–	92
Infantry: 17,122		
Cavalry: 3,700		
Guns: 28		

Note: IV/35th Ligne detached to Palmanova.

In the rear

3rd Division: GD Grenier (GB Abbé, GB Teste)		
IV/1st Léger (detached to Palmanova)	1	–
1st Ligne	4	2,456
52nd Ligne	4	2,892
102nd Ligne	4	2,744
		(Total 8,092)
IV/Napoleon Dragoons (Italian)	1	156
10 guns	–	282
4th Division: GD Lamarque (GB Huard, GB Almeras)		
13th Ligne	4	2,371
29th Ligne	4	2,642
112th Ligne (I, II, III)	3	2,104
		(Total 7,117)
IV/42nd Ligne (detached to Palmanova)	1	–
10 guns	–	270
5th Division: GD Barbou (GB Moreau, GB Roize)		
8th Léger (III, IV)	2	1,404
18th Léger (III, IV)	2	1,544
5th Ligne (III, IV)	2	1,406
11th Ligne (IV)	1	981

23rd Ligne (III, IV)	2	1,365
60th Ligne (III, IV)	2	1,035
79th Ligne (III, IV)	2	1,312
81st Ligne (III, IV)	2	1,182
		(Total 10,229)
12 guns	–	184

6th Division: GD Durutte (GB Valentin in temporary command)

22nd Léger (III, IV)	2	1,178
23rd Léger	4	2,782
62nd Ligne	4	2,993
		(Total 6,953)
6 guns	–	136

1st Italian Division: GD Severoli (GB Bonfanti, GB Peyri)

1st Italian Line	4	3,208
IV/2nd Italian Line	1	787
7th Italian Line (II, III, IV)	3	1,745
Dalmatian Regiment (I, II)	2	1,441
		(Total 7,181)
IV/1st Italian Chasseurs Royal Italian	1	191
12 guns	–	483

2nd Italian Division: GD Fontanelli (GB Julhien, GB Bertoletti)

1st Italian Light (III, IV)	2	705
2nd Italian Light (III, IV)	2	814
3rd Italian Line (II, IV)	2	1,272
4th Italian Line (III, IV)	2	927
Istrian Chasseur Battalion	1	685
		(Total 5,883)
2nd Italian Chasseurs Prince Royal (III, IV)	2	296
10 guns	–	384

1st Dragoon Division: GB Guérin d'Etoquigny (awaiting GD Grouchy)

7th Dragoons	4	867
30th Dragoons	4	947
Italian Queen's Dragoons	4	658
		(Total 2,472)
4 guns	–	95

2nd Dragoon Division: GD Pully (GB Poinsot)

23rd Dragoons	4	959
28th Dragoons	4	718
29th Dragoons	4	797
		(Total 2,374)

Royal Italian Guard: GB Lecchi, GB Viani[38]

Honour Guard (mounted)	(five companies)	330
Dragoons	2	356
II/Royal Velites	1	811
Line Infantry of the Guard	2	1,017

Gendarmes d'Elite (mounted)	–	29
		(Total 2,543)
6 guns	–	102
Unattached:		
9th Chasseurs	4	761

Note: The other two battalions of 3rd Italian Line (I, III) were en route from Naples (1,480).

Infantry: 47,283
Cavalry: 6,817
Guns: 70

Garrisons in operational area

Palmanova: GB Schilt (3,112)

IV/1st Léger	1	779
IV/35th Ligne	1	761
IV/42nd Ligne	1	746
III/3rd Italian Light Infantry	1	826

Istria

| II/3rd Italian Light Infantry | 1 | 530 |
| Carabiniers/IV/Dalmatia (Quarnero Islands)(one company) | | c.120 |

Venice (2,707)

V/1st Italian Light Infantry (depot)	1	120
IV/3rd Italian Light Infantry	1	326
V/3rd Italian Light Infantry (depot)	1	145
V/5th Italian Line Infantry (depot)	1	501
III/Dalmatian Regiment	1	367
Venetian Sedentary (Garrison) Battalion	1	648

Osoppo

Four companies of 92nd Ligne (512 men) detached on 11 April (numbers included in Broussier's division above).

Other Troops in the Italian Peninsula

Troops en route to Germany from Italy:

Under GD Bisson (c.2,000 total)

III/3rd Léger	1	c.600
III/2nd Ligne	1	c.800
voltigeurs	?	

Replacement Detachments of

3rd Chasseurs	–	85
14th Chasseurs	–	c.270
Artillery	–	90
Sappers	–	64
2 x 3-pounders?		

Under GD Lemoine (*c*.2,100 total)

IV/67th Ligne	1	
IV/93rd Ligne	1	
March battalion (three companies each of 37th and 56th Ligne)		
	1	
Replacement Detachments of		
19th Chasseurs	–	*c*.100
23rd Chasseurs	–	*c*.100
24th Chasseurs	–	*c*.70
3 x 3-pounders		

Note: Total infantry was approximately 1,700; the companies from the 37th and 56th were absorbed into the other two battalions on 28 April.

Observation Division: GD Miollis

14th Léger (III, IV)	2	1,454
6th Ligne (III, IV)	2	1,352
IV/101st Ligne	1	681
III/*La Tour l'Auvergne* Foreign Regiment	1	840
1st Neapolitan Light Infantry (I, II)	2	983
1st Neapolitan Chasseurs	1	265
Corsican Light Infantry	1	?

Garrisons:

Mantua

V/7th Italian Line Infantry (depot)	1	546
III/1st Neapolitan Line Infantry	1	202
III/2nd Neapolitan Line Infantry	1	304
IV/2nd Neapolitan Chasseurs	1	70

Other

Piombino Battalion	1	?
French depot battalions	9	3,204
Italian depot battalions	5	1,619
French depot squadrons	11	1,762
Italian depot squadrons	4	899
Velites of Florence	1	(in raising)
Velites of Turin	1	(in raising)

Army of Naples: King Joachim Murat

22nd Léger (I, II)	2
10th Ligne	4
20th Ligne	4
101st Ligne (I, II, III)	3
4th Chasseurs	4
La Tour l'Auvergne Foreign Regiment	3

Isenburg Foreign Regiment	3
1st Swiss Regiment	4
Neapolitan Guard Infantry	6
Neapolitan Guard Cavalry	3
III/1st Neapolitan Light Infantry	1
3rd Neapolitan Light Infantry	3
4th Neapolitan Line Infantry	3
5th Neapolitan Line Infantry	3
6th Neapolitan Line Infantry	3
7th Neapolitan Line Infantry	3
1st Neapolitan Chasseurs	3

Army of Dalmatia: GD Marmont[39]
Field Force
1st Division: GD Montrichard (GB Launay , GB Soyez)

5th Ligne	2	1,622
18th Léger	2	1,417
79th Ligne	2	1,575
81st Ligne	2	1,366

2nd Division: GD Clauzel (GB Delzons, GB Deviau)

8th Léger	2	1,495
23rd Ligne	2	1,424
11th Ligne	3	2,094
Light Cavalry	–	292

(8th Company/3rd Chasseurs and 3rd Company/24th Chasseurs)
Infantry: 10,993
Cavalry: 292
Guns: 12

Garrisons:
Ragusa

60th Ligne	1	*c.*850
IV/Dalmatian Regiment (part)	–	175

Zara

60th Ligne	1	*c.*850
IV/Dalmatian Regiment (part)	–	156

Cattaro

I/3rd Italian Light Infantry	1	512
I/Chasseurs d'Orient	1	116

Note: The battalions of the 60th Ligne were the 1st and 2nd, totalling 1,756 effectives; it is not clear which battalion was in which location.

Bavarian Garrison in the Tyrol[40]
(not under Eugene)
Innsbruck (GL von Kinkel)

11th Infantry	2	c.1,600
sqdn/1st Dragoons	1	c.125
3 x guns		
Sterzing (Major von Speicher)		
4th Light Battalion	(2 companies)	c.400
1 x gun		
Brixen (Oberstleutnant von Wreden)		
2nd Light Battalion	1	c.800
4th Light Battalion	(2 companies)	c.400
sqdn/1st Dragoons	1	c.125
2 x guns		
Hall (Oberstleutnant von Bernclau)		
3rd Light Battalion	(2 companies)	c.400
Schwaz to Rattenberg (Major von Theobald)		
Schwaz: 3rd Light Battalion	(1/2 company)	c.100
Strass: 3rd Light Battalion	(1/2 company)	c.100
Rattenberg: 3rd Light Battalion	(1 company)	c.200
Kufstein (Major von Aicher)		
Provisional Light Battalion	1	471
(Depot troops of 1st, 2nd, 5th, 6th Light Battalions)		
Fortress artillery	–	98
60 x guns and mortars		

Orders of Battle for the Battle of Sacile

ARMY OF INNER AUSTRIA, 16 APRIL 1809

FML Archduke Johann[41]

	baons/ sqdns	present under arms
Oberstleutnant Volkmann		
I/*Johann Jellacic* Infantry Regiment No. 53	1	c. 1,040
Company/*1st Banal* Grenz Regiment No. 10	(one company)	c.200[42]
I/*2nd Banal* Grenz Regiment No. 11	1	c.1,200
Ott Hussars No. 5	2	c.260
EH Josef Hussars No. 2	2	c.260
Artillery:		
1/2 x brigade battery		
In support		
Savoy Dragoons No. 5	6	766
Advance guard: FML Frimont[43]		
Brigade: GM von Schmidt		
III/*EH Franz Karl* Infantry Regiment No. 52	1	c.840
I/*Franz Jellacic* Infantry Regiment No. 62	1	c.620
1st Banal Grenz Regiment No. 10 (ten companies)	2	c.1,980
Brigade: GM von Wetzl > Oberst von Fulda		
Ott Hussars No. 5	6	c.740
Hohenzollern Chevaulegers No. 2	4	c.420

Artillery:
1/2 x 3-pounder brigade battery
1 x cavalry battery

VIII Corps: FML Albert Gyulai
Cavalry
Brigade: GM von Splenyi (from IX Corps)

EH Josef Hussars No. 2	6	*c.*720
Frimont Hussars No. 9	4	*c.*470

Left Wing
Brigade: GM Colloredo

Strassaldo Infantry Regiment No. 27	3	3,274
St Julien Infantry Regiment No. 61	3	2,753

Right Wing
Brigade: GM von Gajoli

II and III/*Johann Jellacic* Infantry Regiment No. 53	2	*c.*2,080
II and III/*Franz Jellacic* Infantry Regiment No. 62	2	*c.*1,300
II/2nd *Banal* Grenz Regiment No. 11	1	*c.*1,250

IX Corps: FML Ignaz Gyulai
First Line
Brigade: GM von Marziani

Allvintzi Infantry Regiment No. 19	3	2,710
Ogulin Grenz Regiment No. 3	2	*c.*2,590

Brigade: GM Kalnassy

Simbschen Infantry Regiment No. 43	3	3,418

Brigade: GM Gavassini

Ottocac Grenz Regiment No. 2 (nine companies)	2	*c.*1,940
Reisky Infantry Regiment No. 13	3	3,202

Second Line
Brigade: GM von Kleinmayrn

Szulin Grenz Regiment No. 4	2	*c.*2,760
Sallomon Grenadier Battalion (16, 26, 27)	1	804
Van der Mühlen Grenadier Battalion (53, 62)	1	532
Albeck Grenadier Battalion (13, 43)	1	505
Janusch Grenadier Battalion (19, 52, 61)	1	803

Third Line
Brigade: GM Hager

Hohenlohe Dragoons No. 2	6	714

Infantry: *c.*36,300
Cavalry: *c.*4,440
Guns: 83[44]

Note: Command arrangements for Fulda's and Splenyi's cavalry brigades at the start of the battle are unclear. Fulda very quickly came under Frimont's orders.

Other Austrian Forces in Italy

Left Flank Column: Oberst Gyurkovics

II/*EH Franz Karl* Infantry Regiment No. 52	I	*c*.900
Detachment/*Ottocac* Grenz Regiment No. 2 (three companies)		*c*.600
Frimont Hussars No. 9	2	*c*.230
1/2 x cavalry battery (four guns)	–	–

Note: A three-platoon squadron was en route to Gyurkovics, whereupon a full squadron would join the main army.

Osoppo Blockade Force

I/*EH Franz Karl* Infantry Regiment No. 52	I	*c*.900
detachment/2nd *Banal* Grenz Regiment No. 11	–	?

Palmanova Blockade Force (Oberst Tomassich)

3rd Garrison Battalion (four companies)	I	*c*.320
1st Adelsberg Landwehr	I	1,130
3rd Adelsberg Landwehr (arrived 16 April)	I	929
1st Triest Landwehr (three companies)		*c*.250
2nd Triest Landwehr	I	1,158
Frimont Hussars No. 9	I	*c*.110
1/2 x cavalry battery (four guns)	–	–

Note: A three-platoon squadron of *Frimont* Hussars was en route to join Gyurkovics.

Gradiska Garrison

1st Görz Landwehr	I	934

FRENCH ARMY OF ITALY, 16 APRIL 1809

Viceroy Eugene de Beauharnais[45]

	baons/ sqdns	present under arms
Left flank column: Adjutant-Commandant Bartier[46]		
8th Léger (III, IV)	2	1,404
60th Ligne (III, IV)	2	1,035
2 guns	–	
At Santissima:		
79th Ligne (III, IV)	2	1,312
2 guns	–	
1st Division: GD Seras (GB Gareau, GB Roussel)		
[35th Ligne: combat ineffective]		
53rd Ligne	4	2,912
106th Ligne	4	2,915

6th Chasseurs	4	847
12 guns	–	
2nd Division: GD Broussier (GB Dutruy)		
9th Ligne	4	2,919
84th Ligne	4	2,872
92nd Ligne	3 1/3	c.2,680
25th Chasseurs	4	807
IV/24th Dragoons	1	174
12 guns	–	
3rd Division: GD Grenier (GB Abbé, GB Teste)		
1st Ligne	4	2,456
52nd Ligne	4	2,892
102nd Ligne	4	2,744
IV/11th Ligne	1	981
IV/Napoleon Dragoons (Italian)	1	156
10 guns	–	
5th Division: GD Barbou (GB Moreau, GB Roize)		
18th Léger (III, IV)	2	1,544
5th Ligne (III, IV)	2	1,406
23rd Ligne (III, IV)	2	1,365
81st Ligne (III, IV)	2	1,182
8 guns	–	
1st Italian Division: GD Severoli (GB Bonfanti, GB Peyri)		
1st Italian Line	4	3,208
IV/2nd Italian Line	1	787
7th Italian Line (II, III)	2	1,099
Dalmatian Regiment (I, II)	2	1,441
IV/1st Italian Chasseurs Royal Italian	1	191
12 guns	–	
Light Cavalry Division: GD Sahuc		
6th Hussars	4	c.600?
8th Chasseurs	4	c.930?
2 guns (?)	–	

Infantry: c.39,110
Cavalry: c.2,800 (counting Sahuc as 650 total)[47]
Guns: 60

Notes:
  a. Numbers above for Sahuc are achieved by subtracting losses on the 15th from previous strength reports. French historians give the two regiments an estimated *total* strength of some 650 effectives on 16 April.
  b. Severoli was under Seras's orders. The company and chasseurs detached on 15 April had returned to Severoli.
  c. IV/7th Line (646 men) in Este as garrison.

Forces in the Tyrol, Late April

AUSTRIAN ARMY, 24–7 APRIL 1809[48]

FML Chasteler

Note: Tyrolian Schützen and Landsturm not included. Strengths are estimated; Landwehr in particular may have been much weaker than shown.

	baons/ sqdns	present under arms
North of the Brenner Pass: GM von Buol		
II/*Hohenlohe-Bartenstein* Infantry Regiment No. 26	1	*c.*1,100
4th Company/9th Jäger Battalion	(1 company)	*c.*130
Hohenzollern Chevaulegers No. 2	1/2	*c.*50
Oberstleutnant Taxis		
III/*de Vaux* Infantry Regiment No. 45	(2 companies)	*c.*320
2nd Inner Austria Volunteers (Salzburger Jäger)	(4 companies)	?
2nd Salzburg Landwehr	(2 companies)	?
O'Reilly Chevaulegers No. 3	(platoon)	*c.*30
Oberstleutnant Reissenfels (Kufstein)		
III/*de Vaux* Infantry Regiment No. 45	(4 companies)	*c.*650
Artillery:		
Austrian: 3 x 6-pounders, 2 x 3-pounders		
Captured: 2 x 6-pounders, 2 x 3-pounders		

South of the Brenner Pass: FML Chasteler
(GM Fenner, GM Marchal)

	baons/ sqdns	present under arms
Hohenlohe-Bartenstein Infantry Regiment No. 26 (I, III)	2	*c.*2,000
Lusignan Infantry Regiment No. 16	3	3,000
Hohenzollern Chevaulegers No. 2	2 1/2	*c.*280

9th Jäger Battalion	(4 companies)	*c.*500
1st Klagenfurt Landwehr	1	868
1st Bruck Landwehr	1	1,401
Hauptmann Zuccheri		
Company/*1st Banal* Grenz Regiment No. 10	(1 company)	*c.*200
Schützen/2nd Villach Landwehr	–	*c.*130
Tyrolians	(1 company)	*c.*140
Major Lodron		
1st Villach Landwehr	1	*c.*1,000
2nd Villach Landwehr	1	*c.*1,000
2nd Bruck Landwehr	1	1,173
Major la Notte		
3rd Company/9th Jäger Battalion	(1 company)	*c.*130
Oberst Auracher (en route through Pustertal)		
2nd Klagenfurt Landwehr	1	1,128
3rd Klagenfurt Landwehr	1	884
1st Judenburg Landwehr	1	992
2nd Judenburg Landwehr	1	717

Artillery:
Austrian: 9 x 6-pounders, 6 x 3-pounders, 3 x cavalry guns
Captured: 2 x howitzers
Note: Zuccheri seems to have remained under direct control of army headquarters.

AUSTRIAN ARMY, 28 APRIL 1809

FML Chasteler

	baons/ sqdns	present under arms
Right Wing (North): GM von Buol		
II/*Hohenlohe-Bartenstein* Infantry Regiment No. 26	1	*c.*1,100
4th Company/9th Jäger Battalion	(1 company)	*c.*130
Hohenzollern Chevaulegers No. 2	1/2	*c.*50
Oberstleutnant Taxis		
III/*de Vaux* Infantry Regiment No. 45	(2 companies)	*c.*320
2nd Inner Austria Volunteers (Salzburger Jäger)	(4 companies)	?
2nd Salzburg Landwehr	(2 companies)	?
O'Reilly Chevaulegers No. 3	(platoon)	*c.*30
Oberstleutnant Reissenfels (Kufstein)		
III/*de Vaux* Infantry Regiment No. 45	(4 companies)	*c.*650

Artillery:
Austrian: 3 x 6-pounders, 2 x 3-pounders
Captured: 2 x 6-pounders, 2 x 3-pounders

Reserve: FML Chasteler

(GM Fenner)

Lusignan Infantry Regiment No. 16	3	3,000
Hohenzollern Chevaulegers No. 2	1 1/2	*c.*170
9th Jäger Battalion	(2 companies)	*c.*260
1st Klagenfurt Landwehr	1	868
1st Bruck Landwehr	1	1,401
2nd Villach Landwehr	1	*c.*1,000
Oberst Auracher (joined main column at Mühlbach, 30 April)		
2nd Klagenfurt Landwehr	1	1,128
3rd Klagenfurt Landwehr	1	884
1st Judenburg Landwehr	1	992
2nd Judenburg Landwehr	1	717

Artillery:

Austrian: 3 x 6-pounders, 4 x 3-pounders, 3 x cavalry guns

Captured: 2 x howitzers

Left Wing (South): GM Marchal

Hohenlohe-Bartenstein Infantry Regiment No. 26 (I, III)	2	*c.*2,000
Hohenzollern Chevaulegers No. 2	1	*c.*110
9th Jäger Battalion	(3 companies)	*c.*390
1st Villach Landwehr	1	*c.*1,000
2nd Bruck Landwehr	1	1,173

Artillery:

Austrian: 6 x 6-pounders, 2 x 3-pounders

FRENCH ARMY, 17–27 APRIL 1809[49]

GD Baraguey d'Hilliers

GD Vial

112th Ligne	3	2,104
IV/67th Ligne	1	*
IV/93rd Ligne	1	*
March battalion (three companies each of 37th and 56th Ligne)		
	1	*
* All infantry from Lemoine's column	–	*c.*1,775
Replacement Detachments of		
19th Chasseurs	–	*c.*100
23rd Chasseurs	–	*c.*100
24th Chasseurs	–	*c.*70
IV/7th Dragoons	1	203
2nd Italian Division: GD Fontanelli (GB Julhien, GB Bertoletti)		
1st Italian Light (III, IV)	2	705

2nd Italian Light (III, IV)	2	814
3rd Italian Line (II, IV)	2	*c*.1,200
4th Italian Line (III, IV)	2	927
Istrian Chasseur Battalion	1	685
2nd Italian Chasseurs *Prince Royal* (III, IV)	2	296
7th Dragoons (I, II, III)	3	664

Artillery: 10 guns

Note: IV/2nd Italian Line (787) was apparently attached to Fontanelli for a few days (approx. 25–7 April).

FRENCH ARMY, 28 APRIL 1809

GD Rusca

IV/67th Ligne	1	*
IV/93rd Ligne	1	*
* Both French battalions total	–	*c*.1,775
1st Italian Light (III, IV)	2	705
2nd Italian Light (III, IV)	2	814
4th Italian Line (III, IV)	2	927
Istrian Chasseur Battalion	1	685
Chasseur Replacement Detachments	2	*c*.270
IV/7th Dragoons	1	203

Artillery: 10 guns

Note: 67th and 93rd Ligne had absorbed the other march battalion and totalled approximately 1,775.

Orders of Battle for the Battle of the Piave

ARMY OF INNER AUSTRIA, 8 MAY 1809

FML Archduke Johann[50]

	baons/ sqdns	present under arms
Rear Guard: FML Frimont		
Brigadier: GM von Splenyi		
EH Franz Karl Infantry Regiment No. 52	3	c.1,950
Ogulin Grenz Regiment No. 3	2	c.2,000
EH Josef Hussars No. 2	6	c.480
Frimont Hussars No. 9	7	c.560
Artillery:		
1/2 x 3-pounder brigade battery (4 guns)		
2 x cavalry batteries (12 guns)		
VIII Corps: FML Albert Gyulai		
Cavalry		
Ott Hussars No. 5	8	c.640
Brigade: GM Colloredo		
Strassaldo Infantry Regiment No. 27	3	c.1,350
St Julien Infantry Regiment No. 61	3	c.1,350
1 x 3-pounder brigade battery (8 guns)		
Brigade: GM von Gajoli		
Franz Jellacic Infantry Regiment No. 62	3	c.1,350

1st Banal Grenz Regiment No. 10 (eleven companies)	2	*c.*1,800
1/2 x 3-pounder brigade battery (4 guns)		
Note: One company of *1st Banal* Grenz with Zuccheri.		

IX Corps: FML Ignaz Gyulai

Cavalry:

EH Josef Hussars No. 2	2	*c.*160
Dragoon Brigade: FML Wolfskeel, GM Hager		
Hohenlohe Dragoons No. 2	6	*c.*600
Savoy Dragoons No. 5	6	*c.*600
1 1/2 x cavalry batteries (9 guns)		
Brigade: GM Kalnassy		
Reisky Infantry Regiment No. 13	3	*c.*1,950
Simbschen Infantry Regiment No. 43	3	*c.*1,950
1 x 3-pounder brigade battery (8 guns)		
Brigade: GM Marziani		
Allvintzi Infantry Regiment No. 19	3	*c.*1,950
1 x 3-pounder brigade battery (8 guns)		
Brigade: GM Gavassini		
Ottocac Grenz Regiment No. 2	2	*c.*2,000
Brigade: GM Kleinmayrn		
Szulin Grenz Regiment No. 4 (ten companies)	1 2/3	*c.*1,600
Sallomon Grenadier Battalion (16, 26, 27)	1	*c.*600
Van der Mühlen Grenadier Battalion (53, 62)	1	*c.*400
Albeck Grenadier Battalion (13, 43)	1	*c.*400
Janusch Grenadier Battalion (19, 52, 61)	1	*c.*600
1 x 3-pounder brigade battery (8 guns)		
Note: Two companies of II/*Szulin* detached in Belluno valley under Zuccheri.		

Attached to army:

4th Inner Austrian Volunteer Battalion (Major du Montet)		
(in raising)		?
At Conegliano (did not participate in combat):		
Brigade: GM Sebottendorf		
1st, 3rd, 5th Graz Landwehr	3	*c.*3,000

Regular Infantry: *c.*21,250
Cavalry: *c.*3,040
Landwehr: *c.*3,000
Guns: 61 (the presence of all brigade batteries not confirmed)

Detached on Right Flank: GM von Schmidt

Main Body:

Johann Jellacic Infantry Regiment No. 53	3	*c.*2,000
2nd Banal Grenz Regiment No. 11 (eight companies)	2	*c.*1,350

Hohenzollern Chevaulegers No. 2	3 1/2	c.280
6 x 3-pounders		
Detachment: Hauptmann von Bianchi		
Local Landsturm (ten companies)	–	c.1,000
Division/2nd Banal Grenz Regiment No. 11	(two companies)	c.350
Hohenzollern Chevaulegers No. 2	1/2	c.40
Detachment: Hauptmann Zuccheri		
Company/1st Banal Grenz Regiment No. 10	(one company)	c.200
II/Szulin Grenz Regiment No. 4	(two companies)	c.350
Schützen/2nd Villach Landwehr	–	c.130
Tyrolians	(one company)	c.140

Notes:
a. The other two companies of 2nd Banal Grenzer had been destroyed at Bassano on 4/5 May.
b. Bianchi's ten companies of Landsturm totalled some 1,600 to 2,000 in late April (many unarmed); it is not clear how many were still with the colours at this time.

Garrisons and blockading forces in operational area

Palmanova: FML von Zach		
3rd Garrison Battalion	(four companies)	c.320
1st Trieste Landwehr	(three companies)	c.250?
2nd Trieste Landwehr	1	1,158?
1st Adelsberg Landwehr	1	1,130?
2nd Adelsberg Landwehr	1	1,328?
2nd Görz Landwehr	1	782?
Frimont Hussars No. 9	1	c.110
1/2 x cavalry battery (four guns)		
Osoppo: GM von Lutz		
1st Marburg Landwehr	(four companies)	c.880?
2nd Marburg Landwehr	1	1,294?
Udine:		
1st Marburg Landwehr	(two companies)	c.440?
1st Görz Landwehr	(four companies)	c.600?
Kordon troops	(detachment)	–
Near Tarvis/Karfreit:		
1st Graz Landwehr	1	934
2nd Graz Landwehr	1	1,357
Präwald GM von Munkaszy:		
2nd Neustadtl Landwehr	1	871?
Replacement detachment for Infantry Regiment St Julien	–	500

Notes:
a. Major Cazzan en route to Palmanova from Istria with his small command (Appendix 10).
b. The 3rd Adelsberg Landwehr had been disbanded owing to massive desertion

and lack of equipment.

c. Landwehr strengths likely much lower than indicated.

d. The two Cilli Landwehr battalions had been sent to the northern border of Styria. Other Landwehr troops were escorting prisoners, stationed in Carinthia/Carniola, or still attempting to organise.

FRENCH ARMY, 8 MAY 1809

Viceroy Eugene de Beauharnais[51]

	baons/ sqdns	present under arms
Advance Guard: GB Dessaix[52]		
1st Combined Voltigeur Regiment (Colonel Nagle/92nd Ligne)	3	–
2nd Combined Voltigeur Regiment (Major Vautré/84th Ligne)	3	–
9th Chasseurs	4	739
4 guns (Lt. Noël)		

Note: Strengths of the voltigeur battalions (eight companies each) are included in home regiments. However, a rough estimate places each battalion between 700 to 800 men, giving Dessaix an infantry strength of approximately 4,800, though it may have been as high as 6,000.

Right Wing: GD MacDonald

Division: GD Broussier (GB Dutruy, GB Quétard)		
9th Ligne	4	2,076
IV/11th Ligne	I	707
84th Ligne	4	2,503
92nd Ligne	3 1/3	2,347
12 guns	–	
Division: GD Lamarque (GB Alméras, GB Huard)		
18th Léger (III, IV)	2	1,176
13th Ligne	4	2,268
23rd Ligne (III, IV)	2	816
29th Ligne	4	2,419
12 guns		

Centre: GD Grenier[53]

Division: GB Abbé (awaiting GD Pacthod)		
8th Léger (III, IV)	2	1,538
1st Ligne	4	1,726
52nd Ligne	4	2,292
102nd Ligne	4	2,234

IV/*Napoleon* Dragoons (Italian)	1	260
12 guns	–	
Division: GD Durutte (GB Valentin)		
22nd Léger (III, IV)	2	1,176
23rd Léger	4	2,626
60th Ligne (III, IV)	2	866
62nd Ligne[54]	4	2,919
6 guns	–	

Left Wing: GD Baraguey d'Hilliers

Division: GD Fontanelli (GB Bonfanti)		
1st Italian Line	4	1,623
IV/2nd Italian Line	1	536
3rd Italian Line (II, IV)[55]	2	c.1,200
7th Italian Line (II, III)[56]	2	662
I/Dalmatian Regiment[57]	1	622
112th Ligne	3	1,873
IV/1st Italian Chasseurs *Royal Italian*	(detachment)	80
6 guns		

Note: Rusca's division detached.

Army Reserve

Division: GD Seras (GB Gareau, GB Roussel)		
[35th Ligne: combat ineffective][58]		
53rd Ligne[59]	3	1,794
79th Ligne (III, IV)	2	1,157
106th Ligne	4	2,388
10 guns		
Royal Italian Guard: GB Lecchi, GB Viani[60]		
Honour Guard (mounted)	(5 companies)	330
Dragoons	2	356
II/Royal Velites	1	811?
Line Infantry of the Guard	2	1,017?
6 guns		

Cavalry

Light Cavalry Division: GD Sahuc (GB d'Avenay)		
6th Hussars	4	555
6th Chasseurs	4	577
8th Chasseurs	4	931
25th Chasseurs	4	645
4 guns		
1st Dragoon Division: GD Grouchy (GB Guérin d'Etoquigny)		
7th Dragoons	3	647
30th Dragoons	4	833

Italian *Queen's* Dragoons	4	645
2nd Dragoon Division: GD Pully (GB Poinsot)		
23rd Dragoons	4	635
28th Dragoons (one squadron detached on 5 May)	3	492
29th Dragoons	4	639
4 guns		

Attached to army headquarters		
IV/24th Dragoons	1	196

Infantry: 44,388 (not including 35th Ligne)
Cavalry: 8,560
Guns: 60

Detached on left flank:

Division: GD Rusca (GB Julhien, GB Bertoletti)		
1st Italian Light (III, IV)	2	852
2nd Italian Light (III, IV)	2	1,101
4th Italian Line (III, IV)	2	756
Istrian Battalion	1	*c.*650
IV/67th Ligne	1	934
IV/93rd Ligne	1	786
IV/7th Dragoons	1	211
10 guns		

Garrisons in operational area

Venice: GD Vial		
5th Ligne (III, IV)	2	1,406
81st Ligne (III, IV)	2	1,182
IV/7th Italian Line	1	*c.*600?
Dalmatian Regiment (II, III)	2	*c.*850?
V/1st Italian Light Infantry (depot)	1	120
IV/3rd Italian Light Infantry	1	326
V/3rd Italian Light Infantry (depot)	1	145
V/5th Italian Line Infantry (depot)	1	501
Venetian Sedentary (Garrison) Battalion	1	648
IV/1st Italian Chasseurs *Royal Italian*	1	*c.*100
Palmanova: GB Schilt		
IV/1st Léger	1	779
IV/35th Ligne	1	761
IV/42nd Ligne	1	746
III/3rd Italian Light Infantry	1	826
Osoppo: Col. Ferrand		
Four companies of 92nd Ligne	–	512

Orders of Battle for the Battles on the Frontier, 14–17 May 1809

ARMY OF INNER AUSTRIA, MORNING OF 16 MAY 1809

FML Archduke Johann[61]

	baons/ sqdns	present under arms
MAIN ARMY		
'Mobile Corps': FML Frimont (Villach)		
Brigade: Oberst Lamezan[62] (Arnoldstein)		
Allvintzi Infantry Regiment No. 19	3	
Strassaldo Infantry Regiment No. 27	2 1/2	
St Julien Infantry Regiment No. 61	3	
Brigade: GM Kleinmayrn (Villach)		
1st Banal Grenz Regiment No. 10 (eleven companies)	2	
Sallomon Grenadier Battalion (16, 26, 27)	1	
Van der Mühlen Grenadier Battalion (53, 62)	1	
Albeck Grenadier Battalion (13, 43)	1	
Janusch Grenadier Battalion (19, 52, 61)	1	
Brigade: GM Sebottendorf		
1st, 3rd, 5th Graz Landwehr (Arnoldstein)	3	*c.*3,000
2nd, 4th Graz Landwehr (escorting trains to Laibach)	2	*c.*2,000
Cavalry Brigade: Oberst Boros		
EH Josef Hussars No. 2 (Villach)	7	
Ott Hussars No. 5 (Arnoldstein)	4	

VIII Corps: FML Albert Gyulai (Tarvis)

Brigade: GM von Gajoli

Reisky Infantry Regiment No. 13	2	
Franz Jellacic Infantry Regiment No. 62	3	
Brigade: GM Marziani		
Ogulin Grenz Regiment No. 3	2	
(two companies in Malborghetto fort)		
Ott Hussars No. 5	4	
Brigade: GM Lutz		
1st and 2nd Marburg Landwehr	2	
One each cavalry, brigade, and position battery		
Detachment in Raccolana valley:		
Strassaldo Infantry Regiment No. 27	1/2	214
Detachment in Isonzo valley:		
I/*Szulin* Grenz Regiment No. 4	1	
(one company in Predil fort)		
EH Josef Hussars No. 2	(one platoon)	
Four guns		

Notes:

a. One battalion of *Reisky* captured on 11 May.

b. Lutz was supposed to receive up to eight additional Landwehr battalions: those of Cilli, Bruck, and Villach (in Styria), one Laibach (Kronau), 1st Adelsberg (in Drava valley); he was also to have the depots of *Hohenlohe* Infantry, and the Villach and Klagenfurt Landwehr. None of these ever reached him.

c. I/*Szulin* detached from Kalnassy, technically under Marziani's command.

FML Jellacic (Salzburg area)

Brigade: GM von Ettingshausen

Esterhazy Infantry Regiment No. 32	3
De Vaux Infantry Regiment No. 45	3
Warasdin-Kreuz Grenz Regiment No. 5	2
Salzburg Landwehr (remnants)	4
O'Reilly Chevaulegers No. 3	3/4

DETACHED

VIII Corps: FML Chasteler (Tyrol)

Brigade: GM Marchal

Lusignan Infantry Regiment No. 16	3
Hohenlohe Infantry Regiment No. 26	3
Brigade: GM Schmidt	
Johann Jellacic Infantry Regiment No. 53	3
2nd *Banal* Grenz Regiment No. 11	2
Brigade: GM Fenner	
9th Jägers	1
Hohenzollern Chevaulegers No. 5	7

Detachment: Hptm Zuccheri
Company/*1st Banal* Grenz Regiment No. 10   (one company)
II/*Szulin* Grenz Regiment No. 4   (two companies)
II/*EH Franz Karl* Infantry Regiment No. 52   1 (much reduced)
Ordered back to Styria: (the three Klagenfurt battalions were not sent back)

1st and 2nd Bruck Landwehr	2
1st and 2nd Judenburg Landwehr	2
1st, 2nd, 3rd Klagenfurt Landwehr	3

IX Corps: FML Ignaz Gyulai
In Laibach

Cavalry Brigade: GM von Splenyi		
Hohenlohe Dragoons No. 2	6	
Savoy Dragoons No. 5	6	
Frimont Hussars No. 9	5	
Brigade: GM Gavassini		
Ottocac Grenz Regiment No. 2	2	
III/*EH Franz Karl* Infantry Regiment No. 52	1	
FML Zach (Präwald)		
II/*EH Franz Karl* Infantry Regiment No. 52 (Ogrissovich)	1	*c.*870
3rd Garrison Battalion	1	*c.*430
1st and 5th Kordon Companies (two companies)		*c.*250
1st Adelsberg Landwehr	1	
2nd Adelsberg Landwehr	1	60
2nd Görz Landwehr	1	
1st and 2nd Triest Landwehr	2	
Frimont Hussars No. 9	3	
GM Munkacsy (Präwald garrison):		
2nd Neustadtl Landwehr	1	286
Replacement detachment for *St Julien*	–	500
GM Kalnassy (Podkraj)		
II/*Szulin* Grenz Regiment No. 4 (four companies)	2/3	
Simbschen Infantry Regiment No. 43	2	
Total infantry:		1,861
EH Josef Hussars No. 2 (three platoons)		76
Other troops:[63]		
3rd Adelsberg Landwehr (Drava valley)	1	
1st Görz Landwehr	1	
2nd Laibach Landwehr (Kronau)	1	
1st, 3rd Neustadtl Landwehr	2	
4th Inner Austrian Volunteer Battalion	1	

Note: Two companies of II/*Szulin* detached in Belluno valley under Zuccheri.
Simbschen reduced to two battalions owing to losses.

Croatian Insurrection in process of formation: ten battalions, twelve squadrons.

GM Stoichevich (Dalmatia)

Licca Grenz Regiment No. 1	2
Reserve Battalion/*Licca* Grenz Regiment No. 1	1
Reserve Battalion/*Ottocac* Grenz Regiment No. 2	1
Reserve Battalion/*Ogulin* Grenz Regiment No. 3	1
Reserve Battalion/*Szulin* Grenz Regiment No. 4	1
Grenz Landwehr Half-Battalions (x 8)	4
4th Garrison Battalion	1
Hohenzollern Chevaulegers No. 2	1
Mounted Serezaner	1

Artillery:
   1 x 6-pounder position battery
   1 x 3-pounder brigade battery

FRENCH ARMY, MORNING OF 16 MAY 1809

Viceroy Eugene de Beauharnais[64]

	baons/ sqdns	present under arms
Advance Guard: GB Dessaix[65]		
2nd Combined Voltigeur Regiment (Major Vautré)	3	–
8th Léger (III, IV)	2	
9th Chasseurs	4	739
4 guns		
Right Wing: GD MacDonald		
Division: GD Broussier (GB Dutruy, GB Quétard)		
9th Ligne	4	2,076
IV/11th Ligne	1	707
84th Ligne	4	2,503
92nd Ligne	4	2,347
12 guns	–	
Division: GD Lamarque (GB Alméras, GB Huard)		
18th Léger (III, IV)	2	1,176
13th Ligne	4	2,268
23rd Ligne (III, IV)	2	816
29th Ligne	4	2,419
12 guns		
2nd Dragoon Division: GD Pully (GB Poinsot)		
23rd Dragoons	4	635
28th Dragoons	3	492
29th Dragoons	4	639
4 guns		

6th Hussars	3	400
Detachment: GB Schilt		
79th Ligne (III, IV)	2	1,157
6th Hussars	1	100
2 guns		

Centre: GD Grenier
Division: GD Pacthod (GB Abbé)

1st Ligne	4	1,726
52nd Ligne	4	2,292
102nd Ligne	4	2,234
IV/*Napoleon* Dragoons (Italian)	1	260
12 guns	–	

Division: GD Durutte (GB Valentin)

22nd Léger (III, IV)	2	1,176
23rd Léger	4	2,626
60th Ligne (III, IV)	2	866
62nd Ligne	4	2,919
6 guns	–	

Left Wing: GD Baraguey d'Hilliers
Division: GD Fontanelli (GB Bonfanti)

1st Italian Line	4	1,623
IV/2nd Italian Line	1	536
3rd Italian Line (II, IV)[66]	2	c.1,200
7th Italian Line (II, III)	2	662
I/Dalmatian Regiment	1	622
112th Ligne	3	1,873
IV/1st Italian Chasseurs *Royal Italian*	(detachment)	80
6 guns		

Division: GD Rusca (GB Julhien, GB Bertoletti)

1st Italian Light (III, IV)	2	852
2nd Italian Light (III, IV)	2	1,101
4th Italian Line (III, IV)	2	756
Istrian Battalion	1	c.650
IV/67th Ligne	1	934
IV/93rd Ligne	1	786
IV/7th Dragoons	1	211
10 guns		

Army Reserve
Division: GD Seras (GB Gareau, GB Roussel)

IV/1st Léger	1	779
IV/35th Ligne	1	761
IV/42nd Ligne	1	746

53rd Ligne	4	2,202
106th Ligne	4	2,388
10 guns		

Royal Italian Guard: GB Lecchi, GB Viani[67]

Honour Guard (mounted)	(5 companies)	330
Dragoons	2	356
II/Royal Velites	1	811
Line Infantry of the Guard	2	1,017
6 guns		

Cavalry

Light Cavalry Division: GD Sahuc

6th Chasseurs	4	577
8th Chasseurs	4	931
25th Chasseurs	4	645
4 guns		

1st Dragoon Division: GD Grouchy (GB Guérin d'Etoquigny)

7th Dragoons	3	647
30th Dragoons	4	833
Italian Queen's Dragoons	4	645

Attached to army headquarters

IV/24th Dragoons	1	196

French Army of Italy, reorganised as of 21 May 1809

Viceroy Eugene de Beauharnais[68]

	baons/ sqdns	present under arms
Right Wing: GD MacDonald		
Division: GD Broussier (GB Dutruy, GB Quétard)		
9th Ligne	3	1,780
84th Ligne	4	2,358
92nd Ligne	4	2,324
6th Hussars	4	515
12 guns	–	
Division: GD Lamarque (GB Alméras, GB Huard)		
18th Léger (III, IV)	2	920
13th Ligne	4	1,997
23rd Ligne (III, IV)	2	634
29th Ligne	4	2,393
12 guns	–	
2nd Dragoon Division: GD Pully (GB Poinsot)		
23rd Dragoons	4	538
28th Dragoons	3	383
29th Dragoons	4	549
4 guns	–	
Präwald: IV/11th Ligne	1	616
Trieste: GB Schilt		
79th Ligne (III, IV)	2	c.1,000

Note: Three companies of 9th Ligne were escorting prisoners from Laibach.

Detachment: GD Grouchy
  Division: GD Pacthod (GB Abbé)

8th Léger (III, IV)	2	1,083
1st Ligne	3	1,792
52nd Ligne	4	2,069

  Light Cavalry: GD Sahuc

8th Chasseurs	4	796
25th Chasseurs	4	428
Artillery: 4 guns (Noël)	–	

Centre: GD Grenier[69]
  Division: GD Seras (GB Gareau, GB Roussel)

IV/1st Léger	1	702
IV/35th Ligne	1	964
IV/42nd Ligne	1	665
53rd Ligne	4	2,211
106th Ligne	4	2,255
9th Chasseurs	4	707
10 guns	–	

  Division: GD Durutte
    Brigade: GB Valentin

22nd Léger (III, IV)	2	684
23rd Léger	4	1,622

    Brigade: GB Dessaix

62nd Ligne	4	2,612
102nd Ligne	4	2,101
Cavalry: 6th Chasseurs	4	471
Artillery: 2 guns	–	
Detached: 60th Ligne (III, IV)	2	724

Left Wing: GD Baraguey d'Hilliers
  Division: GD Severoli (GB Bonfanti)

1st Italian Line	3	2,030
IV/2nd Italian Line	1	618
3rd Italian Line (II, IV)[70]	2	c.1,100
II/7th Italian Line	1	705
I/Dalmatian Regiment	1	466
112th Ligne	3	1,782
IV/*Napoleon* Dragoons (Italian)	1	259

  Division: GD Rusca (GB Julhien, GB Bertoletti)

III/1st Italian Light	1	650
III/2nd Italian Light	1	726
III/4th Italian Line	1	662
Istrian Battalion	1	627
IV/67th Ligne	1	891

IV/93rd Ligne	1	729
IV/1st Italian Chasseurs *Royal Italian*	1	168
10 guns	–	

Army Reserve

Royal Italian Guard: GD Fontanelli (GB Lecchi, GB Viani)

Honour Guard (mounted)	(5 companies)	137
Dragoons	2	339
II/Royal Velites	1	575
Line Infantry of the Guard	2	753

1st Dragoon Division: GB Guérin d'Etoquigny

7th Dragoons	4	607
30th Dragoons	4	848
Italian *Queen's* Dragoons	4	629

Attached to army headquarters

IV/24th Dragoons	1	195

Notes:

a. Some artillery was still en route, having been held up by the fort at Predil: Pacthod, Durutte, Severoli, Guard.[71]

b. Many Italian units had been reduced by one battalion owing to inadequate numbers: 1st, 4th, and 7th Line; 1st and 2nd Light.

APPENDIX 16

Orders of Battle for The Battle of St Michael, 25 May 1809

AUSTRIAN ARMY[72]

Division of FML Jellacic

	baons/ sqdns	present under arms
Brigade: GM von Ettingshausen		
Esterhazy Infantry Regiment No. 32	2	*
De Vaux Infantry Regiment No. 45	2	*
Brigade: GM von Legisfeld		
Warasdin-Kreuz Grenz Regiment No. 5	2	*
III/Reuss-Greitz Infantry Regiment No. 55	1	*
Recruit detachment/EH Karl Infantry Regiment No. 3	-	c. 400
Salzburg Landwehr (remnants)	1	c. 300
O'Reilly Chevaulegers No. 3	3/4	c. 60
Detachment: Oberst Ruiz	-	c. 300

(fugitive elements of *Lusignan* Infantry, 9th Jägers, and a few *O'Reilly* Cheaulegers) four 3-pounders

* These battalions probably numbered approximately 1,000 each.

In vicinity:

Trofaiach: I/*Esterhazy* Infantry Regiment No. 32	1	c. 1,000

Vicinity Rottenmann: Oberstleutnant von Plunquet

1st ober dem Manhartsberg Landwehr	(three companies)	
3rd ober dem Wiener Wald Landwehr	1	
4th ober dem Wiener Wald Landwehr	(three companies)	
1st Cilli Landwehr	1	
2nd Cilli Landwehr	1	
2nd Judenburg Landwehr	1	
1st Inner Austrian Volunteers (forming)	1	c. 400
1st Traunviertel Landwehr	(two companies)	c. 40
two Judenburg Landwehr depots	-	c. 250
two Bruck Landwehr depots	-	c. 250
two Graz Landwehr depots	-	c. 250
two 3-pounders		

Bruck an der Mur: Reserve under FML Lippa

Depots of *Lusignan* and *Strassaldo* Infantry Regiments	-	500
Depot Division/*de Vaux* Infantry Regiment, Nr. 45	-	?
Reserve Squadron/*Frimont* Hussars Nr. 9	-	31
1st Bruck Landwehr	1	c. 1,000
two guns		

FRENCH ARMY OF ITALY[73]

Viceroy Eugene de Beauharnais

	baons/ sqdns	present under arms
Centre: GD Grenier		
Division: GD Seras (GB Garreau, GB Roussel)		
IV/1st Léger	1	702
IV/35th Ligne	1	964
IV/42nd Ligne	1	665
53rd Ligne	4	2,211
106th Ligne	4	2,255
9th Chasseurs	4	707
10 guns		-
Division: GD Durutte		
Brigade: GB Valentin		
22nd Léger (III, IV)	2	684
23rd Léger	4	1,622
Brigade: GB Dessaix		
62nd Ligne	4	2,612
102nd Ligne	4	2,101
Cavalry: 6th Chasseurs	4	471
Artillery: 2 guns	-	

Note: 60th Ligne (III, IV) detached from Durutte (724 men).

Abbreviations

AG   Archives de la guerre, Service historique de la armée de terre

AN   Archives Nationales, *Secrétairerie d'État Impériale: Guerre*

du Casse, *Eugène*   Eugene de Beauharnais, *Mémoires et Correspondance*, ed. Albert du Casse, Paris: Lévy, 1858–60.

Correspondance   Napoleon I, *Correspondance de Napoléon Ier publiée par ordre de l'Empereur Napoléon III*, Paris: Imprimerie Impériale, 1858–70.

GLA   Generallandesarchiv Karlsruhe

HStAS   Hauptstaatsarchiv Stuttgart

Hiller   Manfried Rauchensteiner (ed.), 'Das sechste österr. Armeekorps im Krieg 1809. Nach den Aufzeichnungen des FZM Johann Freiherr v. Hiller (1748–1819)', in *Mitteilungen des österr. Staatsarchivs*.

KAFA   Kriegsarchiv, Alte Feldakten

MOL   Magyar Orszagos Leveltar

ÖMZ   *österreichische militärische Zeitschrift* or *Streffleurs österreichische militärische Zeitschrift*

Stadion   Hellmuth Rössler, *Graf Johann Philipp Stadion: Napoleons deutscher Gegenspieler*, Vienna: Herold, 1966.

Notes

PROLOGUE

1 Dunan, p. 239.

CHAPTER 1: ON TO VIENNA!

1 'Proclamation a l'Armée', 24 April 1809, *Correspondance*, no. 15111.

2 In my opinion, he was *inclined* towards Vienna, but *not inflexibly determined* to seize the Austrian capital. Bonnal overstates this argument, a key thesis in his work. I have no doubt that Napoleon would have altered his plans instantly had he seen good strategic reasons to do so. See subsequent discussion.

3 Koch, *Massena*, vol. VI, p. 167.

4 Buat, vol. I, p. 22.

5 Proponents of this viewpoint often cite one of the letters written by Grünne to Prince de Ligne during the armistice in which he describes the Hauptarmee being in a state of near collapse after Regensburg. However, this letter was probably written with the purpose of vindicating Charles in the face of severe criticism of his performance, and its value as an accurate summary of the army's condition is suspect. The letter, dated 30 September 1809, can be found in Hormayr, *Das Heer von Innerösterreich*, pp. 398–400.

6 The list of authors who chastise Napoleon for not pursuing Charles after Regensburg includes Bonnal (pp. 260, 345–51); Buat (vol. I, pp. 16–22); Petre (pp. 201–6); and James R. Arnold in *Crisis on the Danube*, New York: Paragon House, 1990, p. 215, and in *Napoleon Conquers Austria*, London: Arms and Armour, 1995, pp. 3–4. Gunther Rothenberg called Napoleon's decision 'a mistake' in his *Napoleon's Great Adversaries* (p. 136), but later softened this critique (*The Emperor's Last Victory*, London: Weidenfeld & Nicolson, 2004, p. 76).

7 From FML Ferdinand von Bubna's account of a conversation he had with Napoleon in Vienna during the armistice in early September. Recounted in Friedrich M. Kircheisen, *Gespräche Napoleons*, Stuttgart: Lutz, 1912, vol. II, p. 73.

8 Napoleon could have constructed an ad hoc bridge, but this would have meant more delay.

9   Napoleon to Davout, 26 April 1809, 3 p.m., *Correspondance*, no. 15124; and 27 April 1809, 9 a.m., *Correspondance*, no. 15130.

10 Bonnal uses this phrase (p. 349) but intends it as evidence of Napoleon succumbing to prideful delusion. Camon, on the other hand, writes admiringly that Napoleon designed his strategy 'according to the model of all his *manoeuvres sur les derrières*: using the Danube as cover, he would gain Vienna on the march, cross the river there, and place himself on the rear of the archduke's army, that would still be in Bohemia' (*La Manoeuvre de Wagram*, Paris: Berger-Levrault, 1926, p. 5).

11 Camon, *La Manoeuvre de Wagram*, p. 75.

12 Ibid.

13 Napoleon to Eugene, 25 April 1809, *Correspondance*, no. 15116.

14 For instance: Napoleon to St Marsan (ambassador in Prussia), 29 April 1809, *Correspondance*, no. 15135.

15 'Note sur Passau', 1 March 1809, *Correspondance*, no. 14828.

16 In addition to Bonnal, Buat, Chandler, Petre, Arnold, and Rothenberg, who disagree with Napoleon's decision, this section is founded on my reading of those who found the march on Vienna 'the only sage resolution' (Thiers, vol. X, p. 226): Camon, *La Manoeuvre de Wagram*, pp. 4–5, 72–7; *Krieg*, vol. III, pp. 98–103; Lt. Col. Edmond Ferry, *La Marche sur Vienna*, Paris: Chapelot, 1909, pp. 1–5; Antoine Henri Jomini, *Life of Napoleon*, West Point: U.S. Military Academy, 1939, vol. II, pp. 38–44; Koch, *Massena*, vol. VI, pp. 179–81; Michel Molières, *Napoléon en Autriche: La Campagne de 1809: Les Opérations du 24 Avril au 12 Juillet*, Paris: Le Livre Chez Vous, 2004, pp. 17–21; Pelet, vol. II, pp. 148–54; Thiers, vol. X, pp. 219–26; Yorck von Wartenburg, pp. 147–8; Anton Freiherr von Bechtolsheim, '"Activité, Activité, Vitesse!" Operativer Gegenangriff aus der Versammlung', *Wehrwissenschaftlicher Rundschau*, 1959. Note that Yorck von Wartenburg criticised Napoleon severely for not pushing harder on the night of 22 April, but once Charles had escaped, he regarded an advance on Vienna as 'the only correct course'. Authors who discuss the emperor's decision process, often in great detail, without offering a specific conclusion include: Epstein, *Napoleon's Last Victory*, pp. 73, 97; Vincent J. Esposito and John R. Elting, *A Military History and Atlas of the Napoleonic Wars*, New York: Praeger, 1968, map 100; Laborde, pp. 50–1; C. de Renémont [General Auguste Clément Gérome], *Campagne de 1809*, Paris: Charles-Lavauzelle, 1903, pp. 36, 196–9; and Scott Bowden and Charles Tarbox, *Armies on the Danube*, Chicago: The Emperor's Press, 1989, p. 66. It is also important to read the Ninth Bulletin of the Army of Germany, 19 May 1809, *Correspondance*, no. 15239.

17 See Volume I, Chapter 6. Subsequent examples include Napoleon to Eugene, 26 April 1809, *Correspondance*, no. 14828: 'I cannot imagine that my troops were beaten by that rabble of Austrians'; and Duroc (writing on Napoleon's behalf) to Eugene, 26 April 1809: 'Their troops have in general fought poorly' (Albert Du Casse, *Mémoires et Correspondance Politique et Militaire du Prince Eugène*, Paris: Lévy, 1858–60, vol. XIII, p. 150). During the armistice, Napoleon reportedly told Austrian GM von Wimpffen that the Austrian army, contrary to his expectations, had risen from its ashes like a phoenix (Grünne to de Ligne, 30 September 1809, in Hormayr, *Das Heer von Innerösterreich*, p. 399). Buat (vol. I, pp. 17–20) correctly notes Napoleon's disdain for the Austrians, but he overstates his case;

he highlights, for instance, a 24 April letter from Berthier to Bernadotte (in full in Saski, vol. III, p. 13), but I read this as a blatant attempt to spur the querulous and quarrelsome Prince of Ponte Corvo into action rather than as indisputable evidence of Napoleon's debilitating underestimation of his foe.

18 Elting, *Swords*, p. 130.

19 Charles Esdaille provides a tidy summary of a sordid business in 1801 involving personal glory, status with First Consul Bonaparte, Murat's honour, the Guard's budget, and Caroline Bonaparte ('The Misnamed Bayard', in David G. Chandler (ed.), *Napoleon's Marshals*, New York: MacMillan, 1987).

20 Castellane quoted in Pigeard, *Etoiles*, p. 43.

21 Napoleon to Bessières, 22 April 1809, 3.30 a.m., Saski, vol. II, p. 338.

22 The actions and dispositions of 8th Hussars from 19 to 24 April are clouded in obscurity. At least one squadron fought at Regensburg on the 23rd, but one or two squadrons are also mentioned at Neumarkt on the 24th, so it appears that parts accompanied Jacquinot at some stage in the campaign.

23 In the course of its miniature odyssey, Steigentesch's command broke into three pieces, but most returned safely to Austrian lines by 24 April. See Volume I, Chapter 6.

24 Specifically Unterrohrbach, shown as 'Rohrbach' on the maps.

25 Bessières to Berthier, 24 April 1809, Saski, vol. III, pp. 11–12.

26 Bessières to Molitor, 23 April 1809, Saski, vol. II, pp. 370–1.

27 Forces at Inn crossings on 23 April included the following (all of Reinwald's troops joined his brigade at Obertürken or Hiller's main force on 24 April):
   • Braunau: one and one-half battalions of *J. Mittrowsky* and three platoons of *Stipsicz* Hussars from Reinwald's brigade; 4th, 5th, 6th Vienna Volunteers; III/*Czartoryski*; III/*Beaulieu*; 6th *EH Karl* Legion; 2nd and 3rd Traunviertel Landwehr (plus replacement detachments for *EH Ludwig*, *W. Colloredo*, and 6th Jägers).
   • Obernberg: 4th Hausruck Landwehr.
   • Mühlheim: 2nd Mühlviertel Landwehr.
   • Marktl: III/*J. Mittrowsky* (four companies) and two platoons of *Stipsicz* Hussars from Reinwald's brigade; 1st Traunviertel Landwehr.
   • Burghausen: three companies of *J. Mittrowsky* and one platoon of *Stipsicz* Hussars from Reinwald's command; 2nd Innviertel Landwehr.

28 *Krieg*, vol. III, p. 82.

29 Hiller to Franz, 23 April 1809, *Krieg*, vol. III, p. 650.

30 For some egregious barbs at Charles and lengthy self-justification, see Hiller's report to Franz, 24 April 1809, 8:30 p.m., *Krieg*, vol. III, pp. 662–4. In fairness to Hiller, it should be noted that he also routinely reported to Charles as his immediate superior and that it was completely reasonable of him to send frequent updates to the Kaiser in Schärding given the situation and the distance to Charles.

31 Binder lampoons Hiller's disposition as 'practically monstrous ... in part irrelevant, in part nearly incomprehensible' (vol. II, p. 22).

32 Stutterheim, pp. 298–9. It is not clear how Vincent's troopers and the French 2nd Chasseurs at Stetten failed to discover one another that night. Vincent's movements between 21 and 23 April are not known in detail, nor is it clear why

someone of his rank, nominally a division commander, was left in charge of a lone cavalry regiment.

33 From the official history of Marulaz's division, Saski, vol. II, pp. 368–9.

34 This account is drawn largely from *Krieg*, vol. III, pp. 33–5. The timing of the Austrian advance is from Bessières's report to Napoleon, 24 April 1809, Saski, vol. III, p. 11.

35 Bessières had sent the 13th Infantry south of the Rott as a precaution when he learned of the Austrian advance.

36 One battalion of *Esterhazy* Infantry, two squadrons of *O'Reilly* Chevaulegers, and a half battery of 3-pounders.

37 Provenchères was to join him at Wasserburg.

38 The following relies heavily on the thorough account in *Krieg*, vol. III, pp. 35–61, supplemented by Saski, Binder (vol. II, pp. 21–5), regimental histories, and other sources indicated below. Reports on the battle from Bessières, Molitor, and Wrede are in Saski, vol. III, pp. 8–12. An earlier version of this account appeared in *First Empire*, no. 11, May/June 1993. See also Gill, *Eagles*, pp. 102–4.

39 Significant extracts from Hiller's disposition are given in Johann Baptist Schels, 'Das Treffen bei Neumarkt an der Roth am 24. April 1809', *ÖMZ*, 1846.

40 As usual, III/*Stain* did not participate in the advance, but remained south of the Inn with the trains.

41 It is not clear where the remnants of the *Levenehr* Dragoons were. The authors of *Krieg* (vol. III, p. 29) speculate that they may have made their way to Braunau with other shattered units. Note that the Neumarkt map in vol. III of *Krieg* (Beilage 2) incorrectly lists the left column commander as Hohenfeld; the text is correct.

42 Albert Bessières, *Le Bayard de la Grande Armée: Le Maréchal Bessières*, Paris: Charles-Lavauzelle, 1941, pp. 153–4. Rocamadour is a goat's cheese unique to Cahors.

43 Johann Schnierer, *Aus der Franzosenzeit*, *Innviertler Volksbücher*, nos. 4 and 5, Braunau: Stampfl, n.d., p. 9.

44 Heilmann, *Wrede*, p. 141. See also Max Ruith and Emil Ball, *Kurze Geschichte des K. B. 3. Infanterie-Regiments*, Ingolstadt, 1890, p. 163.

45 Bakonyi quoted in *Krieg*, vol. III, pp. 49–50.

46 Bessières to Berthier, 24 April 1809, Saski, vol. III, pp. 11–12.

47 Hiller, p. 165.

48 The authors of *Krieg* (vol. III, pp. 55–6) attempt to make the case that the Austrian numerical superiority was slim. They are not convincing. They exaggerate Molitor's strength and deduct too many units from Hiller's available force; the fact that Hiller was incapable of, or unwilling to, commit his troops more effectively does not diminish their numbers. The Austrian quantitative advantage was most evident in their ability to feed new units into the fight continually where Wrede soon exhausted his slender reserves.

49 Casualties derived from *Krieg*, vol. III, pp. 59–60.

50 Cynthia Joy Hausmann and John H. Gill (ed.), *A Soldier for Napoleon*, London: Greenhill, 1998, p. 83.

51 *Krieg*, vol. III, p. 58. Binder condemns Hiller's decision to attack, deriding Hiller as 'over-rated', vol. II, pp. 25, 41–2.

52 Franz to Hiller, 24 April 1809, *Krieg*, vol. III, p. 665.

53 Schnierer, p. 11.

54 This compressed account follows *Krieg*, vol. III, pp. 80–5. The 1st and 2nd Hausruck retreated as directed, but the 3rd Innviertel for some reason received no instructions at first.

55 Troops were also en route to Jellacic: a large replacement detachment for the *Esterhazy* Infantry and III/*Reuss-Greitz*; the latter reached Moosbach on 27 April and marched south the following day, but did not join Jellacic until mid-May (Wilhelm Wachtel, 'Die Division Jellacic im Mai 1809', *Mitteilungen des K. und K. Kriegsarchivs*, Vienna, 1911, pp. 170–1).

56 This was the second tranche of 1st *EH Karl* Legion, the initial group participated in the fighting south of Regensburg with III Corps, suffering heavily in the process. This second group arrived in Waitzenkirchen on 24 April along with 1st Moravian Volunteers. Hiller ordered the Moravians to join the army at Altheim, but sent the Legion battalion, poorly equipped and utterly untrained, back across the Danube to complete its preparations.

57 Napoleon to Clarke, 28 February 1809, *Correspondance*, no. 14822.

58 The provisional battalion consisted of one depot company each from the 6th, 9th, 10th, and 14th Regiments.

59 Sinzendorf's four Mühlviertel battalions, ten battalions from Richter's Bohemian brigade, and the six companies under Oberst Nesslinger. It seems that the remaining companies of Nesslinger's two battalions later joined the force at Passau and Innstadt.

60 Richter's other battalions found employment in Bohemian border defence under Oberst Gustav von Rosenhayn.

61 The Grenzer arrived on 16 April with 2,157 men under arms. The three Prachin battalions appeared on the 15th, but Dedovich sent them away on the 16th. Sinzendorf's men crossed the Danube on the night of 16/17 April and marched for Schärding that day.

62 The siege train was supposed to consist of twelve 24-pounders, ten 18-pounders, eight 12-pounders, ten 10-pound howitzers, thirty mortars (six 60-pound, twelve 30-pound, and twelve 10-pound), and four 60-pound stone bombards serviced by some 750 artillerists, specialists, and labourers (*Krieg*, vol. III, p. 87). It is not clear how many of these actually appeared at Passau.

63 The description of the Oberhaus blockade is drawn from *Krieg*, vol. III, pp. 85–97.

64 Piré had 16th Chasseurs and about half of 8th Hussars (the rest of the latter were with Jacquinot). Demont initially marched with Lefebvre (24 April) towards Landshut before coming under Lannes's orders.

65 Infantry Regiment *Phull* was in Regensburg with two guns as city garrison and *Neubronn* was still at Landshut. Of the cavalry, *Herzog Heinrich* was serving with Imperial headquarters and the Leib Chevaulegers would be sent to support Boudet on the 26th.

66 Davout to Napoleon, 25 April 1809, 11 p.m., Saski, vol. III, p. 16. For Boudet, see his reports to Berthier on 25 April (6 p.m.) and 26 April (12.30 a.m.) Saski, vol. III, pp. 18, 32.

67 Berthier's messages to Bernadotte on 24 and 25 April urged entry into Bohemia, but this changed with the note of 26 April 1809, 7 a.m. (Saski, vol. III, pp. 13, 25–6, 28).

68 Napoleon to Davout, 26 April 1809, 3 p.m., *Correspondance*, no. 15124. Note that an earlier message from Berthier to Davout suggests that Bernadotte would be 'called to the battle that will occur to arrive in Vienna' (Berthier to Davout, 26 April 1809, 7 a.m., in Saski, vol. III, pp. 28–9). As the afternoon letter is directly from the emperor to Davout, this comment in the earlier missive is almost certainly an error on Berthier's part (the accompanying letter to Bernadotte says nothing of the Saxons joining in a battle, but does mention that Davout 'will move to his right' as soon as Bernadotte is in position). It is very clear from all correspondence (1) that Napoleon expected a battle in the Danube valley before reaching Vienna; (2) that Davout was to be available for that decisive battle; and (3) that Bernadotte was to cover Regensburg.

69 Stendahl [Henri Beyle], letter to his sister dated 29 April 1809, in *To the Happy Few: Selected Letters of Stendahl*, New York: Grove Press, 1952, p. 111.

70 The Hessian Chevaulegers and 19th Chasseurs rode ahead of Molitor, while 3rd and 23rd Chasseurs aimed for Ampfing.

71 With its many detachments, Vandamme's 'corps' consisted of three infantry regiments (*Camrer*, *Kronprinz*, and *Herzog Wilhelm*), the four light battalions, the two Jäger-zu-Pferd regiments (*Herzog Ludwig* and *König*), and twenty of its twenty-two guns. Regiments *Phull* and *Neubronn* were serving as city garrisons in Regensburg (with two guns) and Landshut respectively, while the Leib Chevaulegers were with Boudet and *Herzog Heinrich* supported Imperial headquarters.

72 The available guard troops included: approximately 240 Horse Grenadiers, 260 Dragoons, 400 Chasseurs, 50 Elite gendarmes, the 1st Battalion of the Foot Chasseurs, the Fusilier-Chasseurs Regiment, and a foot battery. *Krieg*, vol. III, p. 109. The Fusilier-Grenadiers (1,100 men) would arrive on the 27th, and an initial detachment of Polish chevaulegers (490 men) caught up on the 28th.

73 False reports of a large Austrian force near Erding also caused some confusion in various Allied headquarters; these were soon proved to be bogus.

74 Reichold, p. 102.

75 Fourth Corps marched from Straubing to Plattling on the 24th, and from Plattling to Vilshofen the following day. A French cavalry detachment, scouting along the north bank of the Danube, skirmished with a squadron of *Hessen-Homburg* Hussars west of Deggendorf, inflicting fifteen casualties on the Austrian horsemen (*Krieg*, vol. III, p. 134).

76 The Hessian brigade marched along the river road while the corps main body took the inland route.

77 It is not clear why Massena selected Claparède's raw division for this task; perhaps he sought to give them greater experience in a relatively confined situation where the likelihood of success was high.

78 The three companies were those of the 6th, 9th, and 14th Infantry Regiments; the 10th Infantry's depot company remained in the little fortress (Schubert/Vara, p. 187).

79 Massena's report lists the Tirailleurs du Po, but others credit the Tirailleurs Corses with this feat, stating that a sergeant approached the battalion commander and offered to lead some volunteers across (Dominique Buresi, *Les Corses au Combat sous Trois Drapeaux 1792–1815*, Ajaccio: Editions DCL, 2003, p. 95).

80 Quote from Massena's report to Berthier, 26 April 1809, Saski, vol. III, p. 40; also Chambarlhiac's detailed account (p. 41).

81 Massena to Napoleon, 26 April 1809, Saski, vol. III, p. 40.

82 Massena reported a loss of only three men (report to Berthier in ibid.).

83 Key sources for the seizure of Innstadt include: Fabrice, pp. 253–6; *Krieg*, vol. III, pp. 135–8; Markgraf Wilhelm, pp. 74–5; Saski, vol. III, pp. 40–1; Schubert/Vara, pp. 185–8.

84 Coëhorn to Sophie, 28 April 1809, cited in Napoléon Joseph Ernest Baron de Méneval, *Le Général Baron de Coëhorn: Un Bayard Alsacien*, Paris: Fischbacher, 1912, p. 176. Coëhorn's name is spelt in several ways, I have chosen that used in this biography written by his grandson.

85 This calculation is based on information from 28 and 29 April. The 28 April data refer to a strength return for regular forces, noting that 1,330 of these were not prepared for combat ('undienstbar')—which must have indicated a very low level of readiness indeed given the poor state of training and equipment among all of Dedovich's troops. Most notable was that the entire 3rd *EH Karl* Legion (760 men) was listed as unfit for combat. The information on the Landwehr is dated 29 April showing each of Sinzendorf's three remaining battalions with approximately 600 men. For the purposes of this calculation, I have estimated that 3,000 Landwehr were available under Sinzendorf at Schärding on 26 April. See *Krieg*, vol. III, p. 156.

86 Quote from *Souvenirs de Guerre du Général Baron Pouget*, Paris: Plon, 1895, p. 145. Baden Captain Freydorf's report is cited in an editor's note, Markgraf Wilhelm, p. 75.

87 Meier, pp. 35–6.

88 For the crossing at Schärding, see Charles Louis Joseph Olivier Gueheneuc, 'Historique du 26e Léger pendant la Campagne de 1809', manuscript, AG/MR1843 'Notes Brahaut', August 1810; *Krieg*, vol. III, pp. 138–43; Zech/Porbeck, pp. 55–7.

89 Massena to Berthier, 26 April 1809, Saski, vol. III, pp. 40–1.

90 Napoleon to Lannes, 27 April 1809, 6.30 a.m., Saski, vol. III, p. 49.

91 Berthier to Massena, 27 April 1809, 2 a.m., and Massena to Berthier, 28 April 5 a.m., Saski, vol. III, pp. 53, 60–1.

92 Montélégier reached Rosenheim on 28 April. Berthier sent orders to Lefebvre regarding Kufstein on 24 April, 4 p.m., and 27 April, 7.45 p.m., both in Saski, vol. III, pp. 5, 50 (quote from the latter message). Lefebvre's response was sent on 28 April 1809 7 a.m., Saski, vol. III, p. 64.

93 Reichold, pp. 102–3. Marching statistics from *Krieg*, vol. III, p. 188.

94 The following day (28 April), Dedovich marched to Reid for logistical reasons and then returned to his previous position near St Martin, even though he had been ordered to outpost the army's right flank towards the Linz road. This inexplicable behaviour earned him the Kaiser's ire. *Krieg*, vol. III, pp. 175, 210.

95 The locations of Dedovich's Landwehr battalions during this period are unclear.
96 As one example of Hiller's misappreciation of his covering troops, see *Krieg*,
    vol. III, p. 215. Binder (vol. II, p. 58) excoriates Hiller for indulging in this spasm
    of detachments, as does Stutterheim ('Der Feldzug 1809 zwischen Oesterreich
    und Frankreich', *ÖMZ*, vol. III, 1849, p. 264). In a further complication, Mesko
    reported himself ill on 28 April owing to problems with a wound he had received
    earlier: the *Brod* Grenzer seem to have come under Radetzky while the *Kienmayer*
    Hussars went to Schustekh.
97 Hiller was considering attaching some of Jellacic's horse to his main body and
    therefore wanted these four squadrons placed at Laufen.
98 Schnierer, pp. 11–12; Pirquet, p. 82.
99 *Krieg*, vol. III, pp. 208–11.
100 Massena to Berthier, 29 April 1809, 7 p.m., Saski, vol. III, pp. 73–4.
101 The best summaries of this reconnaissance are *Krieg*, vol. III, pp. 219–25;
    Stutterheim, 'Der Feldzug 1809', *ÖMZ*, vol. III, 1849, pp. 264–5. There is very little
    from the French side beyond Massena's report, so it is not clear which infantry
    units participated nor how many. The mention of Legrand's voltigeurs (suggested
    in *Krieg*) is from Pierre Pelleport, *Souvenirs Militaires et Intimes du Général Vicomte
    de Pelleport*, Paris: Didier, 1857, p. 261.
102 Massena to Berthier, 29 April 1809, 7 p.m., Saski, vol. III, pp. 73–4.
103 *Krieg*, vol. III, p. 257.
104 Hiller to Schustekh, 30 April 1809, 6.15 p.m., *Krieg*, vol. III, p. 239.
105 See summaries and analysis of these reports in *Krieg*, vol. III, pp. 239–43, 249–50.
    One of Radetzky's reports (30 April 1809, 9 a.m.) included the results of prisoner
    interrogation: according to this, Napoleon was already in Bohemia and the forces
    on the Inn were awaiting reinforcements from Spain. I have no way to prove it, but
    this reeks of intentional disinformation perpetrated by the French; the topic of
    such disinformation during the Napoleonic era is worthy of further investigation.
106 Franz to Hiller, 29 April 1809, *Krieg*, vol. III, p. 684.
107 Franz to Hiller, 30 April 1809, and Charles to Hiller, 26 April 1809, *Krieg*, vol. III,
    pp. 685–6. Franz complained of Hiller's inaction in a letter sent to Charles the
    same day (ibid., p. 253).
108 Quoted in Zehetbauer, p. 256.
109 Hiller to Franz, 30 April 1809, 5.45 p.m., *Krieg*, vol. III, p. 683.
110 *Krieg*, vol. III, pp. 239, 275.
111 Hiller to Charles, 1 May 1809, 2 p.m., *Krieg*, vol. III, p. 689.
112 Jules Antoine Paulin, *Les Souvenirs du Général Baron Paulin*, Paris: Plon, 1895,
    p. 175.
113 Quotes and details of this scene are also from Paulin, pp. 174–7.
114 Berthier to Daru, 30 April 1809, 6 a.m., Saski, vol. III, p. 66.
115 First quote from Stendahl, letter to his sister dated 29 April 1809, in *Selected Letters*,
    p. 114. Second quote from Bial, p. 217.
116 Napoleon to Eugene, 25, 26, 27, and 30 April 1809, *Correspondance*, nos. 15116, 15128,
    15131, and 15144. Napoleon to Eugene, 30 April 1809, in Lecestre, vol. I, pp. 307–8
    (quote from this letter). Napoleon to Lefebvre, 29 April 1809, in Saski, vol. III,
    pp. 70–1.

117 Napoleon to Kellermann, 29 April 1809, *Correspondance*, no. 15139.
118 Napoleon to Friedrich, 25 April 1809, *Correspondance*, no. 15120.
119 For the Bavarians, see Gill, *Eagles*, ch. 7.
120 Napoleon to Kellermann, 29 April 1809, *Correspondance*, no. 15139; and Napoleon to Clarke, 4 May 1809, *Correspondance*, no. 15152. See also John H. Gill, 'Impossible Numbers: Solving Rear Area Security Problems in 1809', in The Consortium on Revolutionary Europe, Donald D. Horward, Michael F. Pavkovic, and John Severn (eds), *Selected Papers 2000*, Tallahassee: Florida State University, 2000 (note that the title should read 'Imaginary Numbers', reflecting Napoleon's use of deception).
121 Napoleon to Jerome, 29 April 1809, *Correspondance*, no. 15143. He used similar words in replying to his ambassador to Prussia: Napoleon to Saint Marsan, 29 April 1809, *Correspondance*, no. 15135. See also Napoleon to Jerome, 29 April 1809, *Correspondance*, no. 15142; and Napoleon to Jerome, 29 April 1809, Lecestre, vol. I, pp. 306–7.
122 Johann Baptist Skall, 'Feldzugsreise des Kaisers Franz I. von Oesterreich im Jahre 1809', *Mitteilungen des K. und K. Kriegsarchivs*, Vienna, 1907, p. 210.
123 Franz to Hiller, 27 April 1809, 9 a.m., *Krieg*, vol. III, p. 674.
124 *Krieg*, vol. III, p. 510.
125 The replacement detachment was destined for *Josef Mittrowsky*.
126 Only seven *Ferdinand* squadrons went with Stutterheim. He departed Cham on 26 April. *Krieg*, vol. III, pp. 254, 331; vol. IV, p. 37.
127 *Krieg*, vol. III, pp. 254–5. There were also complaints about abuses perpetrated on the local Austrian citizenry by the personnel of Hiller's baggage train and its escorts.
128 *Krieg*, vol. III, pp. 506–10.
129 Memoirs of Graf Eugen von Czernin und Chudenic (a young boy at the time), in Friedrich M. Kircheisen, *Feldzugserinnerungen aus dem Kriegsjahre 1809*, Hamburg: Gutenberg, 1909, p. 25.
130 Maria Louise to Franz, 25 April 1809, in Joseph Alexander Freiherr von Helfert, *Maria Louise, Erzherzogin von Oesterreich, Kaiserin von Frankreich*, Vienna: Braumüller, 1873, p. 36.
131 First quote from Czernin und Chudenic in Kircheisen, *Feldzugserinnerungen*, p. 25. See the army's sobering 'Eleventh Daily Report' (MOL/P300/1/104).
132 Diary of Joseph Carl Rosenbaum in Wertheimer, 'Geschichte Wiens', p. 174.
133 *Krieg*, vol. III, p. 509.
134 Skall, p. 196.
135 See also Karl August Schimmer, *Die Französischen Invasionen in Oesterreich und die Franzosen in Wien in den Jahren 1805 und 1809*, Vienna: Dirnböck, 1846, pp. 71–2.
136 Chef d'Escadron Margueron's report to Jacquinot, 28 April 1809, Saski, vol. III, p. 62; *Krieg*, vol. III, p. 191.
137 The Bavarians captured between seven and twenty-three Austrians (*Krieg*, vol. III, p. 193). Information from the prisoners allowed Wrede to send a very accurate report to imperial headquarters: Wrede to Berthier, 28 April, 6 p.m., Saski, vol. III, p. 63.
138 Berthier to Wrede, 28 April 1809, 1 p.m., Saski, vol. III, p. 62.

139 The replacement detachment had come up the river from Hiller. It numbered some 530 men and was formed into two companies.

140 Jellacic to Hiller, 30 April 1809, in Gedeon Freiherr Maretich von Riv-Alpon, 'Die Gefechte in der Umgebung von Salzburg in den Jahren 1800, 1805 und 1809', *ÖMZ*, January 1893, p. 73. The 1st, 3rd, and 4th Battalions combined still counted 1,340 men in their ranks on 30 April (Wachtel, p. 240).

141 *Krieg*, vol. III, p. 201.

142 Stutterheim, 'Der Feldzug 1809', *ÖMZ*, vol. III, 1849, p. 259.

143 For the Bavarian advance on Salzburg, see Gill, *Eagles*, pp. 104–7; *Krieg*, vol. III, pp. 188–202; Maretich, 'Salzburg', pp. 58–75.

144 Landwehr troops defending the Saalach were the 3rd Salzburg, 2nd Hausruck, and at least part of 3rd Innviertel. The 2nd (four companies only) and 4th Salzburg were stationed behind the city supposedly in support positions.

145 These were: 8th Infantry, I/4th Infantry (2nd Battalion was with Montélégier), a squadron of 1st Dragoons, and two guns from Wagner's battery.

146 Montbrun to Berthier, 24 April 1809, Saski, vol. III, p. 4.

147 GB Barbanègre remained on the Trinity Hill above Stadtamhof with 48th Ligne; the regiment moved to Etterzhausen on the 25th, but returned to its previous position the following day to work on fortifying the heights.

148 The order of battle information Montbrun passed was nearly perfect in its accuracy. Not all of Montbrun's conclusions were correct, but it was not his fault that Davout, apparently unaware that an adequate road ran from Cham north into Bohemia, believed Charles would march on Passau from Cham: Davout to Napoleon, 25 April 1809, 11 p.m., Saski, vol. III, p. 16.

149 Davout to Napoleon, 26 April 1809, 1.30 p.m., Saski, vol. III, p. 130.

150 The 1st Battalion of 111th Ligne that had been assigned to Colonel Guyon, returned to its regiment on the 24th at Regensburg (as did, presumably, the two companies of the 15th Léger).

151 Napoleon to Davout, 1 May 1809, Saski, vol. III, p. 96.

152 Napoleon to Clarke, 11 April 1809, *Dernières Lettres Inédites de Napoléon Ier*, ed. Léonce de Brotonne, Paris: Champion, 1903, p. 179.

153 Marbot, vol. II, p. 513.

154 Ameil had arrived during the Battle of Abensberg and accompanied the main army as far as Landshut. He led a detachment of 200 replacement troopers (2nd March Squadron) destined for Pajol's brigade from Landshut, evidently exchanging these for veterans from 12th Chasseurs on reaching Montbrun. Note that another light cavalry replacement squadron was temporarily assigned to Rouyer at this point and may have come under Ameil briefly.

155 Davout to Ameil, 30 April 1809, 11.30 p.m., in Auguste Jean Joseph Gabriel Ameil, *Notes et Documents provenant des Archives du Général Baron Ameil*, Paris: Teissedre, 1997, pp. 132–3 (originally published in the *Carnet de la Sabretache* in 1906–7).

156 Angeli (vol. IV, p. 412) claims that Charles had 93,360 men, but the authors of *Krieg*, point out that this figure is for 28 April (rather than 25 April) after many stragglers had returned and some replacements had arrived (vol. IV, p. 32).

157 Diary of Oberleutnant Potier quoted in *Krieg*, vol. IV, p. 11.

158 Extract from a IV Corps order, dated 24 April 1809, in *Krieg*, vol. IV, p. 12.

159 Briefing to the Kaiser, *Ausgewählte Schriften*, vol. VI, p. 302.
160 Charles to Franz, 24 April 1809, *Krieg*, vol. IV, p. 731.
161 Franz to Charles, 24 April 1809, in Criste, *Carl*, vol. III, p. 78.
162 Instructions for Friedrich Stadion in Wertheimer, *Geschichte*, vol. II, p. 310. In addition to Wertheimer, see Criste, *Carl*, vol. III, pp. 77–9; Rauchensteiner, *Kaiser Franz und Erzherzog Carl*, pp. 99–100; Rössler, *Oesterreichs Kampf*, vol. II, pp. 11–15; Rössler, *Stadion*, vol. II, pp. 46–9; and Rothenberg, *Adversaries*, p. 136.
163 Criste, *Carl*, vol. III, pp. 105–7; Damas, p. 101; Guglia, p. 68; Rauchensteiner, pp. 100–1; Rothenberg, p. 136; Wertheimer, vol. II, pp. 309–11.
164 Espinchal, pp. 242–3.
165 Text in *Krieg*, vol. IV, pp. 47–8. Foibles of translation are my own.
166 Charles to Franz, 27 April 1809, Criste, *Carl*, vol. III, pp. 75–7 (written before Stadion's arrival in Cham).
167 Charles to Albert, 28 April 1809, Criste, *Carl*, vol. III, p. 479.
168 Ibid.
169 F. A. Brandner, *Aus dem Tagebuch eines österreichischen Soldaten im Jahre 1809*, Lobau: J. Breyer, n.d., p. 51. With thanks to Peter Harrington and the Anne S. K. Browne Collection.
170 Montbrun's force thus consisted of 5th and 7th Hussars, 12th Chasseurs, and one battalion of 13th Léger.
171 Napoleon to Davout, 1 May 1809, Saski, vol. III, p. 96.
172 Paulin, p. 176. See also Kergorre, p. 32; Jean Michel Chevalier, *Souvenirs des Guerres Napoléoniennes*, Paris: Hachette, 1970, p. 94.
173 Vandamme was at Winhöring because the painful wound received at Eggmühl had re-opened when his carriage overturned. He was the target of a stinging rebuke from Berthier when the Major General saw that he was still in Winhöring and mistakenly assumed that 8th Corps had not advanced to Braunau as ordered. See Albert du Casse, *Le Général Vandamme et sa Correspondance*, Paris: Didier, 1870, p. 279; and the exchange between Berthier and Vandamme on 30 April, Saski, vol. III, p. 89.
174 Bial, p. 217.
175 Wrede to Berthier, 30 April 1809, 6.45 p.m., Saski, vol. III, p. 87.
176 Davout to Napoleon, 20 April 1809, 11 p.m., and Bernadotte to Napoleon, 26 April 1809, Saski, vol. III, pp. 42–3, 66–7. The enclosure to Bernadotte's message was Paszkowski to Bernadotte, 21 April 1809, Fedorowicz, pp. 316–18.
177 Castex, letter of 30 April 1809, *Carnet de la Sabretache*, 1903, p. 181.
178 This description is taken almost entirely from *Krieg*, vol. III, pp. 256–63. In addition to the captured Grenzer (927) and Jägers (249), the Austrians lost forty-four lancers. French losses, other than twelve prisoners from Colbert's regiments, are unknown but evidently very light. Two *Brod* Grenz companies that had been detached on the left flank made their way safely to Nordmann's brigade.
179 Friedrich Wilhelm von Bismark, *Reuter-Bibliothek*, Karlsruhe: Müller, 1825, pp. viii–xii; and *Aufzeichnungen*, Karlsruhe, 1847, pp. 55–6.
180 I have related this in some detail because of the interesting tactical aspects. The fight is described in Zech/Porbeck, pp. 64–8; Rau, pp. 18–19; Markgraf Wilhelm, p. 76. The Zech/Porbeck account matches the regimental war diary almost word for word (GLA 48/4271).

181   The Baden dragoons lost one man killed and two wounded; the Württemberg Leib
       Chevaulegers had two dead and ten wounded; the French voltigeurs probably lost
       a few men as well.

182   My paraphrase of *Krieg*, vol. III, p. 270: 'Schustekh wusste nicht, was er tun sollte'.

183   It is not clear exactly what transpired for this battalion to have lost so many
       men (casualties from *Krieg*, vol. III, p. 270). One is left to suspect that there
       was widespread desertion. The French regimental commander said that he lost
       one voltigeur killed and thirteen wounded during the afternoon engagement;
       Trenqualye reported that 'Nothing happened during this brief combat' (Saski, vol.
       III, p. 107).

184   Sources for the engagement at Riedau include *Krieg*, vol. III, pp. 266–71; Louis Léger
       Boyeldieu, 'Itinéraire et Notes Historiques du 4e Régiment de Ligne', published in
       Loy, 'Le Général de Division Baron Boyeldieu', *Carnet de la Sabretache*, vol. 260,
       August 1914–May 1919; Gill, *Eagles*, pp. 148–9, 190; extracts from Trenqualye's two
       after-action reports are in Saski, vol. III, pp. 106–7.

185   'Feldzug der 2ten Division', p. 619.

186   Scheibler to Hiller, 2 May 1809, 2.40 a.m., in *Krieg*, vol. III, pp. 273–4.

187   'Feldzug der 2ten Division', p. 619.

188   Scheibler to Hiller, 2 May 1809, 2.40 a.m., in *Krieg*, vol. III, pp. 273–4.

189   For only two of several examples: III/*Czartoryski* (albeit an orphan unit) was
       forgotten at Braunau on 28 April, and the Vienna Volunteers, whom the Kaiser
       desired to see committed to the defence of the capital, received no orders on 1
       May (it was adventitious that they ended up at Ebelsberg). Hiller and his staff
       repeatedly referred to Schustekh as if he had light infantry under his command
       (in fact only the *Kienmayer* Hussars were actually under his orders), Reinwald and
       Hohenfeld were shuttled willy-nilly all about the theatre, and command relations
       among Kienmayer, Schustekh, and the various light brigade commanders (Gratze,
       Mesko, Nordmann, Radetzky, Bianchi)—not to mention Dedovich's role—were a
       complete farrago after a few days. See the often-understated comments in *Krieg*,
       vol. III, pp. 144–296. Binder and Heller excoriate Hiller.

190   Hiller to Franz, 2 May 1809, 2.30 a.m., *Krieg*, vol. III, p. 691.

191   Radetzky, whose Grenzer were still south-west of the town, instantly recognised
       that his men would be cut off and cut up if he could not delay the French light
       cavalry. Inventing a request from Hiller as a pretext, he sent an officer to negotiate
       with the French commanders. Piré, who should have known better after his own
       'hussar escapade' with Hohenzollern on 19 April, took the Austrian major to
       Bessières, while Radetzky used the time thus gained to slip through Lambach
       to a new position north of town. Napoleon, arriving on the scene around 2 p.m.,
       immediately penetrated Radetzky's ruse. Furious, he declared the Austrian officer a
       prisoner of war and ordered the advance to resume at once.

192   See *Krieg*, vol. III, pp. 296–304.

193   Meier, p. 37.

194   Trenqualye also noticed the unhappy state of the Grenzer and chose this moment
       to order two squadrons of the Baden Dragoons and a platoon of 14th Chasseurs
       to charge. Forced to stay on the road, most of the horsemen quickly recoiled, but
       Heimrodt with ten of his own men and a dozen French chasseurs attempted to

capture two guns that were hurriedly bouncing down the road towards Raffelding. The supporting troops abandoned the guns and the crews were cut down, but Heimrodt's men received no help and did not have time to drag the guns to safety before they were chased off. The same two guns fell into Allied hands a second time shortly thereafter, but Scheibler's desperate charge saved them. For a detailed account, see Zech/Porbeck, pp. 68–72.

195 These figures, taken from *Krieg*, vol. III, p. 315, are low as they do not count wounded in most cases. The authors acknowledge this and also note that in the case of *Gyulai*, the army's 'Standeslisten' give a total of dead, captured, and missing as 70 more than the 162 here.

196 Sources for this series of engagements include: *Krieg*, vol. III, pp. 307–15; Trenqualye's report in Saski, vol. III, pp. 114–15; Rau, pp. 19–20; Gill, *Eagles*, pp. 149, 190–1. Unfortunately, the *Historique du 99e Régiment d'Infanterie de Ligne*, manuscript, AG, 1889, only repeats the sketchy account in Massena's memoirs (the 99th was the tradition-bearer for 24th Léger).

197 Marulaz, campaign summary, Saski, vol. III, p. 113. The history of the 3rd Chasseurs lists one trooper killed during the day (Bonie).

198 Karl von Zimmermann, *Geschichte des 1. Grossherzoglich Hessischen Dragoner-Regiments (Garde-Dragoner-Regiments) Nr. 23*, Darmstadt: Bergsträsser, 1878, pp. 140–1.

199 Marulaz, campaign summary, Saski, vol. III, p. 113. The presence of *Klebek* is based on *Krieg*, vol. III, pp. 315–16.

200 The events involving Schustekh's command are covered in *Krieg*, vol. III, pp. 315–18. Marulaz's account and the Hessian regimental history are listed above.

201 Berthier to Massena, 1 May 1809, 2 p.m., Saski, vol. III, pp. 105–6.

202 Berthier to Lannes and Berthier to Bessières, 3 May 1809, 5 a.m., Saski, vol. III, p. 127.

203 Edmond Buat, 'Vingt-Quartre Heures au Grand Quartier Général de l'Armée d'Allemagne (2–3 Mai 1809)', *Journal des Sciences Militaires*, Paris, 1908, p. 86. This is a slightly expanded portion of his book-length study, see Buat, vol. II, p. 106.

204 Buat, vol. II, pp. 106–7.

205 Many writers (eg Binder, Heller), have maintained that Hiller was pulled in different directions by the Kaiser and Charles, the former demanding a defence of Linz and the approaches to Vienna south of the Danube, the latter insisting on a retreat north of the great river. The letters and orders Hiller received from his two superiors, however, do not offer much evidence to support this conclusion and the careful analysis in *Krieg* removes all doubt (vol. III, pp. 318–31). Charles certainly would have preferred to unite with Hiller via Linz, but he repeatedly mentioned other options as well. The Kaiser's priorities, once the line of the Inn was undone, were for Hiller to risk nothing, but to gain time for Charles to arrive and for the monarchy's defences south of the Danube to solidify. The relevant correspondence among these three is in *Krieg*, vol. III, pp. 665–99; note, however, that the 30 April order from Charles is on p. 320.

206 Radetzky to Hiller, 1 May 1809, in Riedl, p. 57.

207 Hiller to Charles, *Krieg*, vol. III, p. 698. See also Hiller, pp. 167–8.

208 'Redoubt' from *Krieg*, vol. III, p. 347.

209 This description is taken from *Krieg*, vol. III, pp. 346–9.

210 Petre (p. 233) gives the width of the bridge as 'fifteen to sixteen feet' or approximately five metres as in Saski, vol. III, p. 139. *Krieg* does not provide a width. A more recent summary that otherwise follows the official history closely, states that the bridge was thirteen metres wide (Rudolf Walter Litschel, *Des Gefecht bei Ebelsberg am 3. Mai 1809*, Militärhistorische Schriftenreihe Heft 9, Vienna: Bundesverlag, 1968). Extended extract from Litschel in Kulturverein Schloss Ebelsberg, 'Das Gefecht bei Ebelsberg am 3. Mai 1809', Ebelsberg, 1989.

211 This insignificant action gave rise to exaggerated descriptions of Radetzky courageously holding off overwhelming numbers of elite French troops, apparently because one account erroneously stated that *several* light brigades *and the two cuirassier divisions* had taken part in the fight. Although these were under Bessières's command according to the order of battle, as we have seen, only Piré was actually on hand that morning. See the clear explanation in *Krieg*, vol. III, p. 358. Heller exemplifies the heroic hyperbole surrounding this exchange; Binder ridicules it. Radetzky was awarded the Commander's Cross of the Maria Theresa Order in 1810 for his actions west of the Traun, but his biographers, if also perhaps excessively laudatory, cite the fighting between Lambach and Wels as the relevant action (Viktor Bibl, *Radetzky: Soldat und Feldherr*, Vienna: Günther, 1955, pp. 94–5; Oskar Regele, *Feldmarschall Radetzky: Leben, Leistung, Erbe*, Munich: Herold, 1957, pp. 74–6).

212 It is not clear which French cavalry accomplished this feat. The 16th Chasseurs, according to their history (Chevillotte), were involved in the surrender of 'a considerable number of the enemy', but the histories of the other contenders (3rd Chasseurs, 8th Hussars, and the four regiments of Espagne's cuirassier division) make no mention of any action on 3 May. It could have been the 16th alone or in combination with any of these units.

213 Marulaz, campaign summary, Saski, vol. III, p. 133.

214 Radetzky, 'Erinnerungen', pp. 65–6.

215 Austrians, including Schustekh: 8,450 infantry and 2,550 cavalry. French: 7,500–8,000 infantry and 3,000 cavalry. All figures approximate, especially on the French side. I have used a higher number for Claparède than *Krieg* (they estimated 7,200–7,500) to speculate at a march attrition rate of some 10 per cent. It is important to note that only Coëhorn's brigade (3,200–3,600) was engaged on the French side as far as infantry was concerned. Figures from *Krieg*, vol. III, pp. 417–18.

216 Casualty estimate from *Krieg*, vol. III, Anhang XLVII.

217 Brinner, pp. 63–4. The Austrians had removed the railings along the sides of the bridge, making things all the more dangerous for those trying to cross.

218 The 1st Battalion was reinforced on 2 May by a company of volunteers known as the Kronprinz Erzherzog Ferdinand Scharfschützen. Raised at his own expense by a Croatian nobleman named Svetich, the company consisted of one hundred jägers, eleven officers and two drummers. *Krieg*, vol. III, p. 353.

219 *Krieg*, vol. III, p. 353.

220 Dedovich had only III/*Stuart*, 3rd *EH Karl* Legion, and his Landwehr in this position as his other 'third battalions' were behind Hammer, south of the highway.

221 Pirquet, p. 83 (for Ebelsberg and subsequent events, Pirquet shifts from diary entries to memoirs composed sometime after his wounding on 3 May).

222 For flank protection, Kienmayer placed the *Kirchenbetter* Grenadiers and a half-squadron of dragoons at St Florian, a dragoon platoon at Tillysburg, and another just south of Enns on the west bank of the Enns.

223 Curiously, this battalion, composed entirely of recruits, had been consistently protected during the entire campaign thus far. Similar units, such as the third battalions behind Hammer, were not so carefully shepherded about the battlefield. Perhaps this was simply a case of inertia: having been treated with tender care early in the war, the habit remained in place. In any event, someone had to guard the artillery park.

224 This description of Austrian deployments is summarised from *Krieg*, vol. III, pp. 350–6.

225 Franz Kurz, *Geschichte der Landwehre in Oesterreich ob der Enns*, Linz: Haslinger, 1811, pp. 227–8.

226 The curate's wonderful account is in *Krieg*, vol. III, pp. 711–7.

227 Pelet, vol. II, p. 207.

228 Jean François Antoine Marie Castillon, 'Mémorial Militaire', *Carnet de la Sabretache*, 1902, p. 342.

229 Ibid.

230 Pirquet, p. 84.

231 De Moreton de Chabrillan letter to Claparède, 11 June 1842, Saski, vol. III, pp. 134–5.

232 Radetzky in *Krieg*, vol. III, p. 375.

233 For a summary history of the Tirailleurs du Po and their commander, see www.histoire-empire.org/persos/morandini/morandini by Jean-Pierre Poiron.

234 Incredible as it seems, more than three days passed before the Austrians were aware of the French Emperor's presence on Habsburg terrain—a clear indication of the poor state of Austrian intelligence at this stage in the war.

235 Many sources erroneously state that Hiller's retreat was prompted by news of Lannes crossing at Wels. The Austrian official history carefully and convincingly dismantles this argument (*Krieg*, vol. III, pp. 397, 409).

236 Hiller had sixty-three battalions on hand on the evening of 2 May; one of these (II/*Klebek*) was destroyed on the morning of 3 May; two (Nordmann's *Warasdin-St Georg* Grenzer) were too distant to count at Ebelsberg. The following figures are my calculations based on *Krieg*, vol. III, p. 385 and Anhang XLII. Committed in/around Ebelsberg: *Wallach-Illyria* (2), 4th through 6th Vienna Volunteers (3), I and III/*J. Mittrowsky* (2), III/*Stuart* (1), *Beaulieu* (3), *Lindenau* (2). Available: *Deutschmeister* (3), *Kerpen* (2), II/*J. Mittrowsky* (1), 5th and 6th *EH Karl* Legion (2), *Duka* (3), *Gyulai* (3), 1st through 3rd Vienna Volunteers (3). Four third battalions were also on hand, but *Krieg* rates them as not combat-worthy: *Czartoryski*, *Würzburg*, *Württemberg*, *Chasteler*. It is not clear why the authors concluded that these were any less capable than several others (say, 5th and 6th Legion), but including them would give a total of twenty-one available battalions. Unavailable owing to exhaustion or disorder after the fighting west of the Traun: *Klebek* (2), *Jordis* (3), *Gradiska* (2), *Benjovszky* (3), *Splenyi* (3). Kienmayer's six battalions, six

Landwehr battalions, 3rd *EH Karl* Legion, and III/*Stain* were already in the rear (a total of fourteen battalions).

237 This discussion of Hiller's thinking draws heavily on *Krieg*, vol. III, pp. 382–6.
238 Zech/Porbeck, pp. 78–80.
239 Baden contingent's journal, entry for 3 May, GLA 48/4286.
240 Pouget, pp. 144–5.
241 Pelleport, p. 261.
242 Zech/Porbeck, p. 84.
243 *Krieg*, vol. III, pp. 387–8. Some French soldiers erroneously concluded that the Austrians had prepared a trap for the attackers and intentionally allowed the French to enter Ebelsberg in order to ensnare them by setting the town afire (François-Joseph Jacquin, *Carnet de Route d'un Grognard de la Révolution et de l'Empire*, Paris: Clavreuil, 1960, p. 69); others heard a rumour that the French themselves had started the blaze in revenge for being fired upon by the inhabitants (Louis Frèche, *Mémoire de mes Campagnes (1803–1809)*, Levallois: Centre d'Etudes Napoléoniennes, 1994, p. 119).
244 Wilhelm, p. 79. Some writers claim that Massena *ordered* the wounded and dead thrown off the bridge; Pelet objects strongly to this assertion (vol. II, pp. 222–3).
245 A fellow general approached Legrand to offer advice on the local area, but Legrand curtly dismissed him saying, 'I did not ask you for advice, just space for the head of my column!' (Lejeune, vol. I, p. 242; Pelet, vol. II, p. 211). The first two battalions of the 26th moved directly on the Schloss from the town, but III/26th split in half: the first three companies went left in an effort to get around the castle; the other three companies participated in the assault on the Enns gate and the exploitation beyond the town (Gueheneuc, 'Historique du 26e Léger').
246 Pouget, letter to Pelet in 1842, Saski, vol. III, p. 136.
247 Identification of III/18th Ligne is from Gachot, p. 131.
248 Pelleport, p. 262.
249 Legrand's report in Saski, vol. III, p. 136; Pouget claimed 500 prisoners (p. 147).
250 Ledru, letter dated 14 May 1809, Saski, vol. III, p. 141.
251 Ibid.
252 Schnierer, p. 14.
253 *Krieg*, vol. III, p. 405.
254 The battalions at Bruck were *Brzezinski* and *Puteany*; the battalion at St Florian was Kirchenbetter's. Adding up the elements of the *Knesevich* Dragoons, one and one-half squadrons remain unlocated; *Krieg* vol. III assumes that these were assigned to guard the trains and artillery parks.
255 My calculation based on 450 men in the two depot companies and approximately 180 in the two line companies (see *Krieg*, vol. III, Anhang XLII).
256 First quote from Lieutenant Boniface de Castellane, (*Journal du Maréchal de Castellane*, Paris: Plon, 1895, p. 52) who entered the town that evening. Second quote from Wilhelm, p. 80.
257 Meier, p. 40.
258 Charles A. Faré, letter dated 3 June 1809, *Lettres d'un Jeune Officier a sa Mère*, ed. H. Faré, Paris: Delagrave, 1889, p. 201.
259 Ledru, letter of 14 May 1809, Saski, vol. III, p. 142.

260 Lejeune, vol. I, p. 244. Lejeune and Savary (vol. IV, pp. 99–100) provide some of the most grisly depictions of the battle's aftermath: the veritable slough of charred, crushed human remains that constituted Ebelsberg's streets and the highway on the edge of town. Chevalier noted that the sight was enough 'to make the most intrepid tremble' (p. 97). Boulart, Gassicourt, Kergorre, Marbot, Paulin, and Stendahl are some of the others who proffer the modern reader terrifying glimpses into this horror.

261 Maurice de Tascher, *Journal de Campagne d'un Cousin de l'Imperatrice (1806–1813)*, Paris: Plon, 1933, p. 214.

262 Girault, p. 158.

263 Savary, vol. IV, p. 100. See also Chlapowski, p. 133.

264 Gustav Ritter Amon von Treuenfest, *Geschichte des Kaiserlich Königlich Infanterie-Regiments Hoch und Deutschmeister*, Vienna: 1879, p. 416; 'Die Geschichte des k. k. 49. Linien-Infanterie-Regiments Baron Kerpen in den Feldzügen von 1809, 1813, 1814 und 1815', *ÖMZ*, 1821, p. 11; Leopold Auspitz, *Das Infanterie-Regiment Freiherr von Hess Nr. 49*, Teschen: Prochaska, 1889, p. 23.

265 Binder (vol. II, pp. 122–6) and, after him, Petre (pp. 241–2): 'not worthy of the name of a general'.

266 Buat, vol. I, p. 115.

267 During the 1840s, an unseemly public quarrel erupted between Claparède and Ledru (Legrand was already dead) over who would have the credit for the capture of Ebelsberg (Pelleport, p. 261).

268 While Legrand famously rebuffed the general who attempted to advise him (see above), he complained to Colonel Berthezène of the 10th Léger about Claparède: 'When I crossed the bridge, I found that general sheltering with some troops behind the ruins of the houses and it was only with difficulty that I obtained some vague information' (Berthezène, p. 222).

269 Massena, 'Rapport de l'Affaire d'Ebersberg', 5 May 1809, Saski, vol. III, p. 138; and Pelet, vol. II, p. 451.

270 Savary, vol. IV, p. 97.

271 Napoleon to Lannes, 4 May 1809, Saski, vol. III, p. 146.

272 Buat, vol. I, pp. 116–22. See also Binder, vol. II, p. 126; Chandler, p. 695.

273 Lannes had detailed 9th Hussars to cover his left flank as he marched for Steyr. As so often during this war, Jacquinot's actions are unclear. *Krieg*, vol. III places his brigade under Durosnel, but Buat, vol. II has him riding north with Bessières. This account follows *Krieg* as the most likely.

274 Jacquin, p. 69.

275 Napoleon thus had no plan to trap Hiller between two fires at Ebelsberg. He did not think Hiller would retreat over the Traun in the first place. Given the unexpectedness of Hiller's withdrawal behind the Traun (instead of over the Danube) and French dispositions on the morning of 3 May, there was little likelihood of catching the Austrians in the flank while Massena attacked from the front. The absence of timely, detailed reporting from Massena, however, eliminated all possibility of a strike against Hiller's left in the position at Ebelsberg or during his retreat to the Enns.

276 Other troops were located as follows. Montbrun: collecting at Regen in preparation for rejoining 3rd Corps. Dupas and 4th Rheinbund en route to Passau. Rouyer at Straubing; II/5th Rheinbund in Regensburg. The 3rd Baden and Hessian Leib Regiment were billeted east of Braunau; GB Marion's march brigade and the Württemberg *Camrer* Infantry were in Braunau. Other Württemberg regiments: *Phull* in Passau; *Herzog Heinrich* with Imperial headquarters; *Neubronn* in Neumarkt an der Rott. The Portuguese Legion was still in Munich.

277 Nordmann had the *Warasdin-St Georg* Grenzer (1,000), two companies of *Brod* Grenzer (270), four squadrons of *Liechtenstein* Hussars (400), three guns, and a platoon of pioneers. The *Brod* Grenzer left to join Hiller's main force sometime between 3 and 5 May. *Krieg*, vol. III, pp. 429, 700.

278 *Krieg*, vol. III, pp. 436–9.

279 The detachment consisted of one Grenz company, four weak Landwehr companies, and a platoon of hussars.

280 *Krieg*, vol. III, p. 408; Kurz, p. 286.

281 The detachment, consisting of III/*Deutschmeister* and a division of *Liechtenstein* Hussars, rejoined the main body on the night of the 4th.

282 Charles to Hiller, 3 May 1809, *Krieg*, vol. III, p. 430; see also Charles to Albert, 4 May 1809, Wertheimer, vol. II, pp. 312–3.

283 Mesko, report of 5 May 1809; and Radetzky, report of 5 May 1809, *Krieg*, vol. III, pp. 458–9.

284 Paraphrased from *Krieg*, vol. III, pp. 458–9.

285 Berthier to Daru, 4 May 1809, 9 p.m., Saski, vol. III, p. 156.

286 Chevalier, p. 96.

287 Charles Louis Cadet de Gassicourt, *Voyage en Autriche, en Moravie et en Bavière fait a la suite de l'Armée Française pendant la Campagne de 1809*, Paris: L'Huillier, 1818, p. 63. Although it adds little to the history of 1809 in specific, one should also consult the fine new biography of Cadet de Gassicourt for the role of an army pharmacist in general and imperial court life in particular: Jean Flahaut, *Charles-Louis Cadet de Gassicourt: Bâtard Royal, Pharmacien de l'Empereur*, Paris: Teissedre, 2001 (pp. 211–23 for 1809).

288 Writing to his wife on 5 May, Coëhorn related that Napoleon 'asked me to accompany him over the field of battle yesterday [4 May]. He seemed most satisfied; he even said something most flattering: "This crossing is worthy of that of the bridge at Lodi."' That which gave me the most lively pleasure', he continued, 'was the spontaneous cheers of my entire brigade . . . soldiers and officers cried together: "Long live our general! Long live General Coëhorn!" with an enthusiasm so true that I could not repress a thrill that went to the bottom of my soul' (Méneval, pp. 188–9).

289 Pouget, pp. 150–3. Pouget's regiment was the first to be reviewed, and other colonels sent officers to observe the proceedings so that they might be prepared for the emperor's questions and mood.

290 See also Castillon, p. 342; Barsewisch, p. 72; 'Feldzug der zweiten Division', p. 622; Wilhelm, p. 80. Napoleon summarised the utility of reviews in a letter to Marmont, 12 March 1804, *Correspondance*, no. 7616.

291 Roos, pp. 248–9. See also Herre, pp. 14–15; and Peter, p. 15. The troops were deeply disturbed after passing through Ebelsberg, so the cavalry officers called forward all

of the trumpeters, musicians, and singers to perform. A series of well-known, often martial melodies helped raise the spirits of the men.

292 Unterleutnant Karl Christoph von Martens of *Kronprinz* Infantry in Paul Dorsch (ed.), *Kriegszüge der Württemberger im 19. Jahrhundert*, Calw: Vereinsbuchhandlung, 1913, pp. 45–6.

293 Vandamme to Napoleon, 10.30 a.m., 5 May 1809, Saski, vol. III, p. 167.

294 Vandamme to Friedrich, 6 May 1809, HStAS, E270aBü86. For details of the engagement, see *Krieg*, vol. IV, pp. 98–9, 181–5; Gill, *Eagles*, pp. 149–50; and Vandamme's two 5 May reports (10.30 a.m. and 4.30 p.m.) in Saski, vol. III, pp. 167–8.

295 Entry for 4 May 1809, François Duriau, *Carnet de Route*, extract from *Mémoires de la Société Dunkerquoise*, 1907, p. 61. There are several similar descriptions in the rich treasure of French memoirs; I selected this one because it is the only spot in Duriau's march journal for the year 1809 where he lavishes any description on the sights he saw—even Aspern and Wagram rate only passing mention.

296 Lannes to Napoleon, 5 May 1809, Saski, vol. III, pp. 162–3. The 9th Hussars rejoined Colbert during the day.

297 Relevant correspondence: Napoleon to Clarke, 4 May 1809; Berthier to Beaumont, 4 May 1809; and Napoleon to Berthier, 9 May 1809 (two letters); all in Saski, vol. III, pp. 159–61, 218–20.

298 Berthier to Lefebvre, and Berthier to Wrede, both 6 May 1809, 8 p.m., Saski, vol. III, pp. 175–6. Drouet to Wrede, 7 May 1809, evening, ibid., p. 196.

299 Two squadrons at Lambach, one each at Schwanenstadt and Gmunden, Wrede to Berthier, 8 May 1809, Saski, vol. III, p. 196.

300 Hiller to Minister of War Colloredo and Archduke Maximilian, 6 May 1809, 4 and 4.30 a.m. respectively, in *Krieg*, vol. III, p. 464.

301 My estimate based on 100 men per infantry company.

302 The combatants observed a brief cease-fire for approximately one hour sometime around 10 a.m. to allow a pair of Austrian envoys to interact with the French. The mission of this delegation is not clear: the Austrian official history offers several possible explanations ranging from a local effort by Radetzky to secure the release of the staff officer detained by the French at Lambach on 2 May to the re-delivery of Charles's 29 April letter to Napoleon (Charles, of course, having as yet heard nothing in reply from the French Emperor); the latter seems the most likely cause. See *Krieg*, vol. III, pp. 466–7.

303 The estimates of Austrian strength here and with Wilgenheim are mine based on the reduced strength of the Grenzer and uhlans. The *Karl* Uhlans at this point totalled only some 580 men, the Grenzer probably no more than 1,200 to 1,400 (that regiment had been reduced from twelve to ten companies). The Erzherzog Ferdinand Sharpshooters previously attached to Oberst Gratze's *Wallach-Illyria* Grenz Regiment had been shifted to the *Gradiska* Regiment as the regiment's eleventh company (40 men).

304 Denis Charles Parquin, *Napoleon's Army: The Military Memoirs of Charles Parquin*, London: Greenhill, 1987, p. 91.

305 French accounts often refer to this affair as 'Amstetten' as in G. Bertin, 'Combat d'Amstetten', *Carnet de la Sabretache*, 1901. This article describes a painting

purporting to show the achievements of General Lauriston's young son Auguste in single combat against an uhlan at Blindenmarkt, but the tale later proved much embroidered.

306 French losses are unknown, but were doubtless heavy, especially from 20th Chasseurs.

307 History of Saint Hilaire's division, Saski, vol. III, p. 172.

308 A rear guard of two *Klebek* battalions and two *Gradiska* companies had initially remained in Mautern under, as usual, Radetzky.

309 Collecting up stragglers and replacement detachments as it retired along the north bank, Hardegg's detachment had swollen to 1,534 men: 212 *Levenehr* Dragoons, 96 from *Jordis*, 220 from *Josef Mittrowsky*, 712 from *Lindenau*, 162 Jägers, and 132 stragglers from various infantry outfits (*Krieg*, vol. III, p. 503).

310 *Krieg*, vol. III, p. 505. The authors do not detail the losses ('sicher über 12,000 Streiter'), but their careful attention to such matters leads me to trust this estimate. Ebelsberg and Blindenmarkt alone had cost the army approximately 8,400 casualties. This figure does *not* include the enormous losses to desertion among the Landwehr as these units likely would have disintegrated in any case. Note that Charles had initially ordered Hiller to leave the '8,000 to 10,000 man detachment' south of the river in his 1 May 1809 letter (ibid., p. 430).

311 Most of the information on the defence of Vienna is drawn from *Krieg*, vol. III, pp. 506–51. See Andreas Graf Thürheim, *Geschichte des k. k. achten Uhlanen-Regimentes*, Vienna: Hof- und Staatsdruckerei, 1860, p. 102, for the movements of Provenchères's little command.

312 *Krieg*, vol. III, p. 528.

313 Wertheimer, 'Zur Geschichte Wiens', pp. 176–8.

314 Girault, p. 160.

315 Lejeune, vol. I, p. 250.

316 Colbert to Berthier, 8 May 1809, Saski, vol. III, p. 190.

317 *Krieg*, vol. III, p. 547. The Austrian rear guard consisted of the *Wallach-Illyria* Grenzer, the remnants of the *Brod* Grenzer (one consolidated company), and one and one-half squadrons of *Stipsicz* Hussars, all under command of the recovered Mesko. The bulk of these casualties, 108 officers and men captured, came from the *Wallach-Illyria* Regiment, a circumstance that does not speak well of the regiment's cohesiveness (especially when considered in combination with its dubious performance at Eferding and Ebelsberg).

318 Bruyère to Berthier, 8 May 1809, Saski, vol. III, p. 192.

319 Savary to Napoleon, 8 May 1809, 7.30 p.m., Saski, vol. III, pp. 190–2. The following day, Savary's command changed to: St Hilaire's combined voltigeur battalion, Württemberg Leib Chevaulegers, 150 troopers of the Württemberg *Herzog Heinrich* Chevaulegers from army headquarters, a squadron of 8th Hussars, and Espagne's horse battery. The detachment was disbanded on 10 May with the troops returning to their original commands; the Württemberg Leib Chevaulegers, however, apparently stayed along the Danube until approximately 13 May (Starklof, *vierten Reiterregiment*, p. 43). Bessières had been sent towards Mautern on 7 May with Piré's light regiments and Espagne's heavies supported by St Hilaire's voltigeurs. St Hilaire received orders to take his entire division to the Mautern crossing point

early on the morning of 9 May, but these instructions were rescinded shortly thereafter when it became clear that the Austrians had withdrawn across the river (Saski, vol. III, p. 198).

320 Napoleon to Davout, 9 May 1809, 6 p.m., Saski, vol. III, p. 211.

321 There is a tidy summary of these deployments in *Krieg*, vol. III, pp. 558–9.

322 Pelet, vol. II, p. 250.

323 There are several versions of the extent and cause of Tharreau's injury; this one is from *Krieg*, vol. III, p. 561.

324 A Baden grenadier captain named Heusch, quoted in *Krieg*, vol. III, p. 565.

325 O'Reilly's notes cited in *Krieg*, vol. III, p. 567.

326 See Appendix 5.

327 Saski, vol. III, pp. 223–4.

328 Schimmer, p. 87.

329 Maximilian's cursory note to O'Reilly and a message from 'Feldwäbl Wageritsch' reporting the destruction of the bridge are in Wertheimer, 'Zur Geschichte Wiens', p. 184.

330 Complete list is in *Krieg*, vol. III, pp. 747–8. The bulk of the prisoners came from three units: *Kerpen* (1,070), 6th Vienna (866), and *Deutschmeister* (742).

331 Karoline Pichler, 'Aus den Denkwürdigkeiten einer Wiener Schriftstellerin', in Kircheisen, *Feldzugserinnerungen*, p. 251.

CHAPTER 2: MARAUDERS, MILITIAS, AND MAJOR ACTIONS

1 Berthier to Davout, 12 May 1809, noon, Saski, vol. III, pp. 244–5.

2 Davout to Berthier, 14 May 1809, Mazade, vol. II, pp. 535–6.

3 Tascher, p. 216.

4 Davout to Berthier, 7 May 1809, Saski, vol. III, p. 185.

5 Order of the Day, 14 May 1809, *Correspondance*, no. 15205.

6 Buat, vol. I, pp. 152–3.

7 Napoleon to Davout, 5 May 1809, 8 a.m., and 7 May 1809, 10 a.m., Saski, vol. III, pp. 163–4, 182–3. Things began badly for Davout and Vandamme in Linz, the marshal feeling himself slighted when Vandamme did not report to him in proper military fashion, the general (unaware that Napoleon had placed him under Davout's orders) believing himself slighted when Davout gave his chief of staff a frosty reception. Vandamme wrote a stiff note to Davout offering an explanation but not much of an apology and immediately sent a long complaint to Napoleon about Davout's allegedly poor behaviour. Fortunately for French interests, the two quickly patched up their differences and worked well together for the remainder of the war. See Vandamme's correspondence to Davout and Napoleon on this contretemps in du Casse, *Vandamme*, pp. 283–6. See also John G. Gallaher, *Napoleon's Enfant Terrible: General Dominique Vandamme*, Norman: University of Oklahoma Press, 2008, pp. 191–4.

8 Strength from *Krieg*, vol. IV, Anhang X. Note that I/*Camrer* moved to Enns on 14 May (with one company each at Steyr and Kronstorf); its four companies were reunited at Enns by 16 May; and it would later (21 May) march off to join Imperial

Headquarters; in the meantime, of course, it was in the immediate vicinity of Linz and could have been called upon if needed. The only missing elements at this point (12 May) were the Leib Chevaulegers (near Mautern), the *Herzog Heinrich* Chevaulegers (with Imperial Headquarters), and II/*Camrer* (two companies each at Ried and Braunau).

9   Davout to Vandamme, 10 May 1809, Saski, vol. III, pp. 228–9. The two French companies departed to join their regiment on the road to Melk on 14 May; they were replaced by the Grenadier Company of I/*Camrer*, which was deploying to the Enns. One of the battalion's companies was placed at Kronstorf and the other two at Enns. Both of the detached *Camrer* companies returned to their battalion at Enns on by 16 May. See *Krieg*, vol. III, pp. 195, 218, 220. Note that Nübling's description (p. 100) seems incorrect.

10   The Hessian companies were from 1st Leib Fusilier Battalion as was the detachment at Melk Abbey. The Baden Light Dragoons supplied a detachment to Ybbs and the Württemberg Leib Chevaulegers one to Wallsee. See Gill, *Eagles*, pp. 227, 237. They remained in these locations until mid-June.

11   Castellane, p. 52.

12   These were the long-marching 3rd Baden Infantry and Hessian Leib Regiment; Davout placed them under the command of GB Gilly along with a battalion of 15th Léger. Four of Friant's companies (probably also 15th Léger) were conducting reconnaissance from Melk towards Mautern.

13   For Savary at Mautern, see *Krieg*, vol. III, pp. 573–5; and vol. IV, p. 145; the orders for Savary to force the bridge's destruction (9 May) and Savary's detailed reports of 9 and 10 May are in Saski, vol. III, pp. 200–1, 213, 224–5 (quote from his 10 May report, 224); Savary, vol. IV, pp. 102–3.

14   Montbrun to Davout, 12 May 1809, Saski, vol. III, p. 249. Later that day, Schustekh's 1st Moravian Volunteers gave evidence of their rawness when their outposts panicked and retreated upon the appearance of several civilian boats full of fleeing refugees (*Krieg*, vol. IV, p. 149). For these incidents on 10 and 12 May, see the original French reporting in Saski, vol. III and the Austrian accounts in *Krieg*, vol. II, pp. 274–5, and vol. IV, pp. 147–9.

15   Menninger, an officer with *Erzherzog Franz* Cuirassiers, had an ad hoc group comprised of 120 troopers from four regiments (his own as well as *Ferdinand* Hussars, *Klenau* Chevaulegers, and *Vincent* Chevaulegers), along with some 100 men from 7th and 8th Jäger Battalions (*Krieg*, vol. IV, pp. 150–1).

16   The first quote is from Napoleon to Davout, 15 May 1809, 10 a.m. This letter was sent after the fact, when Napoleon had learned of Ameil's ambush and near-capture. Even before the affair at Ebersdorf, however, Napoleon had sent a stiff note admonishing Davout and Vandamme for what he deemed a 'senseless' act (without actually naming Ameil). Berthier's pedantic note, clearly taken from dictation when the Emperor was in a foul humour, was sent the same day—that is, before headquarters knew of the miniature near-disaster (Napoleon to Davout, 13 May 1809, and Berthier to Davout, 13 May 1809, 10 a.m., Saski, vol. III, p. 267). The image of Berthier lecturing Davout on the art of war remains as ridiculous and insulting today as it appeared to Davout at the time: 'I cannot possibly stoop so

low as to tolerate such a style' (Davout to Napoleon, 15 May 1809, Mazade, vol. II, p. 539). See also, Buat, vol. I, pp. 192–3.

17 Ameil would become a général de brigade in late 1812 and would briefly hold the rank of général de division in July 1815.

18 For Ebersdorf and Emmersdorf, see *Krieg*, vol. III, pp. 150–7; as well as Davout's and Ameil's detailed reports of 12 and 13 May, in Saski, vol. III, pp. 276–80.

19 See Gill, *Eagles*, pp. 149–50.

20 The best outline of these deployments is Wachtel, pp. 170–2. Lippa, commander of the Styrian Landwehr, had been charged with the defence of the province's northern borders after the defeat in Bavaria. Kerpen, though nearing seventy years of age, was apparently quite energetic.

21 Bruyère's account as published in 'Notices Historiques et Topographiques sur les Marches et Combats des Troupes aux Ordres du Général Bruyère en 1809', *Carnet de la Sabretache*, vol. 198, 1909, p. 358. Bruyère places this combat on 14 May.

22 *Krieg*, vol. IV, pp. 624–6.

23 Berthier to Vandamme, 16 May 1809. 2 p.m., Saski, vol. III, p. 298. News of Duppelin's success and the engagement at Linz obviated Vandamme's proposed march south.

24 Bernhard Gottlieb Freiherr von Hingenau to Johann, 21 May 1809, in Hans von Zwiedineck-Südenhorst (ed.), 'Zur Geschichte des Krieges von 1809 in Steiermark', *Beiträge zur Kunde steiermärkischer Geschichtsquellen*, no. 23, 1891.

25 Davout to Napoleon, 18 May 1809, 7 p.m., Saski, vol. III, pp. 317–18. Duppelin and the 85th departed on 19 May, but Davout left GB Lacour with 13th Léger and 200 of Bruyère's men in garrisons from Mariazell to Lilienfeld as a precaution. For detailed descriptions of the fighting see French reports in Saski, vol. III, and *Krieg*, vol. III, pp. 617–24. Also useful are contemporary reports from local Habsburg officials published by Karl Altmann in *Blätter des Vereines für Landeskunde von Niederösterreich*, Wien, 1901: 'Die Franzosen in Türnitz 1809' and 'Die Franzosen in Annaberg 1805 und 1809'.

26 In a long letter to Archduke Johann on 9 May, Kaiserin Maria Ludovica wrote: 'while two victorious armies advance, one to the Adige the other as far as Danzig [sic!], the strongest retreats, exposes the capital and the Fatherland, without giving any reasonable cause other than this one: we have hands and feet, but neither head nor energy' (Hans von Zwiedineck-Südenhorst, *Erzherzog Johann von Oesterreich in Feldzuge von 1809*, Graz: Styria, 1892, pp. 20–4).

27 Charles to Albert, 1 May 1809, in Criste, *Carl*, vol. III, p. 480.

28 Charles to Franz, 3 May 1809, in *Krieg*, vol. IV, p. 734.

29 All quotations in this paragraph are from Charles to Franz, 3 May 1809, in *Krieg*, vol. IV, p. 734.

30 'Such an undertaking appeared too risky', Charles, 'Denkschrift', *Ausgewählte Schriften*, vol. VI, p. 340.

31 *Krieg*, vol. IV, pp. 84, 94, 108, 135.

32 Order of the Day, 3 May 1809, published in *Beiträge zur Geschichte des österreichischen Heerwesens*, Vienna: Seidel & Sohn, 1872, vol. I, pp. 219–20. See also Hiller to Franz, 29 April 1809, 7.30 a.m., vol. III, pp. 679–80.

33 Charles to Albert, 1 May 1809, in Criste, *Carl*, vol. III, p. 479. Three days later, Charles remarked that 'the notorious roads of this region . . . could not have been any worse in the times of Ziska [Jan Ziska, Hussite military leader, 1360–1424] than they are at present' (Charles to Albert, 4 May 1809, in ibid., vol. III, p. 481).

34 One of the two *Schwarzenberg* Uhlan squadrons that had been detached in Bohemia evidently rejoined its regiment during its passage through the province.

35 Rauchensteiner, *Franz und Carl*, pp. 100–2; *Krieg*, vol. IV, pp. 91–9.

36 The possibility of a French threat from the Passau area towards the Linz-Budweis road arose several times, largely owing to Ameil's tiny detachment (which was doubtless spreading exaggerated claims all about as it scouted the frontier area). See *Krieg*, vol. IV, p. 111.

37 Josef Veigl, 'Erinnerungen eines Veteranen aus dem Jahre 1809', *ÖMZ*, vol. II, 1860, p. 97.

38 Charles, 'Beitrag zur Geschichte', *Ausgewählte Schriften*, vol. VI, p. 347.

39 These replacements were destined for the following regiments (4,009 total): *Manfredini* (1,300), *Koburg* (762), *Kaiser* (763), *Kaunitz* (762), *Ludwig* (143), *Rohan* (130), *Bellegarde* (103), *Czartoryski* (40), *Reuss-Greitz* (6).

40 *Krieg*, vol. IV, pp. 112–13.

41 *Krieg*, vol. IV, pp. 105–6, 108, 119–20. See also Criste, *Carl*, vol. III, pp. 108–10. A sample of a daily march order from this period is printed in a footnote in *Krieg*, vol. IV, pp. 132–3.

42 Criste, *Liechtenstein*, p. 109 (including quotation).

43 Anonymous eyewitness quoted in Criste, *Carl*, vol. III, p. 110. Similar words appear in *Krieg*, vol. IV, p. 112 suggesting that the source was a remark from Oberleutnant Potier's diary in the army's operations journal.

44 Wimpffen was not only more competent and more original in his thinking, his promotion also meant, as Rauchensteiner notes, that he could no longer pull and push from behind the scenes but would himself bear the responsibility for the army's most important decisions (Rauchensteiner, *Franz und Carl*, p. 102).

45 Charles to Kolowrat, 9 May 1809, *Krieg*, vol. IV, p. 754; quoted in part on p. 122.

46 Having passed through Neu-Pölla (11th), Horn (12th), and Wetzdorf (13th), the Hauptarmee found itself south-west of Göllersdorf on 14 May.

47 For the Tulln planning, see *Krieg*, vol. IV, pp. 135–45.

48 The regulars were as follows. Under GM Am Ende: III/A. Mittrowsky, III/Erbach, one squadron of *Schwarzenberg* Uhlans, one company of 1st Jägers. Under Oberst Rosenhayn: III/Froon, two companies of II/Froon, two platoons of *Schwarzenberg*.

49 Charles to Kolowrat, 9 May 1809, *Krieg*, vol. IV, p. 754. The first indication that Kolowrat might have to perform a more offensive mission came in a letter from Charles dated 7 May (reached the II Corps commander the same day). *Krieg*, vol. IV, p. 201.

50 *Krieg*, vol. IV, p. 210.

51 For the Saxon army in 1809, see Gill, *Eagles*, ch. 6.

52 Schauroth, p. 12.

53 This biographic sketch is drawn from Gill, *Eagles*, pp. 256, 273. For more detail see: Sir Dunbar Plunket Barton, *Napoleon and Bernadotte 1763–1810*, London: John Murray, 1921; Sir Dunbar Plunket Barton, *The Amazing Career of Bernadotte*,

London: John Murray, 1929; Elting, *Swords*, pp. 126–8; T. A. Heathcote, 'Bernadotte', in David G. Chandler (ed.), *Napoleon's Marshals*, New York: Macmillan, 1987; Hans Klaeber, *Marschall Bernadotte Kronprinz von Schweden*, Gotha: Perthes, 1910; Alan Palmer, *Bernadotte*, London: John Murray, 1990; Léonce Pingaud, *Bernadotte et Napoléon*, Paris: Plon, 1933. For defences of Bernadotte see Friedrich Wencker-Wildberg, *Bernadotte: A Biography*, trans. Kenneth Kirkness, London: Jarrolds, 1936 (blaming Berthier); and Christian Desplat, 'Bernadotte—Soldat und Feldherr', in *Jean Baptiste Bernadotte: Bürger—Marschall—König*, catalogue of an exhibition at Schloss Mainau, Boras: Kulturreferat Schloss Mainau, 1998 (blaming Napoleon).

54 Carl Buhle, *Erinnerungen aus den Feldzügen von 1809 bis 1816*, Bautzen: Schlüssel, 1844, pp. 3–4. See also Moritz Exner, *Die Antheilnahme der Königlich Sächsischen Armee am Feldzuge gegen Oesterreich und die kriegerischen Ereignisse in Sachsen im Jahre 1809*, Dresden: Baensch, 1894, p. 15; Ferdinand von Funck, *In the Wake of Napoleon, Being the Memoirs (1807–1809) of Ferdinand von Funck, Lieutenant-General of the Saxon Army and Adjutant-General to the King of Saxony*, ed. Oakley Williams, London: Lane, 1931, p. 247; and André Bonnefons, *Un Allié de Napoléon, Frédéric-Auguste Premier Roi de Saxe et Grand-Duc de Varsovie*, Paris: Perrin, 1902, p. 297.

55 Gutschmid's advance guard force consisted of three hussar squadrons, the lone squadron of *Herzog Albrecht* Chevaulegers, and 200 infantrymen (the Schützen and others from Infantry Regiment *König*); the *Prinz Clemens* Chevaulegers joined the advance guard on 1 May. For a vivid description of Gutschmid, see Albrecht Graf von Holtzendorff, *Geschichte der königlich sächsischen Leichten Infanterie*, Leipzig: Giesecke & Devrient, 1860, p. 10.

56 Both patrols were carried out by Saxon Hussars: 5 May near Haid, 6 May near Klentsch (Moritz von Süssmilch, gen. Hörnig, *Geschichte des 2. Königl. Sächs. Husaren-Regiments*, Leipzig: Brockhaus, 1882, p. 64).

57 *Krieg*, vol. IV, p. 232; Gill, *Eagles*, p. 278.

58 Berthier to Bernadotte, 5 May 1809, Saski, vol. III, pp. 169–70.

59 The 9th Corps route of march took the Saxon main body through Weimar (23 April), Schleiz (28 April), Plauen (30 April), Hof (1 May), Weiden (4 May), Nabburg (5 May), and Rötz (6 May), towards Waldmünchen (7 May). The 1st Division and the advance guard crossed the Danube at Straubing (9 and 10 May respectively); the 2nd Division crossed at Regensburg (Gill, *Eagles*, p. 278).

60 Quoted in Georg von Schönberg, *Geschichte des Königl. Sächsischen 7. Infanterie-Regiments*, Leipzig: Brockhaus, 1890, p. 6.

61 Bernadotte to Napoleon, 15 May 1809, Saski, vol. III, p. 286.

62 A different version of this section appeared in Gill, *Eagles*, pp. 150–5, 282–6; in addition to the citations above, this revision has been supplemented by re-readings of *Krieg*, vol. IV, pp. 235–66; Bernadotte's report of 18 May in Saski, vol. III, pp. 316–20; Vandamme to Friedrich, 18 May 1809, HStAS, E270aBü86; and regimental histories.

63 One source questioned the durability of the bridge, claiming that it 'was so weak and swayed so much that most probably it would have collapsed under the press of a night time retreat', from 'Das Gefecht bei Linz am 17. Mai 1809', *Zeitschrift für Kunst, Wissenschaft und Geschichte des Krieges*, vol. IV, 1828 (this anonymous essay

clearly stems from the pen of an eye-witness, probably a Saxon or Württemberger officer).

64 This figure does not include I/*Camrer* in the Württemberg totals. Subtractions for the Austrians include Oberdorf's reserve and the Hellmonsödt detachment (4,550), Saint Julien (3,832), and the three companies (one-half battalion) sent towards Ottensheim and Rohrbach (my estimate at 300). See *Krieg*, vol. IV, pp. 236–7.

65 Paraphrase from *Krieg*, vol. IV, p. 242.

66 Two companies and one and one-half squadrons went towards Rohrbach; one company and one uhlan platoon towards Ottensheim.

67 Major Hugo von Kerchenawe, the author of this portion of *Krieg*, comments that this decision effectively abandoned the advance guard to overwhelming Württemberg attack (vol. IV, p. 247).

68 Leutnant Stadlinger of *Neubronn*, in Dorsch, p. 54.

69 Johann Jacob Otto August Rühle von Lilienstern, *Reise mit der Armee im Jahre 1809*, Rudolstadt: Hof- Buch- und Kunsthandlung, 1810, entry for 18 May 1809, p. 263.

70 Quote extracted from Neil Litten, 'The Battle of Linz 17th May 1809', p. 10.

71 'Gefecht bei Linz', p. 57.

72 Schönberg, vol. II, pp. 7–8.

73 'Die leichte württembergische Brigade Hügel in dem Gefechte bei Linz, im Jahre 1809', *Archiv für Offiziere aller Waffen*, vol. III, 1847. p. 94.

74 Theobald to Friedrich, 18 May 1809, HStAS, E270aBü83.

75 Approximately half of the Austrian losses (more than 365) came from Somariva's column, some 12 per cent of the force he dragged to the top of the Pöstlingberg.

76 Vandamme's order of the day, 18 May 1809, HStAS, E289aBü72; Nübling, p. 106 for Bernadotte.

77 *Krieg*, vol. IV, p. 266.

78 Stadlinger in Dorsch, p. 54. Rühle von Lilienstern observed 'The enemy was too lackadaisical in advancing and using the small advantages he won at the beginning' (p. 262).

79 This apparently was comprised of 6th Jägers, II/*Peterwardein*, four squadrons of hussars, and a few guns.

80 Somariva's force consisted of 5th Jägers, two companies of *W. Colloredo*, and a platoon of uhlans. Stettner had one company of *Neuffer* Jäger, fifty musketeers from *Herzog Wilhelm*, and fifty troopers each from the two mounted Jäger regiments. The Württembergers lost one man killed and a handful wounded; Austrian losses are unknown. *Krieg*, vol. IV, pp. 267–71; Gill, *Eagles*, p. 155.

81 This record of the events on 19 and 20 May is taken primarily from Saxon regimental and contingent histories as in Gill, *Eagles*, pp. 286–8 (Exner, pp. 32–3; *Geschichte des Königl. Sächs. Königs-Husaren-Regiments No. 18*, Leipzig: Baumert & Ronge, 1901, pp. 166–7; Schuster/Francke, pp. 274–5; *Schützen-Regiment*, p. 10; Süssmilch, pp. 66–9; and *Krieg*, vol. IV, p. 275). My assessment differs from the account in *Krieg* with regard to actions at Neumarkt in the early hours of 20 May: as portrayed in *Krieg*, the Austrians retreated undisturbed and abandoned Neumarkt to the Saxons; Saxon sources clearly relate a fight in front of the town.

82 Berthier to Bernadotte, 19 May 1809, 8 p.m., Saski, vol. III, p. 330.

83 Bernadotte to Berthier, 20 May 1809, and Bernadotte to Napoleon, 21 May 1809, Saski, vol. III, pp. 341, 347–8.

84 Curiously, he placed one brigade from each division on either side of the Danube: Boxberg and Lecoq on and below the Pöstlingberg, Hartitizsch and Zeschau in/around Linz. Gutschmid's advance guard contained the hussars, the *Prinz Clemens* Chevaulegers, the *Egidy* Schützen, and, after the 21st, the new 'light' battery. Gill, *Eagles*, p. 314.

85 Napoleon to Davout, 17 May 1809, 8 a.m., Saski, vol. III, p. 304.

86 Bernadotte to Vandamme, 19 May 1809, Du Casse, *Vandamme*, p. 301. Napoleon's evolving instructions for Vandamme are in Berthier's letters of 16 May, 2 p.m. and 19 May, 7 p.m., Saski, vol. III, pp. 298, 330–1. See also Napoleon's letter to Bernadotte, 15 May 1809, 11 a.m., ibid., p. 286.

87 Württemberg movements from 18 to 21 May are painfully tangled, but by the latter date, the corps was disposed as follows. Enns: corps headquarters, GM von Franquemont, *Herzog Wilhelm*, three companies of *Neuffer* Jäger, 1st Horse Battery. St Florian: GL von Neubronn with the *König* Jäger zu Pferd. Kremsmünster: GL von Wöllwarth, *Herzog Louis*, *Brüsselle* Light Infantry, half of the 2nd Horse Battery. Steyr (or en route): GM von Hügel, *Kronprinz*, *König* Jäger zu Fuss, *Wolff* Light Infantry, one company of *Neuffer* Jäger, 100 detached cavalry, and the other half of the 2nd Horse Battery; this force was charged with patrolling south and south-east into the mountains. Linz: GM von Scharffenstein, *Neubronn*, I/*Phull*, 200 foot Jägers, 50 troopers from the *König* Jäger zu Pferd, foot battery, and artillery park. Wallsee and Ybbs: II/*Phull*. In addition, the following were detached: I/*Camrer* (en route to Imperial Headquarters), II/*Camrer* (split between Ried and Braunau), Leib Chevaulegers (Vienna garrison), *Herzog Heinrich* (Vienna and line of communications). Recall that the 1st Fusilier Company of II/105th Ligne was still in Wels (Saski, vol. III, p. 265). See *Krieg*, vol. IV, p. 279 (which relied on HStAS, E289aBü97); and Gill *Eagles*, pp. 155–6.

88 *Krieg*, vol. IV, pp. 281–2. Schneller had III/*Froon*, III/*J. Colloredo*, and two squadrons of hussars; he was reinforced on 21 May with 5th Jägers, a battalion of *Peterwardein* Grenzer, and two squadrons of uhlans. Somariva's new command was comprised of 6th Jägers, a *Peterwardein* battalion, the *Würzburg* Infantry Regiment, a battalion of *Württemberg*, four Landwehr battalions, and four squadrons of *Merveldt* Uhlans. Kolowrat had hoped to have some support from Schustekh, but received a negative reply.

CHAPTER 3: ASPERN

1 Pelet, vol. II, p. 255. This succinct statement is actually part of the description of Chapter IX, summarising the contents discussed in detail on pp. 299–302.

2 Berthier to Songis, 11 May 1809, 11.30 p.m., Saski, vol. III, p. 236.

3 Buat, vol. I, p. 182.

4 Berthier to Massena, 13 May 1809, noon, Saski, vol. III, pp. 261–3.

5 Songis to Berthier, 13 May 1809, Saski, vol. III, pp. 260–1. For Napoleon's desire to have *two* bridges, see Berthier to Songis, 13 May 1809, ibid., p. 260; and Pelet, vol. III, p. 262.

6 Weissenwolff had *Kerpen* (1,736 effectives), *Deutschmeister* (1,353), and 4th and 5th Vienna Volunteers (674). From Alexander Kirchhammer, *Das Gefecht in der Schwarzen Lacken-Au am 13. Mai 1809*, Vienna: Seidel & Sohn, 1903 (extract from *Danzer's Armee-Zeitung*, vol. 22, 28 May 1903). Major Obergfell's Landwehr probably numbered between 500 and 600 men (estimate).

7 The specific companies of the 105th were the voltigeurs of 1st and 3rd Battalions, and the following from 2nd Battalion: Grenadiers, 2nd, 3rd, 4th Fusilier Companies. See St Hilaire to Berthier, 14 May 1809, Saski, vol. III, p. 265. Strengths are my estimate based on average company strengths on 1 May: 92 for 72nd Ligne and 104 for 105th Ligne.

8 Napoleon to Berthier, 15 May 1809, *Correspondance*, no. 15210. Key sources for this battle include: *Krieg*, vol. IV, pp. 289–317; Kirchhammer, *Das Gefecht in der Schwarzen Lacken-Au*; Pelet, vol. III, 258–64; Saski, vol. III, pp. 256–65 (including St Hilaire's detailed report and accounts by other French officers). See also: Auspitz, pp. 23–5; 'Episoden aus der Geschichte des k. k. 49. Infanterie-Regiments Baron Hess', *ÖMZ*, vol. VII, 1861; 'Geschichte des k. k. 49. Linien-Infanterie-Regiments Baron Kerpen', *ÖMZ*, vol. VII, 1821; note that these three Austrian histories use O'Brien's manuscript as their source and misidentify the French as Oudinot's men.

9 Pelet, vol. III, p. 261.

10 Napoleon to Bernadotte, 15 May 1809, Saski, vol. III, pp. 285–6.

11 Napoleon, 'Proclamation aux Hongrois', 15 May 1809, *Correspondance*, no. 15215. This interesting issue is beyond the scope of the current study, see as starting points: Ladislas Lanyi, 'Napoléon et les Hongrois', *Annales Historiques de la Révolution Française*, no. 141, October–December 1955; and Domokos Kosary, *Napoléon et la Hongrie*, Budapest: Akademiai Kiado, 1979, ch. IV.

12 This counts Piré, Jacquinot, and the Hessian light troops under Montbrun. Insurrection troops near Raab included two cavalry regiments (Pest, Eisenburg), two squadrons of Neograd Hussars, 2nd Eisenburg Infantry, and two companies of Komorn Infantry. South along the Raab were the Szala Hussars, the Veszprem Hussars (four squadrons), the Oedenburg Hussar Division, and three infantry contingents (1st Eisenburg, Szala, Stuhlweissenburg); the Sümegh Hussars joined this grouping on 24 May.

13 Major Anton Demuth, 'Journal des G. Q. M. Stabes über die Ereignisse der könig. hungrischen Insurrection', 1 May 1810, KAFA, *Operativen Akten*, Kart. 1388; Oberst Janos von Lipsky, 'Relation der Vorfallenheiten bei der königl. Ungarisch. Insurrection vom Angang Mai bis nach der Schlacht von Aspern 1809', 18 April 1810, KAFA, *Operativen Akten*, Kart. 1388; Kisfaludy manuscript.

14 The Primatial and Neutra Hussars with the Hauptarmee had come from Davidovich. He had eighteen infantry companies and eight squadrons available on 18 May. Hadik was at Eger (Erlau) with four battalions and most of his cavalry; GM Gabor Hertelendy had five companies of Abaujvar Infantry No. 19 and four and one-half squadrons of Zemplin Hussars at Dukla Pass for approximately 1,600 men (Ludwig

Freiherr von Welden, *Der Krieg von 1809 zwischen Oesterreich und Frankreich von Anfang Mai bis zum Friedensschlusse*, Vienna: Gerold, 1872, p. 10).

15 Napoleon to Berthier, 14 May 1809, Saski, vol. III, pp. 272–4.

Lauriston's force initially consisted of the 1st and 2nd Baden Infantry Regiments (minus the four companies of the latter guarding Massena's trains), the Jäger Battalion, the light half-battery, and 300 riders of Colbert's 20th Chasseurs. The rest of the 20th joined Lauriston several days later. The Baden 3rd Infantry, foot battery, and Light Dragoons remained with Massena.

16 Sources for these operations: *Krieg*, vol. III, pp. 515, 534, 624–32; Saski, vol. III, pp. 272–4, 282, 293–4, 316, 326; Zech/Porbeck, pp. 124–9.

17 Meier, p. 47.

18 Kerpen to Johann, 15 May 1809, in Zwiedineck-Südenhorst (ed.), 'Zur Geschichte des Krieges von 1809 in Steiermark'. A village chronicle recorded that the militia 'assembled with muskets, halberds, threshers, and every possible sort of deadly weapon', hardly the type of combatants to set against veteran regulars (Rudolf Reichel, 'Mittheilungen aus einem Gerichtsprotokolle des Marktes Deutsch-Feistritz', *Mittheilungen des historischen Vereines für Steiermark*, vol. XXXVIII, 1890).

19 *Krieg*, vol. IV, pp. 330–5, 369. Two squadrons of Neutra Insurrection Hussars were soon added to Hoffmeister's command, but these were posted upstream at Angern on the Marchfeld.

20 Reuss' promotion incited Hiller's indignation. 'It could only be painful for me that Fürst Reuss, who had up to then stood under my command, was promoted to FZM without any mention being made of me; but even this insult did not cool my zeal for duty' (Hiller, p. 182).

21 Kisfaludy manuscript.

22 Charles to Liechtenstein, 19 May 1809, *Krieg*, vol. IV, p. 365, as noted in Appendix 8. Note that the former *Erzherzog Johann* Infantry No. 35 was now *Argenteau*; and the vacant (*Gottesheim*) Cuirassiers No. 6 was now *Moritz Liechtenstein*. Commanders of several grenadier battalions also changed as noted in the appendices.

23 Pelet, II, p. 301, commenting on Napoleon's need to end the war quickly. See also Ségur, *Histoire et Mémoires*, vol. III, p. 341; Thiers, vol. X, p. 292. Key analysis is in Buat, vol. I, pp. 209–10.

24 Wimpffen, 'Denkschrift', 17 May 1809, published in *Krieg*, vol. IV, pp. 739–40.

25 Manfried Rauchensteiner, *Die Schlacht von Aspern am 21. und 22. Mai 1809*, Militärhistorische Schriftenreihe Heft 11, Vienna: Bundesverlag, 1986, p. 3.

26 Both quotes from Franz to Johann 15 May 1809, *Krieg*, vol. IV, p. 738. This was not the first reference to Johann carrying out a diversion through the Tyrol, Franz had mentioned a diversionary action as one of several options in an order Johann received on 5 May in Italy (Johann, *Feldzugserzählungen*, pp. 104–5); the 15 May order, however, was direct and definitive.

27 Ibid.

28 This discussion draws primarily on Criste, *Carl*, vol. III, pp. 116–19; *Krieg*, vol. IV, pp. 166–8, 170–4; Rauchensteiner, pp. 102–4. Note that *Krieg*, vol. IV also contains relevant memoranda by Liechtenstein and Bellegarde (pp. 741–5).

29 Johann, *Feldzugserzählungen*, p. 129. Johann sent a long explanatory note to Charles on 24 May from Graz (in Hans von Zwiedineck-Südenhorst, 'Das Gefecht bei

St Michael und die Operationen des Erzherzogs Johann in Steiermark 1809', *Mittheilungen des Instituts für österreichische Geschichtsforschung*, vol. I, pp. 40–3).

30 Bernadotte to Napoleon, 18 May 1809, Saski, vol. III, p. 320.

31 Capitaine Galbois to Berthier, 16 May 1809, 4.50 a.m. (first quote); Montbrun to Bessières, 16 May 1809 (second quote); both in Saski, vol. III, pp. 290–1.

32 Pelet, albeit in reference to forces as far away as Johann and the Insurrection, writes that 'The Emperor wanted to profit by the absence of these troops' (vol. III, pp. 270–1).

33 Charles lamented Napoleon's deployments after the war, 'Beitrag', *Ausgewählte Schriften*, vol. VI, p. 368. See also Buat, vol. I, pp. 215–18 for a fine analysis.

34 Berthier to Lefebvre, 17 May 1809, 9 a.m., Saski, vol. III, p. 308.

35 Berthier to Beaumont, 17 May 1809, 9 a.m., Saski, vol. III, p. 309.

36 Napoleon to Eugene, 10 May 1809, 5 a.m., Lecestre, vol. I, p. 309. Subsequent correspondence on 12 and 17 May did not change these basic guidelines.

37 Napoleon to Eugene, 17 May 1809, *Correspondance*, no. 15224.

38 Napoleon to Eugene, 17 May 1809, *Correspondance*, no. 15224; Berthier to Lefebvre, 17 May 1809, 9 a.m., Saski, vol. III, p. 308.

39 Savary, vol. IV, pp. 112–13.

40 Girault, p. 168.

41 Charles to Liechtenstein, 20 May 1809, 6 a.m., *Krieg*, vol. IV, p. 370, n. 2.

42 Röder was treated to a full display of his king's displeasure after the war. Found negligent by a court martial, he was punished with several months of imprisonment.

43 *Krieg*, vol. IV, pp. 372–4. In addition to 33rd Ligne, sent by Friant on his own initiative, Napoleon despatched GD Savary with a brigade of cuirassiers (probably one of St Sulpice's); by the time the cuirassiers arrived, the incident had already ended. The men from *Deutschmeister* were involved in this expedition because one battalion of the regiment was posted at Jedlersee in close support of Nordmann.

44 Girault, p. 168.

45 Berthier to Davout, 19 May 1809, 4 p.m., Saski, vol. III, p. 328.

46 Buat, vol. I, pp. 213–14.

47 Girault, p. 169.

48 That is 8th Hussars and Bruyère's two regiments. Note that Bruyère reported engaging in this combat with his brigade alone because Napoleon had held back Piré to allow Molitor to cross ('Notices Historiques', *Carnet*, 1909, p. 361).

49 For this engagement, see *Krieg*, vol. IV, pp. 380–8. I suspect that *Krieg* overstates the possible results of any reconnaissance Lasalle might have carried out during the night, but the French might have taken some knowledgeable prisoners.

50 Coëhorn, letter to his wife, 21 May 1809, Méneval, p. 192.

51 Molitor (6,150), Legrand (5,550), Boudet (5,180), Lasalle (2,100), and an unknown number of Guard troops. As *Krieg* (vol. IV, p. 376) points out, the movements of the Guard are difficult to decipher; this estimate is based on the Old Guard infantry and Fusiliers being present across the Danube with 150 cavalry as the emperor's escort.

52 For the 21st, Morand was to move to the following locations: Melk (30th Ligne), Mautern (61st Ligne), St Pölten (division headquarters and 17th Ligne), 13th Léger

(Lilienfeld). The Portuguese Legion was in St Pölten with instructions to march to Vienna. Pajol was to leave one squadron of 5th Hussars at Mautern and another at Tulln. With the remaining troops (including 7th Léger) he was to assemble at Tulln on the 21st (*Krieg*, vol. IV, p. 362).

53 Although there are numerous primary and secondary accounts of the Battle of Aspern (or Aspern-Essling), original sources are vague or silent on many critical points. This problem in sourcing is compounded by the confused nature of the fighting, leaving the historian to cope with many gaps and contradictions. By far the most comprehensive study is the one in the fourth volume of *Krieg 1809*, and my narrative relies heavily on the thorough research and analysis carried out by this admirable team of Austrian authors (*Krieg*, vol. IV, pp. 397–728).

54 C. von Decker, 'Besuch der Insel Lobau und der Schlachtfelder von Aspern (Eslingen) und Wagram im Sommer 1835', *Zeitschrift für Kunst, Wissenschaft und Geschichte des Krieges*, vol. VII, 1836, pp. 154–5. The description of the battlefield is taken from this detailed and near-contemporary article by an experienced military professional. The author, Carl von Decker (1784–1844), was a Prussian officer who had seen action against the French in 1806–7, 1809 (with Brunswick), 1813–14, and 1815. The description in *Krieg*, vol. IV, follows Decker closely. A. von P., 'Die Lobau im Jahre 1809', ÖMZ, vol. III, 1893, is unsatisfactory as far as Aspern is concerned.

55 This is certainly Decker's opinion (p. 167).

56 The comparison of Aspern-Essling to a fortress appears in many accounts, one of the earliest is *Abriss von der Schlacht bei Esling und Gross-Aspern am 21. und 22. May 1809*, Weimar: Geographisches Institut, 1810.

57 Lejeune, vol. I, p. 266.

58 Pelet, vol. III, p. 278.

59 Wilhelm, p. 85.

60 Pelet, vol. III, p. 284; and Koch, vol. VI, pp. 232–3. Lejeune is ambiguous (vol. I, p. 266), but Wilhelm (p. 85) very clearly states that Massena rejected his suggestion that the bulk of the Austrian Army was nearby. See also Buat, vol. I, pp. 242–3; *Krieg*, vol. IV, pp. 392–3.

61 Pelet, vol. III, p. 284; and *Krieg*, vol. IV, p. 400.

62 The order of the day is printed in full in *Krieg*, vol. IV, p. 396. Petre says of it: 'The order is a palpable imitation of Napoleon, but somehow it seems to miss the electric fire, the touch of personal appeal which characterised the heart-stirring words of the Emperor, and the thrilling Trafalgar signal of Nelson' (p. 272).

63 *Krieg*, vol. IV, pp. 401–2.

64 The disposition is printed in *Krieg*, vol. IV, Anhang XXI with the corrections made at the time of issue. The initial draft left Bellegarde, Hohenlohe, and Rosenberg with little or no cavalry; their vigorous protests earned them the squadrons shown in the appendix. The title of the disposition may be rendered as 'Disposition for the attack on the portion of the enemy army between Gross-Aspern and Essling that has crossed over and is in the process of marching on Hirschstetten'.

65 This scene, including the quote from the Baden eyewitness, is from *Krieg*, vol. IV, p. 414.

66 *Krieg*, vol. IV, p. 421; quote from the 23 May 1809 report of Oberstleutnant Beroldingen to King Friedrich.

67 This count includes: Massena's three divisions (16,880), the Old Guard and Guard Fusiliers (5,428), light cavalry under Lasalle and Marulaz (3,225), Espagne's division (2,579), two squadrons of Guard Chevaulegers, two squadrons of Guard Chasseurs, and *Herzog Heinrich* (937).

68 Decker, p. 154.

69 Lejeune, vol. I, p. 271. *Quos ego* refers to a threat of punishment for disobedience from Virgil's portrayal of the wrathful Neptune in *The Aeneid*, Book I.

70 Rauchensteiner, *Aspern*, p. 9.

71 Brandner, pp. 55–6.

72 Lejeune, vol. I, p. 268.

73 Quote from the Reserve Corps' account in *Krieg*, vol. IV, p. 446.

74 Rauchensteiner questions the quality of the Austrian cavalry's training in *Aspern*, p. 9.

75 *Krieg*, vol. IV, p. 450. Criste's biography of Liechtenstein glides over this phase of the battle. For some reason, Lederer's brigade did not intervene in the combat.

76 Pelet, vol. III, p. 301.

77 Hiller, p. 184.

78 Castellane, p. 54.

79 Note that only half of the Baden regiment participated in this charge. The regiment had split in two during the withdrawal through Aspern earlier in the afternoon and the other portion was south-east of the village when Marulaz launched his attack. See *Eagles*, p. 196. I have deducted several hundred from the French side for losses earlier in the day.

80 Captain von Schlotheim (ed.), *Die Schlacht bey Gross-Aspern am 21ten und 22ten Mai 1809, von einem Augenzeugen*, Gotha, 1809, p. 9.

81 August Menge, *Die Schlacht von Aspern am 21. und 22. Mai 1809*, Berlin: Stilke, 1900, pp. 47–8.

82 *Krieg*, vol. IV, p. 455.

83 Quotes from *Krieg*, vol. IV, pp. 472–3. The troops at the wooden house were I/*Klebek*, I/*Jordis*, and 2nd Jägers.

84 Höppler's recollections in Josef Mühlhauser, *Museum Aspern 1809*, catalogue, Vienna: Dassler, n.d.

85 The Austrian infantry attacking from the north included II/*Kolowrat* and three companies of II/*Argenteau*; two companies of III/*Argenteau* provided supporting musket fire until they were called forward to support Bellegarde's batteries north-east of Aspern.

86 Brandner, p. 62. Similarly, the French sent individual companies into the town in dispersed order to engage the enemy (Boyeldieu, p. 495).

87 Hiller only committed his Grenzer (686 men) and four companies of *Gyulai* (perhaps 500 to 600) in this area. The two Vienna Volunteer battalions were deployed along the Danube on 21 May.

88 The available Austrian cavalry was *Klenau* Chevaulegers, *Vincent* Chevaulegers, *Albert* Cuirassiers, and two squadrons of *Kronprinz* Cuirassiers. The *Albert* Cuirassiers would soon contribute to the repulse of Marulaz's advance north of Essling. The Habsburg infantry in support of the two batteries: III/*Kolowrat*, III/*Argenteau*, and three companies of II/*Argenteau*.

89 The reserves were the *Blankenstein* Hussars (six squadrons) and the *Riesch* Dragoons, supplemented by the *Albert* Cuirassiers and the other two squadrons of *Blankenstein*; this made a force of more than 2,000 horsemen. The Austrian first line also numbered approximately 2,000: *Knesevich* Dragoons with *Kaiser, Liechtenstein,* and *Franz* Cuirassiers. This contrasts with Marulaz who could hardly have had more than 1,200 to 1,400 effectives.

90 A recent study places 3rd Léger in the Long Garden as well: Gilles Boué, *Essling: Napoleon's First Defeat?*, Paris: Histoire & Collections, 2008, p. 46.

91 Lederer only had ten squadrons; for unknown reasons, two squadrons of *Kronprinz* remained with the Cavalry Reserve (*Krieg*, vol. IV, p. 457).

92 This figure includes Boudet (5,180), Lasalle (2,240), Lagrange's cuirassier brigade (1,110), and the *Herzog Heinrich* Chevaulegers (160) who had joined Piré behind Essling. Given losses to Lasalle and Boudet, the number was almost certainly smaller.

93 Quoted in *Krieg*, vol. IV, p. 490.

94 Ibid.

95 Marbot, vol. I, pp. 337–8; *Krieg*, vol. IV, pp. 491–5.

96 Hauptmann Waida, 'Geschichte des 21. Linien-Infanterieregiments Prinz Victor Rohan (dermalen Albert Giulay) im Feldzug 1809', *ÖMZ*, vol. IX, 1819. The French cavalry apparently turned on this wandering battalion after Espagne's death near the end of the action (L. Picard, *La Cavalerie dans les Guerres de la Révolution et de l'Empire*, Paris: Teissedre, 2000, vol. II, p. 34).

97 Grueber, p. 75.

98 Savary, vol. IV, p. 118; Thiers, vol. X, pp. 314–15.

99 Lejeune, vol. I, p. 275.

100 The admiring authors of *Krieg* use the word 'übermenschlich' for the French engineers several times, for example, vol. IV, p. 377.

101 Strength calculations follow. Davout: 7,100 for Friant from 8,620 (minus three battalions), and 4,780 for Gudin from 9,702 (minus 7th Léger, 85th Ligne and one battalion of 25th Ligne). Nansouty: 1,136 for the carabinier brigade, 587 for 9th Cuirassiers, circa 250 for 2nd Cuirassiers. Colbert: approximately 680 for 9th Hussars and 510 for 7th Chasseurs. Guard cavalry: Dragoons (219), Grenadiers (254). The 7th Léger (2,442), 17th Ligne (2,048), and 85th Ligne (2,009) were to march to Vienna on 22 May as was the Portuguese Legion (1,471 infantry, 133 cavalry), and most of Montbrun's command (740 light cavalry, 970 Hessian infantry); these forces, however, would not have reached the bridges until after dark on the 22nd. The remaining troops of 3rd Corps (Gudin and Pajol) guarded the Danube from Nussdorf to Melk.

102 The disposition is printed in *Krieg*, vol. IV, p. 772.

103 *Krieg*, vol. IV, pp. 502–6, 514–16; Rauchensteiner, *Aspern*, p. 15.

104 Girault felt himself fortunate to discover some goose hearts and livers that he turned into a hasty, but hardly adequate, repast (pp. 169–70).

105 Veigl, p. 97.

106 *Krieg*, vol. IV, p. 503.

107 Wacquant's brigade (six battalions) plus *A. Mittrowsky* (two), *I/Argenteau*, half of *II/Argenteau*, 7th Jägers, 8th Jägers (the two Jäger battalions from II Corps); all under FML Ulm.

108 *EH Karl* had remained with the cavalry during 21 May; it returned to IV Corps during the night and took up a position between the 4th and 5th Columns (Stanka, pp. 437–8).

109 Pelet and Ségur state that St Hilaire contributed troops to the fighting around Essling early in the morning and *Krieg 1809* follows their analysis. This is logical, but Castillon, commander of IV/76th Ligne, in his detailed memoirs, clearly states that he fought in Essling (pp. 342–4). Although Castillon errs in associating Tharreau's entire division with the defence of Essling, it seems likely that his battalion, and perhaps his demi-brigade or brigade, were engaged there from the early morning hours.

110 My numerical calculation here rather gives the benefit of the doubt to Rosenberg. There were some 13,000 Austrians in the 5th Column and 900 cuirassiers with Lederer. Counting all of Boudet with Lasalle, Lagrange, and the two Guard brigades (who did not fire a shot), but not including any of St Hilaire's men, we get a total of some 13,000 French as well.

111 Savary, vol. IV, p. 119; Chlapowski, p. 153.

112 Pelet, vol. III, p. 313. Pelet is also the source of the misleading intelligence about Landwehr in the Austrian centre; the prisoners, brought in that morning by probing French cavalry, probably belonged to the 2nd *Karl* Legion of II Corps.

113 Lannes to Rogniat, cited in *Krieg*, vol. IV, p. 535.

114 The exact composition of the attacking cavalry elements is not clear. Specifically, there are almost no clues concerning the actions of Lagrange's and Bruyère's brigades; that is, whether they stayed near Essling or participated in the attacks in the centre. The latter seems more likely, but readers should note the paucity of information on this aspect of the battle, as on so many others.

115 Liechtenstein's operations journal quoted in *Krieg*, vol. IV, p. 540, n. 1; this is very similar to remarks in a letter by Liechtenstein's adjutant, Oberstleutnant Alois Freiherr Gollner von Goldnenfels, Criste, *Liechtenstein*, p. 119.

116 *Krieg*, vol. IV, p. 538.

117 Hiller, p. 185.

118 Rogniat's recollections quoted in Alexander Kirchhammer, 'Aspern', *Beilage des Fremden-Blatt*, no. 148, 31 May 1902.

119 Both quotes from Jacques Jouan, 'Souvenirs du Général Jouan', *Miscellanea Napoleonica*, Serie III-IV, 1898, pp. 546, 551. Jouan commanded IV/96th Ligne. Similarly, Savary regretted the absence of the old veterans of the Boulogne Camp who could 'ploy and deploy boldly under fire without fear of disorder' (Savary, vol. IV, pp. 121-2); Pelet, points out that the attack's failure did not result from 'the vice of deploying in columns' rather from the loss of the bridges (vol. III, p. 321).

120 Vladimir Ivanovich Baron Löwenstern, *Mémoires*, Paris: Fontemoing, 1903, vol. I, p. 114.

121 Eduard van der Nüll and Anton Dominik Fernkorn.

122 Lieutenant Aubier, *Un Régiment de Cavalerie Légère,* Paris: Berger-Levrault, 1888, pp. 182-3. It is difficult to say when Colbert crossed, his own account says 1 p.m., but the severe damage to the bridges during the morning suggests that he followed immediately after Demont.

123 The battalions were *Brzezinski, Puteany, Scovaud, Scharlach* (*Krieg*, vol. IV, p. 555).
In the cover letter to his account of the battle, d'Aspre regretted the 'punishable
disorder' into which these battalions had fallen (published in Alexander
Kirchhammer, 'Zur offiziellen "Relazion" über die Schlacht von Aspern 1809',
Beilage des Fremden-Blatt, no. 273, 4 October 1902). 'Only the presence of the
archduke brought his [d'Aspre's] grenadiers to a halt' (Schlotheim, p. 14). For
Boudet, Pelet, vol. III, p. 328.

124 Boué (pp. 56-7) places this action on St Hilaire's right against cuirassiers, but the
division history locates it on the left (Saski, vol. III, p. 351) and *Krieg* (vol. IV, p.
557) states that the cavalry was *O'Reilly* Chevaulegers. This work follows Saski and
Krieg.

125 Marbot, vol. I, p. 343; and Berthezène, p. 236.

126 Some accounts place the withdrawal order around 9 a.m., I have followed here
the conclusions in *Krieg 1809* (vol. IV, pp. 550–3), which seem more logical and
factually based.

127 Mühlhauser, *Museum Aspern*.

128 Ledru, letter to his sister, 27 May 1809, p. 69.

129 Quotes from Wilhelm, p. 86 (first), and Pelet, vol. III, p. 322 (second). See also
Boulart, pp. 215–16.

130 Pelet, vol. III, p. 323.

131 Pelet, vol. III, p. 324.

132 The maximum number of guns was 190, but it is not clear how many were still
functioning and actually participated in this fearful barrage: I Corps (sixty-eight),
II Corps (sixty-two), Grenadiers (twenty-four), Cavalry Reserve (eighteen), VI
Corps (eighteen). From *Krieg*, vol. IV, p. 590.

133 Boulart, p. 217.

134 Coignet, pp. 176–8.

135 Württemberg Oberst Hügel to King Friedrich, 23 May 1809, *Krieg*, vol. IV, p. 602.

136 Dedovich: two battalions of *Koburg*, III/*Ludwig*, with the Grenzer as skirmishers
in advance and 2nd Moravian in reserve.

137 Rohan: *Chasteler*, the first two battalions of *Bellegarde* and I/*Hiller*. Hohenlohe:
Sztaray along with the other two battalions of *Hiller*.

138 From Dedovich: *Ludwig, Koburg*, and *Czartoryski* in regimental columns in the first
line, *Reuss-Greitz* behind and 2nd Moravian in reserve. Riese: *Chasteler* and the first
two battalions of *Bellegarde* with I/*Hiller* in the second line.

139 Jean Rapp, *Memoirs of General Count Rapp*, London: Colburn, 1823; Ken Trotman
reprint, Cambridge, 1985, pp. 137–8; Laurent Goergler, *Georges Mouton Comte de
Lobau*, Drulingen: Scheuer, 1998, pp. 52–3.

140 Chlapowski, p. 161.

141 Fusilier Faiseau-Sauloy to his family, 8 August 1809, in Alain Pigeard, *Les
Campagnes Napoléoniennes*, Entremont-le-Vieux: Quator, 1998, vol. II, p. 433;
François Roguet, *Mémoires Militaires*, Paris: Dumaine, 1865, p. 49.

142 Many Austrians criticised Rosenberg for his performance on 22 May. Liechtenstein's
operations journal was especially severe, referring to the retreat as 'completely
without cause' (*Krieg*, vol. IV, p. 619). The Württemberg regiment's report is in
E270aBü93, dated 26 May 1809.

143 *Krieg*, vol. IV, pp. 620–2, 626–7. GB Dorsenne urged Napoleon to advance after the Austrians, but the emperor rejected this rash advice.

144 Hiller, p. 186.

145 Lejeune, vol. I, p. 291.

146 Chevalier, p. 108.

147 Quote from Chevalier, p. 106. The scene is assembled from Marbot (who helped carry Lannes), vol. I, pp. 345–7; Dumas, vol. II, p. 194; Castellane, p. 55; Paul Triare, *Dominique Larrey*, Tours: Mame, 1902, pp. 474–8; Robert G. Richardson, *Larrey: Surgeon to Napoleon's Imperial Guard*, London: John Murray, 1974, pp. 136–9; Zins, pp. 267–8. The timing of Lannes's injury is given variously as before or after the 'council of war' that Napoleon held late in the evening; in this account I have taken the timing as outlined in *Krieg*, vol. IV, pp. 633–34, 651–2; and Dumas: that Lannes was wounded before the generals' conclave.

148 Chevalier, p. 107. 'We gave them a knock on the head with our swords and sent them back to their regiments', wrote the outraged Szymanowski, p. 38.

149 Dumas, vol. II, p. 193; Castellane, p. 56.

150 Weiss (*Vogelsang*) was commanding in place of the wounded Wacquant. Weiss was promoted to GM, but Vogelsang was pensioned off immediately after the battle (*Krieg*, vol. IV, pp. 637–8).

151 Hiller took *EH Rainer* and (apparently) *Reuss-Plauen* on this attack. The II Corps battalions were I/*Zach*, III/*Zedtwitz*, and one of *J. Colloredo* (*Krieg*, vol. IV, pp. 638–42).

152 Ségur, *Histoire et Mémoires*, vol. III, 358.

153 Cited in *Krieg*, vol. IV, p. 650.

154 'Persuade' is from Ségur, vol. III, pp. 355–6. Thiers (vol. X, pp. 335–40) offers a detailed account of this conclave, that the authors of *Krieg* (vol. IV, p. 654) closely followed. See also Pelet, vol. III, pp. 330–3; and Savary, vol. IV, pp. 128–9.

155 Pelet, vol. III, p. 332 (translation taken in part from Harold T. Parker, *Three Napoleonic Battles*, Durham: Duke University Press, 1983, pp. 74–5).

156 A contemporary observed: 'Everywhere therefore at the end of the second day of battle: defensive measures, passive behaviour … They were satisfied that the enemy withdrew' ([Rühle von Lilienstern], 'Gedanken über die beiden Schacht auf dem Marchfelde bei Wien', *Minerva*, vol. XI, 1809).

157 Berthier to Daru, 1 a.m., 23 May 1809, Saski, vol. III, p. 357; Savary, vol. IV, pp. 130–1. The food delivery included 750 sheep to be shipped across the Danube, a challenging prospect to be sure.

158 The notion that Napoleon slept for thirty-six hours after the battle is a myth as explicated in detail in *Krieg*, vol. IV, p. 659.

159 Dumas, vol. II, p. 195. Massena made a point of leaving nothing behind that was at all accessible (Pelet, vol. III, p. 340; Castellane, p. 56; Paulin, p. 190).

160 Timing of the retreat is unclear; a good summary is in *Krieg*, vol. IV, pp. 661–2. Pelleport, p. 275; Castellane, p. 56.

161 This paragraph is drawn from *Krieg*, vol. IV, pp. 645–50. The quote is from a marginal note Lindenau penned about the operations journal (p. 646).

162 'Bemerkungen über den gegenwärtigen Feldzug', *Minerva*, June 1809.

163 Brandner, pp. 84–5.

164 Casualties for both sides are taken from the detailed analysis in *Krieg*, vol. IV, pp. 689–705.

165 Blücher to his friend Bonin, 6 June 1809, G. Blasendorf, 'Fünfzig Briefe Blücher's', *Historische Zeitschrift*, vol. 54, 1885, p. 210; and Rössler, *Oesterreichs Kampf*, vol. II, p. 22.

166 Karl August Varnhagen von Ense, *Denkwürdigkeiten des eigenen Lebens*, Leipzig: Brockhaus, 1843, vol. II, p. 82. It is hardly surprising that Napoleon attempted to disguise the repulse any more than it is to be expected that Austria and its sympathisers would not promote extravagant accounts of triumph.

167 Davout to his wife, 23 May 1809, Adélaïde-Louise d'Eckmühl, Marquise de Blocqueville *Le Maréchal Davout*, Paris: Didier, 1879, pp. 349–50.

168 Girault, pp. 174–80; Löwenstern, pp. 115–16; Scheltens, p. 93.

169 Delmarche, p. 22.

170 Coignet, p. 181; Larrey provides a number of harrowing technical analyses in *Mémoires de Chirugie Militaire et Campagnes de D. J. Larrey*, Paris: Smith, 1812, vol. III, pp. 280–314.

171 Löwenstern, pp. 115–16; *Krieg*, vol. IV, p. 726.

172 Girault, p. 180.

173 Charles to Albert, 24 May 1809, Wertheimer, vol. II, p. 325.

174 Parker, p. 83.

175 Much is often made of the supposedly low quality of some of the French infantry at Aspern. Although it is true that Oudinot's two divisions could not manoeuvre and deploy like Davout's and St Hilaire's veterans, their skill was not a major factor in the outcome. More tactically able troops likely would perhaps have suffered fewer losses, but Napoleon simply needed more men—with guns and ammunition—to change the course of the fight.

176 Observing the broken bridges on 22 May, Bertrand told Dumas 'See on what the success of the best combinations depends?' (Dumas, vol. II, p. 191).

177 Pelet, vol. III, p. 339. As to the view among the troops, Pelleport wrote of 21 May: 'The soldiers understood perfectly this horrible position and were not discouraged: Napoleon was with them' (p. 267).

178 Buat, vol. I, pp. 280–6; Chandler, p. 707; Petre, p. 298. Thiers (vol. X, p. 345) also criticises Napoleon's decision to cross hastily; he further objects to Napoleon's 'true fault, his eternal fault, which was this politics without limits'.

179 It is not amiss to imagine how commentators would have exhausted themselves in praising Napoleon's boldness had the gamble paid off.

180 Chandler (p. 707) observes, 'in 1809 he could still learn from his mistakes.' Chandler's point remains valid even if one takes a more charitable view of Napoleon's decision to risk the crossing that led to Aspern.

181 In addition to those in the notes above, other sources include: Carl Bleibtreu, *Aspern und Wagram in neuer Beleuchtung*, Vienna, Seidel & Sohn, 1902; Johann Baptist Schels, 'Die Schlacht bei Aspern am 21. und 22. Mai 1809', *ÖMZ*, 1843; Ferdi Irmfried Wöber, *1809: Schlacht bei Aspern und Essling*, Vienna, 1992; Gustav Smekal, *Die Schlacht bei Asparn und Esslingen*, Vienna: Seidel & Sohn, 1899; Ad. Strobl, *Aspern und Wagram*, Vienna: Seidel & Sohn, 1897; Anton Pfalz, *Die Marchfeldschlachten von Aspern und Deutsch-Wagram im Jahre 1809*, Korneuburg:

Kühkopf, 1900; Dr. Zelle, 'Welche Truppentheile Napoleon's fochten bei Aspern', *Allegemeine Militär-Zeitung*, no. 47, 23 November 1901; Kirchhammer's publication of unit battle reports in *Beilage des Fremden-Blatt* in 1902 is especially useful.

182 *Krieg*, vol. IV, p. 727.

CHAPTER 4: OVER THE ALPS

1 See Chapter 2 of this work and discussion in *Krieg*, vol. II, pp. 3–17.

2 Based on Johann's assessment, *Krieg* (vol. II, p. 13) gives most of the Landwehr battalions a fairly good rating. Zehetbauer, however, lists a host of deficiencies similar to the rest of this institution (pp. 241, 243–4). All agree that the Adelsberg and Neustadtl units were the worst, see Johann, *Feldzugserzählungen*, pp. 45, 51, 56. Note that Johann actually said all eight Adelsberg and Neustadtl battalions were unready and thus deducted 8,000 men from his strength calculations. In fact, however, he used the 1st Adelsberg, whatever its quality, from the beginning of the war as shown in the order of battle, thus leaving only 6,880 considered utterly unfit at first.

3 Note that these figures differ considerably from those in *Krieg*, vol. II, pp. 9, 438–40. See order of battle appendix for explanation. Not listed here are some 3,000 in line regiment depot divisions, a lone reserve (depot) squadron, approximately 2,200 Grenz-Kordon troops, and the Landwehr depot companies.

4 D. Fedotoff White, 'The Russian Navy in Trieste', *American Slavic and East European Review*, vol. VI, 18–19 December 1947. The squadron consisted of four ships of the line (80, 80, 74, 66), two 44-gun frigates, and a corvette of 24. Another Russian refugee squadron was in Venice under the aptly named Lieutenant Commander Salti: one frigate (32), three corvettes (28, 24, 18), a cutter (20), and three (possibly four) 16-gun brigs. Many of these ships were in poor condition, potentially unseaworthy. For a comprehensive list of Russian vessels, see Robert Goetz, 'Russian Naval Forces in the Mediterranean: 1805–1809' at www.napoleonseries.org. The local Austrian commander, FML Zach, had orders to seize the Russian ships at Trieste if they appeared to break neutrality or if they were about to fall into French hands (Just, *Politik oder Strategie?*, p. 21).

5 Johann, *Feldzugserzählungen*, pp. 31–9.

6 Jacques Chevillet, letter of 5 April 1809, *Ma Vie Militaire*, Paris: Hachette, 1906, p. 145; also Jean-Claude Barat, 'Les Mémoires du Commandant J.-C. Barat', *Revue du Nivernais*, vol. XIII, 1908–9.

7 Eugene to Napoleon, 8 March 1809, du Casse, *Eugène*, vol. IV, pp. 365–6.

8 Napoleon to Eugene, 29 March 1809, *Correspondance*, no. 14971. Convinced that the Austrians would not attack before mid-May, Napoleon thought he had adequate time to create a new command structure in Italy.

9 The viceroy did, however, place two divisions near the Tyrol under Baraguey d'Hilliers as one of his first acts (Eugene to Napoleon, 10 April 1809, du Casse, *Eugène*, vol. IV, pp. 441–2).

10 Eugene to Napoleon, 19 February 1809, du Casse, *Eugène*, vol. IV, pp. 346–7. For Italian troops, see Frederick C. Schneid, *Soldiers of Napoleon's Kingdom of Italy*,

Boulder: Westview, 1995, pp. 28–9, 36; and his *Napoleon's Italian Campaigns*, Westport: Praeger, 2002, pp. 60–1.

11 Eugene to Napoleon, 24 January 1809, du Casse, *Eugène*, vol. IV, p. 323.

12 Guillaume de Vaudoncourt, *Histoire Politique et Militaire du Prince Eugène Napoléon*, Paris: Mongie, 1828, vol. I, p. 136.

13 Napoleon to Eugene, 16 March 1809, *Correspondance*, nos. 14908 and 14909.

14 Napoleon to Eugene, 14 March 1809, *Correspondance*, no. 14900. For a post-First World War assessment from one of Eugene's detractors, see Gellio Cassi, 'Napoléon et la Défense de l'Italie sur la Piave', *Revue des Etudes Napoléoniennes*, XIX, July–December 1922.

15 Eugene to Napoleon, 24 March 1809, du Casse, *Eugène*, vol. IV, pp. 405–6.

16 Five 'reserve regiments' (four French and one Italian) were also supposed to be created, but it seems unlikely that these ever came into existence (Napoleon to Eugene, 17 March 1809, *Correspondance*, no. 14917).

17 Eugene to Auguste, 10 April 1809, du Casse, *Eugène*, vol. IV, p. 442.

18 Johann, *Feldzugserzählungen*, p. 59 (editor's note). Zuccheri's name is sometimes spelled 'Zuccari'.

19 The Tyrolian experience in 1809 has spawned a large literature. Josef Hirn's opus remains the classic treatment: *Tirol's Erhebung im Jahre 1809*, Innsbruck: Haymon, 1983 (reprint of 1909 edition). F. Gunther Eyck provides a good introduction for English language readers with *Loyal Rebels*, Lanham: University Press of America, 1986. See Gill, *Eagles*, ch. 7 for an overview.

20 Attempting to detail the numbers of insurgents at any point is a nearly hopeless exercise, but reasonable estimates can be offered in some cases; a good rule of thumb seems to be approximately 100–200 men per company. Readers should recognise, however, that the numbers fluctuated from day to day as men came and went almost continually.

21 The Passeiertal, the valley of the River Passer, runs from Meran north-north-east to St Leonhard and then north-west to the Timmelsjoch (a pass leading into the Oetztal).

22 Hans Magenschab, *Andreas Hofer: Zwischen Napoleon und Kaiser Franz*, Graz: Styria, 1984, pp. 193–5.

23 Journal of Chasteler's command quoted in Max Gruber, *Bruneck und das westliche Pustertal im Jahre 1809*, Innsbruck: Wagner, 1952, p. 21.

24 Napoleon to Eugene, 22 March 1809, du Casse, *Eugène*, vol. IV, p. 398.

25 Napoleon to Berthier, 10 April 1809, *Correspondance*, no. 15044.

26 The bridge was near a small town called St Lorenzen (not shown on map) four kilometres west of Bruneck.

27 The similarity with General von Wrede's name has misled many historians. Wreden died in 1812 of wounds received at the First Battle of Polotzk.

28 They would thus approach Pieve di Cadore from different directions.

29 Taxis: two (possibly three) companies of III/*de Vaux*, four companies of 2nd Inner Austrian Volunteers (Salzburger Jäger), one company of 2nd Salzburg Landwehr, a company of Tyrolian Schützen, and one platoon of O'Reilly Chevaulegers. Taxis marched from Salzburg via Berchtesgaden, Zell am See, and Mittersill, then through the Zillertal to the Inn valley and on to Innsbruck.

30 Reissenfels had four companies of III/*de Vaux*.
31 For an overview of the capture of the Tyrol, see Gill, *Eagles*, pp. 326–38.
32 Johann, *Feldzugserzählungen*, pp. 60–61; also Hormayr, *Innerösterreich*, p. 54.
33 One battalion (I/*Franz Karl*), led by Hauptmann Josef Lenardini of the General Staff, marched via the Raccolana valley to join Volkmann just north of Villanova. Additionally, a small detachment (unidentified) made its way south through the Aupa valley to Moggio.
34 Description from Jean-Louis Lacorde, a sergeant in 84th Ligne, *Lieutenant Lacorde: Journal Historique*, Paris: Clavreuil, 1992, p. 72.
35 'Journal de marche et d'opérations du Général Dessaix', AG, *Manuscrits*, MR 743.
36 'Journal historique de la Division Broussier, pendant le Campagne de 1809', AG, *Armée d'Italie—Correspondance*, C4/10.
37 *Krieg*, vol. II, p. 52.
38 *Krieg*, vol. II, p. 53.
39 Johann, *Feldzugserzählungen*, p. 66.
40 Severoli left IV/7th Line (646 men) behind to garrison Este; and Lamarque, when he finally marched, would do so without 112th Ligne. Baraguey d'Hilliers arrived in Verona on 13 April from Venice where he had been serving as governor.
41 The Landwehr were 1st Triest (three companies), 2nd Triest (eight companies), 2nd Adelsberg, and 2nd Görz. The 3rd Adelsberg joined Tomassich on 16 April. One of the *Frimont* squadrons had only three platoons as one was detached in Istria.
42 Gyurkovics: II/*Franz Karl*, three companies of *Ottocac* Grenzer, two squadrons of *Frimont* Hussars, and half a cavalry battery. The complex dispersion of *Franz Karl* is taken from *Geschichte des k. und k. 52. Linien-Infanterie-Regiments*, Wien: Hof- und Staatsdruckerei, 1871, pp. 240–5; see also Wilhelm Bichmann, *Chronik des k. k. Infanterie-Regiments Nr. 62*, Vienna: Mayer, 1880, pp. 76–8.
43 Frimont: III/*Franz Karl*, I/*Franz Jellacic*, *1st Banal* (ten companies—one was with Zuccheri, one with Volkmann), II/*2nd Banal*, two squadrons of *Hohenzollern* Chevaulegers, six squadrons of *Ott* Hussars, a cavalry battery, and half a brigade battery (*Krieg*, vol. II, pp. 56, 66).
44 Eugene to Napoleon, 14 April 1809, du Casse, *Eugène*, vol. V, pp. 134–6. Epstein highlights Eugene's concerns about his Tyrolian flank in his study of the Viceroy's operations, Epstein, *Prince Eugene*, pp. 53, 67.
45 Barbou had only twelve of his fifteen battalions: IV/11th Ligne with Grenier and two battalions of 79th Ligne at Santissima (*Krieg*, vol. II, Pordenone map; Vaudoncourt, vol. I, p. 152).
46 Chevillet, letter of 14 April 1809, p. 152.
47 Sahuc was to return 35th Ligne to Seras and avoid any serious engagement during his reconnaissance; if attacked, he was to retire to a position between Vigonovo and Fontanafredda (Vaudoncourt, vol. I, pp. 152–3).
48 Johann Baptist Schels, 'Der Feldzug 1809 in Italien', ÖMZ, 1844, p. 242.
49 Left column (GM Wetzl) on the road through Torre: I/*1st Banal* (four companies), I/*Franz Jellacic*. Centre column (Oberstleutnant Gabriel Freiherr Collenbach) between Torre and the highway: III/*Franz Karl*, two squadrons *Ott* Hussars. Right column (GM Josef Freiherr von Schmidt) on the highway: II/*1st Banal*,

two squadrons *Hohenzollern* Chevaulegers. Reserve on highway: four squadrons *Ott* Hussars, one cavalry battery, one-half brigade battery. Note that II/*2nd Banal*, previously under Frimont (11–14 April), was evidently left with VIII Corps and did not participate in the engagement.

50 Three companies of *J. Jellacic* marched along the foothills on Volkmann's right. A *Frimont* squadron (only three platoons) from Palmanova was to join Gyurkovics, whereupon he was to return one of his squadrons to the main army (*Krieg*, vol. II, pp. 71–2).

51 *Krieg*, vol. II, p. 75.

52 Consensus among the historians cited here puts one battalion just west of Pordenone, but it is possible that it was in Rorai Grande (*Krieg*, vol. II, p. 77).

53 Chevillet, letter of 15 April 1809, p. 156.

54 *Krieg*, vol. II, pp. 85–6; Franz Joseph Adolf Schneidawind, *Das Leben des Erzherzogs Johann von Oesterreich*, Schaffhausen: Hurter, 1849, p. 121. Another version of this story states that Breissand lost his sword in the fighting and that Johann promised to hand over his own blade if the colonel's could not be located (G. Rondol and V. Jannesson, *Historique du 35e Régiment d'Infanterie de Ligne*, AG, 1893).

55 'Rapport Historique de la Division Pacthod', AG, C4/10.

56 Casualty figures from *Krieg*, vol. II, p. 86, confirmed by French records ('Situation de l'Armée d'Italie', 6 May 1809, AN, AF*/IV/1377, *Livrets des armées: Situations des troupes en Italie*; and 'Armée d'Italie: Etat Général des Pertes Eprouvées, AG, C2/93). Comparing French returns before and after the battle: 8th Chasseurs lost some 30 men, 6th Hussars as many as 300 (on *both* 15 and 16 April), and 35th Ligne more than 2,050. Note that Austrian sources claim the capture of all four of Sahuc's guns. Vaudoncourt admits the loss of only two (vol. I, p. 157). I have listed two owing to the statement of Capitaine Jean Nicolas Auguste Noël who took command of Sahuc's battery on 23 April and mentioned that two guns (only) had been lost at Pordenone (*Souvenirs Militaries d'Un Officier du Premier Empire*, Paris: Berger-Levrault, 1895, p. 59). Noël's insightful memoirs have been reprinted by Greenhill as *With Napoleon's Guns*, edited by Rosemary Brindle, London, 2005.

57 Margon, *Historique du 8e Régiment de Chasseurs*, Verdun: Renvé-Lallemant, 1889, pp. 117–20; C. Voisin, *Historique du 6me Hussards*, Libourne: Maleville, 1888, p. 66.

58 Key sources for Pordenone include: *Krieg*, vol. II, pp. 70–88; du Casse, *Eugène*, vol. V, pp. 12–17; Chevillet, pp. 147–59; R. Duplessis, *Combat de Pordenone 15 Avril 1809: Une Page de l'Histoire du 35me Régiment d'Infanterie*, Belfort: Devillers, 1907; [Oskar Criste], 'Die Offensiv-Operationen des Erzherzogs Johann in Italien im Jahre 1809', *Organ der militär-wissenschaftlichen Vereine*, 1898; Schels, 'Feldzug 1809 in Italien'; Vaudoncourt, vol. I, pp. 151–7; Alois Veltzé, 'Aus den Tagen von Pordenone und Sacile', *Mitteilungen des K. und K. Kriegsarchivs*, 1904 (often clearer than the official history); Martin Vignolle, 'Historique de la Campagne de 1809 (Armée d'Italie)', *Revue Militaire*, 16, July 1900; regimental histories as noted.

59 *Krieg*, vol. II, pp. 89–91.

60 Eugene to Napoleon, 17 April 1809, du Casse, *Eugène*, vol. V, p. 137.

61 *Krieg*, vol. II, pp. 90–2. According to Teste, Eugene rejected Grenier's suggestion that the army slip away during the night, but it is important to bear Teste's disdain

for Eugene in mind while reading his account ('Souvenirs du Général Baron Teste', *Carnet de la Sabretache*, 1911, pp. 594–5).

62 Eugene to Napoleon, 17 and 23 April 1809, du Casse, *Eugène*, vol. V, pp. 137, 145–6. Eugene never did report the Pordenone disaster in writing. On his thinking, see *Krieg*, vol. II, pp. 92–5; Epstein, pp. 55–6; Schneid, *Napoleon's Italian Campaigns*, pp. 72–3.

63 Frimont deployed his men as follows: two Grenz companies in Palse, two in Talponedo, one in Porcia, one with Wetzl, III/*Franz Karl* behind Spinazzedo, the rest of the infantry (I/*F. Jellacic*, four Grenz companies) and two *Ott* squadrons north-west of Porica; Wetzl at Rorai Grande; and Splenyi at Rorai Piccolo (Veltzé, 'Pordenone und Sacile', p. 171). Veltzé indicates that the companies in Palse were from III/*Franz Karl*; they may have been Grenzer ('Taktische Betrachtungen über die Schlacht bei Sacile am 16. April 1809', *ÖMZ*, vol. II, 1861, p. 345). For some reason, the two *Hohenzollern* squadrons that had been with Volkmann were shifted to Frimont while two squadrons of *Josef* Hussars were assigned to Volkmann (*Krieg*, vol. II, p. 71).

64 The *Ott* Hussars and *Hohenzollern* Chevaulegers had been under GM von Wetzl's command, but Frimont placed him in charge of Porcia as the French advance began; Fulda, colonel of the *Ott* Hussars, thus took command of the brigade.

65 Léon-Michel Routier, *Récits d'un Soldat de la République et de l'Empire*, Paris: Editions du Grenadier, 2001, p. 77.

66 Bartier had two guns. The two battalions of 79th Ligne remained at Santissima with two guns.

67 The Austrian figure includes both Frimont and Splenyi.

68 As one Austrian commentator notes, it is difficult to imagine how such a small Austrian force overthrew Severoli's division. One must assume that the terrain led to crowding, confusion, and uncertainty among the troops, so that once the lead elements began to fall back, the rest dissolved in disorder ('Taktische Betrachtungen', p. 345).

69 This regiment (nine companies) arrived sometime after 1 p.m. in response to a request Albert Gyulai sent to his brother.

70 Routier, pp. 78–9.

71 Johann, *Feldzugserzählungen*, p. 78.

72 II/*J. Jellacic* attacked Ronche, II/*2nd Banal* Villadolt.

73 'Rapport Historique de la Division Pacthod'; and 'Rapport-Journal des Marches de la Division de M. le Gal Pacthod pendant la Campagne de 1809', both AG, C4/10.

74 Criste, 'Die Offensiv-Operationen', p. 207.

75 Given the chaos in Sacile, some of Broussier's men made their way down the Livenza to Brugnera.

76 *Krieg*, vol. II, p. 122.

77 J. L. Henckens, *Mémoires*, La Haye: Nijhoff, 1910, p. 63; Pierre Robinaux, *Journal de Route du Capitaine Robinaux*, Paris: Plon-Nourrit, 1908, pp. 70–1.

78 Barat, p. 26.

79 Lacorde, p. 74.

80 French losses from Vaudoncourt, vol. I, p. 173. The Austrian official history calculated that the figures were likely 4,000 and 6,000 respectively, but Eugene's strength report

for 6 May (which includes an incomplete report of losses for the 15th and 16th), coincides fairly well with Vaudoncourt as does a general comparison of individual regimental strengths between the 15 April and 6 May reports. Some Austrian sources claim the capture of nineteen guns (rather than fifteen) and an eagle; the latter claim seems incorrect (Regnault, p. 120).

81 Vaudoncourt, vol. I, p. 173.

82 Eugene to Napoleon, 17 April 1809, du Casse, *Eugène*, vol. V, pp. 137–8.

83 'Notes et Documents Provenant des Archives du Général de Division d'Anthouard' *Carnet de la Sabretache*, 1906, p. 304. GB Charles d'Anthouard was Eugene's senior aide-de-camp.

84 'Taktische Betrachtungen', p. 352. Quote from Routier, p. 79.

85 'Souvenirs du Général Baron Teste', *Carnet de la Sabretache*, 1911, p. 598.

86 Vaudoncourt, vol. I, p. 174.

87 *Krieg*, vol. II, pp. 134–9.

88 Key sources for Sacile include du Casse, *Eugène*, vol. V, pp. 18–30; Criste, 'Die Offensiv-Operationen', pp. 201–12; *Krieg*, vol. II, pp. 89–139; Schels, 'Feldzug 1809 in Italien'; 'Taktische Betrachtungen'; Vaudoncourt, vol. I, pp. 161–75; Veltzé, 'Aus den Tagen', pp. 171–99; Vignolle; Felice Turotti, *Storia dell'Armi Italiane dal 1796 al 1814*, Milan: Boniotti, 1856; and Alessandro Zanoli, *Sulla Milizia Cisalpino-Italiana cenni Storico-Statistici dal 1796 al 1814*, Milan, 1845, vol. II, pp. 84–5. Writers such as Pelet, Petre, and Thiers are scathingly critical of Eugene in this campaign; see Epstein, *Prince Eugene*, and Schneid, *Napoleon's Italian Campaigns*, for much more balanced appraisals.

89 Barat quotes, p. 27. Note that it is not clear when the rains resumed, sources vary from the night of the 16th to late on the 17th.

90 Routier, p. 80.

91 Zuccheri left a detailed account of skirmishing with a fairly significant French force, but there is no mention in the French references (*Krieg*, vol. II, pp. 149–52).

92 Barbou's force included: 5th, 23rd, 60th, 81st Ligne (two battalions each); 7th Italian Line (three battalions, including the one that had been in Este); the Dalmatian Regiment (two battalions); and the chasseurs (minus 100 men left with Bonfanti). Two weak battalions (IV/3rd Italian Light and III/Dalmatian) were already in Venice with three depots and a city garrison battalion.

93 One of these, IV/2nd Line, seems to have been detached to Fontanelli in the Tyrol for a few days, returning on 27 April.

94 *Krieg*, vol. II, pp. 164–6; S. Bouchard, *Historique du 28e Régiment de Dragons*, Paris: Berger-Levrault, 1893, pp. 109–11; Schneidawind, *Eugen*, p. 138.

95 Eugene left the two battalions of 18th Léger to garrison Legnago and most of the component parts of Durutte's division were still several days' march from their assembly point at Isola della Scala.

96 Frimont: *Ogulin* Grenz Regiment, two squadrons of *Hohenzollern* Chevaulegers, nine platoons of *Frimont* Hussars, one and one-half cavalry batteries, and the *Ottocac* Grenz Regiment in reserve half-way to Sacile.

97 The identity of the French with whom Zuccheri skirmished is not clear; *Krieg* (vol. II, pp. 149–52) speculates that it was the two battalions of 79th Ligne making a roundabout retreat after Sacile.

98 Zuccheri's reports quoted in *Krieg*, vol. II, p. 151.

99 For Austrian operations after Sacile, see *Krieg*, vol. II, pp. 144–70.

100 Austrian losses are not known, but were clearly more numerous than the stated twenty, if not perhaps as high as the 600 claimed by the French (*Krieg*, vol. II, p. 159).

101 Johann, *Feldzugserzählungen*, p. 82.

102 Mackesy, p. 319; William James, *The Naval History of Great Britain*, London: Bentley & Son, 1878, vol. V, pp. 27–9. Ships involved in the 23 April attack were *Spartan* (38), *Amphion* (32) under Captain William Hoste, and *Mercury* (28); the other ships in the upper Adriatic at the time were *Thames* (32) and *Redwing* (18).

103 Splenyi had two squadrons of *Josef* Hussars, a *Frimont* squadron, a battalion of *Ogulin* Grenzer, and a half-battery of cavalry guns; Rittmeister Nagy commanded the *Ott* squadron (*Krieg*, vol. II, pp. 171, 174).

104 This was three companies of II/*Ottocac* Grenzer, a wing of *Frimont* Hussars, and, until 29 or 30 April, a squadron of *Savoy* Dragoons (*Krieg*, vol. II, pp. 162, 164, 208).

105 Johann, *Feldzugserzählungen*, p. 91.

106 As noted above, IV/2nd Italian Line was apparently attached to Fontanelli for a few days, perhaps 25–27 April.

107 Vial to Charpentier, 14 April 1809, *Correspondance du Général Vial*, AG, C4/80.

108 The 1st Villach and 2nd Bruck went to the Piave valley; 2nd and 3rd Klagenfurt were marching for the central Tyrol with the two Judenburg battalions ('Tirol im Jahre 1809', *ÖMZ*, 1833).

109 Not only had d'Hilliers's group been sparring with insurgents for several days (17–19 April), he feared being outflanked through the Val Sugana (Vaudoncourt, vol. I, pp. 198–9).

110 GM Fenner with two Jäger companies, a cavalry platoon, and 400–500 Tyrolians under Hofer made for Torbole on Lake Garda, while Leiningen took his battalion, another cavalry platoon and two guns down the west bank of the Adige; neither force (some 1,350 regulars plus the rebels) played a role in the fighting.

111 Sous-Lieutenant Louis Armand Hazon de Saint-Fermin quoted in Eugène Cruyplants, *Histoire Illustrée d'un Corps Belge au Service de la République et de l'Empire: La 112e Demi-Brigade*, Brussels: Spineux, 1902, p. 133.

112 Vaudoncourt, vol. I, pp. 200–4. Austrian sources do not mention this fighting on the west bank, probably because regular troops were not much involved.

113 The history of the 112th provides the best detail of Volano from the French perspective; 'Tirol im Jahre 1809', *ÖMZ*, 1833 is exhaustive from the Austrian side.

114 The war in the southern Tyrol receives spotty and often narrow coverage. 'Tirol im Jahre 1809', *ÖMZ*, 1833–4 is the best military chronicle with enormous detail on the Austrian side; Schemfil provides a good summarisation; also helpful is Conrad Nüschler, 'Rückblick auf die kriegerischen Ereignisse in Tirol im Jahre 1809' *Organ der militär-wissenschaftlichen Vereine*, 1879; Kasimir Freiherr von Lütgendorf, *Die Kämpfe in Südtirol*, Wien: Seidel & Sohn, 1911 is somewhat disappointing. Vignolle's 'Historique de la Campagne du Tyrol en 1809' and 'Campagne d'Italie' are key for Franco-Italian actions. Other French sources include: Gabriel A. Robinet de Clery *En Tyrol*, Paris: Olldendorff, 1897; Lieutenant Morel, *Insurrection au Tyrol*

en 1809, AG, *Manuscrits*, MR 736; and Victor B. Derrécagaix, *Nos Campagnes au Tyrol*, Paris: Chapelot, 1910.

115 The term is Clausewitz's (see Clausewitz, pp. 566–73); see also *Krieg*, vol. II, p. 197.

116 Zach had replaced Tomassich.

117 Eugene to Napoleon, 27 April 1809, and to his wife, same date, 5 p.m., du Casse, *Eugène*, vol. V, pp. 154–5.

118 Etienne Jacques MacDonald, *Recollections of Marshal MacDonald*, London: Bentley & Son, 1892, Worley reprint, 1987, pp. 295–307.

119 Vaudoncourt, vol. I, pp. 187–8; Vignolle, 'Italie'. Additionally, IV/24th Dragoons was assigned to army headquarters on 1 May.

120 Vaudoncourt, vol. I, p. 207; Vignolle, 'Italie'. The authors of *Krieg* (vol. II, pp. 188–9) assert that the 'reconnaissance in force' interpretation was a subsequent invention of French historians attempting to disguise the weaknesses of Eugene's attack plan, but Eugene specifically describes it as a 'reconnaissance' in a 1 May letter to Napoleon (Du Casse, *Eugène*, vol. V, p. 161).

121 Austrian observation, *Krieg*, vol. II, p. 189. Eugene had detached two squadrons of 23rd Dragoons south along the Adige on learning that GM Splenyi had appeared on the east bank near Arcole with a battalion of *Ogulin*, a squadron of *Frimont*, and two squadrons of *Josef* Hussars. The other two squadrons of 23rd Dragoons joined their fellows during the day. The two battalions of 18th Léger garrisoned Legnago and the scattered elements of Durutte's division were still approaching Isola della Scala. Also absent from the French order of battle were 52nd Ligne and the Italian Guard cavalry; these were posted about half-way between Caldiero and Verona.

122 Johann, 'Gedrängtes Journale zur Uebersicht der Ereignisse bei der Armee unter höchsten Befehlen Sr. kaiserlichen Hoheit des Erzherzogs Johann in dem Feldzug vom Jahre 1809', Alois Veltzé, ed., *Mitteilungen des K. und K. Kriegsarchivs*, vol. V, 1907, p. 285.

123 *Krieg*, vol. II, p. 197.

124 Ibid., p. 198.

125 *Simbschen* and one battalion of *Reisky*. It is not clear which battalion Fellner detached towards Pasquaro.

126 Both quotes from Vignolle, 'Italie'.

127 *Geschichte des K. K. 53. Infanterie-Regimentes*, Tulln, 1881, p. 172.

128 *Krieg*, vol. II, p. 205.

129 Ibid.

130 Ibid., p. 207.

CHAPTER 5: FROM THE ADIGE TO THE DANUBE

1 Franz to Johann, 24 April 1809, *Krieg*, vol. II, pp. 462–3.

2 Frimont's force on 2 May (after GM Splenyi had ridden in from near Arcole) included: *Josef* Hussars, five squadrons of *Frimont*, *Ogulin* Grenzer, *Allvintzi* Infantry, I/1st *Banal*, one and one-half cavalry batteries. The *Hohenzollern* Chevaulegers had been with Frimont on 1 May, but were detached to GM Schmidt on the 2nd.

3   Eugene to Napoleon, 1 May 1809, du Casse, *Eugène*, vol. V, p. 161. The advance guard consisted of one battalion each of 52nd and 93rd Ligne, a combined voltigeur battalion (one company each of 9th, 13th, 29th, 84th, 106th, 112th), a sapper company, II/6th Chasseurs, III/8th Chasseurs, 30th Dragoons, and four guns (Charpentier to MacDonald, 1 May 1809, Vignolle, 'Italie', pp. 780–1).

4   Durutte had 18th Léger (two battalions), 22nd Léger (two battalions), 23rd Léger (four battalions), and 62nd Ligne (four battalions) for infantry. The 23rd Dragoons marched between his division and the main body. One squadron of 7th Dragoons was in the Tyrol, the other chasseur squadron was still en route to the army.

5   From Gyurkovics, Hirsch was given the other three companies of II/*Ottocac*, the other half of the hussar squadron, and, briefly, I/*Ottocac*.

6   These were two each of 23rd Ligne, 60th Ligne, and 7th Italian Line, as well as I/Dalmatian. There were two anomalies. First, each battalion was supposed to have been reinforced to a minimum of 600 men, but the 2nd and 3rd of the Italian 7th Line barely exceeded 600 together. Second, each regiment was supposed to contribute two battalions, but the Dalmatian Regiment could only provide one.

7   French losses are not known. On the Austrian side, Gyurkovics had taken ill; he was replaced by Oberstleutnant von Collenbach. It is not clear how Nagy's squadron of *Ott* Hussars (that had been screening Durutte's march from Legnago) rejoined the army.

8   I/*Ottocac*, making its way to the army from the Padua area where it had temporarily come under Hirsch, was set upon by French cavalry and likely would have been destroyed had not Austrian horsemen rushed to its assistance.

9   Schmidt's detachment (under pensioner Hauptmann Ottavio Bianchi) added two companies of 2nd *Banal* and a half-squadron of *Hohenzollern* Chevaulegers to Zuccheri's force (*Krieg*, vol. II, pp. 164, 239, 255). Local militia were also sporadically plentiful, but their numbers and activities are difficult to relate with any accuracy.

10 *Krieg*, vol. II, pp. 232–6, 245, 260; 'Tirol im Jahre 1809', *ÖMZ*, vol. IV, 1833, p. 84.

11 Chasteler, alarmed at the fall of Trient, sent III/*Lusignan*, I/*Hohenlohe*, 2nd Villach, a half-squadron, and a half-battery of 6-pounders to reinforce Marchal (*ÖMZ*, vol. IV, 1833, p. 86).

12 Marziani and Gavassini only had one regiment each; technically speaking, Gajoli had two regiments, but one of these (*1st Banal*) was withheld as corps reserve.

13 Eugene to Napoleon, 7 May 1809, du Casse, *Eugène*, vol. V, p. 173.

14 In addition to personal, archival, and regimental accounts cited below, principal sources for the battle include: du Casse, *Eugène*, vol. V, pp. 69–79; Johann, *Feldzugserzählungen*, pp. 109–14; *Krieg*, vol. II, pp. 266–308; *ÖMZ*, vol. V, 1833, pp. 124–44; Vaudoncourt, vol. I, p. 228–44; Vignolle, 'Italie', pp. 795–814; Alois Veltzé, 'Die Schlacht an der Piave', *Mitteilungen des K. und K. Kriegsarchivs*, vol. IV, 1906.

15 Aymar Oliver Le Harivel de Gonneville, *Recollections of Colonel de Gonneville*, Felling (Tyne & Wear): Worley, 1988, vol. I, p. 262.

16 Chevillet, p. 197.

17 Eugene to Napoleon, 7 May 1809, du Casse, *Eugène*, vol. V, p. 172.

18 'Ordre de mouvement pour le 8 mai', Vignolle, 'Italie', pp. 796–8.

19 Eugene referred to a 'false attack' at Nervesa in his 7 May letters to Napoleon and Clarke (du Casse, *Eugène*, vol. V, pp. 172–5), but this is not specifically mentioned in the written orders for 8 May.

20 Veltzé, 'Schlacht an der Piave', p. 131.

21 *Krieg*, vol. II, pp. 261–2.

22 The hasty reactions to news of the French probe gave rise to an illuminating incident concerning the Austrian army. Frimont ordered the *Ott* Hussars from the VIII Corps camp to the highway south of Boca di Strada without informing their superior, FML Albert Gyulai. Gyulai, asked to report on the situation to his front, thus replied that he did not know the locations of the outposts and had no cavalry to gather intelligence; he therefore declared himself 'under no circumstances responsible for the reported crossing of the enemy' (*Krieg*, vol. II, pp. 266–7).

23 Robinaux, pp. 75–6.

24 Dessaix's journal, AG; Noël, pp. 61–2.

25 François Louis Zaepffel, 'Rapport sur la Passage du Piave & la Combat de 8 Mai 1809', 18 May 1809, AG, C4/10. Zaepffel, one of Napoleon's staff officers, had arrived on 7 May and was present at the battle.

26 Robinaux, p. 78.

27 Chevillet, p. 202.

28 Gonneville, vol. I, p. 266.

29 Noël, p. 61.

30 Gonneville, vol. I, p. 267.

31 *ÖMZ*, vol. V, 1833, p. 130.

32 Broussier's journal, AG.

33 Gonneville, vol. I, p. 272.

34 French: Dessaix, 9th Ligne (Broussier), Sahuc, Grouchy, and Pully for 6,500–7,000 infantry, 7,300 cavalry, and twenty-nine to thirty-one guns. The first three battalions of 84th Ligne in the process of crossing: 1,800. Austrian: Splenyi, Colloredo, *1st Banal*, *Ott* Hussars, Wolfskeel (twelve dragoon and three hussar squadrons), Kalnassy (including three hussars squadrons), IX Corps infantry for 16,950 infantry, 3,000 cavalry, and forty-eight guns; Gajoli's lone regiment represents the additional 1,300. Not counted among the Austrians are the three Landwehr battalions and Frimont's river guard detachments (four battalions, two hussar squadrons, two hussar wings, a cavalry battery, four 3-pounders).

35 Gonneville, vol. I, p. 264.

36 *Krieg*, vol. II, pp. 278–80.

37 Gonneville, vol. I, p. 265.

38 Johann, *Feldzugserzählungen*, p. 112.

39 Chevillet, p. 205.

40 Wolfskeel's dragoons and Pully's were probably almost equal in numbers (approximately 1,000 each). These figures include two dragoon regiments (28th, 29th), three chasseur regiments (6th, 9th, 25th), and one chasseur squadron IV/8th) for the French; for the Austrians: two dragoon regiments and thirteen and one-half hussar squadrons (four of *Josef*, four of *Ott*, five and one-half of *Frimont*). Three and one-half additional Austrian squadrons (two *Josef*, one and one-half *Frimont*) were nearby at Campana (*c.* 280 men), while the French held three squadrons of 8th

Chasseurs in reserve (*c.* 700 men). Although the traditional accounts of this cavalry battle do not include the rest of 8th Chasseurs, Chevillet's letter of 9 May provides good evidence that the entire regiment was engaged in at least part of the fighting (Chevillet, pp. 204–7).

41 Henckens, p. 67; Robinaux, p. 79.

42 Johann, *Feldzugserzählungen*, p. 112.

43 'Rapport-Journal de la Division Pacthod', AG, C4/10. The composition of the two elite battalions is not certain. As they were commanded by chefs de bataillon from the 52nd and 102nd, it seems likely that they were composed exclusively of men from Abbé's division; after deducting the eight voltigeur companies contributed to Dessaix, Abbé had six voltigeur companies (approximately 500 men) and fourteen grenadier companies (1,200) from which he could have constructed two battalions of some 800 men each.

44 *Krieg*, vol. II, p. 286. Johann knew from prisoners that the French had not bridged the Piave.

45 This description is based on the campaign history of Abbé's division ('Rapport-Journal de la Division Pacthod', AG, C4/10) and differs from that presented in *Krieg*, vol. II.

46 *Krieg*, vol. II, p. 293.

47 ÖMZ, vol. V, 1833, p. 141.

48 Zaepffel, 'Rapport sur la Passage du Piave', AG, C4/10.

49 Veltzé, 'Schlacht an der Piave', p. 130.

50 *Krieg*, vol. II, pp. 295, 303.

51 'Season daring with caution' is from a work of fiction: Jack Vance, *Madouc*, New York: Ace Books, 1990, p. 223.

52 *Krieg*, vol. II, pp. 303–8.

53 Grouchy's 9 May report in his *Mémoires*, Paris: Dentu, 1873, vol. III, p. 21.

54 Routier, p. 82; or Horemans, p. 8: 'The 23rd was proud as it was avenged.'

55 Frimont had III/*Franz Karl*, *Ogulin* Grenzer (minus two companies posted at Pinzano), *Ott* Hussars, *Josef* Hussars (seven squadrons), and *Frimont* Hussars (five squadrons). One and one-half squadrons of *Frimont* had been sent towards the Isonzo/Udine on 10 and 11 May.

56 Space limitations preclude a description of this incredible odyssey: see *Krieg*, vol. II, pp. 296–300, and the battalion's report in Hermann and Kesch, *Geschichte des k. und k. 52. Linien-Infanerie-Regiments*, Vienna: Hof- und Staatsdruckerei, 1871, pp. 254–8.

57 Franz hinted at placing Jellacic under Johann on 2 May and made the arrangement clear on 7 May (*Krieg*, vol. II, pp. 468–71).

58 *Krieg*, vol. II, p. 324, and Johann's instructions for Ignaz Gyulai, 11 May 1809, pp. 479–80.

59 Johann to Maria Louise, 14 May 1809, Zwiedineck-Südenhorst, *Erzherzog Johann im Feldzuge von 1809*, pp. 24–5.

60 Pully evidently detached the regiment to the north while the rest of his division headed towards Udine (*Krieg*, vol. II, p. 328; Edouard Hache, *Historique du 23e Régiment de Dragons*, Paris: Hachette, 1890, pp. 96–7).

61 *Krieg*, vol. II, p. 331.

62 The two Marburg Landwehr battalions had maintained a very hesitant blockade until relieved by a battalion of *Reisky* on 11 May.

63 Du Casse, *Eugène*, vol. V, pp. 192–5; Vignolle, 'Italie', pp. 68–9.

64 Casualties taken from the two Austrian regimental histories: *Geschichte des k. k. Infanterie-Regiments Leopold II.*, *König der Belgier Nr. 27*, Vienna: Mayer, 1882, p. 497; August Hofmann von Donnersberg, *Geschichte des k. u. k. Infanterie-Regimentes Nr. 61*, Wien: Kreisel & Gröger, 1892, p. 73. Note that *Krieg*, vol. II, p. 341 gives the total Austrian loss as 200.

65 *Krieg*, vol. II, p. 342.

66 Johann to Franz, 12 May 1809, *Krieg*, vol. II, pp. 481–3. Kalnassy would hold the upper Isonzo.

67 *Krieg*, vol. II, p. 350.

68 See letters from Franz to Johann, 24 April, 29 April, 2 May, and 7 May 1809, as well as extracts from instructions from Charles in *Krieg*, vol. II, pp. 244, 462–3, 468–71, 477–8.

69 *Krieg*, vol. II, p. 337. The batteries were one position, two brigade, and one-half cavalry.

70 Strength estimates from *Krieg*, vol. II, p. 349 (plus my own for Landwehr and cavalry). Three companies of *Strassaldo* were also in the area on 15 May, but Johann had ordered these back to their regiment with Frimont. One of the ten battalions (I/*Szulin*) was an unexpected addition after Johann learned that Kalnassy had left it in the Isonzo valley.

71 Napoleon to Eugene, 1 May 1809, *Correspondance*, no. 15150 (emphasis in original).

72 Dessaix's journal, AG. The two voltigeur battalions rejoined their divisions at Udine on 14 May. Note that this interpretation is from Dessaix's journal (and Georges E. Pitot, *Historique du 83e Régiment d'Infanterie*, Toulouse: Privat, 1891, pp. 102–3), but other sources state that *three* of Dessaix's voltigeur battalions returned to their parent divisions (including Seras), and that 23rd Léger (rather than 8th) replaced them.

73 Noël was describing his actions after receiving orders to move to Malborghetto at 2 p.m. on 16 May (Rosemary Brindle's translation in Noël, p. 63).

74 *Krieg*, vol. II, p. 356; Johann Baptiste Schels, 'Überfall auf eine französische Kolonne bei Wolfsbach, am 15. Mai 1809', *ÖMZ*, vol. XII, 1843.

75 Paraphrased from Gyulai's report, *Krieg*, vol. II, p. 354.

76 *Krieg*, vol. II, p. 356.

77 Dessaix's journal, AG.

78 Vaudoncourt, vol. I, p. 275. Vaudoncourt was with Fontanelli's column.

79 Cruyplants, p. 112.

80 Johann to Franz, 16 May 1809, *Krieg*, vol. II, pp. 503–4.

81 *Krieg*, vol. II, pp. 373, 403–4.

82 Gyulai to Johann, 16 May 1809, 7.15 p.m., *Krieg*, vol. II, p. 410.

83 *Krieg*, vol. II, pp. 408–11.

84 Eugene to Napoleon, 17 May 1809, 11 p.m., Du Casse, *Eugène*, vol. V, pp. 209–11; *Krieg*, vol. II, p. 412.

85 *Krieg*, vol. II, pp. 413–18. One battalion of *1st Banal* did cross the mountains into the upper Sava valley late in the afternoon.

86 This section draws from the analysis in *Krieg*, vol. II, pp. 418–23; and Johann, *Feldzugserzählungen*, pp. 124–5. Quotes from orders to Chasteler and Jellacic, 17 May 1809, *Krieg*, vol. II, pp. 506–7.

87 *Krieg*, vol. II, p. 425.

88 In addition to 309 from *Ogulin*, there were forty-one artillerymen, miners, officers, and others; at least forty were killed, the remainder became prisoners. For Malborghetto, see J. W. Ridler, 'Die Thermopylen der kärnischen Alpen', *Archiv für Geographie, Historie, Staats- und Kriegskunst*, no. 51, April 1811; J. W. Riedler, 'Die Erstürmung des Forts von Malborghetto 1809', *ÖMZ*, vol. V, 1813, and *Neue militärische Blätter*, no. 2, 1813; G. von Fircks, 'Ausgezeichneter Muth der Heldenjünglinge Herrmann und Hensel bei der Vertheidigung der Blockhäuser auf dem Predill und zu Malborghetto, am 17ten Mai 1809', *Militair-Wochenblatt*, no. 88, 28 February 1818; 'Die Vertheidigung der Blockhäuser Malborghet und Predil im Jahre 1809', *Mittheilungen über Gegenstände des Artillerie- und Geniewesens*, 1901; Alois Veltzé, *Österreichs Thermopylen 1809*, Vienna: Stern, 1905; Karl Neuhofer, *Malborghet 1809*, Salzburg, 1997. The official history expends fifteen pages on this action (*Krieg*, vol. II, pp. 374–89). With thanks to Vladimir Brnardic for providing some of these sources.

89 Estimating Austrian troop strength here is challenging. The official history gives a total infantry strength of 3,500 before the arrival of *Strassaldo* and credits the latter with only 1,000 effectives. Based on deducting battle casualties (only) according to their regimental histories, *Reisky* and *Strassaldo* should have numbered at least 1,200 each; likewise, if the three *Strassaldo* companies in the Raccolana totalled 214 men, we may assume the average company strength was 70 for approximately 1,260 in the regiment. On the other hand, the history of *Franz Jellacic* claims each battalion counted only 200 or so in the ranks (thus 600 to 700 total for the regiment). The four companies of *Szulin* on the field (recalling that one was in Predil, and one wandering near Predil) probably numbered between 300 and 400 (70 to 100 per company); and *Ogulin* certainly had 1,000 men in its ten companies (beyond the two in Malborghetto), with perhaps as many as 1,500 (150 per company). Two hundred Marburg Landwehr were in the redoubt with I/F. *Jellacic* (also claimed to be 200), but we have no other information on the militia strength; they can probably be estimated at 400–500 for the two battalions total.

90 I estimate French infantry and cavalry strength to have been at most 22,000 (based on Eugene's 25 May strength report), probably rather less. Although Eugene gives the number of French guns as four (the advance guard's battery); I have used the figure of six based on Vaudoncourt and Noël's memoirs (he commanded the guns).

91 The 3rd Italian Line supported the 1st and 60th, all under Fontanelli; d'Hilliers led IV/2nd, I/Dalmatia, and 112th Ligne (Vaudoncourt, vol. I, p. 284).

92 *Krieg*, vol. II, p. 426.

93 Ibid.

94 This was apparently 2nd Laibach.

95 Eugene to Napoleon, 17 May 1809, 11 p.m., Du Casse, *Eugène*, vol. V, pp. 209–11.

96 In addition to the studies of both Malborghetto and Predil mentioned earlier, see: *Krieg*, vol. II, pp. 389–99; and Franz Pfau, 'Die Vertheidigung und der Fall

des Blockhauses auf dem Predil, im Jahre 1809, ÖMZ, vol. X, 1843. The assaulting French units were: IV/1st Léger, IV/35th Ligne, a battalion each of 53rd and 60th Ligne, and the division's combined grenadiers. The force sent by Eugene consisted of 60th Ligne, a voltigeur battalion, and two guns under Major Grenier.

97 Most of this section is taken from Hermann Sallagar, 'Die Verteidigung der Position von Präwald im Jahre 1809', ÖMZ, vol. VI, 1908.

98 Ogrissovich marched via the Trieste road and did not arrive until late on the 16th.

99 These were: Simbschen (two battalions—its three had been consolidated into two), four companies of I/Szulin Grenzer, and three platoons of Josef Hussars.

100 My estimate based on 360 for the two battalions of Simbschen alone (54 dead, 306 wounded and captured). Friedrich Dengler, Kurzgefasste Geschichte des kaiserlichen und königlichen Infanterie-Regiments Rupprecht Prinz von Bayern Nr. 43, Wien: Stern, 1908, p. 63.

101 Hermann/Kesch, pp. 261–3; Vignolle, 'Italie', p. 84. According to Vignolle, forty men died of bayonet wounds.

102 These were: II and III/Franz Karl and effectively one of Simbschen (as the regiment was reduced to one combined battalion after the fighting on the 17th).

103 Johann listed the garrison as one weak battalion of Simbschen, a Landwehr battalion, and four companies of Szulin for a total of 1,189 (Feldzugserzählungen, pp. 127, 136); see also August Dimitz, Geschichte Krains, Laibach: Kleinmayer & Bamberg, 1876, p. 278; sources vary greatly on the number and composition of the garrison between this minimum and French figures of 4,000 prisoners.

104 One may estimate the strength as 1,500 to 2,000 regular infantry (III/Franz Karl, Ottocac, some Szulin Grenzer, and Simbschen remnants), 1,000 to 1,200 cavalry (dragoons, Frimont, three platoons of Josef), and an unknown number of Landwehr, depot troops, and stragglers; probably no more than 5,000 total.

105 Charpentier to MacDonald, 22 May 1809, Vignolle, 'Italie', p. 105. Grouchy's vanguard and MacDonald's 6th Hussars united at Marburg on 26 May (Pacthod was still at Mahrenberg). Broussier and Pully (23rd and 28th Dragoons) arrived late on the 27th; Lamarque and 29th Dragoons were in Gonobitz.

106 Mackesy, p. 320; Johann, Feldzugserzählungen, p. 127; Friedrich von Seidel, 'Die Operazionen des von dem Banus von Kroazien, Feldmarschall-Leutnant Grafen Ignaz Gyulai befehligten östreichischen neunten Armeekorps im Feldzuge 1809', ÖMZ, vol. V, 1837, p. 147; Simeone Addobbati, Il Reggimento Reale Dalmata, Zara: Artale, 1899, p. 32.

107 Collingwood to Amherst, 25 May 1809, Collingwood, Correspondence, p. 385.

108 These instructions were dated 15 May and Johann received them in Klagenfurt on 18 May, see Ch. 2.

109 Johann to Charles, 24 May 1809, Zwiedineck-Südenhorst, 'Das Gefecht bei St Michael', pp. 40-3; and Johann 'Disposition for 25 May', 24 May 1809, Zwiedineck-Südenhorst (ed.), 'Zur Geschichte des Krieges von 1809 in Steiermark'.

110 Details of the composition of Grouchy's advance guard are unclear, but it evidently included one battalion each of 8th Léger and 52nd Ligne as well as the two chasseur regiments.

111 Bouchard, pp. 118-9; Hache, pp. 97-8.

112 Being several days' march behind the main body, this demi-regiment was not present for St Michael.

113 Wachtel supplies as thorough an account as possible, pp. 167, 188-92. The Austrians comprised members of *Lusignan* and 9th Jägers (including both unit commanders), as well as a few *O'Reilly* Chevaulegers.

114 Johann's 17 and 19 May orders to Jellacic are in Zwiedineck-Südenhorst, 'Das Gefecht bei St Michael', pp. 37-9.

115 Wachtel, p. 253.

116 Napoleon indeed ordered Lefebvre to pursue Jellacic, and GM von Rechberg duly set out with I/1st Infantry and a squadron of 1st Chevaulegers. Marching through Radstadt, Rechberg reached Steinach on 26 May, but had no contact with the enemy and was recalled after Aspern as the emperor drew more troops into the Danube valley. The little column joined 1st Division in Schwanenstadt on 29 May as the division marched north towards Linz.

117 Specifically at a pass called the Pötschenhöhe just west of Aussee, at the road intersection west of Steinach, and at the Mandling Pass east of Radstadt (not shown on maps). Plunquet's name is sometimes spelled 'Plunkett'.

118 Ettingshausen's memoirs in Zwiedineck-Südenhorst, 'Das Gefecht bei St Michael', p. 30.

119 Among the unwise decisions was Jellacic's order for the division to disperse into billets, thus making the morning recall procedure much more time-consuming. The key friction was provided by a staff officer who gratuitously told the advance guard Grenzer to delay their departure.

120 'Liesingberg' is taken from modern maps; older maps refer to this height as the 'Fresenberg'.

121 The only missing element at this stage was his rear guard Grenz battalion.

122 Ettingshausen's memoirs in Zwiedineck-Südenhorst, 'Das Gefecht bei St Michael', p. 32.

123 Ruiz's small detachment seems to have joined the tail of Jellacic's column, but its involvement (if any) in the fighting is unknown.

124 The 106th Ligne was with Roussel, the 53rd in front of the Platte; how the other three battalions were distributed is not clear.

125 Most accounts place two battalions of 62nd Ligne across the Mur (Gaillard and Fleuriot, Historique du 62e Régiment d'Infanterie, Paris: Berger-Levrault, 1899, p. 111), but this history follows Dessaix's detailed letter to Seras, dated 28 May and contained in his journal. Similarly, many accounts refer to Dessaix's command of 102nd Ligne, but he makes no mention of this regiment in the battle. The location of the two 22nd Léger battalions is unknown; one modern author speculates that they remained behind in Kaiserberg (Anton Hugo Wagner, *Das Gefecht bei St. Michael-Leoben am 25. Mai 1809*, Vienna: Bundesverlag, 1984, p. 61).

126 Ettingshausen's memoirs in Zwiedineck-Südenhorst, 'Das Gefecht bei St Michael', p. 33.

127 Dessaix's journal. AG.

128 Ettingshausen's memoirs in Zwiedineck-Südenhorst, 'Das Gefecht bei St Michael', p. 34.

129 Wagner, *Gefecht bei St. Michael-Leoben*, pp. 40-1.

130 Johann, Feldzugserzählungen, p. 135.
131 Eugene to Auguste, 26 May 1809, 6 a.m., du Casse, Eugène, vol. V, p. 223.
132 'Proclamation', Correspondance, 27 May 1809, 15264.
133 Eugene to Auguste, 17 May 1809, midnight, du Casse, Eugène, vol. V, pp. 213-4.
134 Routier, p. 81.
135 Chevillet describes his regiment menacing the enemy cavalry with 'ferocious joy' (p. 204).
136 Routier, p. 82.
137 Krieg, vol. II, p. 324.

INTERMEZZO

1 Pelet, vol. III, p. 332.

APPENDICES

1 From Krieg, vol. III, Anhänge V and VI, unless otherwise noted.
2 Though present on the field, Vincent did not serve as division commander during the battle.
3 The figures for Allied troop strength given in vol. III of Krieg seem too high. Molitor is credited with 8,600 when the division's initial strength was only 6,831 infantry and 308 artillery/train. Wrede is counted as 7,100 when his total infantry was probably under 7,000.
4 From Krieg, vol. III, Anhang I (for 24 April) with adjustments from the text for 25 and 26 April.
5 The troops at Rohrbach, opposite Passau, at Wernstein, and at Schärding were all under Dedovich.
6 This battalion arrived in Moosbach on 27 April and marched off to join Jellacic the next day. The Allied advance, however, prevented it from linking up with Jellacic until mid-May.
7 These battalions had suffered considerably during their retreat and also lacked the two companies of the 2nd Battalion under Steigentesch. Steigentesch made his way through Passau to Engelhartzell on the Danube.
8 Krieg, vol. I, pp. 83-4.
9 From Krieg, vol. III, Anhänge XLII and XLIII, unless otherwise noted.
10 For comparison purposes, Krieg, vol. III, p. 418 gives Claparède a strength of 7,000 to 7,500; Piré and Marulaz some 3,000; and Ledru 4,000. I estimate that Claparède was closer to 8,000 strong (the Krieg figure is not impossible, but would mean 15 to 20 per cent march attrition); the number for the light cavalry seems too low; it was probably closer to the 3,700 in Binder (vol. II, p. 120); but 4,000 is probably close for Ledru.
11 From Krieg, vol. III, pp. 617-24, Anhänge XLII and XLIII; Wachtel, pp. 169-75.

12 According to Stutterheim, Sinzendorf commanded the regular troops and Ulbrecht the Landwehr (theoretically the Vienna Volunteers as well): Stutterheim ('Der Feldzug 1809', ÖMZ, vol. IV, 1849, pp. 26–7).

13 From Krieg, vol. III, Anhang LVIII.

14 From Krieg, vol. III, pp. 545, 550, and Anhang LV.

15 From Krieg, vol. III, Anhänge XLII and XLIII.

16 Krieg, vol. IV, Anhänge X and XI.

17 From Krieg, vol. IV, Anhang XXII; this source gives the type of batteries assigned to each column but does not always state the calibre of the position guns (pp. 409–12).

18 Former EH Johann, the regiment changed Inhaber to FML Eugen Graf Argenteau on 1 May.

19 Two squadrons had been detached in Bohemia at the start of the war, but one evidently rejoined the regiment when it passed through Bohemia during its long retreat. It seems that a squadron was again dispatched to Bohemia in June (placing two in Bohemia during July).

20 From Krieg, vol. IV, Anhang XXIII, unless otherwise noted. Though dated, the arguments in Carl Bleibtreu's works are interesting, if only for their asperity: Aspern & Wagram in neuer Beleuchtung, Vienna: Seidel & Sohn, 1902; and Die Grosse Armee, vol. II, Stuttgart: Krabbe, 1907.

21 As of 18 May. Saski, vol. III, p. 396; Emile François Litre, Les Régiments d'Artillerie à Pied de la Garde, Paris: Plon, 1895, p. 48.

22 From 8th Corps situation report, 31 May 1809, AG, Armée d'Allemagne—Situations, C2/508; 20 May 1809, HStAS, E289a Bü 86; 26 May and 1 June reports from the regiment (HStAS, E289a Bü 88, E270a Bü 93).

23 Strengths for Oudinot's and Demont's divisions present a puzzle: there are simply no strength returns for these formations in the period immediately prior to the battle. The problem arises because march battalions with thousands of conscripts arrived in Vienna during May. It is evident that at least some substantial number of replacements reached their destination units, and the present work follows the Austrian official history in assuming that some 11,000 conscripts were incorporated into Oudinot's divisions before Aspern (approximately 11,000 men destined for Oudinot's battalions passed through Strasbourg between 10 and 16 April). In his memoirs, the commander of IV/96th Ligne suggests this conclusion. He records that replacements he received took his battalion to 1,150 men, in other words, more than 300 over his authorised strength. He further states that the other battalions were one-third less (that is 800–900 or approximately at the authorised level of 840). See Jouan, pp. 545–6, 548, 566. However, it is not clear whether or not such large replacement detachments reached all of Oudinot's battalions. In St Hilaire's case, some of his scheduled replacements arrived but others did not. The same problem occurs in Demont (see below). Taking the maximum figures gives Oudinot approximately 21,000 for his two divisions combined and 4,800 for Demont, but readers should keep in mind that the figure could have been several thousand less. This book follows the analysis in Krieg, vol. IV, pp. 682–3 with supporting material from Saski, vol. I, and Jean Lochet in Empires, Eagles, and Lions, no. 52, January 1981. Castle (Aspern & Wagram, p. 17), on the other hand, gives much lower strengths for Tharreau (7,000), Claparède (5,800), and Demont (4,300); Thiers (vol. X, p. 302) puts Oudinot at 11,000 to 12,000 and Demont at 3,000.

24 Information for St Hilaire's division is based on the 1 May returns in 'Livret de Situation', May 1809, AG, *Armée d'Allemagne—Livrets*, C2/674. The *Livret* includes replacement detachments en route to the division, and the numbers given in this appendix assume (a) that the replacements arrived with few march losses and (b) that they were not detained en route (at Augsburg, for example). An additional 1,290 men were slated to leave Strasbourg by 1 May for the division, but it seems unlikely (though not impossible) that they would have arrived in time for Aspern. Note that *Krieg* (vol. IV, pp. 682, 781) speculates that as many as 1,400 replacements might have arrived before Aspern; this, however, is a simple guess based on the assumption that all ten of the division's missing companies *might* have joined prior to the battle (at 140 men each for 1,400 total); it is not supported by the archival record (which the Austrian authors did not use).

25 For French troops: 4th Corps situation report, 15 May 1809, AG, *Armée d'Allemagne—Situations*, C2/507. For German troops: *Krieg*, vol. IV, p. 780.

26 Note that Thiers (vol. X, p. 301) only credits Carra Saint-Cyr with 6,000 men.

27 Saski, vol. III, p. 403.

28 From *Krieg*, vol. IV, Anhang XXVI.

29 Returns (1 May) in 'Livret de Situation', May 1809, AG, *Armée d'Allemagne—Livrets*, C2/674; and Saski, vol. III, pp. 399–400.

30 Lauriston situation report, 13 June 1809, AG, *Armée d'Allemagne—Situations*, C2/510; Pelet, army situation, 1 June 1809, vol. IV, annex.

31 Saski, vol. III, p. 403; Gill, *Eagles*, pp. 228, 235; John H. Gill 'Les armées de la Confédération du Rhin en Hongrie, en 1809', Robert Ouvrard, trans., June 2004, *Histoire du Consulat et du Premier Empire*, www.histoire-empire.org/1809/raab/confederation.htm.

32 From 8th Corps situation report, 31 May 1809, AG, *Armée d'Allemagne—Situations*, C2/508.

33 Organisational structure taken from *Krieg*, vol. II, pp. 20–3, 438–42. Landwehr strengths from ibid., p. 433. Strengths of regulars from 'Haupt Stand und Dienst Tabelle der kaiserlich königlichen Armee auf den Kriegs Fuss mit Ende März 1809', KAFA, *Stand- und Dienstabellen*, Kart. 3729. The figure used here for IX Corps is considerably larger than that given in *Krieg*, vol. II, pp. 9, 438–40: 33,283 infantry/cavalry compared to 24,690. The difference is Knesevich's Dalmatian detachment. The authors of *Krieg*, vol. II, listed Knesevich's eight battalions with IX Corps totals, but forgot to include his troop strength (*c.* 8,000). This leaves the anomaly of thirty Austrian battalions totalling only 22,290 infantrymen for an average of 743 men per battalion, when each full strength battalion (as these were) should have numbered some 1,300 men. Deducting Knesevich's 8,000 brings the IX Corps total to 25,270, only some 580 more than the 24,690 in *Krieg*. Similarly, the figure from the archives for VIII Corps (including Chasteler) is only 1,000 higher than that in *Krieg*. This consistency lends credibility to the archival data; the figures I have calculated are also close to those in Johann Baptist Schels, 'Der Feldzug 1809 in Italien', ÖMZ, 1844. As a final note, readers should be aware that many accounts of the Italian campaign do not include Landwehr in the totals for Johann's forces, or they state the Landwehr numbers separately; readers must thus exercise caution in noting which troops are included/excluded from various totals.

34 *Krieg*, vol. II, p. 12; Johann, *Feldzugserzählungen*, pp. 62, 69.

35 Emil von Woinovich, *Kämpfe an der Lika, in Kroatien und Dalmatien*, vol. VI of *Das Kriegsjahr 1809 in Einzelldarstellungen*, Vienna: Stern, 1906, p. 10.

36 *Krieg*, vol. II, p. 442.

37 Strengths from 'Situation de l'Armée d'Italie', 15 April 1809, AN, AF*/IV/1377, *Livrets des armées: Situations des troupes en Italie*. See also Vignolle, 'Italie'; *Krieg*, vol. II, Anhang XI.

38 The Royal Guard infantry was composed of the curiously-named 'Line Infantry of the Guard' (one battalion each of grenadiers and chasseurs) and the Royal Velites; the latter included one grenadier battalion (the 1st; it was in Spain in 1809) and two chasseurs battalions (2nd and 3rd) of which the 2nd Battalion served with the field army while the 3rd remained in Milan. See J. P. Perconte's superb website: www. histunif.com.

39 'Situation' of 15 April 1809, AG, *Armée de Dalmatie*, C6/15; guns from Marmont, *Mémoires*, vol. III, p. 133.

40 Other than Aicher, these strength estimates are taken from J. Heilmann, 'Feldzug in Tirol'; they are obviously full strength tallies that are best regarded as estimates; Baur credits 11th Infantry with only 1,200 men (C. Baur, *Der Krieg in Tirol während des Feldzugs von 1809*, Munich, 1812, p. 8).

41 See Appendix 10 for sources. Frimont's organisation taken from Veltzé, 'Pordenone und Sacile', p. 171.

42 This company's presence is not confirmed. Zuccheri left one of his two companies behind, probably with Volkmann, but it does not appear in Austrian orders of battle for Sacile.

43 My estimate of Frimont's losses on 15th subtracted.

44 In a complex note, the authors of *Krieg* (vol. II, p. 97) explain that Johann should have had eighty-three guns (ninety-one minus four each detached with Gyurkovics and Tomassich). However, they can only account for fifty-five to sixty-one that actually might have been involved in the battle.

45 Sources as before (15 April 1809 strengths).

46 The disposition of Barbou's troops is my best guess based on *Krieg*, regimental histories, and losses as recorded in the army's 6 May 'Situation' (AN, AF*/IV/1377). *Krieg* shows Bartier with 60th and 81st Ligne, but the regimental history clearly states that the 81st fought near Porcia and the losses (155) are too high for Bartier's role in the battle; I therefore substituted 8th Léger as having the least losses (33) among the remaining four battalions (not counting 79th at Santissima per *Krieg*).

47 The estimate in *Krieg* (vol. II, p. 96) gives Eugene only 2,050 horsemen; my figure uses a higher count for all regiments/squadrons except Sahuc's (650).

48 'Tirol im Jahre 1809', ÖMZ, 1833–4.

49 Vignolle, 'Campagne du Tyrol'; René de Cosse-Brissac, *Historique du 7e Régiment de Dragons*, Paris: Leroy, 1909.

50 From *Krieg*, vol. II, pp. 208, 472–3, with strengths estimated at 450 per infantry battalion in VIII Corps, 650 per infantry battalion in IX Corps, 1,000 per Grenz battalion, 80 per light cavalry squadron, 100 per dragoon squadron.

51 Source: Army of Italy, 'Situation', 6 May 1809, AN 1377; supplemented by the 1 May order of battle in Vignolle's 'Italie'; number of guns from *Krieg*, vol. II, pp. 474–6.

52 Composition of the provisional regiments follows (contributing regiments in parentheses). 1st Regiment: 1st Battalion (9th, 11th, 84th, 92nd Ligne), 2nd Battalion (18th Léger, 13th, 23rd, 29th Ligne), 3rd Battalion (35th, 53rd, 79th, 106th Ligne). 2nd Regiment: 1st Battalion (8th Léger, 1st, 52nd, 102nd Ligne), 2nd Battalion, (22nd Léger, 23rd Léger, 60th, 62nd Ligne), 3rd Battalion (112th Ligne, 1st, 2nd, 3rd Italian Line). Dessaix's journal, AG.

53 Grenier formed two elite battalions to lead the way across the river. These were apparently taken from Abbé's division alone and likely consisted of the division's grenadiers and remaining voltigeurs (after deducting those sent to Dessaix) for some 800 men per battalion.

54 It is not clear whether all four battalions were present: *Krieg* states that at most 1st and 4th Battalions were on hand (vol. II, p. 475), while the regimental history suggests that all four had been united (Gaillard and Fleuriot, *Historique du 62e Régiment d'Infanterie*, Paris: Berger-Levrault, 1899, p. 106).

55 The army's situation report for 6 May lists all four battalions with this regiment, but it is likely that only two were present at the Piave (as shown). The other two (I and III) ended up fighting in the Tyrol later in the year. If all four had been present, total strength would have been 2,216.

56 Details are limited on the Italian regiments, but it seems 7th Line was technically considered two battalions despite having the strength of one; it would soon be reduced to its 2nd Battalion with cadres sent to rebuild the 3rd.

57 Drafts from II/Dalmatia were used to bring 1st Battalion up to a strength of 635, so the depleted battalion was left behind to recover.

58 The French continued to treat this regiment as one battalion, albeit of remnants. The 6 May 'Situation' lists it with 789 effectives, but makes no mention of those detached to Palmanova (whether included in this figure or not). Curiously, the battered regiment contributed one company to the 3rd Battalion of Nagle's 1st Combined Voltigeur Regiment.

59 One battalion (408 men) detached at an unknown location.

60 The numbers shown for the Italian Guard are the same as in the previous official 'Situation', but total infantry strength was probably only 1,300 after heavy losses at Castelcerino.

61 Taken from *Krieg*, vol. II, pp. 484–5, but modified to show actual dispositions.

62 Replacing the wounded Colloredo.

63 Note that 4th Neustadtl was still organising and 3rd Laibach had been disbanded. Identity of 2nd Laibach is my estimate.

64 Sources: Army of Italy, 'Situation', 6 May 1809, AN 1377; with updates from Vignolle's 'Italie'. The III/3rd Italian Light Infantry (826) remained in Palmanova.

65 Composition of the provisional regiment as in Appendix 13. As noted in the text, sources differ regarding the composition of the Advance Guard at this point; the organisation shown follows Dessaix's journal with one exception: the journal does not mention the battalion from Seras's division, but it seems likely that this had returned to its parent formation just like those for MacDonald's corps.

66 As noted above, the army's situation report for 6 May lists all four battalions united, but it is likely that only two were present at Tarvis (as shown). The other

two (I and III) ended up fighting in the Tyrol later in the year. If all four had been present, total strength would have been 2,216.

67 The numbers shown for the Italian Guard are the same as in the previous official 'Situation', but total infantry strength was probably only 1,300 after heavy losses at Castelcerino.

68 Sources: Army of Italy, 'Situation Sommaire' as of 25 May, in Army of Germany, 'Livret de Situation', 1 June 1809, AG C2/675. The III/3rd Italian Light Infantry (826) remained in Palmanova. 1st Ligne had been reorganised to three battalions owing to losses; cadres of IV/1st were sent to the regimental depot to rebuild (Lt. Brasier de Thuy, *1er Régiment d'Infanterie*, Cambrai: Deligne et Lenglet, 1889, p. 141).

69 Strengths shown apparently have losses for 25 May Battle of St Michael subtracted.

70 The situation report for 25 May ('Livret de Situation', June 1809, AG, *Armée d'Allemagne—Livrets*, C2/675) lists all four battalions united, but it is likely that only these two were in Styria. Strength of all four battalions was 2,126.

71 According to Vaudoncourt, the guns arrived on 22 May, but Eugene reported that this did not occur until the 26th.

72 Wachtel.

73 Army of Italy, 'Situation Sommaire' as of 25 May, in Army of Germany, 'Livret de Situation', 1 June 1809, AG C2/675; losses for the battle (approximately 700) apparently subtracted from this report.

Bibliographic Note

Although a complete bibliography is slated to appear in the third volume of this study, the following will provide some of the key sources for analysis of the war between Regensburg and Aspern as well as the campaign in Italy. As in Volume I, full citations for all sources here employed are included in the endnotes. Note that sources cited in the Volume I 'Bibliographic Note' are not repeated here.

For the war in the Danube valley, the starting points on the Austrian side are volumes III and IV of *Krieg 1809*, unparalleled in detail and thoroughness; Kirchhammer's various pieces add significantly to the official account. Pelet, Buat, and Saski remain key for information from the French perspective.

For the campaign in Italy, the second volume of *Krieg 1809* provides the foundation for the Austrian narrative, but must be supplemented by the *österreichischer militärische Zeitschrift* (1833–4) for operations in the Tyrol. Johann's accounts are also central to the Austrian side as is Wachtel's thorough study of Jellacic's operations; Hans von Zwiedineck-Südenhorst provides a host of key documents and insightful analysis on the Army of Inner Austria and operations in Styria. There is a wealth of material on the French side, beginning with Vaudoncourt (a participant), Vignolle (joined the Army of Italy *after* the opening campaign, but wrote the formation history in 1810), and du Casse. The journals of Dessaix's, Broussier's, and Pacthod's [Abbé's] divisions provide important nuance and detail.

Memoirs and regimental histories, carefully considered, supplement these general accounts, and have been used with archival data to complete the order of battle appendices.

Abriss von der Schlacht bei Esling und Gross-Aspern am 21. und 22. May 1809, Weimar: Geographisches Institut, 1810.

Arnold, James R., *Napoleon Conquers Austria*, London: Arms & Armour, 1995.

Boué, Gilles, *Essling: Napoleon's First Defeat?*, Paris: Histoire & Collections, 2008.

Buat, Edmond Alfonse Léon, *1809 De Ratisbonne à Znaïm*, Paris: Chapelot, 1909.

Camon, Hubert, *La Manoeuvre de Wagram*, Paris: Berger-Levrault, 1926.

Castle, Ian, *Aspern & Wagram 1809: Mighty Clash of Empires*, Osprey Campaign Series No. 33, London: Osprey, 1994.

[Criste, Oskar], 'Die Offensiv-Operationen des Erzherzogs Johann in Italien im Jahre 1809', *Organ der militär-wissenschaftlichen Vereine*, 1898.

Decker, C. von, 'Besuch der Insel Lobau und der Schlachtfelder von Aspern (Eslingen) und Wagram im Sommer 1835', *Zeitschrift für Kunst, Wissenschaft und Geschichte des Krieges*, vol. VII, 1836.

Du Casse, Albert, *Mémoires et Correspondance Politique et Militaire du Prince Eugène*, Paris: Lévy, 1858–60.

Epstein, Robert M., *Prince Eugene at War*, Arlington, TX: Empire Press, 1984.

Exner, Moritz, *Die Antheilnahme der Königlich Sächsischen Armee am Feldzuge gegen Oesterreich und die kriegerischen Ereignisse in Sachsen im Jahre 1809*, Dresden: Baensch, 1894.

Eyck, F. Gunther., *Loyal Rebels*, Lanham: University Press of America, 1986.

Ferry, Lt. Col. Edmond, *La Marche sur Vienna*, Paris: Chapelot, 1909.

'Das Gefecht bei Linz am 17. Mai 1809', *Zeitschrift für Kunst, Wissenschaft und Geschichte des Krieges*, vol. IV, 1828.

Gill, John H., 'The Battle of Neumarkt, 24 April 1809', *First Empire*, no. 11, May/June 1993.

Gruber, Max, *Bruneck und das westliche Pustertal im Jahre 1809*, Innsbruck: Wagner, 1952.

Hirn, Josef, *Tirol's Erhebung im Jahre 1809*, Innsbruck: Haymon, 1983 (reprint of 1909 edition).

[Hormayr, Joseph], *Das Heer von Innerösterreich unter den Befehlen des Erzherzogs Johann im Kriege von 1809 in Italien, Tyrol und Ungarn*, Leipzig and Altenburg: Brockhaus, 1817.

Johann, Archduke of Austria, 'Gedrängtes Journale zur Uebersicht der Ereignisse bei der Armee unter höchsten Befehlen Sr. kaiserlichen Hoheit des Erzherzogs Johann in dem Feldzug vom Jahre 1809', Alois Veltzé (ed.), *Mitteilungen des K. und K. Kriegsarchivs*, vol. V, 1907.

Kirchhammer, Alexander, 'Aspern', *Beilage des Fremden-Blatt*, no. 148, 31 May 1902.

—— 'Zur offiziellen "Relazion" über die Schlacht von Aspern 1809', *Beilage des Fremden-Blatt*, no. 273, 4 October 1902.

—— *Das Gefecht in der Schwarzen Lacken-Au am 13. Mai 1809*, Vienna: Seidel & Sohn, 1903.

Litschel, Rudolf Walter, *Des Gefecht bei Ebelsberg am 3. Mai 1809*, Militärhistorische Schriftenreihe vol. 9, Vienna: Bundesverlag, 1968.

Lütgendorf, Kasimir Freiherr von, *Die Kämpfe in Südtirol*, Vienna: Seidel & Sohn, 1911.

Mackesy, Piers, *The War in the Mediterranean 1803–1810*, Westport: Greenwood, 1981.

Magenschab, Hans, *Andreas Hofer: Zwischen Napoleon und Kaiser Franz*, Graz: Styria, 1984.

Menge, August, *Die Schlacht von Aspern am 21. und 22. Mai 1809*, Berlin: Stilke, 1900.

Molières, Michel, *Napoléon en Autriche: La Campagne de 1809: Les Opérations du 24 Avril au 12 Juillet*, Paris: Le Livre Chez Vous, 2004.

Morel, Lieutenant, *Insurrection au Tyrol en 1809*, AG, Manuscrits, MR 736.

Nüschler, Conrad, 'Rückblick auf die kriegerischen Ereignisse in Tirol im Jahre 1809', *Organ der militär-wissenschaftlichen Vereine*, 1879.

Rauchensteiner, Manfried, *Die Schlacht von Aspern m 21. und 22. Mai 1809*, Vienna: Bundesverlag, 1986.

Robinet de Clery, Gabriel A., *En Tyrol*, Paris: Olldendorff, 1897.

Sallagar, Hermann, 'Die Verteidigung der Position von Präwald im Jahre 1809', *ÖMZ*, vol. VI, 1908.

Savary, Anne-Jean-Marie-René, *Mémoires du Duc de Rovigo*, Paris: Bossange, 1828.

Schels, Johann Baptist, 'Der Feldzug 1809 in Italien', *ÖMZ*, 1844.

Schemfil, Viktor, 'Das k. k. Tiroler Korps im Kriege 1809', *Tiroler Heimat*, vol. XXIII, 1959.

Schneid, Frederick C., *Soldiers of Napoleon's Kingdom of Italy*, Boulder: Westview, 1995.

—— *Napoleon's Italian Campaigns*, Westport: Praeger, 2002.

Seidel, Friedrich von, 'Die Operazionen des von dem Banus von Kroazien, Feldmarschall-Leutnant Grafen Ignaz Gyulai befehligten östreichischen neunten Armeekorps im Feldzuge 1809', *ÖMZ*, 1837.

'Tirol im Jahre 1809', *ÖMZ*, 1833–4.

Turotti, Felice, *Storia dell'Armi Italiane dal 1796 al 1814*, Milan: Boniotti, 1856.

Vaudoncourt, Guillaume de, *Histoire Politique et Militaire du Prince Eugène Napoléon*, Paris: Mongie, 1828.

Veltzé, Alois, 'Taktische Betrachtungen über die Schlacht bei Sacile am 16. April 1809', *ÖMZ*, vol. II, 1861.

—— 'Aus den Tagen von Pordenone und Sacile', *Mitteilungen des K. und K. Kriegsarchivs*, 1904.

—— *Österreichs Thermopylen 1809*, Vienna: Stern, 1905.

—— 'Die Schlacht an der Piave', *Mitteilungen des K. und K. Kriegsarchivs*, vol. IV, 1906.

Vignolle, Martin, 'Historique de la Campagne de 1809 (Armée d'Italie)', *Revue Militaire*, vol. 16, July 1900.

Wachtel, Wilhelm, 'Die Division Jellacic im Mai 1809', *Mitteilungen des K. und K. Kriegsarchivs*, Vienna, 1911.

Wöber, Ferdi Irmfried, *1809: Schlacht bei Aspern und Essling*, Vienna, 1992.

Zanoli, Alessandro, *Sulla Milizia Cisalpino-Italiana cenni Storico-Statistici dal 1796 al 1814*, Milan, 1845.

Zwiedineck-Südenhorst, Hans von (ed.), 'Zur Geschichte des Krieges von 1809 in Steiermark', *Beiträge zur Kunde steiermärkischer Geschichtsquellen*, no. 23, 1891.

—— *Erzherzog Johann von Oesterreich in Feldzuge von 1809*, Graz: Styria, 1892.

Addenda

178 In exile on St Helena, Napoleon—while claiming to have won the battle—wrote that his initial plan was for the Young Guard to support Lannes's attack by debouching from Essling to strike the Austrian left ('Dix-Huit Notes sur l'Ouvrage Intitulé Considérations sur l'Art de la Guerre', *Correspondance*, vol. XXXI, pp. 376–9). See additional note for p. 414 below.

191 In his post-war journal, Hiller claimed that at roughly 7 p.m. he was preparing to 'pursue' the enemy and open an artillery bombardment against the French on Lobau Island. He states that messengers from headquarters recalled his troops without his knowledge, leading to an angry exchange with Wimpffen when the two met near Aspern (Hiller, pp. 187–8). This is rather different from the notion that Hiller was 'poised for the kill and could have rolled up the French line' (Rothenberg, *Great Adversary*, p. 197). Although they did not dismiss the possibility that Hiller had an attack in mind, the authors of *Krieg 1809* could find no contemporary indication that he was preparing for such offensive action, rather they located a 7.30 p.m. message wherein he mentions positioning himself to repulse a possible French advance (vol. IV, p. 648).

195 Note that the Austrians again succeeded in breaking the restored bridge three days after Aspern–Essling by sending floating mills against it as they had during the battle. The success of this technique forces one to ask why Charles did nothing to exploit the new damage to the bridge or why he did not plan an attack on the Lobau in conjunction with further attempts against the bridges. Even if the attack had occurred after most the French troops had evacuated the island, the destruction of a lone corps or several divisions trapped on Lobau could have had significant repercussions for Napoleon.

195 How much the French soldiery knew about the state of the bridges is unclear. At least one, an officer in the 46th Ligne, believed that 'If we had known, on 22 May 1809, that the bridges over the Danube were broken, we would not have won the Battle of Essling' (an interesting commentary on two counts!). See Jean Frédéric Auguste le Mière de Corvey, *Des Partisans et des Corps Irréguliers*, Paris: Anselin et Pochard, 1823, p. 230.

195 A young Württemberg lieutenant on his first campaign described Lobau in a letter to his parents on 6 June: 'Imagine our entire army squeezed together on an island in the Danube. Living, dead, dying, broken cannons, horses that limped about on three legs or with their stomachs torn open—all that lay jumbled together . . . It was terribly hot; stinking fumes from the Danube and the thousand-fold stench of corpses drifted through the air; the entire shoreline was covered with thousands of badly wounded who had dragged themselves here to await the restoration of the bridge. Added to that was a raging hunger. Occasionally a boat arrived with bread; but what was that for an army!' *Denkmal Friedrichs von Harpprecht*, Stuttgart: Cotta, 1813, p. 15.

198 On Napoleon's thinking about the fate of the Habsburg monarchy, see 'Précis de la marche des negotiations qui ont amené le traité de Vienne', in Klinkowström, p. 157.

201 For an excellent modern biography of Johann that emphasises his role in 1805 and 1809 as well as his desire to remake Austria, see Mark van Hattem, *Voor een Nieuw Oostenrijk*, Leiden: University of Leiden, 2011.

202 Looking back ruefully as he considered future operations in Italy in 1813, Radetzky noted that nothing should be undertaken there unless the circumstances were 'exceptionally favourable'. 'The greatest activity and exertion would be required,' he observed, noting that, 'In the war of 1809 we failed in this or simply paid no attention, and we were punished for it.' See 'Einige Gedanken über die Ergreifung der Offensive aus Innerösterreich gegen Tirol und Italien', June 1813, in *Denkschriften militärisch-politischen Inhalts*, Stuttgart: Cotta, 1858, p. 138.

205 Lamarque stated that there were not enough artillery horses, that the army lacked a pontoon train and that logistics were in such disarray that 'we lived by pillage' until more regular distributions began in early May (see his review of Pelet's history of the 1809 war in the *Spectateur Militaire*, vol. III, 1827, pp. 457, 463).

215 Lamarque complained that his orders and those for the dragoon divisions were not sent by courier, but by the regular post and did not reach him in Verona until 2 a.m. on 13 April (Lamarque, *Spectateur Militaire*, vol. III, 1827, p. 457).

233 Fortogna is on the Piave approximately twelve kilometres north of Belluno.

264 The acerbic Lamarque offers 'severe reproaches' concerning Eugene's performance at the Piave: for 'slowness and indecision' and particularly for not cutting the road near Conegliano. Thus, in his view, 'we did not profit from victory' (Lamarque, *Spectateur Militaire*, vol. III, 1827, pp. 463–4).

266 Sacco is a suburb of San Daniele, where the *Reisky* unit symbol is shown on Map 38.

286 *Mercury* also raided Rotti (near Bari) on the east coast of Naples on 15 May (James, vol. V, pp. 259–60).

290 Source for the quote about Jellacic is Johann's memoirs as printed in extract in Zwiedineck-Südenhorst, 'Das Gefecht bei St Michael', p. 45.

300 Map 48: insurrection commander should be Davidovich (not Duka).

370/N18 On Franz, see also Adam Wolf, *Kaiser Franz von der Stiftung der österreichischen Kaiserwürde bis zum Ausbruch des russisch–französischen Krieges*, Vienna: Prandel & Ewald, 1866.

372/N32 See also Gustav Just, *Als die Völker erwachten*, Vienna: Stern, 1907.

414 Rogniat's remarks in notes 113 and 118 are from his *Réponse aux Notes Critiques de Napoléon sur l'Ouvrage Intitulé Considérations sur l'Art de la Guerre*, Paris: Anselin et Pochard, 1823, p. 163. See also his *Considérations sur l'Art de la Guerre*, Paris: Anselin et Pochard, 1820, and Marbot's refutations in *Remarques Critiques sur l'Ouvrage de M. le Lieutenant-Général Rogniat Intitulé Considérations sur l'Art de la Guerre*, Paris: Anselin et Pochard, 1820. This issue, part of a larger 'Rogniat Controversy', is summarised in *The Naval and Military Magazine*, vol. IV, December 1828, followed by *The United Service Journal*, parts I and II, 1829.

Index

The Publisher's authorised representative in the EU for product safety
is Authorised Rep Compliance Ltd, Ground Floor, 71 Lower Bagot St,
Dublin, Ireland, D02 P593 www.arccompliance.com

Printed and bound by CPI Group (UK) Ltd, Croydon, CR0 4YY

04/06/2026

02128172-0001